POLITICAL
SCIENCE
DICTIONARY

POLITICAL SCIENCE DICTIONARY

JACK C. PLANO Western Michigan University

MILTON GREENBERG Roosevelt University

ROY OLTON Western Michigan University

ROBERT E. RIGGS University of Minnesota

THE DRYDEN PRESS
Hinsdale, Illinois

Jay, Gregory, and Vicki Plano · Anne and Nancy Greenberg · Bertrand and Leslie Olton · Robert, Richard, Russel, Rodney, Raymond, and Reisa Riggs

PREFACE

The Function of Language in Political Science

Technical and scientific language has evolved in the natural sciences over a period of several centuries, but the development has gained its greatest momentum during the third quarter of the twentieth century. This vast philological and lexicographical explosion is, only a reflection of the dramatic achievements of scientists in gaining new understandings of the physical world.

In somewhat the same—although comparatively modest—way the discipline of political science has enjoyed a period of feverish intellectual activity over the past twenty-five years. During this period the discipline has made its greatest collective effort and has achieved some of its most significant advances toward understanding the political world. Much of the success of these recent, continuing efforts of the political science discipline have in fact been part of the spillover from those great gains made in the "pure" sciences. These have offered political scientists new methods and techniques with which to carry on research and analyze data, and have increasingly provided potential analogies that help in understanding political behavior and systems.

What, then, is the function of language in the development of a discipline like political science? There are many roles, actual and potential, that language plays in such a context. First, language development may tend to encourage the kind of rigor and precision that is essential to the application of the scientific method in behavioral studies. Second, it will help to provide means for building the cumulative storehouse of knowledge on which every discipline rests. Thus, the individual scholar, when undertaking research and teaching activities, can use the technical language of political science to think abstractly and work out applications. In this way he can recall the properties, attributes, and relationships of concepts, and apply them to new and changing situations as he proceeds with his scholarly activities. Third, he can use the growing body of terminology to communicate new ideas and research results to other persons, particularly political and social scientists. The progress of a discipline like political science might be measured, among other things, by the extent to which members of the profession can communicate with one another on technical topics, and by the level of exactitude transmissible in these communications.

The Scope and Objectives of This Dictionary

The *Political Science Dictionary* offers concise and accurate definitions for approximately two thousand key terms that comprise the working language of political science. The authors believe that these concepts constitute the building blocks of the discipline. They have been painstakingly culled from the extensive literature of politics in the conviction that some kind of selection process is required for a work of this kind. In the difficult and obviously subjective task of gathering, picking, choosing, and rejecting, some omissions become inevitable. It is the hope of the authors that there have been neither critical omissions nor frivolous inclusions. The authors urge readers to call any apparent sins of omission or commission to their attention by writing them in care of The Dryden Press.

The language of political science can be divided into several diverse categories based on inherent properties and attributes, or on specific actions, theories, or events. Without trying to be typologically exhaustive, the following set of categories found in the *Political Science Dictionary* should convey some idea of the range of terms included:

1. Political philosophies and ideological systems (Democracy, Communism, Fascism, Trotskyism, Jeffersonianism, and so on)
2. Historical events which continue to have an impact on contemporary politics (Atlantic Charter, Constitutional Convention of 1787, Yalta Agreement, and others)
3. U.S. governmental agencies, legislative enactments, and Supreme Court decisions (Council of Economic Advisers, National Environmental Policy Act of 1969, *New York Times v. United States*, and so on)
4. Methodologies, techniques of analysis, relationships with other disciplines, and the state of the discipline of political science (Historical Approach, Macro-micro Analysis, Political Anthropology, Postbehavioralism, . . .)
5. Theories that seek to explain types of political phenomena or behavior (Elitist Theory, Functionalism, Organization Theory, . . .)
6. Political activities, forms, rules, and characteristics (Lobbyist, Liberalism, Denaturalization, Voting Behavior, . . .)
7. Institutions and processes of the American political system (Political Party, Electoral College, Advice and Consent, . . .)
8. Major foreign political institutions and processes (Chinese Communist Party; Federal System, Soviet Union; Party System, Italy; . . .)

9. Global and regional political, economic, social, and security organizations and processes (World Health Organization, European Community, United Nations Force in Cyprus, . . .)
10. Concepts borrowed from other disciplines but essential or helpful to the understanding of the functioning of political systems (Regressive Tax, Homeostasis, Culture, Demographic Cycle, . . .)

The prime target of this volume is the student pursuing a college major or minor in political science or international relations. Other readers, especially students taking introductory political science courses and nonstudents who are motivated to gain a better understanding of the world of politics, should find it helpful. It is hoped that this dictionary will enable anyone with an interest in politics to tackle the literature of the field with greater understanding and confidence, and to build an awareness of the need for precise expression in the discipline.

Politics and the field of political science suffer more than most disciplines from semantic confusion. The problem stems at least in part from the fact that while few people consider themselves experts in fields like chemistry and botany, millions believe that they *have* been vested with special insights for discovering political truths. These sentiments, while probably useful in encouraging mass participation in a democratic system, tend to produce conflicting definitions and a popularized language that lacks definitional rigor and precision. The same concept may be used with entirely different meaning by the citizen, the student, and the professional; and interpretive differences may exist within each group as well. The result of such "definitional pluralism" is that often persons interested in political study and research fail to communicate effectively with each other and with the general public because they do not "talk the same language."

The *Political Science Dictionary* also functions as a teaching tool. Many textbooks fail to take account of the reader's lack of familiarity with the technical language of the discipline. This can lead to fuzziness in the student's thinking as he tries to understand a political event or situation that is discussed in technical terms. It can also lead to numerous interruptions and distractions during class periods when students ask for definitions of terms found in the text or used in lectures. By placing a political dictionary in the student's hands a teacher may enhance the student's perception of the political situation under study. The *Political Science Dictionary* is addressed to these varied needs.

Acknowledgments

In preparing the definitions the authors have tried to present the best current usage as accurately and clearly as possible. A vast debt, therefore, is owed to many specific sources and, in general, to all members of the political science profession and related social science disciplines who have contributed to the development and precision of the working language of politics and political analysis. The authors accept full responsibility for any inaccuracies that may occur.

The authors also extend thanks to many people who, over the past decade, have offered advice on their specialized dictionary projects.* This omnibus volume has obviously benefited from their suggestions.

A Note on How to Use This Book

The *Political Science Dictionary* utilizes a comprehensive, yet simplified, reference system that facilitates the finding of entries. Features available to the reader searching for a term or concept that may be discussed under one of several possible topical entries include:
1. Straight A through Z alphabetical listing of all major terms.
2. *See also* references found at the end of most entries, which offer the reader the opportunity of seeking additional related information
3. *See* references that are interspersed between major entries.

Western Michigan University   JCP
Roosevelt University   MG
Western Michigan University   RO
University of Minnesota   RER
January 1973

---

* These include: Jack C. Plano and Milton Greenberg, *The American Political Dictionary* (New York: Holt, Rinehart and Winston, Inc., 1962, 1967; Hinsdale, Ill.: The Dryden Press Inc., 1972); Jack C. Plano and Roy Olton, *The International Relations Dictionary* (New York: Holt, Rinehart and Winston, Inc., 1969); and Jack C. Plano and Robert E. Riggs, *Dictionary of Political Analysis* (Hinsdale, Ill.: The Dryden Press Inc., 1973).

POLITICAL
SCIENCE
DICTIONARY

AAA, *see* Agricultural Adjustment Acts of 1933, 1938.

Ability Theory   The belief that taxes should be based upon the individual's ability to pay, as indicated by income, property, consumption, or wealth. *See also* PROGRESSIVE TAX.

Ableman v. Booth, 21 Howard 506 (1859): Established that a state court may not issue a writ of habeas corpus to a prisoner in federal custody.

Absentee Voting   Provisions of state laws or constitutions that enable qualified voters to cast their ballots in an election without going to the polls on election day. If a person expects to be unable to vote on election day, he obtains a ballot within a specified period preceding the election, marks it, has it notarized, and returns it to the proper official.

Absolute Majority   Any number over 50 percent of the total votes cast by *all* the voters participating in a given election. A *simple* majority, in contrast, is any number over 50 percent of the votes cast on any single issue in an election, even though many voters who go to the polls may not vote on the specific issue. A *plurality* consists of sufficient votes to win an election, but not necessarily a majority. *See also* PLURALITY.

Absolutism   Unrestrained powers exercised by government. Absolutism is the opposite of constitutionalism, which provides for government limited by law. *See also* TOTALITARIANISM.

Abstention, Security Council, *see* Veto (International Organization).

Academic Freedom   The principle that teachers and students have the right and the duty to pursue the search for truth wherever the inquiry may lead, free of political, religious, or other restrictions except those of accepted standards of scholarship.

1

Important corollaries to the principle are that alleged violations of academic freedom will be investigated under procedures consonant with due process, and that the tenure of teachers will not depend upon adherence to any orthodoxy.

Access, *see* Articulation of Interests.

Accession, *see* Adherence or Accession

Accidental War   An unintended armed conflict touched off by incidents caused by human error or mechanical failure. Accidental war in the nuclear age relates to the possibility that an all-out nuclear exchange between major powers could be triggered by a misinterpretation of intentions or by the accidental delivery of a weapon of mass destruction. Events that could precipitate a major war, for example, include the inadvertent destruction of a major population center, an error on a radar screen that leads to the belief that an attack is under way, or the actions of a demented military commander who orders a major attack. *See also* WAR.

Accountability   The concept underlying democratic representative government that elected officials are responsible to the people for their actions. Accountability under law is one of the features distinguishing governments based on the concepts of liberal democracy from those embracing the principles of absolutism. *See also* DEMOCRACY, REPRESENTATIVE GOVERNMENT.

Accretion   Acquisition of title to territory created through the slow depositing of materials by rivers and seas, which vests in the mainland or riparian state. The principle of accretion—that natural additions to the original territory come under the same jurisdiction—can be traced back to Roman law through the work of Hugo Grotius. Such additions may occur on river banks or ocean shores or may take the form of islands or deltas.

Acheson-Lilienthal Report, *see* Baruch Plan.

Acquittal   Formal certification by a court of the innocence of a person charged with a crime. Ordinarily this occurs after a trial and a finding of not guilty by a judge or jury. An acquittal may also take place before trial because the charges are improper or the evidence insufficient.

Action   An independent agency established in 1971 to bring together a number of voluntary action programs of the national government. Action is headed by a director appointed by the President with Senate consent. Most prominent of the programs brought into Action are the Peace Corps (from the Department of State) and Volunteers in Service to America (from the Office of Economic Opportunity). Other programs include Foster Grandparents and Retired Senior Volunteer Program (from the Department of Health, Education, and Welfare), Office of Volunteer Action (from the Department of Housing and Urban Development), and the Service Corps of Retired Executives and Active Corps of Executives (from the Small Business Administration).

Action Theory, *see* Political Action.

Activism versus Self-restraint   Two approaches to judicial decision making in the American political system. Activists hold that a judge should use his position to promote desirable social ends. Proponents of self-restraint counter that in deciding cases a judge should defer to the legislative and executive branches, which are politically responsible to the voters, and not indulge his personal philosophy. Both schools of thought recognize the policy-making nature of judicial decisions on major social questions, but they differ on how that power should be used.

Activist, *see* Political Activist.

Act of Chapultepec   A declaration by American states that an attack against any of them by a nonhemispheric state would be considered an act of aggression against all. The Act of Chapultepec was signed in Mexico City on March 6, 1945, by the representatives of twenty-one American republics. This declaration was the forerunner of the Rio Treaty of Reciprocal Assistance of 1947. *See also* RIO TREATY.

Actor, *see* Political Actor.

Adherence or Accession   The procedure by which a nonsignatory state becomes a party to a treaty previously negotiated by other states. The conditions for adherence or accession are established by the original contracting parties and specified in the treaty. Adherence becomes effective immediately upon deposit of the instrument of adherence unless the acceding state indicates that its constitutional processes require formal ratification of the treaty to make its adherence effective. Some publicists use the term, adherence, when a state accepts only certain provisions of a treaty, and the term, accession, to indicate acceptance of the entire treaty.

Ad Hoc Conference, *see* Conference Diplomacy.

Adjournment   To terminate a session of a legislative body. Adjournment sine die means to end the session without definitely fixing a day for reconvening. It is used to end a congressional session officially. Neither house of Congress can adjourn for more than three days without the concurrence of the other. *See also* SESSION.

Adjudication   A legal technique for settling international disputes by submitting them to determination by an established court. Adjudication differs from arbitration in that the former involves an institutionalized process carried on by a permanent court whereas the latter is an ad hoc procedure. The first international court of general competence was the Permanent Court of International Justice (PCIJ), which functioned as part of the League of Nations system from 1920 until the demise of the League in 1946. It was succeeded by the present International Court of Justice (ICJ), one of the principal organs of the United Nations. *See also* INTERNATIONAL COURT OF JUSTICE.

Administration   The procedure by which laws are enforced and public policy is carried out. *Public* administration, as distinguished from private or business administration, is largely the function of the executive branch of government. It carries out the policies established by the legislative branch subject to the oversight and review of both the legislative and judicial branches. Administration is the art or science of managing public affairs with emphasis on such factors as organization, personnel, and finance.

Administrative Behavior, *see* Organization Theory.

Administrative Law   That branch of law that creates administrative agencies, establishes their methods of procedure, and determines the scope of judicial review of agency practices and actions. The term also describes the rules and regulations made by administrative agencies. Administrative law deals with rate-making, operating rules, the rights of persons and companies regulated by administrative agencies, and the power of the courts to review. *See also* ADMINISTRATIVE PROCEDURE ACT.

Administrative Office of the United States Courts   An agency that handles administrative matters for all federal and territorial courts except the Supreme Court. The Office, established in 1939, is headed by a director who is appointed by the Supreme Court. Its functions include supervision of administrative personnel of the courts, the fixing of compensation of such personnel, preparation of the budget for the operations of the court system, and care of court funds, books, equipment, and supplies. The Office also gathers statistics on dockets, and supervises administration of bankruptcy and federal probation.

Administrative Order   A directive, issued by an administrative agency, that has the force of law. An order is generally distinguished from a "rule" or "regulation" in that an order is specifically directed to an individual or group to correct infractions of a rule. An example would be an order of the National Labor Relations Board to a union or an employer to cease violation of a labor practice that the Board had declared to be unfair. Orders are issued after a hearing conducted by the agency which resembles the procedures of a court of law. Appeals may be brought to the regular courts. Orders of federal agencies are published in the *Federal Register. See also* HEARING EXAMINER, *Opp* case, ADMINISTRATIVE PROCEDURE ACT, CEASE AND DESIST ORDER.

Administrative Procedure, *see* Cease and Desist Order, Certificate of Public Convenience, Interest, and Necessity, Hearing, Quasi-Judicial, Quasi-Legislative.

Administrative Procedure Act of 1946 A major law governing the procedures of regulatory agencies and providing for standards of judicial review of administrative determinations. The Act requires that every agency publicize its operations, give advance notice of proposed rules, and permit persons to testify, to be accompanied by counsel, and to cross-examine witnesses. The Act provides further that the same official may not act as both prosecutor and judge and that persons may appeal decisions of these agencies to the courts. The courts are authorized to set aside any agency ruling that is arbitrary or unsupported by substantial evidence. *See also* HEARING.

Administrative Reorganization The reform of administrative agencies and procedures to improve efficiency, economy, and responsibility. Reorganization movements have generally had as their major purposes the concentration of authority and accountability by: (1) integrating agencies with similar functions to eliminate overlapping and waste; (2) fixing responsibility in some hierarchical arrangement; (3) establishing advisory and centralized housekeeping agencies to aid the chief administrator; (4) eliminating multiheaded boards or commissions and elective officers engaged in purely administrative work; and (5) improving personnel, budget, and auditing procedures. *See also* REORGANIZATION ACT.

Admiralty Jurisdiction Authority vested in federal courts to hear cases involving shipping and commerce on the high seas and on the navigable waters of the United States. It is a highly technical body of law based on tradition, congressional statutes, and international law. Typical cases involve maritime contracts, collisions, and crimes committed on vessels. *See also* JURISDICTION, NAVIGABLE WATERS.

Admission (International Organization) The process of accepting a state for membership in an international organization. In the United Nations, the admission of new members requires a recommendation by the Security Council followed by a two-thirds vote in the General Assembly. Any permanent member of the Council may block an application since the veto is applicable to membership questions. The Charter specifies that states desiring admission to membership: (1) be peace loving; (2) accept the obligations contained in the Charter; and (3) in the judgment of the Organization, be able and willing to carry out these obligations. All of the current members of the United Nations except the fifty-one original members have been accepted through the process of admission. International public unions, such as the specialized agencies of the United Nations, generally require a two-thirds vote of the organization to admit a new member. Regional groups, such as the European Economic Community, usually require a unanimous vote to admit. *See also* SUSPENSION, EXPULSION, WITHDRAWAL, TWO CHINAS PROPOSAL.

Admission of New States   The Constitution empowers Congress to admit new states to the Union (Art. IV, sec. 3). Limitations on this power are that no state may be created within an existing state, nor may any state be formed by the union of two or more states or parts of states without the consent of the states concerned and of Congress. The usual procedure for admission is (1) the people of the territory through their territorial assembly petition Congress; (2) Congress passes an "enabling act" that, when signed by the President, authorizes the territory to frame a constitution; (3) Congress passes an act of admission approved by the President. Though Congress and the President may insist upon certain conditions for admission to the Union, a state, once admitted, is equal with all other states. No state may constitutionally withdraw from the Union. *See also Coyle v. Smith,* TERRITORY.

Ad Valorem Duty   A customs duty levied on an imported commodity according to its value. A 10 percent ad valorem duty on an item valued by customs authorities at $100 would result in a tax of $10. Other types of customs duties include those based on weight or quantity, and fixed duties levied on specific articles of commerce. *See also* TARIFF.

Ad Valorem Tax, *see* Property Tax.

Adversary System   A concept underlying judicial procedure in the United States that assumes that, from the contest of opposing views, justice will emerge. Each side in a civil or criminal trial is expected to press its point of view with vigor and do all it can to refute the opposition's witnesses, evidence and arguments. *See also* TRIAL.

Advice and Consent   The power vested in the United States Senate by the Constitution (Art. II, sec. 2) to give its advice and consent to the President in treaty making and appointments. A two-thirds vote of the senators present is required for treaties. Appointments are confirmed by a simple majority vote. The Senate may give its advice through consultations between Senate leaders and the President, by resolutions setting out its position, or by delegating some of its members actually to sit in on treaty negotiations. *See also* CONFIRMATION, RATIFICATION (EXECUTIVE ROLE), RATIFICATION (LEGISLATIVE ROLE).

Advisory Opinion   An opinion given by a court, though no actual case or controversy is before it, on the constitutionality or legal effect of a law. No advisory opinions are rendered by federal judges. A few states, however, do authorize the highest state court to give such opinions upon the request of the legislature or governor. An advisory opinion is not binding except in the state of Colorado. The International Court of Justice also renders advisory opinions on requests from the General Assembly and Security Council, and from other organs and specialized agencies authorized by the General Assembly to submit them.

Advisory Referendum, *see* Referendum.

AFL-CIO, *see* Labor Unions.

African Development Bank, *see* Regional Development Banks.

Afroyim v. Rusk, 387 U.S. 253 (1967): Declared unconstitutional a law providing that native born citizens forfeit their citizenship by voting in a foreign election. The Court stressed that in the United States, where the people are sovereign, the citizen has a constitutional right to remain a citizen unless he voluntarily relinquishes it. *See also* EXPATRIATION.

Agency for International Development (AID)   A semi-independent agency within the Department of State that directs economic and technical assistance aid programs to foreign nations. AID was created by Congress in the Act for International Development of 1961, replacing the International Cooperation Administration (ICA). AID administers the foreign aid program through developmental loans and grants, investment surveys and guarantees, and developmental research. AID is headed by an administrator who has a dual role as chief of the operating agency and political adviser to the Secretary of State and the President. *See also* FOREIGN AID.

Agenda   A list of specific items of business to be considered at a legislative session or at a conference or meeting. The agenda of the Congress is based on the various calendars used by the two chambers in conducting their business. *See also* CALENDAR.

Aggregate Data, *see* Survey Research.

Aggregation of Interests   The process by which two or more political actors combine their demands to seek a common political objective. Aggregation of interests within political systems is commonly performed by political parties that seek, amid a welter of individual interests, some common denominator of principles, policies, and demands upon which all or most party members can agree. This function may also be performed by interest groups, governmental bodies, or any other agency capable of receiving and combining demands. At the international level aggregation of interests is facilitated by the use of international conference machinery. *See also* ARTICULATION OF INTERESTS, GROUP, STRUCTURAL-FUNCTIONALISM.

Aggression   An unwarranted attack by one state against another. Much of the literature of international law is concerned with the problem of identifying aggression and differentiating it from self-defense. The cold war has been characterized by nations arming and concluding alliances to protect themselves from aggression. The United Nations collective security system was established to protect states from aggression. *See also* COLLECTIVE SECURITY, SANCTIONS.

Agréation, *see* Agrément.

Agreement, Interstate, *see* Interstate Compact.

Agrément   The formal indication by one country of the acceptability of a diplomat to be sent to it by another. The *agrément* by the intended receiving state is a response to inquiries initiated by the sending state prior to the formal nomination of the diplomat under consideration. The procedure followed by the two states is called *agréation. See also* PERSONA GRATA.

Agricultural Act of 1970   The basic farm plan that incorporates national governmental agriculture policies. The Agricultural Act of 1970 continued many of the programs of aid to farmers that have kept outlays during the 1960s and 1970s at about $4 billion annually. These include price supports for wheat, cotton, feed grains, dairy products, and wool; extension of the Food for Peace program of selling surpluses abroad at low prices for local currencies; and idling certain amounts of tillable land in order to be eligible for government support payments. One new feature of the plan was that of limiting the amount of subsidies that individual farmers can receive under the price support system for each major crop. *See also* PRICE SUPPORT.

Agricultural Adjustment Acts of 1933, 1938   Broad agricultural programs sponsored by the Roosevelt Administration and enacted by Congress to maintain farm income through parity price supports and production controls for basic crops. After the first Agricultural Adjustment Act (AAA) had been declared unconstitutional by the Supreme Court in *United States v. Butler*, 297 U.S. 1 (1936), a second AAA, containing much of the first program but eliminating or modifying those sections that had failed the constitutionality test, was adopted in 1938. The 1933 Act was held to be an invalid use of the taxing power, whereas the 1938 Act was upheld as a valid exercise of the commerce power (*Mulford v. Smith*, 307 U.S. 38 [1939]). *See also Mulford v. Smith.*

AID, *see* Agency for International Development.

Aid to Education, *see* Federal Aid to Education.

Aid to Families with Dependent Children (AFDC)   Financial aid provided under the categorical assistance program of the Social Security Act of 1935 for children who lack adequate support but are living with one parent or relative. Some provision also has been made for support of children in foster homes. The program is administered by the states with the assistance of federal funds and under regulations established by the national government. The program is supervised by the Social and Rehabilitation Service of the Department of Health, Education, and Welfare. *See also* CATEGORICAL ASSISTANCE.

Aid to the Blind   Financial aid given to the needy blind under the categorical assistance program of the Social Security Act. Payments are made by the states with funds provided by the states and the national government to persons whose eyesight deficiencies make it impossible for them to engage in normal work. The program is supervised by the Social and Rehabilitation Service of the Department of Health, Education, and Welfare. *See also* CATEGORICAL ASSISTANCE.

Aid to the Totally and Permanently Disabled A program inaugurated in 1950 as part of the categorical aid program of the Social Security Act, which provides for financial aid to persons over eighteen whose physical condition makes it impossible to engage in gainful employment. The program is administered by the states with the assistance of federal funds under the supervision of the Social and Rehabilitation Service of the Department of Health, Education, and Welfare. *See also* CATEGORICAL ASSISTANCE.

Air Force Intelligence (A2), *see* Intelligence (United States).

Airspace Jurisdiction The sovereignty of a state over the airspace above its territory. Jurisdiction over the national airspace was recognized by the Chicago Convention on International Civil Aviation (1944) and is limited only by the bilateral and multilateral treaties to which a state may be a party. The Chicago conference established the International Civil Aviation Organization to implement the principles of the Convention and to develop rules for international air travel. Freedom of the air as a general principle exists only over the high seas and any other portions of the earth's surface not subject to the control of any state, such as Antarctica. Military and other state aircraft not common carriers always require special authorization before using the airspace of another state. *See also* INTERNATIONAL CIVIL AVIATION ORGANIZATION, OUTER SPACE JURISDICTION.

Albertson v. Subversive Activities Control Board, 382 U.S. 70 (1965): Struck down as a violation of the privilege against self-incrimination a requirement under the Internal Security Act of 1950 that individuals register as members of the Communist party. In 1961, in *Communist Party v. Subversive Activities Control Board,* 376 U.S. 1, the Court upheld provisions of the law requiring the registration of organizations found by the Subversive Activities Control Board to be controlled by a foreign power. No one subsequently registered for the party. In the *Albertson* case, the Court ruled that a party member could not be compelled to register because of laws, such as the Smith Act, that penalize such membership. *See also* INTERNAL SECURITY ACT.

Alderman A member of a city council. The term originated in England and was used in the American colonies to designate officials chosen by the common council of the city to exercise judicial power and to share in the governing of the city. In the nineteenth century, when bicameral legislatures were common in cities, one house was designated as the Board of Aldermen, the other, as the Common Council.

Alien An individual who is neither a citizen nor a national of the state in which he is living. Aliens generally owe allegiance to a foreign power, but may acquire citizenship by following prescribed procedures. *See also* ALIEN REGISTRATION ACT, *Truax v. Raich.*

Alien and Sedition Laws   Acts passed in 1798 authorizing the President to deport undesirable aliens and making it a crime to criticize the government or its officials. Through these Acts, the Federalist party sought to silence opposition. About twenty-five persons were jailed or fined for criticizing President John Adams. These Acts were a major reason for the defeat of the Federalist party in the election of 1800. Thomas Jefferson, the winner of that election, pardoned those convicted under the Acts.

Alienation   An individual's estrangement from society. Political alienation results when individuals believe they have lost their ability to participate effectively in the political process and to influence its outcome. Individuals tend to suffer political alienation when their government is unresponsive to their needs or hopes, or fails to quiet their fears. Alienation may involve feelings of distrust, scorn, or fear toward a political system that may produce anomie (a collapse of the social structures governing society) and a rejection of the entire political system.

Alien Registration Act of 1940 (Smith Act)   A major sedition law requiring the annual registration of aliens and prohibiting the advocacy of violent overthrow of the government. The major provisions of the Act make it unlawful to teach, advocate, or distribute information advocating the forcible overthrow of government or to knowingly organize or join an organization that so advocates. Other provisions outlaw activities designed to create disloyalty in the armed forces or to encourage participation in a violent revolution or in the assassination of public officials. *See also Dennis v. United States, Scales v. United States.*

Alliance   A multilateral agreement by states to improve their power position by joining together in defense of their common interest. Most alliances are now characterized by an agreement to regard "an attack upon any member of the alliance as an attack upon all." Hence, an alliance is a way of informing friend and foe that an attack against any individual nation will precipitate a general war. Balance of power systems tend to encourage the growth of alliances. *See also* BALANCE OF POWER.

Alliance for Progress   A program of foreign aid for Latin America developed by the Kennedy Administration. Congress authorized $500 million in 1961 to initiate the program. Nineteen Latin American countries—all except Cuba—have participated in Alliance programs. Continued aid to these nations is offered if internal economic reforms are instituted and if social progress moves forward with economic development. The Inter-American Development Bank was created in 1961 to play a major role in implementing the program through development loans. Its efforts are supplemented by the Development Loan Fund, the Export-Import Bank, and the Agency for International Development. *See also* ORGANIZATION OF AMERICAN STATES.

All-Union Party Congress (Soviet Union)   The Communist party organ to which all others in the party hierarchy are constitutionally responsible. The All-Union Congress is supposed to meet at least every four years. Delegates are chosen indirectly, by party conferences ranging from the city or local district level to the national level. The

Congress is charged with deciding party rules, making party program revisions, establishing party policy lines, selecting the Central Committee membership, and hearing reports from that body. The Congress is composed of approximately five thousand delegates, with each representing an average of 2500 party members or candidate members.

Ambassador The top-ranking diplomat sent by the government of a sovereign state as its official representative to another state. An ambassador is the head of an embassy in the capital city of the foreign state. Official relations between governments are carried on mainly through an exchange of ambassadors. *See also* DIPLOMATIC IMMUNITY, PERSONA NON GRATA.

Amendment (Legislative) An action of a legislative body to delete, alter, or revise the language of a bill or an act. Bills in Congress may be amended by either house at any one of a number of stages in the legislative process. Generally, amendments are printed, debated, and voted upon in the same way as a bill. Most laws enacted by Congress are, in fact, amendments to existing laws. *See also* AMENDMENT (CONSTITUTIONAL).

Amendment (Constitutional) Changes in, or additions to, a constitution. In the United States Constitution, Article V spells out the methods. Amendments may be proposed by a two-thirds vote of both houses of Congress or by a convention called by Congress at the request of the legislatures of two-thirds of the states. Only the first method has been used. Such proposals must be ratified by either the legislatures of three-fourths of the states or by conventions called for that purpose in three-fourths of the states, as determined by Congress. Only the Twenty-first Amendment (repealing prohibition) was submitted to conventions. The President may not veto an amendment proposal. Congress may stipulate a time limit, usually seven years, within which a proposal must be ratified. A state that has rejected an amendment may change its mind, but once a proposal is ratified by a state legislature, it stands. Ratification by a state may not be accomplished by a referendum of the people, but only by the legislature or convention. Though thousands of proposals have been made in Congress to amend the Constitution, only thirty-three have received endorsement from both houses; of these twenty-six have been adopted. Amendments are appended to the Constitution and not placed within the article or section that may have been changed, as is done in some state constitutions. *See also* AMENDMENT (LEGISLATIVE), CONSTITUTIONAL AMENDMENTS, STATE, *Coleman v. Miller.* (See also specific amendments.)

Amendment Process (International Organization) Procedures by which formal changes in the constitutions of international organizations are proposed and ratified. The League Covenant provided in Article 26 that amendments would take effect when ratified by all Council members and by a majority of the Assembly, and that any member refusing to accept such amendments would cease to be a member of the League. The United Nations Charter provides that the General Assembly may propose amendments by a two-thirds vote of its members (Article 108), or a General

Conference may be called by a two-thirds vote in the Assembly and by any nine members of the Security Council to propose alterations in the Charter (Article 109). Amendments, however proposed, must be ratified through national constitutional processes by two-thirds of the United Nations members, including all of the permanent members of the Security Council, before they come into force.

American Civil Liberties Union (ACLU), *see* Civil Rights Organizations.

American Farm Bureau Federation, *see* Farm Organizations.

American Jewish Congress, *see* Civil Rights Organizations.

American Legion, *see* Veterans Organizations.

American Veterans Committee, *see* Veterans Organizations.

Amicus Curiae   A legal term meaning "friend of the court." As *amicus curiae,* individuals or groups not parties to a lawsuit may aid or influence the court in reaching its decision. The court may at its discretion give permission to or request persons to appear as *amicus curiae.* Often a party will seek to appear as *amicus curiae* when the decision in the case will affect his rights as well as the rights of those directly involved. In some states, a friend of the court is permanently attached to a court to help it reach decisions in cases involving minors, divorce, or criminal offenders.

Amnesty   Power exercised by the President to grant a blanket pardon to all members of a group who have violated national law. Amnesties have also been occasionally granted by Congress. *See also* PARDON.

Analogy   The similarity that exists between the characteristics of two otherwise different things that makes a comparison between them possible and useful. Analogy is used in political analysis in hope of gaining a better understanding of the newer or less familiar by comparing it with a related but better known or better understood phenomenon. Thus, for example, some foreign affairs observers have tried to explain or understand the Vietnam conflict by drawing an analogy to the Great Power confrontation at Munich in 1938. Others, by contrast, have compared it with the Spanish Civil War. *See also* COMPARATIVE STUDY.

Analysis   Mentally separating an object of inquiry into its constituent parts to study its nature and to determine the relationship of the parts to each other and to the whole. Analysis may include measurement, explanation, and prediction. It is sometimes contrasted with *synthesis,* the process of combining separate parts into a coherent whole. Analysis is often used as a synonym for systematic interpretation of data without regard to the distinction between analysis and synthesis.

Analytic Political Philosophy, *see* Political Philosophy.

Analytic Statement, *see* Tautology.

Anarchism The doctrine that government is an unnecessary evil and should be replaced by voluntary cooperation among individuals and groups. Anarchists regard the state as an instrument used by the propertied classes to dominate and exploit the people. Anarchist thinking varies from individualism to collectivism, from pacifism to advocacy of violent revolution. All anarchists, however, hold the state's coercive system responsible for the warping of man's personality and look to the day when every form of government will be abolished. *See also* NEW LEFT.

Annapolis Convention A conference called by the Virginia legislature in 1786, whereby states were invited to send delegates to Annapolis, Maryland, to discuss trade regulations. Only five states were represented. Under the leadership of Alexander Hamilton and James Madison, the group urged Congress and the states to call another convention in Philadelphia in 1787 to consider revision of the Articles of Confederation. *See also* ARTICLES OF CONFEDERATION.

Annexation The addition of territory to a unit of government. Annexation usually denotes the addition by a city of land adjacent to it, to meet the problems of metropolitan expansion. Procedures for annexation are established by state law and generally require an affirmative vote of both the central city and of the area concerned. In a few states, as in Virginia and Texas, areas may be annexed by action of the city alone or through judicial procedures. *See also* METROPOLITAN AREA.

Anomic Group, *see* Group.

Antarctic Treaty An agreement to prevent the militarization of the Antarctic continent and to remove it from Cold War conflicts. Signed in December, 1959, the Antarctic Treaty came into force in June, 1961, following ratification by its twelve signatories—Argentina, Australia, Belgium, Britain, Chile, France, Japan, New Zealand, Norway, South Africa, the Soviet Union, and the United States. The major provisions of the treaty include: (1) the prohibition of all military activity on the Antarctic continent, with each signatory accorded the right to aerial surveillance; (2) the prohibition of nuclear explosions or dumping of radioactive wastes on the continent; (3) the right to inspect each other's installations to safeguard against violations; (4) the nonrecognition of existing territorial claims, and agreement that no new claims may be made; and (5) the responsibility to settle disputes peacefully and to cooperate in scientific investigations on the continent. The provisions apply to all land south of sixty degrees south latitude, and the Treaty is subject to review after thirty years.

Anthropology, *see* Political Anthropology.

Anti-Ballistic Missile (ABM), *see* Strategic Arms Limitation Talks.

Anti-Communism (Fascist Theory)   The belief and widely applied propaganda technique of fascism that holds that only a united, totalitarian state headed by a supreme leader (dictator) can defeat the threat posed by the conspiratorial tactics of "world communism." The anti-communism of fascism exploits the fear of communism prevalent in all classes in the advanced states, using it both to win and to hold power. Political enemies are often disposed of by a fascist regime by labeling them "Communists" or agents of international communism. Fascist theory promises to defeat communism by establishing a "true" socialism that eliminates class struggle by reconciling the interests of all groups in common support for and service to the nation.

Antifederalists   Persons who opposed adoption of the United States Constitution framed in Philadelphia in 1787. They opposed the centralist tendencies of the Constitution and attacked the failure of the framers to include a bill of rights. The group included many who had signed the Declaration of Independence or had strongly supported the Revolution.

Antitrust Division   One of the major divisions of the Department of Justice, which has responsibility for enforcement of the antitrust laws.

Antitrust Laws   Laws intended to regulate or prohibit unfair competition and combinations in restraint of trade, including monopolies, cartels, trusts, and interlocking directorates. *See also* MONOPOLY, TRUST, ANTITRUST DIVISION, SHERMAN ANTITRUST ACT.

Antitrust Policies, United States, *see* Clayton Act of 1914, Holding Company, Interlocking Directorates, Merger, Monopoly, Sherman Antitrust Act of 1890, Trust, Webb-Pomerence Act of 1918.

ANZUS Pact   A tripartite security treaty concluded in 1951 among Australia, New Zealand, and the United States. The ANZUS treaty, which has no terminal date, declares that an attack upon any of the members would constitute a common danger and each would act to meet it according to its constitutional processes. *See also* ALLIANCE.

Apartheid   The South African doctrine of the separate development of the races. Apartheid is the basic tenet of social organization in the Republic of South Africa and supports the system of white supremacy. Through such policies as the establishment of native reserves (Bantu Areas) and restrictive legislative and administrative practices, the black majority is denied political, social, economic, and legal rights exercised by the white minority. International opposition to apartheid policies has produced substantial criticism in the United Nations, disturbed relations with many African and Asian states, and was largely responsible for South Africa's withdrawal from the Commonwealth of Nations in 1961.

A Posteriori   Pertaining to knowledge or modes of reasoning based on observation and experience. A posteriori reasoning is inductive in that it starts with securing an understanding of particular events or data and their effects, which are then used to determine causes and arrive at general conclusions. *See also* A PRIORI, INDUCTION.

Appeal   Taking a case from a lower court to a higher tribunal by the losing party. The term also identifies those types of cases brought to the United States Supreme Court as a matter of right; these include cases from federal courts and highest state courts when state or federal laws are declared in conflict with the Constitution or a treaty. Such cases are brought to the Supreme Court "on appeal." An appeal is generally a complex and costly process. Simplified provisions are made for filing of appeals *in forma pauperis* by indigent appellants in criminal cases. *See also* APPELLATE JURISDICTION.

Appeasement   A term used to describe concessions made to a warlike potential enemy in the hope that these will satiate his appetite for expansion, and that peace will be secure. Prime Minister Neville Chamberlain's agreement at Munich to accept Adolf Hitler's demand for the partition of Czechoslovakia is a classic example of appeasement.

Appellate Jurisdiction   Authority of a court to review decisions of an inferior court. In the federal court system, the courts of appeals and the Supreme Court have power to review decisions of district courts and other tribunals. All states have courts of appellate jurisdiction to review decisions of lower state courts. The losing party in a lawsuit generally has the right to appeal the decision to an appellate court. *See also* JURISDICTION.

Applied Statistics, *see* Statistics.

Appointment Power   The authority vested in a public official to fill a vacancy in a governmental office or position. The appointment power is usually shared by the chief executive, who nominates the candidate, with the legislative body, which confirms the appointee. In the national government, the President possesses the full appointing power for some positions but must obtain the Senate's "advice and consent" for others. Positions filled by presidential appointment include those in the executive branch, the federal judiciary, commissioned officers in the armed forces, and members of the independent regulatory commissions. Governors and most mayors share a limited appointment power with their state senates and city councils, respectively. The President and governors may make recess appointments between Senate sessions. *See also* CONFIRMATION, RECESS APPOINTMENT, REMOVAL POWER.

Apportionment   The allocation of legislative seats. The Constitution (Art. I, sec. 2), and the Fourteenth Amendment (sec. 2) provide that representatives shall be apportioned among the several states according to their respective numbers. Under the Apportionment Act of 1929, Congress fixed the number of house seats at 435 and provided that the Census Bureau after each decennial census redistribute the seats among the fifty states, subject to congressional control. Each state, however, is assigned one representative before a population formula is applied. Under the 1970 reapportionment, nine states lost, and five states gained, seats in the House. California led with an increase of five seats. *See also* GERRYMANDERING, REDISTRICTING.

Apportionment Problems and Policies, United States, *see Baker v. Carr*, Census, Gerrymandering, *Gray v. Sanders*, Redistricting, *Reynolds v. Sims*, *Wesberry V. Sanders*.

Approach   A scholarly strategy or mode of analysis which provides a set of intellectual tools for the study and understanding of political phenomena. An approach, in political inquiry, may provide for an expeditious means of gathering, arranging, extracting meaning from, establishing relationships among, and evaluating data; in its most sophisticated forms it may in itself constitute a major body of theory or it may take the form of a simulation model. The main objective of an approach is to give order to a diverse range of political phenomena by fitting them within a limited set of concepts. *See also* CONCEPTUAL SCHEME, PARADIGM.

Appropriation   A legislative grant of money for a specific purpose. First, authorization bills, establishing a specific program, are enacted by Congress. Then, an appropriation bill must usually be passed to provide the money to carry out the program. Appropriation bills originate in the House of Representatives by custom; revenue bills must originate in the House under the Constitution. *See also* AUTHORIZATION, DEFICIENCY APPROPRIATION, POWER OF THE PURSE, SUPPLEMENTARY APPROPRIATION.

A Priori   Pertaining to knowledge or modes of reasoning based on self-evident principles independent of experience and observation. A priori reasoning is deductive in that it starts with general ideas or theories which can be known through reason or intuition, and then proceeds to the logical determination of the results or effects of these ideas. Thus, for example, one may take the intuitively derived proposition, "man ought to be free," and from it deduce a catalog of political ethics applicable to particular situations. *See also* A POSTERIORI, DEDUCTION.

Arab League   A regional group formed in 1945 to coordinate the members' political activities, safeguard their independence and sovereignty, and encourage cooperation in economic, social, and cultural matters. The thirteen Islamic members of the League of Arab States are independent Middle East and North African states. The original members, Egypt, Iraq, Jordan, Lebanon, Saudi Arabia, Syria, and Yemen, have since been joined by Algeria, Kuwait, Libya, Morocco, Sudan and Tunisia. The supreme decision organ of the League is the Majlis, or Council, that meets twice each year and is composed of a representative from each member. Binding decisions can be made only by unanimous vote, as in a decision to repel aggression, but those reached by a majority "bind only those that accept them." In addition, seven permanent committees function under Council authority to study economic and social matters and to elicit support for joint projects and programs. A secretariat headed by a secretary-general is located at League headquarters in Cairo. *See also* REGIONALISM (INTERNATIONAL).

Arab Refugee Relief, *see* United Nations Relief and Works Agency.

Arbitration　A method of settling a dispute whereby the parties to the dispute select the arbitrators and agree to accept their decision as binding. A number of states authorize arbitration and make decisions enforceable by the courts. *See also* ARBITRATION (INTERNATIONAL), ARBITRATION (LABOR-MANAGEMENT).

Arbitration (International)　A method of settling a dispute between states by judges selected by the parties to the dispute. The judges, who have standing as international jurists, must render a decision or award based on international law, and the parties agree in advance to accept the decision as binding, Arbitration dates back many centuries, but its modern use began with the famous *Alabama Claims* settlement between the United States and Great Britain growing out of Civil War controversies. *See also* PACIFIC SETTLEMENT OF DISPUTES.

Arbitration (Labor-Management)　The submission of a labor-management dispute to an impartial board or individual whose decision is binding upon the parties to the dispute. A few states have passed statutes requiring compulsory arbitration of disputes in public utility enterprises, such as electric, gas, and water. *See also* MEDIATION AND CONCILIATION.

Aristocracy　The exercise of political power by a small ruling clique of a state's "best" citizens. The selection of the aristocrats may be made on the basis of birth, wealth, or ability.

Armed Forces Policy Council, *see* Joint Chiefs of Staff.

Armistice　A temporary cessation of hostilities agreed to by belligerents. Sometimes called a "truce," an armistice may be general in scope or may apply only to specific areas. Under international law, an armistice does not affect the legal status of the war, which may be continued in all aspects other than those provided for in the truce agreement.

Arms Control　Measures undertaken unilaterally or through agreement among states to reduce the danger of war by such means as partial disarmament, security arrangements to avoid accidental war, and the stabilization of force levels. Arms control measures are aimed at restricting only certain aspects of the arms race, as, for example, prohibiting certain types of weapons, restricting nuclear testing, or demilitarizing geographical areas.

Arms, Right to Bear, *see* Right to Bear Arms.

Army Intelligence (G2), *see* Intelligence (United States).

Arraignment A stage in criminal proceedings in which the accused is brought before the court to hear the formal charges against him as prepared by a grand jury or prosecutor. The accused is then asked to plead guilty or not guilty. The Supreme Court has ruled that there must be no unnecessary delay between arrest and arraignment. A confession or other evidence obtained as a result of such delay will be barred as evidence (*Mallory v. United States*, 354 U.S. 449 [1957]). *See also McNabb v. United States.*

Arrest Warrant An order issued in writing by a court or magistrate authorizing the detainment of a person. The Fourth Amendment to the Constitution specifies that such warrants are to be issued only upon "probable cause," supported by oath, describing the person to be seized. All state constitutions have similar provisions. *See also* SEARCH AND SEIZURE.

Articles of Confederation The compact made among the thirteen original American states to form the basis of their government. Though prepared in 1776, the Articles were not officially adopted by all states until 1781 and were replaced in 1789 by the United States Constitution. The Confederation was a league of sovereign states. Each state had one vote in a one-house legislature. No provision was made in the Articles for a separate national executive or judiciary. The congress was assigned a limited number of powers, but the approval of nine states was necessary for effective action. The central government lacked significant powers, including the powers to tax, to regulate commerce or the currency, or to make its laws directly applicable to the people without further state action. In short, the congress could not force states or individuals to comply with its decisions, resembling, in many respects, an international organization. Any amendments to the Articles required the unanimous approval of the thirteen states. *See also* CONFEDERATION.

Articulation of Interests The making of a demand on a political system. Articulation of interests is the means by which attitudes, opinions, and beliefs are transformed into expressed demands for governmental action (or inaction). Within national or subnational systems, interests are articulated by private individuals and groups as well as by governmental decision makers. In the international system most articulation is carried on by official representatives of states, but the development of international organizations—governmental and nongovernmental—has increased the opportunity for interest articulation by private groups. Articulation of interests is unlikely to be effective unless the group or individual concerned has access to political decision makers.

"Access," in this sense, means the ability to get a hearing for a political demand. *See also* AGGREGATION OF INTERESTS, GROUP, STRUCTURAL-FUNCTIONALISM.

Ascription, *see* Recruitment.

ASEAN, *see* Association of Southeast Asian Nations.

Ashcraft v. Tennessee, 322 U.S. 143 (1944): Ruled that a confession obtained from a suspect after prolonged interrogation under hot lights by a relay of officers is not admissible in a state trial. Such coercive methods to obtain confessions violate the Fourteenth Amendment. *See also* CONFESSION.

Ashwander v. TVA (Judical Powers), 297 U.S. 288 (1936): Upheld the right of the TVA to sell surplus electric power. Furthermore, the case is well-known for the concurring opinion by Justice Louis D. Brandeis in which he attempted to sum up the rules that the Court had developed in considering the constitutionality of the acts of the legislative and executive branches. Among these were: (1) the court will not decide questions of a constitutional nature, unless absolutely essential to dispose of the case; (2) the Court will not pass upon a constitutional question if the case can be disposed of on some other ground; (3) the Court will not formulate a constitutional rule broader than is required by the precise facts of the case; and (4) the Court will try to construe a statute so as to avoid ruling on constitutional questions, even if serious doubts exist as to its constitutionality. *See also Ashwander v. TVA,* JUDICIAL REVIEW.

Ashwander v. TVA (Legislative Powers), 297 U.S. 288 (1936): Upheld the construction of major dams by an agency of the national government under the war and commerce powers, and upheld the authority of such an agency to build transmission lines and to sell electrical energy generated at the dams. The Court held that Congress could properly build huge dams if needed for national defense and to improve navigation, and that it could, under the Constitution, sell property belonging to the United States, such as electric power.

Asian and Pacific Council (ASPAC) A regional organization established in 1966 to encourage economic, social, and cultural cooperation among members. Unlike most Asian regional organizations, ASPAC's membership includes only Asian nations: Australia, Japan, Malaysia, New Zealand, Philippines, South Korea, South Vietnam, Taiwan, and Thailand. The initiative to establish ASPAC originated with South Korea. ASPAC conferences are held annually in major cities of member states. Between general conferences, the ambassadors of member states to Thailand meet monthly in Bangkok as a standing committee under the chairmanship of the Thai foreign minister. Thailand also provides the secretariat for the organization.

Asian Development Bank, *see* Regional Development Banks.

ASPAC, *see* Asian and Pacific Council.

Assembly, Freedom of, *see* Freedom of Assembly.

Assembly, League, *see* League of Nations.

Assembly of Heads of State, *see* Organization of African Unity.

Assembly, United Nations, *see* General Assembly.

Assessed Valuation   Value assigned to property for tax purposes. The general property tax levied by local governments in the United States is based on the valuation placed upon real estate (land, buildings, and other improvements) and personal property, both tangible (machinery, livestock, merchandise) and intangible (stocks, bonds, bank accounts). The tax paid on property is based on the assessed valuation and the millage or tax rate applied to the assessed value. The assessed valuation is based on a proportion of the actual value of each piece of property assessed within a taxing district, usually 30 to 50 percent of true market value, although some political units currently assess at 100 percent value. Assessments can be changed by reappraisals, adjustment of individual inequities by a board of review, adjustment of unequal valuations for different assessment districts by a county or state board of equalization, or by a general revaluation of all assessments within a district. *See also* PROPERTY TAX.

Assessor   A public official who determines the value of real and personal property for purposes of taxation. Assessors are commonly elected in towns, townships, or counties. In some midwestern townships, the supervisor serves as the assessor. About 15 percent of city assessors are still elected and the remainder are political or merit system appointees. *See also* PROPERTY TAX.

Associated States, *see* European Economic Community.

Associational Group, *see* Group.

Association, Freedom of, *see* Freedom of Association.

Association, Measures of, *see* Correlation.

Association of South East Asian Nations (ASEAN)   A regional organization established in 1967 to accelerate economic growth, social progress, and cultural development in South East Asia. The members of the ASEAN group are Indonesia, Malaysia, Philippines, Singapore, and Thailand. The regional organization is an expanded version of the Association of Southeast Asia (ASA) established in 1961 by Malaysia, Philippines, and Thailand.

Assumption   A proposition that is taken to be true without the benefit of proof. A proposition assumed to be true by one person may, however, be subjected to verification by someone else. An assumption may relate to a question of fact, such as a statement that all people in political life are guided by the principle of self-interest. Or it may relate to values, as the assumption that poor people ought to be assisted by governments. Some assumptions are openly expressed; others are not expressly spelled out, but, nevertheless, are logically implicit in whatever is being said. Advocates of limited nuclear war, for example, assume that nuclear war can, in fact, remain limited. Even if they do not say so, the assumption is implicit in their position. *See also* HYPOTHESIS, PROPOSITION, THEORY.

Asymmetry   A condition of imbalance or lack of equal proportion. Asymmetry implies either a quantitative or a qualitative inequality among the parts that make up a whole unit or system. Political asymmetries relate to the various heterogeneities, inequalities, and conflicts in individual and group behavior that have a direct impact on the stability of political systems. *See also* EQUILIBRIUM.

Atlantic Charter   The joint declaration issued by President Franklin Roosevelt and Prime Minister Winston Churchill in August, 1941, following their historic meeting aboard ship in the mid-Atlantic. The Atlantic Charter proclaimed the principles that were to guide the two countries in their search for a just peace and a stable world after the destruction of the Nazi regime. These included: (1) freedom from fear and want; (2) the application of the principle of self-determination to all territorial changes; (3) the right of all peoples to choose the form of government under which they live; (4) equal access to the trade and raw materials essential to prosperity, and economic collaboration among all nations; (5) peace with security for all states; (6) freedom of the seas; and (7) renunciation of the use of force, establishment of a permanent system of general security, and disarmament of all nations that threaten the peace. *See also* PROPAGANDA, PSYCHOLOGICAL WARFARE.

Atlantic Community   The concept of a partnership among the states of Western Europe and North America to solve common security, economic, social, and political problems. The Atlantic Community idea, based on a common Western cultural heritage, received added impetus in its development from the threat of aggression from Eastern Europe. Although no regional organization includes all Atlantic Community states, the Organization for Economic Cooperation and Development (OECD) and the Council of Europe have memberships that include most of the twenty-five states in the region. Other groups that have helped to integrate the policies of the states in the region include the North Atlantic Treaty Organization (NATO), the European Community, and the European Free Trade Association (EFTA). *See also* POLITICAL COMMUNITY.

At Large   The election of members of a legislative body by the voters of an entire governmental unit rather than from subdivisions thereof. Congressmen at large are elected by the whole electorate of the state when a state legislature fails to redistrict after a decennial census. United States Senators and Electoral College Electors are elected at large in each state. On the local level, members of city commissions are, in some cases, elected at large by the voters of the entire city rather than from wards, especially under the commission and city manager forms.

Atomic Energy Acts of 1946, 1954   The Act of 1946 created the Atomic Energy Commission (AEC) to control and develop the uses of atomic energy. Private mining of fissionable materials was permitted, but all other aspects of atomic energy were kept under strict governmental control. The Act of 1954 modified the public monopoly by permitting private development and operation of atomic power plants and the use of nuclear fuels and the sale of by-products by private firms under government licensing. *See also* ATOMIC ENERGY COMMISSION.

Atomic Energy Commission (AEC)   An independent agency of the United States government with responsibility to foster research and development of atomic energy for both civil and military purposes, and to regulate all private efforts in the field. The AEC consists of five commissioners appointed by the President with the Senate's approval for five-year terms. Responsibility for enforcement of the Atomic Energy Acts of 1946 and 1954 is vested in the Commission. *See also* ATOMIC ENERGY ACTS.

Atoms for Peace Plan   A proposal presented by President Dwight Eisenhower before the Eighth General Assembly in 1953 that would provide for cooperation among the nuclear states and other nations in the peaceful development and application of atomic energy. The Atoms for Peace Plan called for the establishment of an international agency under the United Nations to promote cooperation in the atomic field, and it urged nuclear states to divert fissionable materials from their weapons stockpiles by contributing them for peaceful research and development projects. *See also* INTERNATIONAL ATOMIC ENERGY AGENCY.

Attaché   A military, commercial, agricultural, or other official with diplomatic rank who is attached to an embassy or foreign mission.

Attitude   An interrelated, persisting set of beliefs that predisposes a person to respond in a particular way to some object or situation. Political attitudes relate to political issues, leaders, ideas, institutions, or events. An attitude is psychological in nature and may or may not be reflected in observable political actions. Although attitudes are more enduring than a momentary state of mind or mood, they tend to change over time and with changing circumstances, and they tend to be affected by diverse sets of motives. Groups of related attitudes and beliefs concerning the nature of man and society that posit an ideal political, economic, and social system constitute an *ideology*. *See also* DISPOSITIONS, PUBLIC OPINION.

Attitude Scaling   A technique for measuring and comparing attitudes, in which verbal statements, usually elicited by written or oral questionnaires, are arranged according to their intensity on a given attitudinal dimension. Such questionnaires typically offer the respondent choices ranging from "Agree Strongly" to "Disagree Strongly," or statements that range, for example, from extremely liberal to extremely conservative. Political scientists have also applied attitude scaling to legislative and judicial behavior by treating the votes of legislators or the decisions of judges as "yes" and "no" replies to attitudinal statements. *See also* GUTTMAN SCALE, QUESTIONNAIRE, SCALE, SEMANTIC DIFFERENTIAL.

Attorney General The head of the Department of Justice and a member of the President's Cabinet. He serves as legal advisor to the President and to all agencies of the executive branch and is the chief law-enforcement officer of the United States. The Attorney General directs the work of federal district attorneys, United States Marshals, and federal penal institutions. Criminal investigations and the conduct of lawsuits involving the United States fall under his charge. An attorney general is also found in each of the states, where he is frequently an elected official. He, too, serves as legal advisor and law-enforcement officer. *See also* DEPARTMENT OF JUSTICE, ATTORNEY GENERAL.

Attorney General (State) The chief legal officer of the state. The office of attorney general is elective in forty-two states. He serves as legal adviser to the governor and to state agencies, represents the state in legal proceedings, and may have general supervisory powers over local prosecuting attorneys. *See also* ATTORNEY GENERAL.

Attorney General's List A list of organizations, deemed to be subversive, compiled by the Attorney General of the United States. The Attorney General's list was drawn up as part of the loyalty program established by President Truman in 1947. Membership in any listed organization has been taken into account in determining the loyalty of governmental employees. In *Joint Anti-Fascist Refugee Committee v. McGrath*, 341 U.S. 123 (1951), the Supreme Court declared that an organization could not be listed without being given notice and an opportunity to be heard.

Auditor An official, usually an agent of a legislative body, who checks on the expenditure of appropriated funds to determine that they will be or have been spent for the purposes approved by the legislature in its appropriation acts. The federal auditor, the Comptroller General, is appointed by the President with the Senate's approval; state and local auditors are either appointed or elected by the voters. *See also* COMPTROLLER GENERAL.

Auditor, State, *see* State Auditor.

Australian Ballot A secret ballot prepared, distributed, and tabulated by government officials at public expense. Voting machines are mechanical adaptations of the Australian ballot.

Australia, New Zealand, United States Security Pact, *see* ANZUS Pact.

Autarky   National economic self-sufficiency. Since such a policy lessens dependence on other states, a state may adopt a policy of autarky in anticipation of war or to correct a serious deficit in its balance of payments. A government that adopts a policy of autarky will, typically, curtail imports, encourage the development of substitutes and synthetics to replace imports, and subsidize production for the domestic market.

Authoritarianism   Concentration of political authority in one man or a small group. Authoritarian regimes emphasize obedience by the people to their rulers and the absolute power of rulers over their subjects. Individual freedoms and rights are completely subordinated to the power of the state. *See also* ABSOLUTISM.

Authority   Influence derived from willing acceptance by others of one's right to make rules or issue commands and to expect compliance with them. Authority may be characterized as influence based on legitimacy: A has authority over B (and therefore influence) because B regards A's claims upon him as legitimate or rightful. The authority relationship is subjective, psychological, and moral in nature, as contrasted with forms of influence based on the use of material resources or physical coercion. Authority is also voluntaristic in operation—a person complies voluntarily because it is the right or appropriate thing to do. Authority in a political system means that people are willing to follow rules, accept results, and abide by the judgment of governing officials. The sources of authority in a political system, according to Max Weber's often cited typology, are tradition, law, and the charismatic qualities of political leaders. *See also* COERCION, INFLUENCE, LEGITIMACY, POWER.

Authorization   A legislative action that establishes a substantive program, specifies its general purpose and the means for achieving it, and indicates the approximate amount of money needed to implement the program. An authorization bill is ordinarily enacted before the appropriation bill covering the program is considered by Congress. State legislatures also require authorizations prior to the enactment of appropriation measures. *See also* APPROPRIATION.

Autocracy   Any system of government in which political power and authority are focused in a single individual. *See also* FASCISM, TOTALITARIANISM.

Auxiliary Agency   A governmental unit that services other governmental agencies. Typical auxiliary agencies include central purchasing, personnel, and accounting. They perform what is sometimes called housekeeping or technical services. *See also* CIVIL SERVICE COMMISSION, GENERAL SERVICES ADMINISTRATION.

Availability   The qualifications of a potential candidate which are analyzed by his party in making its selection of a nominee. A candidate whom the party believes has the qualities and background to make him a winner is "available."

Avery v. Midland County, Texas, *see* County Board.

Avulsion   The sudden divergence of a river from its original channel, as when a great flood cuts a new channel. When avulsion occurs, an international boundary, originally based on the thalweg, remains where it was before the sudden shift. Avulsion is thus distinguished from erosion and accretion which involve a gradual shifting of a boundary caused by slow changes in the thalweg. *See also* THALWEG.

Award   A judgment in the form of an indemnity or compensation of a monetary nature handed down against a state by an international arbitral tribunal, court, or claims commission. An award can be made in favor of an individual or his government. If the award is made to a government, its distribution becomes a matter of domestic jurisdiction. *See also* ARBITRATION, COMPROMIS.

Bad Tendency Rule   A test used by the Supreme Court to determine the permissible bounds of free speech. The bad tendency rule holds that speech or other First Amendment freedoms may be curtailed if there is a possibility that they might lead to some evil. Judges who hold this view feel that it is the legislature's duty, not the Court's, to determine what kind of speeches have a bad tendency. It is to be distinguished from the "clear and present danger" doctrine, which holds that an individual's liberty may not be curtailed unless it presents some imminent danger of illegal action. *See also Dennis v. United States*, CLEAR AND PRESENT DANGER RULE.

Baghdad Pact   An alliance to safeguard peace and security in the Middle East that served as the base for the development of the Central Treaty Organization. The Baghdad Pact was concluded in 1955 by Iraq and Turkey and acceded to by Britain, Pakistan, and Iran in the same year. All members of the Arab League and major Western powers concerned with the maintenance of security in the Middle East were invited to join the Pact, but none did. In 1959 the Baghdad Pact was renamed the Central Treaty Organization (CENTO) following the formal withdrawal of Iraq in the wake of its 1958 revolutionary change of government. *See also* ALLIANCE, CENTRAL TREATY ORGANIZATION.

Bail   Funds provided as assurance that a person will appear in court at the proper time. Bail is permitted after arrest and before trial, as well as after conviction pending appeal or sentencing. Bail is usually denied in capital cases. The Eighth Amendment to the Constitution forbids excessive bail; wide discretion is left the courts to determine the amount in relation to the severity of the offense, the record and resources of the defendant, and the likelihood of his reappearing in court. A defendant may appeal a denial of release on bail or the amount of the bail.

Baker v. Carr, 369 U.S. 186 (1962): Ruled in an epic Supreme Court decision that federal courts have jurisdiction over lawsuits challenging the apportionment of legislative districts, on the ground that malapportioned districts may violate the equal protection clause of the Fourteenth Amendment. The case had the effect of overturning *Colegrove v. Green*, 328 U.S. 549 (1946) in which the Court held that the issue of malapportioned legislative districts was a political question and relief should be sought through the political process. The *Baker* case involved a suit to compel the Tennessee legislature to redistrict state legislative districts on a population basis, a provision of the Tennessee Constitution that the legislature had ignored for over sixty years. *See also* REDISTRICTING.

Balance of Payments   The net balance between total income and expenditures of a nation in its business and trade relations with the rest of the world. A balance of payments includes all debit and credit monetary transactions, such as imports and exports of goods, tourist expenditures, investments, and income from investments. *See also* ECONOMIC NATIONALISM.

Balance of Power   A system of power alignments in which peace and security may be maintained through an equilibrium of power between the rival blocs. States participating in a balance of power system enter into alliances with friendly states in attempts to protect and enhance their power positions. *See also* ALLIANCE.

Balance of Terror   The equilibrium of power among nuclear states stemming from common fear of annihilation in a nuclear war. The balance of terror between the United States and the Soviet Union rests on the mutual understanding that each side possesses various types of delivery systems armed with massively destructive power that cannot be prevented by defensive actions from wreaking mass destruction upon the other's population centers. The knowledge that a surprise first strike could not destroy the other's protected and widely dispersed retaliatory capability has reinforced the deterrence created by the balance of terror. The balance of terror standoff tends to be strengthened rather than altered by the efforts of both sides to produce deadlier weapons and more dependable delivery systems. *See also* BALANCE OF POWER, DETERRENCE.

Balance of Trade   A nation's annual net trade surplus or deficit, based on the difference in the value of its total imports and exports. The balance of trade is to be distinguished from the balance of payments; the trade balance is only one part of the many debits and credits that comprise a nation's balance of payments. In a carryover from the days of mercantilism, a surplus of exports over imports is often called a "favorable"—and imports over exports an "unfavorable"—balance of trade. *See also* BALANCE OF PAYMENTS.

Balancing Doctrine   A concept used by judges to weigh the competing interests or values in a case. Typically this involves striking a balance between the interests that society seeks to preserve and the rights of the individual. *See also* POLICE POWER.

Baldwin v. New York, *see* Jury.

Ballot, Office-Block, *see* Office-Block Ballot.

Ballot, Party-Column, *see* Party-Column Ballot.

Bandwagon Effect   A tendency in politics for some individuals to associate themselves with a cause, party, or candidate that they believe will prevail. The bandwagon effect is identified with emotional or nonrational behavior, rather than with rational calculation that one's interests will be served by joining forces with the expected winner. In elections, for example, polls published prior to election day may change the outcome because some voters affected by the "herd instinct" seek to "climb aboard the bandwagon" of the candidate they expect to win. *See also* VOTING BEHAVIOR.

Banking Systems   The national and state banking systems, which exist side by side in the United States. Congress was not granted the specific power to charter banks, but the power is implied from granted powers that can best be carried on through banks, such as the borrowing and currency powers. Both national and state chartered banks are privately owned financial institutions, which are regulated and have their accounts audited by the respective chartering government. National banks, chartered by the national government since 1863, are supervised by the Comptroller of the Currency in the Treasury Department, and are required to join the Federal Reserve System. Most state banks accept Federal Reserve membership and thereby come under a measure of national as well as state regulation. The citizen can usually distinguish between a national and state chartered bank by their names, such as First National Bank or Industrial State Bank. *See also* FEDERAL RESERVE SYSTEM.

Bankruptcy   A procedure for discharging unpaid obligations through a court action that frees the individual from further liability for his debts. Bankruptcy proceedings may be initiated either by the insolvent debtor (voluntary bankruptcy) or by a required number of his creditors (involuntary bankruptcy). Such cases are usually handled by federal district courts under equity jurisdiction. The court appoints an officer who sells the bankrupt's assets and pays his creditors on a prorated basis.

Barron v. Baltimore, 7 Peters 243 (1833): Held that the Bill of Rights limits only the national government and not the state governments.

Barter   An agreement between governments for the exchange of goods. Under a barter agreement, quantities of goods are exchanged at an agreed ratio without any monetary transactions. Barter arrangements, typically, are entered into by nations to overcome foreign exchange problems that hinder trade between them. *See also* BILATERAL TRADE.

Bartkus v. Illinois, 355 U.S. 281 (1958): Denied a claim of double jeopardy appealed from a conviction in a state court for bank robbery following acquittal by a federal court for the same bank robbery. *See also* DOUBLE JEOPARDY.

Baruch Plan A proposal for atomic control and disarmament submitted by the United States to the United Nations Atomic Energy Commission in 1946. Based on the recommendations of a special Board of Consultants (Acheson-Lilienthal Report), the plan was presented by elder statesman Bernard Baruch as the official proposal by the United States to give up its monopoly of atomic weapons under an international security system. Major points incorporated in the Baruch Plan included: (1) establishing an International Atomic Development Authority to control all phases of the development and use of nuclear energy; (2) granting unlimited inspection powers to the Authority to safeguard against violations; (3) applying stiff penalties for any violations related to the use of fissionable materials for weapons development; (4) terminating the manufacture of atomic weapons and destroying all existing stockpiles after the Authority had established control; and (5) changing the voting system in the Security Council so that the veto power could not be used to prevent the punishment of violators.

Battle Act (Mutual Defense Assistance Control Act of 1951) An act to prohibit trade with Communist countries in strategic goods and to deny American foreign aid to any nation that carried on such trade. The President is empowered to make exceptions if cutting off foreign aid would be contrary to American interests.

Behavioralism An approach that emphasizes the application of scientific methods and perspectives to the study of politics and government. Behavioralism focuses on the actual behavior of individuals and groups rather than their formal roles or the institutions and structures within which they function. Although consensus on the exact outlines of behavioralism is lacking, there is wide agreement on some basics. Behavioralists, for example, try to be rigorous and systematic in their research, and seek precision by the quantification and measurement of data. They attempt to discover uniformities or regularities in political behavior through formulation and testing of empirical hypotheses. Behavioralism sees an essential relationship between theory and empirical research. Theory should be verifiable by reference to actual behavior, and the search for facts should be guided by theory. Behavioralism is also concerned with the integration of knowledge about human behavior, and it posits a close working relationship with other disciplines, especially other social sciences. Behavioralism is to be distinguished from *behaviorism*, which is a formal school of psychology instituted by John B. Watson. The latter embodies a theoretical view that only overt data in the form of stimuli and responses are meaningful for analysis, whereas mental factors such as attitudes, opinions, and beliefs are meaningless. *See also* POSTBEHAVIORALISM, SCIENTIFIC METHOD, TRADITIONAL APPROACH.

Behavioral Science, *see* Social Science.

Behaviorism, *see* Behavioralism.

Behavior Pattern Any regular or recurring form of human activity. Political behavior patterns may range from those based on largely internal, psychological responses (thought, perception, judgment, attitude, opinion, belief) to overt, observable physical responses (voting, protesting, lobbying, caucusing, campaigning). *See also* POLITICAL BEHAVIOR.

Behavior, Political, *see* Political Behavior.

Belligerency   The recognition by foreign states that a condition of civil war exists within a state. The determination of the point at which an armed rebellion is accorded the legal status of belligerency is a political, not a legal, question. The effect of such recognition is to confer on the insurgents a de facto international status with regard to the rights and duties of legal warfare. Recognition of belligerency also acknowledges that the antigovernment forces have a right to govern those areas of the state which are under their de facto control. *See also* INSURGENCY, CIVIL WAR.

Benefit Theory   The belief that individuals should be taxed in proportion to the benefits they derive from governmental services. Taxes based on the benefit theory are often earmarked for special purposes, thus reducing the flexibility of government policy makers. *See also* EARMARKING, SPECIAL ASSESSMENT.

Benelux   A customs union agreement established by Belgium, Luxembourg, and The Netherlands to eliminate trade barriers, establish a single external tariff, and foster economic union among the three. The agreement, which was signed in London during World War II and entered into effect on January 1, 1948, abolished most internal tariffs and established a common external tariff. A treaty to harmonize the fiscal and monetary policies of the three by establishing an economic union came into force in 1960. Benelux countries have also agreed to negotiate and enter into economic and trade treaties and arrangements as a unit, with no separate national treaties to be concluded. Benelux organization includes a Conference of Cabinet Ministers, a Council for Economic Union, an Administrative Council on Customs Duties, an Administrative Council to provide for a common foreign economic policy toward other states, and a secretariat located at Benelux headquarters in Brussels. *See also* CUSTOMS UNION.

Benton v. Maryland, *see* Double Jeopardy.

Berger v. New York, 388 U.S. 41 (1967): A decision in which the Supreme Court brought wiretapping within the protection of the Fourth Amendment search and seizure provisions. The Court declared unconstitutional a New York law which authorized a judge to issue an eavesdrop order but which did not require indication of any specific offense, conversation, or special circumstance. *See also* WIRETAPPING.

Berlin Blockade, *see* Blockade.

Betts v. Brady, *see Gideon v. Wainwright.*

Biased Sample   Selection for survey purposes of a slice or sample of a population that is not drawn randomly and does not accurately represent the population as a whole. A biased sample is slanted toward the inclusion of some members of the group and against the inclusion of others, with the result that the finding obtained will produce distortion when applied to the group. Statistical tests may be applied to determine the degree of randomness achieved. *See also* RANDOM, SAMPLING.

Bicameralism   The principle of a two-house legislature, in contrast to unicameralism, or a legislature based on one house. At the Philadelphia convention of 1787, the Founding Fathers adopted a compromise solution for representation in Congress. This "Connecticut Compromise" established a balanced bicameral legislature with one house (House of Representatives) based on population and the second (Senate) based on equality of states. In the states, the Nebraska legislature is the only unicameral legislature. In a bicameral legislature, all bills must pass both houses before becoming law. *See also* UNICAMERALISM, CONNECTICUT COMPROMISE, *Reynolds v. Sims*.

Biennial Session   A regular meeting of a legislature held every two years. Thirty-one state legislatures convene in regular session once every two years, while nineteen meet annually. In biennial session states, typically, legislatures hold their sessions in the odd-numbered years. *See also* SESSION.

Bilateral Aid, *see* Foreign Aid.

Bilateral Security Pact   A treaty between two nations pledging military support for each other in case of an attack by a third state. Bilateral security pacts may provide for immediate and unconditional assistance in case of an attack upon one of the parties, or they may merely call for consultation between the parties. They also may apply against any third state that attacks either party, or they may be limited in their application to attacks launched by specific states named in the pact. *See also* ALLIANCE, JAPANESE-AMERICAN SECURITY TREATY.

Bilateral Trade   An understanding between two states to foster cooperation in trade and related economic matters. A bilateral economic agreement may take the form of a clearing arrangement in which payments for imports and exports are paid through a single central bank account, or a payments agreement that includes all financial transactions between the two countries. In its simplest form, a bilateral agreement may provide for a barter arrangement whereby two countries exchange goods in specified amounts with no payments in foreign exchange. The most common use of economic bilateralism is in the conclusion of trade agreements providing for a mutual reduction in tariffs or other trade barriers. *See also* BARTER.

Bill   A proposed law. Most legislative proposals before Congress are in the form of bills. Members of the House officially "introduce" bills by dropping them into a "hopper"; in the Senate, bills are introduced by verbal announcement. All bills introduced during a two-year congressional term are designated "HR" in the House and "S" in the Senate, with consecutive numbers assigned in the order in which they are introduced in each chamber. Each bill must have three readings in each house, be approved by a majority vote in each house, and, normally, be signed by the President to become law. A bill passed in one house is called an "engrossed bill," and the final authoritative copy of a bill passed by both houses and signed by their presiding officers is called an "enrolled bill." Public bills deal with matters of general concern and may become public laws. Private bills are concerned with individual matters and become private laws if approved. *See also* PRIVATE BILL, READINGS.

Bill Drafting   The process of formulating legislative proposals. Congress and many state legislatures have staff agencies to aid members in this process. In Congress, members seeking assistance in study and research have access to a Congressional Research Service in the Library of Congress. Aid in drawing up bills is supplied by legislative counsel. *See also* CONGRESSIONAL RESEARCH SERVICE.

Bill of Attainder   A legislative act that declares the guilt of an individual and metes out punishment without a judicial trial. The state legislatures and Congress are forbidden to pass such acts by Article I, sections 9 and 10 of the Constitution. *See also* United States v. Lovett.

Bill of Rights   The first ten amendments to the United States Constitution. Bills of rights, sometimes called declarations of rights, are also found in all state constitutions. They contain a listing of the rights a person enjoys that cannot be infringed upon by the government. Many important rights, such as trial by jury and the guarantee of habeas corpus, are stated in other parts of the United States Constitution. All bills of rights contain provisions designed to protect the freedom of expression, the rights of property, and the rights of persons accused of crime.

Bipartisanship   Close cooperation between the two major American political parties in dealing with foreign problems. Bipartisanship usually takes the form of frequent consultations between the leaders of both parties in Congress, and between these leaders and the President. During time of war or threat of war, when bipartisanship typically comes into vogue, the President may appoint members of the opposition party to key Cabinet posts.

Bipolarity   A rigid balance-of-power system in which decisive power is polarized in two rival power centers. Bipolarity is the converse of polycentrism, which describes the development of a number of power centers offering greater flexibility for keeping the balance system in equilibrium. The bipolar model tends to evolve when, because of security, ideological, or political dependence, states are forced to commit themselves and group together within the power configuration dominated by either of the single great powers. *See also* BALANCE OF POWER, POLYCENTRISM.

Birth Control, *see* Population Control.

Bivariate Analysis, *see* Variable.

Bloc   Members of a legislative body, not necessarily of the same party, who have common aims and goals. Some examples include the "farm bloc," "high tariff bloc," "silver bloc," and the "anti-civil rights bloc." *See also* FARM BLOC.

Blockade   A naval action aimed at preventing supplies from reaching an enemy. A blockade may be directed against troops in the field or at denying resources and food to an entire civilian population. A pacific blockade, considered not an act of war but a reprisal for a legal wrong, may be levied by one state on another during peacetime to deny the latter's ships but not those of other nations access to the blockaded nation's ports. A land "blockade" to deny transit across a nation's territory may also be established during peacetime. In the case of the Berlin Blockade, for example, ground access across East Germany to the beleaguered city of Berlin was denied to Allied forces, necessitating an airlift. Blockade enforcement under international law permits confiscation of ships and cargoes of belligerent and neutral registry that are seized while in the act of attempting to run the blockade. *See also* MEASURES SHORT OF WAR.

Blue Laws   Laws on the books of many states that prohibit certain business operations on Sunday. Blue laws often make exceptions for amusements or essential activities and for persons who observe a sabbath day other than Sunday.

Blue Sky Laws   State laws to protect investors in securities from misrepresentation and outright fraud. Blue sky laws commonly require that companies selling securities be certified by a state agency and furnish detailed information concerning their financial position.

Board   A group of persons, usually three or more, who are charged with responsibility for directing a particular governmental function. The term "commission" is frequently used interchangeably with board.

Board of Aldermen, *see* Aldermen.

Board of Commissioners, *see* County Board.

Board of Education   The state or local governing body for public education. State boards of education establish statewide educational and teacher certification standards, determine curricula, and control state educational funds. Most state boards are appointed by the governor; others are elected by the people or appointed by the state legislature. Each state board of education works closely with a state superintendent of schools who is in many cases elected by the people, although the trend is toward appointment by the board. Local school boards are chosen by popular vote in school districts in most states, with a few appointed by the city council. The local school board determines policy but leaves much responsibility in the hands of a school superintendent whom they appoint. Local school boards determine teacher salaries, curricula, and building needs. *See also* SCHOOL DISTRICT.

Board of Governors, Federal Reserve System   A board composed of seven members that determines general monetary and credit policies and oversees the operations of the twelve district Federal Reserve banks and member banks throughout the country. Board members are appointed for fourteen-year terms by the President with the Senate's confirmation, with consideration given to geographical and major business interests in the selection process. The Board is, by statute and practice, independent of the President. *See also* FEDERAL RESERVE SYSTEM.

Board of Immigration Appeals   A board appointed by the Attorney General to hear appeals from decisions of the Immigration and Naturalization Service relative to the exclusion or deportation of aliens. *See also* DEPORTATION.

Board of Review   Public officials charged with the duty of reviewing individual tax assessments on property. The review function is to be distinguished from "equalization," which is the comparison and adjustment of assessments between entire tax-imposing units. The board of review may be elected or composed of local government officials serving ex officio. *See also* ASSESSED VALUATION, ASSESSOR, PROPERTY TAX.

Board of Supervisors, *see* County Board.

Bolling v. Sharpe, 347 U.S. 497 (1954): Declared, in one of the school segregation cases, that segregation in the public schools of the District of Columbia violated the due process clause of the Fifth Amendment. *See also* EQUAL PROTECTION.

Bond   A certificate of indebtedness issued by a borrower to a lender as a legal promise to repay the principal of the loan plus accrued interest. Bonds are issued by private corporations, by all levels of government, and by many governmental agencies and corporations. Most bonds have limited negotiability in the security markets. *See also* BORROWING POWER.

Bonn Constitution   The Basic Law of the Federal Republic of Germany. In 1948, the Western occupation powers, concerned with the reconstruction of the German economy and its role in European recovery, agreed to self-government for West Germany. The Bonn constitution was drafted by a Parliamentary Council called by the Allied military governors and the minister presidents of the eleven German states in the American, British, and French occupation zones. The sixty-five delegates chosen by the states were apportioned among the Christian Democratic, Social Democratic, Free Democratic, Centrist, German, and Communist parties according to party strength. Representatives from Berlin were also invited. The Basic Law was approved by the allies and ratified by the states in 1949. The document shows strong influences from the post-World War I, pre-Hitler Constitution of the Weimar Republic. At Allied insistence, however, the highly organized, detailed, and lengthy document created a federal system rather than the centralized government desired by the delegates. Its main features include a bicameral legislature with the major legislative power located in the Bundestag or lower house, a strong chancellorship (prime minister), and a weak presidency. The capital was established at Bonn until reunification of the divided state makes possible a return to Berlin. *See also* CONSTITUTION.

Bonneville Power Administration, *see* Department of the Interior.

Borough   A municipal corporation, generally smaller than a city. Boroughs are found mainly in Pennsylvania, Connecticut, and New Jersey, and resemble villages or towns of other states. Borough is also the named assigned to major local government divisions in Alaska, comparable to counties. The city of New York is divided into five boroughs: Manhattan, Brooklyn, Queens, Bronx, and Richmond.

Borrowing Power   The authority of a government to finance budget deficits that result when expenditures exceed income. The Constitution (Art. I, sec. 8) provides Congress with full borrowing power, free from restrictions. Most state constitutions, however, severely limit the authority of state governments to incur indebtedness, permitting state borrowing only when authorized by constitutional amendment or by a vote of the people. Local units of government are restricted by state constitutional or statutory limitations on their borrowing power. *See also* DEBT LIMIT, PUBLIC DEBT.

Boss   A political leader who dominates a highly disciplined state or local party organization that tends to monopolize power in its area. Political bosses retain power through patronage disposition, control over nominations, use of "honest" and dishonest graft, and manipulation of voting and elections. Sometimes the term "boss" is used to discredit the successful leader of an opposing party. *See also* POLITICAL MACHINE.

Boundaries   The limits within which a state exercises territorial jurisdiction. Boundaries, as delimitations of jurisdiction, relate not only to a specific portion of the earth's surface but to territorial waters, airspace, and subsurface resources as well. Boundaries may be fixed by negotiation, arbitration, adjudication, plebiscite, allocation by some international body, such as the United Nations, and cession through purchase or war. Various types of, and reasons for, particular boundaries include: (1) natural separators, as in the case of rivers and mountains; (2) cultural differences, such as the communal distinctions that served as the basis for drawing the boundaries between India and Pakistan; (3) historical and political considerations, as in the case of many of the new African states, whose boundaries were originally drawn by European colonial powers; and (4) those established by military equilibrium, as between Israel and her Arab neighbors, or between North and South Korea.

Bourgeois Class, *see* Class Struggle.

Boycott (International)   refusal to buy products from a particular country or group of countries. A boycott may be government-sponsored or may be initiated by private groups which seek to influence consumers against making purchases of goods from the boycotted nation. Boycotts are usually aimed at changing the behavior of decision makers in the states at which they are directed. *See also* EMBARGO.

Boycott (Labor)   An economic weapon used by labor to curtail the purchase of products from an employer. Two types of boycotts, primary and secondary, may be distinguished. A primary boycott involves withdrawal of patronage, and the urging of others to withdraw their patronage, from an employer with whom a union is having a labor dispute. A secondary boycott involves a refusal to deal with or patronize anyone who deals with the employer with whom there is a dispute. Secondary boycotts are outlawed by the Taft-Hartley Act of 1947 and, with certain exceptions, by the Landrum-Griffin Act of 1959. Most states also outlaw secondary boycotts.

Brainwashing   A psychological technique for reorienting the individual's thinking so that it will conform to a predetermined mode. The term "brainwashing" is derived from the Chinese colloquialism of *hsi nao* (wash-brain) and relates to the Communist goal of "thought reform." Brainwashing is carried out by the strategy of first obtaining a confession of wrongdoing, followed by a process of reeducation. The means used to effect brainwashing upon an individual include a combination of extremely harsh and lenient treatment, with an interspersing of physical and psychological punishments and rewards aimed at breaking traditional patterns of thought and instituting new ones. *See also* PSYCHOLOGICAL WARFARE.

Bretton Woods Conference   The United Nations Monetary and Financial Conference that drafted the Articles of Agreement for the International Bank for Reconstruction and Development (IBRD) and the International Monetary Fund (IMF). Called at the initiative of President Franklin Roosevelt, the conference met at Bretton Woods, New Hampshire, July 1–22, 1944, with forty-four nations represented. *See also* INTERNA-TIONAL BANK FOR RECONSTRUCTION AND DEVELOPMENT, INTERNATIONAL MONETARY FUND.

Bricker Amendment   A proposed amendment to the United States Constitution, introduced in Congress by Senator John Bricker of Ohio in 1953 and in 1954. The proposed Bricker amendment was designed to strengthen the role of Congress in treaty making, limit the President's power to conclude executive agreements, and insure the primacy of the Constitution over the provisions of any treaty. The proposal was killed when it failed by one vote to secure the necessary two-thirds majority in the Senate. *See also* MISSOURI CASE.

Brief   A document prepared by an attorney for presentation to a court, containing arguments and data in support of a case. The brief will embody points of law, precedents, and, in a case involving major social issues, relevant economic, sociological, and other scientific evidence. Despite its connotation, a brief may be quite lengthy.

British Commonwealth of Nations, *see* Commonwealth of Nations.

British Political System, *see* Cabinet Government, Conservative Party, Constitution, Crown, Foreign Secretary, Govenor-General, House of Commons, House of Lords, Labour Party, Liberal Party, Monarch, Parliament, Party Government, Party System, Prime Minister, Role of Opposition, Royal Commission.

Brown v. Board of Education of Topeka, 347 U.S. 483 (1954); 349 U.S. 294 (1955): Established in a major decision that segregation of the races in public schools violates the equal protection clause of the Fourteenth Amendment. The Supreme Court in 1954 overruled the "separate but equal" doctrine that had been in effect since 1896, noting that "Separate educational facilities are inherently unequal." In 1955, the Court ordered desegregation to proceed "with all deliberate speed," leaving it to the federal district courts to determine implementations of the ruling in specific cases brought before them. *See also* SEGREGATION.

Brown v. Maryland, 12 Wheaton 419 (1827): Established the "original package" doctrine, which holds that the authority of Congress over foreign commerce does not end until the merchandise arrives at its ultimate destination, the contents of the package are sold or removed for the purpose of selling, and they become commingled with the general property of a state. The case invalidated a law of Maryland that had required importers of foreign goods to obtain a license before being permitted to sell them. *See also* ORIGINAL PACKAGE DOCTRINE.

Brussels Pact, *see* Western European Union.

Budget   An estimate of the receipts and expenditures needed by government to carry out its program in some future period, usually a fiscal year. The President is responsible for formulating the national budget under the Budget and Accounting Act of 1921, and governors of most states likewise operate under an "executive budget" system. The budget process begins with the lengthy and detailed process of preparing estimates, followed by a central review in which budget officers hold hearings during which agency officials defend their estimates. Next, the budget is approved by the chief executive and submitted to the legislative body in a "budget message." After study and the holding of hearings by appropriations committees, the budget is enacted as an appropriation act. This is followed by budget execution, the actual spending of the money during the fiscal period by executive officials. The final step is a post-audit check on the validity of expenditures. Some states and cities use a separate capital budget for financing major public works projects, which are often paid for on a long-term bonding or self-liquidating basis. *See also* PERFORMANCE BUDGET, BUDGET AND ACCOUNTING ACT, OFFICE OF MANAGEMENT AND BUDGET.

Budget and Accounting Act of 1921   A law that established a national budget system and created the Bureau of the Budget (now the Office of Management and Budget), and the General Accounting Office. It provides for the formulation of an annual executive budget by the Bureau under direction of the President, and for the auditing of all government expenditures by the General Accounting Office under the direction of the Comptroller General as an agent of Congress. *See also* OFFICE OF MANAGEMENT AND BUDGET, GENERAL ACCOUNTING OFFICE.

Budget Bureau, *see* Office of Management and Budget.

Budget Message The receipt and expenditure estimates recommended by the President to the Congress for the next fiscal year. In January of each legislative session, the President sends his annual budget message to Congress as required by the Budget and Accounting Act of 1921. Unlike the State of the Union message, which precedes it, the budget message is not usually delivered in person by the President but is sent to Congress in writing to be read to each chamber by its clerk. Many governors, especially of those states that have undergone recent reorganization, also deliver or send to the legislature annual or biennial budget messages. *See also* BUDGET AND ACCOUNTING ACT OF 1921.

Budget, United Nations, *see* United Nations Finance.

Buffer States Weak states, located between or on the borders of strong states, that serve the security interests of the latter. Buffer states often exist only at the sufferance of their more powerful neighbors, who desire a "crush zone" between themselves and their rivals.

Bundesrat (Federal Council) The upper chamber of the West German parliament. The Bundesrat is composed of forty-one voting members and four nonvoting members from Berlin. Each German state *(Land)* appoints a delegation composed of state officials. Representation is weighted but is not fully proportional to population. Each state has a minimum of three delegates, those with a population over 2 million have four, and those over 6 million receive five. Delegations are bound by the instructions of their state governments and their votes are cast *en bloc.* The political situation at the local governmental level is reflected in the Bundesrat at the national level in that the party process in the states produces the cabinets and coalitions which instruct the delegations to the upper house. Standing committees of the Bundesrat must scrutinize all government bills for their possible effects on the *Länder* before the government submits them to the Bundestag (lower house). This serves as a check on the central government in the German federal system. The Bundesrat can only delay final passage of ordinary legislation by the Bundestag. On financial measures and constitutional amendments, its power is equal to that of the lower house in that passage requires a two-thirds majority in each chamber.

Bundestag (Federal Diet) The lower and legislatively more powerful chamber of the bicameral West German parliament. The Bundestag is composed of approximately five hundred voting members apportioned on the basis of population among the states of the federal union. There are also about twenty representatives from Berlin, who participate in virtually all legislative activity except voting in plenary sessions. In each voting district approximately half of the seats are filled by direct election and the rest by a system of proportional representation. The basic Law specifies that candidates must be at least twenty-five years old, that they are to be chosen in "universal, direct, free, equal and secret elections," that they represent the entire people, and that they cannot be "bound by orders and instructions and are subject only to their own conscience." The chamber is arranged in the French manner of a political spectrum from Left to Right and is dominated by moderate parties, particularly the Christian Democratic Union and the Social Democratic Party. The life of a Bundestag is four years unless the Chancellor demands and fails to receive a vote of confidence. In that event the national President, on the proposal of the Chancellor, can dissolve the chamber so that a general election can establish the basis for creating a new government. Although floor debate may be more significant than in the United States, detailed legislative activity and necessary compromise is worked out in several dozen standing committees. Membership ranges between fifteen and thirty, and the party groups *(Fraktionen)* in the Bundestag are represented on the committees in proportion to their strength in that house. The work of the chamber is largely organized and controlled by a twenty-man steering committee, the Council of Elders, composed of the chamber president and vice presidents and the leaders of the parliamentary party groups. The Council advises the presiding officer, proposes the calendar, chooses committee chairmen, and allots time for debate. Its function is somewhat analogous to that of the Rules Committee in the U.S. House of Representatives. Once the house has elected the Chancellor, its power to control him is strictly limited. Ultimately he can be brought down, but only by a procedure called the "constructive vote." That is, when the Bundestag votes to request the national President to dismiss the Chancellor, it must simultaneously elect his successor so as to avoid the dangers of executive instability and recurrent Cabinet crises.

Bureau   A major working unit of a department or agency. Bureaus are generally assigned specific functions and their heads are responsible to the head of the entire department. Well-known examples include the Federal Bureau of Investigation (FBI) in the Department of Justice and the Census Bureau in the Department of Commerce. Bureaus are usually subdivided into various divisions, branches, or sections, each with responsibility for specialized activities.

Bureaucracy   Any administrative system, especially of governmental agencies, that carries out policy on a day-to-day basis, that uses standardized procedures, and that is based on a specialization of duties. Bureaucracy also connotes a system wherein excessive growth of administrative agencies is accompanied by concentration of power in administrative officials, excessive red tape, dedication to routine, and resistance to change. The term "the bureaucracy," is often used simply to designate the administrative or executive branch of government.

Bureau of Indian Affairs, *see* Department of the Interior.

Bureau of Intelligence and Research (I & R), *see* Intelligence (United States).

Bureau of Land Management, *see* Department of the Interior.

Bureau of Mines, *see* Department of the Interior.

Bureau of Outdoor Recreation, *see* Department of the Interior.

Bureau of Reclamation, *see* Department of the˙Interior.

Bureau of Security and Consular Affairs   The part of the State Department that supervises the issuance of passports and visas. The Bureau was established by the Immigration and Nationality Act of 1952 and, under its supervision, consular agents abroad determine whether foreigners will be permitted to enter the United States. *See also* PASSPORT, VISA.

Bureau of the Budget, *see* Office of Management and Budget.

Business Affected with a Public Interest   Any privately owned and operated selling or service activity that, as a matter of public policy, has been brought under the regulatory power of government. Businesses affected with a public interest, such as public utilities, are regulated by government boards and commissions in regard to their services and rates. *See also* PUBLIC UTILITY, *Munn v. Illinois.*

Business and Professional Organizations   Groups organized to promote the interests of business and the professions. The leading nationwide organizations of businessmen are the Chamber of Commerce of the United States and the National Association of Manufacturers (NAM). The Chamber is a federation of more than 3000 local chambers of commerce representing almost three million businessmen. The NAM represents about 20,000 large industrial firms. Another powerful business organization, the Business Council, is composed of the chief executives of the largest American corporations and functions as an unofficial adviser to national policy makers. In addition, businessmen are organized according to their trade or industry interests in numerous national and local trade associations. Leading professional associations include the American Medical Association (AMA), the American Bar Association (ABA), and the National Education Association (NEA). *See also* PRESSURE GROUP.

Business Council, *see* Business and Professional Organizations.

Business Cycles   The rhythmic fluctuation of a free economy as changes occur in business activity. Business cycles, typically, involve movements from prosperity to recession or depression, followed by economic recovery and the completion of the cycle by a return to the previous high point of economic activity. A new cycle then begins. *See also* DEPRESSION, FISCAL POLICY, MONETARY POLICY.

Cabinet (Britain)   That group of officials charged with running the state: hence, the government of Britain. Varying in size from approximately fifteen to twenty of the most important ministers, the Cabinet is chosen by the Prime Minister from among the top political leaders in the majority party in the House of Commons. Thus, a Cabinet Minister must be a member of Parliament (MP). Members of the House of Lords are rarely appointed to Cabinet posts because they cannot defend government policies before the Commons. A typical cabinet includes the Chancellor of the Exchequer (Treasury), Foreign and Home Secretaries, Lord Chancellor, and the Ministers of Defense, Employment, Agriculture, Fisheries, and Food. Men of proven administrative ability or national political importance may be given unspecified Cabinet posts as Ministers Without Portfolio and charged with various temporary but important assignments by the Prime Minister. A shadow cabinet, or government in waiting, leads the opposition party in its challenge to government policies and programs.

Cabinet (France)   The ministers constitutionally charged with determination and direction of national policy, execution of the laws, operation of the government, and responsibility for national defense in the Fifth French Republic. The President of the Republic selects the Premier (prime minister), who in turn suggests the ministerial appointments to be made by the President. The government thus created is technically responsible to the National Assembly. Under Articles 49 and 50 of the Constitution, however, the power of the legislature to control the life of the government through votes of confidence or censure is seriously restricted. *See also* CABINET GOVERNMENT (BRITAIN).

Cabinet (Germany)   The institution that together with the chancellor constitutes the government of the Federal Republic. The Cabinet is composed of approximately twenty ministers, most selected by the Chancellor from his own party. The remaining appointments are the result of hard bargaining between the Chancellor and the leaders of other parties when their support is required to form a coalition. The Cabinet meets in frequent formal executive sessions and the agenda is not publicized. Meetings are attended by ministers, State Secretaries (the highest level civil servant in each ministry whose role corresponds to that of the British Permanent Secretary), the head of the Office of the Federal President, the Chancellor's personal aide, the head of the Press and Information Office, the Secretary of the Cabinet, and any experts invited to a particular meeting. Only ministers vote and a quorum of one half of the ministers is necessary to do business. The Chancellor conducts Cabinet meetings according to established rules for formalizing government policies and for considering the problems of the individual ministries. Ministers may introduce bills in the Bundestag and about three fourths of all legislation originates in the ministries. Although ministers are expected to support government policies in public, some have not always done so, and a few have suffered public rebuke by the Chancellor. The Chancellor and most ministers are elected members of the Bundestag and are subject to questioning by members of that house.

Cabinet Government (Britain) A system based on a fusion of executive and legislative powers in the hands of a cabinet operating in conjunction with the principle of ultimate parliamentary supremacy. Selected from among the leaders of the majority party, the Cabinet has collective responsibility for (1) establishing and implementing domestic and foreign policy; (2) coordinating the operations of government agencies; (3) dealing with emergency situations; and (4) establishing long-range policy objectives. Cabinet-approved measures are introduced and defended in the House of Commons by the appropriate minister. Passage is to be expected because the Cabinet leads the party which controls the House. Since any division within the Cabinet would be seized upon by the opposition, Cabinet unity and collective responsibility for all decisions are essential to the success of the system. A dissenter would therefore have to resign from the Cabinet. Defeat in Commons on a major issue would require the resignation of the entire Cabinet. In this event, the Monarch would request the Leader of the Opposition to form a new government, or, more likely, the Prime Minister could ask the Monarch to dissolve Parliament. In the latter case, a general election would decide whether the Prime Minister was to be returned to power or whether his opposite number in Her Majesty's loyal opposition would become Prime Minister and form a new government.

Cabinet (United States) An advisory group selected by the President to aid him in making decisions. President Washington instituted the Cabinet idea when he began regularly to call together the heads of the four executive departments and the Vice President to consult on matters of policy. The Cabinet remains an informal group, with its membership determined by tradition and presidential discretion. By custom, the heads of the major departments (State; Treasury; Defense; Justice; Interior; Agriculture; Commerce; Labor; Health, Education, and Welfare; Housing and Urban Development; and Transportation) are members of the Cabinet, and the President may also invite the Vice President and other officials to sit in on Cabinet meetings.

Calendar An agenda or list that contains the names of bills or resolutions to be considered before committees or in either chamber of the legislature. When a standing committee of the House of Representatives reports out a bill it is placed on one of the five possible calendars: *Consent* (noncontroversial bills), *Discharge* (discharge petitions), *House* (nonfiscal public bills), *Private* (private bills), and *Union* (appropriation and revenue bills). In the Senate, all bills reported out go on a single calendar, although nonlegislative matters (treaties and confirmations) are placed on the *Executive* calendar.

Calendar Wednesday A procedure of the House of Representatives whereby Wednesdays may be used to call the roll of the standing committees for the purpose of bringing up any of their bills for consideration from the House or the Union Calendars. General debate on each bill called up in this way is limited to two hours. Calendar Wednesday is not observed during the last two weeks of a session and, by a two-thirds vote, may be suspended any Wednesday, which usually is the case. *See also* CALENDAR.

Calvo Clause   A clause sometimes inserted by Latin American governments in public contracts with aliens. The Calvo clause requires that, in case of differences arising under the contract, the alien party will rely solely on local remedies and will not appeal to his government for diplomatic interposition on his behalf. International arbitral tribunals and mixed claims commissions have split in their decisions as to whether, under international law, the inclusion of the clause in such a contract can prevent the foreign government from entering the dispute. The clause is named after Carlos Calvo, the Argentine jurist who wrote extensively on the subject. *See also* DRAGO DOCTRINE.

Campaign   The competitive effort of rival candidates for public office to win support of the voters in the period preceding an election. Candidates use diverse means for reaching the voters—television, radio, telephone, the mails, door-to-door solicitation, speeches, coffee hours, factory visits—and various kinds of propaganda appeals aimed at influencing the thinking, emotions, and, ultimately, the voting actions of the public. *See also* PROPAGANDA.

Candidacy, *see* Filing

Cantwell v. Connecticut, *see* Jehovah's Witnesses Cases.

Canvassing Board   An official body, usually bipartisan, that tabulates the election returns and certifies the election of the winners. When the polls close on election day, the returns from each precinct are forwarded to city and county canvassing boards. These consolidate the returns and forward them to the state canvassing authority, which, usually in a few days, certifies the election of the winners. The local group is the county board of supervisors or county board of election. The state canvassing board consists of several ex officio members of the state government, headed by the secretary of state. Each election winner receives a certificate of election from the county or state board.

Capability Analysis   An assessment of a state's ability to achieve an objective vis-à-vis other states through the application of military, political, economic, psychological, or other forms of power and influence. Capability analysis involves the efforts of state leaders to measure or evaluate tangible and intangible factors that impinge upon a state's capacity to act effectively in a given time, place, and situation. While the tangible factors are empirically verifiable and quantitatively measurable, the intangibles do not lend themselves to precise measurement and are usually matters of subjective judgment. *See also* INFLUENCE, POWER.

Capital   That one of the factors of production—along with land and labor—that is expressed in terms of money and producer goods. The application of capital to the expansion of productive capacities depends upon profits, the amount of profits saved, and the extent to which savings are channeled into investments in the form of capital goods. Advanced capitalist states encourage capital formation through security markets, extensive banking systems, and governmental fiscal and monetary policies. Communist states provide in their national planning for directing a large portion of national income into capital goods development. Sources of capital for underdeveloped states include local savings, private investment from abroad, trade, and foreign aid. Capital provides such essential elements in the economic equation as buildings, machines, tools, supplies, power, and transportation facilities. *See also* INTERNATIONAL BANK FOR RECONSTRUCTION AND DEVELOPMENT, REGIONAL DEVELOPMENT BANKS.

Capitalism   An economic system based on private ownership of the means of production and on a supply-demand market economy. Capitalism is based on the laissez-faire theory, which emphasizes the absence of governmental restraints on ownership, production, and trade. *See also* LAISSEZ-FAIRE, CONVERGENCE THEORY.

Capital Punishment   The death penalty for conviction of a serious crime, such as murder, rape, kidnapping, or treason. Electrocution is the most commonly used method of execution; lethal gas and hanging are also employed. In Utah, the condemned person may choose to be hanged or shot. Fourteen states bar or severely restrict the imposition of capital punishment: Alaska, Hawaii, Iowa, Maine, Michigan, Minnesota, New Mexico, New York, North Dakota, Oregon, Rhode Island, Vermont, West Virginia, and Wisconsin; Puerto Rico, Guam, and the Virgin Islands do likewise. In 1972, the California Supreme Court declared the death penalty to be cruel and unusual punishment. Several states have reinstated the death penalty after having once voted to abolish it. In some states, the death penalty is mandatory for certain crimes while in others the jury may recommend life imprisonment instead of the death penalty. Since 1968, no one may be excluded from a jury because of opposition to capital punishment (*Witherspoon v. Illinois*, 391 U.S. 510).

Career Service   A professionalized civil service wherein employment is based on merit, opportunity is afforded for advancement, and guarantees are provided against arbitrary dismissal. *See also* MERIT SYSTEM, FEDERAL SERVICE ENTRANCE EXAMINATION, ROGERS ACT.

Cartel   An agreement among independent businessmen to restrict competition. A cartel arrangement is based on a contractual understanding concerning prices, limited production, and the division of the market. The term "cartel" originated in Germany during the 1870s (from the Latin *charta*, meaning "contract"). Cartels are employed mainly in mass production industries where exclusiveness is protected by patents or quality differences are minor. The market for primary commodities, especially agricultural products, is highly competitive and does not lend itself to cartelization, resulting in deterioration of commodity prices in the terms of trade relative to manufactured products. *See also* MONOPOLY, TRUST.

Case Study   Research aimed at uncovering detailed information about a particular political event or phenomenon. The case study deals with a single case or event, as contrasted with comparative studies or the sampling of many cases through some form of survey research. The case researcher ordinarily does not rigidly observe the canons of scientific method. Rather, the effectiveness of the case study depends upon the common sense and imagination of the investigator, the pertinence of the subject of investigation to the understanding sought, and the thoroughness and objectivity with which the study is carried out. *See also* COMPARATIVE STUDY, DESCRIPTION, SURVEY RESEARCH, TRADITIONAL APPROACH.

Caste, *see* Social Stratification.

Categorical Assistance   Welfare programs provided under the Social Security Act. These programs include: (1) old age assistance; (2) aid to the blind; (3) aid to dependent children; and (4) aid to the totally and permanently disabled. Persons who fall within these categories and are in need of financial assistance may receive aid from their state from funds supplemented by federal grants. The programs also extend to the District of Columbia, Puerto Rico, Guam, and the Virgin Islands. *See also* SOCIAL SECURITY ACT, FAMILY ASSISTANCE PLAN, *Goldberg v. Kelly.*

Categoric Group, *see* Group.

Caucus (Nominating)   A closed meeting of party leaders to select party candidates. In the early days of the Republic, party members in Congress and in the state legislatures selected their party's candidates for national and state office. Presidential candidates were chosen by party caucuses in Congress. Locally, leading members of each party met behind closed doors to select candidates for various local offices. Some local candidates are still nominated by caucus. The term "to caucus" is also commonly used to describe any private meeting of politicians seeking to reach agreement on a course of political action. *See also* CAUCUS (LEGISLATIVE).

Caucus (Legislative)   A meeting of party members in one of the houses of a legislative body for the purpose of making decisions on selections of party leaders and on legislative business. Republicans in Congress prefer to call their party meeting a "conference." The term "to caucus" is also commonly used to describe any informal meeting of legislators seeking to reach agreement on a course of legislative action. *See also* CAUCUS (NOMINATING).

Caucusing Group (United Nations)   Representatives of member states whose common interests impel them to meet regularly to determine group approaches on substantive and procedural issues arising in the General Assembly. Nine caucusing groups are active in the Assembly: the Afro-Asian, Arab, African, Benelux, Commonwealth, Latin American, Scandinavian, Soviet, and Western European and "other" (Canada, Australia, and New Zealand) states. A considerable overlap in membership exists, especially among the Afro-Asian, Arab, African, and Commonwealth states. A few states—China, Israel, South Africa, the United States, and Yugoslavia—do not caucus with any group. A caucusing group may be distinguished from a voting bloc in that members of the former are not bound to vote in the Assembly according to the caucus decision and exhibit less cohesion.

Caudillismo   The principle of personal or "boss-type" political rule in Latin American politics. The *caudillo* depends on the personal loyalty of his followers. Founded in the feudal systems of Spain and Portugal, *caudillismo* serves as a substitute for the formal institutions of government from the local to the national level. *See also* DICTATORSHIP, PERSONALISMO.

Causality   The relationship, usually imputed by an observer, which can link two or more political variables together in temporal sequence to generate a particular event. An analysis of causality seeks to identify the antecedent action or change in one variable, called the independent variable, that produces or helps to produce a change in a second variable, the dependent variable. Causality can seldom be "proved" in the strictest sense, but is usually inferred from observed sequential relationships. *See also* DETERMINISM, EXPLANATION, PREDICTION.

Caveat Emptor, *see Caveat Venditor*

Caveat Venditor   A term meaning literally, "let the seller beware." *Caveat venditor* involves the acceptance by government of a responsibility to regulate business operations for the protection of consumers. It can be contrasted with the philosophy of *caveat emptor* ("let the buyer beware") that typified the free wheeling business practices of the nineteenth-century period of laissez-faire. *See also* UNFAIR TRADE PRACTICE, CONSUMERISM.

Cease and Desist Order   An administrative order directed to an individual, firm, or labor union to refrain from violating the law or the rules and regulations established by an administrative agency. *See also* ADMINISTRATIVE ORDER.

Censorship   The curbing of ideas either in speech or in writing *before* they are expressed. Accountability *after* expression is provided by laws regulating libel and slander, obscenity, incitement to crime, contempt of court, or seditious utterance. Except in time of war or other national emergency, any prior restraint upon freedom of speech or of the press is forbidden. *See also Near v. Minnesota, Freedman v. Maryland, Roth v. United States,* FREEDOM OF THE PRESS.

Censure   A power vested in each chamber of a legislative body by which the chamber can discipline its own members. Under the Constitution, "Each house may . . . punish its members for disorderly behavior, and, with the concurrence of two-thirds, expel a member." (Art. I, sec. 5). *See also* EXPULSION.

Census A decennial enumeration of the total population of the United States, conducted by the Bureau of the Census. The Constitution provides that the population count be used for the purposes of apportioning direct taxes and representatives among the several states (Art. I, sec. 3). Since the first census in 1790, new ones have been taken every ten years. Approximately one-half of the states conduct a mid-decade census along the same lines as the federal census. The Census Bureau also collects data on a wide variety of subjects useful to Congress and the general public on such matters as business, housing, and units of government. *See also* APPORTIONMENT, REDISTRICTING.

Census Bureau, *see* Department of Commerce.

CENTO, *see* Central Treaty Organization.

Central American Common Market (CACM) A regional organization that seeks to promote economic development in member states through a customs union and industrial integration scheme. Five Central American states—Costa Rica, El Salvador, Guatemala, Honduras, and Nicaragua—have ratified an Economic Integration Treaty of 1960 that, together with several protocols and supplementary agreements, provides for a significant integration of their economies. The assumption underlying the common market system is that industrialization and specialization will be encouraged by the broader market and free trade arrangement, so that foreign investment capital in sizable amounts will be attracted to the region. Common Market decisions are made by: (1) the Central American Economic Council, which consists of members' Economic Ministers and develops policies concerning the integration of their economies; (2) an Executive Council, which implements decisions made by the Economic Council; and (3) a secretariat that provides technical and administrative assistance at the Guatemala City headquarters. The Central American Bank for Economic Integration functions within the system by helping to finance the development program. *See also* ORGANIZATION OF CENTRAL AMERICAN STATES.

Central American Organization, *see* Organization of Central American States.

Central Committee (China (PRC)) The vehicle through which the decisions of the party directorate are tested and transmitted. According to the rules of the Chinese Communist Party (CCP), the Central Committee is "the highest leading body of party organization . . . when the National Party Congress is not in session." During these intervals, it is charged with directing the entire work of the party. The ninety-six members of the Central Committee are elected by the National Party Congress. The committee is composed of: (1) representatives of virtually all provinces and autonomous regions; (2) the chairman and vice chairman of the republic; (3) the chairman of the State Supreme Conference; (4) the premier, twelve vice premiers, and secretary general of the State Council; (5) certain ministers and commission chairmen; (6) representatives of the National Defense Council, the armed services, and the People's Liberation Army; (7) a large delegation from the Standing Committee of the National

People's Congress; and (8) representatives of the legal arm of the government and of the court system. The Central Committee meets once or twice annually for a few weeks at a time. The sessions are closed to outside scrutiny and brief communiqués simply announce topics discussed and policies or programs adopted. *See also* CENTRAL COMMITTEE (SOVIET UNION).

Central Committee (Soviet Union) The Communist party organ responsible for directing all party activity between All-Union Congresses. The Central Committee names the members of the Politburo and the Secretariat, the two most powerful decision-making bodies of the party in the Soviet Union. It is composed of 195 members and 165 candidate members. Nominally elected by the Party Congress, the Committee members are actually chosen in advance by party leaders.

Central Intelligence Agency (CIA) An agency, headed by a Director appointed by the President with Senate approval, that functions under the National Security Council to coordinate intelligence activities in the interest of national security. The CIA evaluates raw intelligence data supplied by the Army, Navy, Air Force, State Department, and other intelligence-gathering civilian and military agencies. This information is disseminated among various units of the national government to aid in decision making. The CIA also engages in worldwide intelligence gathering activities. Critics have charged it with engaging in such clandestine activities as political assassinations, coups and revolutions, and extensive surveillance of American citizens. *See also* INTELLIGENCE.

Centralization The tendency for political power and authority to gravitate from state governments to the national government. Though the functions performed by all governments in the United States have increased, the nationwide impact of economic, social, and defense problems has led to an increased assumption of responsibility by the national government.

Centralized Purchasing Vesting authority in one agency to purchase and handle supplies and materials for governmental agencies. This is now done for the national government by the General Services Administration, and the practice has been adopted by most states and many local units of government. *See also* GENERAL SERVICES ADMINISTRATION.

Central Tendency Measurement The use of statistical techniques to identify a representative value located at or near the center of a numerical distribution. Commonly used measures of central tendency in political research include the *mean* (the "average," which is computed by summing all the numerical values and dividing by the number of cases), the *median* (the true "center point," with half the cases having a higher value and half having a lower value), and the *mode* (the most frequent score, number, class, or category in a distribution).

Central Treaty Organization (CENTO) A Middle East alliance adhered to by Britain, Iran, Pakistan, and Turkey. Originally known as the Baghdad Pact, the name was changed to CENTO and headquarters were moved from Baghdad to Ankara when a neutralist government seized power in Iraq in 1958 and withdrew from the alliance. *See also* ALLIANCE.

Certificate of Public Convenience, Interest, and Necessity Permission granted by a regulatory agency to an individual or group to conduct a particular type of business. The standard of "public convenience, interest, and necessity" has been established by Congress and state legislatures to guide regulatory agencies in issuing licenses and permits to public utilities and communication media. *See also* FRANCHISE.

Certification of Eligibles The practice by which a civil service commission provides a hiring officer of an agency with the names of persons who have qualified for a position. This is usually done in accordance with the ranking of individuals on test scores. The practice in most jurisdictions is to certify the top three names, often called the "rule of three."

Certiorari An order issued by a higher court to a lower court to send up the record of a case for review. Most cases reach the United States Supreme Court through the writ of certiorari, as authorized by the Judiciary Act of 1925. The writ is issued at the discretion of the Court when at least four of the nine justices feel that the case should be reviewed.

Cession The transfer of sovereignty over territory by agreement between ceding and acquiring states. Cession may involve all or a portion of the territory of the ceding state. In the former instance, the ceding state disappears by absorption into the acquiring state. Thus, by the treaty of 1910, Korea became Japanese territory. *See also* PLEBISCITE.

Chain of Command, *see* Unity of Command.

Chairman, Committee, *see* Committee Chairman.

Challenge (Jury) Objection to having a prospective juror serve on a jury. A juror may be challenged by either party. A challenge may be either for "cause" or "peremptory." An unlimited number of challenges may be made for cause with approval of the presiding judge. Peremptory challenges, for which no reason need be given, are limited to a specific number, which varies. from state to state, and depends upon the nature of the offense involved. For crimes punishable by death, as many as forty peremptory challenges may be allowed; as few as five may be permitted for minor offenses. *See also* JURY.

Challenge (Voter)   An allegation by a poll watcher that a potential voter is unqualified or that a vote is invalid. Most states provide for a bipartisan group of election judges in each precinct to help decide disputes. An inspector is usually in charge of each precinct and makes the final decision. In some closed-primary states, a voter's party affiliation may be challenged. If he cannot prove his affiliation to the satisfaction of that party's poll watcher, he can be deprived of his vote in the primary. *See also* POLL WATCHER.

Chamber of Commerce, *see* Business and Professional Organizations.

Chamber of Deputies, *see* Parliament (Italy).

Chance   The quality of occurring randomly, or through unknown causes, that makes a particular political event unpredictable. In statistics, chance is related to the concept of probability. If, for example, the chances of predicting accurately some occurrence are ten in one hundred, the odds are nine to one and the probability is ten percent. *See also* PROBABILITY, RANDOM.

Chancellor   The chief executive officer in the West German federal parliamentary system. The Chancellor is formally elected without debate, usually by a new Bundestag after a general election. He is nominated by the Federal President after the latter has negotiated his selection with the various parties. If he receives an absolute majority on the first ballot, he is appointed by the President. If not, the Bundestag has fourteen days to elect a Chancellor of its own choosing, but if no one receives a majority, a third balloting takes place without delay and with only a plurality required. When the third balloting fails to produce a majority, the President has seven days to choose between appointing the successful plurality candidate to the chancellorship or dissolving the Bundestag for a new election. In the absence of a general election, a new Chancellor can come to office through the constitutionally established "positive" no-confidence procedure by which the Bundestag can force the dismissal of a Chancellor only by electing his successor. Unless dismissed, the Chancellor serves for the four-year life of the Bundestag. The Chancellor forms his Cabinet from his own party if it is the majority, or by negotiation with other parties if a coalition government is necessary. The Basic Law makes the Chancellor individually responsible for the determination of the general policy of his government and for the general direction of the work of individual ministries in line with that policy. The Chancellor, his deputy, or an appropriate minister must sign all laws before the President's signature can give them effect, a requirement that has raised the constitutional question of the right to veto. Only the Chancellor has the legal authority to bring about the dismissal of a minister.

Change, *see* Political Change.

Chaplinsky v. New Hampshire, *see* Jehovah's Witnesses Cases.

Chapters VI and VII, United Nations Charter, *see* Security Council.

Charge   A statement by the judge to the jury at the conclusion of a trial to aid the jury in reaching its verdict. The judge instructs the jury in the law governing the case and reviews the evidence. The authority of the judge to comment on the facts of a case, as distinguished from the law involved, varies from state to state; federal judges have wide latitude. *See also* JURY.

Chargé d'Affaires   The Foreign Service official temporarily placed in charge of an embassy or legation in the absence of the ambassador or minister.

Charisma   An attribute of leadership based on personal qualities of the individual. A charismatic leader, typically, has a magnetic personality, a dedication to achieving his objectives, unusual powers of persuasion, and ability to excite and gain the loyalty of supporters. Although a charismatic leader is usually flamboyant, he may have a mystical, withdrawn personality.

Charismatic Authority, *see* Authority.

Charismatic Leadership   Leadership characterized by a mystical (or spiritual), messianic quality that elicits widespread, emotional popular support often bordering on reverence. Charismatic leadership tends to merge with the spirit of nationalism and to become identified with, or symbolic of, the state itself. The charismatic leader, particularly in newly emergent nations, appears to his followers to be the personification of truth, one who is beyond the fears and ambitions of ordinary mortals, and is the chosen instrument for the realization of the nation's destiny. Qualities of charismatic leadership have been found in such diverse but dominant personalities as Nehru of India, Mao Tse-tung of China, Sukarno of Indonesia, Nkrumah of Ghana, Nasser of Egypt, and Kenyatta of Kenya. *See also* NATIONALISM.

Charter   The basic law of a local governmental unit that defines its powers, responsibilities, and organization. Charters are granted, under state constitutional or statutory provisions, to municipal corporations and, in some states, to counties or townships. Charters may be provided by: (1) special act of the legislature applicable to one city, (2) general laws applicable to all cities within a certain classification, (3) optional charter laws whereby a city may choose a charter from a group provided by law, or (4) home rule whereby the people of a city draw up their own charter. *See also* SPECIAL ACT, GENERAL LAWS; OPTIONAL CHARTER, HOME RULE.

Charter Colony   One of the three types of colonial governments—charter, proprietary, royal—found in colonial America. Charter colonies, namely Rhode Island and Connecticut, operated under charters agreed to by the colony and the king. The legislature was elected and was allowed much autonomy by England. The governor was chosen by the legislature.

Charter, United Nations, *see* United Nations Charter.

Chauvinism   Extravagant, demonstrative superpatriotism. Chauvinism implies uncritical devotion to the state, extreme jealousy of its honor, and an exaggerated sense of its glory. The term is derived from the name of Nicolas Chauvin, a Napoleonic soldier who was notorious for his unrestrained devotion to his leader and the Empire. Chauvinism can be described as an extreme form of nationalism that holds that the state can do no wrong. *See also* NATIONALISM.

Checks and Balances   A major principle of the American governmental system whereby each department of the government exercises a check upon the actions of the others. The principle operates not only among the legislative, executive, and judicial branches but between the two houses of the legislature and between the states and the national government. Each department has some authority to control the actions of one or more of the others by participation in their functions. Examples include the President's veto power and the congressional power to override the veto, judicial review of legislative and executive actions, presidential appointment of judges with senatorial approval, and the congressional power to impeach. *See also* SEPARATION OF POWERS.

Chief Administrative Officer, City, *see* Mayor-Administrator Plan.

Chief Diplomat   The role of the chief executive as the nation's highest-level negotiator with foreign powers. The President as chief diplomat is the official medium through which the government of the United States communicates with foreign countries. The President's powers are derived directly and by implication from Article II of the Constitution. Thus he can send and receive ambassadors, grant or withhold recognition, sever diplomatic relations, negotiate treaties, and, through his power as commander in chief, focus the military power of the nation in support of his foreign policy. In the formulation and implementation of foreign policy, the President depends most heavily on the Secretaries of State and Defense and on the executive departments that they head. *See also* DIPLOMACY, NEGOTIATION, SUMMIT DIPLOMACY.

Chief Justice   The highest judicial officer of the United States or of a state. The Chief Justice of the United States is appointed for a life term by the President with the consent of the Senate. He presides over sessions of the United States Supreme Court, assigns the writing of opinions, and performs a variety of administrative duties as head of the federal court system. In the states, the chief justices are chosen in a variety of ways—appointment, election, seniority—usually for a limited term. Their duties are similar to the Chief Justice of the United States, although in many states they lack control over lower court administrative matters.

Chief Legislator   The role of the President in influencing the making of laws. Constitutional powers available to the President to affect legislation include the recommending of legislative programs through messages to the Congress, the veto, and some control over sessions. Informal methods of influencing legislation include the President's personal contacts with congressional leaders, his use of patronage, his ability to arouse public opinion in support of his program, his efforts to influence the election of congressmen sympathetic to his views, and the continuing efforts of executive officials acting as a "presidential lobby" before congressional committees. In addition, the President's legislative powers include the issuing of rules and executive orders having the effect of law under powers delegated to him by the Constitution or by Congress.

Chief of Foreign Policy   The role of the chief executive as the nation's highest policymaker in the field of foreign affairs. As chief of foreign policy, the President is ultimately responsible for the security and well-being of the nation. His responsibilities derive from his constitutional roles as chief executive officer and commander in chief, which require him to formulate, develop support for, and carry out foreign policies calculated to maximize the national interests of the United States. The President's leadership function is exercised largely through the Secretary and Department of State, although he can exert foreign policy leadership in a variety of other ways. These include the drafting of legislation, messages to Congress, personal diplomacy, public addresses, press conferences, and press releases. The Monroe Doctrine, for example, was contained in a State of the Union message, and the Point Four Program was first enunciated in President Harry Truman's inaugural address. Public statements by cabinet and other executive officials and by persons known to speak with the authority of the President constitute an informal channel through which the President can reach the peoples and governments of the world. *See also United States v. Curtiss-Wright Export Corp.*

Chief of Mission, *see* Foreign Service.

Chief of State   The role of the President as ceremonial head of the government of the United States. Duties of the chief of state include greeting foreign dignitaries, acting as host at state dinners, throwing out the first baseball at the start of the season, and bestowing honors.

Child Labor   The employment of children below the legal age limit. The national government and most states prohibit the employment of children below the age of sixteen and, in certain hazardous occupations, below the age of eighteen. Children are permitted to work outside of school in nonhazardous jobs.

China Membership Issue (United Nations), *see* Two Chinas Proposal.

China (People's Republic), *see* Central Committee, Chinese Communist Party, Commune, Cultural Revolution, Maoism, National Party Congress, National People's Congress, Politburo, Red Guard, State Council.

Chinese Communist Party (CCP)   The largest Communist party in the world, with a colossal membership (in excess of seventeen million). This highly disciplined, monolithic party is the vehicle by which the leaders manipulate the world's largest population, for the most part illiterate. It makes all significant decisions and is organized to insure their execution. Its doctrines bind both member and nonmember. It fills every significant office in the country and it permits no organized opposition. Children from the age of nine on are recruited into the Young Pioneers for indoctrination and familiarization with party practice and collective living. This is the main source of members for the Communist Youth League, which includes ages fourteen to twenty-five. The league is supervised by the party and is the principal pool from which new party members are selected. Standards of initiation and indoctrination are strict, but standards of selection of new party members have varied with the military, technical, intellectual, or peasant leadership needs in a given period. The principal organs of the central apparatus of the party start with the National Party Congress whose one thousand members are a vehicle for the enunciation of policy determined at higher levels. The Central Committee of ninety-four members and ninety-three alternates brings together all major leaders for formal discussion, approval and promulgation of policy. The Politburo of nineteen members and six alternates exercises the powers of the Central Committee between sessions. The highest level of authority is found in the Politburo's Standard Committee, whose half-dozen or so members are the most powerful leaders in the party. *See also* CENTRAL COMMITTEE (CHINA (PRC)), NATIONAL PARTY CONGRESS (CHINA (PRC)), POLITBURO (CHINA (PRC)).

Chisholm v. Georgia, *see* Eleventh Amendment.

Church and State, *see* Separation of Church and State.

CIA, *see* Central Intelligence Agency.

Circuit Court   A general trial court in the states, sometimes called a district court or a superior court. In many states, the court serves several counties and the judges go on "circuit" from one county to another according to a schedule. In most states, the judges of these courts are elected by the voters of a particular county or circuit, with terms varying from two to six years. These are courts of "original jurisdiction," where important civil and criminal cases begin, trials are held, and juries are frequently used. Cases from minor courts, such as justices of the peace or municipal courts, may be appealed to the circuit court. From circuit courts, cases may be appealed to higher state courts.

Citizen   An individual who is a native or naturalized member of a state, owes allegiance to that state, and is entitled to the protection and privileges of its laws. Citizenship in the United States is defined in the Fourteenth Amendment to the Constitution: "All persons born or naturalized in the United States, and subject to the jurisdiction thereof, are citizens of the United States and of the state wherein they reside." Citizenship is based mainly on one's place of birth *(jus soli)* but may be acquired through naturalization and, under circumstances defined by Congress, through blood relation *(jus sanguinis). See also United States v. Wong Kim Ark,* NATIONAL, *Jus Soli, Jus Sanguinis.*

Citizenship, *see* Denaturalization, Deportation, Dual Nationality, Expatriation, *Girouard v. United States,* Immigration and Nationality Act of 1952, Immigration Act of 1965, *Jus Sanguinis, Jus Soli,* Naturalization, *Trop v. Dulles, United States v. Wong Kim Ark.*

City   A municipal corporation, chartered by the state, that is usually larger than a village, town, borough, or other incorporated area. The term is a legal concept and exactly what constitutes a city is defined by state law. This is generally based on population but may be based on assessed valuation.

City Charter, *see* Charter.

City Classification, *see* Classification of Cities

City Council   The policy-making and, in some instances, administrative board of a city. The structure and powers of city councils vary with the plan of city government. In the weak mayor and commission plans, the council plays a large role in lawmaking and in the direction and control of administrative departments. In the strong mayor and council-manager plans, the council's job is largely in the realm of lawmaking, with only general oversight of administration. In all cases, the most important jobs of the council are to pass ordinances that determine public policy, and to exercise control over the purse strings. Other functions, which vary from city to city, may include serving as a board of review for tax assessments, issuing licenses, and making appointments. Members of city councils are elected, on a partisan or nonpartisan basis, from wards or districts, at large, or by a combination of both. *See also* COMMISSION PLAN, COUNCIL-MANAGER PLAN, MAYOR-COUNCIL PLAN.

City-County Consolidation   The merger of county government with all other units within the county to form one unit of government. The plan is suggested as one solution to the problems of a metropolitan area, particularly when it coincides with the county boundary. *See also* METROPOLITAN AREA.

City-County Separation   Political separation of the city from the county. Cities are generally part of the county in which they lie and the city residents pay county taxes and receive certain county services. More than thirty cities in Virginia, and the cities of St. Louis, Denver, Baltimore, and San Francisco, are separated from their counties and provide their residents with county services. *See also* METROPOLITAN AREA.

City Government, *see* Commission Plan, Council-Manager Plan, Mayor-Administrative Plan, Mayor-Council Plan, Strong-Mayor Plan, Weak-Mayor Plan.

City Home Rule, *see* Home Rule.

City Manager, *see* Council-Manager Plan.

Civil Aeronautics Board (CAB)   A five-member independent regulatory agency that controls the business aspects of private airlines engaged in domestic and foreign transportation. Board members are appointed by the President with the Senate's approval for six-year terms. The CAB was established under the Civil Aeronautics Act of 1938, which gave it responsibility for the "encouragement and development" of civil aviation. Its functions include both the promotion and regulation of the economic aspects of domestic airlines and the operations of both domestic and foreign airlines in the United States. It grants permission to companies to fly specific routes, exercises jurisdiction over rates and fares, and regulates mergers and other business relations in the interest of maintaining competition. The CAB is supplemented in its regulation of the airlines by the Federal Aviation Administration (FAA), which carries out extensive responsibilities related to the safety of air travel. The FAA is in the Department of Transportation and is headed by an Administrator appointed by the President with Senate approval.

Civil Defense   The protection of civilian populations from enemy attack. Civil defense operations are centered in the Office of Civil Defense (OCD) in the Department of the Army. The Director of Civil Defense, who heads the OCD, is responsible for developing a shelter program, a defense against chemical, biological, and radiological weapons, a warning system, and measures to be undertaken following an attack. OCD has designated numerous structures as fallout shelters for protection against radioactivity following a nuclear attack and has stocked many of them with supplies; but the adoption of a major shelter program in the United States remains a controversial issue.

Civil Disobedience   Refusal to obey a law, usually on the ground that the law is morally reprehensible. Recent examples of civil disobedience include Negro refusals to obey segregation laws and the actions of anti-Vietnam war groups in refusing to honor draft regulations. Civil disobedience ordinarily takes the form of nonviolent resistance and is aimed at arousing public opinion against the law.

Civilian Control   The American constitutional principle of civilian supremacy over the military to safeguard republican institutions. Civilian control is maintained through constitutional provisions that make the President commander in chief of the armed forces and grant Congress power to raise and support armies, make military law, declare war, and appropriate money for military expenditures for no more than two-year periods. The Second and Third Amendments buttress the principle by forbidding the quartering of troops without consent and by granting the people the right to keep and bear arms. Statutory enactments, such as the legal requirement that the Secretary of Defense and the Secretaries of the Army, Navy, and Air Force Departments must all be civilians, also encourage civilian control. *See also Ex Parte Milligan*, MILITARY-INDUSTRIAL COMPLEX.

Civil Law   The code regulating conduct between private persons. It is to be distinguished from criminal law, which regulates individual conduct and is enforced by the government. Under civil law, the government provides the forum for the settlement of disputes between private parties in such matters as contracts, domestic relations, business relations, and auto accidents. The government may be plaintiff or defendant in a civil suit but, in a criminal case, the government is always the prosecutor. Most civil cases in both state and federal courts are tried without jury. Where juries are used, some states authorize trial by a jury of fewer than twelve persons, and decision by less than unanimous vote. *See also* CRIMINAL LAW.

Civil Liberties   Those liberties usually spelled out in a bill of rights or a constitution that guarantee the protection of persons, opinions, and property from the arbitrary interference of governmental officials. Restraints may be placed upon the exercise of these liberties only when they are abused by individuals or groups and when the public welfare requires them.

Civil Rights   Positive acts of government designed to protect persons against arbitrary or discriminatory treatment by government or individuals. Civil rights guarantees are sometimes written into constitutions, but frequently take the form of statutes. Though the term is often used interchangeably with "civil liberties," the latter generally refers to negative restraints upon government as found in bills of rights. The term "civil rights" is also to be distinguished from "political rights," which generally refers to the rights to participate in the management of government through such practices as voting. Civil rights have taken on special importance since the Civil War, as Congress and state and local legislatures have endeavored to secure equal treatment for Negroes.

Civil Rights Act of 1957   The first civil rights law passed by Congress since Reconstruction, designed to secure the right to vote for Negroes. Its major feature empowers the Department of Justice to seek court injunctions against any deprivation of voting rights, and authorizes criminal prosecutions for violations of an injunction. In addition, the Act established a Civil Rights Division, headed by an Assistant Attorney General, in the Department of Justice, and created a six-man bipartisan Civil Rights Commission to investigate civil rights violations and to recommmend legislation.

Civil Rights Act of 1960   A law designed to further secure the right to vote for Negroes and to meet problems arising from racial upheavals in the South. The major provision authorizes federal courts to appoint referees who will help blacks to register after a voter-denial conviction is obtained under the 1957 Civil Rights Act, and after a court finding of a "pattern or practice" of discrimination against qualified voters. Other provisions: (1) authorize punishment for persons who obstruct any federal court order, such as a school desegregation order, by threats or force; (2) authorize criminal penalties for transportation of explosives for the purpose of bombing a building; (3) require preservation of voting records for twenty-two months, and authorize the Attorney General to inspect the records; (4) provide for schooling of children of armed forces personnel in the event that a school closes because of an integration dispute.

Civil Rights Act of 1964   A major enactment designed to erase racial discrimination in most areas of American life. Major provisions of the Act: (1) outlaw arbitrary discrimination in voter registration and expedite voting rights suits; (2) bar discrimination in public accommodations, such as hotels and restaurants, that have a substantial relation to interstate commerce; (3) authorize the national government to bring suits to desegregate public facilities and schools; (4) extend the life and expand the power of the Civil Rights Commission; (5) provide for the withholding of federal funds from programs administered in a discriminatory manner; (6) establish the right to equality in employment opportunities; (7) establish a Community Relations Service to help resolve civil rights problems. The Act forbids discrimination based on race, color, religion, national origin, and, in the case of employment, sex. Techniques for gaining voluntary compliance are stressed in the Act, and the resolution of civil rights problems through state and local action is encouraged. Discrimination in housing is not covered by the law.

Civil Rights Act of 1968   A law which prohibits discrimination in the advertising, financing, sale, or rental of housing, based on race, religion, or national origin. The law covers about 80 percent of all housing. Major exclusions are owner occupied dwellings of up to four units and those selling or renting without services of a broker. Other provisions of the 1968 Act provide criminal penalties for interfering with the exercise of civil rights by others, or for using interstate commerce to incite riots. Administration of the housing provisions is left largely to the Department of Housing and Urban Development which is limited to conciliation and persuasion. Lawsuits may be initiated by the Attorney General or by an individual.

Civil Rights Acts of 1866, 1870, 1871, and 1875   Laws passed by Congress after the Civil War to guarantee the rights of Negroes. The public-accommodation provisions of the 1875 law were declared unconstitutional by the Supreme Court in the *Civil Rights Cases* (109 U.S. 3 [1883]), as a federal invasion of private rights. Other provisions of these laws were struck down by the courts or repealed by Congress. Today, a few major provisions remain from the Acts of 1866 and 1871. One makes it a federal crime for any person acting under the authority of a state law to deprive another of any rights protected by the Constitution or by laws of the United States. Another authorizes suits for civil damages against state or local officials by persons whose rights are abridged. Others permit actions against persons who conspire to deprive people of their rights. *See also Jones v. Mayer.*

Civil Rights Commission   Established by the federal Civil Rights Act of 1957 as a bipartisan commission of six members to investigate the broad area of civil rights. The Commission has conducted investigations and published reports on such matters as voting rights, education, housing, employment, and the administration of justice. The Civil Rights Act of 1964 strengthened the Commission's investigatory power and established it as a national clearing house for civil rights information.

Civil Rights Organizations   Groups organized to promote observance of the Bill of Rights and related constitutional provisions. These include organizations concerned with Negro civil rights as well as those with broader interests and goals. The major Negro civil rights groups include the National Association for the Advancement of Colored People (NAACP), which concerns itself mainly with legislative and legal matters; the National Urban League, which concentrates on economic improvement for the Negro; and the Southern Christian Leadership Conference (SCLC), which concentrates on mass demonstrations, boycotts, and sit-ins. Among the leading general civil rights and liberties groups are the American Civil Liberties Union (ACLU), the National Council of Churches of Christ, most labor unions, and ethnically oriented groups such as the American Jewish Congress. *See also* PRESSURE GROUP.

Civil Service   A collective term for most persons employed by government who are not members of the military services. It is more generally understood to apply to all those who gain governmental employment through a merit system, more correctly called the "classified civil service." Elective officials and high ranking policy-making officers who are appointed by elected officials, and members of the judiciary are not considered civil servants. *See also* MERIT SYSTEM.

Civil Service Acts, *see* Pendleton Act, Ramspeck Act.

Civil Service Commission   The central personnel agency of the national government, established in 1883. It is composed of three members appointed to six-year terms by the President with the Senate's consent. Its principal activities include the recruitment, examination, and preparation of eligible lists of prospective governmental employees. The Commission also administers a variety of laws pertaining to governmental employees with regard to veterans' preference, classification, security checks, political activity, retirement, and insurance programs.

Civil Service Examinations, *see* Federal Service Entrance Examination.

Civil War   A war fought between different geographical areas, political divisions, or ideological factions within the same country. Civil war may involve a struggle between an established government and antigovernment forces, or it may develop during an interregnum period between groups contesting for power and legitimacy as the new government. *See also* BELLIGERENCY, INSURGENCY.

Class, *see* Social Stratification.

Classification   The orderly arrangement of subject matter in categories or classes, according to perceived similarities and differences in the various objects of inquiry. Classification may be based on whatever criteria the investigator deems appropriate to his subject matter and research objectives. Certain sets of categories are so useful, or so obviously appropriate to a given type of research, that they are used repeatedly and become part of the conceptual treasury of a discipline. Thus, in studies of voting behavior, voters are often classified according to age, sex, economic status, education, partisan affiliation, and so on. A systematic classification scheme is sometimes called a *typology* or a *taxonomy*. The science of classification is referred to as *taxonomy*. *See also* CONTINUUM, DICHOTOMOUS CLASSIFICATION.

Classification of Cities   The grouping of cities by a state legislature according to population for the purpose of enacting laws or city charters. The practice of classification results from the requirement found in most state constitutions that the legislature must deal with local governments by general law rather than by special act applicable to one unit. Since general laws may result in putting all cities, large and small, into a uniform mold, legislatures have classified cities and passed general laws applicable to each class. *See also* GENERAL LAWS.

Classification of Persons, *see* Equal Protection of the Law.

Classified Service   Positions of governmental employment that are under the jurisdiction of a civil service commission and that are filled by merit. Congress has permitted some agencies to establish their own personnel systems outside the classified service, such as the Foreign Service, TVA, FBI, and CIA. *See also* SCHEDULES A B, AND C.

Class Struggle (Communist Theory)   The conflict between the proletariat and bourgeoisie that, under capitalism, results from the increasing impoverishment of the workers and a polarization engendered by a growing class consciousness. For Marx, the class struggle emerged out of the basic contradictions identified by the dialectical process as inherent in capitalism as well as in earlier primitive, slave, and feudal social systems. It is, in other words, what communists perceive to be the means by which the transition from capitalism to socialism will occur. Although many revolutionaries antedating Marx had based their doctrines on the class struggle theme, Marx was the first to accord it the central role in a philosophy of historical evolution.

Clayton Act of 1914   A major antitrust act, aimed at increasing competition in business. Provisions of the Clayton Act forbid price cutting and other abuses that tend to weaken competition, restrict corporations from acquiring stock in competing firms or building interlocking directorates, make corporation officers individually liable for violations, and facilitate civil suit procedures by injured parties. Labor unions and agricultural organizations not carrying on business for profit are exempted from the provisions of the Act. *See also* ANTITRUST DIVISION, ANTITRUST LAWS.

Clear and Present Danger Rule   A test used by the Supreme Court to measure the permissible bounds of free speech. The test was formulated by Justice Oliver Wendell Holmes in *Schenck v. United States*, 249 U.S. 47 (1919): "The question in every case is whether the words used are used in such circumstances and are of such a nature as to create a clear and present danger that they will bring about the substantive evils that Congress has a right to prevent. It is a question of proximity and degree." The application of this test has varied a good deal since 1919. *See also* BAD TENDENCY RULE, *Schenck v. United States*.

Cleavage   Critical divisions within a social system that create conflict within a related political system. Cleavages may be based on such factors as differences in wealth and income, ethnic and religious divisions, urban-rural or regional distinctions, and color or class differences. Differences in opinions, beliefs, attitudes, and perceived interests may create additional cleavages or reinforce existing ones. The severity of social conflict may be increased if cleavages reinforce each other, while crosscutting cleavages resulting from overlapping group memberships may reduce conflict. In a democratic state political parties help to promote consensus by peacefully resolving conflict resulting from social cleavages. *See also* CONFLICT, CONSENSUS.

Clientele Agency   A governmental unit organized to serve or regulate a social or economic group. While all agencies have some characteristic of this sort, a clientele agency's function is specifically directed toward its client's interests. Examples include the Department of Labor, the Veterans Administration, and the Bureau of Indian Affairs in the Department of the Interior. *See also* ORGANIZATION.

Climate (Geographic Power Factor)   The effect of weather conditions on national power. The climatic conditions of a state are determined mainly by its characteristic wind, precipitation, and temperature patterns. Historically, the greatest national power developments have taken place in those regions marked by temperate climatic conditions. Adverse climatic conditions are not impossible to overcome, but extremes of heat and cold demand a greater expenditure of human energy and resources to sustain life than is the case in regions of moderate climate.

Closed Primary   The selection of a party's candidates in an election limited to avowed party members. Voters must declare their party affiliation either when they register or at the primary election. *See also* DIRECT PRIMARY, OPEN PRIMARY.

Closed Shop   An industrial plant that agrees to hire only those persons who are members of a labor union. The closed shop is outlawed by the Taft-Hartley Act of 1947, although later legislation has modified this restriction with regard to the building trades. *See also* UNION SHOP, RIGHT TO WORK LAW.

Closed System, *see* Social Stratification, System.

Cloture (or Closure)   A parliamentary technique used by a legislative body to end debate and bring the matter under consideration to a vote. Cloture can be invoked under an amendment to Rule 22 in the Senate which provides the method by which debate can be limited and a filibuster broken. One-sixth of the Senate membership can initiate action under cloture by petitioning the Senate to close debate on a pending measure. If such a petition is approved by two-thirds of the senators voting, thereafter no senator may speak for more than one hour on the bill being considered. Hence, in a short time the measure will come up for a vote and the attempt of the minority to "talk the bill to death" by filibuster will have been defeated. *See also* FILIBUSTER.

Coalition   The fusion of various political elements into a major American party. In multiparty countries, the fusion involves a coalition of a number of individual parties into a working majority. In the United States, however, both major parties combine factions of liberals, moderates, and conservatives.

Coalition Government   A government in which several minority parties form the Cabinet when no single party can command a majority. The leader of the strongest party tries to secure agreement from enough smaller parties so that their combined strength will constitute a majority in the legislature. The price of agreement may include promises to pursue, modify, or abandon certain policies and programs, and cabinet or other posts for all parties in the coalition. Coalition government is most likely when a nation lacks broad social consensus, parties have strong ideological orientations, diverse minority groups feel they cannot entrust their interests to major parties beyond their control, and the electoral system is based on some form of proportional representation. *See also* MULTIPARTY SYSTEM, PARLIAMENTARY GOVERN-MENT.

Coast and Geodetic Survey, *see* Department of Commerce.

Coast Guard, *see* Department of Transportation.

Code   A compilation of laws in force, classified according to subject matter. Federal laws currently in force are collected in the *United States Code,* which is kept up-to-date with annual supplements and is revised every six years. Many states have collected and classified their statutes, including pertinent judicial decisions, under the title *Compiled Laws. See also* STATUTE.

Code of Federal Regulations (CFR), *see Federal Register.*

Codification of International Law   The systematic organization and statement of the rules of international law. Codification is necessary for the progressive development of international law because of the length of time over which rules of state conduct have been accumulating, because of the changing circumstances in which the rules are applied, and because of the differing interests and interpretations of the rules by various states. Codification has been attempted: (1) by setting forth the rules actually in force; (2) by setting forth the rules as amended to conform to present conditions and standards of justice; (3) by re-creating the entire system in accord with an ideal standard of law. *See also* INTERNATIONAL LAW.

Coding, *see* Content Analysis, Reliability.

Coefficient of Correlation, *see* Correlation.

Coefficient of Reproducibility, *see* Guttman Scale.

Coercion   A form of influence characterized by a high level of constraint or compulsion. Coercive policies may range in a spectrum from economic, social, and political intimidation to the threat or use of military force. Some writers distinguish influence, power, and coercion by treating *influence* as the most inclusive concept, embracing all means of inducement or compulsion. In this schema, *power* is a form of influence deriving from compulsion, that is, the threat of severe loss or deprivation for noncompliance. *Coercion*, in turn, is a form of power that confronts the one coerced with the prospect of severe loss or deprivation no matter what he does. Thus, for the one being coerced, noncompliance will evoke the threatened punishment, but compliance will also involve severe loss. Coercion is sometimes contrasted with *authority* on the ground that authority is legitimate influence while coercion is illegitimate compulsion. *See also* AUTHORITY, INFLUENCE, POWER.

Cognitive Structure, *see* Perception.

Cohens v. Virginia, 6 Wheaton 264 (1821): Ruled that state court decisions are subject to review by the Supreme Court if the case involves a question of federal law, treaties, or the Constitution, even though a state is a party to the suit. An appeal brought to a federal court by a defendant who has been convicted in a state court does not constitute a suit against the state contrary to the Eleventh Amendment.

Cohort   An aggregate of individuals who have had some common experience during the same time period. Most *cohort analyses* use date of birth as their identifying event, although some use such events as "voting for the first time," "married same year," or "inducted into military service the same year." *See also* SURVEY RESEARCH.

Cold War   The extreme state of tension and hostility that developed between the Western powers and the Communist bloc of Eastern Europe after World War II. The Cold War period has been characterized by political maneuvering, diplomatic wrangling, psychological warfare, ideological hostility, economic warfare, a major arms race, peripheral wars, and other power contests falling short of an all-out "hot" war. The origins of the Cold War are found in the conflicts over the partition of

Germany, in the reconstruction of a new balance of power at the war's end, in the communization of Eastern European states and their conversion into a Soviet sphere of influence, in the development of an active anticommunist philosophy and policy in the United States, and in the building of alliances and counteralliances that created a pervasive atmosphere of fear and suspicion between the wartime allies. *See also* BIPOLARITY.

Coleman v. Miller, 307 U.S. 433 (1939): A case establishing the principle that the process of amending the Constitution is essentially political in nature and not subject to judicial interference. Specifically, the Supreme Court held that a state legislature may ratify the child labor amendment proposal after once rejecting it, and that whether the pending proposal was still valid after many years is a political question for Congress to determine. *See also* AMENDMENT.

Colgrove v. Green, *see Baker v. Carr.*

Collective Bargaining   Negotiation between an employer and a union representing the employees. It is to be distinguished from negotiation between an employer and an individual employee. The right of workers to organize and to bargain collectively through their representatives has been the official policy of the United States since 1935. Collective bargaining imposes upon the employer and labor union an obligation to confer in good faith with respect to working conditions and to execute a written contract embodying the agreements reached. Refusal to bargain by an employer or a duly recognized union may be adjudged an unfair labor practice. *See also* WAGNER ACT, *NLRB v. Jones and Laughlin Steel Corp..*

Collective Farm   A huge Soviet farm created by forcing the peasants to pool their individual holdings and to work the land in common. Collectivization was forced upon the Russian peasants at great human and material cost during the 1920s and 1930s by Josef Stalin. Collective farms may include as many as a thousand families and several villages. Experimentation to discover the most effective system of farm management has varied from the local soviet and county level up through the provincial and republic level, with policy direction supplied from the national level. *See also* STATE FARM.

Collective Goods   Anything of value that is characterized by "nonrivalness" in its supply and "nonexclusiveness" in its consumption. Goods have "nonrivalness" of supply when consumption by one individual does not appreciably reduce the supply available for others. "Nonexclusiveness" means that the goods, once produced, are available to purchaser and nonpurchaser alike, because the latter cannot feasibly be excluded from consuming them. Military security, air pollution control, and radio broadcasting are examples of collective goods. Collective goods, sometimes called *public goods,* may be contrasted with *private goods,* such as a loaf of bread or welfare assistance, which can be provided to some and denied to others, and whose consumption diminishes the supply available for others.

Collective Security   A worldwide security system by which all or most nations agree in advance to take collective action against any state or states that break the peace by committing aggression. Collective security is based on the assumption that, normally, no nation or group of nations would dare to challenge the power of the world community, but, if an attack should occur, all nations would honor their commitments to take police action. The United Nations embodies the concept of collective security. Under Chapter VII of its Charter, the organization can take such action, including military, as may be necessary to preserve world peace. Primary responsibility is vested in the five great powers (U.S., USSR, Britain, France, China), each having the veto power in the Security Council. Since 1950, the General Assembly also has been empowered under the Uniting for Peace Resolution to authorize collective security action if the Security Council is stymied with a veto. Sometimes, collective security is also used to describe alliances established under a balance of power system. *See also* SANCTIONS, SECURITY COUNCIL.

Collectivism   A generic term that describes various theories and social movements calling for the ownership and control of all land and means of production by the state or groups rather than by individuals. The term is often used synonymously with the more specific doctrines of socialism and communism, for collectivism rejects the economic freedoms and individual rights of capitalism. *See also* COMMUNISM, SOCIAL-ISM.

Colombo Plan   A regional economic aid program providing multilateral consultative machinery to encourage and to coordinate bilateral assistance programs among its members. The Colombo Plan was established at a Commonwealth Conference at Colombo, Ceylon, in 1950. It provided initially for a $5 billion, six-year development program with capital furnished equally by the developed and developing states. More than twenty states participate in the program, including Commonwealth countries (Australia, Britain, Canada, Ceylon, India, Malaysia, New Zealand, Pakistan, and Singapore), other Asian countries and protectorates (Bhutan, British Borneo, Burma, Cambodia, Indonesia, Japan, South Korea, Laos, Nepal, the Philippines, South Vietnam, and Thailand), and the United States. A Consultative Committee for Economic Development in South and Southeast Asia, with all participating states represented, meets annually to review old programs, plan new ones, and discuss the problems of economic development. A Council for Technical Cooperation functions as a secretariat at the Colombo headquarters to facilitate the exchange of technical experts among members. *See also* COMMONWEALTH OF NATIONS, FOREIGN AID.

Colonialism   The rule of an area and its people. by an external sovereignty, that results from a policy of imperialism. Historically, two broad types of colonialism can be identified: (1) that which involved the transplanting of immigrants from the mother country to form a new political entity; and (2) that which involved the imposition of rule over the technologically less-developed, indigenous peoples of Asia and Africa. In either case, the colony was established to advance the military security, economic advantage, and international prestige of the imperial power. *See also* COLONY, IMPERIALISM.

Colony A noncontiguous territorial possession of a sovereign state. Colonies have been established by settlement, cession, and conquest, and their acquisition marks the successful pursuit of a policy of imperialism. Early in the twentieth century, much of Asia and almost all of the continent of Africa had been carved up into colonies by Britain, France, Belgium, Germany, Spain, Portugal, and The Netherlands. Colonies differ from other dependent territories—such as protectorates, spheres of influence, and leaseholds—in that the imperial power possesses full sovereignty over a colony. *See also* COLONIALISM, IMPERIALISM.

Colorado River Compact An interstate agreement concluded among seven states concerning their respective rights to the waters of the Colorado River and its tributaries. The Colorado River Compact was concluded in 1922 after years of negotiation and was approved by Congress in 1927. Parties to the compact are Arizona, California, Colorado, Nevada, New Mexico, Utah, and Wyoming. *See also* WATER CONSERVATION.

Columbia River Compact An interstate agreement concluded in 1925 among four states—Idaho, Montana, Oregon, and Washington—concerning their respective rights to the waters of the Columbia River and its tributaries. *See also* WATER CONSERVATION.

COMECON, *see* Council for Economic Mutual Assistance.

Comity Courtesies extended between nations in their formal relations with each other. Examples of comity include extradition of fugitives in absence of a treaty, and immunity of diplomats.

Commander in Chief The role of the President, as provided in Article II, section 2 of the Constitution, as supreme commander of the military forces of the United States and of the state national guard units when they are called into federal service. As commander in chief, the President exercises a vast array of "war powers." During periods of war or threat of war, he exercises both military and civilian powers related to defense. *See also* PRESIDENT, WAR POWERS.

Commerce The buying and selling of commodities, transportation, and commercial intercourse, and the transmission of radio, television, and telephonic and telegraphic messages. The Constitution grants Congress the power to regulate interstate and foreign commerce, and commerce with the Indian tribes. The states retain the power to regulate intrastate commerce. *See also* COMMERCE POWER, *Cooley v. Board of Wardens, Gibbons v. Ogden.*

Commerce and Slave Trade Compromise An agreement reached at the Constitutional Convention of 1787, giving the national government power to regulate foreign commerce, requiring the consent of two-thirds of the Senate to treaties, and prohibiting the national government from taxing exports or interfering with the slave trade until 1808.

Commerce Power   The authority granted to Congress by the Constitution (Art. 1, sec. 8) to regulate commerce with foreign nations and among the states. The term "commerce" has been interpreted to include the production and buying and selling of goods as well as the transportation of commodities. Any of these functions are subject to national regulation and control if they affect more than one state. *See also* COMMERCE, *Gibbons v. Ogden.*

Commission, *see* Board.

Commission, European Community, *see* European Community.

Commission on Human Rights, *see* European Convention on Human Rights, Universal Declaration of Human Rights.

Commission Plan   One of the forms of city government in the United States wherein both legislative and executive powers are exercised by a commission of three to nine members. Variations in structure are found around the country, but the essential ingredients of the commission plan include: (1) the concentration of legislative and executive powers in a small group elected at large on a nonpartisan ballot; (2) the collective responsibility of the commission to pass ordinances and control the purse strings; (3) the individual responsibility of each commissioner to head a city department, such as public works, finance, and public safety; and (4) the selection of the mayor from among the commissioners but reducing the office to that of ceremonial leadership. *See also* CITY COUNCIL.

Committee Chairman   The member of the majority party who heads a standing or select legislative committee. In Congress, the chairmen of the twenty-one House and sixteen Senate standing committees are selected automatically under the rule of seniority, although since 1971 the party caucuses must give routine approval in the House. In most state legislatures, the committee chairmen are appointed by the Speaker in the lower house and are usually selected by a committee on committees in the upper chamber. *See also* STANDING COMMITTEE.

Committee of the Whole   An informal procedure used by a legislative body to expedite business by resolving the official body into a committee for the consideration of bills and other matters. In Congress, this procedure is used only by the lower house, which becomes "The Committee of the Whole House [of Representatives] on the State of the Union." A temporary chairman is appointed by the Speaker and the formal rules are suspended.

Committee on Committees   Party committees that determine the assignments of party members to standing committees in the House of Representatives. The Republican Committee on Committees consists of one representative from each state having Republican members in the House. In voting within the Committee on

Committees, each member casts the number of votes equal to the number of Republican members his state has in the House. The Democrats in caucus first choose their party's members of the House Ways and Means Committee and this group then determines the party's standing committee assignments. In the Senate, where only one-third of the seats are filled in each biennial election, a majority party Steering Committee makes the necessary adjustments for each standing committee. In the state legislatures, committees in the lower house are appointed by the Speaker of the House. In the upper house, the procedure varies: selections may be made by the presiding officer, by the chamber as a whole, or by a committee on committees. *See also* STANDING COMMITTEE.

Committee on Political Education (COPE)   The political action organization of the AFL-CIO. COPE combines the political tactics developed over the years by the CIO Political Action Committee (PAC) and the AFL League for Political Education. These were the political action organizations of the two labor federations prior to their merger into the new AFL-CIO in 1955. Funds for COPE's activities are raised through voluntary contributions of trade union members.

Committees, Congressional, *see* Committee Chairman, Conference Committee, Foreign Affairs Committee, Foreign Relations Committee, Investigating Committee, Joint Committee, Rules Committee, Select Committee, Standing Committee, Watchdog Committee, Ways and Means Committee.

Commodity Agreement   An international contract by which signatory states strive to establish an orderly world marketing system for a primary commodity. Commodity agreements are sought mainly by producer states to overcome the destructive competition that emerges from gross overproduction and results in a world "buyers' market." Through a commodity agreement, states establish production controls, regulate exports, establish minimum and maximum world export prices, and provide for reserve stocks of the commodity. States heavily dependent on imports of the commodity may also join in an agreement. Commodity agreements have been concluded for such nonmanufactured products as coffee, olive oil, sugar, wheat, tea, cotton, rubber, tin, and beef. *See also* TERMS OF TRADE.

Commodity Credit Corporation, *see* Department of Agriculture.

Commodity Exchange Authority, *see* Department of Agriculture.

Common Carrier   Any company that offers its services to the public for the transportation of goods or persons. Common carriers include airlines, railroads, bus companies, taxicabs, ships, pipe lines, and trucking lines.

Common Law   Judge-made law that originated in England from decisions shaped according to prevailing custom. Decisions were reapplied to similar situations and, thus, gradually became common to the nation. Common law forms the basis of legal procedures in American states, except in Louisiana, where certain French legal traditions are preserved. There is no federal common law, since the national government is one of delegated powers; however, federal judges apply state common law in cases involving citizens of different states, where there is no applicable federal statute. A statute overrides the common law, but many statutes are based upon the common law and are interpreted according to the common law tradition. *See also* EQUITY, *Erie Railroad v. Tompkins.*

Common Market, European, *see* European Economic Community.

Common Organization of Africa and Malagasy (OCAM)   A regional group formed by French-speaking African states in 1965 to constitute a political force and to promote common economic and social objectives. The Organization Commune Africaine et Malgache includes the member states of Cameroon, the Central African Republic, Chad, the Congo (Brazzaville), Congo (Dem. Rep.), Dahomey, Gabon, Ivory Coast, Malagasy, Niger, Rwanda, Senegal, Togo, and Upper Volta. Mauritania, sponsor of OCAM's charter meeting, withdrew from the organization in mid-1965. OCAM's structure consists of a Conference of Heads of State and of Government that meets annually and functions as the "Supreme Authority," a Council of Ministers that also meets annually to work out programs for member cooperation, and a secretariat chosen for two-year periods that is responsible for general administration.

Commonwealth Aid Program, *see* Colombo Plan.

Commonwealth of Nations   A voluntary association of independent states that were once parts of the British Empire. The Commonwealth's thirty-one members (1972) include some from Europe, Asia, Oceania, and the Western Hemisphere. Queen Elizabeth is recognized as "the symbol of the free association of its independent member nations and as such the Head of the Commonwealth." Several members—India, Pakistan, Malaysia, Cyprus, and Ghana—have become republics and no longer accept the British sovereign as their national head of state. The essence of the Commonwealth system is free cooperation engendered through consultations among members. No formal treaty ties or permanent institutions exist, except for a secretariat. Adherence to the Commonwealth is encouraged by trade preferences and sterling bloc membership, capital and technical assistance grants by advanced members to developing states, military aid to those whose security is threatened, and common institutions and language. Consultations are carried on at many levels, with meetings of the Commonwealth Prime Ministers held whenever necessary. *See also* COMMON-WEALTH PREFERENCES.

Commonwealth Preferences   A system by which Britain and other Commonwealth countries reciprocally grant preferential trade treatment to one another. Imperial preferences originated in 1919, when Britain had no general tariff, as an arrangement whereby members of the Empire granted Britain economic preferences in exchange for the protection by the British fleet. The system was expanded in 1932 when Britain adopted a general tariff and, in the Ottawa Agreement, granted special treatment for the Dominions to sell their primary commodities in the British market in exchange for continued preference for British manufactures in their markets. To protect infant industry in the Dominions, their tariffs were raised on all entering manufactured goods, but rates which applied to Britain were kept much lower, though still protective. *See also* COMMONWEALTH OF NATION, PREFERENTIAL TRADE ARRANGEMENT.

Commune Primary unit of Chinese Communist social organization designed to maximize production through a reorganization of work and living patterns. Communes were established to replace traditional units of local administration in the interest of integrating industrial, agricultural, commercial, cultural, military, and police functions. Private and cooperative property and equipment were to be communalized, and all labor from housekeeping through local agricultural and industrial production and management was to be carried on as a function of the collectivity. Work was to be performed by variously named production teams patterned in echelons like a military organization (squad, company, batalion, regiment, and so on).

Communication, *see* Mass Media, Political Communication.

Communication, Political, *see* Political Communication.

Communications Theory A body of thought that seeks to explain processes of information sending, receiving, storing, and utilization as they relate to a political system. Communication is the means by which a political system receives and acts upon inputs and develops outputs. The system receives *information* that is analyzed and reacted to. The changing environment continually produces new demands, which are communicated to the system and which determine the *load* that challenges the efficacy of the system. The time interval between receipt of the communication and reaction to it is referred to as *lag. Distortion* occurs when information received by the system is changed or misinterpreted before it can be acted on, while *gain* measures the effective action in terms of changes wrought as a result of communications received. Information concerning the effectiveness of system outputs on the environment is termed *feedback,* and the extent to which the system is able to adjust to feedback information helps to determine its effectiveness as a political system. Information communicated to the system is stored so that it may be used in making future decisions. Communications theory also relates to the ways in which attitudes and images are built up in the minds of decision makers and the way they affect perception, values, goal seeking, and decision making. *See also* CYBERNETICS, POLITICAL COMMUNICATION.

Communism A political, economic, and social theory based on a collectivistic society in which all land and capital are socially owned and political power is exercised by the masses. Modern communism is based on the theories and practices of Karl Marx, V. I. Lenin, Josef Stalin, Nikita Khrushchev, and contemporary Soviet leaders, with some new variations provided by Mao Tse-tung and the Chinese Communists. Communism in theory espouses the doctrines of historical inevitability, economic determinism, labor value, the "inner contradictions" of capitalism, class conflict, capitalist colonialism and imperialism, world wars resulting from competition for markets, the destruction of the bourgeoisie, the dictatorship of the proletariat, the socialist revolution, and the final "withering away" of the state. Plato and other political theorists have also advocated communism in the form of communal living and various church and social groups have practiced it. *See also* ECONOMIC DETERMINISM, CONVERGENCE THEORY.

Communism (Communist Theory)   The final stage of the dialectical process, in which the "new Communist man" lives in a classless, stateless society, accepts a new and higher morality, and spontaneously cooperates with his fellow man. Marx anticipated that pure communism would follow the transitional stage of proletarian dictatorship because the proletarian state would simply "wither away" as the classless society was achieved. Communism would constitute man's final and highest stage of social development since the energizing force of class conflict would no longer exist, nor would there be a need for further evolutionary progress. The production and distribution of material wealth under communism, according to Marx, would change from a socialist basis of "from each according to his ability, to each according to his work" to a system based on the communist principle of "from each according to his ability, to each according to his needs."

Communism (United States Policies), *see Albertson v. Subversive Activities Control Board,* Alien Registration Act of 1940, *Dennis v. United States,* Deportation, Guilt by Association, Immigration, Immigration and Nationality Act of 1952, Internal Security Act of 1950, Loyalty Oath, Naturalization, Passport, *Scales v. United States,* Sedition, Subversive Activities Control Board, Treason.

Communist Control Act of 1954   An act of Congress that deprives the Communist party of the rights and privileges of other legally organized bodies or political parties and declares it to be a clear and present threat to the security of the United States. The law does not make it a crime to be a Communist.

Communist Front, *see* Internal Security Act of 1950.

Communist Party of the Soviet Union (CPSU)   The ruling institution in the Soviet state. According to the rules adopted by the Twenty-second Party Congress in 1961, "The Communist Party of the Soviet Union [CPSU] is the tried and tested militant vanguard of the Soviet people, which unites, on a voluntary basis, the more advanced, the politically more conscious section of the working class, collective-farm peasantry and intelligentsia of the USSR" and "is the highest form of sociopolitical organization, and . . . the leading and guiding force of Soviet society." The CPSU pervades every facet of life in the Soviet Union and serves as the vehicle for control from the top. Education for life in Marxist-Leninist society begins early and progresses by age groups through indoctrination and recruitment organizations—the Little Octobrists, the Young Pioneers, and the Young Communist League. Membership through succeeding organizational levels is highly selective; only about 5 percent of the population achieve the ultimate goal of full party membership. At the base of the CPSU structure, the All-Union Party Congress represents the rank-and-file party members but is too large and meets too infrequently to exercise real power. It formally elects the Central Committee to direct party activities between congresses. The Central Committee meets twice a year and is also too large to be an effective, continuing decision-making body. It nominally elects the members of the Politburo, who have been selected in advance by the party leaders. The Politburo tops the pattern of party organization on the national level. It is the supreme policymaking body in the country and consists of eleven members and five candidate members. All party activities are coordinated through the Secretariat. *See also* ALL-UNION PARTY CONGRESS, CENTRAL COMMITTEE, POLITBURO, SECRETARIAT OF THE CENTRAL COMMITTEE.

Communist Party v. Subversive Activities Control Board, *see Albertson v. Subversive Activities Control Board.*

Communist Theory, *see* Class struggle, Communism, Contradictions of Capitalism, Democratic Centralism, Dialectical Materialism, Dictatorship of the Proletariat, Economic Interpretation of History, Historical Inevitability, Imperialism and Colonialism, New Communist Man, Revolution, Socialist Program, Surplus Value.

Community   A social group having a sense of common identity, self-awareness, and shared interests. Generally, members of a community reside in a specific geographical area, utilize common institutional machinery, and carry on a volume of social transactions large enough to create a consciousness of common interests. Communities vary in size and complexity from rural village and urban centers to massive, politically integrated groups in the modern state. Some political analysts have also recognized the existence of "political" and "security" communities on the international level. *See also* POLITICAL COMMUNITY.

Community Action Program   A "war on poverty" program created by the Economic Opportunity Act of 1964 to stimulate communities to mobilize their resources against poverty. Federal aid is given to local public and private agencies to undertake antipoverty programs that involve the poor themselves in operating the programs. Possible projects include literacy instruction, job training, vocational rehabilitation, homemaker services, job development and health services. *See also* ECONOMIC OPPORTUNITY ACT.

Community, Atlantic, *see* Atlantic Community.

Community, European, *see* European Community.

Community (France)   An institution designed to maintain ties and foster cooperation between France and her former colonies. The Community in 1958 replaced the Fourth Republic's French Union which had been established in 1946 as the successor to the pre-World War II French Empire. The Constitution of the Fifth Republic enables the members of the Community to share in the election of the President of France, who is also designated President of the Community. Areas of cooperation and coordination were to include foreign affairs, defense, and monetary, financial, and economic systems. The Executive Council, presided over by the President, is composed of the French Premier, the heads of government of the member states, and ministers responsible for common Community affairs. The Constitution also provides for a Senate composed of representatives of legislatures of the members, and for a court of arbitration.

Community, Political, *see* Political Community.

Community Power Studies, *see* Community, Elitist Theory, Power.

Community Relations Service   Established by the Civil Rights Act of 1964 to help communities resolve civil rights problems. The Service is part of the Justice Department, headed by a director responsible to the Attorney General. The facilities of the Service are made available either upon request or through its own initiative. It is directed by law to seek the cooperation of state and local agencies and to carry on its work without publicity.

Comparative Advantage   A theory, first advanced by David Ricardo in 1817, that explains why each country tends to specialize in the production of those commodities for which its costs are relatively lowest. The concept of comparative advantage or comparative cost modified Adam Smith's theory of an international specialization based on *absolute* national advantage. In rebutting Smith's doctrine, Ricardo noted that few countries have a clear cost superiority in the production of goods for the world market, and that labor, capital, and enterprise are relatively immobile internationally and are unlikely to move to those places where absolute advantage could be maintained. *See also* LAISSEZ-FAIRE.

Comparative Study   A form of inquiry which involves the determination of differences and similarities between two or more units of analysis. A political event or case can be compared with other similar cases, with hypothetical cases, or with cases occurring in a time sequence. *See also* CASE STUDY.

Competitive Bid Contract, *see* Defense Contract

Compiled Laws of the United States, *see* Code.

Compromis   A preliminary agreement by the parties to a dispute which establishes the terms under which the dispute will be arbitrated. The *compromis* specifies the jurisdictional limits of the arbitral tribunal by: (1) defining the subject of the dispute; (2) setting forth the principles that are to guide the tribunal; and (3) establishing the rules of procedure to be followed in deciding the case. Specific questions relating to its jurisdiction are decided by the tribunal under the terms of the *compromis*. An award or decision by the arbitrators may, however, be null and void if the tribunal exceeds its authority as laid down by the parties in the *compromis*. *See also* ARBITRATION.

Comptroller General   The federal official responsible for auditing the accounts of all national government agencies. Functioning as the financial adviser to Congress, the Comptroller General heads the General Accounting Office (GAO), and is appointed by the President with the Senate's approval for a fifteen-year term. The Comptroller General (pronounced con-troller) also has power to validate all payments to ensure that they fall within the purposes and limits of congressional appropriations acts and to standardize accounting systems of government agencies. He can be removed from office by impeachment or by joint resolution of Congress. *See also* GENERAL ACCOUNT-ING OFFICE.

Compulsion, *see* Coercion.

Compulsory Jurisdiction   The power of an international court to hear and decide certain classes of cases without the necessity of both parties agreeing to accept the jurisdiction of the court in each case. The Statute of the International Court of Justice provides for compulsory jurisdiction in its "Optional Clause" (Article 36), which specifies that "The states parties to the present Statute may at any time declare that they recognize as compulsory ipso facto and without special agreement, in relation to any other state accepting the same obligation, the jurisdiction of the Court in all legal disputes concerning: (a) the interpretation of a treaty; (b) any question of international law; (c) the existence of any fact which, if established, would constitute a breach of an international obligation; (4) the nature or extent of the reparation to be made for the breach of an international obligation." *See also* CONNALLY AMENDMENT, INTERNA-TIONAL COURT OF JUSTICE, JURISDICTION (COURT).

Computer Simulation, *see* Simulation.

Concept   A mental image or construct formed by generalizing from the characteristics of a class of things. A concept is an abstraction to which a descriptive label is attached, and the label may then be applied to individual members of the class to which the concept refers. Concepts can represent relatively simple abstractions, such as "President" or "voter," or more complex ones like "integration," "influence," and "decision making." Conceptualizing, the process of constructing or forming the concepts needed to to carry out an investigation, is followed by the development of a conceptual scheme or framework to facilitate systematic study and analysis. Because of the difficulty of developing political concepts that accurately and uniformly describe intricate relationships, an "operational definition" is often inferred from observable properties and used to delimit the applicability of the concept to a specific problem. Thus an investigator may operationally define "integration" in terms of the volume of trade or other transactions occurring between two or more political units. *See also* CONCEPTUAL SCHEME, VARIABLE.

Conceptual Scheme   A set of related concepts that provides an analytic framework in political research and gives an investigator an overview of his research material. A conceptual scheme consists of those concepts, together with theories and assumptions relating the concepts to one another, which an investigator plans to use in his analysis. It might be likened to an umbrella under which concepts can be systematically arranged, or to a sieve which is used to sort out data so that they may be systematically examined. *See also* APPROACH, CONCEPT, PARADIGM.

Concert of Europe   An ad hoc system of consultation among the great powers developed after the Napoleonic wars. The Concert met sporadically during the nineteenth century to settle major issues that threatened to disrupt the peace. It included Austria, England, France, Prussia, and Russia, later joined by Germany and Italy, and smaller powers when they were directly involved in the matter under discussion. The concert system functioned mainly through international conferences called at the initiative of a great power that believed that the peace was threatened. The result was the establishment of great power hegemony that functioned effectively until the unity of the great powers was destroyed by a rigid polarization of its members into two rival alliances—the Triple Entente (Britain, France, and Russia) and the Triple Alliance (Germany, Austria-Hungary, and Italy).

Conciliation (International)   A peaceful settlement procedure in which the representatives of a group of states establish the facts in a dispute and use them as the basis for recommending a solution. Conciliation, which is often linked with inquiry, can be viewed as group mediation. Commissions of conciliation may be established *ad hoc* and are also included in the peaceful settlement provisions of many bilateral as well as multilateral treaties. Such provisions are included, for example, in the Pact of Bogota of the Organization of american States (1948) and the Brussels Treaty, signed the same year by Belgium, Britain, France, Luxembourg, and The Netherlands. *See also* PEACEFUL SETTLEMENT.

Conciliation (Labor), *see* Mediation and Conciliation (Labor-Management).

Conciliation (Private)   A method by which a third party attempts to settle a controversy between disputants outside the courtroom. It is similar to arbitration, except that the decision is not binding upon the parties nor enforceable in court. A number of large cities have established a conciliation branch in their judicial structure.

Concurrent Jurisdiction   Authority vested in two or more courts to hear cases involving the same subject matter. The term is generally used to indicate those instances in which both federal and state courts may hear the same kind of case. For example, the Congress has conferred concurrent jurisdiction upon state and federal courts in suits between citizens of different states where the amount in controversy exceeds $10,000. The parties to such a suit may choose to have their case heard in either a federal or state court. Suits involving less than $10,000 must be heard in state courts. *See also* JURISDICTION.

Concurrent Majority   The political doctrine, expounded by John C. Calhoun of South Carolina prior to the Civil War, that democratic decisions should be made only with the concurrence of all major segments of society. Without such concurrence, Calhoun argued, a decision should not be binding on those groups whose interests it violates. *See also* NULLIFICATION.

Concurrent Powers   Authority possessed by both the national and state governments. Examples include the powers to tax, to maintain courts, and to charter banks. The states exercise concurrently with the national government any power that is not exclusively conferred on the national government by the Constitution and that does not conflict with national law. *See also* DELEGATED POWERS, RESERVED POWERS.

Concurrent Resolution   A special measure, designated "H Con Res" or "S Con Res," that requires approval by both houses of Congress but does not need the President's signature. *See also* JOINT RESOLUTION, SIMPLE RESOLUTION.

Concurring Opinion   An opinion of one or more judges, usually of an appellate court, that supports the conclusions of a majority of the court but offers different reasons for reaching those conclusions. Concurring opinions are quite common in the United States Supreme Court. *See also* DISSENTING OPINION.

Condominium   A dependent territory governed jointly by two or more sovereigns. In a condominium the legal systems of the states exercising control operate side by side, and questions of jurisdiction are governed by an agreement between the sovereigns. Examples of joint control through condominium arrangements include the Sudan (Britain and France, 1914) and Canton Island and Enderbury Island (Britain and the United States, 1938).

Confederation   A league of independent states. A central government or administrative organ handles those matters of common concern delegated to it by the member states. The central unit may not make laws directly applicable to individuals without further action by the member units. The governments under the Articles of Confederation and the Confederate States of America are two examples from American history. The United Nations is often referred to as a confederation. *See also* ARTICLES OF CONFEDERATION, FEDERALISM.

Conference Committee   A special joint committee appointed to reconcile differences when a bill passes the two houses of Congress in different forms. A joint conference committee consists of three to nine "managers" appointed by the Speaker of the House and the President of the Senate. Efforts are directed toward a compromise version of the bill, which must be approved by a majority of the managers for each house voting separately. This compromise version, in the form of a "conference report," then goes for approval to each house. It cannot there be amended, and, if rejected by either house, it may go back to conference for further negotiation.

Conference Diplomacy   Large-scale multilateral diplomatic negotiation conducted at international meetings. Historically associated with the establishment of peace after a major war, conference diplomacy dates from the beginning of the Western state system at the Congress of Westphalia (1642–1648), which ended the Thirty Years' War. Used with increased frequency in the eighteenth and nineteenth centuries, conference diplomacy was institutionalized and systematized on a global scale with the creation of the League of Nations in 1919. As the successor to the League, the United Nations constitutes a world diplomatic conference in permanent session, theoretically capable of dealing with any international political, legal, social, economic, cultural or technical problem. Regularized conference diplomacy also occurs on a limited topical or geographical basis, as in the case of meetings held by the International Monetary Fund, the North Atlantic Treaty Organization, or the Organization of African Unity. Similarly, ad hoc conference diplomacy was employed by the nonaligned Afro-Asian countries at the Bandung Conference of 1955. The knowledge explosion and its attendant technological advances have produced a number and variety of both ad hoc and institutionalized conferences, many of them called by specialized agencies of the United Nations. The formal and quasi-parliamentary nature of conference diplomacy involves selection of a chairman, adoption of standard working procedures, the establishment of a committee structure to expedite the work, and some system for reaching decisions. *See also* DIPLOMACY, NEGOTIATION.

Conference of Experts   A meeting of scientists and technicians to explore complex questions in a specified field to make recommendations to help diplomatic negotiators reach agreement. The conference-of-experts approach, for example, was used twice in 1958 in the disarmament field when Eastern and Western leaders established: (1) a conference of experts to study the possibility of detecting violations of an agreement on the suspension of nuclear tests; and (2) a conference of experts for the study of possible measures which might be helpful in preventing surprise attack. The former was composed of experts from four Eastern countries (Czechoslovakia, Poland, Rumania, and the Soviet Union) and four Western countries (Britain, Canada, France, and the United States), and the latter included representatives from the same nations but added Albania to the Eastern group and Italy to the Western. The reports of both conferences were submitted to the governments involved and to the United Nations. The conference-of-experts approach has also been applied to other areas of negotiation where agreement on technical and scientific issues is a necessary forerunner to political agreement.

Conference of the Committee on Disarmament (CCD) A body originally created as the Eighteen Nation Disarmament Committee (ENDC) by the Sixteenth General Assembly in 1961, to "undertake negotiations with a view to reaching . . . agreement on general and complete disarmament under effective international control." The CCD was established in 1969 when the United States and the Soviet Union agreed to expand the membership of the Committee from eighteen to twenty-six in response to demands from nonnuclear states for a more equitable geographical and political balance on the Committee. Membership on the CCD includes Western bloc states (Argentina, Brazil, Britain, Canada, France, Italy, Japan, Mexico, Netherlands, Pakistan, and the United States). Eastern bloc states (Bulgaria, Czechoslovakia, Hungary, Mongolia, Poland, Romania, and the Soviet Union), and Nonaligned states (Burma, Ethiopia, India, Morocco, Nigeria, Sweden, United Arab Republic, and Yugoslavia). The CCD convenes regularly in Geneva with the objective of bringing the arms race under control by negotiating agreements to limit, reduce, or eliminate nuclear weapons and, ultimately, to secure general and complete disarmament. *See also* STRATEGIC ARMS LIMITATION TALKS (SALT).

Conference, Republican, *see* Caucus.

Confession An admission of guilt by one accused of a crime. *See also Ashcraft v. Tennessee, Miranda v. Arizona, McNabb v. United States.*

Confirmation The power of a legislative body to approve nominations made to fill executive and judicial positions. Nominations for such offices made by the President must be confirmed by the Senate with a majority vote. Many of the appointments made by the governors in the various states must also be approved by the upper houses of the legislatures. *See also* SENATORIAL COURTESY, APPOINTMENT POWER.

Confiscation Seizure of private property by a government, usually without compensation. Confiscation on a large scale may be the result of war or revolution; when it is applied selectively against individuals it typically is the result of law violations on their part. *See also* NATIONALIZATION, EMINENT DOMAIN.

Conflict Antagonistic encounters or collisions of interests, principles, ideas, policies, or programs that characterize many of the interactions carried on within or between political systems. In political analysis the opposing concepts of conflict and cooperation (or consensus) are used to classify the two basic forms of political activity. Many political interactions involve neither in pure form, however, but include some elements of each. Political conflict has many manifestations, ranging from verbal expressions of disagreement to outright physical combat. Within societies, conflict is often mitigated by nonpolitical means, such as social pressures or economic restraints, or is resolved by action of private groups. Serious conflicts that threaten the stability of society or that may result in severe or widespread violence usually require intervention by government. Conflict is especially obvious in the international milieu where political competition in forms ranging from diplomacy to war encourages such encounters and collisions. *See also* COERCION.

Conflict of Interest   The situation that occurs when an official's public actions are affected by his personal interests. A conflict of interest charge usually alleges that an elected or appointed official realized some direct or indirect financial gain from governmental actions he participated in, or that the public decisions he made were motivated by his efforts to protect his personal financial interests or those of close friends or political supporters. *See also* CORRUPT PRACTICES ACTS.

Conflict of Laws (Private International Law)   Legal situations in which the laws of more than one country may be applied. Conflict-of-laws situations typically involve such subjects as torts, contracts, inheritance, acquisition and transmittal of property, nationality, domicile, and marriage and divorce. The conflict-of-laws rules of the state determine whether or not, and to what extent, effect will be given to the acts of another state.

Confrontation Clause   The part of the Sixth Amendment to the Constitution which guarantees that, in criminal prosecutions, the accused shall have the right "to be confronted with the witnesses against him." An important corollary is the right to cross-examine such witnesses. In 1965 the Supreme Court ruled that the right of confrontation of witnesses also applies in state trials under the due process clause of the Fourteenth Amendment (*Pointer v. Texas*, 380 U.S. 400). *See also* WITNESS.

Congo Force, *see* United Nations Operation in the Congo.

Congress   The national legislature of the United States, composed of the Senate and the House of Representatives. The principle of state equality entitles each of the fifty states to two senators who serve six-year terms, with one-third of the senators elected every two years. Membership in the House of Representatives is based on population and all 435 members face the electorate every two years. The foreign relations role of the Congress comprises: (1) its general legislative power in such matters as creating or eliminating agencies and in establishing or changing trade and immigration policy; (2) the executive powers of the Senate in approving treaties and confirming appointments; (3) control over appropriations; (4) power to conduct investigations, particularly in relation to the functioning of old law and the need for new law. Congress is also related indirectly to foreign affairs through: (1) resolutions indicating the "sense of the Congress"; (2) speeches, travels, and other activities of individual members; and (3) political party activity, which can either diminish or increase the distance between the White House and Capitol Hill. *See also* HOUSE OF REPRESENTATIVES, SENATE (UNITED STATES).

Congressional and Senatorial Campaign Committees   House and Senate groups consisting of Republican and Democratic members selected by fellow party members in their respective chambers to organize and to help finance election campaigns. The House Republican Campaign Committee consists of one congressman from each state having Republican representation in the House. House Democrats use this formula also, but supplement it with women members from some states as selected by the committee chairman. Senate Committees consist of six or seven members selected from the Senate.

Congressional Committees, *see* Committee Chairman, Conference Committee, Foreign Affairs Committee, Foreign Relations Committee, Investigating Committee, Joint Committee, Rules Committee, Select Committee, Standing Committee, Watchdog Committee, Ways and Means Committee.

Congressional Directory   A handbook published annually that contains information regarding the organization of Congress and its committees and brief biographical sketches of the senators and representatives.

Congressional District   A political geographical division of a state from which one member of the House of Representatives is elected. A congressional district is usually a portion of a state, but if a state's population entitles it to only one representative, as in the case of Alaska and Nevada, the entire state is the congressional district. *See also* GERRYMANDERING, REDISTRICTING, *Wesberry v. Sanders.*

Congressional Record   A verbatim record of the proceedings (debates, speeches, and votes) in both the House and the Senate, printed daily. Members may edit their remarks and speeches before printing, and they also may insert material, called "extension of remarks," that was not actually delivered on the floor of their chamber. *See also* EXTENSION OF REMARKS.

Congressional Research Service (CRS)   A staff agency of Congress which provides research data to aid committees and members of Congress in their legislative duties. Created as the Legislative Reference Service in the Library of Congress in 1914, it was redesignated Congressional Research Service and given expanded responsibilities by the Legislative Reorganization Act of 1970. Each year, various studies, statistics, charts and the like are provided for congressmen and committees in response to thousands of inquiries. Many state legislatures have created similar staff facilities.

Congressional Township   A six-mile-square area of land established under laws of Congress for the purpose of surveying the land. The system was started by the Confederation Congress in 1785, and was applied to the land in most states. Excluded are the original thirteen states and Maine, Kentucky, Tennessee, Vermont, West Virginia, and Texas. Under the law, land is divided into townships six miles square and each township is divided into thirty-six mile-square sections. Each section is further subdivided into quarter sections and less. By the assignment of numbered base lines, similar to the longitude and latitude patterns on maps, any parcel of land may be easily identified. *See also* TOWNSHIP.

Congressman, *see* Representative.

Congressman at Large   A member of the House of Representatives who is elected by the voters of an entire state rather than by those of a specific district. If a state gains seats following a decennial reapportionment and fails to redistrict, the new seats will be filled by election at large. If a state loses seats and fails to redistrict, then all of the state's congressmen will be elected at large, an arrangement that may result in one party's winning all the seats. States with only one member of the House will, of course, always elect that one at large. Decisions concerning redistricting are made by the majority party in the state legislatures. *See also* AT LARGE.

Congress, Party Role in, *see* Caucus, Committee on Committees, Majority Floor Leader, Policy Committee, Whip.

Congress, Powers of, *see* Constituent Power, Impeachment, Investigating Committee, Power of the Purse, War Powers.

Congress, Voting in, *see* Division, Pair, Record Vote, Teller Vote, Unanimous Consent, Viva Voce Vote.

Connally Amendment   The reservation attached by the United States to its acceptance in 1946 of compulsory jurisdiction under the Optional Clause of Article 36 of the Statute of the International Court of Justice. The Connally Amendment denies the Court compulsory jurisdiction in "disputes with regard to matters which are essentially within the domestic jurisdiction of the United States of America as determined by the United States of America." The practical effect of the Amendment is to destroy the intended compulsory feature of the Court's jurisdiction since the United States is left free to determine what is a domestic matter and therefore beyond the purview of the Court. *See also* COMPULSORY JURISDICTION, INTERNATIONAL COURT OF JUSTICE, JURISDICTION (COURT).

Connecticut Compromise   The agreement reached in the Constitutional Convention of 1787 that resolved the question of representation in the national Congress. Each state is represented in the House of Representatives according to population and in the Senate each state is represented equally. The Compromise, also called the "Great Compromise," satisfied the small states in particular and made it possible for them to agree to the establishment of a strong central government. *See also* BICAMERALISM.

Conscientious Objector   A person who refuses to render military service because of religious training and belief. While the right to religious freedom does not extend to refusal to serve in the military service, Congress has, as an act of grace, authorized noncombatant service or exemption from military service for conscientious objectors. The law does not exempt persons who oppose military service because of "political, sociological, or philosophical views or a merely personal moral code," but the Supreme Court has interpreted this liberally to include nontraditional conscientious objection held with the fervor of religious conviction. *See also* SELECTIVE SERVICE.

Consensus   Agreement within a group on some goal, value, or matter of opinion. Consensus, in relatively small groups and on relatively clear-cut issues, may sometimes be complete. In larger groups, and certainly in whole societies, consensus on an issue is likely to be only partial at any given time and to vary in degree from one time to another. Consensus is frequently contrasted with *cleavage*, which refers to a critical division in a society that may lead to political conflict. Consensus, as a decision-making procedure in a group, means agreement or acquiescence by all members of the group. *See also* CLEAVAGE, CONFLICT.

Consensus of Values   A mutuality of attitudes, beliefs, and aspirations among human beings. When a consensus of values exists, political action may be both motivated by and directed toward the achievement of common goals. When a group possesses a high level of value consensus, it is often described as a "community." *See also* POLITICAL COMMUNITY, VALUE.

Consent Calendar, *see* Calendar.

Consent, Senate, *see* Advise and Consent.

Conservation   The careful management and wise use of natural resources to prevent depletion and to maximize the production of wealth from their use. Conservation involves the protection, preservation, and replenishment as well as the planned use of land, forests, wildlife, minerals, and water by private individuals and national, state, and local governments. Conservationists include those who wish to conserve resources for economic reasons, and those who are mainly concerned with ecological and esthetic considerations. *See also* SOIL CONSERVATION, WATER CONSERVATION, DEPART-MENT OF THE INTERIOR, ENVIRONMENTAL POLITICS.

Conservatism   Defense of the status quo against major changes in the political, economic, or social institutions of a society. The classic statement of the philosophy of conservatism was expounded by the English statesman, Edmund Burke. He held that political stability could be maintained only if the forces of change could be moderated by a slow and careful integration of new elements into time-tested institutions. *See also* LIBERALISM.

Conservative Party (Britain)   Along with Labour, one of the two major parties in British politics. The official title is the Conservative and Unionist Party. Traditionally the party of the aristocracy and middle class, the Conservatives are descended from the old Tories and are sometimes called by that name. Today, the party attempts to draw support from all sectors of the electorate. The party operates under a Leader who exercises extensive personal control over its affairs. He sets party policy, appoints top officials, chooses the shadow cabinet when his party is in opposition, and is not dependent on annual reelection to retain his office. Outside Parliament, the party operates through a hierarchy of institutions that include: (1) local constituency units and associations; (2) the National Union and its Annual Conference; (3) the Central Council; (4) the Executive Committee; and, at the apex of party structure, (5) the Leader. Inside Parliament, the Leader also exercises vast personal power over the Parliamentary Party (all Conservative MPs) as long as he maintains the confidence of his party's nonofficeholding MPs organized in "The 1922 Committee," which could force his resignation. *See also* PARTY SYSTEM (BRITAIN).

Consolidation   The union of two or more units of government to form a single unit. Consolidation is often recommended as a solution to metropolitan area problems, but it is also recommended in rural areas as a means of reducing the large number of local governments in existence. State constitutions or statutes designate consolidation procedures, generally requiring the separate consent of all units. *See also* METROPOLITAN AREA.

Conspiracy   Any agreement between two or more persons to commit an unlawful act. Conspiracy is a crime under numerous criminal statutes; in the realm of business and labor activities the law forbids conspiracies in restraint of trade. The most prominent conspiracy provision in the field of civil liberties is that found in the Smith Act of 1940, which makes it a crime to conspire to teach, advocate, or organize groups that advocate the overthrow of government by force.

Constituency   A voting district or geographical unit represented in a legislature, or the people so represented. The individual voter is called a constituent. Under a single-member district system, a constituency sends one representative to the legislature; under systems of proportional representation, several representatives are elected from each constituency.

Constituent Power   Participation in the process of making, amending, or revising a constitution. The constituent power of Congress consists of its authority to propose amendments to the United States Constitution by a two-thirds vote of both houses, or to call a national convention for this purpose on petition of two-thirds of the state legislatures. Amendment proposals must be ratified by three-fourths of the state legislatures or by specially elected conventions in three-fourths of the states. In the states, the legislatures are usually empowered to propose specific amendments to their state constitutions Extensive revisions of state constitutions are generally done by constitutional conventions established solely for that purpose. Ratification of state constitutional changes is vested in the people of that state. *See also* AMENDMENT, CONSTITUTIONAL CONVENTION.

Constitution   A fundamental or "organic" law that establishes the framework of government of a state, assigns the powers and duties of governmental agencies, and establishes the relationship between the people and their government. Constitutions may be written or unwritten. The English operate under an unwritten constitution, that is, one consisting largely of legislative acts, legal decisions, and customs that have never been comprehensively gathered in one document. American constitutions are written, but much fundamental law is unwritten and is in the form of custom and usage. The United States Constitution went into effect on March 4, 1789, and has been amended twenty-six times. It is the supreme law of the land. Its basic principles include limited government, popular sovereignty, separation of powers, checks and balances, and federalism. *See also* CONSTITUTION, STATE, DISTRIBUTION OF POWERS.

Constitutional Amendment, *see* Amendment.

Constitutional Amendments, State   Changes in or additions to a state constitution. Amendment procedures are detailed in each state's constitution. Generally, two proposal methods are available—legislative, by an extraordinary majority, and initiative of the people. Ratification by the people is usually accomplished by simple majority vote, but a few states require an extraordinary majority. Under the initiative method, permitted in fourteen states, the voters draw up a petition with a specified number of signatures (8 or 10 percent of the voters) requesting the desired change. If the petition is in order, the proposal goes on the ballot for ratification by the people.

Constitutional Commission   A group of citizens selected by the legislature and/or the governor of a state to study the state constitution and to make recommendations for change.

Constitutional Construction   The method of interpreting the Constitution. Some favor a "loose" or "liberal" construction of constitutional phrases; others, a "strict" interpretation. The difference is largely expressed in terms of the interpreter's attitude toward broad grants of power to the national government (loose construction) as opposed to the retention of as much power as possible in the states (strict construction). *See also McCulloch v. Maryland.*

Constitutional Convention   A body selected by the people to rewrite the constitution. Most state constitutions make provisions for the calling of a constitutional convention but, even if no provisions are made, the power to call a convention is considered to be inherent in the people in their sovereign capacity. Eleven states provide for a mandatory, periodic submission to the people of the question of whether they wish to call a convention. The procedures for a constitutional convention generally involve: (1) the placing of the question on the ballot by the legislature, usually by an extraordinary majority unless it be mandatory for that year; (2) the election of delegates, should the people approve the call; (3) the meeting of the convention, which has deliberations similar in method and procedure to legislative bodies; and (4) the submission of the new constitution to the people for ratification.

Constitutional Convention of 1787   The convention held in Philadelphia from May 25 to September 18 that framed the Constitution of the United States. Called by the Confederation Congress to revise the Articles of Confederation, the delegates proceeded to draft an entirely new document. Rhode Island sent no delegates and only fifty-five of the seventy-four men originally appointed as delegates attended. George Washington presided. The deliberations were conducted in secret but have been made known through notes kept by James Madison. The delegates made compromises on various differences between large and small states, North and South, agrarian and commercial interests, and advocates of a strong or a weak central government. They not only ignored their instructions merely to revise the Articles of Confederation, but also ignored the provision of the Articles requiring unanimous consent of the state legislatures for revision by providing that the new constitution would go into effect when nine states ratified it in state conventions. *See also* COMMERCE AND SLAVE TRADE COMPROMISE, CONNECTICUT COMPROMISE, ECONOMIC INTERPRETATION OF THE CONSTITUTION, MADISON'S JOURNAL, NEW JERSEY PLAN, VIRGINIA PLAN, THREE-FIFTHS COMPROMISE.

Constitutional Council (France)   A review body established as a guardian of the Constitution of the Fifth French Republic. The direct antecedent of the Council was the Constitutional Committee of the Fourth Republic, which was to resolve jurisdictional disputes between the two houses of the legislature. The main function of the present Council is to resolve similar difficulties between the executive and the legislature. The constitution also requires that the Council be consulted on the constitutionality of organic laws and on the standing rules of both houses. The President of the Republic must consult the Council on procedures to be followed when he wishes to initiate emergency powers that permit him to rule by decree. The Council supervises referenda and elections and resolves election disputes. The presidents of the two houses, the President of the Republic, and the Premier each have the option of referring ordinary legislation to the Council for review prior to final enactment. The Constitutional Council is composed of nine members who serve nine-year nonrenewable terms, and all former Presidents of the Republic, who are ex officio members for life. The presiding officer is appointed by the head of state.

Constitutional Court   A federal court established under the provisions of Article III of the Constitution. Constitutional courts are limited to the jurisdiction conferred by Article III and their judges are protected as to tenure and compensation. These are to be distinguished from "legislative courts," which are created by Congress under its delegated powers. The major constitutional courts are the district courts, courts of appeals, and the Supreme Court. Congress has conferred constitutional status upon certain specialized courts, such as the Court of Claims, the Customs Court, and the Court of Customs and Patent Appeals. *See also* LEGISLATIVE COURT.

Constitutional Dictatorship   A system in which the executive is empowered to rule by decree, usually for a specified period of time. The scope of the dictator's power is set forth in the instrument that establishes the dictatorship. Constitutional dictatorship usually results from some national crisis and is rationalized as necessary to the ultimate preservation of the democratic constitutional order threatened by the emergency. *See also* DICTATORSHIP.

Constitutionalism   The political principle of limited government under a written or unwritten contract (constitution). Constitutionalism assumes that the sovereign people draw up a constitution, by the terms of which a government is created and given powers. In the American system, the Supreme Court acts as the guardian of the Constitution through its powers to void governmental actions that exceed these limitations (judicial review). The Founding Fathers also incorporated into the system various limitations that restrain the individuals who exercise power. The most significant of these include the separation of powers, checks and balances, federalism, subordination of military to civilian control, and the Bill of Rights. *See also* DEMOCRACY, CONSTITUTION.

Constitutional Law   Law that involves interpretation and application of the Constitution. It is concerned largely with defining the extent and limits of governmental power and the rights of individuals. Final decision as to the meaning of the Constitution is in the hands of the United States Supreme Court. In the case of state constitutions, the highest court of the state renders final decisions, with appeal possible to the United States Supreme Court if conflict with the national Constitution, laws, or treaties can be shown.

Constitutional Monarch, *see* Monarchy.

Constitutional Officer   A public official, usually in the executive branch, whose office is established and required by the constitution. State constitutions generally name numerous state and local officials and designate their terms of office and duties. For example, most state constitutions provide for the election of such statewide officers as secretary of state, attorney general, state treasurer, and state auditor. On the local level, the constitution may require election of such officers as sheriff, county clerk, township supervisor, and highway commissioner.

Constitutional Powers, *see* Concurrent Powers, Delegated Powers, Exclusive Powers, Implied Powers, Inherent Powers, Reserved Powers, Resulting Powers.

Constitutional Referendum, *see* Referendum.

Constitutional Test, *see* Test case.

Constitution (Britain)   That set of fundamental principles which organize the distribution and use of power, set forth the basic organs of government and their operation, and establish the relationship between the individual and the state. In Britain, the Constitution includes: (1) historic documents which have shaped the system, such as the Magna Charta (1215), the Petition of Right (1628), the Bill of Rights (1689), the Act of Settlement (1701), the Reform Act of 1832, and the Parliament Act of 1911; (2) statutes of fundamental importance, such as those which determine the suffrage; (3) judicial decisions which interpret and clarify the principles of the Constitution, especially those based on the common law (in Britain there is no judicial review in the American sense because of the supremacy of Parliament); and (4) customs or conventions of the Constitution. The latter are neither written nor enforceable in the courts; yet they are precedents of such importance as to be binding in the public mind. One such precedent is the requirement that a Cabinet minister must resign before he is free to disagree publicly with government policy. *See also* CONSTITUTION.

Constitution (France)   The fundamental law of the Fifth French Republic. The constitution places great power in the office of the President and, through an emergency procedure, enables him to rule by decree. The President chooses the Premier, who in turn advises the President on Cabinet appointments. The system differs from traditional Cabinet government in that Cabinet ministers cannot serve in Parliament. Details on selection, composition, and organization of Parliament, the judiciary, and administrative agencies are left to be filled in by organic laws and later statutes. The constitution also established the Community to replace the French Union of the Fourth Republic. *See also* CONSTITUTION.

Constitution (Soviet Union)   The formal plan of government in the Union of Soviet Socialist Republics. The constitution establishes a government with features that resemble many found in Western states. The system is federal and representative in nature with a bicameral national legislature (Supreme Soviet) elected by secret ballot on the basis of universal, direct, and equal suffrage. A Presidium performs many of the duties of the Supreme Soviet between legislative sessions. A Council of Ministers exercises executive and administrative functions and, in so far as it is technically responsible to the Supreme Soviet and its Presidium, resembles the French and British Cabinets. The Soviet model varies from Western constitutional theory in that it recognizes the ultimate power not of the people but of the Communist party, which is "the vanguard of the working people in their struggle to build communist society and is the leading core of all organizations of working people, both public and state." The constitutions of 1918 and 1924 were superseded by the present document in 1936, which has since been amended by virtually every Supreme Soviet. The writing of a new constitution is reportedly in progress, initially under the direction first of Nikita Khrushchev and then of Leonid Brezhnev. *See also* CONSTITUTION.

Constitution, State   The organic law of a state that defines and limits governmental power and guarantees the rights of the people. Each state has a constitution and its provisions may not conflict with the United States Constitution. Since state governments have all powers not delegated to the national government, state constitutions, typically, are filled with restrictions on legislative and executive power rather than grants of authority.

Consul   An official appointed by a government to reside in a foreign country in order to assist citizens of the appointing state and to advance their commercial interests. American consuls are members of the Foreign Service.

Consultative Assembly, *see* Council of Europe, Western European Union.

Consumerism   The popular movement in the United States which aims at achieving effective protection for consumers. Consumerism has sought to achieve increased safety standards, truthful advertising, proper labeling, full compliance with regulatory laws and rules, control over food additives and dangerous herbicides and pesticides, consumer credit and pricing protection, and regulation of certain practices carried on by the legal and medical professions. The leader of the American consumer movement, Ralph Nader, has built an organization of young professionals and students, known as "Nader's Raiders," who use the courts and lobbying techniques to increase consumer protection. *See also* CAVEAT VENDITOR, FEDERAL TRADE COMMISSION, UNFAIR TRADE PRACTICE.

Containment   A general policy adopted in 1947 by the Truman Administration to build "situations of strength" around the globe in order to contain Communist power within its existing boundaries. Underlying the containment policy was a belief that, if Soviet expansion could be stopped, communism would collapse of its own internal weaknesses. The policy was first applied in the Truman Doctrine of 1947 in a program of military aid to Greece and Turkey. *See also* TRUMAN DOCTRINE.

Contempt of Congress   Willful obstruction of the legislative process. Authority is vested in both houses of Congress and in their investigating committees to cite for contempt of Congress any subpoenaed witness who refuses to appear or to give testimony under oath. The Supreme Court has upheld this power by asserting: "It is unquestionably the duty of all citizens to cooperate with the Congress . . . to respond to subpoenas . . . and to testify fully with respect to matters within the province of proper investigation." (*Watkins v. United States,* 354 U.S. 178 [1957]). Contempt citations are referred by the presiding officer of the offended chamber to the Department of Justice for criminal prosecution through the federal courts. *See also Watkins v. United States, McGrain v. Daugherty,* INVESTIGATING COMMITTEE.

Contempt of Court   Disobedience of a court order, or any action that operates to impair the authority of a court or to interfere with its proper functioning. Contempt may be civil or criminal. Civil contempt involves a refusal to honor a court judgment in a civil case. Criminal contempt involves any interference with court proceedings. Both may be punished by fine or imprisonment or both. Usually, contempt is punished summarily (without trial), when it is committed in the presence of the court, but if a severe sentence is imposed, a separate trial before a different judge may be ordered. A defendant who flagrantly disrupts a trial may be bound and gagged and even removed from the courtroom (*Illinois v. Allen,* 397 US. 337 [1970]).

Content Analysis   The systematic, objective analysis of written communications for the purpose of making judgments about the communications, their senders, and related political variables. Content analysis may be broken down into a number of related operations, including (1) determination of the kinds of messages to be sampled (such as all foreign policy speeches of United States Presidents from 1949 to 1972); (2) the selection of an adequate sample of the messages; (3) the designation of appropriate units of analysis (words, themes, whole message items, and so forth); (4) the construction of an unambiguous and exhaustive set of categories into which the units will be classified; (5) formulation of explicit *coding* rules for assigning units to categories; and (6) the coding process in which messages are examined and items assigned to categories. The reliability of the coding process may be checked by having several coders analyze the same messages and by comparing the results. The amount of agreement among the coders may be computed and expressed numerically as an *index of intercoder reliability.* Content analysis may be performed through use of computers as well as human coders. Computer analysis is facilitated by the existence of computer-adapted "dictionaries" such as Stone's *General Inquirer,* which provides standardized sets of categories and coding rules for content analysis. The data obtained through content analysis may be subjected to various forms of quantitative manipulation.

Contested Election   Controversy over seating competing claimants to a legislative seat or the qualifications of an elected member. Article I, section 5 of the Constitution states: "Each house shall be the judge of the elections, returns, and qualifications of its own members. . . . " State constitutions have similar provisions. When the election of a member is contested, the chamber concerned sets up a committee to conduct an investigation.

Contextual Analysis, *see* Political Ecology.

Contiguous Zone   An area beyond territorial waters in which a coastal state remains free to enforce compliance with its laws. The extent of the contiguous zone and the jurisdiction of the coastal state are defined in Article 24 of the Geneva Convention on the Territorial Sea and Contiguous Zone (1958) as follows: "1. In a zone of the high seas contiguous to its territorial sea, the coastal state may exercise the control necessary to: (a) Prevent infringement of its customs, fiscal, immigration, or sanitary regulations within its territory or territorial sea; (b) Punish infringement of the above regulations. . . . 2. The contiguous zone may not extend beyond twelve miles from the baseline from which the breadth of the territorial sea is measured." *See also* TERRITORIAL WATERS.

Continental Congress   The body of delegates representing the colonies that first met to protest the British treatment of the colonies and eventually became the government of the United States. The First Continental Congress met in 1774 and drafted a Declaration of Rights. The Second Congress, meeting the following year, adopted the Declaration of Independence, conducted the War of Independence, and served as the national government until the Articles of Confederation went into effect in 1781.

Continuous Voyage Doctrine, *see* Contraband.

Continuum   A continuous range of related phenomena located along a line between two extreme values of the characteristic to which they are related. Thus a conflict-cooperation continuum might range from total war at one extreme position to complete cooperation at the other, with various degrees of cooperation and conflict in between. Unlike a dichotomy that establishes an either-or system for classification into two mutually exclusive categories, a continuum offers the opportunity for more precise classification into a continuous range of categories. *See also* CLASSIFICATION, DICHOTOMOUS CLASSIFICATION.

Contraband   War materials which may not be sold to belligerents by neutrals. International law recognizes the right of belligerents to deny shipments of contraband materials to the enemy, but the international community has never been able to agree on exactly what goods are contraband and which are unrelated to the war effort. Goods shipped to a neutral port, if ultimately destined for shipment to the enemy, may be seized as contraband under the doctrine of continuous voyage or ultimate destination. A category of "conditional contraband" consists of goods normally for peacetime consumption but which may be useful for military purposes. *See also* BLOCKADE, NEUTRALITY.

Contract Clause   Article I, section 10 of the Constitution which prohibits any state from passing laws impairing the obligation of contracts. This clause applies to contracts between individuals and to contracts made by the states. The state may neither weaken the effect of a contract nor make it more difficult to enforce. All contracts, however, are subject to the limitation that they may not endanger the health, safety, and welfare of the people—the areas of the states' "police powers."

Contract Theory   A class of theories that seeks to explain the origin of society and government and to set out the respective authority and responsibility of government and individuals under their contractual obligations. Contract theorists regard man as having lived in a state of nature prior to the organization of civil society. Once a "body politic" has been created through a contract or compact among the people, a government is then founded and empowered through a second contract or constitution concluded between the people and the government. The nature of the relationship established by the governmental contract varies, in these theories, from the individualism of John Locke's popular sovereignty and limited government to the authoritarianism of Thomas Hobbes's *Leviathan*. *See also* CONSTITUTIONALISM, DEMOCRACY, POPULAR SOVEREIGNTY.

Contractual Theory (Presidential Powers), *see* Taftian or Contractual Theory.

Contradictions of Capitalism (Communist Theory)   The fundamental, irreconcilable conflicts inherent in the nature of capitalism that, according to Communist dogma, are instrumental in bringing about its collapse. For Marx, the contradictions of capitalism start at the production stage when the worker receives only a small portion of the value of the article produced in the form of wages, with the rest in the form of surplus value or profits kept by the capitalist. The result is a lack of purchasing power sufficiently large to buy the goods that are produced. This underconsumption, according to Marx, produces increasingly severe economic depressions within nations, an increasing impoverishment of the working class, growing unemployment, a class struggle, and, ultimately, the victory of socialism.

Control Group   In an experimental situation, a group not subjected to experimental treatment, with which the experimental group is compared. Members of a control group are usually selected because of their presumed similarity to the members of the experimental group. Both in fact are likely to be chosen randomly from the same or similar populations. In the experiment the independent variable (experimental treatment) is applied to the experimental group but the control group receives standard treatment or none at all. The control group thus provides a base against which the impact of the independent variable on the experimental group can be measured. *See also* EXPERIMENT, RESEARCH DESIGN, SAMPLING.

Convention   A meeting of party delegates at the national, state, or local levels to decide upon party policy and strategy and to nominate candidates for elective office. Each party holds a national convention every four years to nominate its presidential candidate and adopt a platform. In most states, both parties hold county and state conventions annually. Typically, delegates to the county conventions are selected by party voters in precinct elections; delegates to state conventions are selected by county conventions; and delegates to national conventions are selected by state or district conventions, or, in approximately one-half of the states, by voters in presidential primaries. *See also* NOMINATION, NATIONAL CONVENTION.

Convergence Theory   The view that capitalist and communist systems are evolving in their economic functions and modes of operations in increasingly similar ways. Ultimately, the convergence theory holds, the two systems will become almost indistinguishable in their basic forms, and consequently will no longer constitute a threat to each other. Both systems are being shaped by the same forces of science and technology, cybernetics and automation, industrialization and urbanization, and by cultures shaped by the space age. *See also* CAPITALISM, COMMUNISM.

Conversations   A diplomatic exchange of views between governments. Conversations may be undertaken for information only, or may lead to more detailed negotiations. Conversations are a normal diplomatic activity carried on by an ambassador or members of his staff, but they may also take place through the use of specially appointed diplomatic agents.

Conversion, Monetary, *see* Convertibility.

Conversion Process, *see* Systems Analysis.

Convertibility The free interchange of a national currency into units of foreign currency by private individuals or businesses, without control by the government. A convertible currency, therefore, is one that is not regulated in value or amounts exchanged by a national system of exchange control. *See also* EXCHANGE CONTROL, FOREIGN EXCHANGE.

Cooley v. Board of Wardens, 12 Howard 299 (1851): Upheld the right of the states to regulate interstate commerce if Congress has not covered the field with its regulations and if the subject regulated by the states is not of a nature to require uniform national regulation. The case involved local regulations for port pilots, which were upheld as a reasonable regulation of interstate commerce by a state since such regulation does not need a uniform national policy. *See also* COMMERCE POWER.

Cooling-off Period A period of time, stipulated by the Taft-Hartley Act of 1947, during which parties to a labor-management controversy may not engage in a strike or lockout. Under the Act, an existing collective bargaining contract can be terminated or changed only after sixty days' notice to the other party. If no agreement is reached within thirty days, the Federal Mediation and Conciliation Service must be notified. During the sixty-day period no strike or lock-out is permitted. In the case of disputes threatening the national welfare, the Taft-Hartley Act authorizes the President to seek an injunction from the courts which maintains the status quo for eighty days. During this time, fact-finding and conciliation efforts are to be made and the workers given a chance to vote on the employer's last offer. If at the end of the eighty-day period no solution is reached, a strike or lockout may take place. Similar procedures are provided for the rail and air transport industries in the Railway Labor Act. International dispute settlement procedures have also included use of cooling-off periods as means for avoiding war, as, for example, the mandatory three-month cooling-off period required by the League of Nations Covenant before a disputing state went to war.

Cooperation, *see* Conflict.

Cooperative Federalism A concept that views the states and the national government as cooperating partners in the performance of governmental functions rather than as antagonistic competitors for power. The grant-in-aid programs typify this relationship between the national and state governments. *See also* GRANT-IN-AID, CREATIVE FEDERALISM.

COPE, *see* Committee on Political Education.

Copyright The exclusive right granted by the Copyright Office in the Library of Congress to the creative products of authors, composers, dramatists, photographers, and others. A copyright grant is made to anyone who wants one, following publication of his material and its submission to the Copyright Office. A copyright confers an exclusive privilege for a period of twenty-eight years, with the option of renewal for another twenty-eight-year period. Typical copyrighted items include books, newspapers, magazines, musical compositions, translations, cartoons, sermons, motion pictures, photographs, paintings, maps, and charts. The copyright power is based on the constitutional grant to Congress to promote science and the arts by granting authors "the exclusive right to their respective writings. . . . " *See also* PATENT, TRADEMARK.

Coroner   A county official who investigates deaths that occur by violent means and certifies the cause of deaths unattended by a physician. In the case of violent death, the coroner may conduct an investigation, called an "inquest," to determine if death resulted from a criminal act. A jury of six persons hears evidence presented by the county prosecutor. If the verdict is death by criminal act, the coroner may order the arrest of suspected persons. Most coroners are elected, although a number of states have substituted an appointed medical examiner to perform the duties of the coroner and have transferred his inquest function to the prosecutor.

Corporation   A business unit, chartered under state or federal law, owned by stockholders and legally regarded as an artificial person. Private corporations are owned by individual investors and public corporations are partially or wholly owned by government—national, state, or local. The term "public corporation" is also often used to describe a corporation with broad ownership, such as General Motors, whereas one in which the stock is held by a few people or a family is called a "private corporation." *See also* GOVERNMENT CORPORATION, BOND.

Corporation Income Tax   A national tax levied on corporations, based on their annual net income. The corporation income tax rate in recent years has been a flat 30 percent for the first $25,000 of net income and 52 percent on all net income over that figure. It is, essentially, a tax on the privilege of doing business as a corporation, and, as such, was first enacted prior to the adoption of the Sixteenth Amendment. *See also* EXCESS PROFITS TAX.

Corps of Engineers   A branch of the United States Army charged with planning and constructing public works on navigable waterways. The Engineers construct dams and power-generating facilities on many major rivers and develop extensive flood-control projects. In civil projects the Corps has developed a tradition of autonomy from the Army and Department of Defense, functioning as engineering consultants to the Congress.

Correlation   A relationship between two or more variables. "Correlation" may refer generally to any observed relationships as, for example, between the onset of economic crises and demands for political change. It is most commonly used with reference to a relationship determined by the use of statistical correlation techniques, also called *measures of association*. Such measures produce a *correlation coefficient*, usually between one and minus one, which provides a numerical indicator of the strength of the relationship. A positive coefficient (for example, .61) indicates variance in the same direction; a negative coefficient (for example, -.61) indicates an inverse relationship. Tests of *statistical significance* may be used to determine the likelihood that a relationship of the numerical strength indicated might have occurred by chance, as for example at the .05 level (meaning one possibility in twenty of a chance relationship) or at the .01 level (one possibility in one hundred). Common measures of association are rank order correlation and product moment correlation. *Rank order* techniques involve the ranking of subjects (for example, countries) in descending order of magnitude on each of two variables (for example, gross national product and size of armed forces) and determining the extent to which rank order on one variable is similar to the ranking on the other. Rank order correlation takes into account only the difference in rank. *Product moment* correlation, on the other hand, takes into account the magnitude of the interval between ranks. In the example given it would correlate actual size of GNP and armed forces, not just relative size as indicated by rank position. *Multiple correlation* techniques measure how much of the variation in a dependent variable can be explained by two or more independent variables acting together. *Partial correlation* looks for the association between two variables when other relevant variables are controlled. Correlation methods predict the direction and strength of a relationship as expressed in a positive or negative correlation coefficient. *Regression techniques*, by contrast, measure the amount of change in a dependent variable associated with a given amount of change in the independent variable. Or, in terms of our example, it might measure how much difference in the size of armed forces would be associated with each $100 million increase in GNP. *See also* FACTOR ANALYSIS, STATISTICS, VARIABLE.

Corrupt Practices Acts   Laws that seek to limit and regulate the size and sources of contributions and expenditures in political campaigns. Since 1925, a variety of federal corrupt practices acts were enacted to regulate campaign finance but they proved unrealistic and unenforceable. For example, the Political Activities Act of 1939 (Hatch Act) forbid a political committee to spend more than $3 million in any campaign and limited individual contributions to a committee to $5000, both of which could be circumvented by the creation of additional committees. The Federal Election Campaign Act of 1972 swept aside past laws and instituted a major reform to take into account the problems of reaching a large electorate. The 1972 Act places no limit on overall spending but restricts the amount that can be spent on mass media advertising, including television, limits the amount that candidates and their families can contribute to their own campaigns, requires disclosure of all contributions in excess of $10 and expenditures in excess of $100, and limits the role of labor unions and corporations in political campaigns. In a related action, designed to broaden the base of campaign financing, Congress authorized, beginning with the 1976 presidential election, a system of voluntary one dollar checkoffs on federal income tax returns for a general campaign fund to be made available to major party candidates. State and local political campaign finances are regulated by state laws, which vary considerably. *See also* FEDERAL ELECTION CAMPAIGN ACT OF 1972.

Cost-Benefit Analysis   The appraisal of anticipated expenditures needed to accomplish given objectives, in relation to the value of expected gains. Cost-benefit analysis is a decision procedure used in program planning. Examining the ratio of benefits to costs helps decision makers to determine which among several alternative courses of action may offer the opportunity for the most effective use of resources. *Cost effectiveness* is a related form of analysis that is applied to *ongoing* programs to evaluate their relative progress toward the achievement of goals sought. *See also* ENGINEERING THEORY, POLICY SCIENCES.

Cost-Effectiveness Analysis, *see* Cost-Benefit Analysis.

Cost Plus Contract, *see* Defense Contract.

Council, League, *see* League of Nations.

Council-manager Plan   A form of city government in which the city council appoints a professional administrator, a manager, to act as the chief executive. With variations from city to city, the essentials of this plan are: (1) a small council or commission of five or seven members elected at large on a nonpartisan ballot, with power to make policy and to hire and fire the manager; (2) a professionally trained manager, with authority to hire and fire his subordinates, who is responsible to the council for efficient administration of the city; and (3) a mayor chosen separately or from within the council, but with no executive functions. The council must refrain from bypassing the manager by interfering with his subordinates or in the details of administration, and the manager must follow the policies outlined by the council. A merit system for selection of employees is generally used under this plan. *See also* CITY COUNCIL, MAYOR-ADMINISTRATOR PLAN.

Council (OAS), *see* Organization of American States.

Council of Economic Advisers (CEA)   A staff agency in the Executive Office of the President. It consists of three leading economists who advise the President on measures to maintain stability in the nation's economy. The Council was established by Congress in the Employment Act of 1946 and was given responsibility by that Act to formulate proposals "to maintain employment, production, and purchasing power." The Council's recommendations are included in the President's annual economic report to Congress, in which he sets forth the economic problems facing the nation and recommends legislative solutions. *See also* EMPLOYMENT ACT.

Council Of Europe   A regional quasi-parliamentary organization that encourages political, economic, and social cooperation and seeks to develop a sense of "European" unity among its members. The Council of Europe was established at London in 1949 by Belgium, Britain, Denmark, France, Ireland, Italy, Luxembourg, The Netherlands, Norway, and Sweden. Eight additional states—Austria, Cyprus, Germany (Federal Republic), Greece, Iceland, Malta, Switzerland, and Turkey—have subsequently been admitted to membership. In structure, the Council consists of two chambers—a Consultative Assembly composed of delegates chosen by their national parliaments but free to speak and vote as individuals, and a Committee of Ministers representing member governments. The Consultative Assembly functions as the deliberative organ of the Council, while the Committee of Ministers has sole power to make decisions, with each government having the veto power. The Council makes recommendations to member governments and approves treaties and agreements that, when ratified by member states, constitute a form of international legislation. Both organs are free to debate any matter except military questions. The Committee of Ministers meets monthly; the Assembly meets in spring, autumn, and winter sessions. A secretariat located at Council headquarters in Strasbourg serves both organs. *See also* EUROPEAN CONVENTION ON HUMAN RIGHTS.

Council of Ministers, EFTA, *see* European Free Trade Association.

Council of Ministers, European Community, *see* European Community.

Council of Ministers or Cabinet (Italy)   The government in the Italian parliamentary system. The Council of Ministers is usually a coalition government since no party is strong enough to command a majority in the Parliament. The President consults with political leaders to discover which parties will cooperate in a coalition. He then nominates a chairman of the Council of Ministers (Prime Minister) who in turn suggests the other ministerial nominations to be made by the President. The Cabinet thus formed is responsible to the Parliament, and the Prime Minister has ten days in which to obtain votes of confidence in his government from both the Chamber of Deputies and the Senate. A government ends when it resigns voluntarily, when Parliament is dissolved by the President for a general election, or when a specific motion of no confidence is sustained by either chamber. About twenty ministries are established by statute, but any number of ministers without portfolio can also be nominated for Cabinet posts. Most Cabinet ministers are members of Parliament although this is not a legal requirement.

Council of Ministers (Soviet Union)   The "highest executive and administrative organ of state power" under the constitution. The Council of Ministers is composed of fifty or more members appointed by the Supreme Soviet in accordance with the wishes of party leaders. The Chairman, or Premier, is a high-ranking party member with a seat on the party's Politburo. Most of the individual members administer one of the large government departments. The Council thus resembles the Cabinet in the Western democracies. It is concerned with such usual items as the national budget, foreign affairs, national security, internal order, industry, and agriculture.

Council of Mutual Economic Assistance (COMECON, CMEA, or CEMA)   A regional organization established in 1949 under Soviet direction to integrate the economies of Eastern Europe. COMECON members include Albania (active membership ceased in 1961), Bulgaria, Czechoslovakia, East Germany, Hungary, Mongolia, Poland, Romania, and the Soviet Union. The organizational machinery of COMECON is headed by a Council that functions as the decision-making organ except on matters of basic policy, on which it is limited to making recommendations to member governments. A permanent Executive Committee implements policy decisions, more than twenty standing commissions carry out planning and operations in major commodity fields, and a secretariat headquartered in Moscow functions under the Council's direction. The economic objectives of COMECON include a politically determined specialization of production in member countries, an East European free trade area, accessibility of raw materials, and cooperation in scientific research and technology.

Council of State (France)   An institution of almost two hundred members that stands at the apex of the French system of public administration. Administrative functions of the Council of State cover finance, interior, public works, and social affairs. Its judicial function deals with cases arising out of the impact of administrative law on the rights of individual citizens. In its legislative role, the Council advises the Cabinet on the legality and consequences of legislation, and puts bills into final form. Like the Constitutional Council, the Council of State was designed to aid in keeping executive powers, particularly emergency powers, within constitutional bounds. The Council of State also has a role in settling jurisdictional disputes between the legislature and executive. When the law in question predates the Constitution of the Fifth Republic, the Council of State determines jurisdiction between the executive and legislature, but disputes arising under laws passed under the present constitution are referred to the Constitutional Council.

Council of State Governments   An agency maintained by the state governments to serve as a secretariat, research agency, and clearing house for the improvement of state legislative, executive, and judicial administration. It has encouraged interstate cooperation and the general improvement of federal-state relations and state-local relations. The Council is composed of Commissions on Interstate Cooperation that are found in each of the states and that include legislative and executive officials. The Council serves as the secretariat for the American Legislators Association, The Governors' Conference, and similar organizations of chief justices, attorneys general, court, budget, purchasing, parole, and juvenile officials. It publishes a monthly magazine, *State Government,* and the biennial *Book of the States.* Its headquarters is in Chicago.

Council on Environmental Quality   A staff agency in the Executive Office that advises the President on measures to control or eliminate air, water, and other forms of pollution, and to promote a high quality of life for the American people. The Council, created by the National Environmental Policy Act of 1969, assists the President in drawing up an annual Environmental Quality Report, which he transmits to the Congress annually with recommendations for appropriate legislative action. Three members appointed by the President with the approval of the Senate comprise the Council, with one of the three selected by the President to serve as chairman. *See also* ENVIRONMENTAL PROTECTION AGENCY, NATIONAL ENVIRONMENTAL POLICY ACT OF 1969, ENVIRONMENTAL POLITICS.

Councils of Government   Voluntary organizations of counties and municipalities concerned with areawide problems. Almost 200 regional councils have been established, mainly since 1966, under incentives furnished by federal grants. Most are located in metropolitan areas, and under authority granted by participating units, undertake such tasks as regional planning, community development, pollution control, water systems, and airport construction. Congress has encouraged this development by requiring such Councils to determine the regional effects of programs funded by federal grants. *See also* METROPOLITAN AREA.

Counsel, Right to, *see* Right to Counsel.

Counterintelligence, *see* Intelligence.

Counterinsurgency   Military force employed against a revolutionary group trying to overthrow an established regime. Counterinsurgency operations describe the efforts of American and indigenous military forces to prevent a Communist take-over through revolution, guerrilla warfare, subversion, and related techniques.

Counterpart Funds   Local currencies paid by an aid-receiving country to a donor country for military-, developmental-, or technical-assistance loans. Under grant programs, a recipient country may also be required to appropriate a special fund of national currency to match the amount provided in foreign exchange.

Counterrevolution, *see* Revolution (Communist Theory).

Countervailing Duty   A special assessment levied on imports to offset an advantage or discount provided by a foreign seller or government. A countervailing duty is applied against those products which might provide unfair competition for locally produced articles of commerce as a result of foreign governmental subsidies or other special advantages. The duty levied is in addition to the normal tariff charge. *See also* TARIFF.

Countervailing Theory of Pressure Politics   The concept that in American politics the competition among major business, labor, farm, racial, religious, and other interest groups tends to balance their respective power and influence. *See also* PRESSURE GROUP.

County   The major unit of local government in the United States, except in Connecticut, Rhode Island, and Alaska. Louisiana has county units but calls them parishes. Alaska has a new major division of local government called a borough. Connecticut abolished counties in 1959. In New England, counties are relatively unimportant for governmental purposes. Otherwise, county governments exist as principal agencies of the state for statewide purposes, and as important units of local government. There are over 3000 counties in the United States ranging from three in Delaware to 254 in Texas. Their powers and functions vary from state to state and within states as well. Generally, counties perform such functions as law enforcement and maintenance of courts, highways, schools, and welfare agencies. In urban areas, counties may perform a variety of services usually handled by cities. Counties are governed by a board that differs in composition from state to state. Counties have a large number of elected officials, such as sheriff, clerk, coroner, attorney, auditor, register of deeds, surveyor, and treasurer.

County Agent The local official charged with promoting agriculture under the federal, state, and county cooperative extension program. The Smith-Lever Act of 1914 created the modern extension service under which the county agent program was developed.

County Board The governing body of the county. The official title of this body varies from state to state with as many as twenty-seven different titles used. Most common are "board of commissioners," "board of supervisors," and "county court," but the term county board is the most popular one. Most county boards are composed of three to five commissioners or supervisors who are elected by the voters of the county. In states with township government, the board is composed of township supervisors and representatives of cities within the county, but these are undergoing change to comply with "one man, one vote" rulings of the Supreme Court that have been applied to county boards (*Avery v. Midland County, Texas,* 390 U.S. 474 [1968]). In several states the board is composed of county judges. The board administers state law in the county, levies taxes, appoints numerous officials, and supervises the general affairs of the county.

County Clerk A county official who is popularly elected in more than half the states, His principal duties include acting as secretary to the county board, supervision of elections, issuance of various business certificates and licenses, and handling of birth, marriage, and death records.

County Court, *see* County Board.

County Home Rule, *see* Home Rule.

County-manager Plan A plan patterned after the council-manager plan used in many cities. The county-manager plan envisages a small county board for policy determination and an appointed professional manager to serve as the executive officer of the county. Few of the more than 3000 counties in the United States have adopted the manager plan.

Coup D'État A swift, decisive seizure of government power by a political or military group from within the existing system. A *coup d'état* differs from a revolution in that it is not based on a popular uprising and does not necessarily involve a transformation in the established political and social institutions of the society, although revolutionary changes may be instituted after a *coup*. The organizers of a *coup d'état* usually carry it out by capturing or killing top political and military leaders, by seizing control of key government buildings and public utilities, and by utilizing the mass media of communication to calm the masses and gain their acceptance of the new regime. *See also* REVOLUTION.

Court Calendar, *see* Docket

Court-martial   A military tribunal that conducts trials of military personnel accused of violating military law. A *summary* court-martial consists of a single officer who tries enlisted men for minor offenses. A *special* court-martial, which can only be convened by a commanding general, consists of three officers who may impose moderately severe penalties, such as six months at hard labor, bad conduct discharges, and reductions in rank. A *general* court-martial may be convened by the President or Secretary of Defense. It consists of five or more members, one-third of whom must be enlisted men if they are requested by the accused. Severe penalties, such as the death penalty, life imprisonment, or dishonorable discharge, may be imposed. *See also* COURT OF MILITARY APPEALS, MILITARY LAW.

Court of Appeals   In the national court system, the appellate court below the Supreme Court. A few states also have an intermediate court of appeals, although in Kentucky, Maryland, and New York, the highest state court is called the Court of Appeals. On the national level, there are eleven courts of appeal. The country is divided into eleven "circuits" including the District of Columbia. Prior to 1948, these courts were known as the Circuit Courts of Appeals. The United States Courts of Appeals have only appellate jurisdiction, being empowered to hear appeals from the district courts in their particular circuit and to hear appeals from decisions of independent regulatory commissions, such as the Federal Trade Commission or Interstate Commerce Commission. Each court normally hears cases in panels of three judges but, on occasion, a full court of nine judges will sit. All judges are appointed for life by the President with the Senate's consent.

Court of Claims   A court established in 1855 to hear claims of private individuals against the government for breach of contract, for injuries caused by negligent behavior of government employees, or for recovery of other claims, such as back pay. It also determines claims referred by Congress and the executive departments. The Court of Claims has seven judges who sit "en banc" (together) in Washington, D.C. Evidence is gathered by commissioners who travel throughout the United States. Any awards made by the Court cannot be paid unless Congress appropriates the money, which it usually does. Its decisions may be appealed to the Supreme Court by writ of certiorari. Since 1953 it has held the status of a constitutional court, and its judges are appointed for life by the President with the Senate's consent.

Court of Customs and Patent Appeals A court established by Congress in 1909 which reviews appeals from decisions of the Customs Court, the Patent Office, and the Tariff Commission. The Court has five judges who sit "en banc" (together) in Washington, D.C. They are appointed for life terms by the President with consent of the Senate. Congress designated it a constitutional court in 1958. Decisions may be appealed to the Supreme Court by writ of certiorari.

Court of Justice, *see* European Community.

Court of Military Appeals A court estabished by Congress in 1950 to review court-martial decisions. Composed of three civilian judges appointed for fifteen years by the President with consent of the Senate, the court is judicially independent but is part of the Department of Defense for administrative purposes. The court is obligated to review decisions affecting top military personnel, as well as those imposing the death penalty; it has discretion to review certain other cases upon petition, such as bad conduct discharges or those involving lengthy prison terms. The court applies military law, a special body of rules developed by Congress, rather than ordinary federal criminal law. Appeals may be made to the Supreme Court by writ of certiorari. *See also* COURT-MARTIAL.

Courts, Federal, *see* Constitutional Court, Court of Appeals, Court of Claims, Court of Customs and Patent Appeals, Court of Military Appeals, Customs Court, District Court, Judiciary Act of 1789, Legislative Court, Supreme Court, Territorial Court.

Courts, Jurisdiction of, *see* Ableman *v. Booth,* Admiralty Jurisdiction, Appellate Jurisdiction, *Cohens v. Virginia,* Concurrent Jurisdiction, Diversity of Citizenship, Eleventh Amendment, *Ex Parte McCardle,* Original Jurisdiction.

Courts, State, *see* Chief Justice, Circuit Court, Court of Appeals, Intermediate Court, Judicial Council, Justice of the Peace, Magistrate, Probate Court, Small Claims Court, Supreme Court, Unified Court System.

Covenant A multilateral treaty (Part I of the Treaty of Versailles) that created the League of Nations. The Covenant of the League resembled a national constitution in that it provided for the establishment of major organs and a decision-making system and enunciated principles to guide the actions of its members. *See also* LEAGUE OF NATIONS.

Covenant on Civil and Political Rights, *see* Universal Declaration of Human Rights.

Cox v. New Hampshire, *see* Jehovah's Witnesses Cases.

Coyle v. Smith, 221 U.S. 599 (1911): Established the principle that all states are admitted to the Union on an equal footing. Congress may not enforce conditions that would undermine the equality of the states. In this case, the Court upheld the right of Oklahoma to change its capital city contrary to a requirement in the congressional enabling act that preceded statehood. *See also* ADMISSION OF NEW STATES.

Creative Federalism   A term coined by the Johnson Administration during the 1960s to emphasize joint and mutual decision making as the basis for the planning and management of intergovernmental programs. Creative federalism goes beyond cooperative federalism in that in addition to furnishing funds to state and local units, federal officials consult directly with state and local officials in implementing plans and programs. In addition, creative federalism looks toward the reinvigoration of local responsibility by providing block grants or revenue sharing programs to state and local units with few if any strings attached. *See also* GRANT-IN-AID, REVENUE SHARING.

Credentials Committee   A committee used by political parties in their conventions to determine which delegates may participate. The credentials committee prepares a roll of all delegates entitled to be seated at the convention. Controversy over contested seats arises when rival groups claim to be the official party organization for a county, district, or state. In such cases, the committee makes recommendations to the convention. *See also* NATIONAL CONVENTION.

Crime Control Act of 1970, *see* Organized Crime Control Act.

Crime Control and Safe Streets Act of 1968, *see* Omnibus Crime Control and Safe Streets Act.

Criminal Law   The code that regulates the conduct of individuals, defines crimes, and provides punishment for violations. In criminal cases, the government is always the prosecutor, since all crimes are against public order. The major body of criminal law is enacted by states although the list of federal crimes is growing. Criminal law falls into two categories, felonies and misdemeanors, the former being the more serious. *See also* CIVIL LAW.

Cross-Cultural Analysis, *see* Political Culture.

Crosscutting Cleavages, *see* Cleavage.

Cross-Sectional Analysis, *see* Time Series Analysis.

Crown (Britain)   The executive and administrative machinery of the British government. It is composed of the Monarch, the Cabinet, the Ministers, and the Civil Service. The powers of the Crown are composed of the remaining portions of the royal prerogative and statutory grants by the Parliament. The Crown formulates and executes national policy, issues executive orders and administrative directions, manages public property, and conducts foreign relations. The Crown prepares bills and guides them through the legislative process, appoints judges, and issues pardons and reprieves.

Cruel and Unusual Punishment   Any lingering torture, mutilation, or degrading treatment, or any sentence too severe for the offense committed. The Eighth Amendment to the Constitution forbids such punishment, leaving the scope of the ban to be determined by the courts.

Cult of the Individual   A charge directed by party leaders at individuals who have departed from the Marxist-Leninist principle of collective leadership to establish personal rule through self-deification and totalitarian tactics. The concept of the "cult of the individual" or "cult of personality" was used by Nikita Khrushchev in a speech to the Twentieth Party Congress in 1956 to castigate the totalitarian dictatorship and autocratic rule of Josef Stalin, who had died in 1953. Specifically, he charged Stalin with ignoring the Politburo and the Central Committee and with arbitrary rule that resulted in the purging and death of thousands of party members. Subsequently, Khrushchev was himself charged with indulging in the cult of personality and was removed from power.

Cultural Exchange   International programs carried on by states or by private groups to foster intercultural appreciation of artistic and scientific achievements and understanding of political, economic, and social institutions. Cultural exchange programs are often instruments of foreign policy employed by states to strengthen relations with friendly nations and to contribute to a relaxation of tension between peoples of potentially hostile countries. *See also* CULTURAL EXCHANGE (UNITED STATES).

Cultural Exchange (United States)   Programs aimed at fostering understanding and improving relations between the people of the United States and the peoples of other countries. Although a Division of Cultural Relations was established in the State Department in 1938, the Fulbright Act of 1946 marks the beginning of an intensified program of cultural relations, largely administered today by the Bureau of Educational and Cultural Affairs. The Fulbright Act permits utilization of foreign currencies and credits, obtained from the sale of surplus United States property abroad, to finance study by Americans in foreign universities, and helps foreign students to attend American universities. In addition to student and professorial exchanges under the Fulbright program, the Smith-Mundt Act of 1948 and later programs have made possible the exchange of scientists, businessmen, and governmental and professional leaders. *See also* CULTURAL EXCHANGE.

Cultural Imperialism   Imposing an alien ideology or civilization on an unwilling society. Cultural imperialism as a calculated policy by which a government imposes its values on others should be distinguished from the increasing spread of alien cultural influences resulting from trade, travel, and communication. National leaders who resent or fear foreign influences may brand them as cultural imperialism, but in doing so they are using the term as a propaganda device and not as an objective tool of analysis unless the intent of the foreign government can be demonstrated.

Cultural Pluralism, *see* Pluralism.

Cultural Revolution   The name given by the followers of Mao Tse-tung to their chaotic struggle begun in the mid-1960s against revisionism and betrayal of the revolutionary cause. The Cultural Revolution, according to Maoists, was a mass proletarian movement against either a Western or Soviet type of capitalist restoration and materialism. Constant struggle is necessary because capitalist resistance increases as its end draws near.

Culture   The aggregate of learned, socially transmitted behavior patterns characteristic of a society. The culture of a social group is developed and maintained through formal and informal learning, language, knowledge, folkways, beliefs, customs, traditions, institutions—in sum, the totality of social experience. A political system is shaped by related cultural factors and may, in turn, promote cultural change by influencing other behavior patterns of society. A highly pluralistic society, for example, might be congenial to the maintenance of democratic institutions, and the latter would be likely to provide a setting where cultural diversity flourishes. *See also* POLITICAL CULTURE.

Cumulative Scale, *see* Guttman Scale.

Cumulative Voting   A method of voting in which the individual casts more than one vote in the simultaneous election of several officials, as a means of securing greater representation for minor parties. Each voter is allowed two or more votes, which he can cast for a single candidate or distribute among several. Candidates of minor parties can usually win seats because their supporters concentrate their additional votes for them, whereas major party supporters tend to distribute their votes among several candidates. Cumulative voting is used in electing members of the lower house of the Illinois legislature, with three representatives elected from each district and with each voter casting three votes. *See also* PROPORTIONAL REPRESENTATION.

Curfew   An emergency or wartime order restricting the freedom of movement of the civilian population in a danger zone to specified time periods. Curfews are frequently established to proscribe movement during hours of darkness. They are widely used in fighting insurgencies that utilize guerrilla warfare. *See also* MARTIAL LAW.

Currency, *see* Convertibility, Counterpart Funds, Deflation, Devaluation, Exchange Control, Federal Reserve Notes, Foreign Exchange, Gold Standard, Inflation, International Monetary Fund, Legal Tender, *Legal Tender Cases*, Monetary Policy, Reserve Ratio, *Veazie Bank v. Fenno*.

Currency Control, *see* Exchange Control.

Curtiss-Wright Case, *see United States v. Curtiss-Wright Export Corp.*

Customary Law Rules of international conduct based on practices and usages accepted by states to be obligatory. As customary law is applied over the years, its precepts tend to become clarified and its uncertainties reduced. Often important rules of customary law are transmuted into positive law by their inclusion in treaties. Article 38 of the Statute of the International Court of Justice specifies that "International Custom, as evidence of a general practice accepted as law" is one of the sources of international law to be applied by the Court. *See also* INTERNATIONAL LAW, POSITIVISM.

Customs and Patent Appeals, *see* Court of Customs and Patent Appeals.

Customs Court A special court established by Congress in 1926 to decide disputes that arise over tariff laws and duties levied on imported goods. The Court consists of nine judges appointed for life terms by the President with the Senate's consent. It sits in divisions at principal ports of entry, with its main office in New York City. In 1956, the Customs Court was given constitutional status by the Congress. Its decisions may be appealed to the Court of Customs and Patent Appeals.

Customs Duty, *see* Ad Valorem Duty, Countervailing Duty, Tariff.

Customs Union An agreement among states that provides for free trade among the members and for a common external tariff on imports from outside the union. A customs union arrangement usually provides for the central collection of import duties and their division among the members of the union according to a formula. The common external tariff rates are typically based on an average of pre-union national rates. *See also* BENELUX.

Cybernetics The study of control systems and related communication processes. Cybernetics is concerned primarily with the functioning of the human nervous system and its machine analogues—that is, electronic computers and other self-regulating mechanical systems. Basic to cybernetics is the concept of self-regulation by which a machine or system identifies stimuli, comprehends the information, receives feedback and adjusts itself automatically, and maintains equilibrium as it moves through several possible states or situations. Political and other behavioral scientists seek to gain a better understanding of human behavior by the use of analogical models applied to social systems that are based on their mechanical and electrical counterparts. *See also* COMMUNICATIONS THEORY.

Cyprus Force, *see* United Nations Force in Cyprus.

Danube Commission   An international body that regulates and facilitates traffic on the Danube. The Danube Commission, composed of one representative from each riparian state, sets up uniform traffic regulations and carries out projects to aid navigation and commerce on this major central-European waterway. Although decisions are arrived at by a majority vote, a state may block a Commission project on its territory. The contemporary Danube Commission is the successor to two Commissions established by the Treaty of Paris in 1856 to encourage and control traffic on the Danube.

Darby Case, *see United States v. Darby Lumber Co.*

Dark Horse   A marginal candidate or noncandidate for public office who has little support and almost no chance to win nomination or election. When a consensus cannot be achieved in support of one of the leading candidates, however, the party or voters may suddenly and dramatically shift their support to a dark horse. The role of the dark horse in American politics relates particularly to the presidential nominating conventions of the two major political parties.

Data   The facts, statistics, and other forms of information that provide the raw material for analysis. In the broadest sense data include anything informational that can be perceived through sensory means. Some investigators use "data" in a more restrictive sense to mean facts that have been so classified and ordered that they can be used as a basis for drawing or testing generalizations. Political scientists look for data dealing with the characteristics, attitudes, and opinions of individuals and groups; with political institutions, patterns of actions, and processes; with the situational environment in which interaction occurs; and with the facts that relate to specific political events. *See also* FACT.

Data Access, *see* Access.

Death Penalty, *see* Capital Punishment.

Debt Limit   A constitutional or statutory limitation upon the ability of a government to incur indebtedness. In the national government, the debt limit is fixed by Congress and can be changed to meet new debt needs. All but a few states, however, are restricted by constitutional provisions that usually limit state indebtedness to a specified figure. Debt limitations on local governments generally take the form of restricting total debt to a percentage of assessed valuation or involve state approval of bond issues. *See also* PUBLIC DEPT.

Decentralization   An administrative concept applied by large organizations or departments in assigning decision-making responsibility to subunits on a geographical or subject matter basis. Decentralization usually takes the form of field-service operations or division of tasks through specialization. *See also* FIELD SERVICE.

Decision Makers   Those individuals in each state who exercise the powers for making and implementing foreign policy decisions. Official decision makers may be influenced—sometimes decisively—by private individuals and groups that serve as consultants or function as unofficial members of the nation's "establishment." Opinion élites and the general public may also affect foreign policy actions by setting limits on the decision makers through support for some policies and rejection of others. In most states, the chief of government—whether his title is president, prime minister, premier, or chairman—plays the key role in the decision process. In others, the highest decision maker may be the leader of the single party that controls power, as in many Communist states, or the dictator or oligarchs who hold no official position but control the decision process, as in some Fascist states. Others who function as high-ranking decision makers in most states include the minister of foreign affairs, sometimes called secretary of state, and the bureaucracy that functions under his direction in the state's foreign office. Other ministries, particularly defense, and high military officers contribute to decision making. In many democratic states, key legislators of the majority party or coalition also play a role in making foreign policy decisions, and in some—such as the United States—leaders of the opposition party or parties may also participate in the process. *See also* FOREIGN OFFICE, PUBLIC OPINION.

Decision-making Approach   A mode of analysis used by political scientists to gain an understanding of the way a political system functions through observing and analyzing its decision processes. Decision making involves a sequence of activities by political actors: perception of the problem, marshaling facts and information, considering alternatives, and choosing a course of action calculated to maximize goal achievement. The decision analyst tries to find answers for such questions as what was the decision, who made it, how was it made, why was it made, what impact did the environmental situation have, and what do these answers tell us about the functioning of the political system that produced the decision. *Decision theory* is a body of thought dealing with the nature of the decision-making process. *See also* ORGANIZATION THEORY, POLITICS, PUBLIC POLICY.

Decision Process (International Organization), *see* Egalitarianism, Elitism, Majoritarianism.

Decision Theory, *see* Decision-making Approach.

Declaration of Independence   The document adopted by the Second Continental Congress on July 4, 1776, declaring the independence of the American colonies from Great Britain and justifying the rebellion. It was drafted by a committee composed of Thomas Jefferson, John Adams, Benjamin Franklin, Roger Sherman, and Robert Livingston. The draft was largely the work of Jefferson, who drew heavily from the natural-rights doctrine of the English philosopher, John Locke. The Declaration enumerated the grievances against the Crown and contained an eloquent defense of the rights of man and the right of self-government.

Declaration of Rights, *see* Bill of Rights.

Declaration of War A formal announcement by a nation that a state of hostilities exists with another nation. Constitutionally, only Congress can declare war. Under the usual procedure, the President requests a declaration of war, the Congress adopts it by joint resolution, and the President signs it.

Declaration of War (Congress) A joint resolution adopted by Congress and signed by the President informing the international community that the nation intends to pursue or defend its interests by military action. Technically, the Congress could pass a declaration of war resolution against the wishes of the President; in such a case he would have the option of the veto. Except for the War of 1812, every declaration of war by the United States has come at presidential request. Termination of a state of war is also accomplished by joint resolution or treaty. *See also* DECLARATION OF WAR, COMMANDER IN CHIEF.

Declaration on Outer Space (1963), *see* Outer Space Jurisdiction.

Declaratory Judgment A court procedure used to declare the rights of parties under a contract, will, or other dispute, before any damage occurs. It is a method of preventive justice contrary to the traditional procedure of suing for damages after the damage results. The national government (since the enactment of the Declaratory Judgments Act of 1934) and most of the states permit the use of this procedure.

Deduction The process of reasoning from the general to the particular, drawing conclusions from applicable premises. Deduction can be used to explain a political event by demonstrating that the conclusions concerning the event are the logical consequences of applicable premises. The deductive process starts with a *premise*—a generalization that holds true under specified conditions. The premise is applied to the event to be explained. If there is an orderly, logical connection between the premise and the conclusion, the latter may produce an understanding of the event and add to the body of theory used as a starting point. The validity of the conclusion depends entirely on the validity of the premise and the logical process used to arrive at the conclusion. *See also* A PRIORI, INDUCTION, RATIONALITY.

De Facto Recognition The preliminary recognition of a new state or government by another state. De facto recognition is usually followed by *de jure,* or full, legal recognition with exchange of ambassadors. De facto recognition also refers to a theory advanced by some international jurists (called the declarative theory) that new states and governments should be recognized if, in fact, they do exist. *See also* RECOGNITION.

De Facto Segregation The existence of racially segregated facilities that are, however, not required by law (*de jure*). De facto segregation refers especially to the school system in typical northern communities, in which neighborhood racial patterns lead "in fact" to predominantly Negro and white schools similar to those in the South that, in the past, were segregated by law. *See also Swann v. Charlotte.*

Defense Contract   An agreement between the Department of Defense (DOD) and a private business or industry by which the latter agrees to supply hardware, equipment, supplies, or services to the military. The three types of defense contracts used extensively by the Defense Department are: (1) the *competitive bid* contract, which ordinarily would be awarded to that company offering to provide the hardware or service at the lowest cost; (2) the *negotiated* contract, in which Defense officials discuss and reach agreement with a private company concerning materials or services and their costs; and (3) the *cost-plus* contract, in which the DOD guarantees the private company repayment of all costs involved in producing the hardware or service, plus a stipulated amount or percentage of costs as profit. *See also* DEPARTMENT OF DEFENSE; MILITARY-INDUSTRIAL COMPLEX.

Defense Intelligence Agency, *see* Intelligence (United States).

Defense Reorganization Act of 1958   An act that sought to overcome administrative weaknesses in the Defense Department created by the National Security Acts of 1947 and 1949. The Act of 1958 made it clear that the Secretaries of the Army, Navy, and Air Force were under the direct authority of the Secretary of Defense. A direct line of command from the Secretary to operational units in the field replaced the earlier system whereby the Secretary communicated decisions through the Army, Navy, and Air Force Secretaries. *See also* DEPARTMENT OF DEFENSE, NATIONAL SECURITY ACTS OF 1947 AND 1949.

Defense Support Aid, *see* Foreign Aid.

Deficiency Appropriation   A special bill appropriating funds to make up the difference between an agency's appropriation for the fiscal year and the amount deemed necessary to enable it to continue to operate for the full fiscal year. *See also* SUPPLEMENTARY APPROPRIATION.

Deficit Financing   A technique of fiscal policy that utilizes government spending beyond income to combat an economic slump. The use of deficit financing to "prime the pump" of the free enterprise economy was popularized by the British economist, John Maynard Keynes, in the 1930s. It has since become generally accepted and used as a basic tool of federal economic policy. *See also* FISCAL POLICY, PUBLIC DEBT.

Deflation   An economic condition in which the price level is decreased and the value of money in terms of purchasing power is consequently increased. Deflation may result from either a decrease in the amount of money and credit available or an oversupply of consumer goods. *See also* INFLATION, MONETARY POLICY.

De Jure Recognition   Full legal recognition of a new state or government by another state, usually accompanied by an exchange of ambassadors or ministers. *De jure* recognition also refers to a theory advanced by some international jurists (called the constitutive theory) that only those states and governments that have come into existence through peaceful, constitutional means are deserving of recognition. *See also* RECOGNITION.

Delegate, *see* Presidential Primaries, Washington, D.C.

Delegated Powers Powers granted to the national government under the Constitution. Generally, the delegated powers are those found enumerated in the first three articles of the Constitution, relative to the legislative, executive, and judicial branches of the national government. Article I, section 8 contains the main compilation of these powers. The terms "delegated," "enumerated," "granted," and "specific" may be used interchangeably. *See also* IMPLIED POWERS, RESERVED POWERS.

Delegation of Authority The assignment of decision-making responsibility to subordinate officials. The heads of large agencies find it essential to delegate some of their authority to others, but this must be done within clearly defined standards, subject to review by the head. *See also* HIERARCHY.

Delegation of Power The transfer of authority from one government or branch of government, which has been constitutionally assigned the power, to another branch or specific agency. Generally, delegations of power have involved the transfer of legislative power by Congress to the President, to an executive department or official, or to independent regulatory commissions. *See also Opp Cotton Mills v. Administrator of Wage and Hour Division,* QUASI-LEGISLATIVE.

Demagogue An unscrupulous politician who seeks to win and hold office through emotional appeals to mass prejudices and passions. Half-truths, outright lies, and various means of card-stacking may be used in either subtle or bold-faced attempts to dupe the voters. Typically, a demagogue may try to win support from one group by blaming another for its misfortunes. Another useful demagogic technique is to promise all things to all men.

Demilitarization, *see* Denuclearization, Disengagement.

Democracy A system of government in which ultimate political authority is vested in the people. The term is derived from the Greek words "demos" (the people) and "kratos" (authority). Democracy may be direct, as practiced in ancient Athens and in New England town meetings, or indirect and representative. In the modern pluralistic democratic state, power typically is exercised by groups or institutions in a complex system of interactions that involve compromises and bargaining in the decision process. The Democratic Creed includes the following concepts: (1) individualism, which holds that the primary task of government is to enable each individual to achieve the highest potential of development; (2) liberty, which allows each individual the greatest amount of freedom consistent with order; (3) equality, which maintains that all men are created equal and have equal rights and opportunities; and (4) fraternity, which postulates that individuals will not misuse their freedom but will cooperate in creating a wholesome society. As a political system, democracy starts with the assumption of popular sovereignty, vesting ultimate political power in the people. It presupposes that man can control his destiny, that he can make moral judgments and practical decisions in his daily life. It implies a continuing search for truth in the sense of man's pursuit of improved ways of building social institutions and ordering human relations. Democracy requires a decision-making system based on majority rule, with minority rights protected. Effective guarantees of freedom of speech, press, religion, assembly, petition, and equality before the law are indispensable to a democratic system of government. Politics, parties, and politicians are the catalytic agents that make democracy workable. *See also* ACCOUNTABILITY; CONSTITUTIONALISM; CONTRACT THEORY; DIRECT DEMOCRACY; INDIVIDUALISM; MAJORITY RULE; NATURAL LAW, POPULAR SOVEREIGNTY, REPRESENTATIVE GOVERNMENT, RULE OF LAW.

Democratic Centralism (Communist Theory)   The doctrinally sanctioned method for making and implementing decisions within Communist parties. Democratic centralism, as developed by Lenin, calls for democratic participation through free discussion and deliberation by all Communist party members in the development of party policies. Once decisions have been made, however, further dissent and debate are no longer tolerated, and well-disciplined party members are expected to lend their full support to the execution of policies by the centrally directed party organization. Diversity during the formative stages of policy development, in other words, is to give way to a monolithic unity in support of the party élite in implementing policy.

Democratic Party   A major American party that evolved out of the Democratic-Republican group supporting Thomas Jefferson. Andrew Jackson, regarded by Democrats as cofounder with Jefferson, changed the name to Democratic party in keeping with his ultrademocratic philosophy. Further development of party principles occurred under the more recent leadership of Woodrow Wilson and Franklin D. Roosevelt. Since 1932, the Democratic party has dominated the American political scene, holding the presidency for all but the eight Eisenhower years (1953–1961) and the Nixon years and a majority in Congress for all but four years (1947–1948; 1953–1954). *See also* REPUBLICAN PARTY.

Democratic Socialism   An economic system established by a democratic nation in which the people, through industrial groups or government, take over ownership and direction of basic industry, banking, communication, transportation, and other segments of the economy. The extent of the government's role in the economy is determined by free elections rather than by ideological dogma. Although a private sector of the economy may continue to exist, much effort is expended by government or groups in planning, directing, and regulating it, and in providing welfare services for the needy. *See also* SOCIALISM, WELFARE STATE.

Democratic Theory, *see* Accountability, Civil Liberties, Constitutionalism, Individualism, Majority Rule, Natural Law, Popular Sovereignty, Rule of Law.

Demographic Cycle   The series of changes in births and deaths that affect the size and composition of a society as it experiences technological change. The demographic cycle proceeds in three stages: from a preindustrial base of relative population stability, through a transitional stage of population explosion, to a final stage in which the rate of population growth slows down, stabilizes, and, in some countries, declines. *See also* DEMOGRAPHIC CYCLE, STAGES ONE, TWO, AND THREE.

Demographic Cycle: Stage One   The preindustrial demographic pattern, characterized by high birth and death rates. In stage one, life expentancy is low (approximately thirty years), infant mortality is high, and population increase is steady but slow. This preindustrial population pattern typified the Western societies in the period before the Industrial Revolution and the traditional societies of Asia, Africa, and Latin America prior to the 1930s.

Demographic Cycle: Stage Three   The demographic pattern characterized by the declining rate of natural increase in the population. In contrast to the preceding stage, in which the birth rate remained high while the death rate fell sharply, in the third stage the death rate continues to fall, but more gradually, while the birth rate declines rapidly. The result is a marked increase in the average age of the population. The decline in the birth rate is usually ascribed to a complex of changes in social attitudes and institutions that make large families less desirable, particularly for economic reasons. Stage three of the demographic cycle is associated with such industrialized societies as the Soviet Union, the United States, Japan, and those of Europe.

Demographic Cycle: Stage Two   The demographic pattern characterized by a population explosion. In stage two, the birth rate remains high, but the death rate declines sharply, resulting in rapid population growth. To begin with, a dramatic decrease in infant mortality results in more young adults, who in turn produce additional children, so that the natural rate of increases also rises. Since longevity has not yet increased substantially, the society tends to be biologically young. However, eventually the same technology that makes industrialization possible brings about an additional population increase by reducing the death rate still further, through improved medicine and sanitation.

Denaturalization   The revoking of citizenship that has been acquired by naturalization. This may be done only by court order in accordance with due process of law.

Dennis v. United States, 341 U.S. 494 (1951): Sustained, in a major decision, the conviction of eleven top Communist party leaders for conspiring to teach and to advocate the violent overthrow of the government. The decision upheld the Smith Act of 1940. *See also* ALIEN REGISTRATION ACT.

De Novo, *see* Intermediate Court.

Denuclearization   An agreement to prohibit nuclear weapons in a specific zone, country, or region. The denuclearization of various areas has been extensively discussed for more than a decade in the General Assembly, in the disarmament commissions and committees, and in other international and national bodies. Nuclear-free zones and nuclear test banned areas established by treaty include Antarctica, outer space, Latin America, the seas, the seabed, the atmosphere, and nonnuclear states. Discussions in the United Nations concerning denuclearization have included such geographical areas as the Arctic, the Bering Strait, the Adriatic, the Balkans, the Mediterranean, the Middle East, and Scandinavia, but formal plans and proposals have dealt chiefly with Africa, Central Europe, and Latin America. *See also* DISENGAGEMENT.

Denunciation of Treaty, *see Rebus Sic Stantibus.*

Department   A major administrative unit with responsibility for the conduct of a broad area of government operations. In the national government, the departments are headed by officers who comprise the President's Cabinet. These departments include State; Treasury; Defense; Justice; Commerce; Labor; Agriculture; Interior; Health, Education, and Welfare; Housing and Urban Development; and Transportation. State and local governments also departmentalize major functions. Departments are generally subdivided into bureaus, divisions, sections, and other units. (*See also* specific departments.)

Department of Agriculture   A major clientele department of the national government that provides numerous services for farmers and regulates various aspects of agriculture and related fields in the interest of farmers and the general public. The Secretary who heads the Department is appointed by the President with the Senate's approval and serves as a member of the Cabinet. A variety of activities are carried on by the Department's major operational units. They are (1) Agricultural Research Service which conducts research in crop and livestock production and marketing; (2) Federal Extension Service which works cooperatively with land-grant colleges and county agents to provide research information to farmers; (3) Forest Service which protects the national forests from fire and disease; (4) Soil Conservation Service which conserves soil resources through programs of research, erosion control, reforestation, and flood control; (5) Commodity Exchange Authority which supervises trading on commodity exchanges where agricultural products are bought and sold; (6) Commodity Credit Corporation and the Agricultural Stabilization and Conservation Service which are responsible for the stabilization of agricultural prices; (7) Federal Crop Insurance Corporation which insures farmers against loss or damage to their crops; (8) Farmers Home Administration which makes low-interest loans to low-income farmers to improve their crops or facilities; and (9) Rural Electrification Administration which makes loans to finance the extension of electric power and telephone service to rural areas.

Department of Commerce   One of the eleven major departments of the national administration headed by a Secretary with Cabinet rank. The Department of Commerce and Labor, founded in 1903, was split in 1913 by Congress into the two separate departments of Commerce and Labor. Major units found in the Department of Commerce, and the main responsibility of each, include: (1) the Bureau of the Census, which conducts the decennial census; (2) the National Oceanic and Atmospheric Administration, which monitors the physical and biological environment including weather forecasting; (3) the International Commerce Bureau, which promotes United States business interests abroad; (4) the Maritime Administration, which administers grants to shipbuilders and operators; (5) the National Bureau of Standards, which maintains basic units for testing and measuring in business and industry; (6) the Office of Minority Business Enterprise, which seeks to establish, preserve, and strengthen ownership of business by members of minority groups; (7) the Patent Office, which examines and grants patents and trademarks; (8) the Bureau of Domestic Commerce, which promotes the growth of American industry and commerce; and (9) the Economic Development Administration, which provides aid to areas with substantial and persistent unemployment.

Department of Defense (DOD)   A major department of the national government with responsibility to formulate military policies and to maintain the armed forces of the United States. Since 1961, it has assumed responsibility for civil defense functions. The Secretary who heads the Department of Defense is a civilian appointed by the President with the Senate's approval. He serves as a member of the Cabinet. The three major military departments of the Army, Navy, and Air Force are each headed by a civilian secretary responsible to the Secretary of Defense. The Chiefs of Staff of the Army and the Air Force and the Chief of Naval Operations are the top military officers in each service who advise the civilian secretaries. These three military leaders join with the Chief of Staff to the Secretary of Defense to form the Joint Chiefs of Staff, the nation's highest military advisory body. Other advisers to the Secretary of Defense include the Armed Forces Policy Council, composed of the civilian secretaries, the Joint Chiefs of Staff, the Director of Defense Research and Engineering, and a host of civilian and military individuals, boards, and committees to offer advice on a variety of defense subjects. The Commandant of the Marine Corps also attends meetings of the Joint Chiefs and the Policy Council.

Department of Health, Education, and Welfare (HEW)   A major department of the national government established in 1953 to unify administration of federal activities in the fields of health, education, and social security. The Department is headed by a Secretary who is a member of the Cabinet. Its major operating units include: (1) the Social Security Administration, which administers the Old-Age, Survivors, and Disability Insurance program; (2) the Social and Rehabilitation Service, which administers the categorical aid programs; (3) the Office of Education, which administers grants-in-aid for educational purposes; and (4) the Public Health Service, which carries on far-flung programs in health and hospital care.

Department of Housing and Urban Development (HUD)   A major department of Cabinet status, established in 1965, with responsibility for the housing, home finance, and community-development functions of the national government. The Department, headed by a Secretary, has as its major operational units: (1) Housing Production and Mortgage Credit and Federal Housing Commission, which administers programs related to the production and financing of housing both public and private; (2) Federal Insurance Administration, which protects against losses from riots and civil disorders and natural disasters; (3) Community Development, charged with responsibility for urban renewal, model cities, community planning, new communities development, community facilities, and intergovernmental relations; (4) Housing Management, responsible for the social, physical, and financial aspects of housing management; and (5) Equal Opportunity, to promote civil rights in housing and in employment pertaining to housing and urban development.

Department of Justice   A major department of the executive branch concerned with the enforcement of federal laws. The Justice Department is headed by the Attorney General who is a member of the President's Cabinet. The Department furnishes legal counsel in cases involving the national government, interprets laws under which other executive agencies operate, supervises federal penal institutions, directs United States Attorneys and Marshals, supervises immigration laws, and directs paroles of federal prisoners. The Department includes the Federal Bureau of Investigation (FBI), which is the major police agency for the national government. In 1968 the Law Enforcement Assistance Administration was established within the Department to assist state and local governments to improve their police agencies, courts, corrections and other law enforcement units.

Department of Labor   A major department of Cabinet status that administers laws designed to promote the welfare of wage earners through improved working conditions and employment opportunities. The Department, established originally in 1903 as Commerce and Labor and separated in 1913, is headed by the Secretary of Labor and is divided into five major operational units: (1) Manpower Administration, which appraises national manpower requirements to deal with unemployment, underemployment, the impact of automation, apprenticeship training, and aspects of the war on poverty including the Job Corps, and administers the unemployment compensation program and the United States Employment Service; (2) Labor-Management Relations, which administers laws relating to welfare and pension plans, enforces the Labor-Management Reporting and Disclosure Act relative to internal affairs of labor unions, and provides a wide variety of industrial relations services; (3) International Affairs, which considers the effect of American Labor problems on foreign policy and is responsible for American participation in the International Labor Organization; (4) Employment Standards, which administers the wage and hour laws and seeks to improve working conditions, with special attention to the needs of women, children, and minority groups; and (5) Occupational Safety and Health, which develops and regulates industrial safety and health standards.

Department of State   The agency primarily responsible for making and executing American foreign policy. The Secretary of State, who heads the Department, is the President's official adviser on foreign policy matters. The first responsibility of the Department is to formulate programs and policies for the United States in its relations with other nations. Next in importance are its duties of administering laws relating to foreign affairs and conducting the day-to-day relations with foreign countries. The latter responsibility is carried out primarily by the Foreign Service, which is administratively tied to the Department of State, and has been undergoing a gradual process of integrating its personnel with that of the Department. Specific duties of the Department include: (1) negotiating treaties and agreements with foreign states; (2) carrying on extensive communications with foreign governments and American units abroad; (3) issuing passports and, through consular officials abroad, granting visas; (4) promoting cultural relations between foreign peoples and the American people; (5) carrying on propaganda and information programs overseas; (6) planning and administering economic aid programs. The Department and its Secretary are responsible to the President. Important policymaking and primary contact with field operations and foreign missions are carried on through six regional bureaus. These include the African, Inter-American, European, Far Eastern, Near Eastern and South Asian Affairs Bureaus, and a Bureau of International Orgainization Affairs, each headed by an Assistant Secretary. The Agency for International Development is a semiautonomous agency within the State Department. *See also* ROGERS ACT, SECRETARY OF STATE.

Department of the Interior   A major department of the national government that has responsibility over a variety of affairs concerning the territories and properties of the United States. The Secretary who heads the Department is appointed by the President with the Senate's approval and serves as a member of the Cabinet. Some of the major operating units found in the Interior Department are the: (1) Fish and Wildlife Service, which improves commercial fishing, and hunting and fishing for sport through research and conservation programs; (2) Bureau of Mines, which promotes health and safety in privately owned mines and compiles statistics on mine operations; (3) Geological Survey, which surveys and classifies public lands and conducts geologic research; (4) Bureau of Indian Affairs, which promotes health, welfare, and educational facilities for Indians; (5) Bureau of Land Management, which supervises the exploitation of natural resources of the public domain by private companies; (6) National Park Service, which develops and administers natural beauty spots and historic sites for the enjoyment of the American people; (7) Bureau of Outdoor Recreation, which maintains a continuing inventory and evaluation of recreational needs and resources; (8) Bureau of Reclamation, which constructs and operates public facilities to generate electric power, promote flood control, and provide irrigation; and (9) Alaska, Bonneville, Southeastern, and Southwestern Power Administrations, which market electric power generated by national dams and power stations in different sections of the country. The Department of the Interior also has responsibility for the economic, social, and political development of the territories of Guam, Samoa, the Virgin Islands, and the Trust Territory of the Pacific Islands.

Department of the Treasury   A major department of the national government, responsible for fiscal management and headed by a Secretary with Cabinet rank. The Department of the Treasury was one of the original departments established in 1789. Important administrative units include the Internal Revenue Service, Bureau of Customs, Bureau of Accounts, Secret Service, Bureau of Public Debt, and Office of the Comptroller of the Currency.

Department of Transportation   One of the major departments of the national administration, headed by a Secretary with Cabinet rank. The Department, established in 1966, brought together more than thirty separate agencies and bureaus dealing with transportation. Its major components now include the Federal Aviation Administration, the Federal Highway Administration, the Federal Railroad Administration, the Urban Mass Transport Administration, and the Coast Guard. An autonomous agency within the Department is the National Transportation Safety Board which investigates major air and surface accidents.

Dependent Territory, *see* Colony, Condominium, Leasehold, Mandates System, Protectorate, Trust Territory, Sphere of Influence.

Dependent Variable, *see* Variable.

Deportation   Compulsory expulsion of an alien from a state to his country of origin. Deportation is a civil rather than a criminal proceeding under American law, hence, various constitutional safeguards do not apply. With the exception of naturalized citizens who lose their citizenship, a citizen may not be deported. *See also Fong Yue Ting v. United States.*

Depression   A business cycle period characterized by a serious economic slump, inadequate purchasing power, deflation, and high unemployment. Typically, major depressions have followed peak periods of prosperity when production facilities and credit have been overextended. *See also* BUSINESS CYCLES.

Description   A "word picture" or representation of a particular political phenomenon or class of political phenomena. Description involves a process of selecting and applying appropriate conceptual labels to things observed and experienced, and, when necessary, formulating new descriptive concepts. Description provides the raw material for communication, theory building, and analysis. *See also* ANALYSIS, CONCEPT.

Descriptive Statistics, *see* Statistics.

Design, *see* Research Design.

Détente   A diplomatic term indicating a situation of lessened strain or tension in the relations between two or more countries. A period of *détente* may be established by formal treaty or may evolve out of changes in national strategies and tactics over several years. *See also* RAPPROCHEMENT.

Determinism   The view that all events, including political events, are the direct result of specific causes or conditions. Determinism applied to the discipline of political science means that no political event or phenomenon just happens, that causal relationships are universally present in the social world as in the physical. It is the objective of the political scientist to discover these relationships, determine their causes, and formulate generalizations about observed uniformities. Some deterministic theories, in the context of *free will* versus determinism, emphasize causation inherent in nature or in the social order, thus leaving the individual no freedom of choice. *Indeterminist* doctrines hold that human choice is not wholly determined by causes independent of the individual's will. *See also* CAUSALITY.

Deterrence   Retaliatory capability of a nation's military forces to discourage a potential enemy from launching an attack. The concept implies that a nation's military defenses are so large, diversified, and well protected that a first-strike by an enemy would not cripple its ability to retaliate decisively.

Devaluation   A policy undertaken by a nation to reduce the value of its monetary unit in terms of gold, or its exchange ratio with other national currencies. The United States devalued the dollar by about 59 percent in 1934 by increasing the price of gold to $35 an ounce. The price thereafter remained fixed at $35 an ounce until President Richard M. Nixon agreed in late 1971 to devalue the dollar by changing the official price of gold to $38 an ounce in exchange for agreement by other major nations to realign their currencies by raising their values in relation to the dollar. *See also* GOLD STANDARD, BALANCE OF PAYMENTS.

Development, *see* Political Development.

Development Assistance Committee (DAC), *see* Organization for Economic Cooperation and Development.

Development Bank, *see* Regional Development Banks.

Development Decade, United Nations, *see* Second Development Decade.

Development, Economic, *see* Economic Growth, Underdevelopment.

Development Loans, *see* Export-Import Bank, International Bank for Reconstruction and Development, Regional Development Banks.

Development, Political, *see* Political Development.

Development Theory   Propositions, generalizations, and philosophies of history that seek to explain the process of political, economic, and social transformation or "modernization" of societies and states. Political scientists have been particularly concerned with aspects of development that relate to the nonWestern world, where traditional societies have operated under a minimum of political consciousness and effectiveness. Political development involves a socialization process aimed at building mass support for a national political system, as well as creating institutions to promote more widespread political participation. As development proceeds, government takes on a new image and new responsibilities in the form of directing and servicing functions unknown to the society in the past. Government also begins to promote scientific and technological advances, general public education, fair tax programs, land reform, and other programs of economic and social modernization. A corps of administrators is recruited and trained in modern administrative techniques to provide efficient implementation of government policies. Political development theories relate to the means by which such goals may be achieved. *See also* POLITICAL DEVELOPMENT.

Diachronic Analysis, *see* Time Series Analysis.

Dialectical Materialism (Communist Theory)   The concept that explains how the process involving the union of opposites produces social development. The dialectic, which Marx borrowed from the philosophy of Hegel, postulates a process by which each idea (thesis) produces a contradictory idea (antithesis), leading to a conflict out of which a new, higher idea (synthesis) emerges. Marx adapted the dialectical method to his materialist outlook and used it to describe the process in which the dominant economic classes in each society engage in struggle and produce new economic systems, with the process culminating ultimately in the creation of a pure, classless, stateless society of communism. Lenin described dialectics as "the study of the contradiction within the very essence of things."

Dichotomous Classification   The ordering of phenomena into two mutually exclusive groups. Dichotomous classification requires a precise definition of the two classification categories so that all items under consideration will fall into one or the other and none will fall into both. Examples of dichotomous classification include conservative or liberal, voter or nonvoter, under age thirty or over age thirty. *See also* CLASSIFICATION, CONTINUUM, FACT.

Dictatorship   Arbitrary rule by an individual or junta not constitutionally responsible to the people or their elected representatives. Changes in government can come about only by death, revolution, *coup d'état,* war, or voluntary surrender of power. Characteristics of contemporary dictatorships usually include: (1) a veneer of democratic jargon and institutions; (2) an ideological rationalization; (3) elimination of active opposition; (4) control of the military; (5) an aggressive foreign policy; (6) a charismatic leader who personifies the state; (7) subordination of the individual to the state; (8) control of the mass media of communication and (9) a single party which supports the leader, controls the administration of the state, and transmits government policy to the citizenry. *See also* CONSTITUTIONAL DICTATORSHIP, FASCISM.

Dictatorship of the Proletariat (Communist Theory)   The transitional stage following a proletarian revolution in which Communist power is consolidated, the burgeoisie eliminated as a class, and socialism established. For Marx, the dictatorship of the proletariat meant that the workers would control the machinery of the state and would use it to reorganize society and convert the means of production from private to public ownership to provide for the transformation of society into its final stage of pure communism. For Lenin and Stalin, the dictatorship was vested in the Communist party and its leaders as representatives of the proletariat. For those two leaders, its primary function was to defend the state and the revolution against a renaissance of the bourgeois class, which, they believed, had increased rather than decreased its resistance following the overthrow of its power.

Dilatory Motion   An irrelevant or nongermane motion in a legislative body to delay or prevent action on a bill.

Dillon's Rule   A rule enunciated by Judge John F. Dillon, an authority on municipal corporations, to the effect that a municipal corporation can exercise only those powers expressly granted to it by state law, those necessarily implied from the granted powers, and those essential for the purposes of the organization. If any doubt exists, it is to be resolved against the local unit, in favor of the state.

Diplomacy   The total process by means of which states carry on political relations with each other. The machinery of diplomacy includes a policy-making foreign office (Department of State in the United States) and diplomatic missions abroad (Foreign Service). Diplomacy may be carried on through open or conference negotiations or in secret. Occasionally diplomacy is undertaken by heads of state, a process commonly called "summit" diplomacy. *See also* APPEASEMENT, DOLLAR DIPLOMACY, QUID PRO QUO, PACIFIC SETTLEMENT OF DISPUTES.

Diplomat   An accredited agent of a head of state who serves as the primary medium for the conduct of international relations. Diplomatic titles and order of rank were established by the Congresses of Vienna (1815) and Aix-la-Chapelle (1818) and include: (1) ambassador extraordinary and plenipotentiary, and papal legate and nuncio; (2) envoy extraordinary, minister plenipotentiary, and papal internuncio; (3) minister resident; and (4) *chargé d'affaires,* and *chargé d'affaires ad interim.* Though ambassador is the highest rank a diplomat can hold, both ambassadors and ministers may serve as chiefs of mission, are accredited to the head of the state to which they are sent, and are responsible for the conduct of their official families and staffs. The official quarters occupied by a mission are designated an embassy when headed by an ambassador and a legation if headed by a minister. Virtually all diplomatic missions are now embassies headed by ambassadors. A *chargé d'affaires* accredited to the minister of foreign affairs is the diplomat placed in charge of a mission before an ambassador or minister has been appointed or from which the chief of mission has been withdrawn. The senior diplomatic officer temporarily responsible for a mission because of the absence, disability, or death of the ambassador or minister is designated *chargé d'affaires ad interim*. In the practice of the United States, the title diplomatic agent is used for a representative accredited to the foreign minister of a dependent state. Diplomats take precedence from the date of their arrival at a particular capital. The senior ambassador is the dean (or *doyen*) of the diplomatic corps at that capital and on occasion represents the corps with the foreign office. *See also* ATTACHÉ, LETTER OF CREDENCE, NEGOTIATION, PERSONA GRATA.

Diplomatic Privileges and Immunities   Exemptions of a diplomat from national and local civil and criminal jurisdictions of the state to which he is accredited. Diplomatic privileges and immunities include freedom from arrest, trial, civil suit, subpoena, and legal penalty. His dwelling, offices, and archives may not be entered, searched, or appropriated, and his privileges and immunities also normally apply to members of his official staff and household. Consular officers do not have diplomatic status but, because of their functions, may by law, treaty, and usage enjoy privileges not granted to other aliens. Privileges and immunities enjoyed by United Nations delegates and personnel are governed by an agreement concluded between the organization and the United States as the host country.

Diplomatic Sanctions, *see* Sanctions (Collective Security), Sanctions (International Law).

Direct Approach (Disarmament)   A strategy for seeking agreement on disarmament that places primary emphasis on negotiations for securing arms reduction rather than on related problem areas. The direct approach is best described by its advocates' maxim: "The way to disarm is to disarm." It differs from the indirect approach, which regards armaments as a reflection of major political disagreements that must be resolved before disarmament can become a feasible objective. *See also* INDIRECT APPROACH.

Direct Democracy   A system of government in which political decisions are made by the people directly rather than by their elected representatives. Under direct democracy, the citizens assemble periodically and function as a legislative body, or they vote on public issues to determine government policies. *See also* INITIATIVE; REFERENDUM; REPRESENTATIVE GOVERNMENT.

Directed Interview, *see* Interview.

Direct Election of Senators, *see* Seventeenth Amendment.

Directed Trade   The determination of trade policies by a government in pursuit of a state's economic, political, or security objectives. Directed trade differs from free trade, which permits the supply and demand forces of the marketplace to determine the flow of trade.

Direct Legislation   Electoral devices that enable voters to participate directly in deciding governmental policies. Direct methods include the initiative and the referendum. *See also* INITIATIVE; REFERENDUM.

Direct Primary   An intraparty election in which the voters select the candidates who will run on a party's ticket in the subsequent general election. Primaries are also used to choose convention delegates and party leaders. In a closed primary, the selection process is limited to avowed party adherents; in an open primary, voters participate regardless of party affiliation or the absence of any. Some state and local governments use nonpartisan primaries to reduce the number of candidates for the general election. Candidates get their names on a primary ballot, typically, through petitions signed by a required number of registered voters. Other means include caucus, preprimary convention, and self-announcement. *See also* PRESIDENTIAL PRIMARIES, CLOSED PRIMARY, OPEN PRIMARY, RUNOFF PRIMARY, *United States v. Classic, Smith v. Allwright.*

Direct Tax   Any tax paid directly to the government by the taxpayer. An indirect tax, such as a sales or excise tax, conversely, is paid to private business persons who then remit it to the government. The Constitution, in Article I, section 9, states: "No capitation, or other direct tax shall be laid, unless in proportion to the census or enumeration hereinbefore directed to be taken." This provision means that, for example, the people in a state containing 10 percent of the nation's population would pay 10 percent of any direct tax levied by the national government. *See also Pollock v. Farmers Loan and Trust Co..*

Disarmament, *see* Arms Control, General and Complete Disarmament, United States Arms Control and Disarmament Agency.

Disarmament Agreements, *see* Antarctic Treaty, "Hot Line" Agreement, Non-Proliferation of Nuclear Weapons Treaty, Outer Space Treaty, Partial Test Ban Treaty, Rush-Bagot Agreement, Washington Treaty for the Limitation of Naval Armaments.

Disarmament Approaches, *see* Conference of Experts, Direct Approach, Indirect Approach, Unilateral Disarmament.

Disarmament Commission, *see* United Nations Disarmament Commission.

Disarmament Forums, *see* Conference of the Committee on Disarmament, United Nations Disarmament Commission, World Disarmament Conference.

Disarmament Initiatives, *see* Atoms for Peace Plan, Baruch Plan, Denuclearization, Disengagement, "Open Sky" Proposal.

Disarmament Problems, *see* Enforcement, Inspection, Ratio Problem.

Discharge Rule   A procedure by which a bill in the House of Representatives may be forced out of a committee (discharged) that has refused to report it out for consideration by the House. Bills not reported out within thirty days after referral to a committee may be subject to discharge. The discharge motion must be signed by an absolute majority (218) of the House membership. If the motion to discharge the bill carries by a simple majority vote, consideration of the bill then becomes a matter of high privilege. The Rules Committee may be discharged of a bill after it has held it for only seven legislative days. *See also* STANDING COMMITTEE.

Discrimination, Racial, *see* Civil Rights Acts, De Facto Segregation, Fair Employment Practices Laws, Segregation.

Disengagement   The withdrawal of two potentially hostile military forces from positions of direct confrontation. Almost one hundred disengagement plans for demilitarizing and neutralizing central European areas or states were offered during the late 1950s and early 1960s by Western- and Eastern-bloc statesmen, scholars, and disarmament specialists. Most disengagement proposals call for the neutralization of West and East Germany and part or all of Czechoslovakia and Poland, the acceptance of post-World War II boundary settlements, and the conclusion of a nonaggression pact between NATO and Warsaw Pact countries. *See also* DENUCLEARIZATION.

Disequilibrium, *see* Asymmetry, Equilibrium.

Disfranchise   Taking away the privilege of voting. Persons may be disfranchised if they lose their citizenship, if they fail to reregister when required, or if they are convicted for certain crimes. Many people are disfranchised temporarily when they move, either within the state or from state to state, until they establish new residence. Voters may also be wholly or partially disfranchised indirectly as a result of dishonesty in ballot counts or through political manipulation, such as gerrymandering. *See also* VOTING QUALIFICATIONS.

Dispositions   Personality traits that tend to shape the individual's values, attitudes, and opinions toward political phenomena and his actions in the political arena. *See also* ATTITUDE, PERSONALITY.

Dispute Settlement Procedures (United Nations)   Techniques and tools available for use by agencies of the United Nations in efforts to achieve a peaceful settlement of an international dispute. The Charter (Article 33) provides that the parties to a dispute should "first of all, seek a solution by negotiation, inquiry, mediation, conciliation, arbitration, judicial settlement, resort to regional agencies or arrangements, or other peaceful means. . . . " If these traditional pacific settlement approaches fail or are inappropriate, the dispute may be brought before the Security Council or General Assembly by a member state or by a nonmember if it agrees to accept Charter obligations relating to dispute settlement. The Secretary-General, under the Charter (Article 99), may also bring any situation that threatens peace and security to the attention of the Security Council. Initial actions by the world organization may take the form of an appeal to refrain from aggravating the situation or, if fighting has broken out, a cease-fire order may be issued. The parties to a dispute are given an opportunity to present their cases before the Council or Assembly, and such discussions may be useful to discover common ground for a settlement. "Quiet diplomacy," a blend of public and private negotiations carried on at United Nations headquarters, has proved useful in breaking deadlocks. When mediation and conciliation techniques applied in New York fail, a commission of inquiry and mediation or a United Nations representative or mediator may be appointed to go to the scene of the dispute to establish the facts and try for an on-the-spot settlement. If a great-power confrontation threatens to expand the dispute, "preventive diplomacy" in the form of a United Nations "presence" or police force to fill a power vacuum may be employed. Finally, when it is possible to secure the acceptance of both parties, the legal approaches to settlement—arbitration or adjudication—may be used to settle a dispute. *See also* PEACEFUL SETTLEMENT.

Dissenting Opinion   An opinion of one or more judges, usually of an appellate court, that disagrees with the decision reached by a majority of the court. Such opinions are frequently presented on the United States Supreme Court. *See also* CONCURRING OPINION.

Distortion, *see* Communications Theory.

Distribution of Powers   An underlying principle of the American constitutional system designed to prevent tyranny by assigning powers to different governments and agencies and by checking the exercise of power. The distribution takes the following forms: (1) dividing power between the national and state governments under a federal system; (2) separating power among the three major branches of the government— legislative, executive, and judicial—giving each branch a check upon the operations of the others; (3) selecting the personnel of the three branches by different procedures and electorates, assigning them different terms of office, and making them responsible to different pressures; (4) limiting all governments by specific constitutional restrictions. *See also* FEDERALISM, SEPARATION OF POWERS.

District Attorney   A county official, elected in all but six states for two or four year terms, who represents the state in prosecutions against violators of criminal laws. In some states, he is called the county attorney, county prosecutor, or, simply prosecutor. Prosecutions for the national government are handled by United States Attorneys.

District attorneys also conduct proceedings before grand juries. In states where grand juries are not used, the district attorney brings charges in the form of an information. In addition, the district attorney acts as legal advisor to the county and represents the county in lawsuits. *See also* UNITED STATES ATTORNEY.

District Court   The federal court of "original jurisdiction," where most federal cases begin. It is the only federal court where trials are held, juries are used, and witnesses are called. Both criminal and civil cases arising under federal law are heard. Each state has at least one district court; a few have as many as four, for a total of 88 in the 50 states. District courts are also found in Washington, D.C., and the territories of Puerto Rico, Guam, the Virgin Islands, and the Panama Canal Zone. Each court has from one to twenty-four judges, depending on the volume of business, but each judge holds court separately. Certain cases are heard by a three-judge panel. All judges are appointed for life terms by the President with the Senate's consent, except those serving in Guam, the Virgin Islands, and the Panama Canal Zone, who have eight-year terms. *See also* FEDERAL MAGISTRATE.

District of Columbia   The seat of government of the United States of America, commonly called Washington, D. C. It consists of some seventy square miles of land carved out of the state of Maryland. Article I, section 8, of the Constitution grants Congress exclusive control over the capital. The District is managed by a Commissioner, popularly called Mayor, a Deputy Mayor, and a nine-member council, all appointed by the President with the consent of the Senate. Congress is the legislative body for the District and in effect acts as the city council. Funds for the District are secured largely through local taxation. The District is a highly urbanized area of about one million inhabitants. Under the Twenty-third Amendment to the Constitution adopted in 1961, residents of the District may vote in presidential elections. Legislation enacted by Congress in 1968 authorized the District's first elected school board. In 1970 Congress granted the District a nonvoting delegate in the House of Representatives and established a local court system.

District of Columbia Court Reorganization and Criminal Procedure Act of 1970   A "model anti-crime package" for the nation's capital authorizing stringent law enforcement measures. Among these are provisions that: (1) provide for "no-knock" search and arrest warrants, which allow police to enter without notice if they fear destruction of evidence; (2) authorize pre-trial detention of up to sixty days for defendants whose release would endanger the community; (3) revise the juvenile code to lower to fifteen the age at which a juvenile charged with a felony can be tried as an adult and to eliminate jury trials for juveniles; (4) broaden electronic surveillance procedures by police; and (5) increase penalties for crime. In addition, the Act established a modern court system for the District to have jurisdiction over local matters previously handled in the federal courts.

Diversity of Citizenship   Lawsuits involving citizens of different states. The Constitution (Art. III, sec. 2) confers jurisdiction in such cases on the federal courts, which, generally, apply relevant state law. Congress has conferred exclusive jurisdiction on state courts for suits between citizens of different states if the amount in controversy is less than $10,000, and concurrent jurisdiction if more than $10,000 is involved. *See also Erie Railroad v. Tompkins;* JURISDICTION.

Divine Right   A theory supporting absolutism based on the divinity of a person or his office, or on a right to rule inherited from ancestors believed to have been appointed by a Supreme Being. *See also* ABSOLUTISM.

Division   A method of voting used in a legislative body. In a division or "standing vote," members voting for or against the motion alternately rise and are counted by the presiding officer. *See also* RECORD VOTE, TELLER VOTE, VIVA VOCE VOTE.

Docket   A record of proceedings in a court of justice. The term is usually used to indicate the list of cases to be tried at a specific term of court and may also be known as the calendar of cases. *See also* JUDICIAL COUNCIL, ADMINISTRATIVE OFFICE.

Dollar Diplomacy   A term used by Latin Americans to show their disapproval of the role the American government has played in using diplomatic and military power to open up foreign markets and to safeguard the financial interests of American businessmen. Under the Roosevelt Corollary of the Monroe Doctrine, American Marines were frequently sent into countries of Central America. Protectorates were established over Cuba, Haiti, Nicaragua, and Santo Domingo in the early part of the twentieth century. The term might also be used to describe any use of a state's political or military power to further the economic interests of its citizens abroad. *See also* GOOD NEIGHBOR POLICY.

Domestic Jurisdiction   Those spheres of the national life which are regulated exclusively by national law and within which the validity of international law is denied. Domestic jurisdiction is thus a concomitant of national sovereignty. Article 2 of the Charter of the United Nations provides that "Nothing contained in the present Charter shall authorize the United Nations to intervene in matters which are essentially within the domestic jurisdiction of any state or shall require the Members to submit such matters to settlement under the present Charter. . . . " *See also* CONNALLY AMENDMENT, JURISDICTION (COURT), DOMESTIC JURISDICTION CLAUSE.

Domestic Jurisdiction Clause   The Charter limitation (Article 2) placed upon the competence of the United Nations, which provides that "nothing contained in the present Charter shall authorize the United Nations to intervene in matters which are essentially within the domestic jurisdiction of any state." Collective action to maintain international peace and security is specifically excluded from the limiting clause, but beyond this no definition is provided as to what constitutes an *international* problem (and, hence, a proper subject for United Nations consideration) and what is strictly a *national* or *domestic* question. *See also* DOMESTIC JURISDICTION.

Domino Theory   The doctrine which assumes that if some key nation or geographical region falls into Communist control, a string of other nations will subsequently topple "like a row of dominoes." The Domino Theory was applied by President Dwight D. Eisenhower and his top advisers in 1954 to describe the dangers of Communist expansion in Asia if Indochina were to fall.

Dorr's Rebellion, *see Luther v. Borden.*

Double Jeopardy   The guarantee in the Fifth Amendment to the Constitution that one may not be twice put in jeopardy of life or limb for the same offense. Thus, a person who has been tried may not be tried again for the same crime. The guarantee does not, however, apply to trials by both the national government and a state, or by two different states for offenses growing out of a single criminal act. Trial following a mistrial is not double jeopardy unless the prosecution has deliberately forced a mistrial in order to get better evidence or a more favorable jury. In 1969, the Supreme Court held the protection against double jeopardy applicable to the states through the Fourteenth Amendment (*Benton v. Maryland,* 395 U.S. 784). *See also Bartkus v. Illinois.*

Doyen, *see* Diplomat.

Drago Doctrine   A position in opposition to the use of force by states in the recovery of contract debts. The Drago Doctrine was enunciated in 1902 by the Foreign Minister of Argentina. The doctrine held that a state's defaulting on its public debt owed to aliens did not give another state the right to intervene forcibly on their behalf to collect that debt, or the right to occupy the territory of the debtor state. *See also* CALVO CLAUSE, INTERVENTION, MONROE DOCTRINE.

Dred Scott v. Sanford, 19 Howard 393 (1857): Held, in a famous case, that Negroes could not become citizens of the United States nor were they entitled to the rights and privileges of citizenship. The Court also ruled that the Missouri Compromise, which had banned slavery in the territories, was unconstitutional.

Dual Nationality   Citizenships simultaneously held in more than one country. Dual nationality can occur when an individual acquires citizenship in one country through his parents *(jus sanguinis)* and citizenship in a second country in which he is born *(jus soli).* Dual citizenship also results where a person is a citizen by birth in one country and by naturalization in another when the former does not recognize the right of the individual to renounce his allegiance. *See also* CITIZEN.

Due Process of Law   Protection against arbitrary deprivation of life, liberty, or property. The Fifth and Fourteenth Amendments forbid the national and state governments, respectively, to deny any person his life, liberty, or property without due process of law. While no precise definition of this term has ever been made, it establishes the principle of limited government. Two types of due process—procedural and substantive—have emerged in the course of litigation. Though used sparingly in recent years, substantive due process has been used by the judiciary to strike down legislative and executive acts that are arbitrary or lacking in reasonableness, or that cover subject matter beyond the reach of government. Procedural due process was defined by Daniel Webster as procedure "which hears before it condemns, which proceeds upon inquiry, and renders judgment only after trial." The Supreme Court, in a long series of cases, has marked out the general meaning of the phrase so as to forbid any procedure that is shocking to the conscience or that makes impossible a fair and enlightened system of justice for a civilized people. *See also Moore v. Dempsey; Palko v. Connecticut.*

Dumbarton Oaks Conference   Preliminary conversations over the nature and functions of the anticipated United Nations organization. The Dumbarton Oaks Conference met from August to October, 1944, in Washington, D.C. Delegations from the United States, Britain, and the Soviet Union joined in the first and more important phase of the talks, while China participated with Britain and the United States in the second phase. Views were exchanged, compromises secured, and a preliminary working draft of proposals for the new world organization was hammered out. *See also* YALTA AGREEMENT.

Dumping   Sales of goods in foreign markets at net unit prices lower than those charged domestic consumers. Dumping may involve below-cost sales as a means of reducing large inventories or of trying to drive competitive firms out of the market. State-trading countries may use it as an economic weapon in pursuit of political or ideological objectives.

Duncan v. Louisiana, *see* Jury.

Dunkirk Treaty   A fifty-year security pact concluded by Britain and France in 1947 calling for consultation and joint action against any renewal of German aggression. The Dunkirk Treaty of Alliance and Mutual Assistance provides for continual consultation on economic as well as military matters. *See also* BILATERAL SECURITY PACT, WESTERN EUROPEAN UNION.

Eakin v. Raub, 12 S. & R. 330 (1825): Decided by the Supreme Court of the State of Pennsylvania, this case is famous for an opinion by Judge John B. Gibson against the principle of judicial review. Judge Gibson disagreed with the logic of Chief Justice John Marshall's opinion in *Marbury v. Madison,* 1 Cranch 137 (1803) in which Marshall argued that judges had a special duty to interpret the Constitution and to declare any law in conflict with the Constitution null and void. Judge Gibson argued that the judges had no such duty. Rather, the legislature bore the responsibility for unlawful acts and the people should hold them responsible. *See also Marbury v. Madison.*

Earmarking   Allocation of tax revenues for specific purposes. Earmarking gasoline taxes for highway purposes is the most common example, with about half the states doing so by constitutional provision, and the others by statutory requirement. About half of total state revenue is earmarked for specific purposes, such as highways, education or welfare. Earmarked taxes are often based on the "benefit theory" of taxation. *See also* BENEFIT THEORY.

East African Community (EAC)   A regional economic group that provides a partial common market and shared services for its three members—Kenya, Tanzania, and Uganda. EAC, formerly known as the East African Common Services Organization, was established in 1967 to aid its members in their efforts to modernize.

Eastern European Mutual Assistance Treaty, *see* Warsaw Pact.

ECA, ECAFE, ECE, ECLA, *see* United Nations Regional Commissions.

Eclectic Approach   A mode of analysis that draws from a variety of patterns of thought or methodological approaches rather than focusing on a single, "right" approach. In political science an eclectic approach might combine the appropriate utilization of historical, legal, and institutional approaches with the methods and perspectives of behavioral science. *See also* APPROACH.

Eclectic Functionalism, *see* Functionalism.

Ecological Analysis, *see* Political Ecology.

Ecology, Political, *see* Political Ecology.

Economic and Social Council (ECOSOC)   A major organ of the United Nations concerned with promoting higher standards of living and social justice throughout the world. The Council includes twenty-seven members elected by the General Assembly, nine chosen each year for three-year terms. Responsibilities include: (1) coordinating the activities of the Specialized Agencies, such as the World Health Organization (WHO) and the Food and Agriculture Organization (FAO); (2) administering United Nations functions in economic, social, educational, cultural, and related areas; (3) promoting worldwide observance of human rights and fundamental freedoms.

Economic and Social Council (France)   A national consultative body created by the Constitution to advise the Government on economic and social programs. The Economic and Social Council is a deliberative body of more than two hundred civil servants, representatives of various interest groups, and persons of economic, social, and cultural prominence in French national life. Its members are appointed in part by the government and in part by the groups represented. The Council lacks power to initiate legislation but may be called upon by the Government for its opinion on government bills, ordinances, and decrees, or on parliamentary bills submitted to it. Its advice, for example, has been sought in connection with the national economic "Plan" by which various sectors of the economy have been stimulated with public funds.

Economic Commissions, *see* United Nations Regional Commissions.

Economic Determinism   The theory that the economic factors of the methods of production and exchange of goods control the form of a state's political and social organization and shape the intellectual and moral development of its people. Some economic determinists view history in terms of epochs in which the prevailing economic system pits the servile class against the dominant class, a struggle that eventually results in a new alignment. *See also* COMMUNISM.

Economic Development, *see* Economic Growth, Underdevelopment.

Economic Growth   The increase in a nation's gross national product. Economic growth rates may be measured on an absolute basis in contemporary currency values or may be adjusted to take into account population changes and inflationary or deflationary factors. Economists regard an annual growth rate of 5 percent as satisfactory for most nations. Some have substantially exceeded this rate, but most do not achieve it. Although many developing countries have been able to increase gross national income at a high rate, when the figure has been adjusted for inflation and population growth the net per capita growth rate has seldom exceeded 1 to 3 percent. Some have suffered per capita income losses despite sizable gains in national income. *See also* GROSS NATIONAL PRODUCT, UNDERDEVELOPMENT.

Economic Imperialism   Involvement of one country in the economy of another to the degree that the sovereignty of the latter is impaired. Economic imperialism may result from a conscious policy or from the capital flow of private foreign investment. Through its state-trading practices, the Soviet Union dominated the economies of its East European partners after World War II. Indirect control is illustrated by the "dollar diplomacy" of the United States in the Caribbean area earlier in the century. That a relationship exists between economics and imperialism has been evident since the days of mercantilism. The first well-developed modern theory was formulated by the British economist John Hobson, in 1902, in his book *Imperialism*. Hobson explained imperialism in terms of the search for new markets and capital investment opportunities. Hobson's ideas also influenced V. I. Lenin in developing his communist theory of capitalist imperialism. In his *Imperialism: The Highest Stage of Capitalism* (1917) Lenin presented imperialism as the result of the "monopoly stage of capitalism." He asserted that excess capital accumulated in the home country because of underconsumption. The competitive search for new markets and investment opportunities, he concluded, led to imperialism and to imperialist wars that would hasten the inevitable downfall of capitalism. *See also* LENINISM, IMPERIALISM AND COLONIALISM (COMMUNIST THEORY), DOLLAR DIPLOMACY.

Economic Interpretation of History (Communist Theory)   The assumption that the basic economic system, or "mode of production," of a society determines its political, moral, legal, cultural, and religious superstructure and provides the motive force that guides the development of society from lower to higher stages. Marx's "materialist conception of history" starts with the proposition that man's basic activity relates to the production and acquisition of his means of subsistence. The system for the organization, ownership, and operation of these productive forces and the distribution of food and material wealth produced by them determines the nature of society and through class conflict provides the inner motive power for the society's evolution. The three factors of production identified by Marx as most directly related to social change and historical development are labor, raw materials, and the instruments of production.

Economic Interpretation of the Constitution   The theory that the framers of the Constitution represented the well-to-do classes and that the Constitution was designed to protect their interests. The theory was developed by the distinguished historian Charles A. Beard in his *An Economic Interpretation of the Constitution of the United States* (1913).

Economic Message   The annual Economic Report submitted each January by the President to Congress, as required by the Employment Act of 1946. The economic message is concerned with employment levels, production, purchasing power, inflation and deflation, trends of the nation's economy, and recommendations to Congress on maintaining or improving economic activity. The Economic Report is prepared by the President's Council of Economic Advisers, comprised of three leading economists. A joint congressional Committee on the Economic Report, consisting of seven members from each house, studies the message and makes recommendations for implementing it. *See also* EMPLOYMENT ACT OF 1946, COUNCIL OF ECONOMIC ADVISERS.

Economic Nationalism   An economic policy by which a nation seeks to attain economic prosperity or to correct a disequilibrium in its balance of payments by protecting the home market and/or opening up foreign markets through unilateral or bilateral governmental action. It is the opposite of a multilateral trading system with free flow of trade and free convertibility of currencies. It is characterized by extensive governmental control of trade and the subjection of economic matters to overriding considerations of political or military policy. Techniques employed by states pursuing policies of economic nationalism include: (1) austerity programs; (2) barter arrangements; (3) currency depreciation; (4) exchange controls; (5) export subsidies; (6) licensing; (7) quota restrictions; and (8) tariffs. *See also* TARIFF.

Economic Opportunity Act of 1964   An act to help the poor become productive citizens through a "war on poverty." The Act places stress on education and training through such programs as the Job Corps, Neighborhood Youth Corps, and work-study programs. Community action programs are encouraged under the Act to stimulate local action to meet the needs of low-income people. Loan programs are made available to farmers and small businessmen. VISTA (Volunteers in Service to America) has been established by the Act to aid in community welfare projects. Programs are administered by the Office of Economic Opportunity in the Executive Office of the President, the Department of Labor, the Department of Health, Education, and Welfare, and the Action Agency. *See also* COMMUNITY ACTION PROGRAM; JOB CORPS; VISTA.

Economic Planning   The establishment by government of economic goals and the means for reaching them. Economic planning may be concerned with providing some protection against violent swings of the business cycle in a capitalistic economy. At the other extreme, it may involve total governmental control and direction of investment, production, consumption, and other economic forces. *See also* COUNCIL OF ECONOMIC ADVISERS; PLANNING.

Economic Stabilization Act of 1970   A law authorizing the President to impose controls on the economy, including the freezing of wages, prices, and rents. The Act, which President Richard M. Nixon actively opposed and said he would not use, was invoked by him on August 15, 1971, in the face of unsuccessful efforts by his administration to curb inflation. Thereafter, Congress extended and broadened the Act to authorize additional controls, established a Pay Board and a Price Commission to monitor wages and prices, and provided for judicial review of stabilization orders.

Economic Union   The integration by two or more states of their economies through development of common economic policies. An economic union establishes a common market and a common external tariff, provides for the free movement of labor and capital, harmonizes taxes and subsidies that affect trade within the region, and aims for a general consonance of fiscal and monetary policies. Political institutions for joint economic decision making are essential to an economic union. The European Economic Community (EEC), for example, functions as an economic union through its joint political organs. Other levels of economic integration include free trade areas and customs unions. *See also* EUROPEAN ECONOMIC COMMUNITY.

ECOSOC, *see* Economic and Social Council.

ECSC, *see* European Coal and Steel Community.

Education, *see* Board of Education, Economic Opportunity Act of 1964, Elementary and Secondary Education Act of 1965, Federal Aid to Education, Higher Education Act of 1965, Land-Grant College, National Defense Education Act of 1958, School District, Superintendent of Public Instruction.

EEC, *see* European Economic Community.

EFTA, *see* European Free Trade Association.

Egalitarianism, Élitism, Majoritarianism (International Organization) Concepts which relate to the basic nature and decision processes of international organs. The principle of egalitarianism embodies the traditional equality of states under international law; since each possesses supreme power (sovereignty), all are juridically equal. Élitism, on the other hand, recognizes that great-power politics makes some states in fact "more equal" than others. Majoritarianism offers a decision-making system in keeping with the practices of democratic institutions within states.

Eighteen Nation Disarmament Committee (ENDC), *see* Conference of the Committee on Disarmament.

Eighteenth Amendment, *see* Twenty-First Amendment.

Eighteen-Year-Old Vote, *see* Voting Qualifications.

Eighth Amendment, *see* Cruel and Unusual Punishment.

Elastic Clause, *see* Necessary and Proper Clause.

Election at Large, *see* At Large.

Election Judge, *see* Challenge.

Elections, *see* At Large, Canvassing Board, Challenge, Corrupt Practices Acts, Direct Primary, General Election, Nonpartisan Election, Poll Watcher, Precinct, Proportional Representation, Recall.

Electoral College The presidential electors from each state who meet in their respective state capitals, following their popular election, and cast ballots for President and Vice President. The Electoral College never meets as a national body. The process starts with the nomination of partisan slates of electors by party conventions, primaries, or committees in each state. The number of electors in each state is equal to its number of representatives in both houses of Congress; the Twenty-third Amendment allots three electors for the District of Columbia, making a total electoral vote of 538. In the November presidential election, the slate of electors receiving a plurality of popular votes is elected. The electors usually pledge themselves to vote for their party's candidates for President and Vice President, although the Constitution permits them to use discretion. After casting electoral ballots in their respective state capitals in December, the ballots are counted and certified before a joint session of Congress early in January. The candidates who receive a majority of the electoral votes (270) are certified as President-elect and Vice President-elect. If none receives a majority of the electoral vote, the election of the President is decided by the House of Representatives from among the three highest candidates, with each state having one vote, and that of the Vice President by the Senate from the two highest candidates, with each senator having one vote. Normally, the people of the United States know who has been elected following the popular election in November, and the rest of the process is largely a formality. The rise of political parties that nominate pledged electors has distorted the original intention of the Founding Fathers. They had intended that the electors should be chosen as each state would determine and that they would exercise complete discretion in the selection of the President. *See also* TWELFTH AMENDMENT; ELECTORAL COUNT ACT, MINORITY PRESIDENT, PRESIDENTIAL ELECTION PROCESS.

Electoral Count Act   An 1887 act of Congress that provides for settlement of disputes over the election of presidential electors. When more than one set of electors are certified by different authorities of a single state, Congress, voting as two separate houses, decides which to accept. If Congress fails to agree, the electors certified by the governor are accepted. *See also* ELECTORAL COLLEGE.

Elementary and Secondary Education Act of 1965   The first general federal aid-to-education law enacted by Congress. It provides federal aid to most of the nation's school districts. The Act authorizes aid on the basis of the number of children from low-income families in each district. It applies to both public and nonpublic schools. Other major provisions authorize grants for textbooks and library materials for all schools, educational centers to provide programs that individual schools cannot afford, and grants for improvement of educational research and administration. *See also* SEPARATION OF CHURCH AND STATE.

Elements of National Power   The factors that collectively constitute the power-in-being and the power potentiality of a state. Some elements of national power are natural factors not ordinarily subject to human control or alteration, while others are variables that depend on human impulses, organization, and capacities. Major components in the power equation include: (1) the size, location, climate, and topography of the national territory; (2) the natural resources, sources of energy, and foodstuffs that can be produced; (3) the population, its size, density, age and sex composition, and its per capita relationship to national income; (4) the size and efficiency of the industrial plant; (5) the extent and effectiveness of the transportation system and communications media; (6) the educational system, research facilities and the number and quality of the scientific and technical élite; (7) the size, training, equipment, and spirit of the military forces; (8) the nature and strength of the nation's political, economic, and social system; (9) the quality of its diplomats and diplomacy; and (10) the national character and morale of the people. *See also* POWER.

Eleventh Amendment   An amendment to the Constitution, adopted in 1798, that provides that federal courts do not have authority to hear cases brought against a state by an individual citizen of another state or of a foreign state. The Amendment overruled a decision of the Supreme Court in *Chisholm v. Georgia*, 2 Dallas 419 (1793), which had upheld the right of a citizen of one state to sue another state in federal court.

Elfbrandt v. Russell, 384 U.S. 11 (1966): Struck down a state loyalty oath requirement which bound state employees not to become members of the Communist party. The Court held that a law that applies to membership without specific intent to further illegal aims rests on the unacceptable doctrine of guilt by association. A statute touching First Amendment rights must be narrowly drawn. *See also* LOYALTY OATH.

Elite   Persons who exercise a major influence on, or control the making of, political, economic, and social decisions. Elites achieve their power position through wealth, family status, caste systems, or intellectual superiority. Elites constitute the "power structure" of local and national communities. *See also* OLIGARCHY.

Élitism (Fascist Theory)   The principle that state power should be exercised by a hierarchically structured single party headed by a supreme leader or small group of oligarchs. Fascist élitism rejects democratic processes, constitutional limitations on state power, and pluralism in favor of an organic state in which every group and individual plays the role assigned by the governing élite. Opposition to rule by the élite party group is not tolerated, and the power of the state is used to destroy all resistance to the regime.

Elitism (International Organization), *see* Egalitarianism, Elitism, Majoritarianism.

Elitist Theory   A body of thought aimed at explaining the nature and role of those groups and societies in which decision-making power is highly concentrated. Elitist theorists usually start from the basic premise that in every human institution there is an ordered system of power, with one group directly or indirectly exercising the major share of authority or control. Some sociological studies of American elites have indicated that a single *power elite* drawn from an economic upper class provides leadership for other elements in the political community. Conversely, *community power studies* conducted by political scientists have tended to reject the elitist model in favor of a pluralist model in which power is diffused among many interest groups that compete for power. Other theories have been based on a fusion of the elitist and pluralist theories, holding that although a dominant general elite exists in the typical political system, it encourages other elites and nonelites to develop public policy by building consensus in specific issue areas. *See also* GROUP THEORY, POWER.

Embargo   A government edict prohibiting citizens from trading with one or several countries. The embargo may apply only to certain types of products, or it may be a total prohibition of trade. *See also* BATTLE ACT, BOYCOTT, ECONOMIC NATIONALISM.

Embassy, *see* Ambassador.

Emergency Powers   Powers exercised during a period of crisis by the national government, or those powers conferred by Congress upon the President for a limited period of time. The President's exercise of inherent powers in the field of foreign affairs provides an additional source of power during emergencies. *See also* INHERENT POWERS; *Youngstown Sheet and Tube Co. v. Sawyer*; WAR POWERS.

Emergent Explanation, *see* Reductionism.

Eminent Domain The power inherent in all governments to take over private property, provided that it is taken for a public purpose and that just compensation is awarded. Disputes as to purpose or price are generally settled in the courts. *See also* CONFISCATION.

Empirical Functionalism, *see* Functionalism.

Empiricism Pursuit of knowledge by observation and experimentation. The doctrine of empiricism assumes that man can know only those things that are a direct consequence of perception and experience. In political science empirical theories can be contrasted with normative theories (that is, what *is* in contradistinction to what *ought* to be), and with deductive theories (that is, proof by factual verification in contrast to conclusions logically deduced from premises). In some political writings empiricism is broadly equated with the use of scientific method or the behavioral study of politics. *See also* BEHAVIORALISM, DEDUCTION, FACT, INDUCTION, NORMATIVE, RATIONALITY.

Employment Act of 1946 An act that establishes responsibility for the national government to maintain stability in the nation's economy. A Council of Economic Advisers (CEA) was created by the Act and placed in the Executive Office to advise the President on economic matters. The Act requires the President to make an annual economic report to Congress setting forth the major economic problems confronting the nation and recommending appropriate legislation. *See also* FISCAL POLICY, DEFICIT FINANCING, DEPRESSION, COUNCIL OF ECONOMIC ADVISERS.

Enabling Act An act of Congress authorizing the people of a territory to take the necessary steps to prepare for statehood. This would include calling a convention to frame a constitution. *See also* ADMISSION OF NEW STATES.

En Banc, *see* Court of Claims.

Ends-Means Analysis The systematic attempt to relate rationally selected techniques (means) to desired goals (ends) so as to maximize goal achievement. Ends-means analysis is employed as an aid in problem solving and decision making. In each case the means are tested and evaluated in terms of how well they perform in attaining predetermined ends. Decision makers may pursue ultimate ends, or they may seek proximate ends which, following achievement, become means toward higher or ultimate goals. *See also* COST-BENEFIT ANALYSIS, DECISION-MAKING APPROACH, ENGINEERING THEORY, POLICY SCIENCES, SOCIAL ENGINEERING.

Enemy Alien   A citizen of a foreign state living in a state which is at war with his homeland. The regulation of enemy aliens is covered primarily by customary law, which leaves much discretion to government officials in the state where they reside, subject to the general requirement of humane treatment. *See also* ALIEN.

Enforcement (Disarmament)   The establishment of machinery to provide and administer the sanctions required to implement a disarmament agreement. The enforcement function is related to inspection because any detection of a violation raises questions concerning its political and military consequences. Setting up an enforcement system would be likely to raise such questions as: (1) What should be the composition, powers, and procedures of the enforcement agency; (2) What specific actions would constitute violations; (3) What punishment or sanction would be applied against a violator; (4) Should a state placed at a security disadvantage by a violation be entitled to undertake unilateral measures to restore the power balance; (5) Would a veto power apply to the determination of sanctions against a violator? *See also* INSPECTION, SANCTIONS.

Engineering Statement, *see* Engineering Theory.

Engineering Theory   A body of thought that draws upon the policy sciences to prescribe means of achieving desirable social goals. Engineering theory in political science tries to provide answers to political problems in much the same way that a civil engineer determines the feasibility of building a bridge or highway. If policy makers are faced, for example, with the question of how to deal with rising unemployment, they might develop an *engineering statement* that details the means for meeting that problem. Such a statement would set forth the variables relevant to achieving full employment and the manner in which those variables might be manipulated in order to bring it about. *See also* COST-BENEFIT ANALYSIS, ENDS-MEANS ANALYSIS, POLICY SCIENCES, SOCIAL ENGINEERING.

Engrossed Bill, *see* Bill.

Enrolled Bill, *see* Bill.

Enumerated Powers, *see* Delegated Powers.

Environment   The setting or surrounding conditions within which any object, activity, or system occurs. The environment or *milieu* of a political system includes human and nonhuman factors, both tangible and intangible. Thus, for example, geographical factors, other social systems, ideologies, customs, and institutions may all be features of the environment of a political system. In systems analysis the environment consists of all phenomena that affect the functioning of the system and that are not part of the system. For the purpose of a particular study the investigator is free to define the elements of a political system to suit his own research needs. Thus, of many interacting elements, the investigator determines which shall be regarded as part of the system and which as part of the environment. His definition determines the boundary between system and environment. His definition, of course, is likely to be influenced by patterns set by other researchers. *See also* POLITICAL ECOLOGY, SYSTEMS ANALYSIS.

Environmental Politics   The social and political movement to warn the public about ecological dangers and to encourage the preservation of wild country for esthetic reasons. Environmental politics is aimed at pressuring national, state, and local governments to support policies and programs to end pollution of air, water, and land. Environmentalism starts with the assumption that man is rapidly destroying his life-sustaining ecosystems as a result of the triumph in the modern world of the technological and economic growth ethics. The movement is working for the adoption of governmental policies to clean up pollution, to preserve wild areas, to protect living species, to meet the problem of depletion of natural resources, to deal with population and urbanization problems, and generally to move toward restoring ecological balance. *See also* COUNCIL ON ENVIRONMENTAL QUALITY, ENVIRONMENTAL PROTECTION AGENCY, NATIONAL ENVIRONMENTAL POLICY ACT OF 1969.

Environmental Protection Agency (EPA)   The Agency established by the Presidential Reorganization Plan in 1970 to administer federal programs aimed at controlling pollution and protecting the nation's environment. Headed by an Administrator, the Environmental Protection Agency is concerned with air and water pollution, pesticide research and control, radiation dangers, and basic ecological research. The Agency administers the National Environmental Policy Act of 1969 and those acts that Congress has passed to deal with specific pollution problems. The Clean Air Act of 1970, for example, requires, *inter alia*, that auto-making companies reduce hazardous emissions by 90 percent within five years. The Water Quality Improvement Act of 1970 establishes liability for cleanup costs for ocean spills and provides for extensive control over the Great Lakes and pesticide drainage. Under the Resource Recovery Act of 1970, a major effort is underway to recycle and recover useful materials and energy from solid wastes. *See also* COUNCIL ON ENVIRONMENTAL QUALITY, NATIONAL ENVIRONMENTAL POLICY ACT OF 1969, ENVIRONMENTAL POLITICS.

Envoy, *see* Diplomat.

Equal Employment Opportunity Commission (EEOC)   Established by the Civil Rights Act of 1964 to investigate and conciliate disputes involving discrimination because of race or sex by employers, unions, and employment agencies. EEOC consists of five members appointed for five-year terms by the President with Senate consent. EEOC stresses confidential persuasion and conciliation to achieve its objectives, but may, if conciliation fails, institute legal action. Action by state fair employment agencies is encouraged by the Act. *See also* FAIR EMPLOYMENT PRACTICES LAWS.

Equalization   The review and adjustment of tax assessments among taxing districts in the state. The equalization function may be exercised at the county level to adjust assessments among the townships, cities, and other units of the county and, at the state level, to equalize assessments among counties. If property in one area is assessed at 50 percent of value and in another at 30 percent, some adjustment is necessary to equalize the burdens borne by taxpayers. Equalization differs from the local review of assessments in which individual rather than area assessments are reviewed. *See also* PROPERTY TAX.

Equal Opportunity, *see* Department of Housing and Urban Development.

Equal Protection of the Law   A requirement of the Fourteenth Amendment that state laws may not arbitrarily discriminate against persons. Identical treatment is not required. Classification of persons is permitted provided that the classification is reasonable and bears some relationship to the end sought. Hence, taxation in accordance with ability to pay has been held to be a reasonable classification, whereas classification according to color, religion or social class has been held to bear no reasonable relationship to the functions of government. Current interest in the application of equal protection centers on the desegregation of races in public facilities, equal justice for the poor, inequality in state legislative apportionment, and equality for women. Though the Constitution does not contain a similar restriction on the national government, the courts have read the equal protection concept into the meaning of the due process clause of the Fifth Amendment. *See also Brown v. Board of Education of Topeka, Bolling v. Sharpe.*

Equal Rights   A term used to describe the movement to equalize the rights of men and women. Traditionally in American law, women have not enjoyed the same rights as men. State laws vary widely, although many are protective of women rather than directly discriminatory. Women's suffrage has led to a gradual narrowing of legal differences. *See also* WOMEN'S LIBERATION MOVEMENT.

Equal Time   A regulation under the Federal Communications Act of 1934 which provides that all candidates for a public office be given equal access to the free or paid use of television and radio. The equal time provision means, for example, that during a political campaign if a radio or television station or network provides time for one candidate or party, it must then offer equal time on the same basis for the opposition candidates or parties. The rule is administered by the Federal Communications Commission (FCC) and was upheld by the Supreme Court (*Red Lion Broadcasting Co. v. Federal Communications Commission,* 395 U.S. 367 [1969]). *See also* CAMPAIGN.

Equilibrium   A state of balance ascribed to a political or other system. One form of equilibrium analysis assumes that environmental influences tend to affect the relationships within a system, constantly moving them away from, then back toward, a presumed preexisting point of stability. If the relationships thus affected fail to return to a previous point of stability, it may be assumed that they have moved to a new state of equilibrium, or that a fundamental disruption has occurred within the system. Equilibrium analysis sometimes assumes a dynamic equilibrium in which no fixed point of stability exists. In such case the elements of the system remain in some kind of balance with one another, while the position of equilibrium fluctuates or moves from one point to another. *See also* HOMEOSTASIS, SYSTEMS ANALYSIS.

Equity   A branch of law that provides a remedy where the common law does not apply. The common law is concerned largely with granting of damages after a wrongful action. Equity is designed to provide justice where damages may come too late to be meaningful. In an equity case, the court may order that something be done (specific performance) or forbid certain actions (injunction). In a typical case the court may order a person to fulfill a contract or forbid a union to go on strike under certain conditions. Equity procedures are less formal than regular court procedures and juries are seldom used. *See also* COMMON LAW; INJUNCTION.

Erie Railroad v. Tompkins, 304 U.S. 64 (1938): Ruled that, in diversity of citizenship cases heard in federal courts, the law to be applied is the state law as declared by the state legislature or courts. There is no federal common law. *See also* DIVERSITY OF CITIZENSHIP.

Escalation   Increasing the intensity or geographical extent of hostilities in a war. Escalation may involve an increase in the number of troops engaged in a limited war, participation in hostilities by additional countries, an expansion in the area of operations, a resort to the use of deadlier, more powerful weapons, or a change in the goals sought by the military action. The objective underlying escalation of hostilities in a limited war situation may be that of seeking the defeat and surrender of the enemy, or it may be that of meting out increased punishment to force the enemy to negotiate or to cease an activity that was the initial *casus belli* (an event that results in war). *See also* LIMITED WAR, TOTAL WAR.

Escape Clause   A provision, inserted in a trade agreement, that permits a party to terminate or alter a tariff concession. An escape clause can be invoked only after a specified period of notice has elapsed. In the United States, tariff concessions may be withdrawn if imports substantially threaten or injure a domestic producer. The United States Tariff Commission has established "peril points" at which, when imports reach such levels, the President and Congress are informed of the danger to American producers. The President may then invoke the escape-clause provision in the agreement to reduce the threat of injury. *See also* RECIPROCAL TRADE AGREEMENTS ACT, TARIFF, TRADE EXPANSION ACT, UNITED STATES TARIFF COMMISSION.

"Establishment", *see* Decision Makers, Elite.

Establishment Clause, *see* Separation of Church and State.

Estate, *see* Estate Tax.

Estate Tax   A tax, usually with progressive rates, levied on the property of deceased persons. Estate taxes apply to the total estate, whereas inheritance taxes are levied on the portions of the estate received by the beneficiaries. The national government has regularly levied an estate tax since 1916, and all states except Nevada have an estate or inheritance tax, in most instances, the latter.

Ethnocentrism   The belief that one's own group and culture is superior to all others. Ethnocentrism is a universal social phenomenon that distinguishes "we" from "they." The phenomenon emphasizes the differences between societies, their values, and the states that symbolize those values. The values of the "we" group are the standards by which "they" are evaluated, and since "they" are different, "they" are, by definition, inferior. *See also* NATIONALISM, XENOPHOBIA.

European Atomic Energy Community (Euratom)   A regional organization established by the Treaty of Rome of 1957 that coordinates peaceful atomic research and development, provides for joint power projects, and encourages a pooling of scientific and technical information. Euratom, which became operational in 1958 at the same time that the European Economic Community (EEC) began to function, has the same membership as the European Coal and Steel Community (ECSC) and the Common Market (Belgium, France, Germany, Italy, Luxembourg, and The Netherlands). Decisions of Euratom are made within the common institutional framework of the European Community. *See also* EUROPEAN COMMUNITY.

European Coal and Steel Community (ECSC)   A regional organization established by the Treaty of Paris of 1952 to harmonize production policies and establish a common market for coal, iron ore, and steel. The members of the Community—Belgium, France, Germany, Italy, Luxembourg, and The Netherlands—have agreed on various common domestic policies to encourage production and competitive marketing conditions. Decisions of the ECSC are made within the common organizational framework of the European Community. *See also* EUROPEAN COMMUNITY.

European Common Market, *see* European Economic Community.

European Community   The common political structure established to make economic decisions for the European Coal and Steel Community (ECSC), the European Economic Community (EEC), and the European Atomic Energy Community (Euratom). The European Community institutions include the Council of Ministers, the Commission, the European Parliament, and the Court of Justice. The Council and the Commission constitute a dual executive, with the former directly representing the views of the governments of the Six and the latter functioning as a supranational organ for the Community. Some decisions are made by the Council, some by the Commission, and some by the Council following proposal by the Commission. While the Commission functions as a collegial body, the Council makes decisions by unanimity, by a qualified majority through a weighted voting system (France, Germany, and Italy have four votes each, Belgium and The Netherlands two each, and Luxembourg one).

and by a simple majority of the Six. The European Parliament, first created as the Common Assembly for the ECSC in 1952, serves as a deliberative body and consultative organ to the Community, and as an overseer of its actions. Although it has no power to make laws or decisions binding upon member states, it has served as a source for the initiation of new policies of economic liberalization and political unity. Delegates to the Parliament are appointed by national parliaments and are organized and vote on most issues as three transnational political groups—Christian Democrat, Socialist, and Liberal—rather than as national blocs. The Court of Justice, also established in 1952, functions as the common court to interpret and apply the Community treaties and to resolve disputes between Community organs and member states or within either group. Its powers to interpret and review more closely resemble those of a national supreme court than those of other international courts. *See also* EUROPEAN ATOMIC ENERGY COMMUNITY, EUROPEAN COAL AND STEEL COMMUNITY, EUROPEAN ECONOMIC COMMUNITY.

European Convention on Human Rights A treaty, in force since 1953, that establishes international machinery for the protection of human rights in controversies arising among signatory states. The European Convention, developed under the auspices of the Council of Europe, has been accepted by fifteen states (Austria, Belgium, Britain, Cyprus, Denmark, Germany, Greece, Iceland, Ireland, Italy, Luxembourg, the Netherlands, Norway, Sweden, and Turkey). Only three Council of Europe members—France, Malta, and Switzerland—have not become parties to the Convention. Ten of the ratifying states further agree that appeals on human rights issues by individuals and private groups can be carried beyond their state courts to an international body. Petitions are first reviewed by a Commission on Human Rights composed of fifteen members selected from member states. If the complaint is admissible, the Commission reports its findings and recommends action to the Committee of Ministers of the Council of Europe. The Committee of Ministers, if unable to work out an amicable settlement, may decide the case by a two thirds vote. Finally, a losing party may appeal to the European Court of Human Rights if he is a citizen of one of the ten states that has ratified the optional protocol accepting its jurisdiction. Each of the eighteen members of the Council of Europe is represented on the Court whether it has accepted the protocol or not. Enforcement of Court decisions depends on voluntary compliance by affected states since no sanctions are provided by the Convention. *See also* COUNCIL OF EUROPE, HUMAN RIGHTS.

European Court of Human Rights, *see* European Convention on Human Rights.

European Economic Community (EEC) A regional organization, established by the Treaty of Rome of 1957, which has developed a common market among its members, reached agreement on common Community and national economic policies, and set up a common external tariff wall. Among member countries (Belgium, France, Germany, Italy, Luxembourg, and The Netherlands), goods may flow freely without tariffs or other hindrances, labor and capital are completely mobile, and many national policies relating to production and marketing have been harmonized. Agricultural products, as a result of an agreement reached in 1966, are subsidized by the

Community from a common EEC fund financed from import levies and from contributions by member governments. Eighteen African Associated States, all former colonies of EEC members, are linked with the EEC through the Yaoundé Convention of 1964, and other African and European states have established an associate relationship with the Community. In 1971, Britain was invited to membership in the EEC in 1973, an action which presaged a considerable enlargement of the organization. Decisions of the EEC are made within the common institutional framework of the European Community. *See also* EUROPEAN COMMUNITY.

European Free Trade Association (EFTA)   A regional organization established by the Stockholm Convention of 1959 to eliminate tariffs and other trade barriers among members and to harmonize internal production cost factors. In addition to eliminating industrial tariffs by 1967, EFTA's eight members (Austria, Britain, Denmark, Iceland, Norway, Portugal, Sweden, and Switzerland) agreed to try to reduce trade barriers on agriculture and fish. In 1961, EFTA was joined by Finland as an associate member through the FINEFTA treaty, which provided for extension of the free trade area to Finland, a special council to resolve questions relating to Finnish membership, and the continuance of Finland's special trade arrangements with the Soviet Union. Heading EFTA's simple organizational structure is a Council of Ministers that settles disputes, reviews complaints, makes recommendations to member governments, and serves as the agency for negotiating major decisions. In addition, six standing committees make recommendations to the Council on policy questions, a secretariat functions at the Geneva headquarters, and representatives of EFTA countries to the Consultative Assembly of the Council of Europe meet informally at Strasbourg during annual sessions.

European Investment Bank, *see* Regional Development Banks.

European Parliament, *see* European Community.

European Recovery Program (ERP), *see* Marshall Plan.

Evaluative Structure, *see* Perception.

Ever-normal Granary   The concept behind the national government's farm programs since 1938 that aims at securing a stable supply of, and stable prices for, farm products through governmental action. The ever-normal granary system provides for accumulation of reserves of basic farm products by the government during periods of oversupply as a means of maintaining price levels. During droughts or other times of short supply, when prices rise above support levels, the government reverses the process by selling from its granaries to meet market demand and to stabilize price levels. *See also* PRICE SUPPORT.

Everson v. Board of Education of Ewing Township, 330 U.S. 1 (1947): Decided that it is not a violation of the First Amendment's establishment of religion clause for a state to pay for the transportation of children to parochial schools. The Court found this to be a benefit to the children rather than an aid to the church. *See also* SEPARATION OF CHURCH AND STATE.

Ex Aequo Et Bono   A basis for a decision by an international court on the grounds of justice and fairness. The *ex aequo et bono* concept, set forth in Article 38 of the Statute of the International Court of Justice, can be applied by the Court as the basis for arriving at a decision only if the parties so agree. It is a variation from the more usual bases for reaching decisions in the International Court by applying the rules of positive and customary international law. *See also* INTERNATIONAL COURT OF JUSTICE.

Ex Ante Transfer, *see* Exchange.

Excess Profits Tax   A special tax levied during wartime to supplement the corporation income tax. The excess profits tax is calculated on the difference between business earnings in normal years and earnings during the war years when profits soar. An excess profits tax was levied by Congress during World Wars I and II, and during the Korean action from 1951 to 1953. In the last case, the tax was fixed at 30 percent of the excess profits, with the limitation that the combined corporation income tax and excess profits tax should not exceed 70 percent of net income. The failure to levy an excess profits tax during the Vietnam war contributed to the nation's serious inflation and balance of payments problems of the early 1970s. *See also* CORPORATION INCOME TAX.

Exchange   Interaction characterized by the reciprocal giving and receiving of material goods or of behaviors. Exchanges are arrived at through agreement and consequently are mutually beneficial in that each party considers its position as having been improved by the exchange. Exchanges may involve either a "goods for goods and deeds for deeds" transfer or an exchange of goods for a change in behavior. A developing body of insights called *exchange theory* seeks to explain political behavior in terms of market principles derived from economic models. Politics thus is viewed as a process of resource distribution based on rational calculations of costs and benefits. *See also* COLLECTIVE GOODS.

Exchange Control   Government regulation of the exchange of national and foreign currencies. Exchange control substitutes the arbitrary decisions of administrative officials for the free market forces in the buying and selling of currencies. Control is usually directed toward the objectives of maintaining an arbitrary exchange ratio between the national and foreign currencies, and of permitting exchanges of national into foreign currencies only when national interest considerations are satisfied. Exchange control may range from full regulation over all monetary transactions to a limited supervision over certain types of activities to correct temporary monetary difficulties. *See also* CONVERTIBILITY, ECONOMIC NATIONALISM.

Exchange Programs, *see* Cultural Exchange.

Exchange Theory, *see* Exchange.

Excise Tax   A tax levied upon the manufacture, transportation, sale, or consumption of goods within a country or state. Federal excise taxes are permitted by the Constitution, and such levies have been placed on a variety of consumer goods. The main excise taxes used by the states are sales and use taxes. Heavy excises on what are regarded as socially undesirable commodities, such as liquor and tobacco, are a form of sumptuary tax. *See also* SALES TAX.

Exclusive Powers   Those powers that, under the Constitution, belong exclusively to, and may be exercised only by, either the national government or the governments of the various states. An example of an exclusive national power is that over foreign affairs; an exclusive state power is control over local government. *See also* CONCURRENT POWERS.

Executive Agreement   An international agreement between the President and foreign heads of state that, unlike a treaty, does not require Senate consent. Most notably, trade agreements are concluded under powers granted to the President by Congress. Others are concluded by the President acting under his constitutional powers over foreign relations. The Constitution makes no explicit provision for executive agreements. *See also* TREATY.

Executive Budget, *see* Budget.

Executive Calendar, *see* Calendar.

Executive Office of the President   The top staff agencies that give the President help and advice in carrying out his major duties. President Franklin D. Roosevelt established the Executive Office by executive order under the Reorganization Act of 1939. The components of the Executive Office have changed over the years and today the major staff agencies include the Office of Management and Budget, the White House Office, the National Security Council, the Council of Economic Advisers, the National Aeronautics and Space Council, the Office of Economic Opportunity, the Office of Emergency Preparedness, the Office of Science and Technology, the Domestic Council, and the Council on Environmental Quality. Special offices concerned with trade negotiations, telecommunications policy, international economic policy, consumer affairs, intergovernmental relations, and drug abuse prevention have also been established within the Executive Office of the President.

Executive Order   A rule or regulation, issued by the President, a governor, or some administrative authority, that has the effect of law. Executive orders are used to implement and give administrative effect to provisions of the Constitution, to treaties, and to statutes. They may be used to create or modify the organization or procedures of administrative agencies or may have general applicability as law. Under the national Administrative Procedure Act of 1946, all executive orders must be published in the *Federal Register. See also* QUASI-LEGISLATIVE, DELEGATION OF POWER.

Executive Privilege   The right of executive officials to refuse to appear before or to withhold information from a legislative committee. Executive privilege is enjoyed by the President and by those executive officials accorded the right by the President. No legal means have ever been found by the Congress by which executive privilege could be denied to executive officials. *See also* CHECKS AND BALANCES, SEPARATION OF POWERS.

Executive Session   A meeting of a legislative body or committee that is closed to the public. Executive sessions are used mainly by committees to interrogate witnesses and to discuss controversial bills. Under the Legislative Reorganization Act of 1970, all votes taken in secret committee sessions must be made part of the public record.

Exemption, *see* Tax Exemption.

Exequatur   A formal act by which a receiving country recognizes the official status of a newly appointed consular officer and authorizes him to engage in those activities appropriate to his office. In those countries which issue no formal exequatur or similar document, the consul enters upon his duties when the receiving government publicly recognizes his status by announcement in the official gazette or some other formal act. *See also* CONSUL.

Ex Officio   A Latin term for "by virtue of office." Many persons hold a position on a board or agency by virtue of their holding some other related position. For example, a governor, typically, is a member of numerous state boards and commissions by virtue of his position as governor.

Ex Parte   A judicial proceeding by or for one party without contest by an adverse party. In an ex parte proceeding, there may be no adverse party, or a possible adverse party has had no notice of the case. The term "in re" is sometimes used in place of ex parte.

Ex parte Grossman, 267 U.S. 87 (1925): Upheld a pardon granted by the President to Grossman, who had been convicted of contempt of Court. It was alleged that the independence of the judiciary depends upon the authority of judges to try without jury individuals who violate court orders, and to sentence them for contempt of court free from interference by other departments of government. The Court rejected this argument and upheld the President, holding that he "can reprieve or pardon all offenses after their commission, either before trial, during trial or after trial, by individuals, or by classes, conditionally or absolutely, and this without modification or regulation by Congress." *See also* PARDON.

Ex parte McCardle, 7 Wallace 506 (1869): Declared that the Supreme Court may not exercise appellate jurisdiction over a case when Congress prohibits such jurisdiction. This case arose when Congress repealed an 1867 law that had authorized appeals to the Supreme Court in certain cases involving enforcement of the post-Civil War Reconstruction Acts.

Ex parte Milligan, 4 Wallace 2 (1866): Held that the suspension of the right of writ of habeas corpus and the trial of a civilian by a military tribunal while the civilian courts are operating violate the Constitution. The Court held that neither the President nor Congress could legally deny the accused a civil trial by jury in an area outside an actual theater of war. *See also* CIVILIAN CONTROL.

Expatriation   Voluntary withdrawal of allegiance or residence from the country in which citizenship is held. Since 1865, Congress has expressly recognized the right of expatriation and has set forth specific grounds. Actions that constitute expatriation include: naturalization in a foreign state, taking an oath of allegiance to another state, serving in a foreign army without consent, taking a job open only to citizens of another state, and conviction of treason or attempt to overthrow the government by force. The Supreme Court has taken a dim view of expatriation laws, holding that citizenship is a constitutional right which can be given up only by a truly voluntary act. A citizen living abroad may voluntarily renounce his citizenship before a diplomatic officer but renunciation is permitted within the United States only during wartime with the consent of the Attorney General. *See also Afroyim v. Rusk.*

Experiment   A form of research designed to test a hypothesis under conditions that permit the investigator to control and manipulate one or more independent variables and observe the corresponding changes, if any, in the dependent variables. In an experiment conducted under ideal conditions, the investigator will be able randomly to select subjects for his experiment (known as random assignment of subjects to *experimental groups*), and he will have one or more control groups not subjected to experimental treatment with whose behavior the experimental group may be compared. Presumably the results of the experiment can be checked or verified through replication of the research procedures by others. In a study of the impact of political propaganda on school children, an investigator might randomly select an experimental group and a control group from a given student population. For his experimental treatment he could administer a series of war propaganda movies to the experimental group, but not to the control group. Attitudinal change in members of the experimental group might then be determined by questionnaires administered before and after exposure to the movies. Confidence in the findings would be increased if no comparable change appeared in responses to similar questionnaires completed by the control group. *See also* CONTROL GROUP, RESEARCH DESIGN.

Experimental Design, *see* Research Design.

Experimental Group, *see* Control Group, Experiment.

Explanation   An attempt to clarify a concept (as explaining "power"), to explicate the nature of a thing (as explaining the structure and activities of a political party), or to account for an event or condition (as explaining why blacks tend to vote Democratic). Concept clarification is essentially to explain something by defining it, explication is explaining by description, and accounting for an event means looking for antecedent causes. Although political scientists may use the term "explanation" in all three ways, scientific explanation is primarily concerned with providing answers to "why" and "how" questions, or causal explanation. This involves the use of general explanatory propositions linking the object to be explained with other related events, objects or conditions, under circumstances that permit causation to be inferred. *See also* ANALYSIS, DESCRIPTION.

Export-Import Bank of the United States   A government corporation that guarantees private credit and makes direct loans to foreign and domestic businessmen to promote the flow of trade. The Export-Import Bank, originally chartered in 1934, is governed by a five-member bipartisan board appointed by the President with Senate consent.

Ex Post Facto Law   A criminal law that is retroactive and that has an adverse effect upon one accused of a crime. Thus, an ex post facto law is one that makes an act a crime that was not a crime when it was committed, that increases the penalty for a crime after its commission, or that changes the rules of evidence so as to make conviction easier. Neither the state nor the national governments may enact such laws under provisions of Article I, sections 9 and 10 of the Constitution. The prohibition does not extend to civil laws or to laws favorable to an accused person.

Expropriation   Government seizure of foreign-owned property and transfer of ownership to the state. Although recognized as a rightful exercise of sovereign power, under international law expropriation can be neither retaliatory nor discriminatory and is conditional upon payment of prompt and fair compensation. Expropriation is a form of nationalization, although the latter term refers more broadly to the purchase or expropriation of either foreign- or domestic-owned private property. A declaration of war leads to the expropriation of all properties owned by enemy aliens. *See also* NATIONALIZATION.

Expulsion (Legislative)   The power of a legislative body, usually exercised by each chamber separately, to expel a member as an extreme disciplinary measure. Typical grounds for expulsion include conduct unbecoming a member, disloyalty, and moral turpitude. By Article I, section 5 of the Constitution, each house is empowered to expel a member with the concurrence of two-thirds of the members of that chamber. State constitutions generally vest similar powers in state legislatures. *See also* CENSURE.

Expulsion, Suspension, Withdrawal (International Organization) Procedures by which membership or the rights of membership in an international organization are terminated or temporarily suspended. Expulsion and suspension are potential sanctions that can be applied against recalcitrant members of an international organization, and the right of withdrawal confirms the sovereignty of all members. Under the League of Nations, the Covenant provided: (1) that any member could withdraw from the organization after giving two years' notice, provided that all its obligations were fulfilled (Art. 1); (2) that a member that had violated any covenant of the League could be expelled by a unanimous vote of the Council (Art. 16); (3) that a member that refused to accept an amendment adopted to the Covenant would terminate its membership (Art. 26). The United Nations Charter provides: (1) that the rights and privileges of membership may be suspended by the General Assembly upon Security Council recommendation when preventive or enforcement action has been taken against the member (Art. 5); (2) that a member which is a persistent violator of Charter principles may be expelled by the General Assembly upon Security Council recommendation (Art. 6); and (3) that any member two or more years in arrears in its financial contributions may be deprived of its vote in the General Assembly (Art. 19). Although the Charter does not provide for withdrawal, its framers at San Francisco approved a declaration that admitted the right of withdrawal.

Extension of Remarks Material incorporated into the *Congressional Record* by a member of Congress, although not delivered verbally on the floor of either chamber. Permission to extend remarks is required by the member's house and is ordinarily granted. Material that elaborates on remarks made by the member on the floor follows the text of his speech; other insertions are printed in the appendix. *See also* CONGRESSIONAL RECORD.

Extension Service, *see* County Agent, Department of Agriculture.

Extradition Return by one nation to another of a person accused of a crime. The extradition process resembles that of interstate rendition, which occurs within the United States. In the international field, extradition usually depends upon treaty arrangements between the two nations concerned. Some international jurists regard it as a matter of reciprocal interest covered by customary international law in the absence of any treaty. *See also* INTERSTATE RENDITION.

Extraterritoriality The exercise of jurisdiction by one state within the territory of another. Extraterritoriality is established by a treaty which specifies the persons, the subject matter, and the degree to which local jurisdiction will not be applied to the citizens of the treaty partner. Examples of extraterritoriality antedate the modern state system. "Capitulations" were a form of extraterritoriality which established certain privileges for Christians in countries under Muslim rule. *See also* JURISDICTION (TERRITORIAL).

FAA, *see* Department of Commerce.

Fact　Anything that exists or has existed and can be known by experience or observation. A fact in political analysis is any element or condition in the empirical world that involves or affects political behavior. Facts are sometimes contrasted with values. This is the so-called *fact-value dichotomy*, which emphasizes the distinction between what *is* and what *ought* to be. The former is an objective reference to the world of experience and observation, whereas the latter is a subjective value judgment of what the political world should be like. *See also* DATA, VALUE.

Factor Analysis　A statistical method of reducing a large number of variables to a smaller number of factors or dimensions, each consisting of an interrelated cluster of the original variables. A factor is expressed as a series of numerical "loadings" which indicate the degree of correlation of that factor with each of the original variables. A factor may then be used to "explain" the original variables having high loadings on it, in the sense that the investigator will look for characteristics that the variables with high loadings have in common. Each factor is only a statistical creation, expressing interrelationships among the original variables in a manner dictated by whatever computer program is used. Factors are themselves often treated as variables, however, and their nature is inferred (and an appropriate label assigned) from the characteristics of the original variables with which they have the highest correlations. To illustrate the method, the original variables might be votes cast by 130 United Nations members on 100 UN issues, which could be represented on a table with 100 vertical columns and 130 horizontal rows. By factor analysis the number of columns may be reduced from 100 to perhaps a dozen, more or less. The new columns represent factors which have a numerical loading for each country, the loading representing the extent to which the voting behavior of a country is correlated with a particular dimension or factor. If most of the countries with high loadings on one dimension are Western European, for example, it may be labeled a "Western European" dimension; another factor might show high loadings only for members of the Soviet bloc; and another dimension might show a clustering of states with no obvious common characteristics. Factor analysis does no more than show statistical relationships; the investigator must interpret it as best he can. *See also* STATISTICS, VARIABLE.

Fact-Value Dichotomy, *see* Fact.

Fair Employment Practices Laws　Laws that forbid private and/or public employers, labor unions, or employment agencies to discriminate in hiring or in other personnel policies on the grounds of race, color, creed, or national origin. More than thirty states have enacted such laws. In the Civil Rights Act of 1964, Congress provided for equal employment opportunities in businesses and labor unions engaged in interstate commerce. Equal treatment for women is also required by the Act. *See also* EQUAL EMPLOYMENT OPPORTUNITY COMMISSION.

Fair Labor Standards Act of 1938　An act establishing minimum wages and maximum hours for employees engaged in interstate commerce and outlawing the use of child labor. An eight-hour day at $1.60 per hour is established as the basic requirement, with time and a half for work exceeding forty hours a week. Persons not engaged in interstate commerce are not covered unless state laws make similar provisions. Certain types of work are exempted from coverage, but Congress has progressively increased coverage over the years. *See also United States v. Darby Lumber Co.*.

Fait Accompli   An act by one or several states that creates a new situation vis-á-vis another state or group. Following a *fait accompli*, the other side no longer shares in the power of decision but finds its options reduced to doing nothing or to reacting to the altered situation. *See also* DIPLOMACY.

Family Assistance Plan   A major welfare reform proposal of the Nixon Administration that would guarantee a minimum income to families with unemployable adults and supplemental aid to the working poor. The plan contemplates federal administration of all categorical aid programs. *See also* CATEGORICAL ASSISTANCE, SOCIAL SECURITY ACT.

Farm Bloc   A group made up of both Democratic and Republican representatives and senators from the farm states, who put aside party differences to pass legislation favorable to the farmers. The creation of this voting bloc in the early part of the twentieth century followed the attempts of the farmers to achieve their aims through the creation of various farmers' parties that had been unsuccessful in challenging the two major parties. *See also* BLOC.

Farm Bureau (American Farm Bureau Federation), *see* Farm Organizations.

Farm Credit Administration   An independent agency of the national government that supervises and coordinates the operations of the federal land banks and other corporations and cooperatives that provide credit for farmers in each of the twelve federal farm credit districts. The Farm Credit Administration makes decisions through a part-time thirteen-member Farm Credit Board, appointed by the President and Secretary of Agriculture.

Farmers Home Administration, *see* Department of Agriculture.

Farm Organizations   Groups organized to promote the interests of the farmer. The oldest and most conservative farmers' organization is the National Grange, which was most effective after the Civil War and now has most of its membership in the New England and Middle Atlantic States. The most powerful and energetic spokesman for the farmers' interest is the American Farm Bureau Federation, which represents all types of farmers throughout the country. The Farm Bureau, now a private organization, grew out of the promotional activities of county agents sponsored by the Department of Agriculture through the agricultural extension services. A third major group is the National Farmer's Union, representing the less prosperous farmers. The newest group is the National Farmer's Organization, which seeks to emulate the strike techniques of labor unions by having farmers withhold products from the marketplace to drive prices up rather than depend upon governmental subsidies. *See also* PRESSURE GROUP.

Fascism   The political system of the extreme right, which incorporates the principles of the leader (dictator), a one-party state, totalitarian regimentation of economic and social activity, and the arbitrary exercise of absolute power by the regime. After 1922, Benito Mussolini fashioned the fascist prototype in Italy and was emulated in the 1930s by Adolf Hitler in Germany, Francisco Franco in Spain, and Juan Perón in Argentina. Fascism's glorification of the leader makes the system vulnerable and unstable, and poses serious problems of succession. Unlike communism, fascism retains the private ownership of land and capital, but most economic activity is controlled and regimented by the state through a system of national socialism. *See also* TOTALITARIANISM.

Fascist Theory, *see* Anti-Communism, Elitism, Militarism, Statism, Totalitarianism.

Favorite Son   A state political leader whose name is placed in nomination for the presidency at a national nominating convention by members of his state's delegation. Usually a favorite son is not a serious candidate and his nomination is merely a means of honoring him or of delaying commitment of the state delegation's votes.

FCC, *see* Federal Communications Commission

FDIC, *see* Federal Deposit Insurance Corporation.

Featherbedding   A labor practice requiring an employer to pay for services that are not performed. Featherbedding is considered to be an unfair labor practice and is outlawed by the Taft-Hartley Act. An example of featherbedding is a requirement that a radio station pay musicians who do not play, since phonograph records, rather than "live" musicians, are used. Featherbedding may also take the form of deliberate slowdowns in production or insistence that a job be performed by a particular individual though others can do it as well.

Federal Aid Highway Act   A major example of federal grants-in-aid to the states; the first such grant was given in 1916 for the building of highways. From this time, grants have been given for trunk roads, secondary roads, urban extensions of highways, and, since 1956, an extensive interstate highway system. The states must meet national requirements regarding matching funds, maintenance of roads, location, and engineering details. The 1956 Act provided for a thirteen-year program for the building of 41,000 miles of multilane highways connecting all major cities. In 1968 Congress authorized an additional 1500 miles. The national government is financing 90 percent of the cost. The program is administered by the Federal Highway Administration in the Department of Transportation.

Federal Aid to Education   Various programs of federal grants-in-aid to the states for educational purposes. Such aid has taken the form of land grants for schools and colleges; grants for vocational education and vocational rehabilitation; school lunch programs; scholarship funds for science, mathematics, and other programs in the interest of national defense; grants to veterans to attend school; and grants to areas with a heavy influx of students because of the establishment of a military base or other national facility. In recent years, numerous aids to higher education have been enacted by Congress, and in 1965, the first general aid-to-education bill, providing substantial aid to elementary and secondary schools, was passed. *See also* ELEMENTARY AND SECONDARY EDUCATION ACT, HIGHER EDUCATION ACT, NATIONAL DEFENSE EDUCATION ACT.

Federal Aviation Agency (FAA), *see* Department of Transportation.

Federal Bureau of Investigation (FBI), *see* Department of Justice.

Federal Communications Commission (FCC)   A seven-member independent regulatory commission that controls interstate and foreign communication via radio, television, telephone, telegraph, and cable. The FCC was created by and administers the Federal Communications Act of 1934. Under the Act, the FCC grants licenses to broadcasters, enforces regulations prohibiting indecent language and lotteries, and requires equal time for political candidates. The FCC has no power to regulate rates charged sponsors of radio and television programs, but Congress has designated telephone, telegraph, and cable services as "common carriers" and, therefore, subject to extensive regulation of rates and services. The FCC also implements provisions of the Communications Satellite Act of 1962. *See also* EQUAL TIME.

Federal Council, *see* Bundesrat (Germany).

Federal Crop Insurance Corporation, *see* Department of Agriculture.

Federal Deposit Insurance Corporation (FDIC)   A government corporation established in 1933 that insures depositors' accounts in participating banks up to $20,000 for each account. The FDIC insurance system is financed through annual assessments levied on privately owned banks. Member banks of the Federal Reserve System must participate, and nonmember banks may request to join the program. The FDIC is directed by the Comptroller of the Currency and by two directors appointed by the President with Senate consent.

Federal Diet, *see* Bundestag (Germany).

Federal Election Campaign Act of 1972   An act to control the raising and expenditure of funds for political campaigns. Its major provisions include (1) a limitation on the amount that can be spent for political advertising to 10 cents for every eligible voter—in a congressional district for House contests, statewide for Senate contests, and nationwide for presidential races—with a limit of 60 percent of that sum usable for broadcast advertising; (2) a ceiling on the amount that individual candidates and their immediate families can contribute to their own campaigns—$50,000 for a presidential race, $35,000 for the Senate, $25,000 for the House; and (3) a requirement of complete disclosure of contributions in excess of $10 and expenditures in excess of $100. Other provisions regulate the activities of political campaign committees, labor unions, and corporations, and establish reporting procedures. *See also* CORRUPT PRACTICES ACTS.

Federal Extension Service, *see* Department of Agriculture.

Federal Insurance Administration, *see* Department of Housing and Urban Development.

Federalism A system of government in which power is divided by a written constitution between a central government and regional or subdivisional governments. Both governments act directly upon the people through their officials and laws. Both are supreme within their proper sphere of authority. Both must consent to constitutional change. By contrast, a "unitary" system of government is one in which the central government is supreme and in which regional and local governments derive their authority from the central government. Federal systems are found in the United States, Canada, Switzerland, Mexico, Australia, India, and West Germany, among others. In the United States, the term "federal government" is used as a synonym for the national government. *See also* UNITARY STATE, CONFEDERATION.

Federalism, Cooperative, *see* Cooperative Federalism.

Federalism, Creative, *see* Creative Federalism.

Federalism, Horizontal, *see* Horizontal Federalism.

Federalism, World, *see* World Government.

Federalist Papers A series of eighty-five essays written by Alexander Hamilton, James Madison, and John Jay (all using the name *Publius*), which were published in New York newspapers in 1787 to convince New Yorkers to adopt the newly proposed Constitution drafted in Philadelphia. These essays have been collected and published under the title *The Federalist*.

Federalist Party The first American political party, which evolved during the later phases of George Washington's presidency. Its leaders, Alexander Hamilton and John

Adams, gained the support of the financial, industrial, and commercial interests for the new party. Many of its members had strongly supported the adoption of the new Constitution and the creation of the federal Union.

Federal Magistrate   A minor judicial officer who holds preliminary hearings in federal criminal cases, issues arrest warrants, sets bail, and holds trial over minor federal offenses where a defendant waives his right to trial in a district court. Under the Federal Magistrates Act of 1968, federal magistrates are attorneys appointed for eight-year terms by federal district judges. They serve in various locations, making it unnecessary to bring federal cases to the district court immediately; this is essential since some district courts serve an entire state or other large area. *See also* MAGISTRATE.

Federal Maritime Commission (FMC)   A five-member independent regulatory agency that controls rates and services of water carriers engaged in foreign and domestic off-shore commerce. Members are appointed by the President with the Senate's approval for four-year terms. The FMC's authority includes the approval of routes, the settling of disputes, and the prescribing of working conditions for seamen.

Federal Mediation and Conciliation Service   An agency formerly within the Department of Labor but given independent status under the Taft-Hartley Act of 1947. The Service is headed by a director appointed by the President with the Senate's consent. The Service has no law-enforcement authority but relies upon persuasion to prevent strikes that will impede the free flow of interstate commerce. Professional mediators employed by the Service assist in the settlement of labor-management disputes and try to promote good relations between labor and management. The Taft-Hartley Act requires that employers and unions must file notice of any dispute not settled thirty days after either side has expressed an intention to terminate an existing contract. The Mediation and Conciliation Service then tries to conciliate the dispute, but neither side is compelled to accept the solution suggested by the Service. The Service may also offer to enter a dispute on its own motion or at the request of parties. The Service often helps in the selection of arbitrators when both sides accept arbitration. *See also* MEDIATION AND CONCILIATION.

Federal Open Market Committee, *see* Open Market Operations.

Federal Police Power, *see* Police Power.

Federal Power Commission (FPC)   A five-member independent regulatory commission that controls the production and interstate transmission and sale of electrical energy and the interstate transportation and sale of natural gas. Commissioners are appointed by the President with the Senate's approval for five-year terms. The FPC was created as a Cabinet committee in 1920, and given its independent status by the Federal Power Act of 1930. Its functions include granting licenses to private companies to build hydroelectric plants on navigable waters, determining wholesale rates for electric power transmitted across state lines, regulating security issues of private power companies, planning for multipurpose river basin development, developing power resources at government-built dams, and controlling pipeline transmissions and sales of natural gas.

Federal Register A United States Government publication initiated by the Federal Register Act of 1935, which requires that presidential proclamations, reorganization plans, and executive orders be published. The Administrative Procedure Act of 1946 requires every public agency to publish a statement of its organization, authority, methods of operation, and statements of general policy in the *Federal Register*. Notice of proposed rules and regulations and administrative orders resulting from the adjudicatory functions of the agency must also be published. The *Federal Register* is published five times each week. The documents are codified in the *Code of Federal Regulations* (CFR). Some states have similar publications.

Federal Reserve Notes Currency issued by Federal Reserve banks, backed by deposits with the government of discounted commercial paper (such as promissory notes or bills of exchange), government bonds, and gold certificates.

Federal Reserve System The private-public banking regulatory system in the United States, which establishes banking policies and influences the amount of credit available and the currency in circulation. The Federal Reserve System was created by Congress in 1913. It consists of twelve Federal Reserve banks, each located in one of the twelve Federal Reserve districts into which the country is divided, and a central Board of Governors of seven members appointed by the President and confirmed by the Senate. Each of the Federal Reserve banks is headed by a board of nine directors, six of whom are chosen by the member banks in the district and three by the Federal Reserve Board in Washington. Membership in district Federal Reserve banks is required of all national banks and permitted to state banks, and most of the latter have joined. The Federal Reserve banks are actually privately owned "bankers' banks," with all member banks required to hold stock in them. Buying and selling of commercial paper and government securities is carried on through an Open Market Committee. *See also* BOARD OF GOVERNORS, OPEN MARKET OPERATIONS, REDISCOUNT, RESERVE RATIO, MONETARY POLICY.

Federal Service Entrance Examination A federal civil service examination open to college juniors, seniors, and graduates with broad educational backgrounds who are interested in securing junior management positions in federal service upon graduation from college. The examination tests general intelligence and aptitudes to find promising career servants who can move into management positions in the future. Persons who take the examination may take an additional examination called the Management Internship Examination which, if passed, offers greater opportunities.

Federal Supplement, *see United States Reports.*

Federal System, *see* Federalism.

Federal System (Soviet Union)   The division of power between the Soviet state and its fifteen union republics. The constituent units of the Soviet federal system are: The Russian Soviet Federated Socialist Republic; Ukrainian Soviet Socialist Republic; Byelorussian SSR; Uzbek SSR; Kazakh SSR; Georgian SSR; Azerbaijan SSR; Lithuanian SSR; Moldavian SSR; Latvian SSR; Kirghiz SSR; Tadjik SSR; Armenian SSR; Turkmen SSR; and the Estonian SSR. As understood in the West, federalism implies a formal division of power between the nation and its constituent parts that each is powerless to alter without the participation and consent of the other. In this sense, the Soviet Union is not a federation since observed practice indicates the completeness of centralized authority in the national party and government.

Federal Trade Commission (FTC)   A five-member independent regulatory commission established by Congress in 1914 to promote fair competition in business and to restrict unfair business practices in interstate and foreign commerce. Commissioners are appointed by the President with the Senate's approval for seven-year terms. The FTC enforces the Clayton and the Federal Trade Commission Acts of 1914. It seeks to prevent illegal combinations in restraint of trade, deception, price discriminations, price fixing, interlocking directorates, fraudulent advertising of foods, drugs, and cosmetics, and other business activities that reduce competition or endanger or defraud the consumer. The operations of the FTC include making rules and regulations to establish a code of fair competition, holding hearings concerning alleged violations, and enforcing decisions through cease and desist orders and injunctions granted by federal courts. *See also* CAVEAT VENDITOR.

Feedback   The process by which information about the workings of a system is communicated back to the system so that adjustments and corrections may be made. Within the system feedback inputs may be relayed to control mechanisms which use the information to modify subsequent system behavior. Negative feedback, which may be illustrated by the operation of a thermostat or governor, involves inputs that oppose the direction of the main system. Positive feedback tends to amplify or reinforce existing tendencies in the system, as in the case of popular support for governmental programs leading to expansion of the programs. *See also* COMMUNICATIONS THEORY, HOMEOSTASIS, INPUT, SYSTEMS ANALYSIS.

Fee System, *see* Justice of the Peace, Sheriff.

Felony   A serious crime punishable by death or by imprisonment in a penitentiary for a year or more. The precise character of a felony varies from state to state and is defined by law. Less serious violations of law are called misdemeanors. Felonies generally include murder, arson, robbery, aggravated assault, and forgery. *See also* MISDEMEANOR, JURY.

Field Experiment, *see* Field Study.

Field Service   Decentralized administration typified by local or regional branch offices of a federal or state agency. Operations, personnel, and finance are under the control of the central office in Washington, D.C., or the state capital.

Field Study   Any research project in which the investigator gathers his data directly from the individuals or groups who are the subjects of his inquiry. Field study techniques include personal observation, interviewing, the use of questionnaires, the participant-observer technique, and the case study. In a *field experiment* the political investigator injects an event, condition, or other experimental treatment into an otherwise normal field setting and studies its impact on the situation under scrutiny. *See also* CASE STUDY, INTERVIEW TECHNIQUE, OBSERVATION, PANEL STUDY, PARTICIPANT OBSERVATION, QUESTIONNAIRE.

Field Theory   An approach to social analysis that conceives of individuals and groups as acting within a "field" or "life space"—the actor's behavior being affected by his relationship to the particular configuration of forces in his "field." In political analysis field theory has been primarily a means for ordering variables within a two- or multi-dimensional space (the *field*), so that relationships among the variables may be studied as distances in space. Taking states as objects of analysis, for example, two variables in a simple model might represent the attributes of wealth and population. Countries could then be located in the field, in relation to one another, at the points indicated by their respective wealth and population. Shifts over time in the location of such points, occasioned by attribute change, are indicated by *vectors* (represented on a chart by arrows of appropriate length and direction, or in mathematical models by other appropriate symbols). Primarily a means for ordering data relevant to social relationships, field theory has also been used in efforts to *explain* political behavior. Here the typical field model consists of a number of vectors or dimensions, each denoting the magnitude of a characteristic attributed to one or more political entities. If the entities are states, one such vector might represent population, another wealth, and so on, and states would be arrayed along the vectors at distances appropriate to the magnitude of their respective populations, wealth, and so forth. The theory assumes that the behavior of entities is affected by their distance from one another along the various attribute dimensions. Hence, behavior presumably can be explained if the actor can be located in its field with respect to the relevant attributes and behaviors of other entities.

Fifteenth Amendment   An amendment to the Constitution, adopted in 1870, that forbids a state to deny a person the right to vote because of race, color, or previous condition of servitude. *See also Guinn v. United States, Smith v. Allwright.*

Fifth Amendment   A part of the Bill of Rights that imposes a number of restrictions on the national government with respect to the rights of persons accused of crime. It provides for indictment by grand jury, protection against double jeopardy and self-incrimination, and forbids denial of life, liberty, or property without due process of law. In addition, the Fifth Amendment prohibits the taking of property without just compensation. *See also* GRAND JURY; DOUBLE JEOPARDY; SELF-INCRIMINATION; DUE PROCESS; EMINENT DOMAIN; IMMUNITY.

Fifth Column A subversive movement to weaken a government's defensive efforts during a civil war or an attack by another nation. The term "fifth column" originated during the Spanish Civil War when the rebel forces of Francisco Franco attacked the Loyalists in Madrid with four columns and recognized that a fifth existed within the city to aid their cause. *See also* SABOTAGE.

Fifth French Republic, *see* Constitution (France).

Filibuster A parliamentary device used in the United States Senate by which a minority of senators seek to frustrate the will of the majority by literally "talking a bill to death." Senators are proud of their chamber's reputation for being the world's greatest forum for free discussion. Custom and Senate Rule 22 provide for unlimited debate on a motion before it can be brought to a vote. A filibuster is a misuse of this freedom of debate, since full exploration of the merits and demerits of the pending measure is not its objective. Rather, the minority of senators seeks to gain concessions or the withdrawal of the bill by delaying tactics. These include prolonged debate and speeches on relevant and irrelevant topics, parliamentary maneuvers, dilatory motions, and other tricks of the legislative game. The objective of the minority is to delay action on the measure interminably, until the majority is forced by the press of other business to withdraw it from consideration. *See also* CLOTURE, LEGISLATIVE DAY.

Filing The legal act of declaring candidacy for a public elective office. Most states provide that aspirants first circulate candidacy petitions to be signed by a stipulated number of registered voters. The aspirant presents the petitions, and files for candidacy with the appropriate official (secretary of state, county clerk, or city clerk). The candidate may then run against other candidates of his party for the office in a direct primary election to determine which of them will become the party's standard-bearer in the general election. In some states, persons seeking candidacy for local office may file simply by declaring their intentions before an official. In other states, a candidate may file by depositing a sum of money in lieu of petitions, which may be refunded if the candidate polls enough votes. *See also* PETITION.

Fine A sum of money paid as a penalty for an illegal act. A fine may constitute the total penalty or it may be levied in addition to or as a substitute for imprisonment. The Supreme Court has held it to be a denial of equal protection to either extend a jail sentence for inability to pay a fine (*Williams v. Illinois*, 399 U.S. 925 [1970]) or to put an indigent person in jail for an offense punishable only by a fine (*Tate v. Short*, 401 U.S. 395 [1971]).

First Amendment, *see* Freedom of Assembly, Freedom of Association, Freedom of Religion, Freedom of Speech, Freedom of the Press.

First Strike   The strategy of launching a surprise nuclear attack to destroy or decisively weaken the enemy's capacity to retaliate. The first-strike theory assumes that one side could deliver a paralyzing and devastating blow of such magnitude that it could win a nuclear war before the enemy could recover from the blow. A nation's first-strike capability depends on its arsenal of nuclear warheads and delivery systems, but its employment of a first-strike attack is limited by the potential enemy's second-strike or retaliatory capability. *See also* PREEMPTIVE STRIKE.

Fiscal Policy   The use by government of its financial powers to influence the nation's economy. Decisions on fiscal policy are made largely by the President and Congress, and are concerned with revenue, expenditure, and debt. John Maynard Keynes, the British economist, was one of the first to develop the theoretical basis and sophisticated applications of fiscal policy in combating economic slumps. *See also* MONETARY POLICY, EMPLOYMENT ACT.

Fiscal Year   The twelve-month financial period used by a government for record keeping, budgeting, appropriating, revenue collecting, and other aspects of fiscal management. The fiscal year of the national government runs from July 1 to June 30, but some state and local governments use the calendar year from January 1 to December 31, while a few states use a two-year fiscal period.

Fish and Wildlife Service, *see* Department of the Interior.

Five-to-Four Decision   A decision of the United States Supreme Court in which the justices divide sharply over the decision or interpretation of the Constitution or law. Such decisions tend to attract wide notice and it is sometimes said that one justice, in effect, decides the case.

Floor Leader, *see* Majority Floor Leader.

FMC, *see* Federal Maritime Commission.

Fong Yue Ting v. United States, 149 U.S. 698 (1893): Supported the authority of the national government to deport aliens under its sovereign power in the field of international affairs. The Court upheld a federal law that authorized the deportation of Chinese laborers who had failed to get certificates of residence. Furthermore, the Court held that deportation is not criminal punishment and, therefore, does not require a judicial trial. *See also* DEPORTATION.

Food and Agriculture Organization (FAO)   A specialized agency of the United Nations created in May, 1943. Members agree in the Preamble to FAO's Constitution to work toward "raising levels of nutrition and standards of living . . . efficiency in the production and distribution of all food . . . bettering the conditions of rural populations, and thus contributing toward an expanding world economy. . . . " These goals are sought through: (1) collecting and distributing information; (2) recommending national and international action to improve conservation, production, processing, marketing, and food distribution; and (3) furnishing technical assistance and organizing agricultural missions. Headquarters of FAO are in Rome. *See also* SPECIALIZED AGENCY.

Food and Drug Administration, *see* Department of Health, Education, and Welfare.

Food for Peace Program   The disposition of surplus American agricultural products to improve United States foreign relations and to increase consumption of such commodities abroad. The Food for Peace program (also called Food for Freedom) was established by Public Law 480 in 1954. *See also* FOREIGN AID.

Forecasting, *see* Prediction.

Foreign Affairs Committee   The standing committee of the House of Representatives that has primary responsibility in the field of foreign affairs. The detailed work of the Foreign Affairs Committee is assigned to standing subcommittees whose members develop expertness by their continued involvement with particular geographic and problem areas. The power of the committee in foreign affairs derives from the general legislative power of the House, the power to conduct investigations, and the role of the House in appropriating the funds necessary for all foreign policy activities. Thus, the committee plays an important role in determining the administrative organization, policy orientation, and budget for such bodies as the Agency for International Development, the United States Information Agency, and the Department of State. *See also* FOREIGN RELATIONS COMMITTEE.

Foreign Aid   The granting of economic or military assistance to foreign countries. American economic aid includes disposal of food surpluses, technical assistance, development loans, capital grants, and investment guarantees. The aid has been offered to over ninety countries bilaterally and to additional nations through United Nations and regional programs. Major programs in which the United States participates include the Alliance for Progress, the Peace Corps, the Colombo Plan, the Organization for Economic Cooperation and Development, the Asian and Inter-American Development Banks, the World Bank Group (IBRD, IDA, and IFC), and the United Nations Development Program. Military aid, taking the form of weapons, training, and defense support, and paying civilian costs to make up for the money the aid-receiving country has spent in its own defense, is given on a selective basis to strengthen resistance to external or internal Communist aggression. Foreign economic aid programs are administered by the Agency for International Development (AID), and military aid by the Defense Department.

Foreign Exchange   The buying and selling of national currencies. Foreign exchange is necessary to make purchases of foreign goods or to settle accounts. The price or exchange ratio for national currencies is determined by supply and demand in the international money market or by an arbitrary fixing of the rate of exchange through a national system of exchange control. *See also* CONVERTIBILITY, EXCHANGE CONTROL.

Foreign Office   An executive agency charged with the formulation and implementation of foreign policy. Other names for the foreign office include foreign ministry, ministry of foreign affairs, and department of state. Foreign offices are presided over by a foreign secretary, foreign minister, or secretary of state. In the large states, foreign offices tend to be organized on both geographical and functional lines. *See also* FOREIGN SECRETARY (BRITAIN), DECISION MAKERS, MINISTER OF FOREIGN AFFAIRS (FRANCE), SECRETARY OF STATE.

Foreign Policy   A strategy or planned course of action developed by the decision makers of a state vis-à-vis other states or international entities aimed at achieving specific goals defined in terms of national interest. A specific foreign policy carried on by a state may be the result of an initiative by that state or may be a reaction to initiatives undertaken by other states. Foreign policy involves a dynamic process of applying relatively fixed interpretations of national interest to the highly fluctuating situational factors of the international environment to develop a course of action, followed by efforts to achieve diplomatic implementation of the policy guidelines. Major steps in the foreign policy process include (1) translating national interest considerations into specific goals and objectives; (2) determining the international and domestic situational factors related to the policy goals; (3) analyzing the state's capabilities for achieving the desired results; (4) developing a plan or strategy for utilizing the state's capabilities to deal with the variables in pursuit of the goals; (5) undertaking the requisite actions; and (6) periodically reviewing and evaluating progress made toward the achievement of the desired results. The process seldom proceeds logically and chronologically; often several steps in the process may be carried on simultaneously, and fundamental issues may be reopened when conditions change or setbacks occur. Because situational factors are in constant flux, the policy process is continuous. *See also* REVISIONIST POLICY, STATUS QUO POLICY.

Foreign Policy Objectives   The ends which foreign policy is designed to achieve. Foreign policy objectives are concrete formulations derived from relating the national interest to the prevailing international situation and to the power available to the state. The objectives are selected by decision makers seeking to change (revisionist policy) or to preserve (status quo policy) some state of affairs in the international environment. *See also* CAPABILITY ANALYSIS, NATIONAL INTEREST, SITUATIONAL FACTORS.

Foreign Relations Committee   A standing committee of the Senate that serves as the principal agent of the Senate in the field of United States foreign policy. The Foreign Relations Committee functions largely through standing subcommittees patterned on and coordinated with the geographic and topical divisions of the Department of State. The committee's authority derives from the Senate's general legislative and investigatory powers which are similar to those exercised by the House of Representatives. As a result of the system of checks and balances, however, the Senate has certain powers not given to the House, such as a share in the executive branch's treaty- and appointment-making powers. Article II, Section 2, of the Constitution gives the President power "by and with the advice and consent of the Senate, to make treaties, provided two-thirds of the Senators present concur; and he shall nominate, and, by and with the advice and consent of the Senate, shall appoint ambassadors, and other public ministers and consuls. . . . " The Senate usually accepts the recommendations of its Foreign Relations Committee in these and other foreign policy matters. *See also* FOREIGN AFFAIRS COMMITTEE.

Foreign Secretary (Britain)   A leading member of the Cabinet responsible for the formulation and conduct of foreign policy. The Foreign Secretary defends the government's policy in the House of Commons by participating in debate and by responding to the probing attacks and searching analysis of the Question Hour. He also administers the Foreign and Commonwealth Office, meets with foreign diplomats, and at times represents his country at a variety of international meetings. The Foreign Secretary is assisted by two Ministers of State, two Parliamentary Under-Secretaries of State (all Members of Parliament), and by a Permanent Under-Secretary of State who is the highest-ranking career civil servant in the Diplomatic Service.

Foreign Service   The diplomatic and consular establishment of the United States. Created by the Rogers Act of 1924 and augmented by the Foreign Service Act of 1946, as amended, the career Foreign Service is entered by passing a nation-wide competitive examination and advancement is based on a merit system. Personnel are divided into five broad categories: (1) Chief of Mission (CM), either a senior career officer or a political appointee who serves as an ambassador or as head of a special mission, such as to the United Nations; (2) Foreign Service Officer (FSO), the standard title for the various grades of career diplomatic and consular officers who form the core of the service; (3) Foreign Service Reserve Officer (FSR), a technical expert or specialist, such as a commercial attaché, who may serve for nonconsecutive periods of up to five years at the discretion of the Secretary of State; (4) Foreign Service Staff Category (FSS), which includes diplomatic couriers, executive secretaries, and embassy administrative staff involved in such matters as disbursing, budget, and telecommunications filing; (5) Foreign Service Local Employees (FSL), several thousand noncitizens employed at Foreign Service posts around the world to perform duties ranging from translation to custodial services. *See also* AMBASSADOR, ATTACHÉ, CHARGÉ D'AFFAIRES, CONSUL, DEPARTMENT OF STATE, DIPLOMAT, DIPLOMATIC PRIVILEGES AND IMMUNITIES, PERSONA GRATA, ROGERS ACT, UNITED STATES INFORMATION AGENCY.

Foreign Service Act of 1924, *see* Rogers Act.

Foreign Service Examination   Written, oral, foreign language, and physical examinations that constitute the basis for appointment to the career Foreign Service. The Board of Examiners for the Foreign Service determines the nature, scope, and date of the written examination and selects the panels of officers who will conduct the oral examination of those who pass the written. Physical requirements are similar to those for entrance into military service. Upon successful completion of the first three hurdles, passage of the language examination may be deferred and a provisional appointment to the Foreign Service may be made.

Foreign Service Institute   A division of the Department of State that trains Foreign Service and State Department personnel in the various fields of international relations, administrative operations, management, supervision, and foreign languages.

Foreign Service Officer (FSO)   A United States career diplomatic officer. Foreign Service Officers usually enter the Foreign Service in Class 8 through competitive examination. Promotion by merit goes through Class 1 up to career minister and ultimately career ambassador.

Forest Service, *see* Department of Agriculture.

Fourteen Points   An instrument of psychological warfare composed of idealistic principles which President Woodrow Wilson enunciated in 1918 as a rationale for winning World War I and for maintaining the peace to follow. In his Fourteen Points, Wilson called for open diplomacy, freedom of the seas, disarmament, removal of economic barriers, international supervision of colonies, peaceful change based on self-determination, and the creation of an association of nations that would guarantee the political independence and territorial integrity of great and small states alike. *See also* LEAGUE OF NATIONS, PROPAGANDA, PSYCHOLOGICAL WARFARE.

Fourteenth Amendment   A post-Civil War Amendment (1868) that defines citizenship, restricts the powers of the states in their relations with their inhabitants, requires reduction of a state's representation in Congress for denials of suffrage, disqualifies former officeholders who participated in the rebellion, and invalidates any war debts of rebellious states. The most important provisions are those that forbid a state to deprive any person of life, liberty, or property without due process of law, or deny to any person the equal protection of the law. *See also* DUE PROCESS OF LAW, EQUAL PROTECTION OF THE LAW.

Fourth Amendment, *see* Arrest Warrant, Search and Seizure.

FPC, *see* Federal Power Commission.

Franchise   A privilege conferred by government upon a private company to operate a public utility and to use public property for the welfare or convenience of the public. Franchises are granted by the national, state, and local governments to bus companies, railroads, telephone and electric power companies, pipe lines, and other private companies performing public services. *See also* PUBLIC UTILITY.

Franking Privilege   A policy that enables members of Congress to send material through the mail free by substituting their facsimile signature (frank) for postage. Free mail privileges have also been accorded by Congress to other officials and agencies of the national government.

Freedman v. Maryland, 380 U.S. 51 (1965): Held that motion picture censorship is permissible provided that the procedure followed assures prompt judicial review of the censor's decision. By this decision, the Court affirmed its ruling in *Times Film Corporation v. Chicago,* 365 U.S. 43 (1961) that initial submission of a motion picture to a censoring board may be required, but it held that the board's decision could not be final. *See also* CENSORSHIP.

Freedom, *see* Civil Liberties, Civil Rights.

Freedom from Self-Incrimination, *see* Self-Incrimination.

Freedom of Assembly   The right of the people to congregate for the discussion of public questions and to organize into political parties or pressure groups for the purpose of influencing public policy. The right of assembly does not authorize meetings designed to accomplish an illegal purpose or those that lead to a breach of the peace or resistance to lawful authority. Freedom of assembly is guaranteed by the First Amendment and by state constitutions. In addition, the Supreme Court has ruled that the due process clause of the Fourteenth Amendment protects the individual's freedom of assembly against infringement by state governments. *See also Hague v. CIO.*

Freedom of Association   The right to organize for political, religious, or other social purposes. The Constitution makes no mention of freedom of association, but it is implicit in guarantees of freedom of speech, assembly, and religion. *See also* GUILT BY ASSOCIATION; *Keyishian v. Board of Regents; NAACP v. Alabama; Scales v. United States.*

Freedom of Debate   The right of members of a legislative body in a democratic system of government to freely discuss, deliberate, and act upon matters of policy without fear of legal action. The Constitution (Art. I, sec. 6), provides that "for any speech or debate in either House, they [Senators and Representatives] shall not be questioned in any other place." Utterances that might otherwise be unlawful are privileged, therefore, when made in Congress (*U.S. v. Johnson,* 383 U.S. 169 [1966]).

Immunity to suit does not ordinarily apply to statements made outside of Congress. In all cases, however, whether such statements are made in or out of Congress, members can be held to account through the disciplinary powers of their own house. State constitutions generally provide similar immunity for legislators. Freedom of debate is sometimes used to describe the right under Senate Rule 22 to speak indefinitely on a pending measure in the United States Senate.

Freedom of Religion Freedom of worship and religious practice. The national government under the First Amendment, and the states under their constitutions and the Fourteenth Amendment, may not abridge this right of worship. Any religious practice that is contrary to public peace or morality may be outlawed, such as snake-handling or polygamy. *See also* SEPARATION OF CHURCH AND STATE, *Jehovah's Witnesses Cases, Reynolds v. United States.*

Freedom of Speech The right to speak without prior restraint, subject to penalties for abuse of the right. Abuses include slander, obscenity, incitement to crime, contempt of court, or sedition. By virtue of the First and Fourteenth Amendments and state bills of rights, neither the national government nor the states may abridge freedom of speech. *See also* FREEDOM OF THE PRESS, BAD TENDENCY RULE, CLEAR AND PRESENT DANGER RULE.

Freedom of the Press The right to publish and disseminate information without prior restraint, subject to penalties for abuse of the right. Abuses include libel, obscenity, incitement to crime, contempt of court, or sedition. Freedom of the press is protected by the First and Fourteenth Amendments to the Constitution and by all state constitutions. Major contemporary problems have involved censorship of books and movies for alleged obscenity, restraints on Communist publications, governmental secrecy, and the difficulty of safeguarding both freedom of the press and a fair trial. *See also Near v. Minnesota, New York Times v. Sullivan, New York Times v. United States, Roth v. United States.*

Freedom to Petition, *see* Petition (Right of).

Free Enterprise System,, *see* Capitalism.

Free Trade The elimination of all governmental regulations and controls so as to allow the free flow of commodities among countries. The theory is associated with Adam Smith, who believed that a free trade system would foster an international specialization that would result in higher productivity and standards of living for all nations. *See also* CAPITALISM.

Free Trade Area A region consisting of two or more states in which tariffs and other barriers to trade have been eliminated. A free trade area goes beyond a preferential system that retains tariffs but provides for more favorable rates for members. It does not, however, go as far as a customs union that, in addition to establishing a free trade area, provides for a common external tariff applicable to nonmembers. In a free trade area agreement, members retain full freedom to develop their individual trade policies with the rest of the world. Examples of free trade areas include the European Free Trade Association (EFTA) and the Latin American Free Trade Association (LAFTA). *See also* EUROPEAN FREE TRADE ASSOCIATION, LATIN AMERICAN FREE TRADE ASSOCIATION.

Free Will, *see* Determinism.

French Political System, *see* Cabinet, Community, Constitution, Constitutional Council, Council of State, Economic and Social Council, Gaullism, Minister of Foreign Affairs, National Assembly, Parliament, Party System, Premier, President, Senate.

Friend of the Court, *see Amicus Curiae.*

Frothingham v. Mellon, 262 U.S. 447 (1923): Held that a taxpayer may not bring suit in a federal court to restrain the expenditure of federal funds. The case involved a protest against a federal grant-in-aid to the states for maternity benefits. The Court has since modified the rule to permit taxpayer suits where a specific breach of constitutional power is alleged (*Flast v. Cohen,* 389 U.S. 895 [1968]). *See also Massachusetts v. Mellon.*

FSO, *see* Foreign Service Officer.

FTC, *see* Federal Trade Commission.

Fulbright Act of 1946, *see* Cultural Exchange (United States).

Full Faith and Credit   One of the obligations of each state in its relations with other states. Article IV, section 1, of the Constitution provides that "Full faith and credit shall be given in each state to the public acts, records, and judicial proceedings of every other state." The clause applies to civil but not criminal proceedings. It ensures that rights established under wills, contracts, deeds, and other property rights will be honored in all states. A judicial decision in one state will be honored and enforced in all states. One area of difficulty has arisen with regard to divorce decrees. Some states have refused to recognize uncontested divorces granted by sister states because of questions over domicile (*Williams v. North Carolina,* 325 U.S. 226 [1945]). *See also* HORIZONTAL FEDERALISM.

Function, *see* Functionalism, Structural-Functionalism.

Functional Consolidation (Administrative)   Combining several administrative units that do related work into one major department. *See also* FUNCTIONAL CONSOLIDATION; ADMINISTRATIVE REORGANIZATION.

Functional Consolidation (Local Government)   The cooperation of two or more units of local government in providing services to their inhabitants. Several counties may join together for common administration of health services, or two cities may agree to have a common water supply or sewerage system. *See also* METROPOLITAN AREA; COUNCILS OF GOVERNMENT.

Functionalism (Analytical)   An approach to political analysis characterized by its focus on "functions" performed by or within political systems. Functionalism is an umbrella term covering a variety of analytic modes. It sometimes means no more than the investigation of activities engaged in by some individual, group, or organization within a political system or the purposes served by such activities. This approach has been called *eclectic functionalism* and is characteristic in some degree of most political research. A second variety (variously labeled *functionalism, empirical functionalism,* and *structural-functionalism*) focuses on activities that satisfy needs or demands arising from individuals and groups within a political system and the social structures that perform those activities. The effects or consequences of activities having relevance to the satisfaction of such needs and demands are called *functions*. *Manifest functions* are the purposeful or intended consequences; relevant but unintended or incidental consequences are *latent functions.* The manifest function of a political machine, for example, is to maintain and exercise political power, but its latent functions may include meeting welfare needs and providing channels for social mobility. A third variety, more strictly termed *structural-functionalism,* is theoretically more ambitious than the others. It posits certain functions that must be performed if a whole system is to be maintained or perpetuated and looks for a set of interdependent structures through which these functions are performed. Still a fourth variety, a kind of *international functionalism,* is concerned with the process of international integration through the development of institutions for economic and social cooperation. *See also* POLITICAL INTEGRATION, SPILLOVER, STRUCTURAL-FUNCTIONALISM.

Functionalism (Integrative)   The theory that postulates the building of a world community slowly and cumulatively through progressively expanding programs of economic and social cooperation rather than by political integration. Functionalism is based on the premise that economic and social problems tend to be worldwide in scope and, hence, a coherent attack upon them necessitates common action by members of the state system. Habits of cooperation that result from successful progress toward objectives in one field may be transferred into other areas of needed activity, with a peaceful world the ultimate objective.

Functionalist Theory of Integration, *see* Functionalism (Integrative).

Gag Rule   A legislative rule that arbitrarily limits the time available for consideration of a measure. The term "gag rule" refers generally to any special rule that limits debate on a pending bill or resolution beyond that provided by the chamber's regular legislative rules. *See also* RULES COMMITTEE.

Game Theory   A body of thought dealing with rational decision strategies in situations of conflict and competition, where each participant or player seeks to maximize gains and minimize losses. In game theory the strategy and decisions of one player depend on the strategy and decisions of the other players in the competitive situation. The theory of games assumes "rationality" on the part of the players in ranking their preferences, estimating probabilities, and determining the expectations that each has about the other's choices. Game situations may be described as "two person, zero-sum" in which one player's gain equals the other's loss; "two person, non-zero-sum" in which losses need not equal gains and both players may win or lose; "n-person, zero-sum" in which several players are involved and in which losses must equal gains; and "n-person, non-zero-sum" in which losses and gains among several players need not be equal. Game theory relies heavily on the use of mathematical models of decision structures. *See also* DECISION MAKING, STRATEGY.

Gaming, *see* Simulation.

Garrison v. Louisiana, *see New York Times v. Sullivan.*

GATT, *see* General Agreement on Tariffs and Trade.

Gaullism   The political philosophy of Charles de Gaulle and its impact on French national life since World War II. The essence of Gaullism is the idea of national interest above self-interest, as interpreted by de Gaulle. He altered the emphasis in French politics by downgrading traditionally organized party politics and making the presidency the dominant feature of the government. He tried to shape the concept of an effective national administration run by an apolitical technocracy motivated by his idea of "the reality of an objective national interest." He insisted upon an almost selfless loyalty from his subordinates and earned deep and lasting opposition from those who challenged the philosophy of his regime. Though he demonstrated a readiness to crush obstruction, he also showed a dedication to French constitutionalism, if not to every letter of the constitution. Through dramatic public appearances and masterful domination of the mass media he sought to convey an awesome impression of the President of France standing alone above politics, as the symbol of sovereignty and the guarantor of national independence and integrity.

General Accounting Office (GAO)   An independent agency created by the Budget and Accounting Act of 1921 that controls and audits national government expenditures as an agent of Congress. The GAO is headed by the Comptroller General who is appointed by the President with the Senate's approval for a fifteen-year term and can be removed only through impeachment or a joint resolution of Congress. *See also* COMPTROLLER GENERAL.

General Agreement on Tariffs and Trade (GATT)   An international organization that promotes trade among its members by serving as a forum for negotiating agreements to reduce tariffs and other barriers. GATT first met at Geneva in 1947 to function as an interim arrangement until the proposed International Trade Organization (ITO) could be established as a specialized agency of the United Nations to provide for orderly world trade. When the United States rejected ITO, GATT—which, unlike ITO, is based on executive agreements rather than on a treaty and, consequently, did not have to be approved by the Senate—was developed as the main instrument to encourage freer trade. GATT's membership has increased from the original twenty-three participants to almost one hundred full and associate members, which together carry on more than four-fifths of world trade. GATT's current functions include: (1) negotiating the reduction of tariffs and other impediments to trade; (2) developing new trade policies; (3) adjusting trade disputes; and (4) establishing rules to govern the trade policies of its members. Members negotiate bilaterally and multilaterally at periodic meetings. The most-favored-nation clause incorporated in all agreements concluded at GATT sessions insures that trade concessions will be applicable to every member. Its nondiscrimination rule prohibits members' using quantitative restrictions, quotas, export subsidies, special taxes, or other devices to circumvent the concessions granted. *See also* MOST-FAVORED-NATION CLAUSE, TARIFF.

General and Complete Disarmament   Proposals to eliminate all armed forces and armaments under a system of international control. The first official consideration of proposals for general and complete disarmament during the United Nations era occurred when Premier Nikita Khurshchev of the Soviet Union placed the question on the agenda of the Fourteenth General Assembly in 1959. In the following year, an initial Soviet proposal calling for complete disarmament in three stages within four years, and a British three-stage plan for comprehensive disarmament, were transmitted to the Ten-Nation Disarmament Committee for negotiation on specific points. The Russian proposal and a combined British-American plan have since constituted the substance of the Western- and Eastern-bloc proposals for general and complete disarmament. Both plans provide for complete disarmament in three stages, inspection and control functions vested in an International Disarmament Organization (IDO), and enforcement carried on through the Security Council of the United Nations. *See also* INTERNATIONAL DISARMAMENT ORGANIZATION.

General Assembly   The major organ of the United Nations in which all members (132 in 1972) are equally represented. The Assembly has evolved into the focus for the multifold activities of the United Nations. In one sense, it is a continuing international conference; in another, it is an international forum in which each member nation can discuss its international problems with all others. It is a "Town Meeting of the World," through which world public opinion can be aroused and brought to bear on a problem. Its functions directly or indirectly relate to almost all of the activities carried on by the world organization. Specific responsibilities include: (1) election of some or all members of the other five major organs; (2) an annual review of the activities of all segments of the organization; (3) control over the budget, and (4) decision making and recommendations to members on all subjects within United Nations jurisdiction. Measures are adopted ordinarily by a simple majority vote, but "important questions," as defined by the Charter or as determined by a majority of the Assembly, require a two-thirds vote of members present and voting. The most important power of the Assembly—to deal with acts of aggression and breaches of the peace when the Security Council is stalemated by a veto—was not vested in the Assembly by the Charter, but was assumed by it in 1950 through the Uniting for Peace Resolution.

General Counsel   An official charged with the responsibility for the investigation and prosecution of unfair labor-management practices under the Taft-Hartley Act. His functions include supervision of all regional offices of the National Labor Relations Board and final authority to issue complaints in unfair labor practice cases. These functions were formerly vested in the National Labor Relations Board. The General Counsel is appointed by the President, with the Senate's approval, for a four-year term. *See also* NATIONAL LABOR RELATIONS BOARD.

General Debate (United Nations)   The procedure that permits the representatives of all members of the United Nations to address the General Assembly during the opening weeks of each annual session. Often top leaders of many countries— presidents, prime ministers, monarchs—go to New York to present their nations' views on world problems during general debate. General debate usually absorbs about twenty to forty plenary sessions of the General Assembly each autumn.

General Election   A statewide election, usually held shortly after a primary election, to fill state and national offices. States hold national presidential elections every four years, in November, and national congressional elections in the even-numbered years. Typically, states hold state and county general elections every November in the even-numbered years, although some states elect some important state officials and judges in general elections held in odd-numbered years, frequently in the spring.

General Inquirer, *see* Content Analysis.

Generalization   A statement that attributes some characteristic to a class or category of things. A scientific generalization sets forth an empirical relationship between concepts or variables. The relationships between political phenomena may take the form of universal laws or hypotheses or of probabilistic or tendency statements. *See also* PROPOSITION, TENDENCY STATEMENT, THEORY.

General Laws   Laws applicable to all local government units of a similar type. Most state constitutions now provide that the legislature may pass only laws of general application rather than special acts applicable only to one unit. To allow for variations in the needs of small or large units of government, the legislatures often classify units according to population and then pass general laws applicable to that classification. *See also* CHARTER.

General Services Administration An independent agency established in 1949 to centralize purchasing and property and records management for the national government. The General Services Administration, headed by an Administrator appointed by the President with Senate approval, is assigned responsibility for the procurement, supply, and transportation of property and services for the executive agencies, the acquisition and management of federally owned or leased property, disposal of surplus property, and records management.

General Systems Theory, *see* Systems Analysis.

General Theory, *see* Theory.

General Welfare Clause The clause in Article I, section 8 of the Constitution that authorizes Congress to lay and collect taxes to provide for the common defense and general welfare of the United States. *See also* SOCIAL SECURITY CASES.

Geneva Convention on the Territorial Sea and Contiguous Zone (1958), *see* Contiguous Zone.

Geneva Conventions, *see* Rules of Warfare.

Genocide The destruction of groups of human beings because of their race, religion, nationality, or ethnic background. World concern over genocide was aroused by the mass murders perpetrated by the Nazis against the Jews and other racial and national groups. The United Nations General Assembly in 1948 adopted an International Convention on the Prevention and Punishment of the Crime of Genocide, which became effective in 1951 after 20 nations had ratified it. Categories of crime recognized in the Convention include killing, causing physical or mental harm, inflicting poor conditions of life, enforced birth control, or transferring children from one group to another. Persons committing or inciting acts of genocide are liable to punishment whether they are public officials or private individuals. *See also* GENOCIDE CONVENTION.

Genocide Convention An international treaty that outlaws acts committed by public officials or private individuals whose intent is to destroy, in whole or in part, a national, ethnic, racial, or religious group. The International Convention on the Prevention and Punishment of the Crime of Genocide was written in an ad hoc committee established by ECOSOC and was adopted by the General Assembly in 1948. The Convention specifically makes it an international crime to kill, cause serious bodily or mental harm, inflict harmful conditions upon, impose birth control, or forcibly transfer children from any identifiable group. The Genocide Convention came into force in 1951 after the necessary twenty states had ratified it. *See also* GENOCIDE, HUMAN RIGHTS.

Gentlemen's Agreement, *see* Security Council.

Geographic Power Factors, *see* Climate, Location, Raw Materials, Size, Topography.

Geological Survey, *see* Department of the Interior.

Geopolitics   An approach to foreign policy that attempts to explain and predict political behavior and military capabilities in terms of man's physical environment. Geopolitics, therefore, involves varying degrees of historical determinism based on geography. Friedrich Ratzel (1724–1804) compared the state to a living organism that must expand or die. His disciple Rudolf Kjellen (1864–1922) carried on this process of anthropomorphism, by which the state became more than a legal concept. He developed a body of "laws" on the state as a "geographic organism in space," and gave them the name "geopolitics" in his book *The State as a Form of Life* (1916). Much geopolitical theorizing, although presented in terms of scientific analysis, contains large elements of propaganda. The reputation of geopolitics has suffered because geopoliticians like Karl Haushofer (1869–1946) have frequently been the advocates of particular political ideologies or national policies, which they have sought to explain or justify in terms of geographical causation. The term "geopolitics" may also be used to describe political geography considered in terms of the structure of the world and its component states, or to refer to those aspects of foreign policy planning that must take into account various geographic factors. *See also* HAUSHOFER GEOPOLI-TIK, HEARTLAND THEORY, RIMLAND THEORY, SEA POWER THEORY.

German Political System, *see* Bonn Constitution, Bundesrat, Bundestag, Cabinet, Chancellor, Parliament, Party System, President.

Gerrymandering   The drawing of legislative district boundary lines with a view to obtaining partisan or factional advantage. Gerrymandering is engaged in by partisan majorities in state legislatures when they are drawing up congressional and state legislative districts. The objective is to spread the support for one's own party over many districts and to concentrate the support for the other party in few districts. Gerrymandering is possible because of the pattern of consistency in voting behavior of most Americans. *See also Wesberry v. Sanders, Reynolds v. Sims,* REDISTRICTING.

Gestalt Psychology, *see* Field Theory.

Gibbons v. Ogden, 9 Wheaton 1 (1824): Nullified a state grant giving an exclusive right to use navigable waters within the state. The Court held that congressional control over interstate commerce includes navigation. It was the first case involving the commerce clause, and the powers of Congress to regulate interstate commerce were broadly interpreted by Chief Justice Marshall and the Court. They defined interstate commerce to include not only traffic but all commercial intercourse. *See also* NAVIGABLE WATERS.

Gideon v. Wainwright, 372 U.S. 335 (1963): A landmark ruling that state courts are required by the due process clause of the Fourteenth Amendment to provide counsel to indigent defendants in criminal cases. This had been required in *federal* criminal trials since the 1938 decision in *Johnson v. Zerbst,* 304 U.S. 458, but state courts were required to furnish counsel to needy defendants only in capital cases (*Powell v. Alabama,* 287 U.S. 45 [1932]) or when special circumstances, such as youth, mental incompetence, or inexperience, necessitated the furnishing of counsel to assure a fair trial (*Betts v. Brady,* 316 U.S. 455 [1942]). In *Gideon,* the Court held that defense by counsel is a fundamental right available to all regardless of wealth or status. *See also* RIGHT TO COUNSEL.

Girouard v. United States, 328 U.S. 61 (1946): Established that an alien may be admitted to citizenship even if he refuses, on religious grounds, to swear that he will bear arms in defense of the United States. In this case, the Supreme Court reversed its earlier stand on this question and upheld Girouard's right to become a citizen since he was otherwise eligible and was willing to perform noncombatant duties.

Gitlow v. New York, 268 U.S. 652 (1925): Established, in a landmark case, that the freedoms of speech and press are protected against state impairment by the due process clause of the Fourteenth Amendment. Nevertheless, in this case, the Court upheld a conviction for publishing and circulating materials advocating the overthrow of government by force.

GNP, *see* Gross National Product.

Goal   The condition or end that an individual or group desires to achieve. Political goals may relate to the allocation of rewards within a system, to bringing about a certain event or avoiding it, to changing an intangible element, such as an attitude or opinion, in a desirable way, or to obtaining a tangible object. The nature of a political system, environmental factors, the personalities of decision makers, ideological considerations, and capability analyses help to determine the number and kinds of goals sought by political actors. *See also* ENGINEERING THEORY, PUBLIC POLICY, SOCIAL ENGINEERING.

Goldberg v. Kelly, 397 U.S. 254 (1970): Held that welfare benefits may not be terminated without due process. This requires a pretermination hearing with adequate notice, oral presentation, confrontation and cross-examination, right to retain an attorney, an impartial decision maker, and a decision based on rules and evidence adduced in the hearing. The hearing, said the Court, need not have the characteristics of a trial but should have minimal procedural safeguards adapted to the educational and social characteristics of the welfare recipient. *See also* CATEGORICAL ASSISTANCE; PRIVILEGE.

Gold Standard   A monetary system in which a nation's currency is backed by gold, has a standard of value measured in gold, and can be exchanged for gold. An international gold standard provides for free convertibility of currencies into gold and the unimpeded movement of gold bullion from one nation to another to pay international debts. The gold standard became universally accepted during the nineteenth and early twentieth centuries; the United States adopted it in 1900. In the worldwide depression of the 1930s, the nations of the world discarded it, with the United States going off the gold standard in 1934. After World War II, much of the world functioned under a gold exchange standard system through which central banks bought and sold national currencies backed by gold at a fixed price. Under this system, the American dollar became the major reserve and trading currency since it was freely exchanged into gold at a fixed rate. *See also* DEVALUATION.

Good Neighbor Policy   American policy toward Latin America initiated in the early 1930s. President Franklin Roosevelt described the change in policy in his inaugural address in March 1933 as follows: "In the field of world policy, I would dedicate this nation to the policy of the good neighbor—the neighbor who resolutely respects himself and, because he does so, respects the rights of others. . . . " Although the policy was directed toward the world at large, it soon came into general usage as descriptive of the American policy of treating Latin-American nations as friends and equals. *See also* ORGANIZATION OF AMERICAN STATES.

Good Offices   A method of peaceful settlement by which a third nation seeks to bring two disputing nations into agreement. The state offering its good offices merely seeks to create favorable conditions under which the states in conflict can talk over their differences. Good offices does not include participation in the negotiations nor the offering of a suggested solution, although the disputing states may request them. When they do, good offices is converted into mediation. *See also* PACIFIC SETTLEMENT OF DISPUTES.

Government   The political and administrative hierarchy of an organized state. Governments exercise legislative, executive, and judicial functions; the nature of the governmental system is determined by the distribution of these powers. Government may take many forms, but it must be sufficiently powerful and stable to command obedience and maintain order. A government's position also depends on its acceptance by the community of nations through its diplomatic recognition by other states.

Government Corporation   An agency of government that administers a business enterprise. The corporation form is used when an activity is primarily commercial in nature, produces revenue for its continued existence, and requires greater flexibility than Congress normally permits regular departments. Corporations are used at the national level for such enterprises as electric power distribution (Tennessee Valley Authority), insuring of bank deposits (Federal Deposit Insurance Corporation), and mail service (United States Postal Service). At the state level, corporations (often called "authorities") operate airports, turnpikes, and harbors, the best known being the Port of New York Authority.

Governor   The chief executive officer of a state, In all states, the governor is elected by the people and serves for four years in most and for two years in others. About one-half the states limit the governor to one or two terms in office. A governor's executive powers include the power of appointment and removal (although this is severely restricted in most states), preparation and execution of the budget, the power to issue executive orders, and general law enforcement. In the legislative field, governors enjoy considerable power through exercise of the veto power (in all states but North Carolina), and in all but seven states the governor may veto items in appropriation bills. A governor may call the legislature into special session and, in several states, he may limit the special session to consideration of specified subjects. Like the President, the governor may exercise influence over the legislature through his party leadership, messages, and direct appeals to the people. Most governors have the power to pardon and grant reprieves to convicted persons. They also serve as commanders in chief of the National Guard of the state except when it is called into national service. Governors may be removed from office by impeachment and, in a few states, by the recall.

Governor-General (Britain)   The personal representative of the monarch with comparable duties in those Commonwealth countries which have not become republics. The monarch seeks the advice of local ministers before appointing a Governor-General. In each of the few remaining British colonies a governor is appointed to represent the monarch. *See also* COMMONWEALTH OF NATIONS.

Governor's Conference, *see* Council of State Governments.

Grandfather Clause, *see Guinn v. United States.*

Grand Jury   A body of from twelve to twenty-three members who hear evidence presented by the prosecuting attorney against persons accused of a serious crime, and decide whether or not to present a "true bill" that "indicts" the accused. If indicted, the accused will be bound over for trial; if not, he goes free. The Fifth Amendment requires that this be done for any capital or infamous crime, generally those for which death or imprisonment may result. Unlike a petit or trial jury, a grand jury does not determine guilt or innocence but only whether the evidence warrants bringing the accused to trial; it meets in secret and decides by a majority rather than a unanimous vote. The grand jury may also conduct investigations on its own when a prosecutor is lax or when official misconduct is suspected. In such cases, any resulting accusation is called a "presentment." The grand jury exercises vast powers under the common law, being empowered to subpoena witnesses and records and to compel testimony under oath. More than half of the states have abolished or limited grand jury indictment to capital cases, replacing it with the "information" that permits the prosecutor alone to bring charges. *See also* INDICTMENT; INFORMATION; *Hurtado v. California.*

Grange (National Grange), *see* Farm Organizations.

Granted Powers, *see* Delegated Powers.

Grant-in-Aid   Funds made available by Congress to the state and local governments for expenditure in accordance with prescribed standards and conditions. State legislatures also make such grants to local governments. Some measure of supervision over the expenditure of the funds accompanies the grants. In addition, the receiving government is required to match the contribution dollar-for-dollar or in some other ratio. Highways, airports, agriculture, education, welfare, and health are among the major functions financed through the grant-in-aid device. *See also Massachusetts v. Mellon;* FEDERAL AID HIGHWAY ACT; COOPERATIVE FEDERALISM.

Grants, International, *see* Foreign Aid, United Nations Capital Development Fund.

Graves v. New York ex rel. O'Keefe, 306 U.S. 466 (1939): Held that a state may tax the income of a federal employee and that such a tax does not impose an unconstitutional burden upon the national government. *See also* INTERGOVERNMENTAL TAX IMMUNITY.

Gray v. Sanders, 372 U.S. 368 (1963): Ruled that in a given constituency each person's vote must count equally. The case overturned the Georgia "county unit system" for primary elections for statewide officers whereby the election was decided not by direct popular vote but by a system of county unit votes that discriminated against urban areas. *See also* REDISTRICTING.

Great Compromise, *see* Connecticut Compromise.

Green Revolution   The dramatic increase in cereal production achieved during the 1960s and 1970s as a result of the introduction of high yield seed grains and scientific agricultural technology in many of the poorer countries of the world. The new grains, particularly wheats and rices, are shorter and stiffer stemmed, more responsive to fertilizer, and less sensitive to variations in growing conditions than traditional varieties. Developed by scientists working in Mexico and the Philippines, the new wheat and rice strains together with the new technology may make it possible to double previous yields and achieve self-sufficiency in cereal grains.

Gross National Product (GNP) A measurement of the total annual output of goods and services of a country expressed in terms of its market value. In the United States, the Department of Commerce gathers such data on a quarterly basis and publishes it as an annual figure.

Group A collectivity of individuals distinguished by some common attribute or shared relationship. Groups are categorized in many different ways. A *formal* or *organized group*, such as a political party or an interest group, has recognized goals and structures affecting group interaction. An *informal group* (such as like-minded legislators meeting at lunch to share views) lacks such explicit goals and organizational structure. A *primary group* is a relatively small collectivity that engages in frequent and direct interactions (a family, a work group); the members of a *secondary group* interact infrequently and communicate mainly by indirect and impersonal means (a business association, a political party). The label *categoric group* is sometimes applied to a class of individuals who do not necessarily interact but who share some common characteristic, such as poor people, political activists, or people over thirty. In political studies, group often refers to *interest group* or *pressure group*. A political interest group is a collectivity that seeks to influence governmental policy in favor of some goal or shared concern of the group. Analytically, interest groups are sometimes classified as *associational* (organized interest groups, for example, a labor union or business association); *institutional* (groups based in major social institutions, such as bureaucracies, political parties, legislatures, armies, or churches); *nonassociational* (groups lacking continuity in structure and regular procedures for articulating interests, such as ethnic, regional, or class groups); and *anomic* (largely spontaneous, temporary groups that express discontent through direct action, such as demonstrations or riots). If such a group were to persist, it presumably would cease to be an anomic group and become an associational group that uses violent or unconventional methods. *See also* AGGREGATION OF INTERESTS, ARTICULATION OF INTERESTS, GROUP THEORY, REFERENCE GROUP.

Group of Ten, *see* International Monetary Fund.

Group Theory An approach that seeks to explain political behavior primarily through the study of the nature and interaction of social groups. Group theory deals with both formal and informal groups within which people have membership or interact, or with which they identify. Group theorists in political science regard the group as the primary basis for all political activity and, hence, for political analysis, whereas other investigators view the group as only one of several focal points for the study of political activity. Group theory is often associated with process and equilibrium analyses that offer systemic approaches to the study of group objectives, the balancing of group interests, and the process of "adjustment." *Small group theory* deals with decision making and other interactive processes in small primary groups usually numbering twenty persons or fewer. Such studies include both formal and informal groups, but special attention is given to the informal relationships that supplement formal group procedures. Small groups are studied in both governmental and private settings. *See also* GROUP, REFERENCE GROUP.

Grovey v. Townsend, *see Smith v. Allwright.*

Guarantee Clause, *see* Republican Form of Government.

Guerrilla War   Irregular warfare fought by small bands against an invading army or in rebellion against an established government. Guerrilla war is fought mainly in the rural areas by indigenous elements who know the territory and are often indistinguishable from the rest of the population. The success of the guerrilla movement depends largely on the support accorded to the guerrillas by the local population in supplying food and havens, giving aid in carrying supplies, and refusing to divulge information to the anti-guerrilla forces. Many within the movement function as part-time farmers and part-time guerrillas. Because an outside source of supply is often the key to the success of guerrilla war, the cutting of supply lines becomes a main strategy for the anti-guerrilla units. Guerrilla war is often one phase of a broad political-economic-social-ideological revolution fought against an established order. *See also* CIVIL WAR, INSURGENCY, SABOTAGE, WARS OF NATIONAL LIBERATION.

Guilt by Association   Attribution of criminal or wrongful behavior or beliefs to a person because of the people or groups with whom he associates. *See also Scales v. United States;* FREEDOM OF ASSOCIATION; INTERNAL SECURITY ACT; *Keyishian v. Board of Regents; Elfbrandt v. Russell.*

Guinn v. United States, 238 U.S. 347 (1915): Declared "grandfather clauses" to be unconstitutional under the Fifteenth Amendment. These clauses had been used by many southern states to bestow the franchise upon white voters who had been disfranchised by state tax and literacy requirements intended to keep the Negroes from voting. The grandfather clauses granted the franchise to persons whose ancestors had voted prior to 1867.

Guttman Scale   A technique used to measure attitudes that can be ranked with reference to a common dimension or characteristic that is relevant to a group's behavior. In developing a Guttman scale (also called a cumulative scale) the attitudinal points are distributed in such a way that affirmative responses on any item may be regarded as agreement with all other items of lower rank. If a common dimension is detected, the individuals may be located on a continuum according to their relative positions on that dimension. For example, consider a four item scale designed to measure attitudes toward direct action in politics. The items might be (1) assassination, (2) burning buildings, (3) obstructing traffic, and (4) peaceful sidewalk demonstrations. If these items tap attitudes falling at different points along a single attitudinal dimension, such as a person's tolerance of force and violence in political affairs, they can be used to construct a Guttman scale. Simple inspection suggests that these four items might scale in the order given. Thus, any person willing to tolerate assassination would also be likely to countenance any of the other three forms of action. A person approving the burning of buildings would probably tolerate traffic obstruction and sidewalk demonstrations, but still might boggle at assassination. On the other hand, if a number of respondents approve the first and the fourth items but not the second or third, the items obviously would not scale, at least not in this order. *See also* ATTITUDE SCALING, SCALE.

Habeas Corpus A court order directing an official who has a person in custody to bring the prisoner to court and to show cause for his detention. The Constitution guarantees the right to a writ of habeas corpus, but Congress may suspend it in cases of rebellion or invasion (Art. I, sec. 9). Though President Lincoln suspended the writ on his own volition, Congress subsequently affirmed his action. A number of state constitutions absolutely forbid its suspension.

Hadley v. Junior College District of Kansas City, 397 U.S. 50 (1970): Ruled that the "one man, one vote" principle applies generally to *all*—national, state, and local—elections of governmental officials. The *Hadley* case declared that the "dilution" of the votes of people living in one of the districts comprising the Junior College District of Metropolitan Kansas City violates the equal protection clause of the Fourteenth Amendment. The unconstitutional dilution involved a state apportionment formula whereby 60 percent of the total electorate of the District could elect only 50 percent of the junior college trustees. *See also* APPORTIONMENT; *Baker v. Carr*; REDISTRICTING.

Hague Peace Conferences The first general international conferences, called in 1899 and 1907 to codify and develop rules and procedures related to the problems of armaments and war. The Hague Conferences, with twenty-six states participating in the first and forty-four in the second, produced conventions on the pacific settlement of international disputes, rules for the conduct of war and the treatment of prisoners, the rights and duties of neutrals, and rules regulating action to collect international debts. The conferences, however, produced no general agreement in the crucial areas of disarmament, arms limitation, and compulsory arbitration. *See also* PERMANENT COURT OF ARBITRATION.

Hague v. CIO, 307 U.S. 496 (1939): Declared unconstitutional under the Fourteenth Amendment an ordinance of Jersey City, N.J., that required permission to hold a meeting in or upon public streets, parks, or buildings. Under the ordinance, the officials of Jersey City had molested union organizers of the CIO and had denied them permission to hold meetings or to circulate handbills. *See also* FREEDOM OF ASSEMBLY.

Hare Plan A system of proportional representation, occasionally used in the United States, that is based on a single, transferable vote. Candidates vie in open competition for a number of elective offices. A quota is established and all candidates obtaining sufficient votes to meet it are declared elected. Surplus votes of winning candidates and the votes of candidates eliminated for low-vote totals are distributed according to the second choices expressed by the voters on their ballots. Votes are transferred in this manner until sufficient candidates have been declared elected to fill all elective seats. *See also* PROPORTIONAL REPRESENTATION.

Harriss Case, *see United States v. Harriss.*

Haushofer Geopolitik   The German branch of geopolitics developed by Karl Haushofer (1869–1946), army general, geographer, geologist, historian, and Far Eastern traveler. The *geopolitik* of General Haushofer began with the heartland theory of Mackinder, and with Friedrich Ratzel's and Rudolf Kjellen's concepts of space and of the organic state. He and his disciples at the Institute of Geopolitics in Munich used these ideas to explain German defeat in World War I and to plan future German conquests. As a major general in the German army, Haushofer no doubt viewed Adolf Hitler and the Nazi party as upstarts to be used for the realization of Germany's destiny. Hitler, on the other hand, used Haushofer *geopolitik,* particularly ideas like *lebensraum* (living-space), to suit his own purpose. In line with the heartland theory, Haushofer and his army followers advocated a German-Russian-Japanese bloc, with Germany destined to emerge as the dominant partner. Haushofer also saw that German power would be dissipated in the vastness of Russia should Hitler go through with his plan to invade the Soviet Union. When he tried to dissuade Hitler from this course, he fell from favor, was imprisoned in the concentration camp at Dachau in 1944, released after Germany's defeat in 1945, and committed suicide within a year. *See also* GEOPOLITICS.

Head Start School Program, *see* Office of Economic Opportunity.

Hearing (Administrative)   Adjudication by an administrative or regulatory agency of alleged violations of laws or of rules and regulations administered by it. Hearings are also held to give interested parties an opportunity to be heard prior to the promulgation of a rule. *See also* HEARING EXAMINER, QUASI-JUDICIAL

Hearing (Judicial)   In an equity case, a hearing is a trial, In a criminal case, a hearing is an examination of the accused to determine if he should be held for trial; this is generally referred to as a "preliminary hearing" or "preliminary examination." If a preliminary hearing is held in an equity case, it is called an interlocutory hearing.

Hearing (Legislative)   A public session of a committee of a legislative body to obtain information on a proposed law or resolution. In Congress, public hearings are commonly functions of subcommittees, which report their findings to the full committees. The theory behind hearings is that out of the "combat" between contestants using every ethical means to convince committee members of the wisdom of their positions will emerge the "true facts." The members can then make their decision, much like a judge and jury in a judicial proceeding. The hearings thus serve as a means by which American citizens can "petition" their elected representatives and seek to influence their decision making. *See also* INVESTIGATING COMMITTEE.

Hearing Examiner   An official who conducts hearings for a regulatory agency and makes recommendations to the heads of the agency on issuance of administrative orders. Under the Administrative Procedure Act of 1946, hearing examiners are appointed under civil service rules, are protected against arbitrary dismissal and loss of salary, and may not be assigned administrative duties. *See also* QUASI-JUDICIAL; ADMINISTRATIVE PROCEDURE ACT.

Heartland Theory   The theory that the state that could control the human and physical resources of the Eurasian landmass between Germany and Central Siberia would be in a position to control the world. The heartland theory was developed by the British geographer Sir Halford J. Mackinder (1869–1947) in his paper "The Geographical Pivot of History" (1904) and in his best-know work, *Democratic Ideals and Reality—A Study in the Politics of Reconstruction* (1919). The heartland theory emerged from Mackinder's detailed study of the global relationship between land and sea power. *See also* GEOPOLITICS.

Heart of Atlanta Motel v. United States, 379 U.S. 241 (1964): Upheld the constitutionality of Title II of the Civil Rights Act of 1964, a provision barring discrimination in restaurants, hotels, and other places of public accommodation, on the ground that it is a valid exercise of the power to regulate interstate commerce. In 1883, the Supreme Court struck down a similar federal law (*Civil Rights Cases,* 109 U.S. 3) on the ground that private acts of discrimination could not be forbidden by the national government. In the *Heart of Atlanta* case and its companion case, *Katzenbach v. McClung,* 379 U.S. 294 (1964), the Court found ample power in the commerce clause for the national government to prohibit discrimination against persons in accommodations that serve substantial numbers of interstate travelers or that rely upon interstate commerce for a substantial part of their supplies and materials. *See also* CIVIL RIGHTS ACT OF 1964.

Hegemony   The extension by one state of preponderant influence or control over another state or region. A policy of hegemony may result in a client-state or satellite relationship and the creation of a sphere of influence. *See also* SPHERE OF INFLUENCE.

Helvering v. Davis, *see* Social Security Cases.

Heuristic Device   A model, simulation, or other intellectual contrivance used as an aid to discovery or as a stimulus to investigation in the search for new thought formulations. A heuristic device is used not directly to seek explanations but as a source of insights to uncover new approaches or ways of understanding the subject under investigation. Research with a heuristic purpose seeks to generate tentative ideas and hypotheses. *See also* MODEL, SIMULATION.

HEW, *see* Department of Health, Education, and Welfare.

Hierarchy   A principle of administrative organization in which each person or office is under control of and responsible to the next highest level. In turn, the higher level is responsible to its superior for the conduct of those below. *See also* DECENTRALIZATION; DELEGATION OF AUTHORITY; UNITY OF COMMAND.

High Commissioner for Refugees, *see* United Nations High Commissioner for Regugees.

High Crimes and Misdemeanors   The Constitution provides in Article II, section 4, that the President, Vice President, and all civil officers of the United States are subject to impeachment and removal from office upon conviction for "treason, bribery, or other high crimes and misdemeanors." There has been no attempt to define precisely what acts might constitute high crimes and misdemeanors. Discretion is vested completely in Congress. *See also* IMPEACHMENT.

Higher Education Act of 1965   An act to broaden higher education opportunities through federal aid. Major programs include scholarships, work-study programs, guaranteed low-interest loans, aid to developing colleges, aid to college and university community service programs with emphasis on urban problems, aid for library resources, a National Teachers Corps to work in slum areas, and aid for fellowships for present and future teachers. In addition, the Act increases aid under the Higher Education Facilities Act of 1963, which authorized grants and loans for construction of public and private academic facilities.

High Seas   All of the world's oceans, seas, connecting arms, bays, and gulfs that lie outside of the national territorial waters of coastal states. The high seas are open to commerce and navigation by all countries. States may extend jurisdiction to vessels flying their flags on the high seas but not to the seas themselves. *See also* ADMIRALTY.

Historical Approach   The study of past events within particular time spans in which information is organized and interpreted chronologically. A researcher using the historical approach may be primarily concerned with the narration of events in time sequence, or he may try to recreate a "slice" of history in pursuit of answers to "why" questions. Continuities with earlier epochs may be determined and linkages established between them. The cumulative development of ideas during one time span, for example, may be studied to determine its impact on the institutions and societal changes that occurred during a subsequent period. Or the historical approach may be used to gain an understanding of the uniqueness of a culture, a society, a nation, or an international system. *See also* TRADITIONAL APPROACH.

Historical Inevitability (Communist Theory)   A philosophy of history by which Marx posited the preordained necessity and scientific certainty for the replacement of capitalism by socialism. Historical inevitability, according to Marx, results from the contradictions embedded in society's mode of production, which, under capitalism and preceding primitive, slave, and feudal patterns, has pitted the servile class against the exploiting class, producing an automatic movement from one stage to the next. To an orthodox Marxist, free will and individual initiative are insignificant in the broad sweep of the historical development of mankind.

Hobson's Theory of Imperialism, *see* Economic Imperialism.

Holding Company A corporation whose assets consist of stocks in operating companies, usually a controlling share in each of several allegedly competing companies (subsidiaries). Holding companies, although illegal under the common law, have been legalized by statute in many states. The policies and pricing of subsidiary companies are controlled through stock ownership and the membership of holding company officers on the boards of directors of subsidiaries.

Holism The theory that group properties or characteristics are distinct from those of the individuals who comprise them. Those who espouse the philosophy of holism consequently believe that a social investigator should study systems and structures as whole entities rather than treating them as aggregates of individuals to be studied in terms of individual behavior and psychological characteristics. *See also* REDUCTIONISM.

Homeostasis The tendency toward maintenance of stability in a system through self-adjustments that provide compensating responses to disruptive or destabilizing influences. The existence of homeostasis tends to create a *steady state* equilibrium condition. The role of homeostatic controls in maintaining a political system may be compared to the function of a thermostatically controlled heating system or to the function of the human body in adjusting to the impact of disease, injury, heat, cold, or other kinds of shocks and disturbances. Homeostasis produces a tendency toward an equilibrium condition, but not perfect equilibrium, since the latter could occur only in a closed system not subjected to inputs. *See also* SYSTEMS ANALYSIS.

Home Rule The power vested in a local unit of government, usually a city, to draft or change its own charter and to manage its affairs. Home rule limits legislative interference in local affairs. Most states permit some degree of freedom for cities and an increasing number are granting it to counties. Home rule may be required or permitted by the state constitution or be granted by the legislature without specific constitutional authorization. Under home rule, the voters choose a commission to draft a charter that may be approved or rejected by the voters. This is in contrast to the granting of charters by the legislature under special acts, general laws, or optional plans. The city under home rule has control over its local problems provided it does not violate the state constitution or general laws of the state. *See also* CHARTER, DILLON'S RULE.

Homestead Act of 1862 An historic act in which Congress offered 160 acres of the public domain to any person who would pay a $10 registration fee and live on the land for five years.

Hoover Commission A commission appointed in 1947 to study the organization of the executive branch. The group of twelve persons (four appointed by the President, four by the President pro tempore of the Senate, and four by the Speaker of the House), known as the Commission on Organization of the Executive Branch, was headed by former President Herbert Hoover. It filed its report in 1949. A second Hoover Commission, similarly appointed in 1953, was charged with the responsibility of suggesting which federal functions might be discontinued. *See also* REORGANIZATION ACT.

Hopper, *see* Bill.

Horizontal Federalism   The relationships among the states of the Union either imposed by the Constitution or undertaken voluntarily. This term is used to distinguish state-state relations from national-state relations (denoted by the term "vertical federalism"). Requirements imposed by the Constitution are that each state afford full faith and credit to the public acts, records, and judicial proceedings of other states, grant the citizens of each state the privileges and immunities of citizens of their own state, and return fugitives from justice. Voluntary arrangements include interstate compacts, uniform laws, reciprocal agreements, and cooperation through consultation. *See also* FULL FAITH AND CREDIT, INTERSTATE COMPACT, INTERSTATE RENDITION, PRIVILEGES AND IMMUNITIES, UNIFORM STATE LAWS.

"Hot Line" Agreement   An American-Soviet Memorandum of Understanding signed at Geneva on June 20, 1963, under which an official teletype communications link was established between Washington and Moscow to permit direct contact between heads of government during a crisis. Similar teletype cable links were established between Paris and Moscow in 1966, and between London and Moscow in 1967. The "hot line" agreement was developed out of a fear that nuclear war might be initiated as a result of misunderstanding, miscalculation, accident, or failure to communicate.

Hot Pursuit   The international legal doctrine that permits the apprehension on or over the high seas of vessels or aircraft suspected of having violated national laws within national territorial jurisdiction. Under international law, hot pursuit must be: (1) begun within the jurisdiction of the offended state; (2) engaged in only by the public vessels or aircraft of the territorial sovereign; (3) continuous until the pursued vessel is arrested; or (4) broken off when the vessel has passed into the territorial waters of another state. *See also* INNOCENT PASSAGE, TERRITORIAL WATERS.

House Calendar, *see* Calendar.

House of Commons (Britain)   The lower and more powerful of the two Houses of Parliament. The House of Commons meets more frequently for longer periods and considers a wider and more complex range of topics than the House of Lords. Commons is a representative body and members are elected by universal suffrage from constituencies established by nonpolitical, permanent boundary commissions. Minimum age to vote and to sit in Commons is twenty-one. Of the 630 seats, 511 are from England, thirty-six from Wales, 71 from Scotland, and twelve from Northern Ireland. Members are chosen by general election after dissolution of Parliament or at a by-election when a vacancy occurs.

House Of Lords (Britain)   The upper but less powerful of the two Houses of Parliament and the world's oldest legislative assembly. Lords is descended from the ancient *Curia Regis* or King's Court, nobles summoned by the sovereign to provide him with "aids" (taxes) when the expenses of the kingdom outran his private resources. Later, when representatives of cities, towns, and counties were summoned, the House of Commons began to evolve. Thus representation in Parliament came to be based in one chamber on "name" (title), and, in the other, on election. Peers (lords) are created by the monarch on the advice of the Prime Minister. The major legislative role of the nine-hundred-member House of Lords involves reviewing legislation passed in Commons, approving it, or returning it for revision. The Lords may reduce the workload of the Commons by originating noncontroversial legislation and by considering private bills. Since the Parliamentary Act of 1911, the House of Lords cannot reject a money bill. The Parliamentary Act of 1949 permits a bill to become law over the opposition of the House of Lords if it has been passed by two successive sessions of the House of Commons and if one year has elapsed since the second reading. The House of Lords, the highest judicial tribunal in the nation, does not possess the United States Supreme Court's power to review the constitutionality of legislation because of parliamentary supremacy and the fusion of powers.

House of Representatives   The lower house of the bicameral Congress, in which representation is based on population. The upper house, the Senate of the United States, is based on the principle of state equality. The House was intended by the Founding Fathers to be the popular chamber of Congress, and it was made larger and more responsive to the public will than the Senate, which was intended to represent the states and to function as the more deliberative body. Each state is guaranteed at least one representative. Since 1910, the House has had a permanent membership of 435. The ratio of population to representatives has been steadily increasing until now it is more than 475,000 per representative. The Constitution vests certain powers exclusively in the House. Among them are: (1) the impeachment power; (2) the initiation of revenue bills; (3) the election of a President if no candidate obtains a majority in the Electoral College; (4) the determination of its own rules of procedure; and (5) the discipline of its members. *See also* SENATE.

Housing Act of 1949   An act providing for federal assistance to local governments for low-rent public housing, slum clearance, and urban renewal. The Housing Act of 1949 continued a program, begun under the Housing Act of 1937, that had been interrupted by World War II. The 1949 Act called for the construction of 810,000 housing units over a period of six years but Congress reduced this figure in subsequent legislation. In amendments to the Act since 1949, additional housing units have been authorized and increased emphasis given to urban renewal and new community development. Various specialized housing programs have been instituted, such as those for college dormitories, housing for the aged, and rent subsidies for the poor. Funds have also been made available for municipal public works, such as sewers and transportation. The Department of Housing and Urban Development supervises administration of the Act. *See also* PUBLIC HOUSING, URBAN RENEWAL.

Human Rights Protection for individuals from arbitrary interference with or curtailment of life, liberty, and the equal protection of the laws by government or private individuals and groups. Domestic guarantees embodied in national constitutions and laws are supplemented by international protection afforded through the actions of international organizations. Many nations also regard the safeguarding of the economic and social rights of individuals—as, for example, the right to employment, to medical protection, to leisure—equal in importance to the older concept of political rights. Several regional organizations also provide guarantees for human rights. *See also* CIVIL LIBERTIES, CIVIL RIGHTS, EUROPEAN CONVENTION ON HUMAN RIGHTS, GENOCIDE CONVENTION, UNIVERSAL DECLARATION OF HUMAN RIGHTS.

Human Rights Commission, *see* Universal Declaration of Human Rights.

Humphrey's Executor [Rathbun] v. United States, 295 U.S. 602 (1935): Upheld the provisions of the Federal Trade Commission Act providing that members of the Commission may be removed from office only for causes specified in the Act. President Roosevelt had removed Humphrey for political reasons, and in this case, decided after Humphrey's death, the Court held that Congress clearly had the authority to limit the President's removal power to instances of "inefficiency, neglect of duty, or malfeasance in office." The Court pointed out that the broad removal powers accorded to the President in *Myers v. United States,* 272 U.S. 52 (1926), pertained only to purely executive officers, whereas members of the Federal Trade Commission exercise legislative and judicial powers as well. *See also Myers* case.

Hurtado v. California, 110 U.S. 516 (1884): Established that a state is not required by the due process clause of the Fourteenth Amendment to provide for indictment by grand jury in felony cases. Indictment by information is consistent with fair procedure. *See also* GRAND JURY.

Hypothesis A statement of an expected relationship between variables that may be tested empirically to determine its validity. A hypothesis may be derived from observation, deduced from a larger body of theory, or based simply on a hunch that the investigator is willing to use as a provisional working hypothesis. A hypothesis is typically presented as an assertive statement to be confirmed or denied, as for example: "Voters in American suburban areas tend to vote Republican." *See also* ASSUMPTION, PROPOSITION, SCIENTIFIC METHOD, TESTING, THEORY.

IAEA, *see* International Atomic Energy Agency.

IBRD, *see* International Bank for Reconstruction and Development.

ICAO, *see* International Civil Aviation Organization.

ICC, *see* Interstate Commerce Commission.

ICJ, *see* International Court of Justice.

IDA, *see* International Development Association.

Idealist Policy, *see* Realist - Idealist Dichotomy.

Ideal Type   A concept whose characteristics are represented in so extreme or pure a form that exact referents for the concept are seldom if ever found in reality. An ideal type nevertheless reflects some aspects of reality and may be used as a base for judging, explaining, or investigating reality. An ideal type, like other types, is an abstraction. The difference is that individuals may readily be found that perfectly satisfy the requirements of an ordinary type. Thus, many individuals meet the requirements of the "politician" as a type. On the other hand the concept of rational decision making is an ideal type. Some human behavior may approximate the model of rational decision making but no example of the perfectly rational decision-making situation ever existed. In principle such an example might exist, but in practice the requirements are too demanding. Other examples of ideal types might be the concept of equilibrium in a political system or the notion of political man.

Ideological Warfare   One of the tactics used by the Communist and free world blocs in the cold war. Each side seeks to achieve ideological conformity among its own people while trying to convert the large masses of mankind outside its borders to its basic values and "way of life." Ideology comprises the ideas and ideals of a political and economic system. The struggle involves competition between Soviet-style communism and western-style capitalism and democracy. *See also* IDEOLOGY, PROPAGANDA.

Ideology   The "way of life" of a people reflected in terms of their political system, economic order, social goals, and moral values. Ideology is particularly concerned with the form and role of government and the nature of a state's economic system. Ideology is the means by which the basic values held by a party, class, or group are articulated. *See also* IDEOLOGICAL WARFARE.

Idiographic Explanation, *see* Nomothetic Explanation.

IDO, *see* International Disarmament Organization.

IFC, *see* International Finance Corporation.

If-then Statement, *see* Prediction.

ILC, *see* International Law Commission.

Illinois v. Allen, *see* Contempt of Court.

ILO, *see* International Labor Organization.

IMCO, *see* Inter-Governmental Maritime Consultative Organization.

IMF, *see* International Monetary Fund.

Immigration   Admittance of a person to a country of which he is not a native for the purpose of establishing permanent residence. Early attempts by seaboard states to regulate immigration into the United States were invalidated by the Supreme Court, which declared immigration to be an exclusive function of the national government, incidental to its power over foreign affairs. Immigration into the United States was unlimited until 1882, when Congress began to impose restrictions on the admission of criminals, the mentally ill, paupers, diseased persons, illiterates, the Chinese, anarchists, and advocates of violent governmental change. In 1924, Congress barred Asiatics and established the "national origins quota" system, which limited annual immigration and assigned a quota to each country based on the numerical contribution it had made to the national stock as of 1920. In 1952, Congress erased racial exclusions but retained the quota system and the annual limit. Restrictions against the admission of Communists or other suspected subversives were increased. In 1965, Congress abolished the national origins quota system and established a new annual limit of 170,000, with preference given to relatives of citizens and persons with special skills. Immigration from the Western Hemisphere was restricted for the first time. Immigration laws are administered by the Department of State and the Department of Justice, and each has been given extensive discretion to determine who may enter the United States. *See also* IMMIGRATION ACT OF 1965, *The Passenger Cases.*

Immigration Act of 1965   A major revision of American immigration policy that eliminated the national-origins quota system. Under the quota system, in effect since 1924, American immigration policy discriminated against Asians, Africans, and southern and eastern Europeans. The overall quota was set at less than 157,000 immigrants per year, with nearly 127,000 assigned to northern and western Europe. It was often criticized as racist in philosophy and as detrimental to the American international position. The 1965 law ended the quota system, established an annual limit of 170,000 immigrants (no more than 20,000 from one country), and gave preference to relatives of citizens and persons with special skills. For the first time, a limit (120,000) was placed on immigrants from the Western Hemisphere. *See also* IMMIGRATION.

Immigration and Nationality Act of 1952 (McCarran-Walter Act)   A major revision and restatement of the immigration and citizenship policies of the United States. The Act maintained the quota system for immigration and placed restrictions upon the immigration and naturalization of Communists and other totalitarians. All racial barriers to immigration were eliminated by the Act, but Asians, Africans, and southern and eastern Europeans were assigned small quotas. (The Immigration Act of 1965, however, eliminated the quota system.) Communists or other persons advocating violent overthrow of the government are denied admission to the United States. Further, such persons residing in this country may not be naturalized, and citizenship may be taken from naturalized persons who join the Communist party or refuse to testify before a congressional committee investigating subversive activities.

Immigration and Naturalization Service   The part of the Department of Justice that administers the laws regarding the admission, naturalization, and deportation of aliens. The Service investigates the credentials of immigrants at ports of entry. Immigration and Naturalization Service officers also patrol the Canadian and Mexican borders to prevent the illegal entry of aliens. Aliens seeking to become citizens are investigated by agents of the Service, who recommend to the courts whether or not the alien should be naturalized. *See also* IMMIGRATION, NATURALIZATION.

Immunity   A privilege granted to a person that exempts him from prosecution for any self-incriminating testimony given by him before a court, grand jury, or investigating committee. Immunity involves an enforced waiver of the constitutional right against self-incrimination, so that an individual can be compelled to give testimony or be punished for contempt. No evidence revealed by a witness who has been granted immunity may be used against him in any criminal prosecution, state or federal, or subject him to any penalty by either level of government (*Murphy v. Waterfront Commission*, 378 U.S. 52 [1964]). Many states and the national government make provisions for the granting of immunity to witnesses. *See also* SELF-INCRIMINA-TION.

Impact Panel, *see* Panel Study.

Impeachment   A formal accusation, rendered by the lower house of a legislative body, that commits an accused civil official for trial in the upper house. Impeachment is, therefore, merely the first step in a two-stage process. In the national government, constitutional authority to *impeach* is vested in the House and the power to *try* impeachment cases rests with the Senate. All civil officers of the United States are subject to impeachment, excluding military officers and members of Congress. The impeachment process begins with the preferring of charges by a representative, followed by referral to either the Judiciary Committee or to a special investigating committee. A simple majority vote of the House is sufficient to impeach. "Articles of impeachment" are drawn up, setting forth the basis for removal. The House appoints managers who prosecute the case in a trial before the Senate. If a President is on trial, the Chief Justice of the United States presides. The procedure during the trial closely resembles that of a court of law. A two-thirds vote of the Senators present is necessary for conviction. The only punishments that may be meted out are removal from office and disqualification from holding any office in the future. Once removed, however, the individual may be tried in a regular court of law if he has committed a criminal act. The President's pardoning power does not apply to impeachment convictions. *See also* HIGH CRIMES AND MISDEMEANORS.

Imperialism   A superior-inferior relationship in which an area and its people have been subordinated to the will of a foreign state. Imperialism can be traced through several chronological stages of development in the modern world. The first stage, which dates approximately from the voyages of Columbus to the end of the Seven Years' War in 1763, was a consequence of the emergence of the European nation-state and the economic philosophy of mercantilism. During this period, much of the New World of the Western Hemisphere was brought under European control by conquest and colonization, and initial imperial forays into Asia were launched by trading companies chartered by European states. In the second stage, from 1763 to about 1870, little imperial expansion occurred because of European preoccupation with the development of liberal nationalism and the Industrial Revolution. The third stage, from 1870 to World War I, saw the last great wave of imperial expansion sweep across Africa and much of the Far East. In this period the industrial states reacted to an increasing competition in international trade by seeking to create protected markets and sources of supply. By World War I imperialism had reached its zenith and began slowly to recede. Following World War II, the process of liquidating empires accelerated as the concept fell into disrepute, the economic costs of imperialism increased, and a wave of nationalism enveloped Asia and Africa. The motives for imperialism have varied over time and with the nations involved, but major arguments have included: (1) economic necessity—markets, raw materials, gold "trade follows the flag"; (2) national security—strategic location, materials, man power; (3) prestige—"manifest destiny," a "place in the sun," "the sun never sets on the British Empire"; and (4) humanitarianism—missionary activity, the "white man's burden," civilizing mission. *See also* COLONIALISM, CULTURAL IMPERIALISM, ECONOMIC IMPERIALISM, IMPERIALISM AND COLONIALISM (COMMUNIST THEORY).

Imperialism And Colonialism (Communist Theory)   An assumption that economic contradictions created by the nature of capitalism lead states into undertaking policies of overseas imperialism and colonialism. Capitalist imperialism and colonialism have been explained by communists since Lenin's time as the means for opening new outlets for investments, for finding new markets for the excess production that cannot be sold on the home market because of the impoverishment of the masses, and for securing cheap raw materials to feed the domestic factories. The need to pursue overseas policies of conquest and control grew out of the changing nature of capitalism, which had moved from the early competitive stage to a "monopoly stage" dominated by cartels and trusts. The result, according to Lenin, would be increasing imperialist rivalry leading to major wars among capitalist states.

Imperialist Policy, *see* Revisionist Policy.

Imperial Preferences, *see* Commonwealth Preferences.

Implied Powers   Authority possessed by the national government by inference from those powers delegated to it in the Constitution. For example, the power to draft men into the armed forces may be deduced from the power delegated to raise armies and navies. The implied power concept derives from the "necessary and proper" clause in Article I, section 8, which empowers the national government to do all things necessary and proper to carry out its delegated powers. This principle was officially enunciated by the Supreme Court in *McCulloch v. Maryland*, 4 Wheaton 316 (1819). *See also* CONSTITUTIONAL CONSTRUCTION, *McCulloch v. Maryland*, NECESSARY AND PROPER CLAUSE.

Important Question (United Nations)   An issue placed before the General Assembly that requires a two-thirds vote to reach a decision. The Charter (Article 18) stipulates that important questions include: (1) recommendations on peace and security; (2) election of members to the three Councils; (3) admission of new members; (4) suspension of rights and privileges and explusion of members; (5) questions relating to the operation of the trusteeship system; and (6) budgetary questions. Assembly proposals for amendments to the Charter (Article 108) also require a two-thirds vote. The determination of additional categories of important questions can be made by a simple majority of members present and voting.

Incidence, *see* Tax Incidence.

Income Support Plan, *see* Family Assistance Plan.

Income Tax   A tax levied on income received from profits, salaries, rents, interest, dividends, and other sources, less deductions permitted by law. The national government's income tax includes a tax on both individual income and corporation income, with different rates applicable to each. Most of the fifty states also levy income taxes, many applicable to both individual and corporate income. Many cities, because of increasing resistance to higher property taxes, have adopted an income tax. *See also* SIXTEENTH AMENDMENT, WITHHOLDING TAX.

Incorporated and Unincorporated Areas   The legal status of a local unit of government. Incorporated units include cities, villages, and, in some states, towns and boroughs. Unincorporated units include counties, townships, New England towns, and school districts. Incorporated areas are also called municipal corporations and unincorporated places are known as quasi-corporations.

Incumbent   An officeholder seeking re-election.

Independent   A voter who disregards party affiliation of candidates running for elective office and casts his ballot for the "best man" or on the basis of issues. Most independents are not party members, but a few retain membership in a party, enabling them to vote in primaries while exercising their own judgment in general elections. Empirical studies of voting behavior tend to show that most independents are politically apathetic and possess less information about candidates and issues than strong party supporters.

Independent Agency   A federal agency that is not part of the eleven executive departments. The term may include independent regulatory commissions, but is generally used to describe agencies which perform service rather than regulatory functions. Examples of independent agencies are the Civil Service Commission, the Veterans Administration, and the General Services Administration. Many independent agencies are organized like regular departments and are headed by persons responsible to the President. Others take the form of boards or commissions, such as the Tariff Commission and the Atomic Energy Commission.

Independent Regulatory Commission   An agency outside the major executive departments charged with the regulation of important aspects of the economy. The Commissions are the Interstate Commerce Commission, Federal Trade Commission, Federal Power Commission, Securities and Exchange Commission, Federal Communications Commission, National Labor Relations Board, Civil Aeronautics Board, Federal Reserve Board, and Federal Maritime Commission. All of these agencies are empowered to establish rules for the particular industries they regulate and to prosecute violators. All are multi-headed, with five or seven members, except for the eleven-member Interstate Commerce Commission. (For specific commissions, *see* Index.)

Independent Variable, *see* Variable.

Indeterminate Sentence   A sentence of imprisonment with minimum and maximum limits set by the court or by statute. Once the prisoner serves the minimum sentence, he may be released upon approval of a parole board or a special commission. This is the procedure now used in most states in place of the fixed sentence. *See also* PAROLE.

Indeterminism, *see* Determinism.

Index of Intercoder Reliability, *see* Content Analysis, Reliability.

Indiana Ballot, *see* Party-Column Ballot.

Indian Affairs, *see* Department of the Interior.

Indictment   The formal accusation, drawn up by the prosecutor and brought by a grand jury, charging a person with the commission of a crime. *See also* GRAND JURY.

Indirect Approach (Disarmament)   A strategy for seeking agreement on disarmament that places primary emphasis on resolving major political and related issues as necessary antecedents to the development of a consensus on disarmament. Advocates of the indirect approach regard disarmament as a secondary rather than an immediate objective, since in their view armaments are a product of the deep insecurities of the state system fostered by conflicts of national interests. The indirect approach differs from the direct approach, which postulates that the arms race itself is responsible for world tensions and, consequently, must be ameliorated first. *See also* DIRECT APPROACH.

Indirect Initiative, *see* Initiative.

Individual Freedom, *see* Civil Liberties.

Individualism The political, economic, and social concept that places primary emphasis on the worth, freedom, and well-being of the individual rather than on those of the group, society or nation. The concept of individualism, may be contrasted with that of collectivism, which describes those systems in which primary emphasis is placed on the rights and welfare of the group. *See also* DEMOCRACY, LAISSEZ-FAIRE.

Indoor Relief Care of the needy in public institutions. Indoor relief is usually provided for the aged, the chronically ill, and the mentally incompetent. Prior to 1935 and the passage of the Social Security Act, many poor but healthy persons were cared for in public almshouses, poorhouses, poor farms, asylums, county homes, or institutions of like names. Indoor relief has largely been replaced by "outdoor relief," which provides money, food, and medical care to persons who continue to live in their own homes. *See also* OUTDOOR RELIEF.

Induction The process of reasoning from the particular to the general, drawing general conclusions from observation of individual cases. Induction thus is used to develop generalizations concerning a class of events by observing particular events and drawing conclusions therefrom. Induction, as a *method of inquiry,* is both empirical (observing events) and logical (drawing conclusions), whereas the *deductive* process of drawing conclusions about specific events from general premises is strictly logical. *See also* A POSTERIORI, EMPIRICISM.

Inductive Statistics, *see* Statistics.

Industrialization, *see* United Nations Industrial Development Organization.

Inference A conclusion reached by reasoning from a previous conclusion or from evidence that plausibly suggests, but does not establish, the conclusion inferred. An inference involves a logical leap from evidence to conclusion, or from one conclusion to another. Intentions, for example, which cannot be observed, may be inferred from a conduct which is observable. Thus, State A may infer from increased arms expenditures in State B that State B is preparing to attack. The inference may not be correct, but decision makers in State A may act on the assumption that it is. *See also* ASSUMPTION.

Inferential Statistics, *see* Statistics.

Inflation   An economic condition in which the price level is increased and the value of money in terms of purchasing power is consequently decreased. Inflation may result from either an increase in the amount of money and credit available or a decrease in the supply of consumer goods. *See also* DEFLATION, MONETARY POLICY.

Influence   The capability of a political actor to affect the behavior of others in a manner favored by the actor. The successful use of influence may induce change (or inhibit undesired change) in predispositions, opinions, attitudes, and beliefs as well as more overt behaviors. The capacity of an actor to influence others depends on many factors. Among them are the political resources at his command, the type and extent of the influence exerted, the domain in which he functions (that is, those who may be subjected to his influence efforts), the competitive attempts by others to influence the same subjects, and the extent of compliance sought. An actor's maximum potential ability to change the behavior of others is seldom employed because of the costs to him or his cause which are likely to result if he commits all his political resources. *See also* AUTHORITY, POLITICS, POWER.

In Forma Pauperis, *see* Appeal.

Information (Legal)   An accusation made under oath by a prosecuting attorney before a court, charging a person with a crime. Though regularly used for minor offenses, more than half the states have substituted the information for indictment by grand jury in serious cases as well. The national government is making increased use of the information for noncapital offenses.

Information, *see* Communications Theory.

Infrastructure Development   The economic, political, and social base to support a society's drive to achieve modernization. Infrastructure development involves institutional change to support a national effort to develop such facilities as roads, dams, power plants, and communication, irrigation, and transportation systems. Once the infrastructure base has been created, a nation's economy may—if capital for industrialization is available—move to the stage of self-sustaining economic growth. *See also* FOREIGN AID.

Inherent Powers   Authority vested in the national government, particularly in the area of foreign affairs, that does not depend upon any specific grant of power in the Constitution. Inherent powers derive from the fact that the United States is a sovereign power among nations. The Supreme Court has pointed out that even if the Constitution made no mention of it, the national government could still, for example, make international agreements or acquire territory. Whether or not the President has inherent powers to meet emergencies in internal affairs by virtue of his position as chief executive, is a matter of dispute. *See also United States v. Curtiss-Wright Export Corp., Youngstown Sheet and Tube Co. v. Sawyer.*

Inheritance Tax, *see* Estate Tax.

Initiative   An electoral device by which interested citizens can propose legislation or constitutional amendments through initiatory petitions signed by the required number of registered voters. The number of signatures varies from 5 to 15 percent of the voters in the different states. The proposition is then voted on by the people. Constitutional amendment proposals usually require a greater number of signatures on the petitions. The "direct" initiative involves a vote of the people following the filing of petitions. The "indirect" provides that the proposal, after being filed, be sent to the legislature; if not approved, it then goes before the voters. *See also* DIRECT LEGISLATION.

Injunction   An order issued by a court in an equity proceeding to compel or restrain the performance of an act by an individual or government official. A "mandatory" injunction demands that something be done, although the term "injunction" generally refers to a restraining order. Violation of an injunction constitutes contempt of court, punishable by fine or imprisonment. *See also* WRIT, EQUITY, INJUNCTION (LABOR).

Injunction (Labor)   A court order to compel or restrain the performance of an act. In the field of labor, the injunction became a weapon in the hands of management to restrain the activities of labor unions during their formative period. For many years, the injunction was used to enforce the Sherman Antitrust Act against unions. The Norris-LaGuardia Act of 1932 outlawed the use of the labor injunction when labor pursues lawful ends by legitimate means. The Taft-Hartley Act of 1947, however, empowers the President to seek an injunction when a labor dispute threatens the national welfare. *See also* INJUNCTION .

Inner Six, *see* European Economic Community.

Innocent Passage   The right of foreign vessels to traverse the territorial waters of another state without capricious interference by the coastal sovereign. Innocent passage includes stopping and anchoring but only when incidental to ordinary navigation or made necessary by *force majeure* (superior force) or by distress. *See also* TERRITORIAL WATERS.

Input   In systems terminology any influence that affects the functioning of a political system. In a political system inputs result in demands upon and support for the system, which converts them into outputs in the form of authoritative policies and implementing actions. Inputs originate in the environment of the system and within the system itself. Inputs originating within the system are sometimes called *withinputs*. Theorists have tended to classify inputs of political systems into generic functional categories, such as political socialization and recruitment, interest articulation, interest aggregation, and political communication. *See also* COMMUNICATIONS THEORY, OUTPUT, SYSTEMS ANALYSIS.

Inquest, *see* Coroner.

Inquiry   Formal, impartial determination of the facts involved in an international dispute. Inquiry procedure involves the establishment of a factfinding commission by the parties to the dispute or by some international body. After conducting its investigation, the commission of inquiry issues a report of its findings to the disputants or to the international agency. Unless inquiry is followed by additional peaceful settlement procedures like mediation or conciliation, the parties to the dispute are left free to determine the use to be made of the findings. *See also* PEACEFUL SETTLEMENT.

Inquiry, Scientific, *see* Research

In Re Gault, 387 U.S. 1 (1967): Held that the due process clause of the Fourteenth Amendment requires the essentials of fair treatment in cases involving juveniles accused of crime. The Court reversed a decision committing a child to an industrial school for six years, holding that in juvenile proceedings: (1) adequate notice of a hearing must be given; (2) the child must be informed of his right to counsel and the privilege against self-incrimination; and (3) he must be given an opportunity to confront and cross-examine witnesses. *See also* JUVENILE DELINQUENT.

Inspection (Disarmament)   The establishment of machinery to verify compliance with or to detect violations of a disarmament treaty. In the negotiation of an inspection system, specific questions to be answered would be likely to include: (1) Should inspections be carried on by a national or international body; (2) What should be the extent of access to each country's territory; (3) What forms of inspection should be utilized; (4) How frequently should inspections be conducted; (5) What powers should be exercised by inspection teams; and (6) What constitutes a violation of the disarmament agreement? *See also* ENFORCEMENT.

Institution   An established pattern of human behavior consisting of structured social interaction within a framework of relevant values. Political institutions on the local, national, and international levels range from constitutions and other basic documents and customs to formal legislative, executive, administrative, and judicial structures and processes. The traditional *institutional approach* in political science emphasizes the study of political structures and processes, utilizing mainly government documents and official records as source materials. *See also* SOCIAL SYSTEM, STRUCTURE, TRADITIONAL APPROACH.

Institutional Approach, *see* Institution.

Institutional Group, *see* Group.

Insurgency   A revolt against an established government not reaching the proportions of a full-scale revolution. Under international law, an insurgency is a rebellion not recognized as a "belligerency" or civil war. An insurgency may result in the issuance of proclamations by other states warning their citizens to exercise caution in commercial and travel relations, but it is regarded as primarily a domestic matter by the international community. If the revolt is not quashed in due time by the lawful government through counterinsurgency actions, however, other states may accord belligerent status to the rebels. *See also* BELLIGERENCY, CIVIL WAR, REVOLUTION.

Intangible Tax, *see* Personal Property Tax.

Integral Nationalism   An intolerant, ethnocentric form of nationalism that glorifies the state as the highest focus of individual loyalties. Integral, or totalitarian, nationalism aggressively concentrates on the security of the state, the augmentation of its power vis-à-vis other states, and on the pursuit of national policies motivated by narrow self-interest. Liberal nationalism began to give way to integral nationalism by the end of the nineteenth century under the impact of industrial, trade, imperial, and military rivalries and as a result of increases in popular pressures for the state to protect the economic and social interests of the masses against foreign competition. Integral nationalism is best typified by the fascist totalitarianism of the 1930s and 1940s. Various mainifestations of the same phenomenon are also observable in the ideological rivalries and national power struggles of the post-World War II period. *See also* FASCISM.

Integration, Political, *see* Functionalism, Political Community, Political Integration.

Integrative Functionalism, *see* Functionalism (Integrative).

Intelligence   Information gathered by a government about other states' capabilities and intentions. Military or strategic intelligence is concerned with uncovering the strength and location of land, sea, and air forces, new weapons and weapons development, troop morale and combat qualities, strategic and tactical plans, secret alliances and agreements, and civilian attitudes and morale. Counterintelligence units are active at the same time in trying to ferret out espionage agents carrying on military intelligence activities for other nations. Nonstrategic intelligence efforts are also carried on by most nations to secure pertinent political, diplomatic, economic, and social data to aid governments in pursuit of national interest objectives. Most intelligence is secured openly through careful scrutiny of public documents and private news and data sources, but the more critical strategic information often requires the use of clandestine "cloak-and-dagger" methods. *See also* CENTRAL INTELLIGENCE AGENCY, INTELLIGENCE (UNITED STATES).

Intelligence (United States)   Gathering information about the capabilities and intentions of foreign governments. Most intelligence is secured by analyzing data found in governmental and private publications, but some requires the use of clandestine cloak-and-dagger methods. American agencies actively engaged in the gathering and/or analysis of intelligence include: (1) the Central Intelligence Agency (CIA), which carries on undercover activities around the globe and serves as a central focus for the receipt and evaluation of intelligence; (2) the National Security Agency (NSA), which engages in coding and decoding operations and electronic surveillance; (3) Army Intelligence (G2), which secures data on ground forces and new weapons; (4) Air Force Intelligence (A2), which covers air and space affairs; (5) the Office of Naval Intelligence (ONI), which ferrets out information on foreign navies and fleet movements; (6) the Bureau of Intelligence and Research (I & R) in the State Department, which obtains economic and political data and forecasts trends; (7) the Defense Intelligence Agency (DIA) of the Department of Defense, which evaluates the capabilities of allies and potential enemies; (8) the Atomic Energy Commission (AEC), which seeks data on nuclear weapons and detects nuclear test explosions; and (9) the Federal Bureau of Investigation (FBI), which obtains information on internal threats to security. The United States Intelligence Board, headed by the Director of the CIA, meets regularly to sift information gathered by intelligence agencies and to give a "national intelligence estimate" to the President. *See also* CENTRAL INTELLIGENCE AGENCY.

Interaction   Reciprocal activity involving two or more individuals or groups in which the actions of each party serve as stimuli for responses from the other(s). Such stimulus and response actions may be continuous, constituting a *pattern* of interaction. All interaction involves some form of contact, either direct in such forms as speech, body actions, and listening or indirect through written or other forms of distant communication. Political interaction occurs between individuals, pressure groups, parties, governmental units, international agencies, states—in fact, within and between all political systems. *See also* POLITICAL ACTION, POLITICAL COMMUNICATION.

Inter-American Conference, *see* Organization of American States.

Inter-American Development Bank   An international banking institution established by the Organization of American States in 1959 to accelerate economic development in Latin America. The Inter-American Development Bank is authorized total resources of $1 billion ($850 million in capital stock and $150 million for a Fund for Special Operations). The United States and all Latin American countries except Cuba are members. Subscriptions are on the same basis as quotas for the International Monetary Fund, with the United States providing approximately forty-one percent of the total authorized capital. Loans are made to members, their political subdivisions, or to private entities. In ordinary operations, loans are repayable in the borrowed currency, but loans from the Fund for Special Operations are repayable wholly or in part in the debtor's currency. *See also* CAPITAL, REGIONAL DEVELOPMENT BANKS.

Inter-American Peace Committee, *see* Organization of American States.

Inter-American Treaty of Reciprocal Assistance, *see* Rio Treaty.

Intercoder Reliability Index, *see* Content Analysis, Reliability.

Interest Group, *see* Group, Pressure Group.

Interest, National, *see* National Interest.

Interests, *see* Aggregation of Interests, Articulation of Interests.

Intergovernmental Maritime Consultative Organization (IMCO)   A specialized agency of the United Nations, established to further cooperation in matters relating to shipping, safety, and passenger service on the high seas. IMCO was established under a 1948 convention that came into force in 1958 after receiving sufficient ratifications. IMCO's structure includes an Assembly that meets every two years, with all members having an equal vote, a Council of sixteen members that functions as an executive body, a Maritime Safety Committee, and a secretariat at its London headquarters headed by a secretary-general. *See also* SPECIALIZED AGENCY.

Intergovernmental Tax Immunity   The exemption of state and national governmental agencies and property from taxation by each other. The doctrine of intergovernmental tax immunity had its origin in the case of *McCulloch v. Maryland,* 4 Wheaton 316 (1819), in which the Supreme Court declared that the states may not burden the national government by the taxation of its agents or functions. This doctrine was later extended to national taxation of state agents and functions. For a time, even the salaries of governmental employees and contractors were exempt from taxation; this is no longer the case. National governmental functions and properties are exempt from state taxation, but where hardship may result, because of extensive federal holdings in a state, payments in lieu of taxes may be authorized by Congress. State or local activities may be taxed by the national government if the function is nongovernmental in character. An example of this is national taxation of state-owned liquor stores. *See also McCulloch v. Maryland, Graves v. New York, South Carolina v. United States,* PROPRIETARY FUNCTION.

Interlocking Directorates   A means by which competing companies reduce or eliminate competition among themselves by having the same individuals as members of the boards of directors of their companies. *See also* CLAYTON ACT.

Interlocutory Hearing, *see* Hearing (Judicial).

Intermediate Court   A court of appeals below the level of the highest court. It is found in about one-fourth of the states, mainly those with large populations. In about half the states, county courts function as intermediate courts as well as trial courts by hearing cases *de novo* (a new trial) appealed from decisions of municipal and justice of the peace courts. In both cases, "intermediate" refers to the fact that these courts exercise appellate jurisdiction with further appeal possible to a higher court.

Internal Revenue Service (IRS)   A unit in the Department of the Treasury that has major responsibility for the collection of all taxes except customs duties. The Internal Revenue Service is headed by a Commissioner and operates through district offices, each headed by a director.

Internal Security Act of 1950 (McCarran Act)   An act designed to place the Communist party and other totalitarian groups, under rigid controls. The Act outlaws any conspiracy, peaceful or violent, that has as its purpose the establishment of a foreign-controlled dictatorship in the United States. A Subversive Activities Control Board has been established to designate Communist "action" groups, "fronts," or Communist "infiltrated" organizations. Once identified, action and front groups must register with the Attorney General, listing their officers and members, financial records, and any printing equipment under their control. Publications of these organizations must be labeled as Communist propaganda. Infiltrated trade unions lose all rights under national labor laws. Individual members of any of these groups may not hold office in a labor union, obtain a passport, or work in any public office, and members of action groups are barred from defense plants. The law also strengthens espionage and sedition laws and immigration requirements and provides for the deportation of Communist aliens. Another provision established procedures for detention of suspected saboteurs in an emergency but was repealed in 1971. *See also* SUBVERSIVE ACTIVITIES CONTROL BOARD.

International Atomic Energy Agency (IAEA)   An agency of the United Nations established in 1957 to foster cooperation among nations in developing atomic energy for peaceful purposes. The IAEA was first proposed by President Eisenhower in his Atoms for Peace proposals before the General Assembly in 1953. *See also* ATOMS FOR PEACE PLAN.

International Bank for Reconstruction and Development (IBRD)   A Specialized Agency of the United Nations, known informally as the World Bank, that makes loans to member nations for economic rehabilitation or developmental purposes. The Bank was created by the Bretton Woods Agreement of 1944 to promote the growth of world trade and higher standards of living by making loans when private capital is not available. The Bank's chief sources of funds are capital subscriptions from member nations and sales of its own bonds to private investors. By 1972, the subscribed capital of the Bank was more than $24 billion of which almost one-third was subscribed by the United States. The Bank operates by making loans to governments or to private companies, although the latter loans must be guaranteed by a government or its fiscal agent. By 1972, over 110 countries were members of the Bank.

International Civil Aviation Organization (ICAO)   A specialized agency of the United Nations established in 1947 to develop and to regulate international air transportation. The ICAO applies the principles and law incorporated in the Convention on International Civil Aviation signed at Chicago in 1944, which supersedes earlier air agreements for member states. An Assembly composed of all members (about 120 in 1973), each having one vote, meets every three years to decide general policies of the Organization. An executive Council composed of twenty-seven members elected by the Assembly for three-year terms meets regularly to adopt navigation standards, to arbitrate disputes among members, and to provide extensive information on air transport. Subsidiary bodies appointed by the Council study all aspects of international air transportation and make reports to the Council. Under the Chicago Convention members have reciprocal privileges to fly across each other's territories without landing and, under varying circumstances, to land and take on passengers and cargo. Headquarters of the ICAO are in Montreal. *See also* SPECIAL-IZED AGENCY.

International Commerce Bureau, *see* Department of Commerce.

International Convention on the Prevention and Punishment of the Crime of Genocide, *see* Genocide Convention.

International Court of Justice (ICJ)   An international tribunal, known as the World Court, established as one of the six major organs of the United Nations to adjudicate justiciable disputes among nations and to render advisory opinions to organs of the United Nations. The World Court was established in 1945 under an agreement that was annexed to the United Nations Charter, and to which all United Nations member states are parties. Nonmembers of the United Nations may adhere to the agreement under conditions set by the General Assembly and the Security Council. Other states may use the Court if they accept its jurisdiction. The Court, with its headquarters at the Hague, has fifteen judges elected by the General Assembly and the Security Council, no two of whom may be nationals of the same state. Decisions rendered by the Court are final and, if any party to a case refuses to heed the judgment of the Court, the other party has recourse to the Security Council, which may decide on a course of action. *See also* INTERNATIONAL LAW.

International Development Association (IDA)   An affiliate of the World Bank. IDA was established in 1960 as a specialized agency of the United Nations to grant "soft loans" to members to promote economic development. By 1972, IDA had more than one hundred members and a subscribed capital of over $1 billion. Although it is a separate institution, its management and staff is the same as that of the World Bank (IBRD). Working funds are obtained from contributions made by capital-surplus states and from loans made to IDA by the IBRD. "Soft loan" features of IDA include the low cost of a loan (no interest, but a small annual service charge), a long repayment period (fifty years), and a slow amortization rate (ten-year period of grace, then one percent of loan repayable annually for next ten years, and three percent repayable annually for next thirty years). *See also* SPECIALIZED AGENCY, INTERNATIONAL BANK FOR RECONSTRUCTION AND DEVELOPMENT.

International Disarmament Organization (IDO)   A verification and control agency that, since 1962, has been proposed by both American and Soviet disarmament plans to supervise the three-stage process to achieve a general and complete disarmament. The Soviet-proposed IDO would consist of a conference and a control council, and the American version would include a general conference, a control council, and an administrator who would manage the IDO under the direction of the control council. Under both plans, the conference would operate as a general policymaking body and the control council would be charged with carrying out the verification, inspection, and enforcement functions. The IDO would be established upon the entry into force of the disarmament treaty and would function under the supervision of the United Nations Security Council. *See also* GENERAL AND COMPLETE DISARMAMENT.

International Finance Corporation (IFC)   A specialized agency of the United Nations, established in 1956. The IFC supplements the role of the World Bank (IBRD) in stimulating economic development by making loans to and direct investments in private companies in developing countries. The IFC's nearly one hundred members have subscribed to capital stock of about $100 million in the same ratio as their capital investments in the IBRD. Working funds are secured from the sale of securities in world capital markets and from loans made to the IFC by the World Bank. *See also* SPECIALIZED AGENCY, INTERNATIONAL BANK FOR RECONSTRUCTION AND DEVELOPMENT.

Internationalism   The theory and practice of national involvement in cooperative interstate efforts to solve common security, political, economic, and social problems. Internationalism aims at achieving maximum levels of interstate cooperation, support for regional and global international organizations, participation in alliance systems, multilateral trade and monetary policies, and support for a common attack on major social problems. *See also* ISOLATIONISM.

International Labor Organization (ILO)   A Specialized Agency of the United Nations that seeks through research and recommendation to improve working conditions throughout the world. Established in 1919, the ILO was the only major agency associated with the League of Nations in which the United States participated. The ILO is concerned with problems of full employment, labor standards, migration of workers, collective bargaining, social security, and workers' health. Its headquarters are in Geneva, and it functions through a General Conference comprised of delegates representing labor, employers, and government. Between annual conferences, an executive Governing Body supervises the operations of ILO committees and commissions and prepares the agenda for future conferences.

International Law   A body of rules and principles that guides the relations among nations and between governements and foreign nationals. Sources of international law include treaties, authority (for example, decisions of international courts), reason, and custom. Treaties and other forms of international agreements are the most important source today, as custom was earlier, in the development of international law. The law has been classified into three categories: peace, war, and neutrality, based on the nature of the law, and into public, private and administrative, based on the different sources of the law. *See also* INTERNATIONAL COURT OF JUSTICE.

International Law Commission (ILC)   An agency created by the General Assembly in 1947 to aid it in carrying out its Charter responsibility (Article 13) to "initiate studies and make recommendations . . . encouraging the progressive development of international law and its codification." The International Law Commission consists of twenty-one experts on international law who represent the world's main legal systems and forms of civilization. Chosen on the basis of equitable geographic distribution, the commissioners serve five-year terms, in their individual capacities rather than as representatives of governments. The ILC has presented a variety of reports to the General Assembly and numerous draft conventions with the recommendations that the Assembly convene international conferences to consider the drafts. When this procedure is followed, the conferences adopt law-making treaties that bind the states which ratify them. The ILC has concerned itself with such subjects as recognition, state succession, jurisdictional immunities, the high seas, territorial waters, nationality, statelessness, aliens, asylum, the law of treaties, state responsibility, and arbitral procedure. *See also* CODIFICATION.

International Legislation   Multilateral treaties or conventions designed to codify, modify, and initiate legal rules to be followed by states in their mutual relations. International legislation can be accomplished only by a law-making treaty since states insist, as a function of sovereignty, that they can be bound only by their consent. Law-making treaties can be written by ad hoc conferences, by regional institutions, and by international organizations, such as the specialized agencies and the General Assembly of the United Nations. A procedure followed by the United Nations for the creation of international legislation includes: (1) a study by the International Law Commission, which results in the writing of draft articles of agreement and their submission to the General Assembly; (2) a resolution by the Assembly calling an international conference to consider the draft; (3) approval and subsequent ratification by the individual states; and (4) registration of the instrument by the Secretary-General of the United Nations. Recent illustrations of international legislation by law-making treaty include the Geneva Conventions on the Territorial Sea and Contiguous Zone (1958) and on Fishing (1958), and the Vienna Conventions on Diplomatic Relations (1961) and Consular Relations (1963).

International Monetary Fund (IMF)   A specialized agency of the United Nations established by the Bretton Woods Monetary and Financial Conference of 1944 to promote international monetary cooperation. The major objectives of the Fund include: (1) promotion of exchange stability; (2) establishment of a worldwide multilateral payments system; and (3) provision of monetary reserves to help member nations overcome short-run disequilibria in their balances of payments. By 1972, more than 110 members had joined the Fund and had subscribed to quotas totaling over $16 billion. The two major stabilizing functions performed by the Fund are (a) regulating currency values by controlling exchange rates and (b) providing a pooling arrangement whereby members may purchase foreign currencies with their own domestic currencies to tide them over periods of serious financial hardship. When a member is able to do so, it repurchases its own currency with foreign exchange, thus replenishing the Fund's available resources. Voting power in the IMF is determined by the size of a member's contribution, with the United States casting about one-fourth of the total. Since 1962, major industrial members have functioned as the Group of Ten to defend currency values and to promote international liquidity. *See also* GOLD STANDARD, SPECIALIZED AGENCY.

International Organization   A formal arrangement transcending national boundaries that provides for the establishment of institutional machinery to facilitate cooperation among members in the security, economic, social, or related fields. Modern international organizations, which began to emerge more than a century ago in the Western state system, have flowered in the twentieth century—the age of international cooperation. Two types of international organizations are active—public arrangements between two or more states, and private associations of individuals or groups known as nongovernmental organizations (NGO). Public international organizations include global political arrangements (the League of Nations and the United Nations), regional groups (NATO, the OAS, and the Arab League), and public international unions (the Universal Postal Union and the World Health Organization). Examples of private international organizations include Rotary International, the International Confederation of Free Trade Unions, and the International Red Cross. *See also* CONFEDERATION.

International Police Force   The anticipated agent for collective security enforcement action called for in the United Nations Charter plan for preserving world peace and security. Article 43 of the Charter provides that member states through prior agreements make armed forces and facilities available to the Security Council on its call. These agreements, the heart of the original peace-keeping plan, failed to materialize when the Council's Military Staff Committee was unable in 1946 to secure the agreement of the great powers concerning the size and character of their contributions. International police forces, however, have been subsequently established under United Nations auspices to function in a different capacity; as agents of pacific settlement using diplomatic and military tactics to restore peace in situations of limited war. *See also* UNITED NATIONS EMERGENCY FORCE, UNITED NATIONS FORCE IN CYPRUS, UNITED NATIONS OPERATION IN THE CONGO.

International Refugee Organization (IRO), *see* United Nations High Commissioner for Refugees.

International Telecommunication Union (ITU)   A specialized agency of the United Nations established to facilitate all types of telecommunications and to harmonize the actions of member states in such fields. The ITU was set up in 1932 as a successor to the International Telegraph Union, which had functioned since 1865. Organs of the ITU include a Plenipotentiary Conference that meets once every five years to decide basic policies, two Administrative Conferences (one for telegraph and telephone, the other for radio and television) that adopt regulations binding on all members, an Administrative Council to implement policies, and a secretariat, headed by a secretary-general located at ITU headquarters in Geneva. Almost all countries of the world, as well as many colonies and protectorates, are members of the ITU. *See also* SPECIALIZED AGENCY.

International Trade, *see* Balance of Payments, Balance of Trade, Barter, Battle Act, Bilateral Trade, Boycott (International), Commodity Agreement, Commonwealth Preferences, Comparative Advantage, Countervailing Duty, Directed Trade, Dumping, Economic Nationalism, Embargo, Escape Clause, Free Trade, GATT, Licensing, Mercantilism, Most-Favored-Nation Clause, OECD, Preferential Trade Arrangement, Protectionism, Reciprocity, Tariff, Terms of Trade.

International Trade Organization (ITO), *see* General Agreement on Tariffs and Trade.

Interposition   A concept that holds that a state may place itself between its citizens and the national government so as to prevent the enforcement of national law upon its citizens. According to this doctrine, each state may be the judge of the legality or constitutionality of national action, and may "interpose" its sovereignty to nullify federal action. This theory was propounded by Thomas Jefferson and James Madison in the Kentucky and Virginia Resolutions of 1799 protesting the Alien and Sedition Acts, and by the South prior to the Civil War. Southern leaders reactivated the theory in the 1950s in opposition to the desegregation rulings of the Supreme Court. The federal courts, however, have rejected the doctrine as contrary to the national supremacy clause of Article VI. *See also* NULLIFICATION.

Interstate Commerce, *see* Commerce, Commerce Power.

Interstate Commerce Commission (ICC)   An eleven-member independent regulatory commission, established in 1887, that regulates the business operations, services, and rates of interstate carriers. Commissioners are appointed by the President and confirmed by the Senate for seven-year terms. The jurisdiction of the ICC extends to railroads, express companies, bus and truck companies, oil pipe lines, intercoastal and inland waterway carriers, and terminal facilities used in transporting goods or persons. The ICC enforces the Interstate Commerce Act of 1887 and six other supplementary statutes, plus numerous amendments. It employs a large staff of attorneys, investigators, economists, examiners, and technicians. Its responsibilities include fixing rates, both maximum and minimum, controlling poolings and consolidations of operating companies, regulating their sales of stocks and bonds, prescribing accounting systems, granting permits and licenses, and providing traffic management. *See also* COMMERCE, COMMERCE POWER.

Interstate Compact   An agreement between two or more states. The Constitution (Art. I, sec. 10) requires such agreements or compacts to have the consent of Congress. Many agreements on minor matters, however, are made without such consent. Generally, any compact that tends to increase the power of the contracting states relative to other states or to the national government requires consent. One of the earliest and best-known compacts was concluded between New York and New Jersey, in 1921, to establish the Port of New York Authority for purposes of regulating the New York harbor and other facilities. A great variety of other compacts are in existence covering a wide range of subjects from flood control to petroleum conservation. Congress has, at times, granted advance blanket approval to certain kinds of compacts, as in civil defense matters and water pollution. *See also Virginia v. Tennessee*, HORIZONTAL FEDERALISM

Interstate Highway System, *see* Federal Aid Highway Act.

Interstate Rendition   The return of a fugitive from justice by a state upon the demand of the executive authority of the state in which the crime was committed. This is one of the obligations imposed upon the states by Article IV, section 2. Though the language of the Constitution is positive on this obligation, the federal courts will not order the governor of one state to deliver a fugitive wanted in another state. Compliance by a governor is viewed as a moral duty. Rendition is routinely followed in most cases but, on occasion, a governor has refused to comply. Refusal may be based on such grounds as the good behavior of the fugitive since his escape, the suspicion that a fair trial will not be granted, or for political or other reasons known only to the governor. Congress has supplemented the requirement by making it a federal crime to flee across state lines to avoid prosecution for certain felonies. When apprehended by federal agents, the fugitive is usually turned over to the state from which he fled. The term "extradition" is used to describe this practice among nations under international law. *See also Kentucky v. Dennison*, HORIZONTAL FEDERALISM, EXTRADITION.

Intersubjectivity   The characteristic of knowledge that makes it transmissible from one person to another. Intersubjectivity used in a scientific context means that investigators using the same conceptual language and scientific research methods are able to transmit their findings to one another and probe the reliability of one another's results. It is thus possible to share knowledge even though each person's research embodies his individual interpretations and perspectives. The level of intersubjectivity in political science helps determine the extent to which the finding of one researcher can be added cumulatively to the findings of another. This obviously promotes the development of generalizations and scientific explanations of political phenomena. *See also* SCIENCE.

Interval Scale, *see* Scale.

Intervening Variable, *see* Variable.

Intervention   Coercive interference in the affairs of a state by another state or group of states to affect the internal or external policies of that state. Under international law, intervention may be legally justified: (1) if the intervening state has been granted such a right by treaty; (2) if a state violates an agreement for joint policy determination by acting unilaterally; (3) if intervention is necessary to protect a state's citizens; (4) if it is necessary for self-defense; or (5) if a state violates international law. Intervention is also justified by the United Nations Charter when it involves a collective action by the international community against a state that threatens or breaks the peace or commits an act of aggression. *See also* DOLLAR DIPLOMACY, INSURGENCY, MONROE DOCTRINE.

Interview   The elicitation of information from people by direct personal inquiry. Systematic interviewing techniques require attention to the construction of a schedule of interview questions directly linked to the hypothesis to be tested or other research problems. Other considerations are the selection of a representative sample of the population to be studied, the minimization of interviewer bias, and attention to the time factor as it relates to the event or issue under investigation. In the structured (*directed* or *standardized*) interview the wording and sequence of the questions are determined in advance by the researcher. In the unstructured (*nondirected* or *unstandardized*) interview the interviewer has much more discretion as to question content and is permitted to discuss the subject freely. *See also* PANEL STUDY, QUESTIONNAIRE, SURVEY RESEARCH.

Intrastate Commerce, *see* Commerce, Commerce Power.

Intuition   Insight or understanding that explains or predicts a political event without dependence upon any conscious reasoning process or evidence. Intuition is often used to make normative judgments, such as those on the nature and quality of justice, goodness, fairness, and the ethical conduct of individuals. *See also* RATIONALITY.

Intuitionism, *see* Rationality.

Investigating Committee   A legislative committee that exercises a fact-finding role as an aid to the law-making process. Investigating committees may compel witnesses to attend and to produce relevant materials. Investigations are conducted by both the regular standing committees and by special committees created for that purpose. The purposes behind investigations include: (1) finding of facts on which to base legislation; (2) discovering or developing of public opinion; (3) overseeing of administrative agencies; (4) uncovering the questionable activities of public officials and private individuals; and (5) sometimes securing personal or partisan political gain. In terms of time, effort, and publicity, the investigatory activities of Congress and of some state legislatures have in recent years rivaled their legislative functions. A legislative body may investigate any subject that is properly within the scope of its legislative powers. *See also McGrain v. Daugherty, Watkins v. United States,* WATCHDOG COMMITTEE.

Involuntary Servitude   Slavery, peonage, or forcing a person to work to fulfill a contract or to work out a debt. The Thirteenth Amendment provides that neither slavery nor involuntary servitude, except in punishment for crime, may exist anywhere in the United States. Certain types of employment are not covered by the prohibition when the public safety is jeopardized, as in the case of policemen, firemen, seamen, and train crews. *See also Pollock v. Williams,* THIRTEENTH AMENDMENT, SELECTIVE SERVICE.

Iron Curtain   A phrase coined by Winston Churchill in 1946 to describe the Soviet policy of isolating the Communist states of Eastern Europe from Western Europe. The term, Iron Curtain, described the barrier established by the Communist nations under Soviet direction, the secrecy and censorship imposed within the region, and the absence of communication with the West. *See also* COLD WAR.

Irredentism   The desire of the people of a state to annex those contiguous territories of another country that are inhabited largely by linguistic or cultural minorities of the first state. Irredentism is a term of Italian origin and comes from the expression, *Italia irredenta,* meaning "Italy unredeemed" or Italians not liberated from foreign control. After the creation of the Kingdom of Italy, the slogan was widely used by nationalists working for the annexation of bordering Italian-speaking communities, particularly those under Austrian rule in Trentino and the Tyrol. *See also* NATIONAL SELF-DETERMINATION.

Isolationism   The theory and practice of noninvolvement in the affairs of other nations. Isolationism as a political ideology is nurtured by geographical, ideological, and cultural separateness. *See also* INTERNATIONALISM.

Isomorphism   Similarity in form or structure. In political analysis "isomorphism" generally refers to the similarity between a conceptual model and the institutional or behavioral attributes that it represents. The similarity must preserve the relationships and interactions among the elements modeled as well as their descriptive features. If two theories or laws exist in a one-to-one corresponding relationship to each other, they, too, may be described as isomorphic. *See also* MODEL.

Italian Political System, *see* Council of Ministers, Parliament, Party System, President of the Council of Ministers, President of the Republic.

Item Veto   The power exercised by the governor in all but a few states to veto sections or items of an appropriation bill while signing the remainder of the bill into law. Governors in several states can reduce appropriation items and in a few states may veto sections of nonfinancial bills. The legislature may override the vetoed items. The President does not exercise the item veto power. *See also* VETO, RIDER.

ITU, *see* International Telecommunication Union.

Jacksonian Democracy   A political and social equalitarian movement in the United States that rejected political aristocracy and emphasized the "common man." The chief apostle of the new equality and democracy was Andrew Jackson, who brought to the presidency the leveling influences of the frontier. *See also* LONG BALLOT, SPOILS SYSTEM.

Japanese-American Security Treaty   A bilateral defense pact that provides for joint consultations if the security of Japan is threatened. The original Japanese-American Mutual Assistance Pact was signed in 1954, and a revised Mutual Security Treaty was signed in Washington in 1960. Under the Treaty, the United States retains the right to maintain land, sea, and air forces in Japan. These forces may be used: (1) without prior consultation, to maintain peace and security in the Far East; (2) following consultation, to defend Japan against an armed attack; and (3) at the express request of the Japanese Government, to help suppress domestic disorders in Japan resulting from the instigation or intervention of an outside power. *See also* BILATERAL SECURITY PACT.

Japanese Constitution: Article Nine   That part of the Constitution adopted in 1947 in which the Japanese "forever renounce war as a sovereign right of the nation and the threat or use of force as means of settling international disputes." Article 9 also provides that, to implement the ideal of permanent peace, "land, sea, and air forces, as well as other war potential will never be maintained." The Japanese Constitution was written under the direct supervision of the American occupation forces commanded by General Douglas MacArthur.

Jeffersonianism   The philosophy of Thomas Jefferson, espousing a democratic, laissez-faire styled agrarianism. Jeffersonianism rejected the Hamiltonian idea that a strong central government be created to spur the growth of urban industrialism and commercialism. The Jeffersonian model incorporates the ideal of an independent republic, democratically governed by an intellectual aristocracy under a strictly construed constitutional system, with a national government of limited powers and with major emphasis on individual freedom and responsibility and states' rights. *See also* MADISONIANISM.

Jehovah's Witnesses Cases   Involved, in a series of cases, the religious sect known as Jehovah's Witnesses, testing the scope of religious freedom under the First and Fourteenth Amendments. Among the various decisions were those that held unconstitutional: (1) laws requiring prior official approval to solicit funds for religious purposes (*Cantwell v. Connecticut*, 310 U.S. 296 [1940]); (2) laws levying license taxes on peddlers of religious tracts (*Murdock v. Pennsylvania*, 319 U.S. 105 [1943]); (3) laws prohibiting door-to-door distribution of religious handbills (*Martin v. Struthers*, 319 U.S. 141 [1943]); (4) laws requiring official approval to hold public worship meetings in public parks (*Niemotko v. Maryland*, 340 U.S. 268 [1951]); and (5) an official requirement that children be compelled to salute the flag contrary to their religious beliefs (*West Virginia State Board of Education v. Barnette*, 319 U.S. 624 [1943]). On the other hand, the Court has held that the sect may not under the guise of religious freedom: (1) hold a parade without permission (*Cox v. New Hampshire*, 312 U.S. 569 [1941]); (2) have a young child sell magazines on a street corner late at night, contrary to state child welfare laws (*Prince v. Massachusetts*, 321 U.S. 158 [1944]); or (3) create a breach of peace in the course of a public meeting (*Chaplinsky v. New Hampshire*, 315 U.S. 568 [1942]). *See also* FREEDOM OF RELIGION.

Jim Crow Laws, *see* Segregation.

Jingoism   Inflamation of national passions to generate support for pugnacious or aggressive foreign policies. Jingoism is associated with the efforts of the Yellow Press, led by the New York *Tribune*, the New York *World*, and the New York *Journal*, to bring on war between the United States and Spain at the turn of the century. Jingoism resulted in the abandonment of accuracy, balance, and objectivity in an effort to promote sympathy for the Cubans and public animosity toward Spain.

Job Corps   A program, authorized by the Economic Opportunity Act of 1964, that enables jobless youths from sixteen to twenty-one to work and study at training centers or in conservation camps. Emphasis is placed upon education, vocational training, and work experiences. The Job Corps is managed by the Department of Labor, which contracts with local public and private agencies to establish training centers. *See also* ECONOMIC OPPORTUNITY ACT.

Johnson v. Zerbst, *see* Gideon v. Wainwright.

Joint Anti-Fascist Refugee Committee v. McGrath, *see* Attorney General's List.

Joint Chiefs of Staff   A top-level military staff agency in the Department of Defense responsible for all matters related to military strategy. The Joint Chiefs of Staff, composed of the Chiefs of Staff of the Army and Air Force, the Chief of Naval Operations, the Commandant of the Marine Corps, and the Chief of Staff to the Secretary of Defense, was created by the National Security Acts of 1947 and 1949. A second staff agency, the Armed Forces Policy Council, composed of the civilian and military heads of the Departments of the Army, Navy, and Air Force, advises the Secretary of Defense on broader policy questions. *See also* DEPARTMENT OF DEFENSE.

Joint Committee   A legislative committee composed of members of both houses. The number appointed to a joint committee is usually divided equally between the two houses, with each member having one vote. On some, such as conference committees, each chamber may determine the size of its membership on the committee, and the two groups vote separately on measures. Joint committees are usually select (special) committees appointed for a specified purpose: typically, to conduct investigations. Congress has created a few standing (permanent) joint committees, such as the Joint Committee on the Economic Report, and the Joint Committee on Atomic Energy.

Joint Committee on the Economic Report, *see* Economic Message.

Joint Resolution   A measure, similar to a bill, that must be approved in both chambers and by the executive. In Congress, joint resolutions are designated "H J Res" and "S J Res" and, if passed by a simple majority in both houses, must be signed by the President to become law. The procedure is identical to that used in passing a bill into law except when the joint resolution is used to propose an amendment to the Constitution. Then the President's signature is unnecessary. About half of the state legislatures also employ the joint resolution in enacting laws and proposing constitutional amendments. *See also* CONCURRENT RESOLUTION, SIMPLE RESOLUTION.

Joint Session   A meeting of the members of both chambers of a legislative body. Congress meets in joint session to count the electoral votes and certify the election of the President, and when addressed by the President or a foreign dignitary. A joint session is never used to consider specific bills. Most state legislatures meet in joint session to receive the governor's annual message.

Jones v. Mayer, 392 U.S. 409 (1968): Held that all racial discrimination, private as well as public, in the sale or rental of property, is outlawed by an 1866 act passed under authority of the Thirteenth Amendment. The 1866 law provides that black citizens have the same rights enjoyed by white citizens "to inherit, purchase, lease, sell, hold, and convey real and personal property." The Court held that Congress has authority "to abolish all badges and incidents of slavery."

Judgement, *see* Award.

Judicial Activism and Self-Restraint, *see* Activism Versus Self-Restraint (Judicial).

Judicial Council   An investigative and advisory agency composed of judges, lawyers, and laymen to promote efficient administration in state courts. Councils are used in about three-fourths of the states. Though their composition and authority vary from state to state, they are generally charged with collecting statistics on court operations and recommending changes in court organization, court procedure, assignment of judges, and other matters to improve the handling of court business. *See also* ADMINISTRATIVE OFFICE.

Judicial Review   The power of the courts to declare acts of the legislative and executive branches unconstitutional. All courts, both state and national, may exercise this authority, though final decision is usually made by the highest state or federal court. Though the United States Constitution is silent on this matter, the Supreme Court asserted the power of judicial review in the famous case of *Marbury v. Madison,* 1 Cranch 137 (1803). Judicial review is based on the assumptions that the Constitution is the supreme law, that acts contrary to the Constitution are void, and that the judiciary is the guardian of the Constitution. *See also* CONSTITUTIONAL LAW, SUPREME COURT, *Ashwander v. TVA; Eakin v. Raub; Marbury v. Madison.*

Judiciary   A collective term for courts and judges. In the United States, the judiciary is divided into the national and state judiciary. Each is independent of the other with the exception that the United States Supreme Court may, under special circumstances involving federal questions, review a state court decision. Jurisdiction of particular courts or judges is determined by either the national or state constitutions and laws.

Judiciary Act of 1789   A law passed by the first Congress to establish the federal court system. The Act determined the organization and jurisdiction of the courts. Over the years, the Judiciary Act has undergone numerous changes, adding and deleting courts, changing jurisdiction of courts, establishing rules of procedure, and providing for a variety of court officers and employees.

Jurisdictional Strike   A strike involving a dispute between unions rather than between a union and an employer, Jurisdictional strikes may occur over the question of which union has the right to represent the workers or over the question of which workers are to do a specific job. For example, both carpenters and metalworkers may claim the right to install metal framed windows, or one union may try to "raid" another union's territory. The Taft-Hartley Act and many state laws make the jurisdictional strike unlawful. *See also* STRIKE.

Jurisdiction (Court)   Authority vested in a court to hear and decide a case. The term literally means power "to say the law." The jurisdiction of national courts is controlled by the Constitution and by Congress. State court jurisdiction is similarly determined by state constitutions and statutes. Jurisdiction may be assigned according to such factors as the amount of money involved or the type of offense. Courts may exercise original or appellate jurisdiction, or both. *See also* ADMIRALTY JURISDICTION, APPELLATE JURISDICTION, CONCURRENT JURISDICTION, DIVERSITY OF CITIZENSHIP, ORIGINAL JURISDICTION, *Ex parte McCardle*.

Jurisdiction (Territorial)   The right of a state or a court to speak or act with authority. Jurisdiction involves the assertion of control over persons, property, subjects and situations in a given juridical, political, or geographic area. Under international law, jurisdiction over territory can be acquired by accretion, cession, conquest, discovery, and prescription. *See also* ACCRETION, ADMIRALTY JURISDICTION, AIRSPACE JURISDICTION, CESSION, CONDOMINIUM, CONTIGUOUS ZONE, HIGH SEAS, OUTER SPACE JURISDICTION, PRESCRIPTION, TERRITORIAL WATERS, THALWEG.

Jury   An impartial body that sits in judgment on charges brought in either criminal or civil cases. A trial jury is also known as a petit jury to distinguish it from a grand jury. Under the common law, a trial jury must consist of twelve persons and their decision must be unanimous. The national government and many states authorize trial by less than twelve in certain cases and a decision by less than a unanimous vote. Jury trials may be waived by the accused. Generally, the jury is the judge of the facts though some states permit the jury to determine the law and the punishment as well as the facts. The jury must be impartial and no specific class of persons may be deliberately and systematically excluded from jury service. The Supreme Court has ruled that due process requires that persons accused of serious crimes are entitled to a trial by jury (*Duncan v. Louisiana,* 391 U.S. 145 [1968]), defined a serious crime as one for which imprisonment for more than six months is possible (*Baldwin v. New York,* 399 U.S. 66 [1970]), and authorized juries of less than twelve for the trial of serious offenses (*Williams v. Florida,* 399 U.S. 78 [1970]). Trial by jury is required by Article III, section 2, and by the Sixth and Seventh Amendments of the United States Constitution. *See also Norris v. Alabama,* PANEL, CHALLENGE, CHARGE, CAPITAL PUNISHMENT.

Jus Civile   The early civil law of the primitive Roman city-state, which applied to citizens only. *Jus civile* may be contrasted with the *jus gentium* which applied to the diverse peoples of the Empire. *See also* JUS GENTIUM.

Jus Gentium   That body of Roman law and equity which applied to all foreigners resident in the Empire. The *jus gentium* governed relations between foreigners and between foreigners and citizens, and was based on common ideas of justice found in the laws and customs of the various peoples of the Empire. Because it was thought to be simple, reasonable, and adaptable, early jurists regarded the *jus gentium* as universal in its applicability. *See also* JUS CIVILE, JUS NATURALE.

Jus Naturale   A Roman adaptation of the Greek stoic concept of a set of principles that ought to govern the conduct of all men. The *jus naturale* or natural law is founded in the explanation of the nature of man as a rational and social being. This law of reason based on what ought to be, when coupled with the universalism of the *jus gentium,* gave Roman law the adaptability and progressiveness that enabled diverse peoples to live together in relative peace in spite of changing conditions. *See also* JUS GENTIUM, NATURAL LAW.

Jus Sanguinis   "Law of the blood"—a principle by which citizenship is determined by parentage rather than by place of birth *(jus soli).*   .

Jus Soli   "Law of the soil"—the basic rule under which American Citizenship is determined by place of birth rather than by parentage *(jus sanguinis). See also United States V. Wong Kim Ark.*

Just Compensation, *see* Eminent Domain.

Justice of the Peace   A judicial officer empowered to try minor civil and criminal cases, such as traffic violations or breaches of peace. In some areas, he conducts preliminary hearings to determine whether a person should be held for trial in a higher court. The justice of the peace is usually elected in rural areas and small towns for a two-year term. He is generally paid through fees. *See also* MAGISTRATE.

Justiciable and Nonjusticiable Disputes (International)   A formulation that results from the assertion of the existence of two distinct categories of international disputes—legal and political. Justiciable disputes are those that lend themselves to legal settlement by arbitration or adjudication. Nonjusticiable disputes are those to which techniques of political settlement are applied by bilateral diplomacy, good offices, mediation, inquiry, or conciliation. *See also* PEACEFUL SETTLEMENT OF DISPUTES.

Justiciable Question   A dispute that can be settled through the exercise of judicial power. For a controversy to be justiciable: (1) it must be an actual case, not a trumped-up suit; (2) the person bringing the suit must have a direct interest at stake and have standing to sue; (3) the case must be ripe for adjudication, other remedies having been exhausted; and (4) the court must have jurisdiction over the subject. A question may be ruled "political" rather than justiciable if the court believes that the other branches of the government are better equipped or constitutionally responsible to handle the matter. *See also* JURISDICTION, POLITICAL QUESTION; *Frothingham v. Mellon.*

"Just War", *see* Wars of National Liberation.

Juvenile Delinquent   A child whose behavior is unlawful and who is subject to governmental custody. The definition of a delinquent child is determined by law and usually applies to persons under sixteen or eighteen years of age. All states have developed special courts to process juvenile cases. Juvenile courts have operated under informal procedures, but recent court decisions have imposed basic constitutional due process requirements upon them. *See also In Re Gault.*

Katzenbach v. McClung, *see Heart of Atlanta Motel v. United States.*

Katz v. United States, *see* Wiretapping.

Kellogg-Briand Pact   A general treaty, concluded in 1928 and subsequently ratified by almost all nations, that sought to outlaw war as an instrument of national policy. Officially titled the General Treaty for the Renunciation of War and also known as the Pact of Paris, it was drawn up by United States Secretary of State Frank B. Kellogg and French Foreign Minister Aristide Briand. The two main articles provided, first, that signatories "condemn recourse to war for the solution of international controversies, and renounce it as an instrument of national policy in their relations with one another" and, second, "that the settlement or solution of all disputes or conflicts, of whatever nature or of whatever origin . . . shall never be sought except by pacific means." In ratifying the Pact, however, many nations attached a reservation that proscribed only "offensive" military actions, not those of a defense character. The United States Senate, for example, stipulated that the Pact did not impair the right of self-defense, including enforcement of the Monroe Doctrine, nor did it obligate the nation to participate in sanctions against an aggressor. *See also* WAR, WAR CRIMES TRIALS.

Kentucky and Virginia Resolutions of 1799, *see* Interposition.

Kentucky v. Dennison, 24 Howard 66 (1861): Decided that the constitutional duty of a governor to return a fugitive to the state from which he fled is only a moral obligation rather than a mandatory one. The Court found that a national statute of 1793 dealing with the return of fugitives provided no means by which a governor could be compelled to perform his duty and, in any case, that the national government lacked authority to coerce a state officer. *See also* INTERSTATE RENDITION.

Keyishian v. Board of Regents of New York, 385 U.S. 589 (1967): Struck down a state law which disqualified from public employment any person who advocated, or was a member of a group that advocated, the overthrow of government by force, violence, or any unlawful means. The law was held to violate First Amendment rights of speech and association and to be void because of vagueness. The Court emphasized the need for precision in laws touching basic liberties and that public employment could not be conditioned on the surrender of constitutional rights. Specific intent to further illegal aims must be proven.

Keynesianism   A philosophy and practice of utilizing the machinery of government, through fiscal and monetary policies, to guide and direct a free enterprise economy. Keynesianism, based on the principles and analyses originally propounded by the British economist, John Maynard Keynes, seeks to improve rather than replace capitalism by providing an orderly, predictable pattern of economic activity based on economic indicators utilized by policymakers. Techniques used by Keynesians to manage a state's economy include government control and direction of such matters as budgeting, spending, tax policy, interest rates, and credit availability. Keynesianism substitutes rational decisions made by state leaders in pursuit of specific social goals for the undirected free interplay of market forces that characterizes a laissez-faire approach. *See also* CAPITALISM, FISCAL POLICY, MONETARY POLICY.

Khrushchevism   Contributions to Marxist-Leninist theory, and applications of communist doctrine in the Soviet Union, made by Nikita S. Khrushchev. Khrushchevism was developed in the years between 1956, when Khrushchev emerged as the dominant leader in the post-Stalin power struggle, and 1963, when he was deposed from power by a party faction headed by Leonid I. Brezhnev and Aleksei N. Kosygin. Khrushchev began his rise to power when he replaced Josef Stalin as First Secretary of the Communist Party after the latter's death in 1953. He consolidated his control in 1958 when he removed Nikolai A. Bulganin as Chairman of the Council of Ministers and assumed that post also. Khrushchev's main contributions to communist doctrine include: (1) repudiation of Stalin's "cult of the individual" and the restoration of the "true" Marxist-Leninist approach of collective leadership; (2) enunciation of the doctrine and policy of "peaceful coexistence" between communist and capitalist states while calling for "wars of national liberation" in the underdeveloped world; (3) denunciation of Stalinist totalitarianism and the institution of less-tyrannical policies within the Soviet state; (4) establishment, for the first time in any Communist country of a specifc timetable (within twenty years) for a Socialist state to complete the historical transition to pure communism; (5) a declaration that, although classes and the state will wither away, the Communist party will remain as a directing force in the future society; and (6) development of the tactical position that communism would defeat capitalism in peaceful competition in the world by proving to be a superior social and productive system. *See also* PEACEFUL COEXISTENCE, CULT OF THE INDIVIDUAL, WARS OF NATIONAL LIBERATION.

Kitchen Cabinet   An informal group of close friends and personal advisers to the President. Members of a Kitchen Cabinet may supplement or substantially replace the formal Cabinet as the President's chief source of advice on domestic and foreign policies. *See also* CABINET.

Knowledge, *see* Sociology of Knowledge.

Knownothingism   Political activity on an uninformed, largely emotional level, which exploits the suspicions, hatreds, ignorance, and fears of American voters. The term is derived from the radical right-wing Know Nothing party of the mid-nineteenth century that functioned in American politics as an anti-foreign, anti-Catholic, secret society. The party's name evolved because members professed ignorance when queried about party activities. *See also* MCCARTHYISM.

Laboratory Approach   The conduct of scientific experiments or tests under conditions arranged or controlled by the investigator. In the laboratory approach the social science researcher typically aims at holding certain variables constant so that he may systematically manipulate, observe, describe, and measure the remaining variables and observe the impact of varying stimuli upon them. The principal applications of the laboratory approach to political science are simulations and small group experiments. *See also* EXPERIMENT, FIELD STUDY.

Labor-Management Relations Act of 1947., *see* Taft-Hartley Act.

Labor-Management Reporting and Disclosure Act of 1959., *see* Landrum-Griffin Act.

Labor Standards, *see* International Labor Organization.

Labor Theory of Value, *see* Surplus Value.

Labor Unions   Organizations of workers that seek to improve the economic status and working conditions of labor through collective bargaining and political action.

The largest and most influential labor organization is the American Federation of Labor-Congress of Industrial Organizations (AFL-CIO), a federation of over 130 unions. The AFL-CIO has over 3 million members comprising about 70 percent of organized labor. The remainder of organized labor is in independent unions, such as the Teamsters, Mine Workers, Longshoremen, Railroad Brotherhoods, and a number of smaller unions. *See also* PRESSURE GROUP.

Labour Party (Britain) Along with the Conservatives, one of the two major parties in British politics. A complex amalgam of trade unions, socialist and other professional groups, cooperative societies, and local constituency parties, the Labour party was formed in 1900 and named in 1906. Broad policy consideration takes place at the annual party Conference. Between Conferences, the National Executive Committee conducts party affairs and directs the central office. The primary focus of power is in the parliamentary Labour party (all Labour MPs), which elects the leader who, when Prime Minister, selects the Cabinet. When Labour is in opposition, the parliamentary party elects the shadow cabinet. As Prime Minister, the Leader has such individual power and influence that he can resist being bound by the wishes expressed at the annual Conference. Nevertheless, effective liaison is usually maintained by the Cabinet with the parliamentary party and the party at large. *See also* PARTY SYSTEM (BRITAIN).

Labour Party, Political Role, *see* Labour Party (Britain).

LAFTA, *see* Latin American Free Trade Association.

Lag, *see* Communications Theory.

Laissez-faire The economic theory, propounded by the French physiocrats and popularized by Adam Smith (*The Wealth of Nations*, 1776), that calls for a "hands-off" policy by government toward the economy. Laissez-faire rejects state control and regulation and emphasizes economic individualism, a market economy, and natural economic laws to guide the production and consumption of goods. Tariffs and other trade restrictions are rejected in favor of a worldwide system of free trade. The economic system becomes self-regulatory in nature and each individual's pursuit of his own self-interest contributes to the well-being of all. *See also* CAPITALISM, FREE TRADE.

Lame Duck Amendment, *see* Twentieth Amendment.

Land-grant College An agricultural and mechanical college, or the agricultural and mechanical school of a state university, established under the provisions of the Morrill Act of 1862. The Morrill Act provided for the granting of land (amounting to nearly 11 million acres) by the national government to the states for the support of colleges to teach agriculture, engineering, and home economics. Since that time, Congress has continued to make money grants to these institutions, supplementing funds given by state and private agencies. Experimental stations for agriculture, and an extension service that carries education directly to the farmer in the rural areas, have also been established at land-grant colleges.

Landrum-Griffin Act (Labor-Management Reporting and Disclosure Act of 1959) Informally known as the Labor Reform Act of 1959, this law strengthens the Taft-Hartley Act's restrictions upon internal procedures of labor unions and provides a "bill of rights" for members of labor unions. The Act requires detailed reports to the Secretary of Labor on union finances and the operations of union constitutions and bylaws, and it makes misuse of union funds a federal crime. Ex-convicts, Communists, and labor officials with conflicting business interests are barred from holding union office. The "bill of rights" provisions secure the secret ballot in union elections, freedom of speech in union meetings, hearings in disciplinary cases, the right of members to sue the union for unfair practices, and authorize member access to union records.

Latent Function, *see* Functionalism.

Latent Opinion, *see* Public Opinion.

Latifundia System (Latifundismo) A Latin American pattern of land tenure based on huge landed estates owned by local gentry, absentee landlords, and domestic or foreign corporations. The latifundia system, developed by the ancient Romans, was transplanted first to the Iberian Peninsula and thence to the Americas. *See also* MINIFUNDIA SYSTEM.

Latin American Free Trade Association (LAFTA) A regional organization that seeks to spur the rate of economic development of member states by removing trade barriers. Eleven Latin American states (Argentina, Bolivia, Brazil, Chile, Colombia, Ecuador, Mexico, Paraguay, Peru, Uruguay, Venezuela) agreed in the Montevideo Treaty of 1960 to liberalize their trade over a twelve-year period to achieve the goal of substantially free trade among member countries. The Treaty, however, includes escape clauses, provides for renegotiation of tariff cuts that cause substantial domestic injury, and gives agriculture a preferred status. Two organs constitute the decision-making machinery for LAFTA: (1) a Conference of the Contracting Parties meets annually to decide basic policies by a two-thirds voting procedure; and (2) a Standing Executive Committee implements trade policies and treaty provisions. A small secretariat attached to the Executive Committee provides technical and administrative assistance to aid the Committee in carrying out its supervisory role.

Law A rule of conduct prescribed by or accepted by the governing authority of a state and enforced by courts. The law may derive from a constitution, legislative acts, and administrative rules, or may develop through custom, as have common law and equity. The law controls relations among men, and between men and their government. Penalties are imposed for violation of law. In political inquiry and analysis, a "law" is a proposition that has survived intensive testing and has acquired certainty. Few, if any, such laws are recognized by the discipline, although great efforts are being expended to move in that direction. *See also* ADMINISTRATIVE LAW; CIVIL LAW, COMMON LAW, CONSTITUTIONAL LAW, CRIMINAL LAW, EQUITY, INTERNATIONAL LAW, ORDINANCE.

Law Enforcement, *see* Attorney General, Coroner, Department of Justice, District Attorney, Marshal, Public Defender, Sheriff, United States Attorney.

Law-Making Treaty, *see* International Legislation.

Law of Humanity, *see* Rules of Warfare.

Law of Nations, *see Jus Gentium.*

Law of the Sea   Those international legal rules that pertain to the maritime rights and duties of states. The law of the sea, which is the oldest branch of international law, has grown out of ancient codes based on customs related to the maritime rights and duties of merchants and ship owners. Precedents include the Rhodian Laws (ninth century), the Tabula Amalfitana (eleventh century), the Laws of Oleron (twelfth century), the Laws of Wisby (thirteenth and fourteenth centuries), and the *Consolato del Mare* (fourteenth century). Sources of the law of the sea include international custom, national legislation, treaties, and the work of international conferences on the subject. *See also* ADMIRALTY JURISDICTION, HIGH SEAS.

Laws of War, *see* Rules of Warfare.

Lawyers' Edition, *see United States Reports.*

Leadership   The combination of personal attributes, respected by others, that enables an individual to shape the collective behavior patterns of a group in a direction determined by his own values. Leadership traits that tend to prove effective in politics include an apparent dedication to high ideals, loyalty to party and friends, a good memory for names and faces, a refusal to be bored, a sense of humor, great energy, some charisma, and a capacity to be impartial in disputes and play the role of honest broker within the group one leads. The effectiveness of political leadership depends on the personal traits of the leader, the general environmental conditions surrounding him and conditioning his role, the way in which he views his own role and status, and the specifics of the situation within which leadership is exercised. A leader whose personal qualities elicit widespread, popular, emotional support for his leadership is said to possess *charisma*. The *charismatic leader*, as conceived by Max Weber, commands support without the benefit of material rewards or coercion. As personal qualities are supplemented by a material base and institutional routine, the character of leadership becomes less charismatic. *See also* AUTHORITY, INFLUENCE, POWER.

League of Arab States, *see* Arab League.

League of Nations   The first general international organization established to preserve peace and security and to promote cooperation among nations in economic and social fields. The League was created by the victorious powers of World War I in 1919 under the leadership of President Woodrow Wilson, but the United States did not join. The organization operated under a constitutional system established through its Covenant, a section of the Versailles peace treaty. A Council and Assembly were the major organs (similar to the Security Council and General Assembly of the United Nations) and subsidiary committees and commissions were established to deal with special problems in areas such as mandates, military affairs, and disarmament. A Secretariat, headed by a Secretary-General and staffed with international civil servants, provided continuity and expertness in record keeping and research. A World Court (the Permanent Court of International Justice, forerunner of the present International Court of Justice) and the International Labor Organization were independent of the League but worked closely with it. Sixty-one nations joined the League and its headquarters were at Geneva, Switzerland.

Learning Theory, *see* Stimulus-Response

Leasehold   An area used by a foreign state under a lease agreement with the territorial sovereign. Leaseholds may be of short or long duration, and the extent of authority exercised by the lessee is established by specific agreement in each instance. Such lease agreements have been concluded freely or under various degrees of duress. By the leasehold technique, for example, major European powers acquired economic rights in China during the nineteenth century.

Lebensraum, *see Haushofer Geopolitik.*

Leftist   An individual or a political group advocating liberal, radical, or revolutionary political or economic programs, an expanded role by democratic government, or empowering the masses. Leftists include such categories as "welfare-statists," democratic socialists, Marxian socialists, Communists, and anarchists. The use of the term stems from the practice in European parliaments of seating radical parties to the left of the presiding officer. *See also* NEW LEFT; RADICAL.

Legal Authority, *see* Authority.

Legal Tender   Any medium of exchange that by law must be accepted in payment of a debt. The Constitution gives the national government full control over the nation's money, and it forbids the states to "make anything but gold and silver coin a tender in payment of debts . . . " (Art. I, sec. 10). *See also* LEGAL TENDER CASES.

Legal Tender Cases (Knox v. Lee; Parker v. Davis), 12 Wallace 457 (1871): Recognized the power of Congress to make Treasury notes (paper money) legal tender in place of gold or silver in payment of debt. *See also* LEGAL TENDER.

Legislative Council   An interim committee employed by some legislatures between sessions to study state problems and to plan a legislative program. In some states, legislative councils have pursued extensive fact-finding research programs. The councils range in size from five members to the entire legislature. Usually, membership is selected from the two houses of the legislature, but, in several states, the governor is authorized to include representation from the executive branch.

Legislative Court   A court established by Congress under its delegated powers rather than under the authority granted in Article III of the Constitution. The judges of legislative courts need not have life tenure, may be assigned nonjudicial functions, and have only that jurisdiction that Congress assigns. For example, the Territorial Courts of Guam, Virgin Islands, and the Panama Canal Zone were created under congressional power to govern the territories. The judges have limited terms, and the courts have regular federal jurisdiction as well as jurisdiction over matters that ordinarily belong in state courts. Another example is the Court of Military Appeals, created under the power to make rules for the armed forces. *See also* CONSTITUTIONAL COURT, UNITED STATES TAX COURT.

Legislative Day   The formal meeting of a legislative chamber that begins with a formal call to order and opening of business and ends with adjournment. A legislative day may cover a period of several calendar days, with the chamber merely recessing at the end of each calendar day rather than adjourning.

Legislative Powers (Congress)   The statute-making authority of the national legislature. Article I, Section 1, of the Constitution provides that "All legislative powers herein granted shall be vested in a Congress of the United States, which shall consist of a Senate and House of Representatives," and these powers are detailed in Article I, Section 8. Through its legislative power, the Congress establishes the need for, creates, empowers, diminishes, and eliminates the agencies of the executive branch through which the President conducts foreign policy. Thus, until Congress provides the machinery of government and operating funds, the President is restricted in his conduct of state policy to those few powers given him in the Constitution. *See also* CHIEF LEGISLATOR.

Legislative Reorganization Act of 1946   An act to strengthen Congress in its organization and operations. The Act was based on the studies of a bipartisan joint committee that was charged with recommending plans "with a view toward strengthening Congress, simplifying its operations, improving its relations with other branches of the United States Government, and enabling it to meet its responsibilities under the Constitution." The Act provided for structural and procedural changes, including: (1) reducing the number of committees; (2) strengthening the operations of the committees; (3) providing for a legislative budget system; (4) reducing the workload of Congress; (5) increasing the professional assistance available to each member of Congress; (6) increasing congressional salaries and fringe benefits; and (7) regulating lobbying activities. *See also* LEGISLATIVE REORGANIZATION ACT OF 1970.

Legislative Reorganization Act of 1970   An act to improve the operations of Congress and make them more responsive to the public will. Provisions of the Act include: (1) modification of the teller vote system (whereby members of the House voted by filing anonymously past a "yes" or "no" recording clerk) so that at the request of one-fifth of a quorum (20 members in Committee of the Whole, 44 in House sessions) each member's vote is now recorded and made public; (2) House committee hearings may be broadcast and televised with the agreement of witnesses and a majority of the committee; (3) votes taken in executive sessions of committees must be made public; (4) a majority of the members of any congressional committee may convene a meeting of the committee over the objection of its chairman; and (5) the Legislative Reference Service was renamed the Congressional Research Service and reorganized to provide increased assistance to members of Congress. *See also* LEGISLATIVE REORGANIZATION ACT OF 1946.

Legitimacy   The quality of being justified or willingly accepted by subordinates that converts the exercise of political power into "rightful" authority. Legitimacy reflects an underlying consensus that endows the leadership and the state with authority, and that offers respect and acceptance for individual leaders, institutions, and behavior norms. Although law serves a legitimating function, the technicality of law alone without widespread social acceptance may provide little support for the power of the lawmakers and enforcers. The consensus that provides the legitimating factor in the exercise of power may be cultivated through the sanctity of tradition, by the devotion of people to a charismatic leader, or by the acceptance of the supremacy of "legal authority" through a general belief in the supremacy of law. *See also* AUTHORITY, INFLUENCE, POWER.

Leisy v. Hardin, *see* Original Package Doctrine.

Lend-Lease   A program of mutual assistance carried on among the nations fighting the Axis Powers during World War II. The United States initiated the program in March, 1941, with the passage of the Lend-Lease Act, which canceled the "cash and carry" provisions of the Neutrality Act of 1937. The Lend-Lease Act empowered the President to sell, transfer, exchange, lease, lend, or otherwise dispose of any item related to support of the Allied cause, including weapons, food, raw materials, machine tools, and other strategic goods. Under the act, executive agreements concluded by the President with Allied nations provided for a mutual balancing of accounts for services rendered to encourage a common war effort, and to facilitate postwar settlements. *See also* FOREIGN AID.

Leninism   The theoretical interpretations and practical applications of Marxist doctrine contributed to the ideology of communism by the Russian revolutionary leader, Vladimir Ilyich Lenin. The main contributions of Leninism include: (1) the theory that imperialism, the highest stage of monopoly capitalism, results from the contradictions of capitalism that force trusts and cartels to seek outlets for surplus capital and production abroad and to bring world sources of raw materials under their control; (2) the theory that imperialist competition between capitalist states generates war; (3) the theory that revolution can take place in a precapitalist colonial society no matter how primitive; (4) a redefinition of the Marxist conception of revolution to include such non-Marxist opportunities as a national disaster that the ruling class cannot deal with or general public discontent with the government; and (5) the utilization of the Communist party, guided by a small, dedicated élite, to lead the revolution and to serve as the instrument for implementing Marx's "dictatorship of the proletariat." A prolific author, Lenin's main ideas are found in his works: *What Is to Be Done?* (1902), *Imperialism—The Highest Stage of Capitalism* (1917), and *State and Revolution* (1918). *See also* DEMOCRATIC CENTRALISM, IMPERIALISM AND COLONIALISM.

Letter of Credence   The formal document by which the head of the sending state introduces his diplomatic representative to the head of the receiving state. The letter of credence attests to the diplomat's representative character, expresses confidence in his ability, outlines his mission and the extent of his powers, and requests that full faith and credit be given to activities undertaken by him on behalf of his government. The letter of credence is usually presented to the chief of state in a formal audience. *See also* DIPLOMAT.

Level of Analysis, *see* Macro-Micro Analysis.

Leviathan, *see* Contract Theory.

Libel and Slander   Defamation of character, written in the case of libel, and oral in the case of slander. Both include statements that expose a person to hatred, contempt, or ridicule, or that injure his reputation by imputing to him a criminal act, or that harm him in his trade or profession. Libel and slander usually involve suits for civil damages, but they may also be punished under criminal laws. Libel is generally considered more serious than slander because the written word is more durable than a passing remark. The reputation of those involved, the nature of the audience, and the conditions under which the words were written or spoken may prove pertinent in a suit for damages. Truth of a statement is generally an absolute defense. *See also New York Times v. Sullivan.*

Liberal Construction, *see* Constitutional Construction.

Liberalism   A political view that seeks to change the political, economic, or social status quo to foster the development and well-being of the individual. Liberals regard man as a rational creature who can use his intelligence to overcome human and natural obstacles to a good life for all without resorting to violence against the established order. Liberalism is more concerned with process, with the method of solving problems, than with a specific program. *See also* CONSERVATISM.

Liberal Nationalism   A form of nationalism that describes the aspirations of a group to achieve statehood and establish government based on popular sovereignty. Liberal nationalism is philosophically connected through the American and French Revolutions with the decline of absolute monarchy as the only legitimate form of government. It is closely associated with the democratic concepts of self-determination, individualism, constitutionalism, natural rights, and popular sovereignty. *See also* DEMOCRACY, NATIONAL SELF-DETERMINATION.

Liberal Party (Britain)   The third party in British politics. The Liberals, descended from the Whig party, were once one of the two major parties. Their decline has resulted from the rise of Labour, the liberalization of Conservative positions, internal disunity, and the lack of a broad socioeconomic base. The Liberals run approximately one hundred candidates in a general election. They also continue to receive a substantial number of votes, but these are spread so evenly that, given the single-member constituency system, the size of their popular vote is not reflected in the size of their parliamentary party. Party organization is roughly analogous to that of the major parties. *See also* PARTY SYSTEM (BRITAIN).

Liberum Veto, *see* Unanimity.

Library of Congress   The national library of the United States, which serves the entire national government and state and local governments as well as the public. The Library of Congress was created in 1800 by Congress and is headed by the Librarian of Congress, who is appointed by the President with Senate approval. Two important divisions of the Library are the Copyright Office and the Congressional Research Service. *See also* COPYRIGHT, CONGRESSIONAL RESEARCH SERVICE.

License   A certificate granted under law by administrative officials, permitting private individuals to engage in certain business or professional activities. Licensing power is exercised primarily by the state and local governments, but the national government also uses it to regulate such fields as atomic materials, securities, market exchanges, and radio and television. *See also* CERTIFICATE OF PUBLIC CONVENIENCE, INTEREST, AND NECESSITY.

Licensing (Trade)   A trade-control device whereby a government grants permission to certain private individuals and companies to engage in importing or exporting commodities, and regulates their activities by the conditions of the license. Under a trade licensing system, administrative officials determine which companies shall be permitted to engage in certain types of trading activity. Licensed companies must comply with state policy and administrative directives or they may have their licenses suspended, revoked, or not renewed. Licensing systems have been used primarily to allocate import quotas among several companies. Licensing thus seeks to avoid the rush to import characteristic of the global quota system that permits any importer to purchase goods up to the limit of the quota. *See also* ECONOMIC NATIONALISM, QUOTA.

Lieutenant Governor   The elective official in thirty-nine American states who succeeds to the governorship when that office is declared vacant. Typically, the lieutenant governor presides over the state senate and casts the deciding vote in case of a tie. He is elected at the same time and for the same term as the governor. In some states he serves as an ex officio member of the governor's administrative council and several boards and commissions.

Limited Government, *see* Constitutionalism.

Limited War   Any war that is fought without the employment of all major weapons and for objectives other than the complete defeat of the enemy. Limited war involves the use of conventional military forces rather than of atomic superweapons. *See also* NIXON DOCTRINE.

Line and Staff   An administrative concept that categorizes the work of an agency as an operating or advisory function. The line carries out legislative programs and deals directly with the people. The executive departments such as Agriculture or Labor are typical line departments. The staff serves in an advisory capacity, aiding the chief executive and the line officials through such activities as planning, coordinating, and budgeting. The Office of Management and Budget is a major staff agency of the federal government. *See also* AUXILIARY AGENCY.

List System   An electoral system based on proportional representation and used in a number of European countries. Each party presents its list of candidates for the seats to be filled. The party determines the order of names on its list and seats are filled starting with the top of the list. The voter chooses between lists, and is thus voting for a party rather than an individual. Each party wins the number of seats equated with its fraction of the total popular vote. *See also* PARTY SYSTEM (FRANCE).

Literacy Test   A suffrage qualification used to determine fitness for voting by means of a reading or "understanding" test. Because literacy tests have been used to discriminate against prospective voters in several states, Congress suspended their use for five years in the Voting Rights Act of 1970. *See also* VOTING RIGHTS ACT OF 1970.

Little Octobrists, *see* Communist Party of the Soviet Union.

Load, *see* Communications Theory.

Loans, International, *see* Export-Import Bank, Foreign Aid, International Bank for Reconstruction and Development, United Nations Capital Development Fund.

Lobbyist   A person, usually acting as an agent for a pressure group, who seeks to bring about the passage or defeat of legislative bills or to influence their contents. Lobbyists, often called the "Third House" of the legislature, are experts who testify before committees and present important facts on legislative proposals to support their clients' interests. Several states and the national government require the registration of lobbyists and the disclosure of information concerning their employers, their salaries, and the amounts spent to influence legislation. Lobbyists are also active in trying to influence decisions made by executive officials and administrators. *See also* REGULATION OF LOBBYING ACT; *United States v. Harriss*, PRESSURE GROUP.

Local Option   Authority vested in local units to approve, reject, or select specific or alternative forms of action. Local option often refers to the power of local units to determine by popular vote whether or not liquor will be served in the community. It may also be used to describe the action taken by communities to select a charter from those made available by state law.

Location (Geographic Power Factor)   The relationship between physical position on the globe and national power. The location of a state is related to national power through climate, access to and from the sea, control over river, sea, and land transportation routes, and the availability of natural resources. The presence or absence of powerful neighbors is also a function of location.

Lockout   Action taken by an employer to close down his plant to keep workers from their jobs in order to force them to accept his position in a labor controversy. Lockouts are lawful unless they violate a collective bargaining agreement or seek a goal that the law declares to be an unfair practice.

Logical Statement, *see* Tautology.

Logrolling   An arrangement by which two or more members of a legislative body agree in advance to support each other's bills. The technique pertains especially to the trading of votes among legislators in order to gain support for appropriations beneficial to each legislator's home district. *See also* PORK BARREL LEGISLATION.

Long Ballot   The typical state and local ballot, sometimes called the "bedsheet ballot" or "jungle ballot," which has a large number of offices to be filled, candidates to be selected, and issues to be decided. *See also* SHORT BALLOT.

Longitudinal Analysis, *see* Time Series Analysis.

Lower Level Theory, *see* Theory.

Loyalty Oath   An oath that requires an individual to disavow or abjure certain beliefs and associations. Such oaths were exacted during the Revolutionary War, the Civil War, and the "red scare" of the 1920s. Recent loyalty oaths, inspired by the cold war, generally require persons to swear that they do not advocate the violent overthrow of government nor belong to any organization so advocating. Loyalty oaths are generally required of public employees, teachers, attorneys, defense workers, and recipients of governmental benefits. The courts have struck down most loyalty oath laws after earlier acceptance, usually on the grounds that the oath did not excuse those whose associations were innocent of illegal intent or because the oath was totally unrelated to any governmental purpose. In 1970, the United States Civil Service Commission dropped the loyalty oath requirement for federal employees. Test oaths for students receiving federal aid, for Job Corps members, and for recipients of medicare have also been dropped. *See also Elfbrandt v. Russell.*

Loyalty-Security Programs   Programs carried on by national and state governments to rid the public service of disloyal persons or persons suspected of being security risks. The national government's loyalty program had its inception in 1947 when President Truman ordered that governmental employees be dismissed if grounds existed to doubt their loyalty. President Eisenhower extended the program to include all "security risks"—disloyal as well as generally untrustworthy people. The programs have also been applied to the armed forces, defense plants, maritime workers, and other government-connected activities. Appeal procedures are provided for discharged persons but do not always permit confrontation with informers. Many persons have been denied jobs without knowing the precise reasons and the programs have resulted in numerous dismissals. Although the Courts have sustained these programs, they have, in recent years, limited their application to persons holding sensitive positions and those whose activities encompass illegal aims. Similar programs have been undertaken in the states, although most states have limited their loyalty requirements to the taking of a loyalty oath. *See also* ATTORNEY GENERAL'S LIST, *Keyishian v. Board of Regents.*

Luther v. Borden, 7 Howard 1 (1848): Held that the question of whether a state has a republican form of government is a political and not a judicial question. The Supreme Court refused to define a republican form of government, holding that Congress and the President must decide. The case arose out of Dorr's Rebellion in Rhode Island in 1841, when rival groups claimed to be the true government of the state. *See also* REPUBLICAN FORM OF GOVERNMENT.

Machiavellian Diplomacy   The pursuit of national objectives by crafty, conspiratorial, and deceitful tactics motivated solely by narrow self-interest. The term derives from the name of Niccolò Machiavelli (1469–1529), the Florentine diplomat and scholar who in his celebrated book *The Prince,* described and advocated unscrupulous tactics to win and hold political power. *See also* DIPLOMACY.

Machine Politics, *see* Political Machine.

Macro-Micro Analysis   Alternative levels of analysis, the micro level consisting of subunits of the higher level macro unit. In macro analysis the researcher directs his attention to the collective, systemic, institutional, composite, or group level. In micro analysis he focuses attention on the parts, subsystems, components, or individuals that comprise the collectivity. A study made of a legislative body by measuring its inputs and outputs, for example, may constitute *macro-level* analysis, whereas the study of its committee structure or the behavior of the individual legislators that comprise the legislature would involve *micro-level* analysis. Level of analysis is a function of context, however, and what constitutes a macro-level unit in one context may be a micro-level unit in another. In the example above the legislative body would be considered as a *micro-level* unit in relation to the larger governmental system of which it is a part.

Madisonianism   The philosophy of James Madison espousing a political system based on checks, balance, moderation, and the fostering of a harmony of interests. The Madisonian model begins with the assumption that the greatest dangers to republican government are those of the divisive power of faction and the threat of tyranny resulting from too great a concentration of political power. Madison's solution to these problems was to establish a powerful national government that could provide balance to the state and local units, with checks and balances within the national government to insure adjustment and moderation in the exercise of power. *See also* JEFFERSONIAN-ISM.

Madison's Journal   Notes kept by James Madison of the proceedings of the Constitutional Convention of 1787. Although an official journal of the convention was kept, it contained only formal motions and votes by states. Madison kept a record of the debates as well. These notes were not published until 1840, four years after Madison's death.

Magistrate   A minor judicial officer, usually elected in urban areas, with jurisdiction over traffic violations, minor criminal offenses, and civil suits involving small amounts of money. Magistrates may also conduct preliminary hearings in serious criminal cases and commit the offender for trial in a higher court. In some areas, the magistrate court is called a police court, and its authority is similar to that of a justice of the peace serving in a rural area. Juries, though rarely used in magistrate courts, may consist of only six jurors. *See also* JUSTICE OF THE PEACE, FEDERAL MAGISTRATE.

Magna Carta   The Great Charter of freedom granted in 1215 by King John of England on demand of his barons.

Majority   Any number greater than one-half of those participating. A majority is utilized typically in democratic decision making to determine the outcome of an election or the resolution of procedural or substantive issues. Most non-electoral decisions in democratic political systems are made by an ordinary majority; in some cases, particularly when voting on constitutional changes, an *absolute majority* (any number greater than one-half of those eligible whether they participate or not) is required. Most election decisions, however, require only a *plurality* of the votes cast. *See also* MAJORITY RULE, PLURALITY.

Majority Floor Leader   The chief spokesman and strategist of the majority party who directs the party's forces in legislative battles. In the House, only the Speaker is usually considered to be more influential. In the Senate, the majority leader is the undisputed leader of his party. Floor leaders seek to carry out decisions of their party's caucus or conference and are aided by party whips. Their counterparts in the other party are the minority floor leaders. Floor leaders are selected by their respective party caucuses. Similar party leadership positions exist in most state legislatures. *See also* WHIP.

Majority Rule   A basic principle of democracy which asserts that the greater number of citizens in any political unit should select officials and determine policies. Majority rule is justified on the grounds that it rests on superior force, that it is commonly accepted in practice, and that, pragmatically, no reasonable alternative exists. *See also* DEMOCRACY, MAJORITY.

Majoritarianism (International Organization), *see* Egalitarianism, Elitism.

Malloy v. Hogan, 378 U.S. 1 (1964): Held that protection against self-incrimination found in the Fifth Amendment to the Constitution applies to the states through the Fourteenth Amendment in the same manner that it limits the national government. *See also* SELF-INCRIMINATION.

Malthusianism   The theory which postulates that population increases geometrically (2, 4, 8, 16, 32, . . .) while the means of subsistence increase only arithmetically (2, 4, 6, 8, 10, . . .). Malthusianism, therefore, asserts that improvement in the standard of living is not possible and that a livable ratio between population and food supply can be maintained only through the corrective intervention of recurring war, pestilence, disease, and famine. Named for its formulator, the economist Thomas Malthus (1776–1834), Malthusianism went out of vogue when the Industrial Revolution made it possible for the countries of Western Europe to have both a rising standard of living and a substantial increase in population. *See also* DEMOGRAPHIC CYCLE.

Management Internship Examination, *see* Federal Service Entrance Examination.

Management Science   The use of scientific and particularly mathematical methods to assess the effectiveness of organizations from the perspectives of managers. Management science emphasizes the measurement of efficiency and economy, as in the determination of dollar costs per unit of item produced or service delivered. Modern versions of management science include a concern for human relations variables in the assessment of effectiveness or productivity. *See also* COST-BENEFIT ANALYSIS, OPERATIONS RESEARCH.

Manager Plan, *see* Council-Manager Plan, County-Manager Plan.

Managers, *see* Conference Committee.

Mandamus   An order issued by a court to compel performance of an act. A writ of mandamus may be issued to an individual or corporation as well as to a public official. In the case of public officers, a writ will be issued only to compel performance of a "ministerial" act—one that the officer has a clear legal duty to perform. If he has discretion to determine whether he will perform an act, the court will not order him to do so. *See also* WRIT.

Mandate   Popular support for a political program. A mandate is assumed to emerge from an election as a result of popular support given to a political party or to elected officials. A mandate may be vague or specific, depending upon the clarity with which alternatives are presented to the voters. *See also* RESPONSIBLE PARTY SYSTEM.

Mandates System   The arrangement whereby the colonial territories of the defeated Central Powers of World War I were placed under the guardianship and tutelage of Allied nations. Each Mandatory Power was responsible to the League of Nations in the administration of its mandate. Mandated territories were classified into three groups according to their relative stages of development. Class A mandates (Arab territories formerly under Turkish dominion) were regarded as ready for independence and self-government after a minimal period of tutelage. Class B mandates (German East and West Africa) were given no promises of early independence and were to be governed as colonies with certain fundamental rights guaranteed. Class C mandates (German South West Africa and Pacific islands) were to be governed as "integral portions of the [Mandatory Power's] territory," with no promise of eventual independence. A Permanent Mandates Commission of ten private experts was established under the Covenant to oversee the administration of the mandates and report its finding to the League Council. *See also* TRUST TERRITORY.

Manifest Function, *see* Functionalism.

Maoism   Interpretations of Marxism-Leninism, and the policies developed and actions taken by the Chinese Communist party under the leadership of Chairman Mao Tse-tung. Maoism's theoretical base is set forth for mass consumption in the aphorisms included in the widely distributed *Quotations from Chairman Mao Tse-tung.* Mao's main theoretical contributions include: (1) a theory for fighting guerrilla war in agrarian colonial and semicolonial countries with the active support of the peasants;

(2) a definition in the Chinese context of democratic centralism to mean that the people should enjoy a measure of freedom and democracy while at the same time submitting themselves to "socialist discipline"; (3) a definition of Marx's "dictatorship of the proletariat" in the Chinese situation as "a people's democratic dictatorship, led by the working class and based on the worker-peasant alliance"; (4) a theory that recognizes contradictions within the people's socialist system as well as between it and the capitalist enemy; (5) rejection of Soviet doctrinal appeals for "peaceful coexistence" in favor of "permanent revolution" throughout the world against the remaining bastions of capitalism; and (6) rejection of the primacy of economic development and material betterment in favor of maintaining the purity of the revolution and the creation of the "new Chinese man" and a new society freed of all contradictions. *See also* CULTURAL REVOLUTION.

Mapp v. Ohio, 367 U.S. 643 (1961): Ruled that a state may not use illegally seized evidence in criminal trials. This decision overruled *Wolf v. Colorado,* 338 U.S. 25 (1949), which held that a state could use evidence secured through an illegal search and seizure. *See also* SEARCH AND SEIZURE.

Marbury v. Madison, 1 Cranch 137 (1803): Struck down, for the first time in American history, an act of Congress as unconstitutional. The Court, speaking through Chief Justice John Marshall, held unconstitutional a portion of the Judiciary Act of 1789 that had added to the original jurisdiction of the Supreme Court, as specified in Article III of the Constitution. The case was essentially a political controversy between the defeated Federalist party and the incoming Jeffersonian party over last minute Federalist party appointments to the federal courts. *See also* JUDICIAL REVIEW.

Margin   The cash down payment made by a customer who purchases stocks or bonds on credit. The margin or amount of down payment required for the purchase of securities is set by the Board of Governors of the Federal Reserve System. The securities purchased usually constitute the collateral for the loan on the balance owed. *See also* BOARD OF GOVERNORS, FEDERAL RESERVE SYSTEM.

Margin of Preference, *see* Preferential Trade Arrangement.

Maritime Administration, *see* Department of Commerce.

Maritime Law, *see* Admiralty Jurisdiction, Inter-Governmental Maritime Consultative Organization.

Marshal   An official of the federal Department of Justice attached to each federal district court. The duties of United States Marshals correspond to those of sheriffs in county governments. They make arrests in federal criminal cases, keep accused persons in custody, secure jurors, serve legal papers, keep order in the courtroom, and execute orders and decisions of the court. Marshals are appointed by the President, subject to the Senate's confirmation, for four-year terms.

Marshall Plan   A proposal made by Secretary of State George C. Marshall in 1947 for a vast program of American economic aid to reconstruct the war-devastated economies of Western Europe. The United States Congress accepted the Plan and, in 1948, established the European Recovery Program under which sixteen nations of Western Europe (later joined by West Germany) received $15 billion in grants and loans from 1948 to 1952. Under the Marshall program, the participating European nations on American request joined together in the Organization for European Economic Cooperation (OEEC) for the purpose of drawing up a collective inventory of resources and requirements. The USSR and other Communist countries were invited to participate, but rejected the offer. *See also* FOREIGN AID.

Martial Law   Military government established over a civilian population during an emergency in which military decrees supersede civilian laws and military tribunals replace civil courts. Martial law may be accompanied by the suspension of the writ of habeas corpus. Although the Constitution does not delegate specific power to declare martial law, it is implied from military and defense powers and can be invoked by the President when necessary for the security of the nation. In the states, the governor as commander in chief of the state militia may declare martial law during an emergency occasioned by internal disorders or a natural disaster. Vast discretion is vested in military officers in enforcing martial law. *See also Ex parte Milligan.*

Marxian Socialism, *see* Socialism.

Marxism   The body of economic, political, and social theories developed by Karl Marx and his collaborator, Friedrich Engels, in the nineteenth century. Marxism offers a comprehensive "scientific" philosophy of history that explains mankind's development dialectically as a series of class struggles which have produced new social orders. Marx viewed capitalism as a system suffering from irremediable internal contradictions with an intensifying class struggle that would culminate in a revolution carried out by the proletariat against the bourgeoisie. A period of "dictatorship of the proletariat" would follow in which capitalists would be stripped of their wealth and power, land and the means of production nationalized, and class distinctions abolished. Then, according to Marx, the state would "wither away," a final stage of pure communism would be ushered in, and man would live in a perfect, classless, stateless society of spontaneous cooperation in which each individual would contribute according to his ability and receive according to his needs. Marx's ideas were developed in *The Communist Manifesto* of 1848 and in his principal work, *Das Kapital,* of which the first volume was published in 1867.

Massachusetts Ballot, *see* Office-Block Ballot.

Massachusetts v. Mellon and Frothingham v. Mellon, 262 U.S. 447 (1923): Rejected claims by a state that the federal grant-in-aid program to protect the health of mothers and infants was an unconstitutional invasion of the reserved powers of the states guaranteed by the Tenth Amendment. In a companion case *(Frothingham v. Mellon),* the Court rejected the claim of Mrs. Frothingham that the grant-in-aid program would take her property under the guise of taxation. *See also Frothingham v. Mellon.*

Massive Retaliation   The threat of a nuclear response to restrain the actions of another state. After the Korean War, the Eisenhower Administration adopted a policy of massive retaliation to cope with the threat of limited, peripheral wars fostered by the Communists. The policy was aimed at preventing such wars by announcing in advance that the United States reserved the right to meet any new peripheral aggression not at the point of outbreak but by a "massive retaliation at places and times" of the nation's own choosing. The concept of massive retaliation underlies American and Soviet contemporary policies of deterrence: both sides accept the premise that neither could destroy the other's retaliatory capability in a surprise first strike and that a massive retaliation would follow. *See also* BALANCE OF TERROR, DETERRENCE.

Mass Media   The technical means of communication with millions of people, exemplified by television, radio, newspapers, motion pictures, magazines, and periodicals. Television, in particular, is used with increasing impact to build an "image campaign" in which special techniques (contrived situations, spot announcements, editing of video tapes, and the like) are used to achieve short-term perceptual shifts in voter behavior. *See also* PROPAGANDA.

Mass Public   The general public as it relates to the making of governmental decisions. The mass public, far from being a single, cohesive unity with common attitudes, prejudices, and views, consists of many publics holding diverse, often conflicting, opinions. The views of the mass public on specific issues may be expressed or divulged in various ways, but they are usually most effectively presented in democratic states through the electoral process or in polls. Mass opinion goes through three stages in the process of influencing governmental actions: formulation, expression, and direct effect upon or embodiment in policy decisions.

Maternal and Child Welfare Program   A feature of the Social Security Act of 1935 that provides for grants to the states for maternal and child health services, crippled children services, and general child welfare programs. Grants are made to the states not for payments to particular persons, as is true under the categorical aid programs, but for support of state welfare programs. Maternal and child health services include care of mothers before and after childbirth, and immunization of children against communicable diseases. Another program seeks to provide therapy and rehabilitation for crippled children whose parents lack independent means to care for them. Child welfare activities include counseling and care of neglected, mentally retarded, and emotionally disturbed youngsters, and care of delinquent children.

Mathematical Model, *see* Model.

Mayflower Compact   An agreement signed in 1620 by all adult males on board the ship *Mayflower,* prior to landing at Plymouth, to form a civil body politic governed by majority rule. *See also* CONTRACT THEORY.

Mayor   The chief executive and/or the ceremonial leader of a city. The role of the mayor varies with the form of city government. Under the strong mayor-council plan, the mayor has extensive executive power including control over appointments and removals of city officials and the veto power. Under a weak mayor-council plan, the mayor has limited executive powers. The mayor in the commission and manager plans is largely a ceremonial figure. *See also* MAYOR-COUNCIL PLAN.

Mayor-administrator Plan   A plan of city government in which an administrative officer is appointed to assist the mayor in managing the affairs of the city. The plan has been adopted in a number of large cities to free the mayor for broader policy-making duties while using expert aid to supervise the routine administration of city government. The administrator, called the chief administrative officer, is appointed by the mayor with or without council approval and may have extensive appointment and removal power over administrative officials. His duties include budget supervision, coordination of city agencies, personnel direction, and the giving of technical advice to the mayor.

Mayor-council Plan   A plan of city government in which the mayor is elected to serve as the executive officer of the city and an elective council serves as the legislative body. Wide variations exist from city to city but the plan usually takes the form of a weak or strong mayor-council plan depending upon the position of the mayor in the system. *See also* STRONG-MAYOR PLAN, WEAK-MAYOR PLAN.

McCarthyism   Unsubstantiated accusations of disloyalty and abuse of legislative investigatory power that engender fear over real or imagined threats to the security of the nation. The term was derived in the early 1950s from the actions of Senator Joseph R. McCarthy of Wisconsin who made repeated charges against public officials and private individuals under the protection of his senatorial immunity.

McCulloch v. Maryland, 4 Wheaton 316 (1819): Upheld, in a landmark decision of the Supreme Court, the power of the national government to establish a bank, and denied the state of Maryland the power to tax a branch of the bank. In the opinion by Chief Justice John Marshall, the Court held that it was not necessary for the Constitution expressly to authorize Congress to create a bank. Rather, the power to do so was implied from Congress' power over financial matters and from the "necessary and proper" clause of the Constitution. Maryland could not tax a legitimate instrumentality of the national government, said the Court, since this would be an invasion of national supremacy. "The power to tax is the power to destroy. . . . " From this was derived the principle of intergovernmental tax immunity. *See also* IMPLIED POWERS.

McGrain v. Daugherty, 273 U.S. 135 (1927): Decided that Congress has the right to compel testimony from private individuals as an aid to its power to pass laws. The *McGrain* case concerned the congressional investigation which arose out of the Teapot Dome scandal involving bribery and other illegal acts by public officials. The Court held that Congress could subpoena a private individual as well as a public official when this action is pertinent to a proper legislative function. *See also* INVESTIGATING COMMITTEE.

McNabb v. United States, 318 U.S. 332 (1943): Held that the federal courts may not convict a person of a crime on the basis of a confession secured while he was unlawfully detained. The Court ruled that a prisoner must be taken before a judicial officer for arraignment without delay. *See also* ARRAIGNMENT.

Mean, *see* Central Tendency Measurement.

Measurement, *see* Attitude Scaling, Biased Sample, Central Tendency Measurement, Guttman Scale, Quantification, Reliability, Sampling, Semantic Differential, Scale, Sociometry, Statistics, Testing.

Measures of Association, *see* Correlation.

Measures Short of War   Actions undertaken by one state against another to protect its legal rights or punish a wrongdoer, without a formal declaration of war. Measures short of war may involve such unilateral state actions as: (1) breaking diplomatic relations; (2) retortion (a legal but unfriendly action taken against a state that had acted in an equally unfriendly but legal way); (3) reprisal (undertaking a normally illegal action to retaliate against a state that had perpetrated a wrong); (4) an embargo or boycott; (5) a blockade; or (6) the occupation of foreign territory. *See also* BLOCKADE, BOYCOTT, EMBARGO, REPRISAL.

Median, *see* Central Tendency Measurement.

Mediation and Conciliation (Labor-Management)   Terms used interchangeably to refer to the attempt of a third party to settle a labor dispute by bringing the parties together and persuading them to reach a compromise. Unlike arbitration, the mediator or conciliator has no power to make his suggested solutions binding upon the parties. *See also* FEDERAL MEDIATION AND CONCILIATION SERVICE, NATIONAL MEDIATION BOARD.

Mediation (International)   A peaceful settlement procedure whereby a third party aids the disputants in finding a solution by offering substantive suggestions. Mediation may be requested by the parties to a dispute or volunteered by a third state. In international practice, the disputants are not entitled, even during the course of hostilities, to view an offer of mediation as an unfriendly act, nor are they obligated to accept an unsolicited offer of mediation. *See also* PEACEFUL SETTLEMENT.

Medical Examiner, *see* Coroner.

Medicare   A health insurance program enacted in 1965 as an amendment to the Social Security Act to provide medical care for the elderly. Two health care programs are involved. One, which is compulsory and financed by increases in the social security payroll tax, covers most hospital and nursing home costs, home health service visits, and diagnostic services for persons aged sixty-five or older. The second is a voluntary supplementary health program for persons over sixty-five, which covers a variety of health services both in and out of medical institutions and pays a substantial part of physician costs. The supplementary plan is financed by a small charge to the person enrolled and by an equal amount paid by the national government out of general revenue.

Megalopolis, *see* Metropolitan Area.

Mental Health Program, *see* National Mental Health Act of 1946.

Mercantilism   The economic philosophy and practice of government regulation of a nation's economic life to increase state power and security. Mercantilism provided the economic model followed by European states from the sixteenth through the eighteenth centuries. Each state sought to build up its treasury by maintaining a surplus of exports over imports, so that the favorable trade balance would result in inflows of gold and silver. Cottage industries were encouraged by government policies over agriculture and mining since finished goods offered lower shipping costs and higher prices. Colonies were utilized as sources of cheap raw materials and as markets for expensive manufactured goods. Governmental regulation and control permeated all sectors of each nation's economy. Wages were kept low to add to the profit for the nation's treasury and to stimulate industriousness among the masses who otherwise, it was believed, were too lazy to work.

Merger   The pooling of assets of two companies to form a single company. Various kinds of mergers are possible, including those between competing companies (horizontal), those aimed at gaining control of raw material suppliers (vertical-backward), those involving retail outlets (vertical-forward), and those of unrelated businesses (conglomerate).

Merit System   The selection, retention, and promotion of government employees on the basis of demonstrated fitness. Though the term is often used interchangeably with "civil service," the merit system emphasizes positive programs of sound personnel management rather than the mere placing of restraints upon the spoils system. *See also* CIVIL SERVICE; CLASSIFIED SERVICE.

Methodology   A body of knowledge and technique relating to the process and assumptions of scholarly inquiry within a discipline. Methodology is concerned with the gathering, analysis, measurement, evaluation, and use of data. Some political scientists have treated methodology as quite narrowly restricted to research methods and techniques used in data analysis. Others regard methodology as concerned not only with technique but also with broader questions of research design, choice of inductive or deductive modes of reasoning, criteria for identification of relevant variables, and standards of acceptable proof and explanation. Much of the effort expended on methodology in political science has been devoted to adapting techniques of inquiry used in other disciplines.

Metropolitan Area   A large city and its surrounding suburbs, which are socially and economically integrated although composed of separate units of government. The term metropolitan is derived from the Greek terms "mētēr" (mother) and "polis" (city). In 1971, the Bureau of the Census indentified 247 metropolitan areas (including four in Puerto Rico), up from 212 in 1960. These include each county, or group of contiguous counties, containing at least one city having a population of 50,000 or more. The contiguous counties are included if they are densely populated and economically and socially integrated with the central county. The Census Bureau calls these "standard metropolitan statistical areas." New York and Chicago have been identified as "standard consolidated areas" because of the highly complex nature of these regions which combine several contiguous standard metropolitan statistical areas. More than one-sixth of the population lives in a belt from Boston to Washington, D.C. This "megalopolis" is about 450 miles long, 150 miles wide, and contains 34 contiguous standard metropolitan statistical areas. *See also* ANNEXATION, CITY-COUNTY CONSOLIDATION, CITY-COUNTY SEPARATION, CONSOLIDATION, FUNCTIONAL CONSOLIDATION, METROPOLITAN FEDERATION, URBAN COUNTY PLAN, COUNCILS OF GOVERNMENT.

Metropolitan Federation   A proposed solution to the problems of metropolitan areas that would create a central metropolitan government to handle problems of the entire metropolitan region, reserving to the local units control over local matters. The plan is based on the principle of federalism which is in effect at the national-state level. The plan has been put into effect in Toronto, Canada, and the metropolitan government of Dade County (Miami), Florida, resembles a federation. Under a federated plan, the metropolitan or central unit might handle such common problems as highways, air terminals, water supply, sewerage, and air pollution. The local units could continue to act in the areas of police, schools, and other matters which the people desire to retain as strictly local functions. *See also* METROPOLITAN AREA.

Micro Analysis, *see* Macro-Micro Analysis.

Middle Range Theory, *see* Theory.

Migration   Population movements from one state or region to another. "Immigration" is the movement viewed from the receiving state, while population movements out of a country are called "emigration." The record of human migration is as old as recorded history, but perhaps the greatest wave involved the emigration of over 25 million people from Europe between the 1870s and World War I. In Asia during the same period, Chinese emigration averaged 70,000 to 80,000 annually, although civil war in central China caused this figure to go above 200,000 in 1926 and 1927. Most Chinese migrants have gone to the countries of Southeast Asia, where their communal culture has created problems of national integration. Heavy migration declined after World War I and by the 1930s had virtually stopped. One of the major migrations after World War II involved well over 1,000,000 Jews from all over the world, mainly Europe, North Africa, and the Middle East, who flocked to the new state of Israel. The term "migration" indicates voluntary displacement from one country to another and does not refer to populations forcibly removed or transferred by treaty. *See also* OVERSEAS CHINESE, REFUGEE.

Milieu, *see* Environment.

Militarism (Fascist Theory)   The emphasis placed by fascists on military organization and discipline to strengthen the single national party and to provide order and security for the state. Under fascism, typically, militaristic values are inculcated in the young at school and in youth organizations, military heroes are revered, and spectacular ceremonies and parades extolling the virtues of the soldier are used to cultivate an honored role for the military as the defenders of the nation and to encourage acceptance of a well-disciplined social order.

Military Aid, *see* Foreign Aid, Lend-Lease.

Military Appeals, *see* Court of Military Appeals.

Military Government   Temporary government established by conquering military forces over occupied enemy territory. Areas occupied by American forces are governed under statutes enacted by Congress, supplemented by orders issued by the President as commander in chief. The military governor of a territory under military government exercises supreme legislative, executive, and judicial authority. Civil government operates to the extent permitted by the military governor.

Military-Industrial Complex   An informal alliance among key military, governmental, and corporate decision makers involved in the highly profitable weapons-procurement and military-support system. The phrase, military-industrial complex, was coined by President Dwight D. Eisenhower in his final presidential address in which he warned the American people to guard against the growing and excessive militarization of society. The evolution of the military-industrial complex can be determined through such indicators as the growth of the national defense budget, the increasingly militaristic posture of the nation in foreign policy, the magnitude of profits for those corporations engaged extensively in defense business, and the size of subsidies paid by the Pentagon to defense contractors. *See also* CIVILIAN CONTROL; DEFENSE CONTRACT.

Military Law Law, enacted by Congress, that governs the conduct of enlisted men and officers of the armed forces of the United States. Military law also establishes the procedures for trial by courts-martial for alleged infractions. *See also* COURT-MARTIAL.

Military Sanctions, *see* Sanctions (Collective Security).

Military Staff Committee, Security Council, *see* Sanctions (Collective Security).

Militia, *see* National Guard.

Millage, *see* Property Tax.

Mines, Bureau of, *see* Department of the Interior.

Minifundia System (Minifundismo) A Latin American pattern of land tenure based on agricultural units too small to provide the income necessary by local standards to satisfy the basic needs of a family. The minifundia are found as scattered individual units or as communities, and they may also exist in a symbiotic relationship with latifundia. In many areas the *minifundistas* are squatters or tenants, often dependent on the latifundia for markets, credit, and part-time employment. The minifundia system is extensive throughout Latin America, and in such countries as Ecuador, Guatemala, and Peru, accounts for eighty-five to ninety percent of all farms. *See also* LATIFUNDIA SYSTEM.

Minimum Wage Act, *see* Fair Labor Standards Act of 1938.

Minister, *see* Diplomat.

Ministerial Act, *see* Mandamus.

Minister of Foreign Affairs (France) The Cabinet official charged with the development and execution of French foreign policy. The Foreign Minister is appointed by the President at the suggestion of the Prime Minister and is removable by the President. The President determines the extent of the role to be played by the Foreign Minister. The Foreign Minister advises the President and participates in the deliberations of the Council of Ministers. Under President de Gaulle who personally assumed control of foreign affairs, the foreign ministers' duties were largely technical and administrative.

Minority President An elected President who has received less than 50 percent of the total *popular* votes cast for all candidates, although obtaining a majority of the *electoral* votes. A winning candidate is most likely to be a minority president when there are several fairly strong minor party candidates in the presidential contest. *See also* ELECTORAL COLLEGE.

Minority Rights, *see* Majority Rule.

Minor Party   A party movement, often based on a single idea or principle, that usually has little influence on elections because its support is either localized or widely scattered. Some American political observers distinguish a minor party from a third party, a new party based on a protest movement which may influence the outcome of a major election. *See also* THIRD PARTY.

Miranda v. Arizona, 384 U.S. 436 (1966): A major ruling on criminal procedure to secure the privilege against self-incrimination. The Court held that "Prior to any questioning, the person must be warned that he has a right to remain silent, that any statement he does make may be used against him, and that he has a right to the presence of an attorney, either retained or appointed." The defendant may "knowingly" waive these rights. *See also* SELF-INCRIMINATION.

Misdemeanor   A minor criminal offense. The precise nature of a misdemeanor varies from state to state where it is defined by law. It may include such offenses as traffic violations, petty theft, disorderly conduct, and gambling. Punishment is usually limited to light jail terms or fines. Minor courts such as justices of the peace or municipal courts usually hear such cases without a jury. *See also* FELONY.

Mississippi v. Johnson, 4 Wallace 475 (1867): Rejected an attempt by the State of Mississippi to enjoin President Andrew Johnson from enforcing the Reconstruction Acts of 1867. The Court held that the President cannot be restrained by injunction from carrying out his official duties of a political nature, such as the enforcement of an act of Congress.

Missouri Compromise, *see Dred Scott v. Sanford.*

Missouri Plan   A method of selecting state judges used in a few states that combines both appointment and election. In Missouri, judges of the Supreme Court, of courts of appeals, and of courts in St. Louis and Kansas City are appointed by the governor from a list of three names prepared by a commission composed of lawyers and laymen. The judge serves one year and then stands for election on the basis of his record. There is no opposition candidate. If the voters approve, he serves for six to twelve years, depending on the court. If he is defeated, the procedure is started anew. Other communities in the state may come under the plan if the voters approve. A similar plan exists in California; here, however, the governor nominates the candidate subject to approval of, rather than from a list prepared by, the commission.

Missouri v. Holland, 252 U.S. 416 (1920): Upheld the validity of a federal statute based on a treaty with Great Britain for the protection of birds and waterfowl migrating between Canada and the United States. The question was whether the national government could acquire, through a treaty, power to legislate on domestic matters otherwise reserved to the states. A similar federal law, antedating the treaty and the law in question in this case, had earlier been declared unconstitutional by the lower federal courts. *See also* TREATY.

Mixed Economy, *see* Keynesianism, Laissez-Faire.

Mobilization Preparing a nation to meet an attack or to fight a war. Mobilization involves placing the armed forces in readiness, calling up reserves to active duty, putting the nation's economy on a war footing, establishing governmental controls over manpower, production, resources, and prices. Mobilization for modern war involves readying the totality of a nation's manpower and physical resources for military action. The Office of Emergency Preparedness in the Executive Office of the President is responsible for planning the nation's nonmilitary defense effort. *See also* EMERGENCY POWERS, WAR POWERS.

Modal Personality, *see* Personality.

Mode, *see* Central Tendency Measurement.

Model A working intellectual construct by which social or physical situations—real or hypothetical—can be represented. "Model" sometimes connotes an ideal to be achieved or a pattern to be followed, such as a model state constitution. But as it is generally used in political science, such value connotation is lacking. Most models are simply intellectual constructs used to organize thought and direct research. Models typically include sets of categories, assumptions, and postulates, which are used to sort out data, analyze it, determine relationships, and help the model builder to explain or predict. A construct that conceives of politics as a set of input-output relations might be called a system model. Or a construct that depicts the legislative process as a sequence of related operations would be a legislative process model. Political model design is aimed at incorporating or reproducing those elements of the real world of political behavior that the investigator regards as critical for accomplishing his research goal. A model may be expressed in words, charts and graphs, or mathematical symbols. A *mathematical model* is a set of political or other relationships represented in mathematical form. *See also* HEURISTIC DEVICE, ISOMORPHISM.

Model Cities, *see* Department of Housing and Urban Development.

Model State Constitution A proposed state constitution prepared by the National Municipal League. Highlights of the Model include a unicameral legislature, a strong executive, and a unified court system with judges appointed by the governor. It also provides for modern techniques of budgeting, fianancing, auditing, and personnel management; for home rule for cities and counties, the initiative and referendum, simplified amendment and revision procedures, and a brief bill of rights. The Model is brief compared to most state constitutions and is restricted to fundamentals. *See also* CONSTITUTION, STATE.

Modernization, *see* Development Theory, Political Development, Technology.

Modern Society, *see* Political Development.

Monarch (Britain)   The hereditary chief of state of the United Kingdom and British Empire, and the symbol of Commonwealth unity. Prior to the establishment of the ultimate authority of Parliament, the king ruled by the power of the royal prerogative. With the Glorious Revolution of 1688, the primacy of parliamentary statutes was recognized, and today's constitutional monarchy is based on statutes and conventions. The remaining prerogatives are exercised on the advice of the Cabinet and include appointing the Prime Minister, dismissing the government, dissolving Parliament, creating peers, and granting patronage, honors, and mercy. *See also* MONARCHY.

Monarchy   Any form of government in which the supreme powers of the state are exercised, or ceremoniously held, by a king, queen, emperor, or other regal potentate. Monarchs may acquire their position through inheritance or election, although the latter is unusual. Absolute monarchs exercise full ruling powers, whereas constitutional monarchs either share governmental powers with elected parliaments or are mere figureheads. *See also* DIVINE RIGHT.

Monetary Policy   Government policy that aims at affecting the amount of currency in circulation and the availability of credit. The Federal Reserve Board uses "tight money" monetary policies to restrain and prolong boom periods in the nation's economy and to fight inflation. "Loose money" policies are used to check deflation and to fight recessions by making money and credit more freely available. *See also* FISCAL POLICY; FEDERAL RESERVE SYSTEM.

Monopoly   A market condition characterized by the absence of competition and the artificial fixing of prices for services or commodities, unaffected by the supply-demand forces of the market economy. *See also* OLIGOPOLY.

Monroe Doctrine   A unilateral declaration of American foreign policy made by President Monroe in his annual message to Congress in December 1823, opposing any European intervention in the affairs of the American continents. He also reaffirmed the American intention to refrain from interfering in European affairs. The Doctrine was intended to stop the Holy Alliance from aiding Spain in a reconquest of the newly independent Latin-American republics. *See also* RIO TREATY, ORGANIZATION OF AMERICAN STATES.

Moore v. Dempsey, 261 U.S. 86 (1923): Declared that a trial conducted under the influence of a mob, in which public passion dominates the judge, jury, witnesses, and defense counsel, is a denial of due process of law. In this case, the trial of five Negroes was conducted under the duress of a mob, making the outcome a certainty. *See also* DUE PROCESS.

Morning Hour A period reserved in Congress at the start of a legislative day to consider routine business. The Senate sets aside the first two hours of each new legislative day for such matters as committee reports, the introduction of bills and resolutions, and the receipt of presidential messages. In the House, the morning hour is seldom used since most routine business is transacted in the Committee of the Whole.

Morrill Act of 1862, *see* Land-Grant College.

Most-Favored-Nation Clause A provision inserted in a trade agreement that extends tariff concessions agreed to by the signatories to all nations participating in the reciprocal system. The most-favored-nation clause avoids trade discrimination against third states by granting equal treatment to all. Likewise, more favorable tariff arrangements extended to other states by any signatory will automatically apply to the original parties. *See also* GENERAL AGREEMENT ON TARIFFS AND TRADE.

Mulford v. Smith, 307 U.S. 38 (1939): Sustained the constitutionality of the Agriculture Act of 1938, holding that Congress may limit the amount of a crop sold in interstate commerce, and that the delegation of powers to the Secretary of Agriculture by Congress was proper since definite standards were laid down in the Act. It also held that Congress may validly exercise its power to regulate interstate commerce through a regulatory tax. *See also* COMMERCE POWER, REGULATORY TAX.

Multilateral Trade, *see* Customs Union, Economic Union, Free Trade Area, Most-Favored-Nation Clause, Preferential Trade Arrangement.

Multilateral Treaty, *see* Treaty.

Multiparty System An electoral system, usually based on proportional representation, that requires a coalition of several parties to form a majority to run the government. Multiparty systems are typical of continental European democracies. The system can be distinguished from the Anglo-American two-party system not by the existence of numerous parties, but rather in that many parties seriously compete for, and actually win, seats in the legislature. *See also* TWO-PARTY SYSTEM, PROPORTIONAL REPRESENTATION.

Multiple Correlation, *see* Correlation.

Multiple Independently-Targeted Re-Entry Vehicle (MIRV), *see* Strategic Arms Limitation Talks.

Multipolarity, *see* Polycentrism.

Multivariate Analysis, *see* Variable.

Municipal Corporation, *see* Borough, City, Dillon's Rule, Incorporated and Unincorporated Areas, Village.

Munn v. Illinois, 94 U.S. 113 (1876): Held that a state can validly fix maximum rates for a "business affected with a public interest." Regulation of a privately owned grain warehouse by the state of Illinois was upheld on the ground that when a proprietor devotes his property to a public use, he "must submit to be controlled by the public for the common good. . . . " *See also* BUSINESS AFFECTED WITH A PUBLIC INTEREST.

Murphy v. Waterfront Commission, *see* Immunity.

Myers v. United States, 272 U.S. 52 (1926): Upheld the President's removal from office of a postmaster without securing the approval of the Senate to the removal. The Court held that Congress cannot limit the President's power to remove executive officials, and the provisions of a law of 1876 requiring the Senate's concurrence in presidential removals was held to be unconstitutional. *See also Humphrey's* case.

NAACP, *see* Civil Rights Organizations, *National Association for the Advancement of Colored People v. Alabama.*

Namibia (Southwest Africa), *see* Trust Territory.

NASA, *see* National Aeronautics and Space Council.

NASC, *see* National Aeronautics and Space Council.

Nation   Any sizable group of people united by common bonds of geography, religion, language, race, custom, and tradition, and through shared experiences and common aspirations. The term is often used interchangeably with *state,* but not all national groups have achieved statehood, although they all aspire to it. Modern nations began to emerge from feudalism in the ninth century. The community of nation-states was given political and legal recognition by the Peace of Westphalia in 1648. *See also* NATIONALISM, STATE.

National   A person who owes allegiance to a country, though not a citizen thereof. The term is used at times, however, in the same sense as the term "citizen." Under American law, a national is an inhabitant of an outlying possession of the United States to whom Congress has not granted citizenship. Residents of the Philippine Islands were considered nationals until independence was granted, whereas the people of Puerto Rico were granted citizenship in 1917 after a period as nationals.

National Aeronautics and Space Council (NASC)   A staff agency in the Executive Office of the President that advises the President on policies, plans, and programs concerning the American space program. Members include the Vice President of the United States, who serves as Chairman, the Secretaries of State and Defense, the Administrator of the National Aeronautics and Space Administration (NASA), who carries out space program decisions, and the Chairman of the Atomic Energy Commission. The NASC was established under the National Aeronautics and Space Act of 1958.

National Assembly (France)   The lower but dominant house of the bicameral Parliament. All 486 members of the National Assembly are elected as a unit for five-year terms from single-member voting districts under a two-ballot system. To be elected on the first ballot, a candidate must receive a majority that includes at least twenty-five percent of the eligible voters. Otherwise, a second balloting occurs one week later and the candidate receiving a plurality is declared elected. Candidates post a deposit of 1000 francs, which is forfeited unless they poll five percent of the vote. If this figure is met, the deposit is refunded and the state provides an additional 4000 francs toward campaign expenses. Deputies must be at least twenty-three years of age, must have completed their military service, and must have been French citizens for at least ten years. Parliament meets for a three-month spring session and for two and one half months in the fall.

National Association for the Advancement of Colored People v. Alabama, 357 U.S. 449 (1958): Established that a state may not compel the disclosure of the membership lists of an organization that is pursuing lawful ends, if members are likely to suffer physical, economic, and other hostile reprisals from such disclosure. *See also* FREEDOM OF ASSOCIATION.

National Association of Manufacturers (NAM), *see* Business and Professional Organizations.

National Bureau of Standards, *see* Department of Commerce.

National Chairman   The chairman of a political party's national committee, who is generally chosen by his party's presidential candidate, with the national committee ratifying the choice. *See also* POLITICAL PARTY.

National Character, *see* Political Culture.

National Committee   A standing committee of a national political party established to direct and coordinate party activities during the four-year periods between national party conventions. The Democratic National Committee includes two members, a man and a woman, from each state, from the District of Columbia, and from several territories; the Republican National Committee uses the same formula but adds state chairmen from all states carried by the Republican party in the preceding presidential, gubernatorial, or congressional election. National committeemen and committeewomen are chosen every four years by the various delegations to the national convention. Each committee ratifies the presidential nominee's selection of a national chairman who acts as spokesman for his party. *See also* POLITICAL PARTY.

National Communism, *see* Titoism.

National Conference of Commissioners on Uniform State Laws, *see* Uniform State Laws.

National Convention   A quadrennial meeting held by each major party to select presidential and vice presidential candidates, write a platform, choose a national committee, and conduct party business. Presidential candidates have been nominated by the convention method in every election since 1832. Delegates are apportioned on the basis of state representation with bonuses for states showing voting majorities for the party in preceding elections. Delegates are selected by party conventions or committees in approximately one-half of the states and by presidential primaries in the remaining states. Both parties also accredit delegates from the District of Columbia, Puerto Rico, and the Virgin Islands. The nomination of, and voting on, candidates is conducted by a call of the states in alphabetical order. Democratic party conventions no longer authorize use of the unit rule. Both conventions nominate their candidates by an absolute majority vote. *See also* CREDENTIALS COMMITTEE; FAVORITE SON, PLATFORM, PRESIDENTIAL PRIMARIES, UNIT RULE.

National Council of Churches of Christ, *see* Civil Rights Organizations.

National Defense Education Act of 1958   An act to encourage education in science, mathematics, engineering, languages, humanities, social sciences, and teacher education. The Act provides for loans to needy college students, with preference given to those pursuing these courses of study; one-half the loan is forgiven if the student teaches for five years after graduation. In addition, the Act provides funds for graduate fellowships, and for public schools to purchase educational equipment and to improve guidance and testing services.

National Economic Plan, *see* Economic and Social Council (France).

National Environmental Policy Act of 1969   The basic declaration of national policy aimed at encouraging "productive and enjoyable harmony between man and his environment" and promoting efforts that "prevent or eliminate damage to the environment and biosphere and stimulate the health and welfare of man. . . . " The Act established a Council on Environmental Quality in the Executive Office to advise the President. Each year the President is required by the Act to transmit an Enviromental Quality Report to the Congress in which he reviews the current situation and makes recommendations for legislative programs. The Act in effect recognizes that modern technology and the "growth ethic" of capitalism must be redirected so that they function more in harmony with the natural environment. *See also* COUNCIL OF ENVIRONMENTAL QUALITY, ENVIRONMENTAL PROTECTION AGENCY, ENVIRONMENTAL POLITICS.

National Farmer's Union, *see* Farm Organizations.

National Front   The device of alliance with non-Communist groups, utilized by a Communist party to achieve its goals. The national-front approach is often used in underdeveloped countries where the Communists team up with nationalist elements in independence movements or undertake leftist-inspired revolutions against indigenous élites. *See also* WARS OF NATIONAL LIBERATION.

National Government, Powers of, *see* Concurrent Powers, Delegated Powers, Exclusive Powers, Implied Powers, Inherent Powers, *Missouri v. Holland,* Resulting Powers, *United States v. Curtiss-Wright Export Corp.*

National Grange, *see* Farm Organizations.

National Guard   The volunteer armed forces of the states formerly called the militia. The Constitution provides for a cooperative system under which each state is responsible for appointing officers and Congress provides for organizing, arming, and disciplining the Guard. Each governor is commander in chief of his state's national guard and may call it out for emergencies, such as floods, fires, and civil disorders.

National Interest   The concept of the security and well-being of the state, used in making foreign policy. A national interest approach to foreign policy demands "realistic" handling of international problems, based on the use of power divorced from moral principles and values. Conflicts of national interest in the state system are resolved through diplomacy, international law, international institutions, or, ultimately, through war.

Nationalism   Social and psychological forces that spring from unique cultural and historical factors to provide unity and inspiration to a given people through a sense of belonging together and of shared values. Nationalism binds together people who possess common cultural, linguistic, racial, historical, or geographical characteristics or experiences and who give their loyalty to the same political group. Modern nationalism began to make its appearance as a major political and ideological force in the early nineteenth century, particularly in Napoleonic France. *See also* NATION.

Nationality The legal relationship between an individual and a state whereby the individual claims protection from the state and the state in turn requires his allegiance and the performance of certain obligations. Nationality is acquired by birth or by naturalization, although the rules covering each method vary from country to country. The principle that an individual can be divested of his nationality is commonly accepted in the state system, and diverse methods recognized by states include denationalization, denaturalization, expatriation, and renunciation. *See also* CITIZEN, NATION.

Nationalization The transference of the ownership and operation of private enterprises to a national government. Nationalization may result from purchase or confiscation (expropriation), with or without compensation, and may apply to properties owned by citizens or foreign nationals. *See also* CONFISCATION.

National Labor Relations Act of 1935, *see* Wagner Act.

National Labor Relations Board (NLRB) An independent regulatory commission, established in 1935, which administers the Wagner Act and the Taft-Hartley Act relative to unfair labor practices and the designation of appropriate bargaining units. The NLRB consists of five members appointed by the President, with the Senate's consent, for five-year terms, and a General Counsel similarly appointed for a four-year term. The Board is authorized to issue cease and desist orders, to hold bargaining representative elections, and to seek court injunctions and other enforcement orders. The General Counsel conducts investigations, issues complaints, and conducts prosecutions before the Board. Actual hearings are held by trial examiners with final orders issuing from the Board. *See also NLRB v. Jones and Laughlin Steel Corp..*

National Liberation Front, *see* National Front.

National Mediation Board An independent agency established in 1934, under an amendment to the Railway Labor Act of 1926, to mediate differences between management and labor in the railroad and airline fields and to determine bargaining representatives. The Board consists of three members appointed by the President with the Senate's consent. For the settlement of disputes growing out of the application of collective bargaining contracts, the National Railroad Adjustment Board, consisting of representatives of the unions and the carriers, is called into action. In the event of deadlocks in the Adjustment Board, the National Mediation Board appoints a referee. Parties may appeal to the courts for enforcement of any settlements reached through this procedure. If the dispute does not involve a collective bargaining agreement, and the National Mediation Board cannot effect a solution, the law authorizes the President to appoint a special fact-finding board and, if this fails, the President may place the carrier under government operation, *See also* MEDIATION AND CONCILIATION.

National Mental Health Act of 1946 A nationwide program for the care and treatment of the mentally ill. The Act provides for grants-in-aid to the states for psychiatric personnel, community psychiatric services, and research into prevention and care of mental illness. The Act is administered by the Public Health Service in the Department of Health, Education, and Welfare.

National Municipal League, *see* Model State Constitution.

National Origins Quota System, *see* Immigration, Immigration Act of 1965, Immigration and Nationality Act of 1952.

National Park Service, *see* Department of the Interior.

National Party Congress (China (PRC)) The "rubber stamp" institution that represents the rank-and-file party members. The National Party Congress is described by the party's constitution as the "highest leading body of the Party." As in the U.S.S.R.'s All-Union Congress, the approximately one thousand delegates to the National Party Congress are chosen indirectly through a series of municipal, county, and provincial party congresses. In China the delegates, once chosen, serve for four years. Although required to meet annually until the next National Party Congress, the Central Committee has made liberal use of its power to cancel the annual meetings because of "extraordinary conditions." Thus, the Central Committee frees itself of responsibility to the congress and to the rank and file of the party by simply refusing to convene its parent body. At its infrequent meetings the National Party Congress hears party leaders expound previously determined policy, passes previously prepared resolutions, and elects Central Committee members previously selected at the Politburo level. *See also* ALL-UNION PARTY CONGRESS (SOVIET UNION).

National People's Congress (China (PRC)) The policy-validating legislature of the People's Republic of China. The PRC Constitution labels the Congress "the highest organ of state authority in the People's Republic" and "the only legislative authority in the country." Delegates are chosen indirectly, through a series of people's congresses beginning at the local level and ultimately reaching the national level. Ballots are not secret and the voters are presented with a single list of candidates prepared in secret by the local party officials. The only choice occurs when the local party runs more candidates than there are seats at stake. Each year the thousand or more delegates, so chosen for four-year terms, meet in Peking for several weeks to endorse the policies of the party leaders. The NPC also elects its Standing Committee, a body analogous to the Presidium of the Supreme Soviet, to function between congresses. The Chairman of the NPC, who enjoys a status second only to that of the Chairman of the CCP but little authority, is also elected by the NPC and serves as titular head of state. *See also* SUPREME SOVIET (SOVIET UNION).

National Railroad Adjustment Board, *see* National Mediation Board.

National Security Acts of 1947 and 1949   The Act of 1947 provided the nation's most comprehensive reorganization of its defense structure. It established a new National Security Organization and placed the three major military forces—Army, Navy, and Air Force—in a National Military Establishment under a single civilian Secretary of Defense. The National Security Council was established as a top-level advisory body. In the National Security Act of 1949 the National Military Establishment was replaced with a single executive department—the Department of Defense—and the National Security Council was transferred to the Executive Office as a staff agency to the President. *See also* DEPARTMENT OF DEFENSE, DEFENSE REORGANIZATION ACT OF 1958.

National Security Agency, *see* Intelligence (United States).

National Security Council (NSC)   A staff agency in the Executive Office of the President, established by the National Security Act of 1947, that advises the President on domestic and foreign matters involving national security. The Council is composed of the President, the Vice President, the Secretaries of State and Defense, and the Director of the Office of Emergency Preparedness. The Central Intelligence Agency (CIA) functions under the direction of the Council. The Council's main role is to assess and appraise the objectives, commitments, and risks of the United States in the interests of national security and to make recommendations to the President on specific policies and decisions.

National Self-Determination   The doctrine that postulates the right of a group of people who consider themselves separate and distinct from others to determine for themselves the state in which they will live and the form of government it will have. National self-determination is closely linked with the concept of liberal nationalism and is implicit in the American Declaration of Independence and the French Declaration of the Rights of Man and Citizen. It is the vehicle by which national groups seek to insure their identity by institutionalizing it in the form of an independent sovereign state. The name most frequently associated with national self-determination is that of Woodrow Wilson. The doctrine is found in his 1918 peace aims in the form of the famous Fourteen Points. In the 1919 peace settlements it was instrumental in establishing the independence of Albania, Austria, Czechoslovakia, Estonia, Finland, Hungary, Latvia, Lithuania, Poland, Romania, and Yugoslavia. It also figured in the creation of the mandates system and its successor, the trusteeship system. The principle of self-determination has also been associated with the technique of the plebiscite as a basis for solving problems relating to boundaries and territorial sovereignty, as recommended by the United Nations, for example, in the Kashmir dispute between India and Pakistan. *See also* NATIONALISM, PLEBISCITE.

National Style   The characteristic behavior patterns followed by a state as it attempts to deal with its foreign policy problems. National style can be described as a function of ideological values, common historical experiences, traditions, and precedents. Thus, in established countries, a change in regime is not likely to result in a drastically altered approach to international problems. The effort can be made, however, consciously and explicitly to alter the national style. Under the constitution of the Fifth French Republic, for example, the personalized executive leadership of President Charles de Gaulle has weakened legislative dominance in French national life. In the developing countries, by definition, national styles are in the process of creation and evolution.

National Supremacy A basic constitutional principle of American government that asserts the superiority of national law. This principle is rooted in Article VI, which provides that the Constitution, laws passed by the national government under its constitutional powers, and all treaties are the supreme laws of the land. The Article requires that all national and state officers and judges be bound by oath to support the Constitution regardless of any state constitutional or legislative provisions. Thus, any legitimate exercise of national power supersedes any conflicting state action. Determination of whether such a conflict exists rests in the hands of the judiciary, with the final decisions made by the Supreme Court. *See also McCulloch v. Maryland, Cohens v. Virginia.*

National Urban League, *see* Civil Rights Organizations.

NATO, *see* North Atlantic Treaty Organization.

Natural-born Citizen A native of the United States. The term is used in Article II, section 1 of the Constitution, which stipulates that "No person except a natural born citizen" may be President of the United States.

Natural Experiment Research utilizing observation of human behavior or some other phenomenon in the normal field setting without injecting artificial stimuli. In conducting a natural experiment the investigator simply bides his time until the desired stimuli occur in the regular course of events. He then records and measures the extent of the impact on the subject under study. Thus an investigator might wait for a government or political party to carry out a propaganda campaign and then might measure its impact by conducting before-and-after sample surveys of the population affected. *See also* EXPERIMENT.

Naturalization The legal procedure by which an alien is admitted to citizenship. Congress is authorized by Article I, section 8 of the Constitution to establish uniform rules for naturalization. Naturalization may be individual or collective. Collective naturalization confers citizenship upon entire populations by statute or treaty as was done in the cases of Alaska, Hawaii, Texas, Puerto Rico, Guam, and the Virgin Islands. An individual over eighteen years of age may be naturalized after meeting certain qualifications. These include: (1) residence in the United States for five years; (2) ability to read, write, and speak English; (3) proof of good moral character; (4) knowledge of the history and attachment to the principles of American government; (5) neither advocacy of Communist or other subversive doctrine nor membership (unless involuntary) in any subversive or totalitarian organization; and (6) taking of an oath of allegiance to the United States and renunciation of allegiance to his former country. Detailed administration of naturalization is handled by the Immigration and Naturalization Service of the Department of Justice with final examination and administration of the oath by a judge of a federal court or a state court of record. The residence requirement is lowered for spouses of citizens and for aliens who serve in the armed forces. Minors become citizens when their parents are naturalized. *See also Girouard v. United States.*

Natural Law   The concept that human relations are governed by an immutable set of laws, similar to the physical laws of the universe and recognizable through human reason. Such laws are regarded as ethically binding in human society. The theory of *jus naturale* was expounded by the Stoics and was highly developed by the eighteenth-century natural-rights philosophers. *See also* NATURAL RIGHTS, DEMOCRACY.

Natural Monopoly, *see* Franchise.

Natural Rights   An underlying assumption of the American political creed that men are endowed by their Creator with certain rights that may not be abridged by government. *See also* NATURAL LAW.

Navigable Waters   All waters within the boundaries of the United States that are or may be used as highways for interstate or foreign commerce, such as rivers, streams, lakes, and inlets. *See also* ADMIRALTY JURISDICTION, *Gibbons v. Ogden.*

Near v. Minnesota, 283 U.S. 697 (1931): Defined freedom of the press to mean that the press is to be free from prior restraint or censorship. A state may not, under the due process clause of the Fourteenth Amendment, permanently enjoin a newspaper from being published. If a newspaper abuses its privilege, it may be punished subsequently. The Court held unconstitutional a Minnesota statute that authorized officials to forbid publication of "malicious, scandalous and defamatory" newspapers. *See also* FREEDOM OF THE PRESS.

Necessary and Proper Clause   The final paragraph of Article I, section 8, of the Constitution, which delegates legislative powers to Congress. It authorizes all laws "necessary and proper" to carry out the enumerated powers. This clause, sometimes called the "elastic" clause, was used by the Supreme Court in *McCulloch v. Maryland,* 4 Wheaton 316 (1819), to develop the concept of "implied powers." *See also McCulloch v. Maryland,* IMPLIED POWERS.

Negotiated Contract, *see* Defense Contract.

Negotiation   A diplomatic technique for the peaceful settlement of differences and the advancement of national interests. The objectives of negotiation are accomplished by compromises and accommodations reached through direct personal contact. *See also* APPEASEMENT, DIPLOMACY.

Neo-Functionalism, *see* Spillover.

Nepotism   Granting of political favors to relatives, often in the form of appointments to office.

Neutralism   A "third force" in the cold war power struggle comprised of states that pursue policies of nonalignment with the free world and the Communist bloc. Most of the nations of Asia, Africa, and the Middle East and a few states in Europe have refused to join military alliance systems propagated by either the United States or Soviet Russia. Although some of these states profess ideological sympathy toward one side or the other, none has committed itself to any kind of military involvement. *See also* NEUTRALITY.

Neutrality   The legal status of a nation that does not participate in a war between other states. Under international law, such a state is free to defend its territory or neutral waters against attack by belligerents. Although public opinion and even the government of a neutral state may sympathize with one side or the other, to retain its neutral position a state may not engage in action that might favor one side in the war. Some states, such as Switzerland, Sweden, and Ireland, have espoused a doctrine of perpetual neutrality. *See also* NEUTRALISM.

New Communist Man (Communist Theory)   The belief that an evolution of human nature can be produced by changing man's social environment. The concept of the "new communist man" assumes that man's nature—kindly, cooperative, and gregarious—has been warped by the competitive, hostility-prone, and conflict-ridden social environment of capitalist society. When private property is abolished and capitalist institutions are replaced by socialist designs, according to communist theoreticians, man's potential virtue will prevail.

New Community Development, *see* Urban Renewal.

"New Economics", *see* Keynesianism.

New England Town, *see* Town.

New Jersey Plan   A plan submitted by William Paterson of New Jersey to the Constitutional Convention of 1787 representing the views of the small states and states' rights advocates. It was expressly designed as a counterproposal to the strong nationalistic Virginia Plan. The essence of the New Jersey Plan was a single-house Congress with each state having an equal vote. Moreover, the Plan looked toward a moderate modification of the Articles of Confederation rather than toward the drafting of a new document. *See also* VIRGINIA PLAN.

New Left   A contemporary radical-liberal mass movement, particularly of the college young. The New Left subscribes to a multifaceted radical ideology, with many uncoordinated campaigns and organizations challenging the established political, social, and economic order. The main unifying themes of the New Left have been common opposition to the Vietnam war, the draft, the military-industrial complex, racial discrimination, the machinations of the establishment or power structure, the plundering and pollution of the planet, and economic deprivation of poor people. The New Left also provided the vanguard of the cultural revolution of the 1960s and 1970s which changed the attitudes and social practices of millions concerning hair styles, drugs, sex, rock music, religion, education, and pornography. "Participatory democracy," or direct decision making by interested, active elites, became the basic political objective, a means by which the New Left sought to reform what they regarded as the perversion of the democratic process by private interests. *See also* POLITICAL ACTIVIST, WOMEN'S LIBERATION MOVEMENT.

New York Times v. Sullivan, 376 U.S. 254 (1964): Held that a public official could not recover civil libel damages for criticism of his official conduct by a newspaper or other persons. The rule applies even if the criticism is exaggerated or false, unless deliberate malice and reckless disregard for the truth or falsity of the statement can be shown. This principle was extended to suits for criminal libel in *Garrison v. Louisiana,* 379 U.S. 64 (1965). *See also* LIBEL AND SLANDER.

New York Times v. United States, 403 U.S. 713 (1971): Held that any prior restraint of freedom of expression by the government carries a heavy presumption of unconstitutionality. In this case the Court held that the Nixon Administration could not forbid newspaper publication of classified documents on the Vietnam war since the government had failed to bear the heavy burden of justification for censorship. *See also* FREEDOM OF THE PRESS.

Nineteenth Amendment   An amendment to the Constitution, adopted in 1920, that prohibits any state from denying the right to vote to any citizen because of sex. Wyoming took the initiative, in 1869, in granting suffrage to women, but only a few states followed this lead. Suffragette agitation during the early part of the twentieth century culminated in the Nineteenth Amendment, which was adopted in time for women to participate in the presidential election of 1920. *See also* WOMEN'S LIBERATION MOVEMENT.

Ninth Amendment   A part of the Bill of Rights that reads, "The enumeration in the Constitution, of certain rights, shall not be construed to deny or disparage others retained by the people." This provision reaffirms the tradition of the natural rights philosophy, supported by those who feared that a listing of rights in the Bill of Rights might be interpreted to mean that no other rights were held by the people.

Nixon Doctrine   An attitude or general philosophy of American restraint enunciated by the Nixon Administration as a guideline for foreign policy programs and decision making. The Nixon Doctrine was aimed at limiting United States' aid for friendly and allied nations to military supplies and economic assistance while insisting that threatened nations assume "primary responsibility" for their own defense. The Doctrine was first suggested by President Richard M. Nixon in an impromptu press conference on Guam Island in 1969, but was subsequently expanded in statements and actions by President Nixon and his top-level defense and foreign policy advisers.

NLRB, *see* National Labor Relations Board.

NLRB v. Jones and Laughlin Steel Corp., 301 U.S. 1 (1937): Upheld the National Labor Relations Act of 1935, which guarantees labor the right to organize and bargain collectively and establishes the National Labor Relations Board to regulate labor-management relations. The Act was upheld as a valid exercise of Congress' power to regulate interstate commerce. *See also* COLLECTIVE BARGAINING.

No-Knock Search and Arrest Warrant, *see* District of Columbia Court Reorganization and Criminal Procedure Act of 1970.

Nominal Scale, *see* Scale.

Nomination   The official designation of an individual as a candidate for public office. Methods for selecting candidates in the United States have included the rank and file party caucus, legislative and congressional caucuses, the mixed caucus (legislators and party representatives), the party convention, the primary, and petition. Nomination also signifies the first step in the appointment of an executive or judicial official. *See also* AVAILABILITY, CAUCUS, CONVENTION, DIRECT PRIMARY, PETITION, NATIONAL CONVENTION.

Nomological Explanation, *see* Nomothetic Explanation.

Nomothetic Explanation   Explanation based on general propositions applicable to classes of events or objects. Nomothetic explanations, sometimes called *nomological* or "covering law" models, may be contrasted with *idiographic* explanations, which are concerned with specific propositions that explain unique or individual social phenomena. History is often regarded as essentially an idiographic discipline, while political and other social sciences that emphasize explanation by theoretical generalization are more nomological. *See also* EXPLANATION.

Non-Alignment, *see* Neutralism.

Nonassociational Group, *see* Group.

Non-Directed Interview, *see* Interview.

Non-Governmental Organization (NGO)   A private international organization that serves as a mechanism for cooperation among private national groups in international affairs, especially in the economic, social, cultural, humanitarian, and technical fields. Under the United Nations Charter (Article 71), the Economic and Social Council is empowered to make suitable arrangements for consultation with NGOs on matters within its competence.

Nonimmigrant   One who comes to the United States on a temporary basis. This includes visitors, seasonal workers, tradesmen, crewmen, students, members of the press, and accredited representatives of foreign nations. Nonimmigrants must meet many of the qualifications imposed upon regular immigrants.

Nonparametric Statistics, *see* Statistics.

Nonpartisan Election   An election in which candidates have no party designations and political parties are prohibited from running candidates. Nonpartisan elections are typically used to elect state and local judges and municipal officials. They are often preceded by nonpartisan primaries in which the number of candidates for each office is reduced to two.

Non-Proliferation of Nuclear Weapons Treaty   An international agreement to prohibit the diffusion of nuclear weapons among nonnuclear states. The Treaty on the Non-proliferation of Nuclear Weapons was hammered out during four years of intensive negotiations in the Eighteen Nation Disarmament Committee (ENDC) and in the General Assembly's Political and Security Committee, leading to approval of the draft treaty by the Assembly in June, 1968. Under the terms of the treaty, each nuclear-weapon state agrees "not to transfer . . . assist, encourage, or induce any nonnuclear weapon State to manufacture or otherwise acquire nuclear weapons. . . . " Each nonnuclear state agrees "not to receive . . . manufacture or otherwise acquire nuclear weapons. . . . " The eleven-article treaty took effect in 1969 after its ratification by three nuclear powers (Britain, Soviet Union, and United States) and by forty nonnuclear countries. To counter the threat of future "nuclear blackmail," the three nuclear powers have offered to provide "immediate assistance, in accordance with the Charter, to any non-nuclear-weapon State that is the victim of an act or an object of a threat of aggression in which nuclear weapons are used. . . . " *See also* DENUCLEARI-ZATION, PARTIAL TEST BAN TREATY.

Non-Self-Governing Territory, *see* Colony, Condominium, Leasehold, Mandates System, Protectorate, Trust Territory.

Nordic Council   A Scandinavian regional organization composed of elected and appointed delegates who meet as a Council to recommend common policies and programs to the governments of the member states. Established in 1952, the membership of the Nordic Council includes Denmark, Finland, Norway, Sweden, and Iceland. Delegates are chosen by their national parliaments (Iceland is accorded five, the other members sixteen each), with major political groups and opinions represented. Each state may also appoint as many governmental representatives as it wishes, but voting power is limited to the elected delegates. Ordinary sessions of the Council are held annually, but extraordinary sessions may be convoked by two members or twenty-five elected delegates. A Presidium of elected officers directs deliberations which are concerned with economic, social, cultural, legal, and transport matters.

Norm   A rule or value that provides a generally accepted standard of behavior within a group. Norms relate to the powers, rights, and duties of the individual within the group, helping him to identify his role and what he can expect from others. A family norm, for example, might call for deference to the father; a norm of a larger society might dictate fair play in an election. Norms may be embodied in formal rules (explicit norms) or informal understandings (implicit norms). In some contexts "norm" may refer to the typical or average behavior or condition of a group. Thus, in American society, possessing a low level of political information would be the norm. In a related usage "norm" may have reference to a statistical measure of central tendency (that is, mean, median, or mode). *See also* CENTRAL TENDENCY MEASUREMENT, NORMATIVE, SOCIAL CONTROL, VALUE.

Normal Distribution, *see* Statistics.

Normative   Pertaining to value judgments or standards. In political analysis a normative statement or theory expounds a subjective, preferential point of view in contrast to an empirical statement that seeks to describe what actually exists. While normative statements incorporate a "should" or "ought" question or judgment, empirical statements involve an "is" type of statement that can be tested and have its accuracy verified. Normative positions are not subject to scientific testing or verification because they cannot be proved either true or false. They are philosophical positions, culture-centered and relative to time and place, over which reasonable (and sometimes unreasonable) men may disagree. *Prescriptive theory* embodies normative judgments about desirable social goals and how to achieve them. *See also* NORM, POLITICAL THEORY, VALUE.

Norris-LaGuardia Act of 1932   An act that outlawed "yellow-dog" contracts by which workers agreed not to join unions, and limited the use of the injunction in labor disputes. *See also* INJUNCTION.

Norris v. Alabama, 294 U.S. 587 (1935): Held, in what is popularly known as the Second Scottsboro case, that Negroes could not be systematically excluded from jury service. *See also* JURY.

North Atlantic Treaty   A mutual security treaty, signed April 4, 1949, to provide peace and security in the North Atlantic area through joint defense. The North Atlantic Treaty signatories include twelve original parties (Belgium, Britain, Canada, Denmark, France, Iceland, Italy, Luxembourg, The Netherlands, Norway, Portugal, and United States), and three that subsequently ratified (Greece and Turkey in 1952, West Germany in 1955). To implement treaty provisions, the extensive military-political-administrative structure of the North Atlantic Treaty Organization (NATO) was created. The heart of the Treaty is Article 5, which provides: "The Parties agree that an armed attack against one or more of them in Europe or North America shall be considered an attack against them all; and . . . each of them . . . will assist the Party or Parties so attacked. . . . " Since 1969, Article 13 has permitted any signatory to "cease to be a Party one year after its notice of denunciation. . . . " *See also* ALLIANCE, NORTH ATLANTIC TREATY ORGANIZATION.

North Atlantic Treaty Organization (NATO)   An organization established under the North Atlantic Treaty of 1949 to create a single unified defense force to safeguard the security of the North Atlantic area. Members agree under Article V of the Treaty to regard an attack upon any of them as an attack upon all, and, if an armed attack occurs, each will render such assistance as it deems necessary. NATO now includes fifteen members, the original twelve (Belgium, Britain, Canada, Denmark, France, Iceland, Italy, Luxembourg, Netherlands, Norway, Portugal, and the United States) and three states that joined NATO in the 1950s (Greece, Turkey, and West Germany). NATO's members seek, in addition to attainment of mutual security, "the further development of peaceful and friendly international relations . . . and to eliminate conflict in their international economic policies." *See also* ALLIANCE.

Northwest Ordinance   An enactment of the congress under the Articles of Confederation providing for the government of the territory north of the Ohio River and west of New York to the Mississippi River. The Ordinance provided for the eventual statehood of areas of the territory when they acquired 60,000 inhabitants. Liberal provision was made for local self-government, civil and political rights, and education. Slavery was forbidden in the territory. A previous ordinance of 1785, establishing the township system of dividing land and providing for local schools, was reaffirmed in the Ordinance of 1787.

Nuclear-Free Zone, *see* Denuclearization.

Nuclear Non-Proliferation Treaty, *see* Non-Proliferation of Nuclear Weapons Treaty.

Nuclear Proliferation Problem, *see* Non-Proliferation of Nuclear Weapons Treaty.

Nuclear War, *see* Balance of Terror, Deterrence, First Strike, Limited War, Massive Retaliation, Preemptive Strike.

Null Hypothesis   A proposition stating that no relationship exists between the variables in a research problem. For testing purposes the null hypothesis is stated in the form of a *statistical proposition* in which the variables of a substantive proposition are quantitatively expressed so that they are subject to statistical manipulation. The null hypothesis is used by a researcher to make a statistical check of the validity of a substantive hypothesis. In using the null hypothesis, the researcher reverses the normal form of a hypothesis by positing that a certain relationship between the variables does *not* exist. If the null hypothesis is substantiated, it demonstrates that no significant relationship exists between the variables, and the researcher abandons or modifies his hypothesis. If, on the other hand, the null hypothesis is rejected, he may proceed to further exploration of the substantive hypothesis with added confidence that some meaningful relationship may exist between the variables. The null hypothesis typically is applied to samples to determine the likelihood that relationships of the magnitude revealed by the sample might have occurred by chance. If the test of the null hypothesis produces high values that have little possibility of occurring through random error in the sample, the null hypothesis is rejected. If the values are small enough that they might result from chance variation, the null hypothesis is confirmed. *See also* HYPOTHESIS, SAMPLING, SURVEY RESEARCH.

Nullification   A declaration by a state that a national law is null and void, and therefore not binding upon its citizens. South Carolina, in 1832, attempted to nullify the Tariff Acts of 1828 and 1832. The theory of nullification, a logical extension of the theory of interposition, was formulated by John C. Calhoun. The theory holds that the Union is a compact among sovereign states and that the national government is not the final judge of its own powers; a state may nullify any national law and even secede from the Union. *See also* INTERPOSITION.

Null Set, *see* Set.

Nuremberg War Crimes Trials, *see* War Crimes Trials.

OAS, *see* Organization of American States.

OASDI, *see* Old-Age, Survivors, and Disability Insurance.

OAU, *see* Organization of African Unity.

Obiter Dictum   A statement in a court opinion on an issue not precisely involved in the case. Since such statements are not relevant to the conclusions reached in the decision, they are not binding as precedents.

Observation   The purposeful gathering of information by direct sensory contact with the persons or objects being studied. Observation in political research can be carried on by such means as direct viewing or listening, interviewing, and experimenting. Common problems facing the investigator include observer bias (his own failure to observe a political phenomenon in a completely objective and consistent manner) and observer variability (a methodological failure that results in the inability of the investigator to replicate his initial procedures in exactly the same way with the same results). *Replication* means repeating an experiment or other research procedure with the object of checking previous findings. *See also* INTERVIEW, PANEL STUDY, PARTICIPANT OBSERVATION, SURVEY RESEARCH.

OCAM, *see* Common Organization of Africa and Malagasy.

Occupational Safety and Health Act of 1970   A comprehensive industrial safety program which requires employers engaged in interstate commerce to furnish a work place free from hazards to life or health. The Act authorizes the Secretary of Labor to promulgate safety standards, conduct investigations, and to issue citations for noncompliance. An independent agency, the Occupational Safety and Health Review Commission composed of three members appointed by the President with Senate consent, for six year terms, is established by the Act to adjudicate alleged violations contested by either employers or employees and to assess civil penalties. Appeals from Commission orders may be brought to a federal court of appeals. The Act also authorizes federal grants to states to promote occupational safety.

ODECA, *see* Organization of Central American States.

Oder-Neisse Line   The de facto boundary established between East Germany and Poland at the end of World War II. The Oder-Neisse line is named for the two rivers that form the boundary from the Baltic Sea south to the border of Czechoslovakia. Representatives of the Allied Powers met at Potsdam in 1945 to consider, *inter alia,* a provisional German settlement and procedures for drawing up final peace treaties. They agreed that northern East Prussia was to be annexed "in principle" by the Soviet Union, and that, pending a final boundary determination, southern East Prussia and German territory east of the river line were to be "under the administration of the Polish State." The Allies also agreed to an "orderly and humane" transfer of resident ethnic Germans out of Poland, Czechoslovakia, and Hungary. *See also* BOUNDARIES.

OECD, *see* Organization for Economic Cooperation and Development.

Office-block Ballot   A form of general election ballot in which candidates for elective office are grouped together under the title of each office. The "office block" or "Massachusetts ballot" is in contradistinction to the other common type of ballot, the "party column" or "Indiana ballot," in which all candidates of a particular party are arranged in one column. *See also* PARTY-COLUMN BALLOT.

Office of Economic Opportunity (OEO) An agency in the Executive Office of the President established by the Economic Opportunity Act of 1964. The Office coordinates federal antipoverty programs and carries on programs of its own. Its stated purpose is to "eliminate the paradox of poverty in the midst of plenty in this Nation by opening to everyone the opportunity for education and training, the opportunity to work, and the opportunity to live in decency and dignity." Among its programs are urban and rural community action, work and training programs, employment and investment incentives, preschool programs, such as Head Start and day care, and provision of health and legal service to the poor. The Office is headed by a director appointed by the President.

Office of Education, *see* Department of Health, Education, and Welfare.

Office of Emergency Preparedness, *see* Mobilization, National Security Council.

Office of Management and Budget An agency in the Executive Office of the President, headed by a Director who has primary responsibility for efficient and economical conduct of government services and for budget preparation and administration. In addition to budget functions, specific activities carried on by the Office include legislative reference, management and organization, statistical standards, and financial management. The Office of Management and Budget was created by Executive Order in 1970 to replace the Bureau of the Budget and perform its statutory functions. *See also* BUDGET AND ACCOUNTING ACT.

Office of Naval Intelligence, *see* Intelligence (United States).

Office of Territories, *see* Department of the Interior.

Offset Tax, *see* Tax Offset.

Old-age Assistance Financial aid provided under the categorical assistance program of the Social Security Act for the needy aged who are not covered by the Old-Age, Survivors, and Disability Insurance program. Old-age assistance is furnished through the states under grants-in-aid from the national government under supervision of the Social and Rehabilitation Service of the Department of Health, Education, and Welfare. The program is in effect in all states, the amount granted to an individual varying with his need, the responsibility of relatives, and other requirements established under state laws. *See also* CATEGORICAL ASSISTANCE.

Old-Age, Survivors, and Disability Insurance (OASDI) An insurance program, commonly called "social security," administered by the national government under the provisions of the Social Security Act of 1935. Its major purposes are to provide a retirement income for elderly persons, income for workers who are totally disabled, and income for the widows and minor children of deceased wage earners. Specifically exempted from coverage are federal employees under the civil service retirement system, ministers (optional), state and local employees not authorized coverage by state law, and some persons whose incomes are not sufficient to qualify. All other persons are required to contribute a certain percent of their income that is matched by their employer. Self-employed persons also contribute. These contributions are credited to each worker's account and, upon death, retirement, or disablement, funds are allocated in accordance with the formulas provided by law for each eventuality. Retirement usually takes place at the age of sixty-five, but one may retire at sixty-two with reduced benefits. Retired persons may continue to work but may have their benefits reduced if they earn more than $1680 a year. After the age of seventy-two, no limitations are placed on earnings. The program is administered directly by the Social Security Administration in the Department of Health, Education, and Welfare. *See also* SOCIAL SECURITY CASES.

Oligarchy   Any system of government in which a small group holds the ruling power. Oligarchical systems are usually based on wealth, military power, or social position. *See also* ELITE.

Oligopoly   A market condition wherein the supply of a commodity is controlled by a few companies, consequently limiting competition. Oligopoly is sometimes referred to as a situation of partial monopoly, because the market price can be fixed through collusion or passive competition. In such a market, a business enjoys *market power—* that is, its pricing policy is set by managerial discretion without concern for competition rather than by the market forces of supply and demand. *See also* MONOPOLY.

Ombudsman   A special official or commissioner appointed by a legislative body to hear and investigate complaints by private individuals against public officials or agencies. The office of ombudsman, which originated in the Scandinavian countries, is utilized currently in many countries by national, state, and local units of government and other public bodies, including some local agencies in the United States. Typically, the ombudsman has no decision-making authority but is empowered to carry on inquiry and mediation functions.

Omnibus Crime Control and Safe Streets Act of 1968   The first comprehensive national anticrime legislation. Major provisions of the Act: (1) provide for federal block grants to states to upgrade state and local police forces; (2) authorize wiretapping and bugging by police with and without warrants; and (3) alter federal criminal procedures to modify Supreme Court decisions (*Miranda* and *Mallory* cases) so as to make voluntary confessions admissible irrespective of delay in arraignment or failure to inform a suspect of his rights.

"One Man, One Vote", *see Baker v. Carr, County Board, Hadley v. Junior College District of Kansas City, Reynolds v. Sims, Wesberry v. Sanders.*

One-Party System   A system of government in which there is but a single party. One-party systems tend to be authoritarian and dictatorial in their form and substance, although democratic systems may also occasionally be one-party. *See also* CHINESE COMMUNIST PARTY, COMMUNIST PARTY OF THE SOVIET UNION.

ONUC, *see* United Nations Operation in the Congo.

Open Market Operations   Buying and selling government securities, bills of exchange, and other commercial paper by the Federal Open Market Committee. The Committee is composed of the Board of Governors of the Federal Reserve System and five directors of the Federal Reserve banks chosen annually by the boards of directors. *See also* FEDERAL RESERVE SYSTEM.

Open Primary   A direct primary voting system that permits the voter to choose the party primary in which he wishes to vote without disclosing his party affiliation or allegiance, if any. In an open primary, the voter makes his choice in the privacy of the voting booth. He is still limited, however, to casting votes for candidates of only one party. *See also* CLOSED PRIMARY, DIRECT PRIMARY.

Open Shop, *see* Right to Work Law.

"Open Sky" Proposal   A plan, submitted by President Dwight Eisenhower to Premier Nikita Khrushchev at their first summit conference in Geneva in 1955, to reduce the fear of a surprise nuclear attack and to break the deadlock in disarmament negotiations. The "open sky" proposal was developed by a panel of governmental and private experts who met at the United States Marine Base at Quantico, Virginia. It provided for the United States and the Soviet Union to exchange blueprints of their military establishments and to carry on continuous aerial surveillance of each other's territory. The plan was never adopted.

Open System, *see* Social Stratification, System.

Operational Definition, *see* Concept, Research, Variable.

Operations Research   Research that utilizes scientific techniques to provide governmental and business executives with information relevant to decision making. Operations research relies heavily on the construction of models to simulate the real world and test out the consequences of various decisions in executive situations. Mixed teams of scholars from various disciplines—political science, engineering, physics, business management, economics—may attack decision-making problems collectively, studying them from an interdisciplinary perspective and within the context of the organization being examined. *See also* ENGINEERING THEORY, MANAGEMENT SCIENCE, POLICY SCIENCES, SOCIAL ENGINEERING.

Opinion, *see* Public Opinion.

Opinion Élites   Leadership elements influential in developing and shaping public opinion as a force in the political process. Opinion élites that influence foreign policy decisions include business, professional, educational, labor, farm, religious, patriotic, and other interest-group leaders and persons active in upper-echelon political, administrative, and communications areas. Opinion élites compete in seeking to interest and influence both official decision makers and the mass public on contemporary issues of concern to the élites.

Opinion of the Court, *see* Concurring Opinion, Dissenting Opinion, Obiter Dictum.

Opinion Poll, *see* Poll.

Opp Cotton Mills v. Administrator of Wage and Hour Division, 312 U.S. 126 (1941): Declared that the provisions of the Fair Labor Standards Act of 1938 authorizing an administrative determination of minimum wages in a particular industry do not constitute an unconstitutional delegation of legislative power. *See also* DELEGATION OF POWER.

Optional Charter   A plan in effect in about one-third of the states that permits a city to choose a charter from among several provided by state law. Typically, cities may choose various forms of the mayor-council plan, the commission plan, or the council-manager plan. *See also* CHARTER.

Optional Clause   A method outlined in Article 36 of the Statute of the International Court of Justice, by which states may agree in advance to accept the compulsory jurisdiction of the Court in certain circumstances. If a state accepts compulsory jurisdiction, it agrees to submit to the Court all legal disputes involving questions of treaty interpretation, international law, breaches of international obligations, and amounts of reparations to be awarded. *See also* COMPULSORY JURISDICTION, CONNALLY AMENDMENT.

Optional Referendum, *see* Referendum.

Ordinal Scale, *see* Scale.

Ordinance   A legislative enactment of a local governing body. Ordinances have the force of law, but the term is to be distinguished from the statute-making power of national and state legislatures. Ordinances are issued under authority granted by the sovereign power and, in the case of local governments, must comply with state constitutions, charters, and general laws.

Organization   A goal-seeking collectivity of individuals having some kind of structure designed to help achieve the collective goals. Some scholars hold that "organization" may refer to any complex system of human interaction, regardless of the existence of collective goals. In *formal organizations,* role relationships among the members are explicitly stated, while *informal organizations* evolve from repeated contacts among people without any express statement of goals or defining of roles. *See also* GROUP, ORGANIZATION THEORY.

Organization (Administrative)   The arrangement of persons for the most effective achievement of a purpose or objective. Public administration experts are concerned with the problem of the best way to organize the government or a particular agency to eliminate friction and to best accomplish the task assigned. This involves decisions as to the nature of line, staff, and auxiliary agencies, the location of responsibility, and the overall coordination of efforts. Activities may be organized according to major purpose (for example, the Department of Agriculture), process or skills (central purchasing), area (fire and police protection), or clientele (Veterans Administration). The use of a single head or a board is another concern of organization. *See also* ADMINISTRATIVE REORGANIZATION, CLIENTELE AGENCY, HIERARCHY.

Organizational Behavior, *see* Organization Theory.

Organization for Economic Cooperation and Development (OECD)   An international organization created in 1961 to achieve expanded cooperation and joint action between the United States and Western Europe and Canada. The OECD is an outgrowth of the Organization for European Economic Cooperation (OEEC) established in 1948 to decide how American aid granted under the Marshall Plan would be distributed. When the OEEC dissolved in 1960, its membership included eighteen European nations which, with the addition of the United States and three new members, comprise the present membership of OECD. Fifteen of the twenty-two members of OECD are NATO allies—the United States, Canada, Belgium, Britain, Denmark, France, Greece, Iceland, Italy, Luxembourg, Netherlands, Norway, Portugal, Turkey, and West Germany. The other seven are Austria, Finland, Ireland, Japan, Spain, Sweden, and Switzerland.

Organization of African Unity (OAU)   A regional organization established in 1963 to develop unity, end colonialism, foster economic development, and provide security for African states. OAU's membership of thirty-eight includes every independent African state except South Africa and Rhodesia. Its organization consists of an Assembly of Heads of State that meets annually and a secretariat located at OAU headquarters in Addis Ababa. A special Decolonization Committee has been established to aid in the struggle to achieve independence for the Portuguese colonies of Angola, Guinea, and Mozambique, and to overthrow the white-dominated regimes in Rhodesia and South Africa.

Organization of American States (OAS) A regional political organization, comprised of the United States and twenty Latin-American republics, that was created at the Bogotá Conference in 1948. The OAS consists of: (1) the Inter-American Conference, which meets every five years to decide general policies; (2) the Council, with each member state represented by an ambassador, which oversees the implementation of general policies of OAS; (3) the Consultative Meetings of Ministers of Foreign Affairs, which occur whenever urgent problems confront the OAS; (4) the Pan-American Union, which operates through its headquarters in Washington, D. C., as a general secretariat of the OAS; (5) the Specialized Conferences, which are called periodically to enable the members to cooperate in dealing with technical problems; and (6) the Specialized Agencies, which are responsible for eliciting cooperation in economic, social, education, technical, and humanitarian problem areas. The OAS is a regional organization of the type encouraged by the United Nations Charter, Important provisions of the OAS Charter concern the peaceful settlement of disputes among members and procedures for mediation, arbitration, and adjudication. The OAS also implements the Rio Treaty's provision to safeguard the hemisphere from attack. *See also* ALLIANCE FOR PROGRESS, GOOD NEIGHBOR POLICY, MONROE DOCTRINE, RIO TREATY.

Organization of Central American States (ODECA) A regional organization that fosters political, economic, and social cooperation among Central American states. Established under the terms of the 1951 Charter of San Salvador, ODECA's members are Costa Rica, El Salvador, Guatemala, Honduras, and Nicaragua. Panama has been invited to join. A new Charter was negotiated for ODECA in 1962 but has not been fully ratified. ODECA organs include: (1) a Conference of the Presidents of the Central American Republics that functions as the supreme body; (2) a Meeting of Ministers of Foreign Affairs that convenes every two years and serves as the principal decision-making agency, with unanimity required for all substantive decisions; and (3) the Central American Bureau, headed by a secretary-general, that functions as a general secretariat for ODECA. Members of ODECA have established the Central American Common Market (CACM) to promote economic integration. *See also* CENTRAL AMERICAN COMMON MARKET.

Organization Theory A body of thought that seeks to explain the nature and functioning of large, complex, goal-seeking collectivities. "Organization theory" is a broad designation encompassing the study of organization structure or design, decision-making processes or decision theory, group and individual behavior within complex organizations, role theory, group theory, group dynamics, and organizational psychology (sometimes called *administrative behavior*). Organization theory also extends to questions of organizational effectiveness, often labeled *program evaluation* or *policy analysis*. Organization theory as a field of inquiry is sometimes called *organizational behavior*. Organization theory is concerned with the way organizations seek goals and adapt to their environment, as well as with individual behavior occurring within organizations. Many studies have a problem-solving orientation aimed at prescribing courses of action. Organization theorists make use of direct observation, the laboratory approach, simulation studies, and mathematical models, as well as more traditional methods. *See also* DECISION-MAKING APPROACH, GROUP THEORY, MANAGEMENT SCIENCE, OPERATIONS RESEARCH, ORGANIZATION, ROLE.

Organized Crime Control Act of 1970   A comprehensive law designed to strengthen the hands of the federal government to combat organized crime. Major provisions: (1) authorize special grand juries to investigate organized criminal activities; (2) standardize witness-immunity laws for legislative, administrative, and judicial bodies; (3) limit challenges to illegally seized evidence; (4) forbid use of income from organized criminal activity to establish a legitimate business; (5) extend federal jurisdiction over gambling and use of explosives; and (6) authorize increased prison terms, up to twenty-five years, for dangerous offenders.

Original Cost Theory   An approach used by government, in fixing rates, to determine a fair return in profits for public utilities. The original cost theory is based on ascertaining the total investment made by the stockholders when the corporation was organized, plus subsequent capital expansions, less depreciation. *See also* RATE-MAKING; *Smyth v. Ames.*

Original Jurisdiction   The authority of a court to hear a case in the first instance. Generally, courts of original jurisdiction are minor courts or trial courts. They are to be distinguished from courts of appellate jurisdiction, which hear cases on appeal from courts of original jurisdiction. A court that is primarily appellate may have some original jurisdiction. The United States Supreme Court, for example, has original jurisdiction over suits involving ambassadors and those to which a state is a party. *See also* JURISDICTION (COURT).

Original Membership, United Nations, *see* Admission (International Organization).

Original Package Doctrine   A limitation on the state taxing powers that exempts commodities from state jurisdiction so long as they remain in their original shipping containers. The Supreme Court applied the original package doctrine to products imported from foreign countries (*Brown v. Maryland,* 12 Wheaton 419 [1827]) and to those commodities produced in the United States and shipped in interstate commerce (*Leisy v. Hardin,* 135 U.S. 100 [1890]). *See also Brown v. Maryland.*

Outdoor Relief   Financial aid or food and medical care provided needy persons outside of public institutions. Outdoor relief programs are administered by state and local governments under a general relief program or with the aid of the national government under the categorical assistance program. *See also* INDOOR RELIEF.

Outer Space Jurisdiction   International authority over the area beyond the atmosphere. Although no state exercises jurisdiction over outer space, the subject has become one of increasing international concern since the first earth satellite was orbited in 1957. In 1959 the United Nations established a permanent Committee on the Peaceful Uses of Outer Space. In 1961, the General Assembly unanimously proclaimed that "International law, including the Charter of the United Nations, applies to outer space and celestial bodies;" and that "Outer space and celestial bodies are free for exploration and use by all States in conformity with international law, and are not subject to national appropriation." In 1963, these principles were augmented by the Declaration of Legal Principles Governing Activities in Outer Space, which provided that: (1) space exploration and use is to be for the benefit of all mankind; (2) states conducting such activities bear international responsibility for their acts; (3) all space activity shall be guided by the principles of cooperation and mutual assistance; (4) states launching objects and personnel retain jurisdiction over them in outer space and on their return to earth wherever they may land; (5) states are liable for any damages on earth, in the airspace, or in outer space caused by objects they launch into outer space; and (6) astronauts are to be considered envoys of mankind in outer space, and in case of accident, all states are to render them every possible assistance and to return them promptly to the state of registry of their space vehicle. These principles were embodied in the Outer Space Treaty, which was adopted by the General Assembly in 1966 and entered into force for ratifying states in 1967. *See also* AIRSPACE JURISDICTION, OUTER SPACE TREATY.

Outer Space Treaty   An international convention that restrains the arms race, seeks to elicit cooperation, and establishes rudimentary rules of international law for outer space. The Outer Space Treaty was approved by the General Assembly in 1966 without a dissenting vote and was put into force by eighty-four signatory nations in October, 1967—a decade after the launching of the first Soviet sputnik. Major provisions of the treaty; (1) prohibit placing nuclear or other weapons of mass destruction in orbit or on the moon and other celestial bodies; (2) ban military bases and maneuvers on the moon and other planets; (3) provide that all explorations and uses of outer space be for the benefit and in the interests of all countries; (4) forbid claims of national sovereignty in outer space; and (5) encourage international cooperation in exploring space, in assisting astronauts and space vehicles, and in the exchange of scientific information. *See also* OUTER SPACE JURISDICTION.

Output   Activities carried on by a political system in response to demands or stresses placed upon the system in the form of inputs. Outputs usually take the form of governmental policies, programs, decisions, and implementing actions. They may be generically categorized as rule making, rule interpreting, and rule enforcing functions carried on within the larger social system. *See also* COMMUNICATIONS THEORY, INPUT, SYSTEMS ANALYSIS.

Overseas Chinese   People of Chinese ancestry and culture living outside the borders of mainland China and Formosa. Overseas Chinese living in the countries of Southeast Asia exceed 16 million and represent a major problem of cultural assimilation.

Pacific Settlement of Disputes   The peaceful adjustment of international disputes by one or more of the following techniques: negotiation, inquiry, good offices, mediation, conciliation, arbitration, or adjudication. Pacific settlement may be employed through the traditional diplomatic channels, regional organizations or arrangements, or the organs or agencies of the United Nations. Chapter VI of the United Nations Charter sets out in detail the political procedures available to the Security Council and the General Assembly, Chapter XV delegates peaceful settlement responsibilities to the Secretary-General, and Chapter XIV prescribes the legal processes by which the International Court of Justice may attempt to settle justiciable disputes. *See also* ARBITRATION, DIPLOMACY, GOOD OFFICES, INTERNATIONAL COURT OF JUSTICE.

Pacific States Telephone and Telegraph Co. v. Oregon, 223 U.S. 118 (1912): Involved the question of whether the initiative and referendum provisions of the Oregon Constitution destroy the republican form of government guaranteed to all states by the United States Constitution in Article IV, section 4. The Court held it to be a political question not open to judicial inquiry. *See also* REPUBLICAN FORM OF GOVERNMENT.

Pacta Sunt Servanda   The rule of general international law that treaties are binding and should be observed. *Pacta sunt servanda* is the principle that establishes the legal basis whereby treaties constitute binding contracts between signatory states. *See also* REBUS SIC STANTIBUS, TREATY.

Pact of Paris, *see* Kellogg-Briand Pact.

Pair   An understanding reached in advance between two legislators, holding opposing views on a bill, to withhold their votes on a "yea and nay" roll call. In this way, each is assured that his absence from the chamber during the vote will not affect the outcome. In effect, each member of the pair cancels out the other's vote. A "special" pair applies to one or several votes taken on the same subject. A "general" pair, occasionally used in the Senate, applies to all votes taken over a specified period of time. On a question requiring a two-thirds vote, two members must be "paired for" the measure to balance off one "paired against" it. *See also* RECORD VOTE.

Palestine Refugee Aid, *see* United Nations Relief and Works Agency.

Palko v. Connecticut, 302 U.S. 319 (1937): Ruled that the double jeopardy provision of the Fifth Amendment does not apply to the states through the Fourteenth Amendment. In the *Palko* case, the Supreme Court permitted the state to appeal a conviction of a defendant to ask for a more severe sentence. The *Palko* case was overruled in 1969 in *Benton v. Maryland,* 395 U.S. 784.

Pan-American Union, *see* Organization of American States.

Panel   The list of persons summoned for jury duty. A trial jury is "impaneled" when the parties to the case have agreed to the selection of the jurors from the panel. Panels are selected in a variety of ways in different states by jury commissioners or county or township clerks or other officials. Names are usually selected from voting or taxpayer lists. A 1968 law requires random selection from voter lists for federal juror panels. *See also* JURY.

Panel Study   A research technique involving repeated interviews of the same individuals over a planned time period. Through interviews of the same group of respondents at two or more points in time, the panel study permits the investigator to observe changes in individual attitudes that might be attributable to intervening events. The technique was first used by Stuart Rice in 1924 to learn how candidate preferences of college students changed during the course of the presidential campaign. The panel technique, as contrasted with the controlled experiment, is designed to measure changes occurring in a nonlaboratory setting. It may acquire some characteristics of an experiment, however, when the intervening stimulus is introduced by the experimenter. The intervening stimulus, for example, might be a public information campaign conducted between the first and second interviews and planned as part of the study. This kind of study is called an *impact panel. See also* INTERVIEW, SURVEY RESEARCH.

Papal Legate and Nuncio, *see* Diplomat.

Paradigm   A model, pattern, or example that helps organize thought and give direction to research. "Paradigm" may have reference to the design of a particular piece of research, or some aspect of it; to a framework for research in some broad area of a discipline, such as a paradigm for political integration; or, more broadly, to the assumptions and modes of thought characteristic of an entire discipline or major segment of it. At the more specific level, a paradigm may set forth appropriate problems and research methods, identify important variables, and propound a set of research questions. It may also include a theoretical element, that is, a statement of hypothesized relationships among key variables. Some usages of the term suggest that a paradigm, while more than a vague perspective, stops short of setting forth the deductively related set of propositions that would constitute a theory. In political science literature the label "paradigm" may be attached to almost any model having some of the above elements, including a graph, a diagram, or a verbal outline. Two of the most common paradigms in modern political science fall under the rubrics of structural-functionalism and systems analysis. Within these rubrics one might refer to particular formulations, such as the Almond (structural-functional) paradigm or the Eastonian (systems) paradigm. Paradigm is sometimes used in the sense of an example of a class of things rather than a model. *See also* APPROACH, CONCEPTUAL SCHEME.

Parameter   A condition or value that is given or held constant or assumed to be constant in a research problem. Parameters are limiting conditions that serve as boundaries or constraints upon the operation of the variables. Political scientists sometimes use the term more generally to mean the boundaries, limits, or constraints in any situation. Parameter values may be arbitrarily assigned for research purposes. For example, in a study of decision making under conditions of perfect availability of information, perfect information is not in fact available but is arbitrarily assumed as a parameter of the situation. In other instances parameter values may be drawn from actual data. In the terminology of statistics a parameter is a numerical characteristic, such as a mean or median, of a *population* under study. This may be contrasted with a *statistic,* which is a numerical characteristic of a *sample* of the population. *See also* VARIABLE.

Parametric Statistics, *see* Statistics.

Pardon The granting of a release from the punishment or legal consequences of a crime by the proper executive authority before or after conviction. An "absolute pardon" restores the individual to the position he enjoyed prior to his conviction for commission of a crime. A "conditional pardon" requires that certain obligations be met before the pardon becomes effective. The President exercises the complete pardoning power for federal offenses except for convictions in impeachment cases. Pardons are administered for the President by the Office of the Pardon Attorney in the Department of Justice. Thirty states entrust the governor with the full authority for granting pardons. In the remainder, the governor typically shares the power with a pardon board or with the state senate. Pardons are granted usually to provide a remedy for mistakes made in convictions or to release offenders who have been properly rehabilitated. The President and most state governors also have the power to grant *reprieves,* which postpone the execution of a sentence for humanitarian reasons or to await new evidence. *See also* AMNESTY, *Ex parte Grossman.*

Parish, *see* County.

Parity A governmental price policy designed to maintain a level of purchasing power for farmers equal to that of a previous base period that was favorable to agriculture. This means, for example, that if in 1910 a farmer was able to sell ten bushels of wheat and buy a bicycle with the receipts, at full parity today he should be able to work out the same exchange. Parity-support price levels are determined by Congress, and actual parity prices for specific crops are determined each year by the Department of Agriculture. *See also* PRICE SUPPORT.

Parliamentary Diplomacy A form of conference diplomacy that emphasizes the search for agreement through the construction of majorities within continuing international institutions. The term, attributed to United States Secretary of State Dean Rusk, emphasizes similarities between the political process in the General Assembly and other international organs and in national parliaments. Parliamentary diplomacy calls attention to the maneuvering of the various regional and special-interest groups, which resembles legislative caucusing, pork barreling, and log rolling in national assemblies. *See also* DIPLOMACY.

Parliamentary Government A system in which legislative and executive powers are fused. Parliamentary government does not require the separate election of the head of government, as in the American system, where powers are separated. The leadership of the majority in the legislature forms the Cabinet, which exercises executive power. Leadership of the majority party or parties in the cabinet virtually guarantees the passage of government-sponsored legislation. This form of government operates with either a two-party or a multiparty system, such as those found in Britain and in Western Europe. *See also* PARLIAMENT (BRITAIN), PARLIAMENT (FRANCE), PARLIAMENT (ITALY), PARLIAMENT (GERMANY).

Parliamentary Party, *see* Conservative Party (Britain), Labour Party (Britain).

Parliamentary System   A system of government, often based on the British prototype, in which governmental authority is vested in the legislative body (parliament) and in a cabinet headed by a prime minister or premier. The cabinet exercises political leadership and directs the administration. Cabinet ministers are entirely or largely selected from the membership of parliament and the cabinet continues in power so long as it commands the support of a majority of the parliament. Substantial disagreement between the parliament and the cabinet results in either the appointment of a new ministry or the election of a new legislature. *See also* PRESIDENTIAL GOVERNMENT.

Parliament (Britain)   The two-chamber (House of Commons, House of Lords) legislative assembly that is the focus for political power in Britain. The British Parliament, legally supreme, is actually the vehicle for formalizing government policies. The Cabinet, through its control of the majority party, utilizes the power of Parliament to establish such policies. *See also* PARLIAMENTARY GOVERNMENT.

Parliament (France)   The bicameral legislature of the Fifth Republic. The lower house, the National Assembly, consists of 486 members, and the Senate, or upper house, has 273. Parliament sits in two regular sessions each year up to a legal maximum of 170 days. Special sessions are called by the Premier of the National Assembly. Each house is run by a bureau of parliamentary officials and is presided over by a president. The numerous standing committees that characterized previous French systems have been reduced in each chamber to six committees of unwieldy large membership. Attendance at sessions of Parliament is obligatory but irregular even though absence is punishable by forfeiture of pay. The executive controls the work of Parliament; but members of the government are forbidden to occupy a seat in the legislature. While the forms of parliamentary government have been preserved, the substance has been diluted. For example, it is open to question whether Parliament's legal power to bring down a government by censure exists in fact. *See also* PARLIAMENTARY GOVERNMENT.

Parliament (Germany)   The bicameral legislature of the West German Federal Republic. The Bundestag (lower house), composed of 496 deputies plus twenty-two nonvoting deputies from Berlin, represents all of the people of the Republic, and is the more powerful of the two chambers. The Bundesrat (upper house), composed of forty-one delegates from the ten states of the Federal Republic and four nonvoting delegates from Berlin, has a qualified legislative veto and is the guardian of state interests. The Cabinet reports to the Bundestag which, though it cannot dismiss a minister, can bring about the overthrow of the Chancellor by electing his successor. Both houses make extensive use of committees in the legislative process with committee membership based on party strength in the lower house. The committees exercise less control over bills than in the United States but by the same token more actual legislative work is done during floor debate than is the case in the American Congress. Legislation usually follows this course: (1) from the ministry where the bill is written (2) to the Cabinet, (3) which submits it first to the Bundesrat, for initial evaluation, (4) then to the Bundestag for action, and (5) thence back to the Bundesrat for final consideration. *See also* CABINET (GERMANY), CHANCELLOR, BUNDESRAT, BUN-DESTAG.

Parliament (Italy)   The bicameral legislature of the Italian democratic republic created in 1948. By direct universal election, citizens over twenty-one choose the Chamber of Deputies while those over twenty-five elect senators as well. Each member of the Chamber of Deputies (lower house) represents 80,000 people or a major fraction thereof, must be twenty-five years of age, and serves a five-year term. Senators are elected in each of the nineteen regions of the country; each represents 200,000 people or a major fraction thereof, must be at least forty years old, and serves a six-year term. As in the French and West German multiparty systems, Italian legislators are organized into parliamentary party groups, which are the basis for membership on legislative standing committees. The committee structure roughly parallels the pattern of government ministries. Bills are introduced by the government, by members of either house, or by initiative; they must pass both houses to become law. In cases of disagreement, legislation is shuttled between the two houses until a consensus is reached or until Parliament is dissolved. In addition to its normal, legislative functions, Parliament also elects the President of Italy and one third of the members of both the Constitutional Court and the High Judicial Council. *See also* PARLIAMENTARY GOVERNMENT.

Parochial Schools, *see* Separation of Church and State.

Parole   Release from prison prior to the expiration of a sentence. The release is based on the good behavior of the prisoner, who may be returned to prison if he violates the conditions of his parole. In the national government, paroles are administered through the Department of Justice by the Board of Parole, consisting of eight members appointed by the President. In the states, paroles are generally administered by parole boards or by the governors.

Partial Correlation, *see* Correlation.

Partial Test Ban Treaty   A treaty signed at Moscow on August 5, 1963, by representatives of Britain, the Soviet Union, and the United States, which bans nuclear weapons tests in the atmosphere, in outer space, and under water. The Test Ban Treaty permits underground nuclear tests so long as such explosions do not pollute the environment with radioactive debris outside the territorial limits of the state conducting the tests. Article IV of the Treaty establishes the right of each party to withdraw from the Treaty after giving three months' notice if "extraordinary events" jeopardize "the supreme interests of its country." The Treaty entered into force on October 10, 1963.

Participant Observation   A research method by which the investigator becomes a member, or poses as a member, of a group he is studying. Participant observation makes the researcher both a participant in the group and an observer of its behavior. As participant, he tries to become familiar with the perspectives and assumptions of group members and, over a period of time, to acquire the capacity to think and act as one of them. As an observer, he tries to view his own behavior and theirs objectively. He thus becomes socialized to new values and biases yet tries to eliminate these biases from his analysis. The success of this form of inquiry rests heavily upon the investigator's ability to combine the two roles effectively. A variation of participant observation has been used in live simulations of decision-making behavior. In such cases the researcher is less concerned with acquiring the perspectives of the other participants than with influencing their interactions to meet experimental needs. *See also* OBSERVATION, SIMULATION.

Participatory Democracy, *see* New Left.

Partition   The division of territory between two or more sovereign entities. Partition can involve an entire state, a portion thereof, or an area that does not have the status of statehood. Partition may be imposed by a powerful state upon a weaker one by war or threat of war. It might also occur as a result of mutual agreement or as a method of peaceful settlement offered by a third state or international organization, as in mediation or arbitration. Partition may be determined by political elites or by plebiscites or other forms of self-determination. *See also* IRREDENTISM, NATIONAL SELF-DETERMINATION.

Party-column Ballot   A form of general election ballot in which candidates for various offices are arranged in one column under their respective party names and symbols. The "party column" or "Indiana ballot" is in contradistinction to the other common type of ballot, the "office block" or "Massachusetts ballot," in which candidates are grouped under each elective office. *See also* OFFICE-BLOCK BALLOT, STRAIGHT TICKET.

Party Government (Britain)   The decisive role of the majority party in the political decision-making process. In the British system, the party that wins a majority at the polls has the right to form the government. The Prime Minister and the Cabinet as majority party leaders wield the powers of the Parliament to implement their programs. They can continue so long as the government retains the confidence of the Parliament and the electorate.

Party Platform, *see* Platform.

Party, Political, *see* Political Party.

Party System (Britain) The British have basically a two-party system composed of the Labour and Conservative parties. Third parties like the Liberals, the Welsh and Scottish Nationalists, and the Communists exist, however, and contest elections. The tendency to regroup around a two-party norm was demonstrated in the early twentieth century when Labour took the place of the Liberals as a major party. *See also* TWO-PARTY SYSTEM.

Party System (France) Politics in France has historically been organized on a multiparty basis with no one party capable of winning a majority. Governments have traditionally been coalitions, a form which reached a high point of instability during the period of the Fourth Republic. A few parties, such as the Union for the New Republic, the Radical Socialists, the Popular Republicans, the Socialists, and the Communists, are nationwide. Many parties, however, are sectional, and many voters tend to group around individual leaders. Indeed, party loyalty and unity are not highly valued by most Frenchmen, who tend to be independent and individualistic. Party identification for election purposes bears little resemblance to the parliamentary parties. Individual members of Parliament exhibit considerable freedom in attaching themselves to leaders or parliamentary groups in the National Assembly since only parties or groups of thirty or more are entitled to be represented on committees. After these groups are formed, the attempt is made to seat them from Left to Right around the chamber according to their ideological identification in the political spectrum. Major exceptions to this highly individualized approach to politics and parliamentary government have been the Communists and the Socialists. *See also* MULTIPARTY SYSTEM.

Party System (Germany) A multiparty system trending toward bipartyism. The party system emerged with allied permission during the post-World War II occupation period. Except for the subsequent banning of neo-Nazi and Communist parties, the system remains fundamentally the same under the Basic Law of the Federal Republic. Strict electoral laws have curtailed the proliferation of parties that characterized the Weimar experience. The ten parties that competed for power at the end of the occupation period have largely coalesced into two major and one minor party represented in the Bundestag. In the 1966 general election, the Christian Democratic Union (CDU) won 246 seats, the Social Democratic party (SDP) 202 seats, and the Free Democratic party (FDP) forty-nine seats. Since 1949, West Germany has regained an international position of economic and political importance under the leadership of the CDU and its first Chancellor, Konrad Adenauer. The CDU is supported in its slightly right-of-center position by middle-class business interests and by industrial and agricultural workers. As its name implies, the CDU represents a religious approach to politics, but it is not a clerical party. The Free Democratic party is also of the center-right, but unlike the CDU it rejects a role for religion in politics.

The SDP, the second of the two major parties, has survived in Germany since its creation during the Empire period. Support for its left-of-center position comes mainly from the ranks of industrial workers, and its program resembles that of the British Labour party. Splinter groups exist on the extreme Left and Right, but have failed to win seats in the Bundestag because the law requires a party to poll five percent of the national vote or show a majority in a voting district to be represented. The National Democratic Party (NPD), for example, emerged during the 1960s and has steadily increased its support, mainly in local elections, from conservatives and ultranationalists on the Right. *See also* MULTIPARTY SYSTEM.

Party System (Italy)   The continental European type of weak, unstable multiparty system. The governing majority in the Italian party system consists of a ruling centrist party and coalition that support the established constitutional order. The system lacks an effective alternative because the forces on the far Left and Right oppose the existing constitutional order. Hence, the center party or parties continue in office with only minor variations in the composition of the government. The Christian Democratic, or Catholic party, which regularly polls forty to fifty percent of the popular vote, has ruled alone or in coalition with minor centrist parties since 1945. The Christian Democratic party is so large, however, that internal factionalism has limited its ability to provide programmatic leadership. The Communist party, the largest in any non-Communist country, is the second-largest mass party in Italy. Regularly polling twenty to twenty-five percent of the popular vote, the Communists are an anticonstitutional party composed both of ideological militants and of a mass of persons disaffected by the present system because of poverty, corruption, unemployment, and lack of social progress. The Italian Socialist party, founded in the late nineteenth century, polls eight to fifteen percent of the vote and is the smallest of the nation's three mass parties. No longer allied with the Communists, the Socialists continue to draw their major support from the radical proletarian left, particularly from those voters alienated by Communist regimentation of the personal lives of party members and fear of Soviet domination of party policy. The Socialists also have their splinter groups such as the Social Democrats. Minor national parties which collectively poll up to twenty percent of the vote include: The Liberal party, which speaks for conservative upper-income industrial, agricultural, and professional groups; the Radical party which grew out of nineteenth century liberalism and is somewhat analogous to American Progressives and New Dealers; the Italian Social Movement, a remnant of former minor Fascists from the Mussolini era; and the Italian Democratic party (Monarchists), supporters of vested interests, ultraconservatism, and reaction who with the Fascists, make up the anticonstitutional "revolutionary" Right. *See also* MULTI-PARTY SYSTEM.

Party Whip, *see* Whip.

Passport   A certificate, issued by an offical governmental agency, that identifies a person as a citizen of a country and authorizes him to travel abroad. Passports are granted to Americans by the Passport Office of the State Department, by territorial governors, and by diplomatic officials abroad.

Patent　An exclusive grant to an inventor by which the national government extends to an individual or corporation "the right to exclude others from making, using, or selling the invention throughout the United States" for a period of seventeen years. Patent grants are made only for bona fide "discoveries," and not for improvements upon existing inventions. They apply to any new machine, design, process, composition, substance, or plant variety. The Constitution grants Congress exclusive power to grant patents. Patents are granted by the United States Patent Office in the Department of Commerce. *See also* COPYRIGHT, TRADEMARK.

Patent Office, *see* Department of Commerce.

Patronage　The power to make partisan appointments to office or to confer contracts, franchises, licenses, honors, or other special favors. Patronage powers are vested primarily in the President, in governors and other state elective officials, in mayors, and in various county officers. Through senatorial courtesy and similar practices, legislators on all levels of government also share in patronage disposition. *See also* SPOILS SYSTEM, SENATORIAL COURTESY, MERIT SYSTEM.

Pattern, *see* Behavior Pattern.

Patterns of Power　The ways in which individual states organize and use their power to maximize their security and achieve their national interests in competition with other states. The patterns of power involve the characteristic responses available to the state in an international system in which the power of other states represents an actual or potential threat. The patterns include: (1) unilateralism—dependence on one's own power; (2) alliances—the power configuration of group against group; (3) collective security—a universalized power system of "one for all, and all for one"; and (4) world government—a cooperative federal structure, or a world empire dominated by one government. *See also* CAPABILITY ANALYSIS, POWER.

Payroll Tax, *see* Withholding Tax.

PCIJ, *see* Permanent Court of International Justice.

Peace Corps　An agency that administers the foreign aid program, adopted in 1961, under which American volunteers are sent to developing countries to teach and help improve living standards. By 1972, thousands of Peace Corps volunteers were in training or in service in many countries of Asia, Africa, and Latin America. The Peace Corps, established within the State Department in 1961, was transferred to the Action Agency in 1971. *See also* FOREIGN AID.

Peaceful Change, *see* Political Change.

Peaceful Coexistence   A reinterpretation of Leninism that rejects the inevitability of a major war between the leading Western and Communist states. The Communist doctrine of peaceful coexistence was enunciated by Soviet Premier Nikita Khrushchev before the Twentieth Party Congress in 1956. As a basis for Soviet policy, the new doctrine called for both sides to avoid nuclear war and to refrain from exporting revolution or counterrevolution. Competition between states with different social systems, according to Khrushchev, was to continue in all nonmilitary areas until communism proved itself superior and presided at the burial of capitalism. *See also* KHRUSHCHEVISM.

Peaceful Settlement   The resolution of international disputes without resort to force. Pacific settlement involves the procedural techniques by which conflicts over substantive rights and duties of states can be resolved. The two categories of techniques for the peaceful settlement of international disputes are: (1) legal, which involve the application of international law to the facts of the dispute; and (2) political, which involve diplomatic procedures. Arbitration and adjudication comprise the legal methods of pacific settlement, and the political techniques include diplomatic negotiation, good offices, mediation, inquiry, and conciliation. *See also* ADJUDICATION, ARBITRATION, CONCILIATION, DIPLOMACY, GOOD OFFICES, INQUIRY, INTERNATIONAL LAW, MEDIATION, NEGOTIATION, DISPUTE SETTLEMENT PROCEDURES (UNITED NATIONS).

Peace Research   Scholarly investigation, often interdisciplinary in scope, of the nature and causes of international conflict and the conditions of peace. Peace research embraces a wide scope of subject matter, ranging from psychological studies of conflict and aggression in individuals to grandiose plans for world political order. Peace researchers have increasingly shown preference for systematic, empirical investigation, often using advanced research methodologies and statistical techniques. The establishment of numerous institutes for peace research and disarmament studies, and the convening of international scientific conferences on the subject, have given peace research the appearance of an organized movement. In fact, however, the movement is highly amorphous, and many scholars continue to pursue peace research without the benefit of such institutional connections.

Pendleton Act (Civil Service Act of 1883)   This law, as amended over the years, forms the basis for the personnel policies of the national government. The law established the principle of employment on the basis of open, competitive examinations, and created a Civil Service Commission to administer the personnel service. The Pendleton Act extended the merit principle to only 10 percent of national employees, but later laws and executive orders have extended coverage to more than 90 percent of employees.

Peonage, *see* Involuntary Servitude.

People's Republic of China, *see* Central Committee, Chinese Communist Party, Commune, Cultural Revolution, Maoism, National Party Congress, National People's Congress, Politburo, Red Guard, State Council.

Perception   The act of becoming aware of things by means of the senses. Perception involves two related operations—receiving impressions through sight, touch, and other senses, and the interpretation or assignment of meaning to the sensory impressions. Meaning is assigned through the interaction of sensory impressions with a person's *cognitive structure* (relevant beliefs arising from past experience) and his *evaluative structure* (the values that he holds). Perception is not an entirely explicit process, since the reception and evaluation of many sensory cues may occur below the threshold of consciousness. People perceive things selectively, depending on their concerns and motivations and that small portion of the memory that is active at the time information is received. Thus, what people notice, and how they interpret what they notice, are influenced by preconceptions. Studies of *social perception* deal with differences in people's perceptions arising from differences in their cultural and social backgrounds. Among the factors that affect the perception of political phenomena are ideology, personality, past political activity and experience, characteristics of a particular decision situation, potential costs and rewards, available information, and the emotional states of the perceiver. *See also* ATTITUDE, DISPOSITIONS, PERSONALITY.

Peremptory Challenge, *see* Challenge.

Performance Budget   The drawing up of a plan for anticipated expenditures based on the activities, services, and functions (that is, *units* of work) performed by government, rather than allotting funds on the basis of items to be purchased and salaries to be paid by each department and agency. *See also* BUDGET.

Peril Points, *see* Escape Clause, Reciprocal Trade Agreements Act, Trade Expansion Act, United States Tariff Commission.

Periodic Registration, *see* Registration.

Permanent Court of Arbitration   A panel of internationally recognized jurists who stand ready to serve as arbitrators in any international dispute. The Permanent Court of Arbitration, with headquarters at the Hague, was established by the Convention for the Pacific Settlement of International Disputes as adopted and revised by the Hague Peace Conferences of 1899 and 1907. The panel of available arbitrators includes four jurists of recognized competence appointed by each signatory. Each party to a dispute selects two judges, only one of whom may be a national. The four arbitrators so chosen then select a fifth to serve as umpire. Thus, the Court is not a standing body but only a panel from which arbitral tribunals can be selected. The parties identify the points at issue, define the authority of the tribunal, and agree that a decision made within these limitations will be accepted as legally binding. *See also* ARBITRATION, HAGUE PEACE CONFERENCES.

Permanent Mandates Commission, *see* Mandates System.

Permanent Registration, *see* Registration.

Permanent Under-Secretary of State, *see* Foreign Secretary (Britain).

Persona Grata   An expression used to indicate that a particular individual would be, or continues to be, acceptable as an official representative of a foreign state. The concept of *persona grata* implies that a state may also declare a diplomatic representative of another state to be unacceptable *(persona non grata)*. *See also* AGRÉMENT, DIPLOMATIC PRIVILEGES AND IMMUNITIES.

Personalismo   The Latin American political phenomenon of personalizing political power. Traditionally, many Latin American political parties could be described as bands of loyal followers clustered around, and serving as a vehicle for the expression of, some dominant and colorful personality. *See also* CAUDILLISMO.

Personality   The persisting, organized dispositions in a person that lead him to respond in characteristic ways to his environment. Personality, in a technical sense, is usually equated with dispositions underlying behavior rather than with the behavior itself. Personality traits, however, are sometimes regarded not only as dispositions but as acts, or characteristic modes of behaving. Dispositions, or personality traits, are interrelated, although theorists differ on how they are organized within a personality structure. Psychologists generally hold that dispositions precede attitudes, and that personality, therefore, tends to shape attitudes rather than the other way about. The dispositions that shape responses to political stimuli are sometimes called *political personality. Modal personality* refers to personality features most widely shared, or the most prevalent personality type, among a group of people. In a general way personality is often used in political studies to include all nonenvironmental variables that affect an individual's political behavior. Methods of investigating personality characteristics may include interview, observation, content analysis of a person's communications, and examination of biographical materials. *See also* ATTITUDE, DISPOSITIONS.

Personal Property Tax   A tax levied on things of value other than real property. Personal property is usually classified as tangible or intangible, the former including valuables of substance, such as business inventories, machinery, jewelry, and household goods, and the latter a right, claim, or interest of value, such as found in bonds, stocks, and bank accounts. *See also* ASSESSED VALUATION.

Persona non Grata   An unacceptable person. *Persona non grata* relates particularly to the situation in which a nation declares that an ambassador or minister is no longer acceptable and requests his recall by his government.

Perspective   A point of view or way of comprehending things. A perspective embraces a cluster of values, beliefs, and expectations that tend to orient a person's thinking on a given subject. A "political science" perspective, for example, might include notions of the kinds of behaviors that are "political," commitment to the values of scholarship and systematic inquiry, and certain expectations about the rewards and costs of political inquiry. *See also* ATTITUDE, VALUE.

Petition (Nominating)   A method of placing a candidate's name on a primary or general election ballot by submitting a specified number, or percentage, of signatures of registered voters to an appropriate state or local official for certification. Petitions may also be used to commence the initiative and referendum procedures in several states. *See also* NOMINATION, FILING.

Petition (Right of)   A request to a public official that seeks to correct a wrong or to influence public policy. The First Amendment guarantees to the people the right to "petition the government for a redress of grievances." This provision, like all provisions of the First Amendment, is applicable to the states through the Fourteenth Amendment, although most state constitutions contain a similar provision. The right of petition, closely related to freedoms of speech, press, and assembly, is generally exercised through letter writing to public officials and through pressure group activity.

Petit Jury, *see* Jury.

Philadelphia Convention, *see* Constitutional Convention of 1787.

Philosophy of Science   The field of study dealing with science as a way of knowing and a mode of inquiry. The philosophy of science does not add to substantive knowledge within political science or any other discipline, but rather is concerned with the way knowledge is acquired and the nature of what is known. It asks fundamental questions about the nature of scientific theory, the relation of theories to evidence, criteria for evaluating concepts and theories, differences between acceptable and specious scientific explanations, and criteria for making predictions that are justifiable as well as plausible. The philosophy of science deals with all the basic questions on which the validity of scientific inquiry depends, but which are often merely assumed by the practicing scientist. *See also* SCIENCE, SCIENTIFIC METHOD.

Philosophy, Political, *see* Political Philosophy.

Picketing   Patrolling the site of a business establishment by workers who are on strike. Peaceful picketing is a form of free speech protected by the First Amendment (*Thornhill v. Alabama*, 310 U.S. 88 [1940]). Under national and state laws, however, picketing may not be used to promote any purpose which is contrary to law or public policy. The Taft-Hartley Act and the Landrum-Griffin Act forbid picketing for such purposes as encouraging secondary boycotts or trying to force employers to recognize a union other than one already lawfully recognized.

Pigeonhole   To kill a bill in committee by putting it aside and not reporting it out for consideration by the chamber. The term relates to the old-time desks in committee rooms of Congress, which had open "pigeonholes" or cubicles for filing papers. To pigeonhole a bill means, figuratively, to file the bill away and forget it. This usually kills the bill. Killing a bill by pigeonholing is typically accomplished by a committee chairman when a majority of the committee members do not object.

Pivotal States   Those states with large electoral votes that are crucial in winning a presidential election and in which the outcome is doubtful. *See also* ELECTORAL COLLEGE, PRESIDENTIAL ELECTION PROCESS.

Planning   Preparation and execution of projects for the future economic, social, and physical development of a community. Planning may be nationwide or statewide in situations in which it encompasses all types of governmental problems, but it is more often associated with the physical development of municipal governments. This includes planning street layouts, parks, public utility routes, and the zoning of areas for residential and commercial purposes. In recent years, emphasis has turned from purely physical aspects of city planning and beautification to social and economic concerns such as urban redevelopment and housing. In metropolitan areas, stress is now being put on the need for countywide or regional planning to provide orderly development. Sound planning must take into consideration population and economic trends as well as future fiscal needs. Many cities and states have official planning agencies. *See also* ZONING.

Platform   A statement of principles and objectives espoused by a party or a candidate that is used during a campaign to win support from voters. Platforms are typically written by platform committees and adopted by national, state, or county party conventions. *See also* NATIONAL CONVENTION.

Plebiscite   A vote to determine the will of the entire population of an area on some matter of great public interest. Plebiscites have frequently been used in international relations in connection with territorial cessions. Although a specific treaty of cession may stipulate that a plebiscite must be held, there is no customary rule of international law that requires the approval of the inhabitants before sovereignty over a territory can be legally transferred. *See also* CESSION, NATIONAL SELF-DETERMINATION, PEACEFUL SETTLEMENT.

Plessy v. Ferguson, 163 U.S. 537 (1896): Upheld, in a famous decision, a state law requiring segregation of the races in public transportation. The Court held that under the equal protection clause of the Fourteenth Amendment, a state could provide "separate but equal" facilities for Negroes. This case was overruled in *Brown v. Board of Education of Topeka,* 347 U.S. 483 (1954).

Pluralism   The existence in modern society of heterogeneous institutions and organizations that have diversified religious, economic, ethnic, and cultural interests. *Political pluralism* describes a society in which power is widely distributed among numerous groups arrayed in shifting patterns of conflict, competition, and cooperation with one another. Political pluralism may also refer to governmental and other social institutions that make possible such a wide sharing of power. As a political philosophy, pluralism holds that diversity is desirable as a precondition of democracy. *Social pluralism*, emphasizing the role of voluntary groups in an industrial society, is sometimes contrasted with the *cultural pluralism* of premodern or traditional societies in which "natural" groupings based on such factors as race, language, caste, or religion are more important. Social pluralism presumes the clash of group interests but, hopefully, within an overall value consensus, whereas cultural pluralism is a product of basic value cleavages. *See also* GROUP THEORY.

Plurality   The winning of an election by a candidate who receives more votes than any other candidate but not necessarily a majority of the total vote. *See also* ABSOLUTE MAJORITY.

Pocket Veto   A special veto power exercised mainly at the end of a legislative session whereby bills not signed by a chief executive die after a specified time. Under the Constitution, if the President holds a bill for ten days without signing or vetoing it, the bill becomes law if Congress is in session, and it is pocket vetoed if Congress adjourns during the ten days. In about one-third of the states, the governors exercise a similar pocket veto power if they do not approve the measure during a stated period after legislative adjournment. This period varies in these states from three to thirty days. *See also* VETO.

Pointer v. Texas, *see* Witness.

Point Four Program   A program designed to help foster economic development and modernization by making available to the recipient countries American technical knowledge and skills. The Point Four Program resulted from an appeal to Congress to provide foreign technical assistance. The program received its name because it was the fourth major point in President Harry Truman's inaugural address delivered on January 20, 1949. The President advocated the maintenance of peace and freedom by means of "a bold new program for making the benefits of our scientific advances and industrial progress available for the improvement and growth of underdeveloped areas." Implementation was provided in 1950 by the Act for International Development. *See also* FOREIGN AID (UNITED STATES).

Police Court, *see* Magistrate.

Police Power   Authority to promote and safeguard the health, morals, safety, and welfare of the people. In the context of the American federal system, police power is reserved to the states. The national government, exercising only delegated powers, does not possess a general police power. Many national laws enacted under the commerce and postal powers, such as those which prohibit shipment of impure drugs in interstate commerce or mailing of obscene literature, are, however, examples of what may be termed "federal police power." State laws enacted under the police power may legally invade national jurisdiction if such laws are pertinent to the health, safety, or welfare of the people of the state, such as a state law regulating grade crossings for interstate trains.

Policy Analysis, *see* Organization Theory.

Policy Committee   A party committee in Congress that functions as an agent of the caucus or conference in formulating legislative plans and strategy. Although the reorganization of Congress in 1946 provided for policy committees to replace the old steering committees, only the Senate has formally created such bodies. House Republicans unofficially converted their steering committee into a policy committee in 1949, but the House Democratic Steering Committee remains operational. In the Senate, the Democrats retained their steering committee to function solely as a committee on committees to fill vacancies on Senate standing committees.

Policy Foreign, *see* Foreign Policy.

Policy Makers, *see* Decision Makers.

Policy, Public, *see* Public Policy.

Policy Sciences   An emerging interdisciplinary field of inquiry concerned with the application of scientific methods and insights to the improvement of public policy making and the solution of public problems. Policy science(s) (used in both the singular and the plural) thus represents primarily the "applied" as contrasted with the "pure science" aspects of relevant disciplines. Given the wide range of public problems, policy scientists may be drawn from almost any discipline—social, biological, or physical. The disciplines most directly concerned with the policy sciences approach have been political science, sociology, law, business management, history, and public administration. Policy sciences also utilize insights drawn from such fields as systems analysis, operations research, cybernetics, game theory, and general systems theory, which cut across traditional disciplinary boundaries. Policy scientists are particularly concerned with the process by which public policy decisions are made. They bring their insights to bear on the problems of clarifying goals, evaluating alternatives, identifying trends, and analyzing the policy situation. Policy science does not posit basic values, but, rather, is concerned with factual propositions that are subject to empirical inquiry. Nevertheless, policy scientists contribute to goal choice by rendering judgment on the feasibility of means, the range of possible choices, and the possible consequences of alternative choices. *See also* ANALYSIS, COST-BENEFIT

ANALYSIS, ENDS-MEANS ANALYSIS, ENGINEERING THEORY, OPERATIONS RESEARCH, SOCIAL
ENGINEERING.

Politburo (China (PRC))   The chief decision-making body in the Chinese Communist
Party (CCP) and nation. It is composed of twenty full members and six alternates and
is considerably larger than the Russian model. Here issues are settled and policy is sent
on to the hand-picked Central Committee for legitimation and transmittal to the
appropriate action groups in the party or government, or both. *See also* POLITBURO
(SOVIET UNION).

Politburo (Soviet Union)   The focus of supreme decision-making power in the
Communist party and the Soviet state. Called the Presidium of the Central Committee
after 1952, the older name, Politburo, was reinstituted at the Twenty-third Party
Congress in 1966. The Politburo is composed of eleven members and five candidate
members.

Political Action   Any observable, overt behavior of an individual or a social group
carried on within a political system. A political action may be unplanned, random
behavior, or it may be part of a coherent decision process. A response to actions
undertaken by others is a *reaction*. In *action research* in the social sciences an
investigator introduces his own actions as an element in the process he is studying. In
this way he may observe the impact of his behavior on the interactions within the
group under observation. *Action theory* is a body of thought identified with Parsonian
structural-functionalism, in which the basic units of analysis are social actions, that is,
the intended or motivated actions of individuals. *See also* INTERACTION, STRUCTURAL-
FUNCTIONALISM.

Political Activist   An individual who is extensively and vigorously involved in
political activity, either within or outside the party system. Political activists within
the party system typically participate in decision making at various levels, verbalize
their ideas, attend party functions, campaign, work at the polls, help collect funds,
support party candidates, and carry on other forms of activity within the party
framework. Political activists outside the party system typically are protestors who
build their interest and activity around a major issue, idea, or ideological point of view.
Studies of political participation have produced operational definitions and varied
categories of activist behavior. *See also* NEW LEFT.

Political Actor   An individual or social group that affects the decision process within
a political system. As in the theater, the political actor "plays a role" in politics.
Although action is performed only by human beings, in political analysis the capacity
for action is often attributed to corporate entities, such as states. The political
behavior of actors may be described, analyzed, explained, and predicted for political
systems at all levels—local, state, national, or international—and for actors of different
types, as, for example, a state, a top decision maker, a national parliament, or an
administrative agency. *See also* ROLE.

Political Anthropology   The study of governmental institutions and practices among ethnic communities, particularly in primitive and tribal societies. Political anthropology probes the relationship of political behavior to the broader group culture and examines the ways in which political institutions and practices evolve. *See also* PARTICIPANT OBSERVATION.

Political Behavior   Human thoughts and actions related to the governing process. Political behavior embraces internal responses (thought, perception, judgment, attitude, belief) as well as observable actions (voting, protesting, lobbying, caucusing, campaigning). In the broadest sense behavior that is "political" may be found in any institutional setting (family, business, church, and the like), but the term is usually applied to activity occurring within or through the institutional setting of the state. Political behavior also designates an approach to political science that takes the individual actor as the primary unit of analysis. Such studies may focus on the behavior of groups, but with the assumption that groups are the collective interactions of individuals. Studies of legislative, judicial, administrative, or even international behavior are thus distinguished from legal, institutional, or historical approaches to the study of politics. Political behavior is also a label given to a subject matter subfield of political science having such concerns as political personality, political attitudes and public opinion, voting behavior, political parties and interests groups, political socialization, political culture, elite studies, and community power. In a very general sense political behavior is sometimes treated as synonymous with the behavioral study of politics. *See also* ATTITUDE, BEHAVIORALISM, BEHAVIOR PATTERN, POLITICS, PUBLIC OPINION, VOTING BEHAVIOR.

Political Change   Transformation of structures, processes, or goals affecting the distribution and exercise of governing power in a society. Political change may occur as a system adapts to new demands and a changing environment, or as one system—unable to maintain itself—is replaced by another. Within a society political change having widespread and persisting impact on the society may be called revolution. A *coup d' état* (or "palace revolution") is a sudden and unconstitutional change of ruling elites that in itself involves no basic alteration of social relationships. Peaceful political change may be called reform or simply be identified with constitutional change in leadership or the restructuring of political influence within a society. In international affairs the *pacific settlement* of particular disputes is sometimes contrasted with *peaceful change*, which refers to some fundamental alteration in the international order. This alteration may include change in sovereignty over territory, as through cession or decolonization; enduring changes in relationships of domination and subordination, as within power blocs; and basic changes in the accepted rules and norms governing international conduct. *See also* POLITICAL DEVELOPMENT, POLITICAL SOCIALIZATION.

Political Communication   The transmission of meaning having relevance for the functioning of a political system. Political communication, like other communication, requires a sender, a message, some channel or means of transmission, and a receiver. Political communication ordinarily involves the written or spoken word, but it may occur by means of any sign, symbol, or signal through which meaning is transmitted. This communication would include symbolic acts as diverse as burning a draft card, voting, political assassination, or sending a fleet around the world. Much political communication is the province of specialized institutions, such as the mass media, government information agencies, or political parties. It nevertheless is found in every social environment, from face-to-face two-person settings to the chambers of a national legislature. *See also* COMMUNICATIONS THEORY, CONTENT ANALYSIS, CYBERNETICS.

Political Community   A social group characterized by recognition of shared interests, some means for controlling disruptive violence, and institutions for making and implementing joint decisions. A political community may be coterminous with a nation-state or one of its political subdivisions. Within a given society there may be numerous, sometimes overlapping communities, such as a city within a province within the nation. At the international level the term "political community" is sometimes applied to any group of two or more states having shared interests, settled expectations that their differences will be resolved without violence, and diplomatic or other machinery for dealing with matters of joint concern. *See also* COMMUNITY.

Political Culture   The pattern of orientations toward government and politics within a society. Political culture generally connotes the psychological dimension of political behavior—beliefs, feelings, and evaluative orientations. A political culture is the product of the historical experience of the whole society as well as the personal experiences that contribute to the socialization of each individual. Within a national political culture one may distinguish between elite and mass subcultures, reflecting differences in the orientations of political decision makers from those of the less active citizenry. The mass culture may in turn consist of numerous subcultures, based on class, ethnic, regional or other differences. Somewhat similar phenomena have in the past been studied under such labels as national character, temperament, ethos, spirit or myth, political ideology, national political psychology, and fundamental political values. *See also* CULTURE, POLITICAL SOCIALIZATION.

Political Development   Growth and change within political systems, or change from one system to another, generally toward greater governmental capacity to cope with the demands made upon it. Political development has sometimes been equated with the growth of democratic institutions and practices. Recently, it has been more commonly associated with increasing complexity, specialization, and differentiation of political institutions in a society, regardless of their democratic or authoritarian character. *Political modernization* is sometimes used as a synonym for political development. Development, as a generic term, encompasses economic and social as well as political change. The terms *traditional, transitional,* and *modern* are commonly used to designate societies in different stages of political, economic, and social development. In a premodern society political development typically involves a socialization process aimed at building mass support for a national political system, as well as creating institutions to promote more widespread political participation. As development proceeds, government takes on a new image and new responsibilities in the form of directing and servicing functions unknown to the society in the past. Government also begins to promote scientific and technological advances, general public education, and other programs of economic and social modernization. A corps of administrators is recruited and trained in modern administrative techniques to provide efficient implementation of government policies. Political development theories help explain this process and suggest means by which development goals may be achieved. *See also* POLITICAL CHANGE, POLITICAL SOCIALIZATION.

Political Ecology   The study of the relationship of a political system to its environment. There is no general agreement concerning which aspects of the environment should be regarded as having ecological significance for a system. Some writers apparently include the entire physical, cultural, and social environment. Others limit ecology to the physical and nonhuman setting, while still a third view holds that ecology embraces both physical and social aspects of the environment but excludes other political systems. In the third view other political systems are regarded as part of the "context" rather than the ecology of the system being examined; and the study of interaction between a political system and its context is called *contextual analysis* as distinguished from *ecological analysis*. *See also* ENVIRONMENT, SYSTEMS ANALYSIS.

Political Integration   The process by which two or more political units increase their cooperative contact with each other. The political merger of previously separate units is often regarded as a desirable or logical end product of the integrative process. Political integration requires formal or informal institutions for making joint decisions. In addition, integration assumes a high or rising level of transactions between the units, and the growth of perceptions of shared interests and values. Integration is sometimes regarded as a condition as well as a process. Karl Deutsch, in a frequently cited definition, identifies integration with the existence of settled expectations between states that their mutual conflicts will be resolved peacefully. In this view integration is both the condition and the process of attaining it. The condition may also be called *political community*. *See also* FUNCTIONALISM, POLITICAL COMMUNITY, SPILLOVER.

Political Machine   A well-entrenched party organization headed by a boss or small group of autocratic leaders. Political machines usually operate at the city or county level and occasionally on a statewide basis. They may use ruthlessly efficient methods in maintaining themselves in power through such techniques as bribery, patronage, "honest graft," control over nominations, and the rigging of elections. Any successful political organization may, however, be dubbed a "machine" by its opponents. *See also* BOSS.

Political Party   A group of individuals, often having some measure of ideological agreement, who organize to win elections, operate government, and determine public policy. A party differs from a pressure group mainly in its basic objective of winning control of the machinery of government. In the United States, political parties are organized on precinct, county, congressional district, state, and national levels, with most decisions made by conventions, chairmen, and committees at the county, state, and national levels. Unlike parties in most countries, power in American political parties is highly decentralized. *See also* MANDATE, MULTIPARTY SYSTEM, TWO-PARTY SYSTEM, DEMOCRATIC PARTY, REPUBLICAN PARTY, MINOR PARTY, THIRD PARTY.

Political Personality, *see* Personality.

Political Philosophy   The branch of intellectual inquiry dealing with ideas about politics, particularly ideas relating to political values, the nature of political reality, and the intellectual assumptions of political analysis. Political philosophy has several major emphases. First, as normative theory, it seeks to clarify political values, to define what is desirable and moral. The normative philosopher feels free to make moral and ethical judgments, to prescribe desired states of affairs, and to recommend political goals. Second, as speculation about what *is* rather than what *ought* to be, political philosophy is concerned with the essence or basic nature of reality, rather than particular, observable manifestations of it. While not rejecting observation and experience, the philosopher looks for rational interconnections between things as a means of describing and explaining political reality. This contrasts with the empirical scholar who seeks scientifically verifiable hypotheses as the basis of explanation. The philosopher may find truth wherever intuition and rational speculation lead him. Third, as *analytic philosophy*, political philosophy deals with the meaning of words and concepts, the logical consistency of arguments, ways of knowing truth, and the grounds on which a proposition may be taken as true or false. *See also* PHILOSOPHY OF SCIENCE, POLITICAL THEORY.

Political Pluralism, *see* Pluralism.

Political Process, *see* Process.

Political Question   A doctrine enunciated by the Supreme Court holding that certain constitutional issues cannot be decided by the courts but are to be decided by the executive or legislative branches. The doctrine has generally been invoked when the issue would place the courts in serious conflict with other branches, involve the courts in political controversies, or raise serious enforcement problems. Examples of "political questions" include presidential power to recognize foreign governments, congressional power to determine whether constitutional amendments have been ratified within a reasonable time, and congressional and presidential power to determine whether states have a republican form of government. *See also Luther v. Borden, Baker v. Carr.*

Political Recruitment, *see* Recruitment.

Political Right   The right to participate in the management of government and to influence public policy. Typical political rights include the right to vote, to form a political party, and to participate in pressure group activity.

Political Science   The systematic study of government and politics. Political science deals with the making and implementing of public policy by means of decisions regarded as authoritative or binding for a society. Substantively, the discipline has moved in the past century from an emphasis upon formal institutions and legal relationships to a concern for processes, the behavior of individuals and groups, and informal relationships. The preferred criteria for identifying political science subject matter have shifted from the institutional concepts of *state* and *government* to the process or relational concepts of *power, decision making,* and *political system.* Methodologically, political science has supplemented the predominantly legal, historical, and descriptive analysis of an earlier period with the methods and perspectives of modern behavioral science. Although lines of intradisciplinary specialization are not rigidly fixed, the principal subfields of the discipline generally include national and local government, comparative or cross-national analysis, politics and behavior, public law and judicial behavior, political theory, public administration and organizational behavior, and international relations. *See also* BEHAVIORALISM, POLITICS, TRADITIONAL APPROACH.

Political Socialization   The learning process by which individuals acquire orientations (consisting of belief, feeling, and value components) toward government and political life. From the perspective of society, political socialization is the means by which political culture (the pattern of political orientations within the society) is maintained or changed. The range of possible orientations acquired in the socialization process can be very broad. It may include generalized attitudes toward concepts like authority, democracy, and political obligation, and such specific orientations as a preference for a particular political party or an aversion to street demonstrations as a form of political expression. The family and the educational system are generally regarded as important socializing agents. Political orientations may also be shaped by exposure to the mass media, organized groups, informal groups or any other experience having political relevance. *See also* ATTITUDE, POLITICAL CULTURE, VALUES.

Political Sociology   The study of political institutions and processes in their social setting. Political sociology is concerned with ways in which political phenomena influence, and are influenced by, other aspects of society. The macro or whole society approach deals with the social foundations of power, the impact of social class and group conflict upon political institutions, and the reciprocal influence of political institutions upon social stratification (class) and group behavior. The micro approach to political sociology focuses on particular political institutions as social organizations, including their formal and informal structures, leadership patterns, methods of managing conflict, and relationships with other organizations. The term "political sociology" is often used interchangeably with "sociology of politics." Some writers, however, distinguish the two by treating the latter as more specifically a subfield of sociology, while the former suggests a somewhat more cross-disciplinary enterprise that attempts to integrate the perspectives of both disciplines. *See also* ELITIST THEORY, GROUP THEORY, MACRO-MICRO ANALYSIS, ORGANIZATION THEORY, SOCIAL STRATIFICATION.

Political System   The persisting pattern of human relationships through which authoritative decisions are made and carried out for a society. A political system is distinguished from other social systems by four characteristics: it is *universal* in its reach, extending to all members of a society; it claims ultimate control over the use of physical *coercion;* its right to make binding decisions is accepted as *legitimate;* and its decisions are *authoritative,* bearing the force of legitimacy and a substantial probability of compliance. Since these are also characteristics of states, the term "political system" is commonly used as a label for the collectivity of relationships comprising the government and political processes of a state. Some writers define the term more broadly to include almost any social relationship where influence is exercised or authoritative decisions made. Thus, within subsocietal groups, such as a family, church, labor union, or business organization, the group decision-making structure is regarded as a political system. At the international level authority and other influence relationships among states are often said to constitute an international political system, with various geographical (for example, Western Europe), organizational (for example, the United Nations), and national (for example, China) subsystems. *See also* AUTHORITY, COERCION, DECISION-MAKING ANALYSIS, INFLUENCE, LEGITIMACY, POLITICS, POWER, SOCIAL SYSTEM, SYSTEM.

Political Theory   A body of thought that seeks to evaluate, explain, and predict political phenomena. Political theory is also a subfield of political science, concerned with political ideas, values, and concepts, and with the explanation and prediction of political behavior. Political theory in this broad sense has two major branches. One is *political philosophy* or *normative theory,* with its value, analytic, historical, and speculative concerns. The other is empirical theory, with its efforts to explain, predict, guide research, and organize knowledge through the formulation of abstract models and scientifically testable propositions. *See also* EMPIRICISM, NORMATIVE, POLITICAL PHILOSOPHY, POLITICAL SCIENCE, POLITICS, THEORY.

Political Trial   Prosecution directed against alleged enemies of the government or the political system. Sedition laws and other loyalty-security measures are common legislative acts that define political crimes. Prosecutions resulting from such laws are often referred to as "political trials" designed to expose rather than punish. *See also* SEDITION, MCCARTHYISM.

Politics   Human activity concerned with making and implementing decisions vested with the authority of the society for which the decisions are made. No single phrase can capture the many meanings assigned to the word. "Politics" connotes activity or process, whereas "political system" implies the existence of structures or patterned relationships. In a practical setting, politics has been called the "art of the possible," the "art of governing," and the study of "who gets what, when, and how." It is commonly identified with the exercise of influence, the struggle for power, and competition among individuals and groups over the allocation of rewards or "values" within a society. It is also said to involve a social steering process, including the setting and attaining of collective goals. The many faces of politics—the decision-making, value-allocating, goal-setting, social-steering, power-seeking, interest-competing, influence-exerting activities—may appear within any social group. In most political discourse, however, politics refers to *public* policies and allocations rather than the internal processes of *private* organizations. *See also* DECISION-MAKING APPROACH, INFLUENCE, POLITICAL SCIENCE, POLITICAL SYSTEM, POWER.

Polity   The political organization of a society. Polity may refer to the body politic, or citizenry, of a particular country, or it may refer to the institutional forms and processes through which the country is governed. The concept of a polity may apply to a highly organized state like the United States, as well as to a very primitive society in which a recognized political authority figure has barely emerged. In broad terms polity is another name for political system. *See also* POLITICAL SYSTEM.

Poll   An attempt to uncover public opinion or to forecast an election. Public opinion polling has developed from the early newspaper straw-vote poll of its subscribers to the personal interview technique, based on "scientific" quota sampling of the voting population, developed during the 1930s. New polling methods in use today involve probability sampling, in which representative precincts are used as barometers to indicate prevailing opinions. Poll results are checked against the actual voting records of the precincts.

Pollock v. Farmers Loan and Trust Co., 158 U.S. 601 (1895): Held the federal income tax law of 1894 unconstitutional on the ground that it was a direct tax and, therefore, Congress should have apportioned it among the several states according to population as provided in Article I, section 9 of the Constitution. *See also* INCOME TAX.

Pollock v. Williams, 322 U.S. 4 (1944): Decided that a state lends support to slavery or peonage, contrary to the Thirteenth Amendment, when it requires that a person must work to discharge a debt or go to jail. The Court held unconstitutional a law that made it a crime to take money in advance and then refuse to perform the required labor. A state may punish fraud but it cannot make failure to work a crime. *See also* INVOLUNTARY SERVITUDE.

Poll Tax   A special head tax that must be paid as a qualification for voting. The Twenty-fourth Amendment to the Constitution outlawed the poll tax in national, but not state, elections. In 1966, the Supreme Court declared that payment of any poll tax as a condition for voting in *any* election is unconstitutional (*Harper v. Virginia State Board of Elections*, 383 U.S. 663). *See also* TWENTY-FOURTH AMENDMENT.

Poll Watcher   An individual appointed by a political party to be present at a polling place on election day to ensure the honesty of the election. In many states, both major parties have poll watchers present at all polling places during partisan elections. In closed primary elections, poll watchers may also be appointed to prevent "raiding" (Crossing over to vote in the opposition party's primary to influence its outcome). *See also* CHALLENGE, CLOSED PRIMARY.

Polycentrism (or Multipolarity) An international balnce-of-power situation characterized by the existence of a number of power centers. Polycentrism, or a flexible balance multipolar system, is reminiscent of the nineteenth century in that it is composed of a number of active participants. It has taken the place of the post-World War II bipolar balance controlled by the Soviet Union and the United States. *See also* BIPOLARITY, TITOISM.

Polygamy, *see Reynolds v. United States.*

Popular Front, *see* National Front.

Popular Sovereignty The natural-rights concept that ultimate political authority rests with the people and can be exercised to create, alter, or abolish government. In practice, popular sovereignty is ordinarily exercised through representative institutions. *See also* DEMOCRACY.

Population, *see* Demographic Cycle, Random, Sampling, Survey Research.

Population Control Adjustments in population size resulting from national policies and from individual birth control practices. Government measures, historically, have involved efforts to influence the quantity and the quality of population by various techniques. These include: (1) encouraging or discouraging immigration and emigration; (2) fostering or discouraging large families; and (3) carrying out a policy of mass extermination, as in the case of Nazi Germany. The availability of improved contraceptive methods, especially in Western societies, has increasingly made family size a matter of individual choice. *See also* DEMOGRAPHIC CYCLE, MALTHUSIANISM.

Population Explosion, *see* Demographic Cycle, Underdevelopment.

Populist Movement A radical social and political philosophy and grass-roots action program developed by farmers in the South, West, and Midwest. The movement resulted in the emergence of the Populist party in the late nineteenth century which favored government ownership of the railroads, free coinage of silver, a vastly expanded supply of paper money, elimination of monopolies, and a graduated income tax. Populism as a continuing American political characteristic describes the role of large numbers of poor urban dwellers and farmers who seek by democratic means to use the power of government to cope with the financial giants of business, industry, and commerce.

Pork Barrel Legislation Appropriations made by a legislative body providing for expenditures of sums of public money on local projects not critically needed. The term is closely related to logrolling, in that members of the legislative body usually do not question each other's pet project for fear that their own may be voted down. It is frequently a simple matter of *quid pro quo*—that is,"You scratch my back and I'll scratch yours." *See also* LOGROLLING.

Port of New York Authority, *see* Interstate Compact.

Position Classification   The grouping of government employment positions on the basis of duties, responsibilities, and qualifications. A position is classified in accordance with the nature of the job rather than the person holding the position. *See also* MERIT SYSTEM.

Positivism   The doctrine which holds that international law consists only of those rules by which states have consented to be bound. Positivism, which emphasizes the concept of state sovereignty, asserts that consent may be granted expressly in the form of a treaty, or by implication through adherence to international customary practices. *See also* CUSTOMARY LAW, JUS NATURALE, INTERNATIONAL LAW, TREATY.

Postbehavioralism   An intellectual movement in political science, dating from the late 1960s, that asserts the obligation of political scientists to become more "relevant" and concerned with values and to use their special knowledge to improve society. Postbehavioralism is not a well-developed doctrine or school of thought but represents an attitude toward the discipline and the profession held by some political scientists. Essentially, they believe that behavioralist overemphasis on methodology has tended to divorce the discipline from the real substance and issues of politics. Thus, postbehavioralists would reverse some of the priorities associated with the behavioralist movement by placing substance before technique, social relevance before pure science, and political action above academic neutrality. *See also* BEHAVIORALISM, TRADITIONAL APPROACH.

Postdiction, *see* Prediction.

Post Office, *see* United States Postal Service.

Potsdam Conference, *see* Oder-Neisse Line.

Powell v. Alabama, *see Gideon v. Wainwright.*

Power   The capacity to affect the behavior of others in some desired way. Thus, broadly defined, "power" is synonymous with "influence" and embraces the whole range of influence mechanisms. These mechanisms extend from persuasion (influence without promise of reward or threat of punishment by the power wielder) to mild pressure or bargaining (promise of reward, threat of punishment) to extreme pressure, force, or coercion (threat of severe punishment or deprivation). Although "power" and "influence" are often used as synonyms, many analysts regard influence as the broader concept and treat power as a form of influence deriving from the threat of severe punishment for noncompliance and posing a greater probability of compliance. *See also* AUTHORITY, COERCION, INFLUENCE, LEGITIMACY.

Power Elite, *see* Elitist Theory.

Power (National)   Influence and control exercised by one nation over others. Power is both the means used and the goal sought by states in political, military, economic, and social competition with each other. Although not every state action is motivated by power considerations, those directly related to enhancing or defending the national interest are always deeply involved in power politics. The exercise and pursuit of power is carried on by decision makers who utilize the machinery of the state to develop and implement foreign policy. Political power, therefore, involves a psychological relationship between élites who exercise it and those who are influenced or controlled by it. The exercise of power takes many forms, including persuasion, ideological and psychological warfare, economic coercion, moral suasion, cultural imperialism, legally recognized measures short of war, and, ultimately, war. *See also* CAPABILITY ANALYSIS, ELEMENTS OF NATIONAL POWER.

Power of the Purse   The historic power of democratic legislative bodies to control the finances of government. The power of the purse extends to both revenue and appropriation functions. In the national government, the Constitution specifies that "No money shall be drawn from the Treasury, but in consequence of appropriations made by law." (Art. I, sec. 9). New programs must be twice approved, first, through authorization and, second, through appropriation to finance them. Expenditures by the executive must be validated by the General Accounting Office to ensure that such outlays fall within the limits of appropriations made by Congress. Additional checks are carried on through the "watchdog" oversight committees of Congress. *See also* APPROPRIATION, WATCHDOG COMMITTEE.

Power Patterns, *see* Patterns of Power.

Powers (National Government), *see* Concurrent Powers, Delegated Powers, Exclusive Powers, Implied Powers, Inherent Powers, Reserved Powers, Resulting Powers.

Power Structure, *see* Elite.

Preamble   The statement affixed at the beginning of the Constitution, stating the source of its authority and the purposes it is to serve. The Preamble to the United States Constitution is of no legal effect but may serve as a guide to the intent of the framers.

Precedent   A court ruling bearing upon subsequent legal decisions in similar cases. Judges rely upon precedents in deciding cases. The common law is based primarily upon reasoning from precedents. *See also* COMMON LAW, STARE DECISIS.

Precinct   The basic unit in the United States in the election process and for party organization. Cities and counties are divided into precinct polling districts, each containing from 200 to 1000 voters and a polling place. In political organization, each party usually elects or appoints a precinct captain or committeeman who functions as a party leader within the precinct. Precinct leaders in the cities may represent their precincts in party ward committees. The precinct also serves for the election or appointment of delegates to city or county party conventions. *See also* POLITICAL PARTY.

Prediction   A statement of what one expects to happen under given conditions. Prediction in political science may take the form of anticipating future events based on past, observed regularities. Or it may refer to a statement of relationships that one expects to find upon examination of past events—that is, prediction of an expected relationship between variables. The latter is sometimes termed *postdiction*. Scientific prediction does not unconditionally assert that certain events will occur. Rather, it takes the form of a conditional or *if, then* statement. *If* certain conditions are present, *then* certain outcomes may be expected. This is contrasted with *forecasting* which, by some definitions, asserts the probability of future outcomes without specifying any qualifying conditions. Most predictions in political science are stated as probabilities or tendencies. Thus they state that an event is *likely* to occur under given conditions, not that it will *certainly* occur if the conditions are met. If, in the unusual case, the researcher can specify the conditions not only *necessary* to a certain outcome, but also *sufficient* to produce it, the prediction becomes *deterministic* rather than *probabilistic*, although still conditional. A *negative prediction* states that a certain relationship is not likely to exist, or a certain class of events is not likely to happen under specified conditions. *See also* CAUSALITY, EXPLANATION, SCIENCE.

Preemptive Strike   A first-strike nuclear attack undertaken on the assumption that an enemy state is planning an imminent nuclear attack. The concept of a preemptive attack was developed by Soviet military tacticians during the 1950s as a defense measure to transform an enemy's planned first strike into a less dangerous counter-blow. The preemptive attack would be aimed at seizing the initiative to gain the advantage of surprise while a state's offensive power remained undamaged. Also known as a "spoiling" or "blunting" attack, it would be undertaken only after state leaders received intelligence data clearly indicating that the rival state was preparing a nuclear strike. *See also* FIRST STRIKE, PREVENTIVE WAR.

Preferential Primaries, *see* Presidential Primaries.

Preferential Trade Arrangement   An agreement among several states to provide each other favorable trade treatment. Members of a preferential system mutually reduce their tariffs or other trade barriers to an agreed level. The difference between the tariff levels for members and those applied by each member to other states is referred to as the "margin of preference." A preferential system may be multilateral (for example, the Commonwealth of Nations system of preferences) or bilateral (as in the case of the United States–Philippines economic agreement). Any trade agreement between two or more nations that reduces barriers to trade but does not incorporate the most-favored-nation clause to apply these reductions to nonsignatory states is preferential in nature. *See also* COMMONWEALTH OF NATIONS, COMMONWEALTH PREFERENCES.

Preliminary Hearing or Examination, *see* Hearing.

Premier (France)   The constitutional head of government in the Fifth Republic. The President of the Republic, as chief of state, appoints the Premier, who in turn proposes to the President the individuals to be appointed to the Cabinet. The Premier and other Cabinet ministers have no fixed term of office. The President has power to remove ministers from office, although the Constitution makes no mention of the removal of the Premier. The prime criterion for the premiership is the individual's acceptability to the President and, only secondarily, acquiescence by the National Assembly. The Premier is officially charged with the operation of the government, the execution of the law, and the responsibility for national defense. The Constitution is, however, vague concerning the specific functions of the Premier and his Cabinet. Consequently, the personalities of the President and Premier, as well as the nature of the relationship between them, are likely to define the Premier's role.

Premier (Italy), *see* President of the Council of Ministers.

Premise, *see* Deduction.

Prescription   A method recognized in international law whereby one state, through long and uninterrupted dominion, acquires title to territory previously claimed by another state. The prior sovereign's long-term acquiescence in the exercise of jurisdiction by another state constitutes the grounds for the transference of valid title.

Prescriptive Theory, *see* Normative.

Presentment, *see* Grand Jury.

President   The chief executive of the United States and the key official in the American system of government. The Constitution in Article II vests the complete executive power in the President. The President is elected every four years through the Electoral College machinery, and is eligible under the Twenty-second Amendment to one additional term. His chief official advisers are found in the Executive Office of the President and in the Cabinet. The President exercises a broad array of powers, some provided by the Constitution, some based on custom and tradition, some delegated to him by Congress, and others that are simply inherent in the nature of his office. Foremost are those broad and largely undefined powers that he exercises in his role as chief of foreign policy. These include the leadership of the armed forces, the recognition of foreign states and governments, the conduct of diplomacy, the making of international agreements and treaties with the Senate's approval, the initiation of new foreign programs, and the providing of leadership for the United States and the free world. In his role of chief administrator, the President exercises broad appointing and removal powers, directs and supervises the operations of the executive branch, directs the formulation of the annual budget, and sees that the laws are faithfully executed. As chief legislator, the President initiates comprehensive legislative programs, delivers regular and special messages to Congress, summons Congress into special sessions, wields a broad veto power, and influences the course of much legislation in his relations with legislative leaders and by arousing public opinion to support his programs. As chief of his party, the President dispenses patronage, influences the direction and nature of party policies, provides leadership to his party's delegation in both houses of Congress, and generally influences and determines party actions and policies. In his role as chief of state, the President maintains relations with other nations and performs numerous ceremonial functions in the United States. The prestige of his office contributes much to the effectiveness of the President in his many roles. His easy access to the mass media of communication aids him in molding public opinion. His many sources of information keep him well-informed on the complex problems facing the nation. *See also* ELECTORAL COLLEGE, CHIEF LEGISLATOR, CHIEF OF STATE, STEWARDSHIP THEORY, PRESIDENTIAL ELECTION PROCESS.

President-Elect   The candidate selected by the Electoral College to be the next President. Following the November popular election, the winning candidate is unofficially called the "President-designate" until the electors are able to ratify the people's choice. Under the Twentieth Amendment, the President-elect is sworn into office at noon on the twentieth day of January, and if the President-elect fails to qualify at that time, the Vice President-elect then acts as President until a President qualifies. If the President-elect dies, the Vice President-elect is then sworn in as President. *See also* TWENTIETH AMENDMENT.

President (France)   The chief of state of the Fifth Republic. Under the Constitution of 1958, the President of France was elected for a seven-year term by an indirect method involving an electoral college of some 80,000 electors. The bulk of the electors consisted of mayors and other representatives of the smaller communes throughout the country, with some representatives from the Parliament and the overseas territories. De Gaulle changed this method in October, 1962, when he won popular approval on a referendum calling for the direct popular election of the President. Employed in the elections of 1965 and 1969, both De Gaulle and Pompidou failed to win on the first ballot but secured victory on the second ballot as a result of the tendency of the Right and Center to coalesce in the second vote.

President (Germany) The formal head of state of the Federal Republic, who symbolizes national unity but wields little power. The President is elected indirectly by a Federal Convention called by the President of the Bundestag. Consisting of more than one thousand electors, the Federal Convention is made up of the members of the Bundestag and an equal number of delegates chosen proportionally by each state *(Land)* legislature. The convention proceeds without debate and, if no candidate receives a majority on the first two ballots, the person receiving a plurality of the votes on a third ballot is declared elected. The term of office is five years and the law permits reelection to one additional consecutive term. Any German citizen is eligible for the presidency if he has reached forty years of age and is qualified to vote for the Bundestag. The President exercises the normal functions of a chief of state in form but not in fact. New laws and other state papers that require his signature must be countersigned by the Chancellor or an appropriate minister. The President's appointments, foreign relations functions, and other ostensibly discretionary acts are decided for him elsewhere in the executive structure.

Presidential Disability, *see* Twenty-Fifth Amendment.

Presidential Election Process Various steps in the process by which the American people select their President. The presidential election process involves two races, the first in which the aspirants seek to obtain their party's nomination, and the second in which the nominees of the two major parties contest. The climax of the aspirant's race for nomination takes place in the summer of the presidential election year at his party's national nominating convention. This convention is composed of delegates chosen in about one-half of the states by conventions or committees, and in one-half by the voters in presidential primaries. Following the conventions, the autumn campaign between the major party candidates begins in earnest. In the national election, held on the first Tuesday after the first Monday in November, the voters in the fifty states and the District of Columbia cast ballots for their choice for President, although in fact they are legally electing only members of the Electoral College. In early January, a joint session of Congress opens the Electoral College ballots and certifies the winners, who are subsequently sworn into office on January 20.

In brief, here is the typical major party candidate's schedule in a presidential election year: *Late winter:* announce candidacy; *spring:* campaign vigorously in key primary contests, particularly in New Hampshire (the first primary); *early summer:* continue primary races while striving to win delegates at party convention and committee meetings in nonprimary states; *late summer:* marshal all possible party strength for final drive to obtain nomination at party's national nominating convention; *early autumn:* resume campaigning with increasing tempo and a broader focus to attract votes from independents and rival party members as well as from members of candidate's own party; *late fall:* build campaign to a climax, with major speeches and saturation of television and radio with partisan propaganda; *post-election period:* congratulate opponent and go into seclusion, or if victorious, prepare to take over the reins of power in January. *See also* AVAILABILITY, DARK HORSE, ELECTORAL COLLEGE, MINORITY PRESIDENT, NATIONAL CONVENTION, PIVOTAL STATES, PRESIDENT-ELECT, PRESIDENTIAL PRIMARIES, STALKING HORSE, TWENTIETH AMENDMENT, VOTING QUALIFICATIONS.

Presidential Government   A system that features a separation of powers between the legislative and executive branches and the independent election of an executive serving a fixed term. *See also* PRESIDENT.

Presidential Primaries   The election of delegates to a major party's national convention. About one-half of the states and the District of Columbia hold some form of presidential primary in the weeks or months preceding the conventions; delegates are selected in the other states by political party conventions or committees. Delegates selected in the primaries may or may not be "pledged" to vote for a presidential aspirant. In a few states, delegates are selected by the party organization but are bound to support the candidate designated by the voters in a so-called popularity contest. *See also* NATIONAL CONVENTION, DIRECT PRIMARY.

Presidential Succession   The order of eligibility for filling a vacancy in the office of President, as specified in the Constitution and statutes. The Constitution, in Article II, section 1, stipulates that "In case of the removal of the President from office, or of his death, resignation, or inability to discharge the powers and duties of the said office, the same shall devolve on the Vice-President. . . . " Congress is empowered by the same section of Article II to provide for the officer to act as President in case both the President and Vice President are unable to serve. Congress has from time to time provided by statute for the line of succession, with the present order based on the Presidential Succession Act of 1947. This law provides for succession by the Speaker of the House, President pro tempore of the Senate, and members of the Cabinet, with the Secretary of State first in line. Cabinet members serve only until a Speaker or President pro tempore is available. The Twentieth Amendment provides that the Vice President-elect shall become President if the President-elect is unable to assume office on inauguration day. In addition, the Twenty-fifth Amendment provides for the temporary succession of the Vice President to the presidency in cases of presidential disability. *See also* TWENTIETH AMENDMENT, TWENTY-FIFTH AMENDMENT, VICE PRESIDENT.

President of the Council of Ministers or Prime Minister (Italy)   The head of government in the Italian republic. As first among equals, the Prime Minister (or Premier) is responsible for the direction and coordination of government policy. He is appointed by the President of the Republic, who, because of the coalition nature of Italian governments, must first gain acceptance for the nominee from the various party leaders. The Prime Minister then selects the members of his government who are also appointed by the President of the Republic. Because the government is constitutionally responsible to Parliament, the Prime Minister must, within ten days, obtain a vote of confidence in each house. Either house can subsequently force the resignation of the Prime Minister and his Cabinet by a vote of no confidence. In theory, the Prime Minister is the leader and spokesman of the parliamentary majority. Whether he is in fact depends on his ability to maintain cohesion within the coalition. *See also* PRIME MINISTER (BRITAIN), PREMIER (FRANCE).

President of the Republic (Italy)   The head of state of the Italian republic. Presumably above the vicissitudes of partisan politics, the President symbolizes national unity. He is elected indirectly for a seven-year term by a joint session of the Senate and Chamber of Deputies. The parliamentarians are joined on this occasion by three delegates from each of the nineteen constituent regions, and by one delegate from the Valley of Aosta. A two-thirds majority is required, but if no one is elected after two secret ballots, a simple majority on the third ballot is sufficient. The broad constitutional powers granted to the President include: (1) naming the President of the Council of Ministers, five senators for life, and five members of the Constitutional Court; (2) casting a suspensive veto to force Parliament to reconsider a measure it has already passed; (3) authorizing the submission of government bills to Parliament; and (4) dissolving Parliament, calling special sessions, elections, and referenda. The President also ratifies treaties; promulgates statutes, executive orders, and regulations; grants amnesties, pardons, and reprieves; formally declares war; bestows honors; and appoints certain ministers on the suggestion of the Prime Minister. *See also* PRESIDENT (FRANCE), PRESIDENT (GERMANY).

President Pro Tempore   The temporary presiding officer of the Senate in the absence of the Vice President. The President pro tempore is elected by the Senate, following his nomination by the majority party caucus. He is eligible for the presidency of the United States following the death or disability of the President, Vice President, and Speaker of the House. State senates also select presidents pro tempore.

President's Role, *see* Appointment Power, Chief Legislator, Chief of State, Emergency Powers, Pardon, Ratification, Recognition, Removal Power, Veto.

Presidium of the Council of Ministers (Soviet Union)   An executive committee or "inner cabinet" of the Council of Ministers that functions as the top-level decision-making body in the government apparatus. The Presidium is usually composed of the Chairman of the Council, two First Vice Chairmen, and several Vice Chairmen. The Chairman is the head of government, or Premier, of the Soviet Union. The First Vice Chairmen divide the supervision of administrative agencies at the highest level. At the next level, each of the Vice Chairmen supervises a cluster of related ministries.

Presidium of the Supreme Soviet (Soviet Union)   A legislative-executive committee that directs the activities of the Supreme Soviet and exercises many functions of the parent body between sessions. The thirty-odd members of the Presidium are elected by a joint session of both houses of the Supreme Soviet. It is composed of a Chairman, one Vice Chairman from each of the union republics, a Secretary, and sixteen ordinary members. The Chairman, sometimes called the President, acts as the head of state for the Soviet Union. Under the constitution, the Presidium can convene the Supreme Soviet, issue decrees, interpret national laws, conduct nationwide referenda, void acts of the Council of Ministers when they do not conform to law, issue decorations, honors, and pardons, appoint and remove officers of the military high command, order mobilization, appoint and receive ambassadors, and proclaim martial law. Between sessions of the Supreme Soviet, the Presidium can appoint and dismiss ministers on the recommendation of the Chairman of the Council of Ministers, declare war in case of attack, and order the implementation of mutual defense treaties in cases of aggression.

Press, Freedom of, *see* Freedom of the Press.

Pressure Group   An organized interest group in which members share common views and objectives and actively carry on programs to influence government officials and policies. Unlike political parties, which seek to win control of and operate the government, pressure groups are mainly interested in influencing the determination of public policies that directly or indirectly affect their members. Such groups vary considerably in size, wealth, power, and objectives. Their methods, however, are quite similar and include lobbying, electioneering, and propagandizing to influence public opinion. Pressure groups seek to influence decisions in the legislative, executive, and judicial branches. *See also* LOBBYIST, REGULATION OF LOBBYING ACT, BUSINESS ORGAN- IZATIONS, CIVIL RIGHTS ORGANIZATIONS, FARM ORGANIZATIONS, LABOR UNIONS, VETER- ANS ORGANIZATIONS.

Prestige   A state's international reputation for effectiveness in the pursuit of its foreign or domestic policy goals. Prestige implies neither friendly nor unfriendly relations but involves an attitude of respect derived from the recognition by others of the successful use of state power. It is a psychological phenomenon that supplements power and, where prestige is high, may make the application of other more specific forms of power less necessary. Prestige is actively sought, jealously guarded, and is usually an important objective of national propaganda efforts.

Preventive Diplomacy, *see* Dispute Settlement Procedures (United Nations).

Preventive War   A military strategy that calls for an attack by a nation that enjoys a temporary advantage in striking power. The doctrine of preventive war calls for a surprise attack against an enemy that is dedicated to the destruction of the attacking state and is developing a superior force for a crushing future blow. The theory assumes that the other side in an arms race is determined to undertake a future aggression, that time is on its side, and that an immediate decisive strike could destroy that future threat. *See also* PREEMPTIVE STRIKE.

Previous Question   A motion in a legislative body to cease debate and force a vote on a pending measure. In Congress, the rules permit previous question motions in the House but not in the Senate. The motion itself cannot be debated nor laid on the table. If the motion carries before any debate on the bill has occurred, each side is allowed twenty minutes to present its case. State legislatures use similar rules to limit debate.

Price Support   A program of the national government to help stabilize agricultural prices near parity by buying up market surpluses. Price supports, which have been used since 1933, are accompanied by production controls. The Commodity Credit Corporation (CCC) and the Agricultural Stabilization and Conservation Service (ASCS) administer the price support program through outright purchases and, more commonly, by granting loans to farmers, accepting their stored crops as collateral. The individual farmer can, in effect, turn the loan into a government purchase of his crop by simply not paying it off. If, however, the market price of the commodity goes above support level, he may pay off his loan, redeem his stored crop, and sell it on the free market. *See also* EVER-NORMAL GRANARY, PARITY, AGRICULTURAL ADJUSTMENT ACTS, *Mulford v. Smith*, AGRICULTURAL ACT OF 1970.

Primary Commodity, *see* Commodity Agreement, Raw Materials.

Primary Election, *see* Closed Primary, Direct Primary, Open Primary, Presidential Primaries, Runoff Primary, *Smith v. Allwright, United States v. Classic.*

Primary Group, *see* Group.

Primary, Presidential, *see* Presidential Primaries, Presidential Election Process.

Primary, Runoff, *see* Runoff Primary.

Prime Minister (Britain)   The head of government in Britain. In the British system, the Prime Minister's title has meant chief adviser to the Crown. Given the two-party system, it is virtually automatic for the monarch to select as Prime Minister the leader of the majority party in the Commons. The Prime Minister forms "his" government by selecting the members of the Cabinet; he can reshuffle, remove, or call upon them to resign. He also selects the heads of the non-Cabinet ministries and other departments and agencies. As "first among equals" in the Cabinet, he is responsible for framing and coordinating policy and for introducing and passing legislation. As head of government, he is charged with administering the affairs of the nation and with serving as its chief representative in international relations.

Prime Minister (Italy), *see* President of the Council of Ministers.

Private Bill   A bill introduced into a legislative body that deals with specific matters and individuals rather than with general legislative affairs. In Congress, although the number of private bills was considerably reduced by the Reorganization Act of 1946, thousands are still introduced at each session. The main categories include: (1) immigration and naturalization bills applying to specific individuals; (2) claim bills not subject to administrative resolution; and (3) land bills assigning title to individuals. Private bills are introduced by congressmen who are petitioned by their constituents to right a government-inflicted wrong or to deal with a matter not covered by general statute. If enacted, they become private law and apply only to specific individuals named in the act. All state legislatures allow introduction of private bills. *See also* BILL.

Private Calendar, *see* Calendar.

Private International Law, *see* Conflict of Laws.

Private International Organization, *see* International Organization, Non-Governmental Organization.

Privilege   An advantage, benefit, or opportunity granted to an individual or group to which it has no right. The range of privileges bestowed by government is very broad and includes government employment, medicare, public housing, tax exemptions, welfare programs, professional licenses, and veterans benefits. The government may attach qualifications or demands before a privilege is granted, but these must pass the test of reasonableness. Any withdrawal of a privilege from an individual must be done under procedures that afford minimal due process rights, such as notice and hearing. *See also Keyishian v. Board of Regents, Goldberg v. Kelly.*

Privileges and Immunities   Special rights and exemptions provided by law. The Constitution contains two clauses that use the term "privileges and immunities." Article IV, section 2, provides that, "The citizens of each state shall be entitled to all privileges and immunities of citizens in the several states." The Fourteenth Amendment provides that, "No state shall make or enforce any law which shall abridge the privileges or immunities of citizens of the United States." The first provision is considered to be an instrument of federalism, one of the obligations of states in their relations with each other. Basically, it means that a citizen of one state is not to be treated as an alien when in another state; he may not be discriminated against by denial of such privileges and immunities as legal protection, access to courts, travel rights, or property rights. Out-of-state residents, however, may be denied certain political rights, such as voting, or other privileges reserved to that state's residents, such as lower tuition at state universities. The full and precise meaning of the term has never been established by the courts. The Fourteenth Amendment's privileges and immunities clause has, similarly, not received complete definition. It is basically an instrument of civil liberties, placing certain restrictions upon each state in its dealings with United States citizens. The clause has been interpreted to apply only to those privileges that apply to the individual by virtue of his national citizenship (*Slaughterhouse Cases*, 16 Wallace 36 [1873]). These include the rights to travel, to have access to national officials, and to engage in interstate and foreign commerce. As interpreted, the clause confers no new rights upon citizens nor does it affect the citizen in those privileges that he enjoys by virtue of his state citizenship.

Privileges and Immunities (International), *see* Diplomatic Privileges and Immunities.

Probability   The degree of likelihood that a given outcome will occur. Probability in political science is associated with attempts to predict behavior or relationships. There are many theories of probability, none uniquely applicable to political science. Most may be classified as theories of *subjective* or *objective* probabilities. Subjective theories deal with problems of rational choice and belief. Rational belief in an individual is defined in terms of a coherent personal system of probabilities assigned to particular outcomes—that is, the degree of belief or doubt that a particular outcome will occur. Rational choice occurs through interaction of this belief system with personal values, given the alternatives possible in the situation. For example, in deciding to run for office, a potential candidate must consider the *costs* of running and the *value* of winning in relation to the *probability* that he will be elected. If the cost of running is small and the value of the office is great, he may rationally decide to run even though there is only a small probability of success. *Objective* theories of probability are concerned with *actual* outcomes rather than beliefs about *possible* outcomes. These include a priori theories and a posteriori, or *frequency*, theories. The former deal with situations, such as gambling games, where the probabilities that a class of events will occur may be calculated prior to empirical investigation. For example, the probability that "heads" will turn up fifty times in one hundred tosses of the coin can be readily calculated in advance. Frequency theories, on the other hand, are concerned with empirical or statistical probabilities, determined in simplest form by counting the number of times a particular class of events occurs in a given number of cases or trials. Thus, investigation might disclose that the probability or relative frequency of suburbanites voting Republican is fifty-five in one hundred in a given metropolitan area. *See also* CHANCE, CORRELATION, NULL HYPOTHESIS, PREDICTION, RANDOM, STATISTICS.

Probability Statement, *see* Tendency Statement.

Probate Court   A court, used in about one-half the states, with jurisdiction over wills, estates, guardians, and minors. Probate courts are found at the county level; in states without separate probate courts, such matters are handled by regular county courts. In some areas, probate courts are called surrogate courts. Much of the work connected with probate courts is administrative in nature, concerned largely with proper handling of minors and estates by guardians and administrators. Juries are rarely used. Probate judges are generally elected.

Probation   Suspension of the sentence of a person convicted of a crime, permitting him to remain free, subject to good behavior. Persons on probation are subject to supervision by an agent of the court. If the person's conduct justifies it, he will be released from probation after a period of time determined by the court. Failure to observe the terms of probation subjects him to possible imprisonment.

Procedural Decision, *see* Security Council, Veto (International Organization).

Procedural Due Process, *see* Due Process of Law.

Procedural Rights   Protection against arbitrary actions by public officials. Under American constitutional law, no person may be deprived of his life, liberty, or property or of any other right guaranteed him, except under well-defined procedures, including a fair hearing before a judicial tribunal. American procedural rights are generally considered to be those listed in the Bill of Rights, particularly in the Fourth through the Eighth Amendments. *Procedural* rights are to be distinguished from *substantive* rights. The latter include those elements that are considered to be of the very essence of freedom, such as freedom of speech, whereas the former are concerned with the methods by which rights are protected. *See also* DUE PROCESS OF LAW.

Process   A sequence of related actions or operations. "Process" denotes activity, movement, and relatively rapid change, as distinguished from the more stable and slower changing elements in a situation, which are called structures. One may also speak of a "process approach" to the study of society, which views social life as a flow of events over time rather than a condition or set of static relationships. The total social process may be regarded as a combination of political, economic, sociological, and other processes. These in turn may be subdivided analytically into constituent elements, such as the executive or administrative aspects of the political process, and into still more specific subprocesses, such as budgeting, planning, staffing, and coordinating. As a general concept political process embraces all the activities by which people attempt to gain and wield legitimate influence within a society. It is often used as a synonym for "politics." In a more specialized sense it may denote an approach to political studies whose perspectives and concerns overlap substantially with those of political behavior. *See also* STRUCTURE.

Product Moment, *see* Correlation.

Progressive Tax   Any tax in which the tax *rates* increase as the amount to be taxed increases. It is the opposite of a regressive tax, in which tax rates remain uniform or decline as the tax base increases. *See also* REGRESSIVE TAX, ABILITY THEORY.

Prohibition, *see* Twenty-First Amendment.

Projective Methods   A research technique used to measure psychological variables by inducing human subjects to project their inner attitudes, feelings, values, motives, and needs upon external objects. The most common projective methods involve association, construction, completion, and expression. In the use of *association* techniques the subject is asked to respond to a given stimulus with the first idea that occurs to him. The response presumably will be a projection of his attitudes and feelings. Word association and the Rorschach ink blot test are examples of this technique. *Construction* requires the subject to make or produce something, most often a story or a picture, which is then interpreted by the observer as a reflection of the subject's feelings. With the *completion* technique the subject is asked to complete sentences, or to supply the ending to a brief story or incompletely presented situation. *Expressive* techniques permit the attitudes and feelings of the subject to be deduced from his behavior in some activity, such as drawing, finger painting, playing games, role-playing, and so on. The emphasis is on the way he performs the activity rather than on any product outcome (as contrasted with construction). Because of the necessarily subjective interpretation of the subjects' responses, the reliability and validity of the results of projective methods are generally hard to establish. *See also* ATTITUDE.

"Proletarian Democracy", *see* Dictatorship of the Proletariat.

Proletariat Class, *see* Class Struggle.

Propaganda   Communication aimed at influencing the thinking, emotions, or actions of a group or public. The use of propaganda assumes that changes in men's thinking will prompt changes in their actions. Propaganda is not necessarily true nor false; it is based on a careful selection and manipulation of data. *See also* MASS MEDIA.

Property Qualification   A qualification for voting that requires the ownership of property. Historically, the property qualification usually took the form of a state constitutional requirement that a voter in a local election involving a financial issue be a taxpaying owner of real estate. Today, property qualifications may not be imposed as a requirement for voting because, in the words of the Supreme Court, they constitute an "invidious discrimination based on social class."

Property Tax   An ad valorem (according to value) tax levied on real or personal, tangible or intangible property. The general property tax is levied by local units of government throughout the country, and most states make limited use of some form of the tax. The tax process includes assessment of property valuations, determination of tax rates (millage), tax computation, and tax collection. To correct injustices, boards of review on the local level adjust inequalities in assessments. Where the taxing jurisdiction crosses political boundaries, central assessment or equalization is often provided to avoid geographical inequities. *See also* ASSESSED VALUATION, ASSESSOR, BOARD OF REVIEW, EQUALIZATION.

Proportional Representation (PR)   An electoral system that allocates seats in the legislative body to each party or group approximately equal to its popular voting strength. Under a system of proportional representation, for example, a minority party that receives 5 percent of the total vote in an election will win about 5 percent of the legislative seats. The most commonly used systems of PR are the list system, based on voting by party, and the Hare system, based on voting for individuals using the single transferable vote. *See also* HARE PLAN, MULTIPARTY SYSTEM.

Proposition   A statement of relationships, expressed in either verbal or mathematical form. Defined broadly, a proposition may be descriptive, explanatory, or evaluative. The indicated relationship may be either unique (Hitler was a dictator), or generalizable (dictators are tyrannical). Used in the more specific sense of a theoretical proposition, the term refers to an empirical statement of a relationship between variables, not to a value judgment or an assertion applicable only to a unique case. A related set of such propositions may constitute a theory. Some writers suggest that a proposition is a statement of lesser certitude than a law or an axiom. Others treat all statements of relationships, whatever their degree of certitude, as propositions. A *law* (if such were ever achieved in political science) would be a theoretical proposition whose truth is established; a hypothesis is a more speculative proposition. *See also* HYPOTHESIS, THEORY, VARIABLE.

Proprietary Colony   One of the three types of colonial governments—charter, proprietary, royal—found in colonial America. Proprietary colonies were governed by charters issued by the "proprietor," an individual to whom the king had made a land grant. Pennsylvania was established under such a charter bestowed by William Penn. Other proprietary colonies were Delaware and Maryland. Though the lower house of the legislature was elected, the upper house and the governor were chosen by the proprietor, subject to approval of the Crown.

Proprietary Function   A governmental activity involving business-type operations ordinarily carried on by private companies. Proprietary functions include such activities as supplying electricity and gas, recreational facilities, garbage collection, transportation, and operating a liquor business. *See also* INTERGOVERNMENTAL TAX IMMUNITY, *South Carolina v. United States*, REVOLVING FUND.

Prosecutor, *see* District Attorney.

Protectionism   The theory and practice of utilizing governmental regulation to control or limit the volume or types of imports entering a state. Protectionism involves the use of tariffs, quotas, licensing, exchange control, and other devices to reduce or eliminate imports, or to increase the cost for the consumer of foreign trade commodities that compete with domestically produced articles of commerce. The degree of protection afforded domestic producers varies from state to state, but every country utilizes some protective measures. *See also* ECONOMIC NATIONALISM.

Protectorate   A relationship between a strong state and a semisovereign state, or an area or people not recognized as a state. Protectorates have been established voluntarily and by force, normally either to thwart the interests of third states, or to provide for the administration of law and order in territory over which no responsible government exists. The term "protectorate" also applies to the country under protection. The extent to which the alien government exercises sovereign powers in the protectorate is controlled by treaty between the parties.

Prudent Investment Theory   An approach used by government in fixing rates to determine a fair return in profits for public utilities. The prudent investment theory is based on ascertaining the original cost of investments in the utility and subtracting from this figure those that have been imprudent or wasteful. *See also* RATE-MAKING; *Smyth v. Ames.*

Psychological Warfare   Political, military, economic, and social activities carried on during war or Cold War periods aimed at influencing thoughts and actions. The major objectives of psychological warfare are to weaken an enemy's or potential enemy's will to fight, to strengthen the resolve of a nation's people or those of its allies, or to achieve diplomatic objectives. Psychological warfare is conducted mainly through propaganda or ideological campaigns based on carefully planned strategies and tactics directed toward the achievement of specific goals. The "weapons" employed include radio, television, films, public rallies, demonstrations, slogans, posters, books, newspapers and magazines, news conferences, and other means for reaching and affecting the thinking and emotions of opinion élites or mass publics. Psychological warfare may also be carried on at a more limited, sophisticated level in an effort to mislead or confuse policymakers or military commanders. *See also* FOURTEEN POINTS, IDEOLOGICAL WARFARE, PROPAGANDA.

Public Accomodations, *see* Civil Rights Act of 1964.

Public Debt   The total indebtedness, including accrued interest, of a government or of a country, the latter embracing the indebtedness of all its units of government. The public debt of the United States government is usually referred to as the national debt. Whenever expenditures exceed revenue during a fiscal year, the deficit is added to the public debt; when revenue exceeds expenditures, the public debt is reduced by the amount of the surplus. *See also* DEBT LIMIT, DEFICIT FINANCING.

Public Defender   An official whose duty it is to act as attorney for persons accused of crime who are unable to secure their own counsel. Since the Supreme Court ruling in *Gideon v. Wainwright,* 372 U.S. 335 (1963) that indigent defendants must be furnished counsel, many state and local governments have established public defender systems. In 1970, Congress authorized the appointment of federal public defenders by federal courts of appeals or, as an alternative, the establishment of community defender organizations financed by federal grants. *See also* RIGHT TO COUNSEL.

Public Domain   Public lands owned by the United States government. The public domain consists of national parks and forests, grazing districts, Indian reservations, and miscellaneous holdings. The Bureau of Land Management in the Department of the Interior has custody over a large portion of the public domain. *See also* HOMESTEAD ACT.

Public Employment Rights, *see Keyishian v. Board of Regents of New York.*

Public Health Service, *see* Department of Health, Education, and Welfare.

Public Housing Government construction and maintenance of dwellings for low-income families. Since 1937, and with increasing emphasis after 1949, the national government has given assistance to local governments to clear slum areas and to construct housing. Local governments need state authorization to participate in the program and the local community can reject public housing by referendum. A local housing authority must be established. It administers the funds provided by the federal government and floats bonds. Rentals are used to repay the federal loan and private bondholders. Rentals are kept very low and the federal government subsidizes the difference between costs and rental receipts. Only persons with limited incomes are eligible to occupy the housing. Some cities and states have undertaken their own public housing programs without federal aid. *See also* HOUSING ACT, URBAN RENEWAL.

Public International Organization, *see* International Organization.

Public Opinion Beliefs and attitudes of people generally on a social issue. Public opinion may relate to matters of *fact* or matters of *preference*. An opinion expressing preference can be classified in terms of its *direction* (for or against a candidate, action, position) and its *intensity* (the strength of the preference). An opinion actually held or expressed is *active*, while a predisposition to respond in a particular way, once an issue arises, is *latent* opinion. Public opinion is not a unified whole but an aggregate of many, generally diverse, individual opinions. There is, moreover, no single public for all issues. There are many publics, each consisting of the people concerned with a particular issue. Within any given public may be found numerous *subpublics* (with still more numerous crosscutting "sub-subpublics"), each with different opinions on the issue. Viewing society as a whole, students of public opinion distinguish the *mass public*, which is ill-informed and little concerned, from the small *attentive public*, which is aware of significant issues. Some also distinguish a still smaller *informed public*, which is both aware and knowledgeable. Government officials, editors, commentators, and others who generate the flow of communication on public issues are *opinion makers*. Information on public issues tends to move in a *two-step flow* from the opinion makers, who have access to the mass media, to informed *opinion leaders* at all social levels, who pass the word to a wider audience through personal contact. *See also* ATTITUDE, POLITICAL BEHAVIOR, SURVEY RESEARCH, VOTING BEHAVIOR.

Public Opinion (Foreign Policy) Views and attitudes on foreign actions and issues held by the people of a nation, community, or group. Public opinion often fluctuates in response to independent or controlled stimuli in the political and social environment. It may in turn have a considerable impact on the environment by giving direction to the decision makers or by influencing or controlling their actions. In a totalitarian state, public opinion is shaped, manipulated, and controlled by the ruling élite utilizing the mass media, censorship, elimination of opposition, rigged elections, and nationalistic propaganda. In a democracy, no single public opinion prevails; there are, rather, many publics in a pluralistic society holding diverse views on a variety of subjects. Public opinion can be identified and measured with varying degrees of accuracy through elections, plebiscites, the initiative, referendum, and recall procedures, pressure group activities, polls, public demonstrations, and by elected officials

who secure the views of constituents by various means of inquiry. *See also* IDEOLOGI-
CAL WARFARE, MASS MEDIA, PROPOGANDA.

Public Opinion Poll, *see* Poll.

Public Policy Governmental rules and programs, considered individually or collectively, that is, the authoritative decisional output of a political system. Public policy
may be expressed in a variety of forms, including laws, local ordinances, court
decisions, executive orders, decisions of administrators, or even unwritten understandings of what is to be done. *Foreign policy* consists of governmental actions with respect
to foreign governments and their nationals and international agencies. "Policy,"
without the modifier "public," is sometimes regarded as synonymous with "governmental decision," but it is often treated as embracing a set or sequence of decisions
rather than a single decision about a particular governmental action. "Policy" is also
used by some to distinguish decisions about goals or preferences from decisions
relating to the means of achieving goals. Others, however, may treat policy as
embracing both ends and means. Policy in some contexts refers to decisions about
long-range objectives or general directions of governmental action, which serve as
guides to short-run action in specific cases. *See also* DECISION-MAKING, POLICY
SCIENCES, POSTBEHAVIORALISM.

Public Power The production of electrical energy by government-built and operated
dams and power plants. Millions of kilowatts are produced and sold by the national
government, especially from generating plants on the Colorado, Columbia, and
Tennessee rivers. Public power production has become one of the major functions of
the huge governmental dams, along with reclamation, irrigation, navigation, and flood
control. Many cities and towns also produce and sell public power. *See also* TENNESSEE
VALLEY AUTHORITY, *Ashwander v. TVA.*

Public Roads Bureau, *see* Department of Transportation.

Public Service Commission A regulatory agency, found in each of the states, that
regulates the rates and services of public utilities operating within the state. Public
service commissions vary in size from one to seven members, with most states fixing
the number at three. Private utility companies regulated by the commissions include
gas and electric suppliers, buses, interurban railway transit systems, taxicabs, oil and
gas pipe lines, telephone and telegraph services, and in some states, municipal utilities.
Some of the larger cities have also established public service commissions, and in many
other cities the city council functions in this role. *See also* PUBLIC UTILITY.

Public Utility A privately owned business that performs an essential service for the
community and is extensively regulated by government. Congress and the state
legislatures establish general criteria for regulation and create government commissions to perform the regulatory function subject to review by the courts. Typical

examples of public utilities include transportation facilities, electric and gas suppliers, communication services, and water suppliers. *See also* FRANCHISE; RATE-MAKING.

Public Utility Holding Company Act of 1935, *see* Securites and Exchange Commission.

Public Works   Improvements in public facilities financed or built by government for the public welfare and convenience. Public works include such projects as parks, bridges, public buildings, roads, sewers, dams, harbors, housing, hospitals, canals, reclamation, irrigation, and navigation. *See also* FISCAL POLICY; PORK BARREL LEGISLATION.

Publius, *see Federalist Papers.*

Puerto Rico, *see* Naturalization, Territorial Court, Territory.

Pump Priming, *see* Deficit Financing.

Quantification   The assignment of numerical values to political variables so that they may be measured or compared by quantity. Quantification of any political variable may be achieved by the judgmental assignment of numbers to the concept being examined. In creating a ten-point scale of political violence, for example, one might give a value of one to rock-throwing and a value of ten to armed conflict, with intermediate numbers assigned to intermediate forms of violence. When such judgmental assignment is not appropriate, quantification may be achieved by finding numerical indicators to *represent* a political variable or concept that cannot be directly quantified. Gross national product, which can be counted in terms of dollars, may be used as an indicator of national power, which is not directly quantifiable (except by judgmental assignments). Quantification is usually identified with statistical methods of data analysis (quantitative methods) and with attempts to measure political variables precisely. The quantification and measurement of political variables is sometimes called *polimetrics. See also* CONTENT ANALYSIS, CORRELATION, FACTOR ANALYSIS, SCALE, STATISTICS, TESTING.

Quartering of Soldiers   A prohibition found in the Third Amendment against housing soldiers in private homes during time of peace without consent of the owner. In wartime, quartering of soldiers may be done under conditions prescribed by law.

Quasi-Corporation, *see* Incorporated and Unincorporated Areas.

Quasi-judicial   Powers exercised by administrative agencies that have the characteristics of a judicial act. Independent regulatory commissions, as well as other administrative agencies, exercise quasi-judicial powers when they conduct hearings and make decisions having the force of law. *See also* HEARING.

Quasi-legislative Rule-making powers, exercised by administrative agencies, that have the characteristics of a legislative act. Numerous administrative agencies are authorized to issue rules and regulations having the force of law. These include not only the independent regulatory commissions but a host of other agencies, such as the Department of Agriculture, which issues rules relative to crop quotas and other agricultural practices. *See also* ADMINISTRATIVE ORDER.

Question Hour, *see* Foreign Secretary (Britain).

Questionnaire A survey research instrument consisting of a set of questions designed to elicit responses from a selected group of people through personal interview or by mail. Questionnaire items may call for factual responses, expressions of attitudes and opinions, or explanations of attitudes, opinions, and behavior. The questions may be either open-ended or closed. With the *closed* type the respondent must choose among limited alternative answers. The alternatives might, for example, be "yes" or "no," a choice of one among several political candidates, or the expression of preference along a scale of several fixed points ranging from "strongly agree" to "strongly disagree." *Open-ended* questions leave the respondent free to give any answer that seems appropriate to him. A questionnaire administered by personal interview is called an *interview schedule.* A schedule is used in a *structured* or *standardized* interview where wording and sequence of questions must be fixed in advance. An unstructured interview is more flexible and does not call for adherence to a questionnaire. *See also* ATTITUDE SCALING, GUTTMAN SCALE, INTERVIEW, SEMANTIC DIFFERENTIAL, SURVEY RESEARCH.

Quid pro Quo A diplomatic bargaining concept meaning, literally, something for something. Negotiations conducted on a basis of *quid pro quo* depend on mutual compromises for success. *See also* DIPLOMACY.

Quiet Diplomacy, *see* Dispute Settlement Procedures (United Nations).

Quorum The minimum number of members of a legislative chamber who must be present in order to transact business. The Constitution specifies that "a majority of each [house] shall constitute a quorum to do business." (Art. I, sec. 5). This means 218 in the House and 51 in the Senate. In the House, the quorum for the Committee of the Whole is 100. Typically, state legislatures also require a majority of members to be present for the transaction of business.

Quota A quantitative restriction established by a state to control the importation of certain commodities. Variations of the quota system used in different countries provide for: (1) increasing customs duties as large numbers of items are imported, up to the limit of the quota (customs quota); (2) individual quotas for specific countries (allocated quota); (3) a general limit on imports, applicable to all countries (global quota); (4) individual quotas for specific companies (import licensing); (5) reciprocal arrangements for limiting trade (bilateral quota); (6) import limits determined by the relationship of the articles to domestic production (mixing quota). *See also* PROTEC-TIONISM.

Quotations From Chairman Mao Tse-Tung, *see* Maoism.

Racial Discrimination, *see* Civil Rights Acts, De Facto Segregation, Fair Employment Practices Laws, Racism, Segregation, *Swann v. Charlotte-Mecklenburg Board of Education.*

Racism   A belief that differences among people are rooted in ethnic stock. These differences include color, religion, blood line, or national origin. Racism usually involves the assumption that one's own race is superior and that social and political organization should reflect that superiority. Nazi persecution of Jews prior to and during World War II on the theory that German Aryans constituted a superior race is a leading example of racism. In the United States the term, "white racism," is used to describe discrimination against black people in social and political institutions.

Radical   An advocate of substantial political, social, and economic changes. Although no precise use of the term exists, a radical is generally regarded as a leftist or rightist who is extreme in his demands for change. *See also* LEFTIST, NEW LEFT, RIGHTIST.

Radio Free Europe   The miltantly anti-Communist "private" organization that broadcasts programs to the peoples of Eastern Europe. Radio Free Europe is staffed largely by refugees who fled from Eastern Europe during the period of its communization following World War II. Its efforts are supplemented by a second private and equally anti-communist broadcasting group, Radio Liberty, that broadcasts to the people of the Soviet Union. Congressional disclosures in the 1960s indicated that both radio stations were financed largely by the Central Intelligence Agency, casting doubt on the alleged private and voluntary nature of their operations. In 1971, the Nixon Administration proposed the creation of a publicly funded private corporation to finance the operations of both stations in an effort to remove the stigma of CIA control.

Raiding, *see* Poll Watcher.

Railroad Commission of Texas v. Rowan and Nichols Oil Co., 311 U.S. 570 (1941): Refused to overturn a ruling of the Railroad Commission relating to the amount of oil that could be taken from wells in Texas. The Court noted that the issue was too complex for judges to determine and that the Commission's order must stand in the absence of a showing that it was based on insubstantial evidence.

Ramspeck Act (Civil Service Act of 1940) Authorizes the President to place, by executive order, nearly all federal positions under the civil service system. Exemptions include those positions filled by presidential appointment requiring the Senate's approval, and certain special agencies, such as the Tennessee Valley Authority and the Federal Bureau of Investigation, which have merit systems of their own.

Random The quality of occurring by chance, or in no predictable fashion. Paradoxically, although individual random events cannot be predicted, in the aggregate they can often be predicted with considerable accuracy through use of probability theories. Coin tossing is an obvious example. An individual toss cannot be predicted, but in every one hundred tosses approximately fifty will turn up "heads." In research a *random sample* is one which is selected from a larger population, by procedures that give each member of the population an equal possibility of being chosen (and, more technically, all possible combinations are equally probable). A *population* or *universe* refers to all members of any class of things (including people) that might be studied. *See also* CONTROL GROUP, EXPERIMENT, PROBABILITY, RESEARCH DESIGN, SAMPLING.

Random Sample, *see* Random, Sampling.

Ranking Member That member of the majority party on a legislative committee who ranks first after the chairman in number of years of continous service (seniority) on the committee. *See also* COMMITTEE CHAIRMAN, SENIORITY RULE.

Ranking Minority Member The minority party member of a legislative committee with the longest continuous service (seniority) on the committee. *See also* SENIORITY RULE.

Rank Order, *see* Correlation.

Rapprochement A reconciliation of the interests of rival states after a period of estrangement. Rapprochement, in diplomatic parlance, implies a policy of attempting to reestablish normal relations. *See also* DÉTENTE.

Rate-making The determination by governmental regulatory agencies of the charges that public utilities will be permitted to levy for their services to the public. Rate-making agencies usually fix only maximum rates, although minimum rates may be set to avoid rate wars. *See also* ORIGINAL COST THEORY, PRUDENT INVESTMENT THEORY, REPRODUCTION COST THEORY, *Smyth v. Ames.*

Rathbun Case, *see Humphrey's Executor v. United States.*

Ratification (Executive Role) The approval by the President of the version of a treaty that has received Senate consent by a two-thirds vote. Ratification may involve the problem of whether a President will accept amendments and reservations to the treaty affixed by the Senate, which might entail reopening of negotiations with other signatory nations. *See also* RATIFICATION (LEGISLATIVE ROLE).

Ratification (Legislative Role)   A power vested in a legislative body to approve (or reject) agreements entered into with other states and constitutional ammendment proposals. In the states, interstate compacts negotiated by the governors of several states must be ratified or approved by the state legislature of each before becoming effective. Amendments proposed to the United States Constitution must be ratified by legislatures or conventions in three-fourths of the states to become effective. Amendments proposed to state constitutions, however, must be ratified by a vote of the people of that state. The term "ratification" is also popularly used to describe the "consent" function of the United States Senate regarding treaties negotiated by the United States with foreign nations, although here the term more properly applies to the role of the President in accepting or rejecting the Senate approved version of a treaty. *See also* RATIFICATION (EXECUTIVE ROLE), TREATY RATIFICATION, AMENDMENT.

Ratification, Treaty, *see* Treaty Ratification.

Rationalism, *see* Rationality.

Rationality   The capacity to reason logically from premises to conclusions, or to choose the most efficient and appropriate means to achieve goals and maximize values. Rationality in thinking is sometimes called "formal rationality" as distinguished from the "substantive rationality" of action. Some students use Max Weber's distinction between types of rational action: *Zweckrational* (goal oriented) action is concerned with effective use of available means to attain desired ends, while *wertrational* (value oriented) action is directed toward conformity to consciously held values or standards of conduct. In the Weberian scheme, nonrational behavior is classified as *affectual* (based on feeling, emotion) or *traditional* (based on accepted custom and authority). *See also* ASSUMPTION, EMPIRICISM, GAME THEORY, GOAL, INTUITION, VALUE.

Ratio Problem (Disarmament)   Issues that arise in disarmament negotiations over the schedule for disarming, the categories of forces, and other factors related to the future power relationships of participants. The ratio problem can be overcome only if all states involved in negotiating a disarmament agreement can be convinced that their security will not be jeopardized by an imbalance in weapons at any stage of the disarming process.

Ratio Scale, *see* Scale.

"Raw" Empiricism, *see* Fact.

Raw Materials (Geographic Power Factor) The resources of water and soil, their products, and the minerals of the subsoil in relation to national power. Access to raw materials is essential to the standard of living and the security of the state, and dependence upon them relates to the technological developments that create demands for them either at home or abroad. Iron and coal have long been the basis for industrialization, but increasing technological sophistication is creating new demands for other materials, such as uranium as an energy source, titanium for jet engines, and germanium for transistors. The advanced technologies of such fields as space exploration, medicine, and warfare depend on high levels of industrialization requiring a wide diversity of raw materials. The developing countries that are seeking ways to sustain growing populations at improved standards of living are adding to the pressures on diminishing supplies of world resources.

Reaction, *see* Political Action.

Reactionary A person who advocates substantial political, social, or economic changes favoring a return to an earlier, more conservative system. A reactionary believes that most social problems result from democratic excesses favoring the propertyless masses, and usually prefers government by oligarchy. Although the use of the term is not precise, reactionaries are political rightists who are more extreme in their views than are conservatives, and are more likely to adopt militant tactics to achieve their objectives. *See also* RIGHTIST.

Readings The three readings of a bill required at different stages of the legislative process. In Congress, the first reading occurs when the bill is introduced and printed by title in the *Congressional Record*. The second, often a reading in full, takes place when the bill is brought out of committee for consideration before the chamber. The third reading, usually by title only, comes after amendments have been voted on and the bill is up for a final vote. State legislative procedure is similar. *See also* BILL.

Realist Approach, *see* Power.

Realist-Idealist Dichotomy Alternative approaches followed by decision makers in the formation of foreign policy. The realist approach to policymaking is fundamentally empirical and pragmatic, whereas the idealist approach is based on abstract traditional foreign policy principles involving international norms, legal codes, and moral-ethical values. The realist school starts with the assumption that the key factor prevalent in all international relationships is that of power. The wise and efficient use of power by a state in pursuit of its national interest is, therefore, the main ingredient of a successful foreign policy. The idealist, on the other hand, believes that foreign policies based on moral principles are more effective because they promote unity and cooperation among states rather than competition and conflict. Moral power, according to the idealist, is more effective than physical power because it is more durable. It involves not force and coercion but winning over the minds and allegiances of people to accept principles that ought to govern state conduct. *See also* FOREIGN POLICY, FOURTEEN POINTS, MACHIAVELLIANISM, POWER.

Reapportionment, *see* Apportionment.

Reasonable Doubt   The standard for determining the guilt of a person charged with a criminal offense. The prosecution must persuade the judge or jury that the evidence proves guilt beyond a reasonable doubt. Though long accepted as part of the common law tradition, it was not until 1970 that the Supreme Court held "lest there remain any doubt about the constitutional stature of the reasonable doubt standard, we explicitly hold that the Due Process Clause protects the accused against conviction except upon proof beyond a reasonable doubt of every fact necessary to constitute the crime with which he is charged" (*In Re Winship*, 397 U.S. 358 [1970]). The standard applies to both adult and juvenile criminal cases.

Rebus Sic Stantibus   The international law doctrine that an essential change in the conditions under which a treaty was concluded frees a state from its treaty obligations. *Rebus sic stantibus* is a rationalization for unilateral, unauthorized denunciation of a treaty commitment. The doctrine asserts that every treaty contains an unwritten clause to the effect that substantial changes in the conditions that existed at the time the treaty was signed alter the obligations established by the treaty. *See also* PACTA SUNT SERVANDA, TREATY.

Recall   A procedure enabling voters to remove an elected official from office before his term has expired. The required number of valid signatures on petitions results in the calling of a special election. If the majority of voters favor recall, the official is replaced by a successor who is either chosen on the recall ballot or in a subsequent election. Twelve states and numerous local units of government provide for the recall of elected officials.

Recess Appointment   An appointment of a federal official made by the President to fill a vacancy while the Senate is not in session. To prevent the President from postponing appointments until the Senate has adjourned, Congress has by statute prohibited the payment of salary to an officer appointed to fill a vacancy that existed but was not filled while the Senate was still in session. Recess appointments expire at the end of the next congressional session unless the Senate has confirmed the appointed official by a majority vote. Most state constitutions provide for recess appointments by the governors. *See also* APPOINTMENT POWER, CONFIRMATION.

Recession, Economic, *see* Depression.

Reciprocal Trade Agreements Act of 1934   A broad tariff program under which the President negotiates trade agreements with foreign countries that provide for mutual reductions in tariff rates. It incorporates the "most-favored nation" principle, under which concessions contained in agreements apply to all other nations with which we have most favored nation arrangements. The original enactment in 1934 provided that tariff rates of the United States could be lowered or raised up to 50 percent of the existing rates, but renewals have given the President authority to seek additional cuts. Amendments to the Act include "peril-point" and "escape-clause" provisions. The peril-point amendment provides that the Tariff Commission inform the President and Congress at what level a tariff rate might allow imports to threaten or injure a domestic producer. Escape-clause procedures require that tariff rates be raised if they injure domestic producers. The Trade Expansion Act of 1962 expanded the President's tariff-cutting powers, and strengthened the American bargaining position, especially with the European Common Market countries. *See also* TARIFF.

Reciprocity A *quid pro quo* (something for something) basis for international bargaining on tariff rates. While reciprocity is the basis for negotiating mutual trade concessions, it can also imply retaliation for tariff increases by other nations. Tariff rates may be raised unilaterally, but they are seldom if ever lowered without reciprocal reductions. *See also* TARIFF.

Recognition of Governments An official act, such as an exchange of ambassadors, that acknowledges the existence of a government and indicates readiness to engage in formal relations with it. Recognition of a new state cannot be accomplished without recognizing the government in power. For this reason, confusion often arises concerning recognition of states and recognition of governments. Recognition of a state, once accomplished, continues for the life of the state even when a particular government of that state is not recognized. After the Russian Revolution of 1917, for instance, the United States continued to recognize the Russian state even though it did not recognize the Soviet government until 1933. Recognition of a government is not perpetual and may be granted or withheld with each change of regime. A break in diplomatic relations, however, is not a withdrawal of recognition.

Recognition of States The process by which a political entity becomes an international person in international law and is accepted by existing states as a new member of the community. Once recognition of statehood has occurred, this status continues regardless of internal organization or changes in government so long as the sovereign character of the state continues.

Recognition (Presidential Power) The power exercised exclusively by the President to establish diplomatic relations with foreign states. Recognition powers are vested in the President by the Constitution, which grants him the power in Article II, secion 2 to send and receive ambassadors. *See also* RECOGNITION (UNITED STATES)

Recognition (United States) The discretionary function exercised by the President of deciding whether or not the United States shall officially carry on relations with a new state or a new political regime in an existing state. *See also* RECOGNITION (PRESIDENTIAL POWER), DE FACTO RECOGNITION, DE JURE RECOGNITION.

Recommittal   The action of a legislative body of sending a bill back to the committee that had reported it out for consideration. A motion to recommit may instruct the committee to report the bill out again with certain amendments or at a later date. Most motions for recommittal, however, simply call for further study by the committee.

Record Vote   A "yea or nay" roll call vote in a legislative body in which each member's vote is required to be recorded. Those members not voting for or against the measure will either be "paired" or "present." In Congress, the Constitution requires a record vote for overriding a presidential veto, and whenever one-fifth of the members demand it. Record votes are not taken in Committee of the Whole. State constitutions also require record votes on important measures before the state legislatures. *See also* DIVISION, TELLER VOTE, VIVA VOCE VOTE.

Recruitment   The selection of people to fill roles in a social system. *Political recruitment* refers to the filling of formal, legal positions, such as President, legislator, or civil servant, as well as less formal roles, such as lobbyist, party activist, or propagandist. Recruitment may be based on *ascription* (criteria derived from status factors, such as race, birth, or social position), or *achievement* (what a person has done or can do), or some combination of the two. Specific techniques of recruitment may include co-optation, appointment, election, lot, rotation, apprenticeship, examination, seizure, and purchase. Most recruitment involves an element of self-selection by potential recruits who have the desire and the skills necessary to obtain and hold office. Political recruitment is treated as a major category of inputs in structural-functional analysis. *See also* POLITICAL SOCIALIZATION, ROLE, STRUCTURAL-FUNCTION-ALISM.

Red Guard   A largely unorganized, undisciplined, militant mob of students of college and high school age, who were during the late 1960s incited by Maoists in the government and party to search out and destroy bourgeois values and institutions in Chinese society. The Red Guard thus functioned as the instrument of Mao Tse-tung's "great proletarian Cultural Revolution." The Guard physically assaulted individuals and humiliated public leaders in addition to destroying ancient Chinese art treasures and denouncing "high living standards, Hong Kong fashions, and bureaucratic behavior."

Rediscount   Credit granted by a Federal Reserve bank to a member bank on negotiable instruments that had already been discounted (a loan with interest subtracted in advance) when the member bank made loans to its customers. *See also* FEDERAL RESERVE SYSTEM.

Redistricting   The action of a state legislature or other body in redrawing legislative electoral district lines following a new population census. Redistricting occurs after each decennial federal census when congressional seats are reapportioned among the fifty states. In each state that gains or loses seats, the state legislature usually draws up new districts. Additionally, state legislatures are required by most state constitutions to redraw district boundary lines for electing state representatives and senators to the state legislatures following each federal census. *See also* GERRYMANDERING, *Baker v. Carr, Reynolds v. Sims, Wesberry v. Sanders.*

Reductionism   A method of explanation in which the attributes or behaviors of the *whole* are reduced to, or explained by reference to, the attributes or behaviors of its constituent *parts.* A reductive approach might explain the functioning of a political system in terms of personality variables, or by reference to particular components of the system, such as actor characteristics, processes of political socialization and recruitment, political values, and so on. In effect, the nature or behavior of the broader macrosystem is explained in terms of one or more of its component microsystems. This type of *reductive* explanation may be contrasted with *emergent* or *holistic* explanations, which focus on the functioning of the whole system rather than its parts. The emergent systemic pattern is seen as a product of the interaction of system components, not just a larger replica of its individual subsystems or the arithmetic sum of its component parts. *See also* EXPLANATION, HOLISM, MACRO-MICRO ANALYSIS.

Referee   A person, ordinarily an attorney, appointed by the court to conduct a hearing on a particular matter and to report to the court. In federal courts, referees are used often in bankruptcy proceedings to collect information and to present it to the court for final disposition of the case. Under the 1960 Civil Rights Act, the federal courts were authorized to appoint voting referees to help qualified Negroes to register to vote in areas where a pattern or practice of discrimination existed.

Reference Group   Any group of people from which a person adopts attitudes, beliefs, or values that affect his behavior: his behavior is in some way determined by *reference* to theirs. A reference group may be a membership group (to which the individual concerned may or may not belong) or simply a categorical group having no formal membership but sharing one or several common characteristics, such as race, sex, class, or income level. Analytically, reference groups may be either comparative or normative. A *comparative* reference group provides a standard for comparative *self-evaluation,* as, for example, a group of co-workers, co-religionists, classmates, or persons of one's own race or of another race. A *normative* reference group helps to shape the cognitions, values, attitudes, and norms by which the individual *evaluates the world* around him. Although the comparative and normative functions are analytically distinct, one group may be a referent for both purposes. Some normative reference groups may be *negative* rather than *positive.* In such case the affected person is repelled by the norms of the group and adopts contrary norms. *See also* ATTITUDE, POLITICAL SOCIALIZATION, PUBLIC OPINION, VALUE, VOTING BEHAVIOR.

Referendum   An electoral device, available in many states, by which voters can "veto" a bill passed by their legislature. Emergency and financial bills are commonly excluded from referendum action. In states providing for the referendum, bills passed by the legislature do not take effect for a specified period (usually ninety days), during which the bill may be suspended by obtaining the required number of voters' signatures on petitions (usually 5 percent of the total votes cast in a preceding election). A suspended bill is voted on by the electorate and, if disapproved by a majority, it is killed. The *constitutional referendum* gives voters an opportunity to approve or reject amendments or revisions of state constitutions. Many state and local governments may also use the *optional* or *advisory referendum,* by which a legislative body may voluntarily refer a measure to the voters for an expression of popular sentiment. *See also* DIRECT DEMOCRACY, DIRECT LEGISLATION.

Refer to Committee   The sending of a bill that has been introduced into one of the houses of a legislative body to a standing committee. In Congress, public bills are assigned to committees by the parliamentarian under the scrutiny of the presiding officer in each house. Private bills are usually referred to the committee requested by the senator or representative who introduces the bill. *See also* STANDING COMMITTEE.

Refugee   A person who is expelled, deported, or flees from his country of nationality or residence. Since a refugee has no legal or political rights, his welfare has become a matter of concern and action by international bodies. Refugees may be repatriated to their homeland or resettled and assimilated into other societies when governments agree to accept them. *See also* UNITED NATIONS HIGH COMMISSIONER FOR REFUGEES, UNITED NATIONS RELIEF AND WORKS AGENCY.

Regional Aid Programs, *see* Foreign Aid.

Regional Commissions, *see* United Nations Regional Commissions.

Regional Development Banks   Public lending institutions created by governments to foster regional and subregional economic development. Regional development banks have been established in Europe, Latin America, Africa, and Asia. The European Investment Bank, which began to function in 1958, is an institution of the six industrially-developed states of the European Economic Community. Its headquarters are located in Luxembourg and it has a capitalization of $1 billion. The membership of the Inter-American Development Bank, operational in 1960, is composed of twenty-one American republics. Headquartered in Washington, D.C., the bank has an authorized capitalization of $3.15 billion. The African Development Bank, organized in 1965 with headquarters in Abidjan, Ivory Coast, includes most African countries in its membership and has an authorized capital of $250 million. The Asian Development Bank was organized in 1967 with headquarters at Manila and has a capitalization of more than $1 billion. In addition to its Asian and Pacific regional participants, the Bank's members include the United States, Britain, West Germany, Belgium, The Netherlands, Italy, and Switzerland. *See also* INTERNATIONAL BANK FOR RECONSTRUCTION AND DEVELOPMENT.

Regionalism (International)   Limited systems of international organization that enable groupings of states to deal cooperatively with political, economic, social, and military problems. Geographical proximity of states typifies most regional organizations, although a community of common interests alone, such as that found in the Commonwealth of Nations, can be the integrating force behind such movements. Regional organizations include the military alliance systems of both the Western and Soviet blocs, political systems such as the Organization of American States and the Council of Europe, and economic groupings such as the Common Market and the Free Trade Association.

Regionalism (National)   A method of decentralizing power on a geographical basis. In the United States, regionalism is often proposed as an alternative or supplement to the states. For example, the country could be divided into nine or ten regional subdivisions instead of into fifty states. The term is also applied to regional administration of federal projects, such as the Tennessee Valley Authority, and to regional interstate compacts.

Register of Deeds   A county officer, sometimes called recorder of deeds, who is elected in about half the states. His major duty is to record and preserve legal documents relating mainly to real estate ownership and transfers. This function is designed to protect landowners and prospective purchasers of land against flaws in titles to property.

Registration   Enrolling prospective voters prior to their participation in elections. Under a system of *permanent* registration, the voter, once qualified, remains on the eligible list until he dies, moves, or fails to vote in several consecutive elections. *Periodic* registration requires that he enroll at the appropriate local office annually or at fixed intervals. Almost all states now use some form of permanent registration, although in many there is no statewide application. *See also* VOTING QUALIFICATIONS.

Regression Techniques, *see* Correlation.

Regressive Tax   Any tax in which the burden falls relatively more heavily upon low-income groups than upon more wealthy taxpayers. It is the opposite of a progressive tax, in which tax rates increase as ability to pay increases. *See also* PROGRESSIVE TAX.

Regulation of Lobbying Act (Title III, Legislative Reorganization Act of 1946)   The first attempt by Congress to control interest groups, lobbyists, and lobbying activities through legislation. The Act provides for a minimum of *regulation* and a maximum of *publicity*. Specific provisions include: (1) persons or organizations receiving money to be used principally to influence passage or defeat of legislation before Congress must register; (2) persons or groups registering must, under oath, give their name and address, employer, salary, amount and purpose of expenses, and duration of employment; (3) each registered lobbyist must report quarterly full information on his activities, which are then published in the *Congressional Record;* and (4) severe penalties are prescribed, ranging up to a $10,000 fine and a five-year prison term, and including a three-year ban against further lobbying. *See also United States v. Harriss.*

Regulatory Tax   A tax levied for purposes other than the raising of revenue. A protective tariff is a clear example of a regulatory tax. More subtle uses of taxing power for nonrevenue regulatory purposes include restricting the marketing of a product (the heavy tax on oleomargarine many years ago to maintain the butter market), or adding to the government's arsenal against illegal or undesirable activities (a tax on gamblers), sometimes called a sumptuary tax. *See also Veazie Bank v. Fenno.*

Reliability   The extent to which a measurement technique produces the same results time after time, assuming the relevant conditions to be held constant. Reliability implies constancy, dependability, and accuracy of measurement. It does not, however, imply that the measurement technique will accurately measure the variable the researcher is concerned with, in the way he wants it measured. That is a question of *validity.* A biased questionnaire, for example, might *reliably* elicit the same kinds of responses from different samples of the population time after time, but, because of the bias in the instrument, the data would not be a *valid* measure of attitudes or opinions on the subject being examined. A public opinion poll that consistently finds 75 percent of its respondents favoring monarchy in the United States might be very reliable, but it probably would not be a valid measure of the actual state of opinion in the country. Because consistent bias is compatible with reliability as we have defined it, differences in reliability are usually associated with chance or random errors in measurement, not biased or systematic variance from some true value. In many kinds of political science research, such as content analysis, data must be assigned to categories for purposes of analysis. This assignment to categories, usually designated numerically, is called *coding.* If several coders are engaged in the task, a problem of *intercoder reliability* exists. Intercoder reliability is commonly measured by calculating the percentage of agreement among the coders, when they are coding the same data. Often an intercoder reliability test will be run to determine the reliability of the coding system. If a high percentage of agreement exists, the categories as applied to the data may constitute a reliable instrument. *See also* BIASED SAMPLE, CONTENT ANALYSIS, RANDOM, SAMPLING, STATISTICS, SURVEY RESEARCH.

Religion, Freedom of, *see* Freedom of Religion.

Religious Establishment, *see* Separation of Church and State.

Religious Test   A requirement that one profess belief in a particular religious faith or in a Supreme Being as a condition to holding public office. Article VI of the Constitution prohibits such tests. Several state constitutions contain a requirement that public officials profess a belief in God, but in 1961 the Supreme Court held such a Maryland provision unconstitutional (*Torcaso v. Watkins,* 367 U.S. 488). *See also* SEPARATION OF CHURCH AND STATE.

Removal Power   The authority of an executive official to dismiss appointed officials from office. Although the Constitution is silent on the subject, the President has from the beginning exercised the power to remove executive and administrative officials. As a general rule, all officials appointed by the President serve at his pleasure. Federal judges, however, have life tenure, on good behavior, while members of "independent commissions," and merit system employees can be removed only for cause. The removal power of state governors generally compares unfavorably with that of the President because of the number of elective officials in most states and the sharing of the governor's removal power, in many states, by the state senate. *See also Myers v. United States; Humphrey's Executor [Rathbun] v. United States.*

Renunciation of Citizenship, *see* Expatriation.

Reorganization Act of 1949   A grant of power to the President to reorganize the executive branch of the government. Plans for reorganization must be submitted to Congress, and either house may veto the proposal within sixty days. The Reorganization Act has been extended several times since 1949.

Reorganization, Administrative, *see* Administrative Reorganization.

Reparations   Compensation demanded by victor nations of defeated states for wrongs committed by the latter before or during hostilities. Reparations often take the form of capital goods removed from the defeated nation's territory to replace those destroyed during the war, but may also involve monetary payments.

Replication, *see* Observation.

Report   The action of a legislative committee in sending out its findings and recommendations to its chamber following consideration of a bill or investigation of some matter. The report explains the reasons for the committee's actions. Most committee reports are favorable, but on rare occasions a committee will report out a bill with a recommendation that its parent chamber kill the bill. In any case, many reports are not unanimous, and those members of the committee who dissent may file a minority report. If a bill has been amended in committee, the majority report will provide an explanation for this action. *See also* STANDING COMMITTEE, DISCHARGE RULE, RULES COMMITTEE.

Representative   A member of the House of Representatives in Congress or of the lower house of a state legislature. Representatives are elected for two-year terms and, in keeping with the idea that the lower house is to be the more representative of the two chambers, all members' terms are coterminous. The Constitution provides that a representative must be at least twenty-five years of age, a citizen for seven years, and a resident of the state from which he is elected. Vacancies are filled by special election called by the governor. *See also* HOUSE OF REPRESENTATIVES.

Representative Government   Any democratic system of government in which the people elect representatives to act as their agents in making and enforcing laws and decisions. Authoritarian regimes often have a façade of representative institutions, but they lack the vital element of accountability of democratic governments. *See also* REPUBLIC, DEMOCRACY.

Reprieve, *see* Pardon.

Reprisal   A coercive measure short of war, undertaken by one state against another as a means for redressing a wrong or punishing an international delinquency. Reprisals may include a show of force, a boycott, an embargo, a pacific blockade, a freezing of assets, or a seizure of property belonging to the offending state. *See also* MEASURES SHORT OF WAR.

Reproduction Cost Theory   An approach used by government in fixing rates to determine a fair return in profits for public utilities. The reproduction cost theory is based on ascertaining the cost of reproducing the assets of a utility at current prices less depreciation over the period of their use. *See also* RATE-MAKING, *Smyth v. Ames.*

Republic   A form of government in which sovereign power resides in the electorate and is exercised by elected representatives who are responsible to the people. Republican government stands in contradistinction to monarchical or oligarchical government in which the rulers have a vested right to office. It is also to be distinguished from pure democracy in which the people govern directly. *See also* REPRESENTATIVE GOVERNMENT.

Republican Conference, *see* Caucus.

Republican Form of Government   A government that operates through elected representatives of the people. It is generally distinguished from a pure democracy in which the people govern directly. Article IV, section 4 of the Constitution, known as the "guarantee clause," provides that the national government shall guarantee to each state a republican form of government. *See also* Luther v. Borden, *Pacific States Telephone and Telegraph Co. v. Oregon.*

Republican Party   A major American party that emerged in the 1850s as an antislavery party. The Republican party is the successor to two earlier major parties—the Federalist and the Whig. It became firmly established in American politics when its candidate, Abraham Lincoln, won the presidency in 1860 and successfully prosecuted the Civil War. The period from 1860 to 1932 was characterized largely by Republican dominance of the American political scene, but in the years since 1932 the Democrats have dominated the presidency except for the elections of Dwight D. Eisenhower and Richard M. Nixon. *See also* DEMOCRATIC PARTY.

Research   The critical, systematic investigation of a subject to increase knowledge and understanding. The research process includes identification of a research problem, gathering and analysis of data, and formulation of findings and conclusions. The objectives of research may range from careful description and classification of observed phenomena to explanation, prediction, and theory building. Scientific research is commonly said to be concerned with the formulation and testing of hypotheses. Ideally, scientific research begins with a body of theory, gleaned from relevant literature or the researcher's past experience, from which a hypothesis is deduced. The variables in the hypothesized relationship are *operationalized*, that is, defined in terms of, or with reference to, specific kinds of data that are available and can be measured. The data are then gathered and analyzed to determine if they support the hypothesis or not. Whenever possible, the investigator attempts to control for, or rule out, the effects of variables other than those being examined. *See also* HYPOTHESIS, RESEARCH DESIGN.

Research Design   The overall plan for a research project, specifying what the researcher proposes to do and how he proposes to do it. A research design ordinarily includes a statement of the research problem (the questions to be asked, or hypotheses tested), operational definitions of important concepts (at least of the variables in any hypotheses), the kinds and sources of data and how gathered, and methods of data analysis to be used in answering the questions or testing the hypotheses. Designs for hypothesis testing may be experimental or ex post facto. *Experimental designs,* by definition, permit the researcher to manipulate one or more independent variables (the so-called treatment of the experimental group). With *ex post facto* designs the researcher is not able to administer treatment to his subjects but takes as his independent variables events that have already occurred. A *quasi-experimental* design utilizes experimental methods under conditions where full experimental control is not possible. *See also* EXPERIMENT, HYPOTHESIS, NATURAL EXPERIMENT, RESEARCH, VARIABLE.

Reserved Powers   Powers of state governments under the American federal system. The states retain all powers not delegated to the national government, or prohibited to them, by the Constitution. These powers are frequently referred to as "residuary." It is not possible to make a definitive list of state powers since, in the very nature of the federal system, the states may exercise any power that is not delegated to the national government. This usually includes authority over internal affairs of the state and general police power over the health, safety, morals, and welfare of the people. State constitutions may place specific restrictions upon state powers. *See also* DELEGATED POWERS.

Reserve Ratio   The percentage of liquid assets held by a bank as a reserve for its deposits. The *legal* reserve ratio is that percentage set by government to ensure that banks will maintain a safe proportion of ready cash to meet depositors' demands for their money. Under the Federal Reserve System, the legal reserve requirement is set for the member banks within each district by the Federal Reserve Board of Governors. Reserve requirements for state banks are usually set by law in each state. *See also* FEDERAL RESERVE SYSTEM.

Reserves   The Army, Navy, Air Force, Coast Guard, and National Guard units not on active duty but available to supplement the regular military services during emergencies. Reservists are divided into "ready reserves," "standby reserves," and "retired reserves." The ready reserve may be called to active duty by the President or Congress. The standby reserve is a pool of trained military personnel who can be called up only in case of war or an emergency declared by Congress. A third category, the retired reserve, can be recalled to active duty by Congress during a major emergency.

Residence   A qualification for voting based on domicile. Such laws require that a person live in the state for a specified period of time, commonly one year, and within a county and a voting precinct, typically ninety days for the former and thirty days for the latter. In 1972, the Supreme Court declared invalid lengthy state (one year) and local (ninety days) residence requirements and suggested thirty days as sufficient (*Dunn v. Blumstein,* 92 S. Ct. 995). In the Voting Rights Act of 1970, Congress provided that thirty days residence in any state would qualify citizens to vote in presidential elections. *See also* VOTING QUALIFICATIONS, DISFRANCHISE.

Resident Commissioner   A delegate elected by the people of a territory to represent them in the House of Representatives. A resident commissioner may speak in the House and serve on committees, but he may not vote. His salary is the same as that of all congressmen. Guam, Puerto Rico, and the Virgin Islands have resident commissioners. The District of Columbia is also represented in the House of Representatives by a nonvoting delegate.

Residuary Powers, *see* Reserved Powers.

Response, *see* Stimulus-Response.

Responsible Party System   A democratic political system in which parties accept full accountability to the voters in developing policy and operating the government. A responsible party requires internal discipline, so that its members give support to its objectives and platform promises. The real test of responsibility is whether the majority party can redeem its pledges to the voters. *See also* POLITICAL PARTY.

Restraint of Trade   The use in the business world of trusts, monopolies, price fixing, collusion, conspiracy, or other practices that hamper or eliminate a market economy based on free competition. The phrase is used in the Sherman Act of 1890 wherein it forbids any "conspiracy in the restraint of trade. . . . " *See also* SHERMAN ANTITRUST ACT.

Restrictive Covenant   A clause entered in deeds to protect the value of properties by restricting their uses. Some restrictive covenants prohibit the sale of property to Negroes or other minority groups. *See also* CIVIL RIGHTS ACT OF 1968, *Jones v. Mayer.*

Resulting Powers Powers of the national government derived from a combination of delegated or implied powers; hence, powers that "result" from a number of powers, rather than inferred from one of the delegated powers. *See also Legal Tender Cases.*

Retortion, *see* Measures Short of War.

Revenue Bills, *see* Appropriation.

Revenue Sharing A system in which one unit of government automatically and regularly turns over a certain portion of its tax yield to another unit of government, according to a formula established by constitution or statute. Revenue sharing differs from a grant-in-aid program in that the transfers of tax monies are completely or largely free from legal and administrative controls by the grantor government, and receiving governments are not required to match the amount. Under general tax sharing, as distinguished from contributions for specific programs, the receiving government determines how, when, and for what purposes the tax monies will be spent, with minimal direction, control, and oversight carried on by the government that collects the taxes. *See also* GRANT-IN-AID, TAX OFFSET.

Revisionist Policy An analytical term used to describe any foreign policy by which a state seeks to alter the existing international territorial, ideological, or power distribution to its advantage. A revisionist policy is basically expansionist and acquisitive in nature; hence a state will be likely to pursue such a policy if its decision makers are dissatisfied with the status quo and believe that the state has the capability to achieve its objectives. *See also* BALANCE OF POWER, STATUS QUO POLICY.

Revolution A basic transformation of the political, economic, or social principles and institutions in a state, resulting from the overthrow of an established governmental order. A revolution typically involves a popular uprising and the use of violence against the governing élite. If successful, the revolutionary leaders take over control of the government and may then institute basic reforms in accord with revolutionary goals. A revolution differs from a coup d'état in that the latter involves a seizure of governmental power within the élite group without the support of the masses and with little or no basic political change. *See also* CIVIL WAR, COUP D'ÉTAT, INSURGENCY, WARS OF NATIONAL LIBERATION.

Revolution (Communist Theory) The use of force by the masses to win and hold power in the violent climax to the class struggle anticipated by communist doctrine. Marx believed that in democratic states the proletariat could conceivably take power initially by winning the battle of the ballot box, but he forecast that when the proletariat sought to dislodge the bourgeoisie from its control of economic and political institutions, a counterrevolution would be likely to result. Lenin modified Marxism by postulating that the bourgeoisie would never relinquish its dominant role until its power was smashed by a violent proletarian revolution. Nikita Khrushchev, in enunciating a policy of peaceful coexistence, declared in 1961 that communism does not need war to spread its ideals, that its weapon "is its superiority over the old system in social organization, political system, economy, the improvement of the standard of living and spiritual culture." Wars of national liberation fought by the masses in the underdeveloped lands of the world, however, were recognized by Khrushchev, and are accepted by current Soviet leaders, as necessary and just.

Revolution of Rising Expectations   A change in attitude, prevalent among millions in the poor nations of the world, from a fatalistic resignation and acceptance of poverty to an optimism that living conditions can be substantially improved. The revolution of rising expectations is engendered by the improved communications that have brought awareness of better living conditions in the advanced nations and recognition that man can improve his life by altering his environment.

Revolving Fund   An operational fund established for a governmental agency carrying on proprietary (business-type) functions that make the agency financially self-supporting, or nearly so. Income from the agency's operations is not turned in to the Treasury Department but is spent directly by the agency. The Tennessee Valley Authority (TVA), for example, uses its revenue from electric power sales to finance its continuing operations and its expansion programs. *See also* PROPRIETARY FUNCTION.

Reynolds v. Sims, 377 U.S. 533 (1964): A landmark decision that under the equal protection clause of the Fourteenth Amendment both houses of a bicameral state legislature must be apportioned on the basis of population. The Court rejected the "federal analogy" that, like Congress, a state legislature could have one house based on a factor other than population. It held that political subdivisions in states are not sovereign entities (on which equal representation of states in the Senate is predicated). Since both houses of a legislature must agree to enact legislation, representation on factors other than population dilutes the vote of citizens living in heavily populated areas. "Legislators represent people, not trees or acres," said the Court, and an apportionment scheme cannot discriminate on the basis of residence any more than it can on the basis of race or economic status. *See also* BICAMERALISM.

Reynolds v. United States, 98 U.S. 145 (1879): Established that religious freedom does not protect a person who commits a crime or an act contrary to accepted public morals. In this case, the Court upheld the enforcement of anti-polygamy laws against Mormons who, prior to 1890, practiced polygamy as a religious doctrine. *See also* FREEDOM OF RELIGION.

Rider   A provision, unlikely to pass on its own merits, added to an important bill so that it will "ride" through the legislative process. Riders become law if the bills to which they are attached are passed. What may be considered a rider by one legislator may be regarded by another as an important and germane amendment to the bill. *See also* ITEM VETO.

Rightist   An individual or group advocating conservative or reactionary political or economic programs, a restriction on the power of the masses, and oligarchical rule. Rightists tend to favor laissez-faire and strong executive power; the extreme right wing supports fascist dictatorships. The term is derived from the common practice in European parliaments of seating conservative parties to the right of the presiding officer. *See also* REACTIONARY.

Right of Petition, *see* Petition (Right of).

Right to Bear Arms   The guarantee in the Second Amendment of the right to keep weapons, recognizing that "A well regulated militia [is] necessary to the security of a free state." Similar provisions are found in many state constitutions. The keeping and use of arms, however, is extensively regulated. Possession of certain types of weapons, such as machine guns or sawed-off shotguns, is prohibited, and registration of some weapons is required.

Right to Counsel   The guarantee in the Sixth Amendment to the Constitution that a defendant in a criminal case have the assistance of an attorney. The Supreme Court has ruled that the national government (*Johnson v. Zerbst,* 304 U.S. 458 [1938]) and state governments (*Gideon v. Wainwright,* 372 U.S. 335 [1963]) must furnish counsel for indigent defendants. An accused must be permitted to confer with counsel prior to interrogation by the police and at any other critical stage in proceedings against him, such as a preliminary hearing, lineup, or appeal. He may waive his right to counsel, but the waiver must be an intelligent one in which the defendant recognizes the consequences of his action. *See also Gideon v. Wainwright, Miranda v. Arizona;* PUBLIC DEFENDER.

Right to Work Law   A law that prohibits making union membership a qualification for employment. Nineteen states have constitutional or statutory provisions that a person may not be compelled to join a union or to remain a member of a union to hold his job. Right to work laws establish the principle of the "open shop." *See also* CLOSED SHOP, UNION SHOP.

Rimland Theory   The theory that emphasizes the rimlands of Europe, the Middle East, Africa, South Asia, and the Far East as the keys to the security of the United States. The rimland theory was developed by the American geographer and geopolitician Nicholas J. Spykman (1893–1943). In his book *The Geography of Peace* (1944), Spykman developed his theory around the concept of the rimlands, which corresponded to the inner crescent of Mackinder, modified and renamed. It was Spykman's thesis that domination of any of these areas by a hostile power threatened the security of the United States because from such a position the encirclement of the New World became a possibility. Spykman's revision of Mackinder's famous dictum became "who controls the Rimland rules Eurasia, who rules Eurasia controls the destinies of the world." *See also* GEOPOLITICS.

Rio Treaty   The Inter-American Treaty of Reciprocal Assistance of 1947 by which twenty-one American republics agreed "that an armed attack by any State against an American State shall be considered as an attack against all the American States . . . " The Rio Treaty was the first mutual security pact entered into by the United States and it became a model for all subsequent ones. The treaty establishes a hemispheric security zone stretching from the North Pole to the South Pole. If an attack occurs within the zone, members agree to consult about collective measures to be undertaken while retaining freedom to act individually. The treaty also includes principles and means by which conflicts between American states can be settled peacefully. Decisions concerning implementation of the treaty are reached through organs of the Organization of American States. *See also* ALLIANCE, ORGANIZATION OF AMERICAN STATES.

Rogers (Foreign Service) Act of 1924   The basic law that established the organization and functions of the Foreign Service as it exists today. The Rogers Act unified the diplomatic and consular services into an integrated Foreign Service, created a career service based on merit, and established the Foreign Service Institute. Subsequent amendments added in the Foreign Service Acts of 1946 and 1949 have sought to professionalize the Service. Additional changes based on the report of the Wriston Committee in 1954 have sought to "democratize" the Service and integrate its personnel with that of the State Department. *See also* DEPARTMENT OF STATE.

Role   The set of behaviors expected of one who occupies a given position in society. Political roles are the expected behaviors associated with positions such as legislator, party leader, voter, or revolutionary, which relate to making and implementing authoritative decisions for a society. The societal expectations that define a particular role are often so generalized (and perhaps ambiguous or contradictory) that the role occupant may have a wide choice of specific behaviors. The occupant's actual behavior is called *role enactment*. Role enactment is affected by the occupant's perceptions of the role expectations of others, his own interpretation of his role, his sensitivity to demands for specific enactments generated by the situation, and his skills and capacity to respond. A group of roles occupied by a single individual is a *role set*. Roles within a set that make contradictory demands upon the individual produce *role conflict*. The actor or occupant of a given role is called *ego;* his role partner, the person in a related role with whom he interacts, is termed *alter*. The study of roles and role behavior has produced a body of thought sometimes called *role theory. See also* BEHAVIOR PATTERN, CONFLICT.

Role of Opposition (Britain)   The function of the principal minority party in the British political system. Her Majesty's Loyal Opposition subjects government programs to constant questioning and scrutiny. It places on the party in power the constant requirement to lead, to explain its policies, to justify its actions, and to remain responsive to the wishes of the public. The role of the opposition is recognized also by the granting of a state salary to the Leader of the shadow cabinet.

Roll-Call Vote, *see* Record Vote.

Rome Treaty, *see* European Atomic Energy Community, European Economic Community.

Roosevelt Court Packing Plan, *see* Supreme Court Packing Plan.

Roth v. United States, 354 U.S. 476 (1957): Excluded obscenity from the area of constitutionally protected speech and press. The Court held that the proper standard to determine obscenity is "whether to the average person, applying contemporary community standards, the dominant theme of the material taken as a whole appeals to prurient interest." *See also* CENSORSHIP.

Royal Colony   One of the three types of colonial governments—charter, proprietary, royal—found in colonial America. Eight colonies were royal colonies. The lower house of the legislature was elected but the upper house and the governor were appointed by the king. Royal governors exercised almost complete authority over the colony through instructions received from England.

Royal Commission (Britain)   A nonpartisan, ad hoc committee appointed by the government to study a major problem of public interest. A royal commission is assigned a task usually so complex and controversial as to require more time and effort than a regular parliamentary committee could devote to it. The commission is composed of members of Parliament, experts, and private citiznes, with a well-known public figure as chairman and a civil servant from the appropriate ministry as secretary. The commission, which can function as long as necessary, operates by holding hearings, taking testimony, consulting experts, gathering data, and sifting evidence. The final report usually contains recommendations for executive and legislative action. Dissenting members of a commission are free to issue one or more minority reports.

Royal Governor, *see* Royal Colony.

Rule 22, *see* Cloture (or Closure), Filibuster, Freedom of Debate.

Rule-Making, *see* Quasi-Legislative.

Rule of Law   An Anglo-American concept that emphasizes the supremacy of the law and restricts the discretionary power of public officials. The rule of law particularly stresses the protection of individual rights from the arbitrary interference of officials. *See also* DEMOCRACY.

Rule of Three, *see* Certification of Eligibles.

Rules Committee   A standing committee of the House of Representatives that can provide special rules under which specific bills will be debated, amended, and considered by the House. The Rules Committee functions as a valve or sifting device to control the flow of bills from House standing committees to the floor for consideration, a power which can be abused by its selective use.

Rules of Warfare   Principles and practices set forth in international law to govern the conduct of nations engaged in hostilities. The rules of warfare initially took the form of customary law, but since the latter half of the nineteenth century they have been based on major multilateral international conventions. Major instruments that set forth the "laws of war" and their main fields of application include: (1) the Declaration of Paris of 1856, which limited sea warfare by abolishing privateering and specifying that a blockade had to be effective to be legally binding; (2) the Geneva Convention of 1864 (revised in 1906), which provided for humane treatment for the wounded in the field; (3) the Hague Convention of 1899, which codified many of the accepted practices of land warfare; (4) the Hague Convention of 1907, which revised the 1899 Convention concerning the rights and duties of belligerents and of neutral states and persons, and proclaimed rules governing such new weapons as dumdum bullets, poisonous gas, and the use of balloons for bombing; (5) the Geneva Conventions of 1929, which provided for decent treatment for prisoners of war and the sick and wounded; (6) the London Protocol of 1936, which limited the use of submarines against merchant ships; and (7) the Geneva Conventions of 1949, which updated rules concerning treatment of prisoners, the sick and wounded, and the protection of civilians. In addition to these and other minor conventions and regional treaties, belligerents in the contemporary world are bound by customary international law and a "law of humanity" forbidding unwarranted cruelty or other actions affronting public morality but not covered by either customary or treaty law. *See also* INTERNATIONAL LAW, WAR.

Runoff Primary   A nominating system used in eleven southern states, in which a second primary election is held between the top two candidates if no candidate in the first primary polls a majority vote. *See also* DIRECT PRIMARY.

Rural Electrification   The governmental program to bring electric service and telephone lines to rural people not serviced by private enterprise. The Roosevelt Administration initiated the electrification program in 1935 with the establishment of the Rural Electrification Administration (REA) by executive order. The telephone program was added by Congress in 1949.

Rush-Bagot Agreement   A treaty between Britain and the United States to demilitarize the American-Canadian border and the Great Lakes in perpetuity. The Rush-Bagot Agreement was part of the peace settlement for the War of 1812. It permits each country to sail on the Great Lakes only those warships required for patrol duty and customs inspection. It was concluded originally in 1817 as an executive agreement and approved the following year as a treaty.

Sabotage Destruction of military, industrial, communication, and transportation facilities in an enemy's homeland or in enemy-occupied territory, carried on by fifth column elements, guerrillas, or professional agents. Acts of sabotage are aimed at reducing production of military equipment, cutting lines of communication, weakening enemy morale, and forcing the enemy to divert large numbers of troops from the fighting fronts to deal with the saboteurs. The term derives from the *sabot* (wooden shoe) that, during the early part of the Industrial Revolution, French workers threw into the new machines to wreck them so as to avoid unemployment. *See also* FIFTH COLUMN, GUERRILLA WAR.

SACEUR, *see* North Atlantic Treaty Organization.

SACLANT, *see* North Atlantic Treaty Organization.

Sales Tax A tax levied upon the sale of commodities, usually paid by the purchaser. The sales tax may apply generally to all commodities or it may be restricted to certain classifications or specific commodities. Typically, the sales tax is levied on retail sales, but in some cases it is imposed on sales by manufacturers and wholesalers as well. Closely related to the sales tax is the "use" tax, which applies to purchases made outside the taxing jurisdiction and is designed to prevent state residents from avoiding the sales tax through out-of-state purchases. Most of the fifty states levy sales taxes from 2 to 6 percent, and an increasing number of cities also levy sales taxes. A value-added tax is a special type of sales tax in which each stage of production and distribution of the product is taxed, with the consumer paying the ultimate cost of all the value-added taxes.

SALT, *see* Strategic Arms Limitation Talks.

Sampling The selection of part of a population or universe as representative of the whole (a population or universe being all members of any class of things that might be studied). Sampling procedures are of two general types—probability and non-probability. In *probability sampling,* which always has an element of randomness, each member of the population has a known probability of being selected. In the truly *random* sample each individual in the population, and each combination of individuals, has an equal chance of being selected; and each is selected independently of the others. Other probability sampling procedures include: *systematic sampling,* in which every nth (for example, every tenth) item in a list or sequence is chosen; *stratified sampling,* which involves initial division of the total population into strata or categories, followed by random or systematic sampling within each category; and *cluster sampling,* in which the population is divided into many groups or "clusters" (census tracts, for example), and the sample is obtained by random selection of clusters. *Nonprobability procedures* include judgmental, quota, and convenience or opportunity sampling. In *judgmental sampling* someone's judgment is used, usually based on past observation, to determine what units ought to be studied. This procedure is used, for example, in the selection of certain "bellwether" voting precincts by pollsters and television networks for use on election night in predicting the outcome of presidential elections. In *quota sampling* subjects are selected by reference to certain qualities whose incidence in the total population is known. The object is to obtain the same distribution of characteristics (for example, sex, race, or age) as occurs in the population as a whole. The *convenience* or *opportunity sample* consists of subjects selected because they are accessible to investigation, regardless of how representative the sample may be. *See also* BIASED SAMPLE, INFERENCE, PROBABILITY, RANDOM, RELIABILITY, SURVEY RESEARCH.

Sanctions (Collective Security)   A collective punitive action involving diplomatic, economic, or military measures against a state. Under the United Nations Charter (Chapter VII), when the Security Council determines that a threat to the peace, breach of the peace, or act of aggression exists, members may be called upon to invoke military or nonmilitary sanctions against the lawbreaking state. Since the adoption of the Uniting for Peace Resolution in 1950, the General Assembly is also empowered to levy sanctions against an aggressor by a two-thirds vote. Sanctions may include such actions as breaking diplomatic relations, embargo or blockade, and the use of force. *See also* COLLECTIVE SECURITY.

Sanctions (International Law)   Penalties meted out as consequences of illegal conduct. Sanctions in international relations involve the collective effort of the international community to force a law-breaking state to comply with international law when diplomatic and legal techniques of dispute settlement have failed. Authority to impose sanctions was embodied in the Covenant of the League of Nations and in the Charter of the United Nations. *See also* SANCTIONS (COLLECTIVE SECURITY).

San Francisco Conference, *see* United Nations Conference on International Organization.

SBA, *see* Small Business Administration.

Scale   An instrument that provides a means of classifying, ranking, or otherwise measuring objects according to their possession of a given characteristic. A scale may be constructed at one of four levels of measurement: nominal, ordinal, interval, and ratio. A *nominal scale* is the lowest level of measurement. It involves the classification of objects into two or more categories, to which nonnumerical labels are assigned. A two-category scale (for example, voter, nonvoter) is called a *dichotomy;* a scale with three or more categories (for example, Catholic, Protestant, Jewish) is a *polytomy.* An *ordinal scale* permits the numerical rank ordering of phenomena according to whether they possess more or less of a characteristic, as, for example, the ranking of governments on a scale from "most democratic" to "least democratic." *Interval* and *ratio scales* are based on some unit of measurement that permits not only the ranking of objects but also the measurement of distances between them. Technically, a ratio scale has an absolute zero point, while an interval scale need not have one. In the absence of a nonarbitrary (absolute) zero point, as in the case of a thermometer quantities on a scale can be added or subtracted but not appropriately multiplied or divided, or expressed as a ratio of one another (for example, twice as cold, or one third as hot). In practice most interval scales used by political scientists are also ratio scales, so the difference is not often of importance. *See also* ATTITUDE SCALING, GUTTMAN SCALE, QUANTIFICATION, RELIABILITY, SEMANTIC DIFFERENTIAL, SOCIOMETRY, TESTING.

Scales v. United States, 367 U.S. 203 (1961): Sustained that portion of the Smith Act of 1940 that makes it a crime to be a member of an organization that advocates overthrow of the government by force if one knows this to be the purpose of the organization. The Court drew a distinction between active membership and mere membership, noting that only active membership in a party that has illegal aims is not constitutionally protected. *See also* ALIEN REGISTRATION ACT.

Scaling, *see* Attitude Scaling, Scale.

Schedules A, B, and C   Three classes of positions in the federal service that are filled without the usual competitive examinations. Schedule A positions are those for which no practical examination is possible, such as federal attorneys. Schedule B positions are filled by noncompetitive examination, which includes a survey and evaluation of a candidate's experience and qualifications. Schedule C includes positions of a confidential and policy-making character. *See also* CLASSIFIED SERVICE.

Schenck v. United States, 249 U.S. 47 (1919): Upheld a conviction against Schenck, who had circulated materials urging men to resist the call to military service during World War I. The Court held that this was a justified infringement upon the freedoms of speech and press in view of the wartime emergency. *See also* FREEDOM OF SPEECH.

School District   A governmental unit for the maintenance of schools. In about half the states, school districts are administratively and financially independent and do not follow township, city, or county lines. The town or township plan is dominant in New England and the county plan in the South. In Delaware and Hawaii, the entire state comprises one school district. Typically, school districts are governed by elective boards, which choose a superintendent to administer the system. In some areas, the school is part of city government, and the board is selected by the mayor or council. Approximately one-fifth of all local units of government are school districts and they account for almost one-half of all local governmental expenditures. *See also* BOARD OF EDUCATION.

School District of Abington Township v. Schempp, 374 U.S. 203 (1963): Held devotional Bible reading and/or the recitation of the Lord's Prayer in public schools to be an unconstitutional violation of the establishment clause of the First Amendment as applied to the states through the Fourteenth Amendment. The Court reasoned that while the study of religion could be part of a school curriculum, an organ of government (the public school) could not be used for essentially religious purposes.

The Court held that the fact that students could excuse themselves from the devotional exercises was irrelevant, since the exercises in themselves constituted an establishment of religion. "In the relationship between man and religion," said the Court, "the state is firmly committed to a position of neutrality." *See also* SEPARATION OF CHURCH AND STATE.

Science   A systematized body of knowledge; or, the methods and assumptions characterizing the search for verifiable, transmissible knowledge. Science assumes that the world of experience and observation is objectively knowable, that recurring relationships in it are discoverable, and that reliable knowledge about these relationships can be obtained through careful observation, theorizing, and testing of hypotheses. The function of science is to develop theory (statements about relationships between variables) that will explain and, hopefully, permit prediction of events in the observable world. *Pure science* is concerned with knowledge for its own sake; *applied science* aims at using scientific knowledge to achieve particular human ends. Many of the methods and perspectives developed in the natural and social sciences have been applied to political science. *See also* BEHAVIORALISM, INTERSUBJECTIVITY, METHODOLOGY, POLITICAL SCIENCE, SCIENTIFIC METHOD, SOCIAL SCIENCE, THEORY.

Scientific Approach (Political Science), *see* Behavioralism.

Scientific Management, *see* Management Science.

Scientific Method   An approach to the discovery of verifiable, transmissible knowledge. Scientific method is sometimes treated as a mood or posture toward scholarly inquiry, generally connoting an unbiased search for truth using methods replicable by others who may wish to verify conclusions. Some writers have listed series of steps or operations regarded as essential to the scientific method, while others have argued that scientific method does not imply any particular kind or sequence of procedures since scientists, in fact, use a variety of different techniques and methods. Although the steps or procedures advocated by the former tend to vary somewhat in their detail, they usually embrace the following: (1) the clear identification of a research problem, (2) the formulation of a hypothesis expressing a relationship between variables, (3) careful deductive reasoning upon the hypothesis to explore its implications for the problem and its logical adequacy, (4) the gathering of data for empirical testing of the hypothesis, (5) quantitative and qualitative analysis of the data, and (6) acceptance, rejection, or reformulation of the hypothesis. *See also* BEHAVIORALISM, DATA, DEDUCTION, EMPIRICISM, HYPOTHESIS, INDUCTION, METHODOLOGY, RESEARCH, RESEARCH DESIGN, SCIENCE, THEORY, VARIABLE.

Scientific Socialism, *see* Communism.

Seabed Treaty   An agreement reached in 1970 to ban nuclear weapons from the seabed outside any state's twelve-mile territorial waters. The Seabed Treaty was endorsed by the Twenty-Fifth General Assembly and was initially signed by sixty-three nations, including three nuclear powers—the United States, Britain, and the Soviet Union. The Treaty, which took effect after twenty-two nations ratified it, is weakened by the fact that it does not prohibit emplacement of nuclear weapons within the twelve-mile limits of signatory states, and because it lacks the support of two nuclear states, France and the People's Republic of China. The seabeds, which cover 70 percent of the earth's surface, are added to those other areas from which nuclear weapons or tests are excluded by treaty, including the seas, the atmosphere, outer space, non-nuclear states, Antarctica, and Latin America. *See also* DENUCLEARIZATION.

Sea Power Theory   The theory that posits naval power as the key to world power. Sea power as the basis for a geopolitical theory was first developed by an American naval officer, Admiral Alfred Thayer Mahan (1840–1914), through his perception that the seas of the world connected landmasses rather than separated them. The acquisition and defense of overseas empires, therefore, was dependent upon the ability to control the sea. Central features of Mahan's work include: (1) a scholarly analysis of British naval history that explained Britain's role as a world power; (2) a dedication to the idea of an American world mission to be carried out through overseas expansion; and (3) a rationalization of imperialism on the assumption that countries cannot stand still spatially, but must expand or decline. *See also* GEOPOLITICS.

Search and Seizure   Methods by which police officers gather evidence and make arrests. The Fourth Amendment prohibits "unreasonable" searches and seizures. Under ordinary or "reasonable" circumstances, a search warrant must be secured from a judge or magistrate. This is a written order issued under oath; it describes the place to be searched and the person or things to be seized. A warrant is not essential if it can be shown that time or circumstances did not reasonably permit securing it. Evidence gathered through illegal or unreasonable means is not admissible in federal trials nor, under the Fourteenth Amendment, in state trials (*Weeks v. United States*, 232 U.S. 383 [1914], *Mapp v. Ohio*, 367 U.S. 643 [1961]). *See also Mapp v. Ohio*, WIRETAPPING, ARREST WARRANT.

Search Warrant, *see* Search and Seizure.

SEATO, *see* Southeast Asia Treaty Organization.

SEATO Treaty, *see* Southeast Asia Collective Defense Treaty.

SEC, *see* Securities and Exchange Commission.

Secession, *see* Nullification.

Secondary Group, *see* Group.

Second Development Decade   A program adopted by the United Nations General Assembly for the 1970s to foster progress toward modernization in the developing countries. The Second, like the First Development Decade of the 1960s, is aimed at dramatizing, mobilizing, and sustaining support for the measures required of both developed and developing countries to accelerate progress in the latter towards self-sustaining economic growth and social advancement. Growth targets set by the program include an annual 6 percent GNP rate and a 3.5 percent per capita rate of growth for developing countries. For the developed countries, the program established a goal of contributions of financial aid amounting to 1 percent of each nation's GNP, with 75 percent contributed by governments and the rest by private investors. *See also* FOREIGN AID.

Secretariat   An organized body of officials and civil servants who have the responsibility of fulfilling administrative, secretarial, and housekeeping functions for an international organization. The United Nations Secretariat is one of the six major organs of the world organization. Its formal structure includes a Secretary-General and eight Assistant Secretaries-General, each of the latter heading a major Department (Security, Economic, Social, Trusteeship, Legal, Information, General Services, and Administrative and Financial). *See also* SECRETARY-GENERAL.

Secretariat of the Central Committee (Soviet Union)   The chief administrative organ of the Communist party. The Secretariat exercises decision-making power second only to that of the Politburo, and drafts plans and policy proposals for that body. It is headed by a General Secretary (previously First Secretary) and from five to ten Secretaries. These men are leaders of the party with extensive cross-membership in the Politburo. Nominally elected by the Central Committee, they are in fact chosen by top party leaders. Their supervision of every phase of Soviet life is carried on through administrative staffs or sections that, in organization, resemble the ministries of a government. The Central Apparatus, which services the upper echelon of party agencies, is something of a proving ground for younger party members likely to rise to positions of prominence.

Secretary   The title of most of the heads of the major executive departments in the national government and a few major state officials. *See also* DEPARTMENT, CABINET.

Secretary-General   The chief administrative officer of the United Nations who heads the Secretariat. The Secretary-General is chosen by the General Assembly, upon recommendation by the Security Council, for five-year terms. The United Nations Charter, in an attempt to strengthen the office of Secretary-General over its League of Nations predecessor, gave him authority to place security questions before the Security Council. *See also* SECRETARIAT.

Secretary of State   The leading Cabinet officer, who heads the Department of State and is charged with responsibility for formulating policies and conducting relations with foreign states. The Secretary of State has been recognized by statute as first o.

the Cabinet officials in the line of succession to the presidency following the Vice President, Speaker, and President pro tempore. His responsibilities include the direction and supervision of policy-making and administrative functions vested in the State Department in Washington, D.C., the diplomatic and consular services, and special missions and agencies abroad. *See also* DEPARTMENT OF STATE.

Secretary of State (State) A state official elected by popular vote in thirty-nine states and appointed by the governor or legislature in others. His major duties include the preservation of official documents, administration of elections, issuance of business licenses and certificates of incorporation, and registration and issuance of motor vehicle licenses. He is also keeper of the state seal.

Secret Service A law-enforcement division of the Treasury Department, which has full responsibility for protecting the life and security of the President and his family. The Secret Service also performs security functions concerned with treasury matters, and in 1970 it was assigned new responsibilities for protecting foreign dignitaries visiting the United States, and for guarding foreign embassies in Washington, D.C.

Sectionalism The influence of local or regional loyalties on state or national elections, issues, or party unity.

Securities and Exchange Commission (SEC) A five-member independent regulatory commission established by the Securities Exchange Act of 1934 to regulate the buying and selling of securities (stocks, bonds, and so forth). Commissioners are appointed by the President, with the Senate's approval, for five-year terms. In addition to the Act of 1934, the SEC enforces the Securities Act of 1933, which compels full disclosure of information concerning new security issues, and the Public Utility Holding Company Act of 1935 under which the SEC tries to limit mergers and combinations of utility companies. *See also* MARGIN.

Security Council One of the six major organs of the United Nations, which was given primary responsibility for maintaining peace and security in the world. There are five permanent members—Britain, China, France, Soviet Union, and the United States— and ten nonpermanent members elected by the General Assembly for two-year periods, five chosen each year. Procedural and substantive decisions are made by an affirmative vote of nine members but, in the latter case, a negative vote cast by any permanent member constitutes a veto and stops all action. When considering peaceful settlement measures, a Council member that is a party to the dispute must abstain from voting. Nations that are not members of the Council may be invited to participate without a vote in Council deliberations if they are involved in a dispute being considered. Chapter VII of the Charter gives the Security Council the responsibility to "determine the existence of any threat to the peace, breach of the peace, or act of aggression. . . . " The Council can make recommendations or take enforcement action to restore peace and security. *See also* COLLECTIVE SECURITY.

Security Council Veto, *see* Veto (International Organization).

Security Risk, *see* Loyalty-Security Programs.

Sedition   Actions that incite rebellion or discontent against duly established government. Espionage, sabotage, or attempts to overthrow the government constitute sedition, as does advocacy by publication or speech to accomplish these goals. The Sedition Acts of 1798 and 1918 put severe limitations on mere criticism of the government. Recent sedition legislation has been aimed at outlawing Communist conspiracies and advocacy of doctrines aimed at overthrow of government by force. *See also* ALIEN AND SEDITION LAWS, SMITH ACT, INTERNAL SECURITY ACT, COMMUNIST CONTROL ACT, *Dennis v. United States.*

Segregation   The separation of the white and black races in public and private facilities. Laws requiring the segregation of the races (Jim Crow laws) have been or are still on the statute books of several states. In 1896, the Supreme Court upheld such laws under the "separate but equal" doctrine whereby the Negro could be segregated if he were provided with equal facilities (*Plessy v. Ferguson,* 163 U.S. 537). Under this doctrine, a wide pattern of segregation developed in schools, transportation, recreation, and housing. Beginning in the 1940s, the Supreme Court began to weaken the separate but equal doctrine by insisting that the facilities provided for Negroes, particularly in education, be equal, indeed. Finally, in 1954, the Supreme Court struck down the separate but equal formula, holding that segregation based on color denied the equal protection of the laws (*Brown v. Board of Education of Topeka,* 347 U.S. 483). *See also Plessy v. Ferguson, Brown v. Board of Education of Topeka,* CIVIL RIGHTS ACTS, *Swann v. Charlotte.*

Select Committee   A legislative committee established for a limited time period and for a special purpose. Select committees may be created by either house or may include members from both houses (joint committee).

Selective Draft Law Cases, 245 U.S. 366 (1918): Upheld the constitutional authority of Congress to draft men into the military forces. The Supreme Court rejected the argument that conscription is "involuntary servitude" in violation of the Thirteenth Amendment, holding that such service by the citizen was "his supreme and noble duty." *See also* CONSCIENTIOUS OBJECTOR, SELECTIVE SERVICE.

Selective Service   The conscription system under which the national government drafts men for service in the armed forces. Selective service is based on the constitutional provisions which give Congress the powers necessary "to raise" armies and "to provide" a navy. *See also Selective Draft Law Cases,* CONSCIENTIOUS OBJECTOR.

Self-Determination, *see* National Self-Determination.

Self-incrimination   Testimony by a person that reveals facts that may result in a criminal prosecution against him. The Fifth Amendment of the Constitution provides that no person "shall be compelled in any criminal case to be a witness against himself." Though originally applied to persons on trial, the concept has been extended to cover testimony before legislative committees or executive agencies. A person may not refuse to testify in order to protect another person, nor because his answers might bring disgrace upon himself. The guarantee extends only to testimony that might involve the person himself in a criminal prosecution. A person who has been given immunity or a pardon, or who has already been convicted of the particular offense (so that he may not be tried again), may not refuse to testify. No unfavorable inferences may legally be drawn from a refusal to testify. The Fifth Amendment guarantee against self-incrimination applies with equal force to both state and federal proceedings (*Malloy v. Hogan*, 378 U.S. 1 [1964]). *See also Malloy v. Hogan, Miranda v. Arizona,* IMMUNITY.

Semantic Differential   A technique for measuring the connotative meaning that people assign to concepts. The semantic differential consists of several *scales* and one or more *concepts* to be rated on the scales. Each scale consists of a pair of polar opposite adjectives (good–bad, beautiful–ugly, and the like) arranged to permit a seven-point (sometimes five- or nine-point) rating from one pole to the other. The concepts may be anything relevant to a particular research problem—issue concepts like foreign aid and government spending, or person concepts like Richard Nixon or Franklin Roosevelt. The paired adjective scales are supposed to reflect underlying dimensions or factors of connotative meaning. Charles E. Osgood, developer of the technique, found three such basic dimensions, which he labeled *evaluative* (as indicated by pairs such as good–bad, clean–dirty), *potency* (strong–weak, large–small, and so forth), and *activity* (active–passive, fast–slow, and so forth) factors. By asking subjects to rate relevant concepts on the bipolar adjective scales and scoring their responses, the investigator can obtain numerical indexes of the connotations attached by the subjects to the various concepts. *See also* ATTITUDE, ATTITUDE SCALING, SCALE.

Senate   The upper house of the United States Congress and of forty-nine state legislatures. Representation in the United States Senate is based on the principle of state equality, and the Constitution specifies that no state may be deprived of its equal representation in the Senate without its consent. The Senate is comprised of one hundred Senators from fifty states. Most state senates have fewer than fifty members. The Vice President is the presiding officer of the Senate; in the state legislatures, the lieutenant governor normally presides. In the absence of a presiding officer, a president pro tempore elected from the membership assumes that role. *See also* HOUSE OF REPRESENTATIVES.

Senate Approval, *see* Advice and Consent.

Senate Foreign Relations Committee, *see* Foreign Relations Committee.

Senate (France) The upper house or second chamber of the bicameral French Parliament. One third of the 273 senators are elected every three years for nine-year terms. Senators must be at least thirty-five years old. They are elected indirectly by electoral colleges in the various departments. Densely populated areas elect senators by a list system. Smaller departments (administrative districts) with four or less senators use the two-ballot method, by which candidates receiving a majority on the first ballot are elected. Remaining seats are filled the same day by plurality voting on a second ballot. The indirect method of election, designed as a counterfoil to direct popular election of the Assembly, produces a rural rather than an urban political orientation in the Senate. Election success is also more dependent on party loyalty, reputation, and personal connections than in election to the Assembly. The Senate is technically equal in power with the Assembly and, in theory, neither can override the other. In practice, however, an impasse between the houses throws the initiative to the government. If the executive decides to do nothing, the bill is killed by being shuttled back and forth between the two houses. Alternatively, if the government wants the bill enacted, it can manipulate a conference committee procedure which forces reconsideration in both houses on terms established by the government. If necessary, it can maneuver an Assembly vote that overrides the Senate. Unlike the Assembly, the Senate has no power to bring down a government. The President of the Senate may temporarily exercise the duties of the President of the Republic when a vacancy occurs.

Senate (Italy), *see* Parliament (Italy).

Senator A member of the United States Senate or of the upper house in state legislatures. United States senators have been directly elected by the people of their respective states since the adoption of the Seventeenth Amendment in 1913. The term of office is six years, with one-third of the Senate seats up for election every two years. Vacancies are usually filled by appointment by the state's governor, although the legislature may provide for a special election. The Constitution provides that a senator must be at least thirty years of age, a citizen for nine years, and a resident of the state from which he is elected. In the state legislatures, senators are in all cases elected by the people, usually for four years. *See also* REPRESENTATIVE, SEVENTEENTH AMENDMENT.

Senatorial Campaign Committees, *see* Congressional and Senatorial Campaign Committees.

Senatorial Courtesy An unwritten agreement among senators that requires the President to confer with the senator or senators of his party from a state before he makes a nomination to fill a federal office located in that state. The Senate will almost invariably reject a presidential nominee when the senator involved raises a personal objection. When neither senator of a state is of the President's party, the President is apt to consult state party leaders. *See also* CONFIRMATION.

Seniority Rule A custom nearly always followed in both houses of Congress of awarding chairmanships of committees to the majority party member who has the longest number of years of continuous service on the committee. Each party, majority and minority alike, strictly lists its members on the various committees according to the seniority rule. When a high-ranking member leaves the committee, all members of that party move up one notch on the seniority list. Many state legislatures follow the seniority rule, although other political and personal factors may modify or override seniority. *See also* COMMITTEE CHAIRMAN, RANKING MEMBER.

Separate but Equal Doctrine, *see* Segregation.

Separation from Service Termination of employment in the classified service. Separation may be voluntary, as by resignation, or may be the result of retirement laws, a reduction in force, or disciplinary action for conduct unbecoming a public employee. *See also* TENURE.

Separation of Church and State A basic principle of American government that prohibits the mingling of church and state. The principle rests on the First Amendment clause forbidding the passage of any law "respecting an establishment of religion." In a series of controversial cases, the Supreme Court has held that the state must be committed to a position of neutrality and may neither advance nor retard religion. No public funds may be expended on behalf of any church nor may the government favor one church over another. Public schools may not be used for sectarian religious observances and official requirements for Bible reading or prayer recitals are forbidden. Laws that have a predominantly secular effect, such as public bus transportation for parochial schools or Sunday closing laws, have been upheld. The permissible extent of public aid to church-related schools remains, however, unresolved. The national government, under the Elementary and Secondary Education Act of 1965, and many state governments provide for aid to parochial schools. In 1971, the Supreme Court struck down state programs that paid the salaries of teachers in church-related schools, for instruction in nonreligious subjects, as "excessive entanglement between government and religion" (*Lemon v. Kurtzman,* 403 U.S. 602). At the same time, however, the Court upheld federal construction grants to church-related colleges (*Tilton v. Richardson,* 403 U.S. 672). The distinction was made by the Court on the grounds that precollege parochial schools are more involved in religious indoctrination, and that the state programs would involve continuing controversy over public support. *See also* Everson v. Board of Education of Ewing Township, School District of Abington Township v. Schempp, Zorach v. Clauson, ELEMENTARY AND SECONDARY EDUCATION ACT.

Separation of Powers A major principle of American government whereby power is distributed among three branches of government—the legislative, the executive, and the judicial. The officials of each branch are selected by different procedures, have different terms of office, and are independent of one another. The separation is not complete, in that each branch participates in the functions of the other through a system of checks and balances. The separation, however, serves to ensure that the same person or group will not make the law, enforce the law, and interpret and apply the law. *See also* CHECKS AND BALANCES.

Session   The period during which a legislative body assembles and carries on its regular business. Each Congress has two regular sessions based on the requirement in the Constitution that Congress assemble at least once each year. In addition, Congress may be summoned into special session by the President. The first session of a Congress usually begins on January 3 of odd-numbered years, with the start of the terms of all representatives and one-third of the senators. The second session begins on January 3 of even-numbered years. The Congress that assembles in January 1973, for example, is the Ninety-third Congress, first session. Adjournment is left up to Congress, although the Constitution provides that if the two houses cannot agree on a date, the President may adjourn them at his discretion. No President has exercised this authority. In the states, most legislatures convene in regular session every two years, although many have regular annual sessions. Most state constitutions limit the length of legislative sessions either by specifying the number of days or by cutting off pay and allowances for legislators after a certain date. *See also* SPECIAL SESSION, TWENTIETH AMENDMENT.

Set   Any defined collection, category, group, or class of things. A set must be defined so that it is possible to tell which things belong and which do not. This can be done by *listing* all of the objects in the set, or by a *rule* stating criteria for membership in the set. In political science research definition by rule is the more common. A part or sample of a set is known as a *subset*. Thus, Democrats and Republicans may be regarded as *subsets* of a larger *set* of people having political preferences. The *universal set* consists of all the elements of the class being examined, from which any subsets will be drawn. A set without any members in it is an *empty set* or *null set*. *Set theory* is a branch of mathematics devoted to the manipulation of numerical sets. *See also* CLASSIFICATION, VARIABLE.

Set Theory, *see* Set.

Seventeenth Amendment   An amendment to the Constitution, adopted in 1913, that provides for the direct election of United States senators. The Amendment changes those sections of Article I that authorized senators to be chosen by the legislatures of the states. It also provides that, when a vacancy occurs, the legislature may authorize the governor to make a temporary appointment until an election can be held. Most legislatures have so authorized their governors. *See also* SENATOR.

Seventh Amendment   A part of the Bill of Rights that guarantees the preservation of the right to a jury trial in a suit at common law where the value in controversy exceeds $20. It also provides that facts tried by the jury may not be reexamined in any court except in accordance with common law rules.

Severance Tax   A tax levied upon natural resources at the time they are taken from the land or water.

Shadow Cabinet, *see* Cabinet (Britian).

SHAPE, *see* North Atlantic Treaty Organization.

Shared Tax, *see* Revenue Sharing.

Shays' Rebellion   An armed revolt by farmers in western Massachusetts in 1786-1787, seeking relief from debts and possible foreclosures of mortgages. Led by Daniel Shays, a Revolutionary War officer, the group prevented judges from hearing mortgage foreclosure cases and attempted to capture an arsenal. They were repelled by the state militia.

Sheriff   The chief law enforcement officer of a county, an elective position in all the states except Rhode Island. His duties pertain to both civil and criminal actions. In addition to general law enforcement, the sheriff, as an officer of the court, serves papers, enforces orders, maintains the jail, and collects taxes, with particular functions varying from state to state. In many jurisdictions, the sheriff is paid through fees for each job performed rather than on a regular salary basis. Law-enforcement activities are generally limited to areas outside cities and to patrol on county highways.

Sherman Antitrust Act of 1890   The basic federal antimonopoly law that forbids "every contract, combination . . . or conspiracy in the restraint of trade or commerce." Enforcement of the Act is provided through criminal penalties, civil suit action with triple damages to injured parties, injunction, and seizure of property. Responsibility for enforcement is vested in the Antitrust Division of the Department of Justice. *See also* ANTITRUST DIVISION, ANTITRUST LAWS.

Short Ballot   A ballot containing relatively few offices to be filled by election. It is differentiated from the long ballot, which contains numerous elective offices, especially in the executive and judicial branches. Several states, such as New Jersey and Alaska, have reduced the number of statewide elected executive officials to governor and lieutenant governor and have considerably cut down the number of judicial elections. The national election ballot is already a "short" one, providing for the casting of a single vote for President and Vice President, the election of a single representative, and in two out of three elections, of a senator. The longest ballots, typically, are found on the local government level, especially in the county. *See also* LONG BALLOT.

Simple Majority, *see* Absolute Majority.

Simple Resolution   A measure adopted by one chamber of a legislative body. It does not require approval either by the other house or by the President. Simple resolutions are designated either "H Res" or "S Res." *See also* CONCURRENT RESOLUTION, JOINT RESOLUTION.

Simulation   The reproduction, in a laboratory or experimental situation, of selected aspects of a real or hypothetical system. In political simulations the usual model is a decision-making system. Political simulations are usually simplified or scaled-down representations of political behavior, although the simulations of a small group situation, such as a jury, may approach the complexity of reality. Some simulations involve only human interaction; others may be done by computer; and some combine human interaction with programmed features to be executed by a computer (man–machine simulation) or a staff separate from the participants. Computer simulation requires complete specification of the relevant variables and decision rules. With human participants, at least some of the rules governing interplay of model components are left unspecified. If only human participants are involved, the technique is usually called *gaming*. (Gaming, as a technique, should not be equated with *game theory*, which deals with substance rather than method. Simulation is sometimes used to develop game theory.) *See also* GAME THEORY.

Sine Die, *see* Adjournment.

Single-member District   An electoral district from which a single legislator is chosen, usually by a plurality vote. The single-member district voting system is used in the United States and Britain, and differs from the multimember districts typical of most continental European electoral systems based on proportional representation. *See also* PROPORTIONAL REPRESENTATION, CUMULATIVE VOTING, TWO-PARTY SYSTEM.

Situational Factors   The international and national variables considered by decision makers when making foreign policy. Situational factors include: (1) the general international setting or environment, including the attitudes, actions, and national interest considerations of policy officials in other states; (2) the relative power or capability of the state as computed by its decision makers; and (3) the specific actions and reactions undertaken by other states related to the policy decision and its execution. *See also* CAPABILITY ANALYSIS, FOREIGN POLICY.

Sixteenth Amendment   An amendment to the Constitution, adopted in 1913, that grants Congress the power to levy taxes on incomes without apportioning them among the states according to population. The individual income tax levied by the national government is based on the power granted by this Amendment. *See also* INCOME TAX, *Pollock v. Farmers Loan and Trust Co..*

Sixth Amendment   A part of the Bill of Rights that stipulates the basic requirements of procedural due process in federal criminal trials. These include a speedy and public trial, an impartial jury, trial in the area where the crime was committed, notice of the charges, the right to confront witnesses and to obtain favorable witnesses, and the right to counsel. All have been made binding on the states through the due process clause of the Fourteenth Amendment. *See also* TRIAL, JURY, VENUE, WITNESS, RIGHT TO COUNSEL, CONFRONTATION CLAUSE.

Size (Geographic Power Factor) The effect on the power equation of the relationship between the surface areas of states. Enormous variations in size exist among the more than 140 states of the world, ranging from the Soviet Union with approximately 8.6 million square miles to the Vatican with 108.7 acres. China, Canada, and the United States range from 3.8 to 3.6 million square miles. Brazil, Australia, India, and Argentina each have over 1 million square miles. There are fifty-four states in the range from 100,000 to 1,000,000 square miles, thirty from 40,000 to 100,000, more than thirty from 3000 to 40,000, and about twenty with less than 3000 square miles.

Slander, *see* Libel and Slander.

Slaughterhouse Cases, *see* Privileges and Immunities.

Slavery, *see* Involuntary Servitude, *Jones v. Mayer,* Thirteenth Amendment.

Slum Clearance, *see* Urban Renewal.

Small Business Administration (SBA) An independent agency, headed by an Administrator, established to make loans to small businesses and to assist them in obtaining government contracts. The SBA was given temporary status by Congress in 1953, and was expanded and made a permanent agency in 1958. Some of its operations since 1961 have been carried on through small-business investment companies around the nation. Principal functions of SBA include financing plant expansion and modernization, aiding disaster victims, helping businessmen to cut through red tape to secure government procurement contracts, and giving managerial advice to small firms. Applicants for loans must show they have been turned down by private banks.

Small Claims Court A court found in many large cities to expedite minor cases at low cost. Disputes over such issues as fuel or grocery bills or wages are quickly settled by a judge.

Small Group Theory, *see* Group Theory.

Smith Act, *see* Alien Registration Act of 1940.

Smith-Lever Act of 1914, *see* County Agent.

Smith-Mundt Act of 1948, *see* Cultural Exchange (United States).

Smith v. Allwright, 321 U.S. 649 (1944): Established, finally and conclusively, that the "white primary" was a violation of the Fifteenth Amendment. The case arose over the denial of a ballot to Smith, a Negro resident of Houston, Texas, in the Democratic primary of 1940 for nominating candidates for congressional and state offices. The Court recognized that its earlier decision, allowing the exclusion of blacks from "private" party primaries, in the case *Grovey v. Townsend,* 295 U.S. 45 (1935), had been "in error." The Court reasoned that the party was actually performing a state function in holding a primary election and was not acting as a private group. Moreover, the Court pointed out that a primary is an integral part of the election process.

Smoot-Hawley Tariff Act of 1930   An act that imposed extremely high tariff duties on agricultural and industrial imports to the United States. Passage of the bill in Congress resulted from the political pressures exerted by numerous special-interest groups seeking protection. President Herbert Hoover, petitioned by leading economists to veto the bill, permitted it to become law without his signature although personally opposed to it. *See also* PROTECTIONISM.

Smyth v. Ames, 169 U.S. 466 (1898): Declared, in an historic rate-making case, that government regulatory agencies must consider a number of factors in fixing rates, rather than a single one. The facts in the case involved a dispute over rate-setting for Nebraska railroads, in which the governmental agency based its formula chiefly on "reproduction cost," and the railroads demanded that the rate base be "original cost." The Court held that many factors should be considered in determining fair value, including original cost, cost of improvements, value of securities, reproduction cost, earning capacity, and operating expenses. *See also* RATE-MAKING.

Social and Rehabilitation Service, *see* Department of Health, Education, and Welfare, Aid to Families with Dependent Children, Aid to the Blind, Aid to the Totally and Permanently Disabled.

Social Class, *see* Social Stratification.

Social Cohesion   The degree of unity within a national society. Social cohesion depends upon the relationship among economic, social, and religious groups, the extent to which basic values are shared, common nationalistic and ideological impulses, and the nature of social organization. *See also* CONSENSUS OF VALUES.

Social Contract, *see* Contract Theory.

Social Control   The maintenance of order and stability in a society through sanctions that produce conformity to social norms. Social control is achieved through a variety of mechanisms, both governmental and nongovernmental. These may include ethical and religious sanctions, economic rewards and deprivations, social approval and ostracism, and the threat or use of physical force. *See also* COERCION, LEGITIMACY, SOCIAL SYSTEM, STABILITY.

Social Engineering   The application of social science theories to problems of social organization and behavior with the object of improving society. Social engineering combines values or goals, which are not scientifically derived, with the insights of social science, which presumably can suggest practical ways to realize the values and achieve the goals. It may be regarded as social reform with at least a minimal social science basis. Social engineering commonly involves the attempt either to reform government or to use government as an instrument to reform society. *See also* COST-BENEFIT ANALYSIS, ENDS-MEANS ANALYSIS, ENGINEERING THEORY, POLICY SCIENCES.

Socialism   A doctrine that advocates economic collectivism through governmental or industrial group ownership of the means of production and distribution of goods. Its basic aims are to replace competition for profit with cooperation and social responsibility, and to secure a more equitable distribution of income and opportunity. Though these aims are common to all socialists, a wide variety of schools of thought have arisen, distinguished mainly by their approaches to the problem of how best to achieve socialism. These vary from the peaceful and democratic ideas of utopian and Christian socialists to the aggressive, and sometimes violent, approaches of anarchists and Communists. *See also* DEMOCRATIC SOCIALISM, CONVERGENCE THEORY.

Socialist Program (Communist Theory)   The basic changes to be undertaken, following a Communist revolution, that would transform society from capitalism to socialism and prepare the way for transition into the final classless, stateless stage of pure communism. The main objectives of the Socialist program set forth by Marx in the *Communist Manifesto* of 1848 include: (1) abolition of all private ownership of land; (2) a sharply progressive income tax; (3) abrogation of all inheritance rights; (4) state control of all banking and credit; (5) state ownership and operation of all communication and transport; (6) collectivization of agriculture and creation of industrial armies; (7) equal obligation for all to work; (8) abolition of child labor; and (9) free education for all children in public schools. The Socialist program, according to Communist theorists, is to be implemented during the period of transition under the dictatorship of the proletariat.

Socialization, *see* Political Socialization.

Social Matrix   The web of social relationships within which political behavior occurs. The idea of a social matrix implies that political interactions have their origin in, and are shaped by, the social setting. Political roles, thus, are to be examined in relationship to other social roles and to the group and class structure of society. *See* *also* ENVIRONMENT, POLITICAL SOCIOLOGY, SOCIAL STRATIFICATION, SOCIAL SYSTEM, SOCIETY.

Social Mobility, *see* Social Stratification.

Social Pluralism, *see* Pluralism.

Social Science   The application of scientific methods to the study of human behavior, the body of knowledge so produced, or the disciplines, individually or collectively, engaged in such inquiry. Social science is sometimes used more broadly to mean the study of man's social relations, with emphasis on "social" rather than "science." Used in the first sense, social science is essentially synonymous with the newer term, *behavioral science.* Although social science may be regarded as embodying an interdisciplinary approach to knowledge, most scholars have their intellectual base in one of the several social science disciplines—anthropology, sociology, psychology, economics, or political science. History, geography, law, and public administration are sometimes regarded as social sciences. *See also* POLITICAL SCIENCE, SCIENCE, SCIENTIFIC METHOD.

Social Security Act of 1935   The basic social welfare legislation embodying social insurance, public assistance, and child health and welfare services. Social insurance programs include Old-Age, Survivors, and Disability Insurance, Medicare, and unemployment insurance. Public assistance is provided under the categorical assistance program to the needy aged, blind, permanently and totally disabled, and to dependent children. Child health and welfare services are provided under the Act for maternal care, crippled children, and general child welfare services. With the exception of the Old-Age, Survivors, and Disability Insurance and Medicare programs, which are financed and administered exclusively by the national government, all others are administered by the states under grants-in-aid from the national government. Responsibility for overall supervision rests with the Department of Health, Education, and Welfare. In addition, the Social Security Act provides for widespread public health services through grants to the states under supervision of the Public Health Service in the Department of Health, Education, and Welfare. *See also* SOCIAL SECURITY CASES.

Social Security Administration, *see* Department of Health, Education, and Welfare.

Social Security Cases: Two cases in which the Supreme Court upheld the Social Security Act of 1935. In *Steward Machine Co. v. Davis,* 301 U.S. 548 (1937), the Court upheld the unemployment insurance feature of the Act. The Court reasoned that the tax for relief of the unemployed was within the power of Congress to provide for the national welfare and that the states were not coerced to join the plan. In *Helvering v. Davis,* 301 U.S. 619 (1937), decided the same day, the Court upheld the Old-Age, Survivors, and Disability Insurance provisions. The Court recognized the broad power of Congress to promote the general welfare and maintained that the scope of the general welfare was for Congress to determine. The Court denied that the tax on payrolls for Old-Age, Survivors, and Disability Insurance benefited only a particular class of persons or invaded the powers of the states. *See also* SOCIAL SECURITY ACT.

Social Stratification   The division of society into classes or strata, hierarchically ranked according to perceived differences in wealth, prestige, or other social characteristics. Social stratification reflects the uneven distribution among the population of things that a society values. It is produced by people's perceptions of differences in status between broad groups or strata of people, rather than by perceptions of individual differences. The bases of social stratification may differ over time and from one society to another. They include various combinations of such factors as power, property ownership, income, education, religion, inherited position, race, altruism and morality, and associational connections. Movement of individuals from one level to another or the shift in relative position of a whole stratum or class, is known as *social mobility.* In an *open* stratification system, social mobility is common; in a *closed* system, mobility is very limited. The ranks in an open system are generally called *classes;* in a closed system the term *caste* is commonly used. Initial recruitment to both class and caste systems is typically hereditary, but in the former there is mobility based on individual achievement. *See also* POLITICAL BEHAVIOR, POLITICAL SOCIOLOGY.

Social System   An aggregation of two or more persons that interact with one another in some patterned way. Social system, in its generic sense, may refer to the interaction of human beings on any scale—within a small group, a complex organization, or an entire society. Some analysts identify individual human beings, or groups, as the basic elements of social systems (that is, systems of human entities). Others speak of actions, interactions, behavior, or relationships as the system elements (that is, systems of action). Both points of view assume the existence of people and their interaction. All but the simplest social systems embrace a number of *subsystems.* These may be conceived as subgroups of different people (families as subsystems of a larger society, governmental agencies as subsystems of the larger governmental system). Or they may involve the same people or overlapping groups of people, differentiated as separate subsystems by the kinds of interactions in which the people engage, such as economic and political subsystems of a larger national social system. A *social system,* consisting of interacting people, may be distinguished from a *cultural system,* which refers to learned modes of behavior characteristic of a society, and from a *personality system,* which refers to the organized dispositions within a single individual that lead to characteristic responses. *See also* CULTURE, INTERACTION, PERSONALITY, POLITICAL ACTION, POLITICAL SYSTEM, SOCIETY, STRUCTURAL-FUNCTIONALISM, SYSTEM.

Society   An aggregation of people who have certain common attributes that distinguish them as a group and who interact with one another in some characteristic way. Society commonly refers to a group having a distinct culture and living as a distinguishable entity. In sociological literature a society is regarded as a social system that furnishes the primary orientation for people in a given territorial area, recruits members through sexual reproduction, and persists beyond the life-span of its individual members. In practice the boundaries of societies so defined tend to be fixed along political lines, so that a society is likely to mean a national society—that is, the people embraced within a sovereign political system. In a nontechnical sense "society" is used with reference to phenomena as diverse as a specific voluntary association, a group of people distinguished from others by common aims or ways of behaving (as a hippie society, or "high" society), or the social order in general. *See also* POLITICAL COMMUNITY, POLITICAL SYSTEM, SOCIAL SYSTEM.

Sociology of Knowledge The study of the social origins of knowledge. The sociology of knowledge is based on the assumption that what is known, or believed to be true, is conditioned by the economic and social forces at work in society. In its most extreme form this assumption would rule out the finding of objective truth because truth as perceived is always relative to social conditions at a given time and place. There might be some certainty about analytic truth derived from mathematics and systems of logic, which require no validation by reference to physical objects or social behavior. But knowledge of the world, it is suggested, cannot be perceived and interpreted independently of the observer's social biases. *See also* SCIENCE.

Sociology of Politics, *see* Political Sociology.

Sociometry A technique for the analysis of relationships within small groups. Sociometry uses data from a written questionnaire or interview in which each person is asked to indicate, often in rank order, the members of the group with whom he would most like to associate in a particular activity (or, sometimes, in general). Sociometric tests may also ask for negative choices. Data gathered by observation is used in a somewhat related fashion to study associational choice. The graphic representation of choices by means of circles and connecting lines, or some other geometric figures, is called a *sociogram*. *See also* ATTITUDE, ATTITUDE SCALING.

Soft Loan, *see* International Development Association.

Soil Conservation A cooperative program of the national government, states, local units, and individual farmers to preserve valuable top soil from being washed or blown away through erosion and dust storms. Primary responsibility for developing and carrying out a national soil conservation program is vested in the Soil Conservation Service of the Department of Agriculture.

Solicitor General An important official in the Department of Justice who conducts cases on behalf of the United States before the Supreme Court. In addition, his approval is necessary before any appeal may be taken on behalf of the federal government to any appellate court.

Sources of International Law, *see* International Law.

South Carolina v. Katzenbach, *see* Voting Rights Act of 1965.

South Carolina v. United States, 199 U.S. 437 (1905): Upheld a federal tax levied upon wholesale and retail liquor sales by the state of South Carolina on the ground that exemption of states from federal taxes applies only when a state carries on strictly governmental functions, not when it engages in business of a private nature. The state argued unsuccessfully that because all profits from liquor sales went into the state treasury, it was exercising the sovereign power of the state and should be immune from federal taxes. *See also* INTERGOVERNMENTAL TAX IMMUNITY, PROPRIETARY FUNCTION.

Southeast Asia Collective Defense Treaty A mutual security pact signed at Manila in 1954 that calls on the signatories to consult and to meet the common danger in accordance with their constitutional processes. The Treaty applies to both external aggression and internal subversion in Southeast Asia and the Southwest Pacific. Parties to the Southeast Asia Collective Defense Treaty are Australia, Britain, France, New Zealand, Pakistan, the Philippines, Thailand, and the United States. To implement the Treaty's guarantees, in 1955 its signatories estabished the Southeast Asia Treaty Organization (SEATO), which functions through a council and a secretariat located at SEATO headquarters in Bangkok. By a special Protocol to the Treaty, the security area covered was extended to include Cambodia, Laos, and South Vietnam, but the Treaty excludes Hong Kong, South Korea, and Taiwan because the Asian signatories were unwilling to assume responsibility for their defense. *See also* ALLIANCE, SOUTHEAST ASIA TREATY ORGANIZATION.

Southeast Asia Treaty Organization (SEATO) A military-economic arrangement based on the Southeast Asia Collective Defense Treaty of 1954. Members who agree to consult about potential collective action whenever any of their number is threatened by external aggression or internal subversion in southeast Asia are Australia, Britain, France, New Zealand, Pakistan, the Philippines, Thailand, and the United States. SEATO headquarters are in Bangkok and include a council and a secretariat. *See also* ALLIANCE.

Southeastern Power Administration, *see* Department of the Interior.

Southern Christian Leadership. Conference (SCLC), *see* Civil Rights Organizations.

South Pacific Commission An advisory and consultative international organization founded in 1947 to facilitate cooperation in regional and United Nations social, economic, and health programs. Members of the South Pacific Commission and their territories include: Australia (Norfolk Island, Papua and New Guinea), Britain (British Solomon Islands Protectorate, Gilbert and Ellice Islands, and New Hebrides), France (French Polynesia, New Caledonia, New Hebrides, Wallis and Futuna Islands), New Zealand (Cook Islands, Niue, Tokelau Islands), United States (American Samoa,

Guam, and the Trust Territory of the Pacific Islands), Nauru, and Western Samoa. The structure of the Commission includes (1) a Commission composed of two commissioners from each member state; (2) a Research Council appointed by the Commission; (3) a Conference held at least every three years attended by delegates from South Pacific territories and member states; and (4) a Secretariat, headed by a Secretary-General, located at SPC headquarters in New Caledonia.

Sovereignty   The supreme power of a state, exercised within its boundaries, free from external interference. The idea behind sovereignty is an ancient one, but it was first developed into an elaborate doctrine by philosophers of the sixteenth and seventeenth centuries, who sought to justify the absolutism of the kings of the new state system..

Soviet of Nationalities, *see* Supreme Soviet.

Soviet of the Union, *see* Supreme Soviet.

Soviet Political System, *see* All-Union Party Congress, Central Committee, Collective Farm, Communist Party of the Soviet Union, Constitution, Council of Ministers, Presidium of the Supreme Soviet, Secretariat of the Central Committee, State Farm, Supreme Soviet.

Space Treaty, *see* Outer Space Treaty.

Span of Control   An administrative concept concerned with the number of agencies or subordinates that one person can supervise effectively. Experts have different opinions about what constitutes a manageable span of control, but most agree that no person can direct more than twenty agencies or persons.

Speaker of the House   The presiding officer in the House of Representatives and in the lower chamber of state legislatures. His election by the House is a formality that follows his selection by the majority party caucus. As a member of the House, the Speaker may engage in debate and vote on measures.

Special Act   Legislation applicable to one unit of local government. The special act system prevailed from colonial times to the middle of the nineteenth century and is still in use in several states. Through special acts, state legislatures grant charters to municipalities, amend the charters, and pass legislation on a wide variety of purely local problems. *See also* CHARTER, GENERAL LAWS.

Special Assessment   A charge made by a government against a property owner for that part of the cost of public improvements made adjacent to his property that are especially useful or beneficial to his property. Special assessments are different from taxes in that the improvements have been petitioned for by the landowners concerned.

Special District   A unit of local government established to provide a single service. About one-half of the special districts in the United States are for fire protection, soil conservation, water, and drainage. Other common types of special districts provide cemetery, sewer, housing, and mosquito abatement services. A school district may be classified as a special district but the Census Bureau and political scientists classify it separately. Special districts are usually created to meet problems that transcend local government boundaries or to bypass taxation and debt restrictions imposed upon local units by state law. The number of special districts has almost tripled since 1942 (8000 to 21,000), and they now comprise about 20 percent of all local units. The special district is created under state law, usually requiring the consent of the people in the district, and is governed by a small board that has taxing and bonding authority.

Specialized Agency (United Nations)   A functional international organization that has broad international responsibilities in the economic, social, cultural, educational, health, or related fields. Although each of the thirteen specialized agencies operates outside the general United Nations framework, each maintains a relationship with the world organization through a special agreement concluded between the agency and the Economic and Social Council. Each agency has its own budget, although the General Assembly may review it and make recommendations. The common organizational structure of the agencies includes: (1) a general conference or assembly of all members which functions as the chief policymaking organ; (2) an executive council or board that implements policies between sessions of the general conference, performing executive and supervisory functions; (3) a secretariat headed by a director or secretary-general, that performs administrative chores at the agency's headquarters. The agencies propose legislation for national enactment by members, draft treaties on matters of common concern, and carry on extensive research, publication, and informational work for the benefit of members. The specialized agencies include: the Food and Agriculture Organization (FAO); Inter-Governmental Maritime Consultative Organization (IMCO); International Bank for Reconstruction and Development (IBRD); International Civil Aviation Organization (ICAO); International Development Association (IDA); International Finance Corporation (IFC); International Labor Organization (ILO); International Monetary Fund (IMF); International Telecommunication Union (ITU); United Nations Educational, Scientific, and Cultural Organization (UNESCO); Universal Postal Union (UPU); World Health Organization (WHO); and the World Meteorological Organization (WMO). With the exception of the UPU, ITU, and ILO, all of the specialized agencies have been established during the United Nations era with the encouragement of the world organization. *See also specific agencies.*

Specialized Organizations (OAS), *see* Organization of American States.

Special Session   An extraordinary session of a legislative body, convoked usually on the initiative of a chief executive. The Constitution grants power to the President to summon Congress or either house into session "on extraordinary occasions" (Art. II, sec. 3). Although the House has never been called into special session, the Senate has been convoked to act upon executive appointments or treaties. In all fifty states, the governors are empowered to call special sessions of the legislatures. In several states, a stipulated number of legislators may petition the governor to call the legislature into session. In a few others, the legislature can call itself into special session.

Specific Powers, *see* Delegated Powers.

Speech, Freedom of, *see* Freedom of Speech.

Sphere of Influence   An area dominated by the national interests of a foreign power. In a sphere of influence, the foreign power does not possess sovereignty but imposes on the area an international servitude that restricts the free exercise of local territorial sovereignty. Such servitudes may be positive, as in granting the dominant state a monopoly of commercial exploitation, or negative, as in requiring the weaker state to refrain from fortifying a common border.

Spillover   An integrative process by which cooperation between political units in one issue area leads to further cooperation in other areas. Spillover typically arises from the attempt by states to resolve problems created by their previous cooperative acts. More specifically, joint action in one sector may have disruptive consequences in other sectors or be hindered by lack of international coordination in the other sectors, and the states respond by creating new integrative institutions, or expanding old ones. The expansion of the European Coal and Steel Community into a wider European Economic Community is a classic case of such spillover. Cooperation attributable to the example set by earlier cooperative enterprises (the *demonstration effect*), or resulting from goodwill and cooperative habits generated by previous common endeavors, might appropriately be called *learning* rather than spillover. Spillover is often used in a general sense, however, to include learning-induced as well as problem-induced cooperation. *See also* FUNCTIONALISM, POLITICAL INTEGRATION.

Split Ticket   Voting for candidates of two or more parties for different offices. Split-ticket voting is not permitted in primaries. *See also* STRAIGHT TICKET, OFFICE-BLOCK BALLOT.

Spoiling Attack, *see* Preemptive Strike.

Spoils System   The award of government jobs to political supporters and friends. The term derives from the expression, "to the victor belongs the spoils." The spoils system is generally associated with President Andrew Jackson. *See also* PATRONAGE.

Stability   A condition of a system whose components tend to remain in, or return to, some constant relationship with one another. Stability is identified with the absence of basic or disruptive change in a political system, or the confining of change to acceptable or specified limits. In discussions of sampling techniques stability is sometimes used as a synonym for *reliability*. *See also* EQUILIBRIUM, HOMEOSTASIS, RELIABILITY.

Staff, *see* Line and Staff.

Stalinism   The theoretical interpretations and practical applications of Marxist doctrine contributed by Josef Stalin, who dominated the party and governmental machinery in the Soviet Union from the mid-1920s until his death in 1953. The main contributions of Stalinism were in the methods of organizing the Soviet people for achieving industrialization, improving agriculture, defense of the nation against the Nazi attack, and the reconstruction of the war-devastated nation. Stalin demonstrated that, in addition to the Marxist and Leninist prescriptions for the victory of communism, military occupation by a communist great power, as demonstrated in Eastern Europe after World War II, could also accomplish the goal if international circumstances were favorable. In the area of theory, Stalin contributed little to communist doctrine, limiting himself to redefining Marxism-Leninism to apply it to the domestic and international milieu of his day. Stalin predicted in his last published work in 1952, for example, that instead of war between the socialist camp and the capitalist states, Lenin's theory that war may occur between capitalist nations as a result of their imperialistic rivalry was still applicable. He asserted that it could conceivably be applied to predict war between such close allies as the United States and Britain.

Stalking Horse   A candidate for public office whose only role is to function as a cover or decoy on behalf of a stronger but unannounced candidate. The term *stalking horse* comes from the Great Plains states where hunters once used their horses as cover to move in for a close-range shot at bison or other game. Unlike a favorite son candidate, a stalking horse tries to convey the appearance of being a serious candidate so that his impact on the voters can be accurately assessed, and the base prepared for the subsequent candidacy of the party leader for whom he has fronted. Nevertheless, favorite son candidates may also function in the capacity of stalking horses.

Standardized Interview, *see* Interview.

Standing Committee   A regular committee of a legislative body that considers bills within a subject area. In Congress, there are twenty-one House and sixteen Senate standing committees. House committees range in size from nine to fifty-one members and Senate committees from seven to twenty-four members. Representatives are normally assigned to only one standing committee, senators to two. In the House, the leading standing committees include Rules, Ways and Means, Appropriations, Armed Services, Judiciary, Foreign Affairs, Commerce, and Agriculture. In the Senate, influential committees include Foreign Relations, Appropriations, Finance, Judiciary, Armed Services, and Banking and Currency. The majority party in each house holds a majority vote on each committee and the chairmanship. Positions of importance on the committees are determined under the rule of seniority. Under the Legislative

Reorganization Act of 1970, committee votes in executive (secret) sessions must be made public, and committee hearings may for the first time be opened to radio and television coverage if witnesses and a majority of the committee do not object. *See also* COMMITTEE CHAIRMAN, COMMITTEE ON COMMITTEES, SENIORITY RULE.

Standing Vote, *see* Division.

Stare Decisis   A legal term meaning "let the decision stand." It is an important element of the common law whereby a decision applies in similar cases and is binding upon lower courts. Precedents thus established stand until overruled. *See also* PRECEDENT.

State   A political community occupying a definite territory, having an organized government and possessing internal and external sovereignty. Recognition of a state's claim to independence by other states, enabling it to enter into international engagements, is important to the establishment of its sovereignty. The term is also used to describe territorial divisions within a federal system, such as in the United States. *See also* NATION.

State Action   An official act by a state or local governmental agency or officer. The term usually refers to any abridgment of individual rights by state or local governmental agencies, laws, or officials, which is forbidden by the Fourteenth Amendment to the Constitution. Invasions of individual rights by private individuals are not within the purview of the Amendment. For example, a law imposing racial segregation is state action, whereas an individual's discriminatory act does not violate the Fourteenth Amendment, although the individual action may be forbidden by statute. *See also* FOURTEENTH AMENDMENT.

State Aid   Funds provided to local governments by the state in the form of grants-in-aid or shared taxes. State grants go primarily to school districts for educational purposes and to counties for welfare and highway functions. Shared taxes are administered by the state, which gives a portion of sales or income taxes to local units, including cities. *See also* REVENUE SHARING.

State Attorney General, *see* Attorney General.

State Auditor   A state official elected in thirty-one states and appointed by the governor or legislature in others. In some states, the title "comptroller" is used. His major duty is to act as a watchdog over expenditures of state agencies by postauditing accounts. In some states, however, he has preauditing and accounting duties as well. *See also* AUDITOR.

State Central Committee   The principal committee of a political party within a state. State central committees are composed of members representing congressional districts, state legislative districts, or counties. *See also* POLITICAL PARTY.

State Constitution, *see* Constitution, State.

State Constitution, Model, *see* Model State Constitution.

State Constitutional Commission, *see* Constitutional Commission.

State Constitutional Convention, *see* Constitutional Convention.

State Council (China (PRC))   The highest executive decision-making body of the state apparatus, comparable to the Council of Ministers in the Soviet Union. The Chairman of the Republic names the Premier, or head of the State Council of Ministers, who functions as head of government. The members of the State Council include sixteen vice premiers, some thirty ministers, and the heads of various state commissions and bureaus, all named by the Premier and confirmed by the National People's Congress. The State Council meets monthly and is the center of state executive and administrative activity. It also has a standing committee or inner cabinet that meets more frequently and is analogous to the Presidium of the Council of Ministers in the Soviet system. Members of this inner group include the Premier, vice-premiers, and the secretary-general of the Council. *See also* COUNCIL OF MINISTERS (SOVIET UNION).

State Farm   A large-scale Soviet farm owned and operated by the state through the Ministry of Agriculture. State farm labor is hired for wages and farm managers are appointed by the state as in any large industrial enterprise. Many state farms began as experiment stations and demonstration units on public lands. Others have developed out of the "virgin lands" projects, which have taken labor from the cities to open unsettled territory to agriculture. State farms have also absorbed some collective farms and produce specialized crops such as cotton or, on the edges of industrial areas, potatoes and vegetables. *See also* COLLECTIVE FARM.

State Government, *see* Council of State Governments.

State Government, Powers of, *see* Borrowing Power, Concurrent Powers, Exclusive Powers, Police Power, Reserved Powers.

State Legislature, *see* Biennial Session, Constituent Power, Gerrymandering, Legislative Council, Redistricting.

Statelessness   The condition of an individual who is not recognized by any state as one of its nationals. Statelessness may result from dislocations caused by war or revolution, from a conflict of nationality laws, or by some act of denationalization undertaken by a government against some of its citizens. An individual act of expatriation which is not followed by the acquisition of a new allegiance would also result in statelessness. *See also* CITIZEN, EXPATRIATION, NATIONALITY, REFUGEE.

State Militia, *see* National Guard.

State of Nature, *see* Contract Theory.

State of the Union Message   An annual message to Congress in which the President proposes his legislative program. It is based on the constitutional directive that the President "shall from time to time give to the Congress information of the state of the Union, and recommend to their consideration such measures as he shall judge necessary and expedient. . . . " (Art. II, sec. 3). Although the President may choose his time for the message, it has become customary to transmit it at the beginning of a legislative session. *See also* CHIEF LEGISLATOR.

State Police Power, *see* Police Power.

State Sovereignty   Independence of a state from external control. The concept of state sovereignty was an integral part of government under the Articles of Confederation and was part of the great debate on the Union that took place prior to the Civil War. In effect, state sovereignty is a rejection of the principle of national supremacy under the United States Constitution. *See also* STATES' RIGHTS.

States' Rights   A term used to connote opposition to increasing the national government's power at the expense of that of the states. States' rights adherents call for an interpretation of the Constitution that would place limits on the federal assumption of implied powers and give expanded interpretation to the reserved powers of the states. *See also* STATE SOVEREIGNTY.

State Superintendent, *see* Superintendent of Public Instruction.

State Treasurer   A state official popularly elected in forty-one states and chosen by the governor or legislature in others. His major duties are the safekeeping of state funds and the payment of bills on proper warrant. In some states, he has tax collection responsibilities as well.

Statism (Fascist Theory)   The basic concept that sovereignty is vested not in the people but in the national state, and that all individuals and associations exist only to enhance the power, the prestige, and the well-being of the state. The fascist concept of statism repudiates individualism and exalts the nation as an organic body headed by the Supreme Leader and nurtured by unity, force, and discipline. Under this doctrine, the state creates worthy individuals who realize their destiny only by contributing to the glory of the state.

Statistical Significance, *see* Correlation, Probability.

Statistics   The science dealing with the collection, classification, and use of numerical data. As applied to a discipline such as political science, statistical methods are used to summarize data and reduce it to manageable form, to locate and evaluate patterns in the data, and to assist the researcher in making reliable inferences from his data. Statistics may be categorized in a number of ways: descriptive and inferential, theoretical and applied, parametric and nonparametric. *Descriptive* statistics refers to the use of such measures as percentages, means, medians, and frequency distributions to reduce quantities of data to manageable form and make them more understandable. *Inductive* or *inferential* statistics deals with theory and techniques for drawing inferences from observed data and estimating the probability that the inference is correct. Statistical inference ordinarily has reference to the characteristics of populations that may be inferred from known samples of the population. *Theoretical* statistics seeks understanding of the inferential process and the assumptions underlying differing modes of analysis. Methods thus investigated are *applied* to specific research problems and bodies of data. Statistical procedures are *parametric* if they are designed to apply to samples of data having a *normal distribution*—that is, the cases tend to cluster about a mean and progressively decrease in number toward either extreme of measurement. *Nonparametric* statistical procedures do not require normal distribution. A *statistic* is also the name given to a numerical characteristic (for example, mean, median) of a *sample* as contrasted with a *parameter*, which is a characteristic of the larger *population* from which a sample is drawn. *See also* CORRELATION, INFERENCE, NULL HYPOTHESIS, PROBABILITY, QUANTIFICATION, RELIABILITY, SAMPLING.

Status Quo   A descriptive term used by international political analysts to describe the foreign policy of a state that aims at preserving the existing distribution of power in the world. The concept is derived from the diplomatic term, *status quo ante bellum,* which is a clause typically inserted into peace treaties providing for the restoration of prewar conditions.

Status Quo Policy   An analytical term used to describe any foreign policy aimed at maintaining the existing international territorial, ideological, or power distribution. A status quo policy is basically conservative and defensive in nature; hence, a state will pursue such a policy if it enjoys an advantageous position in world politics and seeks stability rather than change, so as to maximize its existing advantages. *See also* REVISIONIST POLICY.

Statute (Act)   A law enacted by Congress or by a state legislature. Simple, concurrent, and joint resolutions adopted by Congress are not considered statutes. Statutes take the form of public and private laws and are numbered consecutively in each session of Congress. *See also* BILL, CODE.

Statute of Limitations   A state or federal legislative act that establishes a time limit within which lawsuits may be brought, judgments enforced, or crimes prosecuted. The time limit varies among different jurisdictions and with the nature of the case, although for certain major offenses, such as murder, no limits are placed on prosecution.

Statute of the World Court, *see* International Court of Justice.

Statutory Construction   Judicial interpretation of legislative enactments. The application of a statute is not always clear from the words of the statute. Judges seek "legislative intent" by consulting legislative committee hearings, floor debates, and legislative journals. If these sources do not reveal the legislature's objectives, the court must then discern the meaning of the law.

Steady State, *see* Homeostasis.

Stereotype   A fixed belief about some object, often based on second-hand knowledge, that is oversimplified and therefore inaccurate. The term "stereotype," as it appears in political science literature, usually refers to a fairly widespread belief among a society or a social group about members of another group. Each member of the other group is seen as possessing the characteristics of the stereotype. Thus there may be a French stereotype of Germans and vice versa, an American stereotype of communists, a white stereotype of blacks, and so on. *See also* ATTITUDE, PUBLIC OPINION.

Sterling Bloc, *see* Commonwealth of Nations.

Steward Machine Co. v. Davis, *see* Social Security Cases.

Stewardship Theory   A view of presidential powers that holds that the President has not only the right but the duty to do anything needed to safeguard the nation and to protect the American people, unless such action is specifically forbidden by the Constitution. The stewardship theory is usually ascribed to Theodore Roosevelt, although other strong Presidents, such as Abraham Lincoln, Woodrow Wilson, and Franklin Roosevelt, followed the basic principle on which the stewardship theory rests. *See also* EMERGENCY POWERS, TAFTIAN OR CONTRACTUAL THEORY.

Stimson Doctrine   The position enunciated by Secretary of State, Henry Stimson, that the United States would not recognize the validity of political changes brought about in violation of international obligations or American treaty rights. The Stimson non-recognition doctrine was enunciated in diplomatic notes to Japan and China in

1932 following the Japanese conquest of Manchuria. Stimson's initiative failed to gain world support but became a policy guideline for American decision makers involved in recognition issues. *See also* RECOGNITION OF GOVERNMENTS, RECOGNITION OF STATES.

Stimulus-Response The mode of explaining human behavior in which political actions are seen as responses to events or conditions in the actor's environment. Stimulus-response models now generally take into account, as part of the explanation, the perceptual and evaluative processes that intervene between environmental stimulus and actor response. This reflects the view that the response is not produced directly by the external event but rather by the actor's perception and evaluation of it. The stimulus-response concept is also a key element in psychological *learning theory*, which regards human learning as a process of strengthening or weakening associations between stimulus and response, as particular responses prove rewarding or punishing. *See also* ENVIRONMENT, PERCEPTION, SYSTEMS ANALYSIS.

Stockpiling The accumulation of strategic raw materials for use during a national crisis. The United States has amassed a stockpile of about eighty essential raw materials and metals that must be obtained abroad or that might be needed quickly during an emergency. Stockpiled materials range from steel and aluminum to natural rubber, industrial diamonds, and such rare items as selenium and tantalum. The storehouse of agricultural products acquired by the national government under its price support program buttresses the strategic materials stockpile.

Straight Ticket Voting for all candidates of a single party for all offices. *See also* SPLIT TICKET, PARTY-COLUMN BALLOT.

Strategic Arms Limitation Talks (SALT) Negotiations between the Soviet Union and the United States aimed at reaching agreement on the control of strategic nuclear weapons, delivery systems, and related offensive and defensive weapons systems. SALT talks, which began in Helsinki in 1969, were initially directed toward reaching agreement to limit or eliminate the costly Anti-Ballistic Missile (ABM) systems which both countries were developing. Subsequently, discussions covered the range of strategic weapons and related systems, including the ABM issue, multiple independently targeted reentry vehicles (MIRV), nuclear testing, and limits on the number of delivery systems with nuclear warheads.

Strategic Materials Raw materials and semifinished and finished products essential for fighting a modern war. The availability of strategic materials is a significant component in the determination of national power. The number of materials considered to be strategic has increased rapidly with the technological revolution in warfare that has occurred since 1940. Some of the most critical strategic materials include foodstuffs, aluminum, cadmium, copper, magnesium, tin, tungsten, mercury, cobalt, uranium, diamonds, petroleum, antimony, and lead. *See also* STOCKPILING.

Strategic Trust, *see* Trusteeship Council.

Strategy   A plan of action to defeat an opponent or to achieve some other goal. "Strategy" usually refers to a comprehensive or long-range plan involving a series of moves directed toward some overall objective. "Tactics," by contrast, consist of single moves or limited sequences of steps toward intermediate goals within a larger strategic plan. In a military context, where the term originated, tactics relate to the maneuvering of forces in a combat situation, while strategy is concerned with the overall conduct of a campaign or war. Strategic and tactical uses of aircraft and missile weaponry are distinguished primarily on the basis of depth of penetration. Strikes deep within enemy territory are called *strategic,* whereas shorter range missions in support of ground operations or against the supply systems of enemy ground forces are *tactical. See also* GAME THEORY.

Stratification, *see* Social Stratification.

Strict Construction, *see* Constitutional Construction.

Strike   A stoppage of work by employees for the purpose of winning concessions from their employer on matters of wages, hours, or working conditions. The right to strike, except for purposes prohibited by law, is considered to be a fundamental right of free workingmen. Government employees, however, are not permitted to strike. National and state laws contain a variety of limitations on the right to strike. For example, strikes may not be used to promote a secondary boycott or other unfair labor practice. Procedures are also provided by law for cooling-off periods, injunctions, fact-finding boards, and mediation services in order to avoid strikes. *See also* COOLING-OFF PERIOD, JURISDICTIONAL STRIKE, LOCKOUT.

Strong-mayor Plan   A plan of city government in which the mayor is given complete executive authority. Its major features include: (1) election of a mayor as chief executive; (2) concentration of administrative power in the hands of the mayor, including powers of appointment and removal; (3) a veto power over the city council; and (4) strong budgetary controls in the hands of the mayor. *See also* MAYOR-COUNCIL PLAN.

Structural-Functionalism   An approach to political analysis that focuses on the functions performed within a political system and on the structures through which they are performed. Structural-functionalism provides a framework for analyzing whole systems. It lays stress upon the interrelatedness of structures and functions within a given system and postulates that certain necessary functions must be performed if the system is to persist or be adequately maintained. A *function,* in this context, means some purpose served with respect to the maintenance or perpetuation of the system; a *structure* could be any set of related roles, including such concrete organizational structures as political parties and legislatures. Structural-functional analysis ordinarily involves the identification of a set of requisite or at least recurring functions in the kind of system under investigation. This is coupled with an attempt to determine the kinds of structures—and their interrelations—through which those functions are performed. *See also* FUNCTIONALISM, POLITICAL ACTION, POLITICAL SYSTEM, SOCIAL SYSTEM, STRUCTURE, SYSTEM, SYSTEMS ANALYSIS.

Structure A pattern of related roles or established relationships among people. Structures are the relatively stable, uniform, or patterned elements in a situation. A political party organization is a formalized pattern of related roles and, thus, a structure. The established relationship between the party organization and the voting public, although less formalized, could also be regarded as a structure. In the structural-functional analysis of systems, structures are action patterns, while functions are the results or consequences of actions. In the study of international politics the pattern of power distribution among states is sometimes called the *structure* of the international system. *See also* INSTITUTION, PROCESS, ROLE, STRUCTURAL-FUNCTIONAL-ISM.

Subpoena An order of a court, grand jury, legislative body or committee, or of any duly authorized administrative agency, compelling the attendance of a witness. A *subpoena duces tecum* requires the witness to produce specific documents. Failure to honor a subpoena may subject the person to prosecution for contempt. *See also* WITNESS.

Subset, *see* Set.

Subsidy Financial or other forms of aid bestowed by government upon private individuals, companies, or groups to improve their economic position and accomplish some public objective. Subsidies may be direct, as in the payment of sums of money to shipbuilders and farmers, or indirect, as in the tariff that protects American business, labor, and agriculture from foreign competition. *See also* TAX EXEMPTION.

Substantive Decision, *see* Security Council, Veto (International Organization).

Substantive Due Process, *see* Due Process of Law.

Substantive Rights Constitutional guarantees essential for personal liberty. These generally include those rights listed in the First, Thirteenth, and Fourteenth Amendments—freedoms of speech, press, religion, assembly, and petition, freedom from involuntary servitude, and the right to equal protection of the law. *Substantive* rights are to be distinguished from *procedural* rights, which are concerned with the manner in which the substantive rights are protected, as by due process and fair trial.

Subsystem, *see* Systems Analysis.

Subversive Activities Control Board An independent agency established in 1950 under the Internal Security Act. The Board is composed of five members appointed by the President, with the consent of the Senate, for five-year terms. Its major function is to conduct hearings, upon the request of the Attorney General, to determine whether an organization is a Communist action, front, or infiltrated group subject to the registration requirements of the Internal Security Act. It also determines whether an individual is a member of a Communist action organization. *See also* INTERNAL SECURITY ACT.

Succession, *see* Presidential Succession.

Suffrage, *see* Voting Behavior, Voting Qualifications.

Summit Diplomacy   Personal diplomacy by heads of state or government as contrasted with diplomacy at the ambassadorial or ministerial level. Summit diplomacy emerged during the era of absolute monarchy and has continued sporadically. Summit diplomacy has experienced a new vogue associated with the perplexing problems of the Cold War, and "summit conferences" between United States and Communist leaders have been held at Geneva (1955), Paris (1960), Vienna (1961), Glassboro, New Jersey (1967), Peking (1972), and Moscow (1972). *See also* DIPLOMACY.

Summons   A complaint made by an individual or a police officer and signed by a judicial officer requiring a person to appear in court to answer charges made against him.

Sumptuary Tax   A tax levied by a unit of government aimed at regulating personal conduct which offends the religious or moral standards of the community. A sumptuary tax may be aimed at promoting frugality and temperance, or at preventing ostentatiousness and vulgarity. *See also* REGULATORY TAX.

SUNFED Proposal, *see* United Nations Capital Development Fund.

Superintendent of Public Instruction   A state official whose function is to supervise the public school system of the state. In some states he is known as superintendent of schools or commissioner of education. He is elected in about twenty states, appointed by the governor in a few, and, in increasing numbers of states, chosen by the state board of education. In most cases, the superintendent serves on the state board of education and acts as its chief administrative officer. His duties generally include the establishment of standards for schools, curriculum development, setting up teacher qualifications, and control of state administered school funds. In some states, his authority extends to other educational institutions, such as state teachers colleges and community colleges.

Superintendent of Schools, *see* Board of Education, Superintendent of Public Instruction.

Supervisor   The chief elective officer of the township (called trustee in some states). The supervisor has overall responsibility for township government and presides over the township board. He may represent his township on the county board and serve as tax assessor. *See also* TOWNSHIP.

Supplementary Appropriation   An appropriation of public money authorized by a legislative body after the regular appropriation bills have been enacted. It differs from a deficiency appropriation in that it is passed prior to the fiscal period in which it will be spent. *See also* DEFICIENCY APPROPRIATION.

Supranationalism   Power exercised by international institutions to make majority-vote decisions that are binding upon all member states or their citizens. Supranationalism involves a transfer of decision-making authority in agreed areas from constituent units to a central body. Members must accept supranational decisions or withdraw from the system. Decisions may be made either by representatives of member governments or by an institution that functions as an integral unit of the international arrangement. Supranationalism in effect establishes a limited federal system with powers divided between the two levels. *See also* POLITICAL COMMUNITY.

Supremacy Clause, *see* National Supremacy.

Supreme Court   The court of last resort in the federal and in most state judicial systems. In a few states, the highest court is called by another title. The Supreme Court of the United States is composed of the Chief Justice of the United States and eight associate justices. The number of justices is established by Congress; it has varied from five to ten, but has been set at nine since 1869. Cases are decided by majority vote. The Supreme Court is the only court specifically provided for in the Constitution, and its original jurisdiction is set therein to include cases affecting ambassadors, public ministers, and consuls, and those to which a state is a party. Its appellate jurisdiction is determined by Congress. Certain cases involving federal questions may be appealed to the Supreme Court from the highest state court. With the exception of certain specified cases involving questions of constitutionality, the Supreme Court determines which cases it will hear through the writ of ceritorari. The Court sits from October to June and its decisions are reported in the *United States Reports*. State supreme courts vary in size and jurisdiction in accordance with state constitutions and laws but, except for cases that may be brought to the United States Supreme Court, they are the courts of last resort in each state. Justices of the United States Supreme Court are appointed by the President, with the Senate's consent, for life terms subject to impeachment. Most state supreme court judges are elected. The United States Supreme Court and some state supreme courts oversee their respective court systems in matters of procedure and administration. *See also* ACTIVISM VERSUS SELF-RESTRAINT, JUDICIAL REVIEW, UNITED STATES REPORTS, *Ashwander v. TVA*.

Supreme Court Packing Plan   A proposal made in 1937 by President Franklin D. Roosevelt that the President be authorized to appoint an additional justice of the

Supreme Court for each justice over the age of seventy who did not retire after ten years of service. The maximum number of appointments was to have been six, thereby possibly increasing the size of the Supreme Court from nine to fifteen. The President claimed that this plan would increase the efficiency of the Court, but it was defeated in the Congress on the ground that Roosevelt was trying to "pack" the court to overcome unfavorable decisions on New Deal programs.

Supreme Court Reporter, *see United States Reports.*

Supreme Soviet   The bicameral national Soviet legislature. The Soviet Constitution describes the Supreme Soviet as the highest organ of state power and assigns it authority to make laws and adopt constitutional amendments. The Soviet of Nationalities, the upper chamber, with approximately 652 deputies, represents the various administrative units of the nation, such as the constituent republics, autonomous republics, autonomous regions, and national districts. Each of the almost eight hundred delegates to the lower house, the Soviet of the Union, represents a district of approximately 300,000 people. In contrast to the All-Union Party Congress, each delegate is directly elected by the people of the unit involved. Many delegates are administrators in the party, government, and military services. There is also a heavy percentage of manual workers and peasants and a scattering of notables in the arts, sciences, and letters. The jurisdiction of both houses is essentially equal. The Supreme Soviet meets every six to eight months in brief sessions and, therefore, cannot be considered a deliberative body in the Western sense. It appoints the Council of Ministers, the working executive of the government apparatus, and elects its own Presidium where policy decisions can be made in the long intervals between sessions of the Supreme Soviet. The Chairman of the Presidium of the Supreme Soviet is the head of state.

Surplus Value (Communist Theory)   The Marxian postulate that the price of any product includes not only the "socially necessary" labor cost of production but also a "surplus value" that takes the form of profit for the capitalist. For Marx, the theory of surplus value meant that the worker who contributes all the value to a product is cheated out of his just compensation while the capitalist profits by exploiting another's labor. The surplus-value concept was developed by Marx by combining the classical labor theory of value expounded by John Locke, Adam Smith, and David Ricardo with the mercantilist doctrine of subsistence wages. The first propounded the idea that all value is based on mixing one's labor with the raw materials of the earth, and the second articulates the philosophy that workers should be paid extremely low wages to provide them with an incentive to work by making their lives a struggle for sustenance.

Surrogate Court, *see* Probate Court.

Survey Research   The investigation of social phenomena by means of interviews and questionnaires administered to a number of respondents. The purpose of survey research is to study people's attitudes, opinions, behavior, and social attributes (such as age, sex, political affiliation, and socioeconomic status) and the relationships among these characteristics. Survey research ordinarily entails the study of samples, from which inferences may be drawn about the whole population under investigation. An entire population, however, might be surveyed. If, for example, a state legislature were the population being studied, every member might be interviewed rather than a sample only. Personal interview is the most common form of data gathering, but other alternatives include the mailed questionnaire, telephone interview, panel study, or controlled observation. Survey research provides data on characteristics of each individual interviewed. This contrasts with *aggregate data,* such as trade or census figures, which provide no information on individual cases but summarize the characteristics or transactions of a number of cases. For example, survey data would report the income of individual members of a community, whereas aggregate data might report the per capita or gross income of all members of the community taken as a group. Aggregate data, of course, may be compiled from survey results. *See also* BIASED SAMPLE, INTERVIEW, PUBLIC OPINION, QUESTIONNAIRE, RANDOM, RELIABILITY, SAMPLING, VOTING BEHAVIOR.

Suspension of Rules   A time-saving procedure used by a legislative body to bring a measure to a vote. In the House of Representatives, a motion to "suspend the rules and pass the bill" requires a two-thirds vote of members present for passage. Debate on the bill is limited to forty minutes and no amendments are permitted.

Swann v. Charlotte-Mecklenburg Board of Education, 402 U.S. 1 (1971): Held that all vestiges of state imposed racial segregation in schools must be eliminated at once, and that federal district courts have wide authority to fashion remedies to accomplish this. Among the remedies approved were busing, racial quotas, and pairing and grouping of noncontiguous school zones. School boards must eliminate racial distinctions in the assignment and treatment of students and faculty and in school construction decisions. *See also* SEGREGATION.

Synchronic Analysis, *see* Time Series Analysis.

Syndicalism, *see* Socialism.

Synthesis, *see* Analysis.

System   Any set of elements that exist in some patterned relationship with one another. A system may be composed of tangible elements, such as the parts of an internal combustion engine, or such intangible ones as a system of ideas. For many analytical purposes, the elements of a system may be specified by the investigator to meet his research needs. Thus, a group of people might be specified as the set of elements making up a political or other social system; or, as is commonly the case, the elements might be specified as political interactions rather than concrete human beings. Either could constitute a system, as long as the elements are identifiable and the relationships among them specifiable. The way in which the investigator defines the elements of the system and the relevant relationships among them will determine the *boundaries* of the system (the analytical line that separates the system from its environment). An *open system* is one whose functioning is affected by inputs from its environment; a *closed system* is unaffected by its environment or, for analytical purposes, is considered as being unaffected. See *also* SYSTEMS ANALYSIS.

Systems Analysis   An approach, sometimes called *systems theory*, that treats politics as a set of interactions occurring within, but analytically distinct from, the larger social environment. Systems analysis provides a number of conceptual categories for describing and analyzing political behavior. Some of the more salient concepts are system, subsystem, environment, boundary, input, output, conversion process, and feedback. *System* implies patterned interactions or persisting relationships among political entities. A system that constitutes an element of a larger system is called a *subsystem*. The setting within which a system occurs is its *environment*. The analytical line that separates the system from its environment is the system *boundary*. A system receives *inputs* from its environment in the form of *demands* upon the system and *supports* for its functioning. Through the operation of the system inputs are subjected to a *conversion process*, which leads to system *outputs* embodying rules to be enforced or policies to be implemented. When system outputs affect the environment so as to modify inputs, *feedback* occurs. Systems that tend, when disturbed, to return to an equilibrium state are said to be *homeostatic*. *General systems theory* is concerned with the development of systems concepts and research methodologies having applicability to many scientific disciplines and pointing ultimately toward a synthesis of human knowledge within a systems framework. In an organizational management context *system analysis* refers to the use of a systems framework to evaluate strategies, alternatives, and program objectives with the object of optimizing resource utilization in the achievement of organizational goals. See *also* COMMUNICATIONS THEORY, CYBERNETICS, ENVIRONMENT, FEEDBACK, HOMEOSTASIS, INPUT, OUTPUT, PARADIGM, POLITICAL SYSTEM, SOCIAL SYSTEM, STRUCTURAL-FUNCTIONALISM, SYSTEM, THEORY.

Systems Theory, *see* Systems Analysis.

Tactics, *see* Strategy.

Taft-Hartley Act (Labor-Management Relations Act of 1947)   A major revision of the Wagner Act of 1935 that seeks to equalize the power of employers and labor unions. The Act places limitations upon labor union practices, regulates certain internal arrangements of unions, and strengthens the position of the individual worker. Provisions of the Wagner Act relative to unfair practices by employers against unions are retained. Among the major limitations placed upon unions by the Taft-Hartley Act are those outlawing the closed shop (but permitting the union shop), jurisdictional strikes, secondary boycotts, political expenditures, and excessive dues. The Act also permits unions and employers to sue each other for contract violations and provides for the use of the injunction and other "cooling-off" procedures in strikes that threaten the national welfare. Internal affairs of unions are regulated by requiring them to file reports on the use of union funds and organizational procedures. The National Labor Relations Board (NLRB) was increased from three to five members and the office of General Counsel was established to investigate and prosecute unfair labor charges.

Taftian or Contractual Theory A view of presidential powers that holds that the President is limited by the specific grants of power authorized in the Constitution and by statute. Supporters of the contractual or Taftian theory, sometimes called "literalists," hold the view that no undefined residuum of power for the office of President exists, and that every executive power must be traced to some specific grant of power or reasonably implied from such a grant. The theory was argued explicitly by President William Howard Taft, who regarded it as the only approach compatible with the separation of powers-checks and balances system of American government. *See also* MADISONIANISM, STEWARDSHIP THEORY.

Tangible Tax, *see* Personal Property Tax.

Tariff A tax levied on imports to help protect a nation's industry, business, labor, and agriculture from foreign competition or to raise revenue. Tariffs are discriminatory if they apply unequally on similar products from different countries, and are retaliatory if motivated by the creation of trade barriers by other countries. *See also* UNITED STATES TARIFF COMMISSION, RECIPROCAL TRADE AGREEMENTS ACT.

Tariff Commission, *see* United States Tariff Commission.

Tate v. Short, *see* Fine.

Tautology A statement that is true by definition, or is necessarily true within a given logical framework. A tautology is logically true rather than factually true. It cannot be confirmed by facts, but neither can it be contradicted, because it tells one nothing about the world of observation and experience. Thus, the statement, "The United States is or is not a political system," cannot be controverted because it includes all logical possibilities; it also imparts no information about the United States. Propositions of mathematics or logic are likewise tautologies because they are necessarily true within their own logical systems. Such tautologies are usually called *analytic* or *logical* statements. *Analytic* statements may be contrasted with *empirical* statements, which are verifiable by reference to fact and experience, and *normative* statements, which relate to values and therefore cannot be proved or disproved. *See also* EMPIRICISM, NORMATIVE.

Tax, *see* Corporation Income Tax, Direct Tax, Estate Tax, Excess Profits Tax, Excise Tax, Income Tax, Personal Property Tax, Progressive Tax, Property Tax, Regressive Tax, Regulatory Tax, Sales Tax, Severance Tax, Sumptuary Tax, Withholding Tax.

Tax Equalization, *see* Equalization.

Tax Exemption   The privilege granted by a government legally freeing certain types of property, sales or income from general taxpaying obligations. *See also* SUBSIDY.

Tax Immunity, *see* Intergovernmental Tax Immunity.

Tax Incidence   The point at which the actual burden of paying a tax falls, regardless of whom the tax is formally levied upon. Those taxes in which the burden cannot be shifted to someone else by the taxpayer are sometimes classified as *direct* taxes; those in which the burden can be passed on are *indirect* taxes.

Tax Offset   A device used by the national government to induce states to adopt certain types of taxes or programs by permitting individuals to deduct such state taxes from the amount of federal tax that they would otherwise pay. *See also* REVENUE SHARING.

Taxonomy, *see* Classification.

Taxpayer Suit   A suit brought by a taxpayer to prevent the expenditure of public funds for a given purpose. Such suits are permissible in most of the states but rarely in federal courts. *See also Frothingham v. Mellon.*

Tax Sharing, *see* Revenue Sharing.

Technical Assistance   The teaching of new technological skills. Technical assistance programs of foreign aid are offered by the advanced states to the underdeveloped states to help them to progress toward the goal of modernization. The transference of skills ranging from the most rudimentary to the highly complex—from teaching simple farming skills to the operation and maintenance of a modern industrial plant—falls within the scope of technical assistance. Technical assistance programs have sought to develop industrial, managerial, educational, public health, agricultural, mining, and administrative skills. *See also* TECHNOLOGY, UNITED NATIONS INSTITUTE FOR TRAINING AND RESEARCH.

Technology   The application of scientific knowledge and human skills to the solution of problems in the field of the practical or industrial arts. The level of technology depends mainly on research and development (R and D)—that is, the acquiring of new basic knowledge and its application to innovation. The process of modernization in the contemporary world involves the transfer of skills from the technically advanced to the underdeveloped societies. *See also* TECHNICAL ASSISTANCE.

Telephone Taps and Bugging Devices, *see* Wiretapping.

Teller Vote   A vote taken in a legislative body in which members are counted as they file past tellers. In Congress, the House but not the Senate uses teller votes, which can be demanded by one-fifth of a quorum (forty-four in the House, twenty in the Committee of the Whole). When a teller vote is called, two tellers, one for and one against, stand in front of the Speaker's desk and count the votes as the members file past. The Speaker or Chairman presiding over the Committee of the Whole then announces the results. Although teller votes have traditionally been anonymous, under the Legislative Reorganization Act of 1970, one-fifth of a quorum may request that members' individual votes be recorded. *See also* DIVISION, RECORD VOTE, VIVA VOCE VOTE.

Tendency Statement   The positing of a relationship between variables as a probability rather than a certainty. A tendency statement usually suggests the direction but not the magnitude of the relationship. It is often in the form of a hypothesis subject to verification or disconfirmation. An example of such a statement might be: "Political participation tends to increase with the citizen's level of education." A tendency statement is sometimes distinguished from a *probability statement* in terms of its degree of certainty. Using this distinction, a tendency statement indicates the probable existence of a relationship (for example, that suburbanites tend to vote Republican), while a probability statement will set forth the anticipated degree of relationship (for example, a probability that suburbanites will vote Republican in six out of ten cases). *See also* HYPOTHESIS, PROBABILITY, THEORY.

Tennessee Valley Authority (TVA)   A major corporation of the national government established by Congress in 1933 to provide for the development of the Tennessee River and its tributaries. The TVA has responsibility for the generation, transmission, and sale of electric power, flood control, improvement of navigation, production of fertilizers, reforestation, reclamation, and soil conservation. The TVA operates under a board of three directors appointed by the President with the Senate's approval. Its operations cover an area of over 40,000 square miles in the states of Alabama, Georgia, Kentucky, Mississippi, North Carolina, Tennessee, and Virginia. Development projects are financed through the issuance of bonds by the Authority and through the sale of electric power to private companies. *See also Ashwander v. TVA.*

Tenth Amendment   The final item of the Bill of Rights in the Constitution, which defines the principle of American federalism: "The powers not delegated to the United States by the Constitution, nor prohibited by it to the states, are reserved to the states respectively, or to the people." *See also* FEDERALISM.

Tenure   The right to hold a position or office free from arbitrary dismissal. Public employees in the classified service and teachers achieve tenure after serving a probationary period. *See also* SEPARATION FROM SERVICE.

Terms of Trade   The relationship between the prices a country receives for its exports and the prices it pays for its imports. The terms of trade serve as a means for measuring the trend of a nation's gains or losses from trade compared to a previous base period by determining the barter or exchange value of commodities bought from and sold to other countries. If, on the average, export prices rise or import prices fall, or both occur, the nation's terms of trade have improved; if on average export prices fall or import prices rise, or both, its terms of trade have worsened. *See also* BALANCE OF TRADE, COMMODITY AGREEMENT.

Territorial Court   A court established by Congress in a territory of the United States. Congress has established district courts in Guam, Puerto Rico, the Virgin Islands, and the Panama Canal Zone, under its power to govern the territories, and has authorized minor courts in some cases. With the exception of Puerto Rico, the federal district courts of the territories also hear cases ordinarily heard in state courts. The two federal judges in Puerto Rico hold life terms while the one judge in each of the other territorial courts is appointed for an eight-year term.

Territorial Jurisdiction, *see* Accretion, Admiralty Jurisdiction, Airspace Jurisdiction, Avulsion, Cession, Condominium, Contiguous Zone, High Seas, Outer Space Jurisdiction, Prescription, Territorial Waters, Thalweg.

Territorial Limits, *see* Boundaries.

Territorial Waters   The belt of water immediately adjacent to the coast of a state over which the state exercises sovereignty. Territorial waters three miles wide are the minimum generally recognized by the states of the world. There is no generally accepted maximum width although a number of states claim twelve miles and, in individual cases, up to two hundred miles. *See also* INNOCENT PASSAGE.

Territory   An area belonging to the United States that is not included within any state of the Union. Though the Constitution does not expressly grant the power to acquire territory, Article IV, section 3, authorizes Congress to make rules respecting the territory of the United States. Power to acquire territory also results from the national government's power to make treaties, to admit new states, and to make war that might result in conquest. The District of Columbia, though not a part of any state, is not considered a territory. Major territorial possessions of the United States now include Guam, Puerto Rico, the Panama Canal Zone, Samoa, the Virgin Islands, and the Territory of the Pacific Islands. The Department of the Interior supervises the territories except for the Panama Canal Zone, which is under the Department of the Army. *See also* ADMISSION OF NEW STATES.

Test Ban Treaty, *see* Partial Test Ban Treaty.

Test Case   A lawsuit initiated to assess the constitutionality or application of a legislative or executive act. Since federal courts and most state courts do not give advisory opinions, it is necessary to institute a suit to obtain a judicial ruling on the act. This may require the deliberate violation of the act to compel a prosecution or a suit seeking to restrain enforcement. The term "test case" also refers to any landmark case that is the first test of a major piece of legislation.

Testing   The attempt to confirm or disconfirm a factual proposition, or hypothesis, by gathering and analyzing relevant evidence. Testing also refers to the use of certain types of measuring instruments, such as intelligence tests, attitude scales, and tests to determine the level at which observed relationships in a sample are statistically significant. *Verification* is another name for testing a hypothesis, although the result will sometimes be disconfirmation rather than verification. *Validation* means establishing the accuracy of the measuring instrument, or the validity of the test, in measuring the relevant variables. An instrument is valid if it measures the characteristics it is designed to measure. Questions on an interview schedule, for example, may need to be validated by pretesting to make sure they evoke the attitudes the investigator wishes to study and not some other attitudes. *See also* ATTITUDE SCALING, HYPOTHESIS, RELIABILITY, SCIENTIFIC METHOD.

Thalweg   The rule of international law which determines the exact location of the boundary between two states separated by a navigable river. The *thalweg*, or "downway," is the middle of the main channel or downstream current.

Theocracy   Any political system in which political power is exercised directly or indirectly by a clergy, and in which church law is superior to or replaces civil law. The implication is that decisions are made by a Supreme Being and are transmitted to man through agents who rule in a theocracy.

Theorem, *see* Theory.

Theoretical Statistics, *see* Statistics.

Theory   An idea or body of thought that purports to explain, predict, or prescribe in any field of inquiry. In *empirical science* (including empirical political science) theory refers to a logically related set of propositions stating relationships between variables for the purpose of explanation or prediction or both. A *single* theoretical proposition or generalization is sometimes called a theory, but the term usually implies the linking together of a number of *related* propositions in some coherent structure, such as a theory of power elites, or a theory of political integration. One commonly used classification distinguishes *lower-level, middle-range,* and *general theories.* A *lower-level* theory consists of one or a few theoretical propositions dealing with a particular subclass of events. A *middle-range theory* embraces a larger class of events, combining and interrelating a number of separate propositions. *General theory,* broadest in scope, combines middle-range theories into a comprehensive structure for integrating knowledge in a large segment of a field or even a whole discipline. Thus, a hypothesis about the relationships between bloc alignment and voting behavior in international organizations might be joined with other lower-level propositions to form a middle range theory of voting behavior in international organizations. This in turn could be combined with related middle-range theories to form a general theory of international organizations. *Empirical theory*, which deals with observable relationships, may be distinguished from *philosophical theory*, which is concerned with value judgments (*normative theory*) and with the discernment of reality by a priori reasoning. Empirical theories and hypotheses may be deduced from existing bodies of theory or from abstract models, or they may be arrived at inductively by generalizing from the observation of particular cases. However derived, empirical theories are tested by reference to the factual situations they purport to explain or predict. A well-established theoretical proposition is called a *law*. An *axiom* is a proposition whose truth is taken to be self-evident, or established. Axioms sometimes appear as a set of interrelated propositions, proven or assumed, that constitute the fundamental postulates of a theory. Propositions deduced from the axioms of a theory are called *theorems*. The truth of theorems may be demonstrated deductively by reference to the axioms, or it may be subjected to empirical testing. *See also* COLLECTIVE GOODS, COMMUNICATIONS THEORY, CONCEPT, DECISION MAKING, DEVELOPMENT THEORY, ELITIST THEORY, ENGINEERING THEORY, FACT, FIELD THEORY, FUNCTIONALISM, GAME THEORY, GENERALIZATION, GROUP THEORY, HYPOTHESIS, ORGANIZATION THEORY, POLITICAL PHILOSOPHY, POLITICAL THEORY, PREDICTION, PROPOSITION, SCIENCE, SCIENTIFIC METHOD, STRUCTURAL-FUNCTIONALISM, SYSTEMS ANALYSIS, TENDENCY STATEMENT, VARIABLE.

The Passenger Cases, 7 Howard 283 (1849): Declared that immigration is the exclusive concern of the national government and is not subject to state control. The seaboard states had sought to regulate the heavy flow of immigrants to their shores by levying a tax on ships carrying immigrants.

Third Amendment, *see* Quartering of Soldiers.

Third Force   A post-World War II concept of an area of power and influence in international politics in addition to those of the United States and the Soviet Union. The idea of a third force has been associated on various occasions with France, West Europe, the nonaligned states, and the Afro-Asian bloc. *See also* BIPOLARITY.

Third House, *see* Lobbyist.

Third Party   A new party, usually comprised of independents and dissidents from the major parties in a two-party system that, typically, is based on a protest movement and that may rally sufficient voter support to affect a presidential election. Some students of government distinguish a third from a *minor* party, a long-standing ideological party that seldom affects a specific election outcome. The objective of American third parties may be to encourage a large protest vote, or to seek to prevent either major party candidate from winning a majority of electoral votes with the result that the election of the President would be thrown into the House of Representatives. *See also* MINOR PARTY.

Third World, *see* Neutralism, Third Force.

Thirteenth Amendment An amendment to the Constitution, adopted in 1865, forbidding slavery or involuntary servitude anywhere in the United States or any place subject to its jurisdiction. It applies to individuals as well as to government. The Amendment is a guarantee against forced labor and, under recent Supreme Court rulings, gives Congress power to legislate against any acts which impose a "badge of slavery" on anyone. *See also* INVOLUNTARY SERVITUDE, *Jones v. Mayer.*

Three-fifths Compromise An agreement reached at the Constitutional Convention of 1787 to count only three-fifths of the slave population in determining representation in the House of Representatives and in apportioning direct taxes.

Tight Money Policy, *see* Monetary Policy.

Tilton v. Richardson, *see* Separation of Church and State.

Time Series Analysis The analysis of numerical data arranged in time sequence, representing quantitative values of the same or similar kinds of events occurring at successive intervals in time. A time series might be constructed, for example, from voter turnout each election year, annual observations of outbreaks of domestic violence over a twenty-year period, or population figures collected at five-year intervals over a half century. The analysis of a time series may consist of examining it for descriptive content, comparing data for different time periods, and looking for trends, uniformities, and deviations. Analysis may also include attempted explanation, often by means of correlating two or more interrelated series. Thus, an analyst might try to explain shifts over time in United Nations voting alignments by reference to time series data on foreign aid patterns. *Diachronic* analysis and *longitudinal* analysis are other names applied to studies having a time dimension. Research dealing with data drawn from a single time period, or examined without reference to time as a variable, is called *synchronic* or *cross-sectional* analysis. *See also* CASE STUDY, COMPARATIVE STUDY.

Times Film Corporation v. Chicago, *see Freedman v. Maryland.*

Titoism The theory and practice of national communism espoused by Josip Broz Tito, Communist leader of Yugoslavia. Titoism emerged as a new doctrine in 1948 when President Tito rejected the monolithic approach to world communism forcefully pushed by Josef Stalin, under which national Communist parties were expected to accept the direction and control of the Communist party of the Soviet Union. For Tito, nationalism and communism are complementary doctrines that should be fused into a new movement that permits each Communist state to retain full political independence and to choose its own "road to socialism."

Tokyo War Crimes Trials, *see* War Crimes Trials.

Topography (Geographic Power Factor)   The effect on national power of the physical features of a state. Topography includes such elements as altitude, river systems, mountain ranges, plains, and marshlands. Such other factors as size, location, raw materials, and climate, when considered together with topography, constitute the geographic element of national power.

Torcaso v. Watkins, *see* Religious Test.

Tort   A wrongful act involving injury to persons, property, or reputation, but excluding breach of contract. The injured party may bring suit against the wrongdoer. This is an important and often used branch of law. A major tort problem concerns the responsibility of governmental units for torts committed by government employees against individuals.

Tory, *see* Conservative Party (Britain).

Totalitarianism   A modern form of authoritarianism in which the state controls nearly every aspect of the individual's life. Totalitarian governments do not tolerate activities by individuals or groups, such as labor unions and youth organizations, that are not directed toward the state's goals. Totalitarian dictators maintain themselves in power by means of a secret police, propaganda disseminated through all media of communication, the elimination of free discussion and criticism, and widespread use of terror tactics. Internal scapegoats and foreign military threats are created and used to foster unity through fear. *See also* ABSOLUTISM, FASCISM.

Totalitarianism (Fascist Theory)   Authoritarian control by the state over individuals and organizations so that all activity is harmonized with the policies and goals of the regime. Fascist totalitarian tactics include utilizing secret police and terroristic operations, eliminating dissent, denying civil rights, and carrying on an all-pervasive propaganda program through state-controlled media of communication. A single political party inspired by the ideology of fascism monopolizes power and uses the machinery of the state to carry out its objectives.

Total War   A modern war fought for unrestricted objectives with all means available for marshaling national power. Total war involves: (1) participation of entire populations in the war effort; (2) terrorization of civilian populations to destroy their will to fight; (3) the use of modern weapons offering a vast range of destructive power; (4) participation of most nations in the war, with fighting carried on globally; (5) gross violations of the international rules of warfare; (6) intense mass emotional attachment to nationalist or ideological ideals or goals that transform the war into a moral crusade for both sides; (7) demand for unconditional surrender; and (8) the political, economic, and social reconstruction of the defeated states according to the dictates of the victors. *See also* LIMITED WAR.

Town   The major unit of local government in New England. The term is used in some states to designate a township or a small urban area but is generally used by political scientists to designate the New England town. With the exception of some incorporated cities, all six states of New England are divided into towns; this division includes both the rural and urban portions of each particular area. The town is responsible for most of those governmental services provided in other states by counties and cities. The town is governed by all the inhabitants through the town meeting and, between meetings, by a board of selectmen and other town officers. In many towns, however, representatives are chosen for town meetings, and some utilize a town manager.

Town Meeting   The governing authority of a town or township. All qualified voters may participate in the election of officers and in the passage of taxes or other legislation. Town meetings are used in New England towns and in many midwestern townships.

Township   A unit of government, usually a subdivision of a county, found in sixteen states, principally in the midwest and in the northeast. The term "midwestern township" is often used to distinguish it from the New England town. Townships vary in shape and size but tend to cover an area of thirty-six square miles as a result of the congressional township system of identifying land. Some townships have an annual town meeting and all are governed by a township board, usually consisting of three members. Municipal areas are usually excluded from the township territory but in some states, villages, or towns remain part of the township. Township functions tend to be rural in nature, such as maintaining roads, cemeteries, and drains, minor law enforcement, and assessment of property. In urban areas, however, townships have taken on numerous urban services, such as police and fire protection and public works. In some states, the township is the unit for school administration. *See also* CONGRESSIONAL TOWNSHIP, TOWN.

Township, Congressional, *see* Congressional Township.

Trade Agreements Act, *see* Reciprocal Trade Agreements Act of 1934.

Trade Balance, *see* Balance of Trade.

Trade Embargo, *see* Embargo.

Trade Expansion Act of 1962 (TEA)   The statute which replaced the Trade Agreements Act of 1934 as the basis for United States trade policy. The Trade Expansion Act retained the principle of reciprocal tariff reductions. The President was given a five-year authority to negotiate tariff reductions, of up to 50 percent, covering broad categories of products rather than on the traditional item-by-item basis. A "trade adjustment" feature in the statute permitted expansion of government programs to help home industries that suffered from foreign competition, and peril-point and escape clauses to provide tariff relief to industries seriously damaged by foreign competition were continued. *See also* ESCAPE CLAUSE, MOST-FAVORED-NATION CLAUSE, TARIFF.

Trade, International, *see* Balance of Payments, Balance of Trade, Barter, Battle Act, Bilateral Trade, Boycott (International), Commodity Agreement, Commonwealth Preferences, Comparative Advantage, Countervailing Duty, Directed Trade, Dumping, Economic Nationalism, Embargo, Escape Clause, Free Trade, GATT, Licensing, Mercantilism, Most-Favored-Nation Clause, OECD, Preferential Trade Arrangement, Protectionism, Reciprocal Trade Agreements Act of 1934, Reciprocity, Tariff, Tariff Commission, Terms of Trade, Trade Expansion Act of 1962, Webb-Pomerene Act of 1918.

Trademark   A name, mark, or symbol used by a manufacturer or dealer to identify his product or service to the consuming public. Trademarks are granted by the Patent Office through a procedure similar to that for obtaining patents. Registered trademarks are valid for twenty years, provided registrants file affidavits with the Patent Office every five years attesting to their use, and are renewable for subsequent twenty-year periods. Trademark protection is left up to registrants who can take civil suit action in the courts when infringements occur. *See also* COPYRIGHT, PATENT.

Traditional Approach   An approach to political inquiry that emphasizes humanist, legal, and philosophical perspectives in contrast to the predominantly scientific and empirical. The traditional approach, thus broadly defined, embraces many divergent attitudes and methodologies. Nevertheless, some commonly attributed characteristics may be summarized as follows: (1) Traditionalists regard both empirical and normative questions as proper subject of inquiry. (2) Research commonly focuses on formal institutions, legal systems, and historical description of political events. (3) Quantitative methods are used sparingly, if at all. (4) Conclusions are drawn from informed judgement after careful study or observation, rather than from statistical probabilities based on many observed cases, (5) Doubt exists that scientific method, in any sense other than careful, systematic inquiry, can be successfully transferred to the study of human behavior. *See also* BEHAVIORALISM.

Traditional Society, *see* Political Development.

Transitional Society, *see* Political Development.

Transnational Society, *see* Society.

Treason   A disloyal act, which, as defined by Article III, section 3 of the Constitution, "shall consist only in levying war against [the United States], or in adhering to their enemies, giving them aid and comfort." The Constitution further provides that one may not be convicted of treason "unless on the testimony of two witnesses to the same overt act, or on confession in open court."

Treasurer, State, *see* State Treasurer.

Treaty   A formal agreement entered into between two or more sovereign states for the purpose of creating or restricting mutual rights and mutual responsibilities. The treaty process includes negotiation, signing, ratification, exchange of ratifications, publishing and proclamation, and treaty execution. Treaties having only two signatory states are called bilateral, whereas those with more than two parties are multilateral. Treaties may expire at the end of a specified time limit, when certain conditions have been met, or by mutual agreement. Renunciation of a treaty by one of its parties may occur when a state of war exists or when conditions have been substantially altered (*rebus sic stantibus*). In the United States, all treaties are negotiated under the direction of the President, with some members of the Senate occasionally participating under the constitutional provision that treaties be made "by and with the advice and consent of the Senate. . . . " Treaties must be approved by a two-thirds vote in the Senate, followed by presidential ratification if the Senate's version is acceptable. *See also* EXECUTIVE AGREEMENT, RATIFICATION, *Missouri v. Holland.*

Treaty Denunciation, *see Rebus sic Stantibus.*

Treaty for the Renunciation of War, *see* Kellogg-Briand Pact.

Treaty Power (Congress)   The participation of the Senate in the executive act of treaty making. The President negotiates treaties, but under the constitutional system of checks and balances he cannot ratify them until the Senate by a two-thirds majority of those present and voting gives its consent. Under its treaty power the Senate may: (1) consent to ratification; (2) refuse consent; (3) consent to ratification after specified amendments have been made; and (4) consent to ratification with specific reservations. In no case, however, is the President legally required to ratify following Senate action. Although the Senate Foreign Relations Committee is the principal focus of the treaty power in Congress, other committees in the Senate and the House also become involved, depending on the treaty's subject matter. The House of Representatives, for example, has no treaty power per se; however, it has assumed an active role through its Appropriations Committee's insistence on a substantive review of treaty provisions before recommending the funds necessary to implement the treaty. *See also* TREATY POWER (PRESIDENT).

Treaty Power (President)   Treaties are negotiated under the President's direction as the nation's chief diplomat and chief of foreign policy. The treaty power is set forth in Article II, Section 2, of the Constitution. Under the system of checks and balances, the President can negotiate but cannot ratify a treaty until the Senate has given its consent in the form of a two-thirds vote of approval. Courses of action open to the President in connection with the Senate's role in the treaty process include these possibilities: (1) normally, he will submit the treaty to the Senate and then ratify it after the Senate has consented; (2) if the Senate is hostile, the President may refuse to submit a treaty and let it die rather than suffer a defeat; (3) under similar conditions, the treaty can be withdrawn from the Senate before a vote has been taken; and (4) if the Senate has approved a treaty with Senate amendments and if the President deems renegotiation inappropriate, he may refuse to ratify. The technical steps in the entire treaty process are negotiation, signature, ratification, exchange of ratifications, publication, proclamation, and execution. *See also* TREATY POWER (CONGRESS).

Treaty Ratification   The act by which a state formally confirms and approves the terms of a treaty. Normally an executive act, ratification is accomplished for each signatory of a treaty in accordance with its constitutional processes. This usually requires the consent of one or more houses of the national legislature. In some countries, legislative participation is pro forma, but in others—such as the United States—it is the critical stage in the treaty process. *See also* TREATY POWER (CONGRESS), TREATY POWER (PRESIDENT), RATIFICATION (EXECUTIVE ROLE), RATIFICATION (LEGISLATIVE ROLE).

Trial   The examination of a civil or criminal action in accordance with the law of the land before a judge who has jurisdiction. A trial must be public, conducted fairly before an impartial judge, and in the case of criminal trials, started without unreasonable delay. *See also Moore v. Dempsey*, SIXTH AMENDMENT.

Troika Proposal (United Nations)   A plan offered by the Soviet Union during the early 1960s to replace the one-man office of Secretary-General of the United Nations with a three-man presidium. Nikita Khrushchev coined the term with reference to a type of Russian vehicle drawn by three horses. Each of the three major world blocs—Western, Soviet, and Neutralist—would be represented on the presidium and each would have the power to veto Secretariat decisions. *See also* SECRETARY-GENERAL.

Trop v. Dulles, 356 U.S. 86 (1958): Decided that the deprivation of citizenship for wartime desertion is a cruel and unusual punishment. The Supreme Court held that native-born citizenship is a basic right and cannot be taken away without voluntary expatriation. The Court noted that desertion does not always indicate disloyalty to one's country. *See also* DENATURALIZATION, EXPATRIATION.

Trotskyism   The theories of Leon Trotsky, a leading Communist revolutionary, who contested for power with Josef Stalin in the Soviet Union after Lenin's death in 1924. After the Bolshevik Revolution of 1917 and the Civil War period, Trotsky argued for using the Communist base in Russia for the achievement of world revolution. Stalin, on the other hand, called for building socialism in one country to give communism a sound base, impregnable to capitalist counterrevolution. Stalin won the power struggle in the late 1920s, ousted Trotsky from the Communist party of the Soviet Union, and exiled him from the country. Trotsky continued his opposition to Stalin and Stalinism in exile, but was assassinated in Mexico in 1940. Trotskyism as an ideology called for unity and common effort among the proletariat of all countries to establish a world Communist commonwealth. Trotsky believed that the Russian Revolution had failed because it had created a bureaucratic ruling class that exploited the workers and betrayed their interests.

Truax v. Raich, 239 U.S. 33 (1915): Declared unconstitutional an Arizona law requiring that at least 80 percent of the employees of any private business must be citizens, as a denial of equal protection of the law. The Court held that a state may not deny a person the right to earn a living, regardless of his race or nationality. *See also* ALIEN.

Truce, *see* Armistice.

True Bill, *see* Grand Jury.

Truman Doctrine   The policy, adopted by President Harry Truman in 1947, that called for American support for all free peoples resisting armed subjugation by internal or outside forces. The policy was aimed expressly at halting Communist expansion in southeastern Europe and was expounded in a speech to Congress in which President Truman asked for an appropriation of $400 million for military and economic aid to Greece and Turkey. *See also* CONTAINMENT.

Trust   Two or more corporations linked together by assigning the voting rights of a majority of stockholders in each corporation to a single group of trustees. The term is also commonly used to describe any huge corporation or group of corporations that pursues monopolistic policies in the production or supplying of goods or services. *See also* SHERMAN ANTITRUST ACT.

Trusteeship Council   One of the six major organs of the United Nations, which helps the General Assembly to supervise the administration of the international trusteeship system. Members of the Council include those nations that administer trust territories, permanent members of the Security Council, and enough elected members to provide for parity between nontrust and trust-administering states on the Council. Trust territories include the: (1) former mandates of the League of Nations; (2) Axis colonies; and (3) colonies voluntarily placed under trusteeship. No colonial power has yet volunteered to place a colony under the system. Council powers include considering reports, accepting petitions, and making periodic visits to trust territories. Administration of "strategic" trust territories is supervised by the Security Council, rather than by the Trusteeship Council, because of their military importance.

Trustee, Township, *see* Supervisor.

Trust Territory   A former League of Nations mandate or a non-self-governing territory placed under the United Nations trusteeship system. All mandates that had not achieved independence became trust territories in 1946, with the exception of South West Africa. Only one additional territory—Italian Somaliland—was placed under trust as a consequence of World War II. Each trust territory was brought into the arrangement by a special agreement drawn up by the administering state and approved by the General Assembly. Supervision over the administration of trust territories is carried on by the Trusteeship Council, utilizing annual reports, petitions from trust peoples, and visiting missions. *See also* MANDATES SYSTEM, TRUSTEESHIP COUNCIL.

TVA, *see* Tennessee Valley Authority.

Twelfth Amendment An amendment to the Constitution, adopted in 1804, that provides for separate ballots to be used by the electors in voting for President and Vice President. Previously, the vice presidency went to the runner-up in the Electoral College vote. The Amendment also reduces the range of choice of the House of Representatives from the five highest to the three highest candidates when none has received an electoral vote majority. The Senate's choice of Vice President under these circimstances is limited to the two highest candidates. *See also* ELECTORAL COLLEGE.

Twentieth Amendment (Executive Provisions) The "lame duck" Amendment to the Constitution, adopted in 1933, which changed the date for beginning the presidential and vice-presidential terms from March 4 to January 20, and that for beginning congressional terms from March 4 to January 3. Other provisions are: (1) if the President-elect dies before taking office, the Vice President-elect shall become President; (2) if a President-elect has not been chosen or fails to qualify by January 20, the Vice President-elect shall act as President until a President is chosen; (3) if neither qualifies, then Congress shall decide who shall act as President until a President or Vice President qualifies; and (4) if the election of the President and Vice President is thrown into the House and the Senate and a candidate dies, Congress shall determine by law what shall be done. *See also* TWENTIETH AMENDMENT (LEGISLATIVE PROVISIONS), PRESIDENT-ELECT.

Twentieth Amendment (Legislative Provisions) An amendment to the Constitution, adopted in 1933, that provides that a new Congress elected in November of even-numbered years will convene on January 3 of the following year unless Congress sets a different date. Prior to its adoption, a newly elected Congress did not convene in regular session until December of the following year—a lapse of thirteen months. The old Congress, meanwhile, with many members who had failed to win re-election ("lame ducks"), met in perfunctory session for four months following the election. The Amendment also changed the presidential term to start a month and one half earlier, on January 20 instead of on March 4. *See also* TWENTIETH AMENDMENT (EXECUTIVE PROVISIONS).

Twenty-fifth Amendment An amendment to the Constitution, adopted in 1967, that establishes procedures for filling vacancies in the two top executive offices, and makes provision for situations involving presidential disability. The Twenty-fifth Amendment specifically assigns to the President the power to fill a vacancy in the office of Vice President, with the approval of a majority of both houses of Congress. In case of presidential disability, the Amendment provides: (1) when the President believes that he is incapable of performing the duties of office, he informs the Congress in writing and the Vice President thereupon serves as acting President until the President can resume his duties; (2) when the President is disabled and unable to communicate, the Vice President and a majority of the Cabinet declare that fact to Congress, and the Vice President then serves as acting President until the President recovers; and (3) when a dispute arises over whether the President is capable of discharging the powers and duties of his office, Congress by a two-thirds vote decides whether the Vice President should continue as acting President or the President should resume his office. *See also* PRESIDENTIAL SUCCESSION.

Twenty-first Amendment   An amendment to the Constitution, adopted in 1933, permitting the sale of intoxicating beverages in the United States. The Amendment protects states that retain prohibition, by barring the importation or transportation of liquor into such states. It repealed the Eighteenth Amendment, which had imposed prohibition on the entire country.

Twenty-fourth Amendment   An amendment to the Constitution, adopted in 1964, that forbids the levying of a poll tax in primary or general elections for national officials, including the President, Vice-President, and members of Congress. The Amendment does not apply to elections for state or local officials.

Twenty-second Amendment   An amendment to the Constitution, adopted in 1951, limiting presidential tenure to two terms for an individual. A Vice President who succeeds to the office may serve as long as ten years as President, provided he has not served more than two years of the uncompleted term of his predecessor. The incumbent President, Harry S Truman, was excluded from the limitations of the Amendment, but he chose not to run for a third term.

Twenty-sixth Amendment   An amendment to the Constitution, adopted in 1971, that lowers the legal voting age to eighteen in the United States. Although eighteen-year-olds had already been accorded the vote in national elections by the Voting Rights Act of 1970, the Twenty-sixth Amendment assured them the vote in *all*—national, state, and local—elections. The amendment proposal was ratified by the necessary thirty-eight state legislatures in record time during 1971 so that the measure could take effect for the 1972 presidential election. Voting opportunities were increased by the Amendment at the time of its adoption for an estimated eleven million young people. *See also* VOTING QUALIFICATIONS.

Twenty-third Amendment   An amendment to the Constitution, adopted in 1961, that enables the people of the District of Columbia to participate in the election of the President. The Twenty-third Amendment allots the District of Columbia three electoral votes. *See also* DISTRICT OF COLUMBIA, ELECTORAL COLLEGE.

Two Chinas Proposal   A solution offered to the problem of Chinese representation in the United Nations that would have admitted Communist China as a new member while continuing membership for Formosa as an independent state. The proposal would have changed the consideration of Communist Chinese membership in the United Nations from that of a question of credentials or "representation" (i.e., since China is an original member, which government, then, is entitled to be recognized as the proper representative for the China seat?) to that of "admission" of a new member. In 1971, the General Assembly decided that the People's Republic be accepted as the legitimate holder of the China seat, but Formosa was not admitted as a new member. This solution resulted in Peking being seated as a permanent member in the Security Council, possessing veto power, with Formosa expelled from the United Nations as a consequence.

Two-House Legislature, *see* Bicameralism.

Two-party System   Division of voter loyalties between two major political parties, resulting in the virtual exclusion of minor parties from sharing in political power. The two-party system is the traditional British system, which has been adopted in many Commonwealth countries and by the United States. *See also* SINGLE-MEMBER DISTRICT, MULTIPARTY SYSTEM, THIRD PARTY.

Typology, *see* Classification.

UEAC, *see* Union of Central African States.

Ultimatum   A formal, final communication from one government to another, requiring the receiving government to comply in some stated fashion with the wishes of the sender or be prepared to take the consequences, ultimately war. An ultimatum indicates that the diplomatic process is but one step short of a breakdown and that one sovereign state is willing to risk the use of force if necessary to impose its will upon another. *See also* NEGOTIATION.

Unanimity   The voting procedure in international organs that provides that no state may be bound by a decision without giving its consent. The rule of unanimity has generally involved the *liberum veto* (a single member, by voting against a proposal, can defeat it), although some organizations' constitutions provide that the dissenting state either accept the decision of a majority or quit the organization. The principle of unanimity is a modern adaptation of the traditional rule of international law that a sovereign state can be bound only by those decisions to which it consents.

Unanimous Consent   A time-saving procedure, also known as "without objection," used by a legislative body to adopt noncontroversial motions, amendments, and bills without submitting them to a vote. Both houses of Congress use the procedure to expedite business. In the House, an objection from a single member results in the tabling of the bill or motion for two weeks.

UNCIO, *see* United Nations Conference on International Organization.

Unconditional Surrender   Termination of hostilities without stipulation of terms. In an unconditional surrender, the vanquished nation places itself fully under the discretionary authority of the victor nation or nations, which may legally impose any terms or conditions considered appropriate. An unconditional surrender would be likely to involve, as a minimum, occupation of the defeated state's territory, punishment of "war criminals," imposition of reparations, and a basic change in political, economic, and social institutions in line with the wishes of the victors.

UNCTAD, *see* United Nations Conference on Trade and Development.

Underdevelopment   A condition characterized by economic, social, and political backwardness when measured by the standards of the advanced societies. Typical features of underdevelopment include: (1) low national and per capita income and productivity; (2) high rates of illiteracy; (3) high birth rates with decreasing death rates, leading to a virtual "population explosion"; (4) a heavy dependence upon subsistence-level agriculture; (5) extensive use of child labor and few educational facilities and opportunities; (6) decentralized political institutions; (7) a rigid class structure with a minimum of social mobility; and (8) rudimentary communication and transportation facilities. *See also* ECOMOMIC GROWTH.

Underdog Effect   A tendency of some voters to feel sorry for a losing candidate and to switch their vote to him.

UNEF, *see* United Nations Emergency Force.

Unemployment Insurance   A program of insurance under the Social Security Act of 1935 that provides for payment of funds for a limited period of time to workers who are laid off or discharged for reasons beyond their control. The program is administered by the states under national supervision. Under the plan, Congress imposes a tax on the payroll of employers of four or more workers. Ninety percent of the revenue from this tax is credited to each state that comes under the act (all do), with the remainder used for administrative purposes. All proceeds of the tax are held by the national Department of the Treasury in separate state accounts to be paid out as needed by each state. Each state determines the amount to be paid to each unemployed person, for how long, and under what conditions. Generally, benefits amount to about $40 per week for twenty weeks and are available to unemployed persons who register with the proper state agency and are willing to accept suitable employment. Most states penalize employers with poor employment records by raising their payroll tax. Overall supervision of state plans is in the hands of the Unemployment Insurance Service in the Department of Labor. *See also Social Security Cases.*

UNESCO, *see* United Nations Educational, Scientific, and Cultural Organization.

Unfair Labor Practice   Activity by a labor union or an employer that is defined by law as constituting a threat to industrial peace. Unfair labor practices are defined in the Taft-Hartley Act of 1947. Employers are forbidden to interfere with the rights of unions to organize, to discriminate against union members, or to refuse to bargain collectively. Unions may not discriminate against or coerce employees who are not union members, or engage in such practices as secondary boycotts, featherbedding, jurisdictional strikes, charging excessive dues or fees, or refusing to bargain collectively. *See also* BOYCOTT, FEATHERBEDDING, JURISDICTIONAL STRIKE, TAFT-HARTLEY ACT.

Unfair Trade Practice   Any business activity that deceives or misleads the consumer and results in his being sold shoddy, dangerous, or overpriced goods or services. Examples of unfair trade practices include false and misleading advertising, misbranding, improper labeling, conspiracies to fix prices, collusive bidding, discrimination against buyers, price cutting to eliminate competition, and other practices in restraint of trade. *See also* FEDERAL TRADE COMMISSION, CLAYTON ACT.

UNFICYP, *see* United Nations Force in Cyprus.

UNHCR, *see* United Nations High Commissioner for Refugees.

Unicameralism   The principle of a one-house legislature, as contrasted with bicameralism, a legislature based on two houses. One state legislature—Nebraska's—is unicameral, as are local governmental policy-determining bodies, such as county boards, city councils, township boards, and school boards. *See also* BICAMERALISM.

UNICEF, *see* United Nations Children's Fund.

UNIDO, *see* United Nations Industrial Development Organization.

Unification   The integration of the military services of the United States. Under the National Security Act of 1947, the Army, Navy, and Air Force were unified under a single Department of Defense. *See also* DEFENSE REORGANIZATION ACT, NATIONAL SECURITY ACTS.

Unified Court System   An integrated statewide or areawide court system, organized into divisions for more efficient distribution of case load and judges. A chief judge, aided by a judicial council or business manager, supervises the operations of the courts, shifts judges about to meet case load demands, and, through collection of significant data, promotes the efficient administration of justice.

Uniform State Laws   Laws proposed by the National Conference of Commissioners on Uniform State Laws, a few of which have been adopted by all or many states. Among those proposals that have had wide adoption are the Negotiable Instruments

Act, the Warehouse Receipts Act, the Stock Transfer Act, others relating to sales, partnerships, bills of lading, and some traffic, criminal, and family matters. The National Conference has proposed over 100 uniform laws since its inception in 1892, but it has met with only minor success. The Conference consists of three Commissioners from each state, usually lawyers, appointed by the governor. The Council of State Governments acts as secretariat for the Conference. *See also* HORIZONTAL FEDERALISM.

Unilateral Disarmament   A strategy advocated by some disarmament protagonists to overcome a continued deadlock in negotiations by undertaking one-sided initiatives. Unilateral disarmament schemes are predicated on the assumption that both sides in an arms race would prefer to disarm but that the fear, tension, and mistrust generated by the search for security through increased armaments stymies the quest. By demonstrating peaceful intentions rather than merely talking about them, unilateral disarmament theorists believe, one side could put the arms-race cycle into reverse by evoking reciprocation of its disarmament initiatives.

Unilateralism   A policy whereby a state depends completely on its own resources for security and the advancement of its national interest. Unilateralism can take a variety of forms: (1) Isolationism or neo-isolationism implies a decision not to participate in or to severely limit participation in international relations. (2) Neutrality involves giving up, by unilateral act or by treaty, the option of military participation in international affairs unless attacked. (3) States which participate actively in international politics but which rely on their own wits and strength are also engaged in unilateralism. (4) Nonalignment is a form of unilateralism that describes the current disinclination, mainly of the developing countries, to commit themselves exclusively to either side in the cold war.

Unincorporated Area, *see* Incorporated and Unincorporated Areas.

Union, *see* Labor Unions.

Union Calendar, *see* Calendar.

Union of Central African States (UEAC)   A regional organization established in 1968 to foster economic and social cooperation among its three members, the Congo (Democratic Republic), the Central African Republic, and Chad. The UEAC charter provides for tariff reductions, travel between the three without visas, improved transport facilities, and the exchange of security information. The secretariat for UEAC is located at Bangui in the Central African Republic.

Union Shop   An establishment in which all newly hired workers must join the union after a specified period of time, usually thirty days. Unlike the closed shop, now outlawed, the employee need not be a member of the union in order to be hired. *See also* CLOSED SHOP, RIGHT TO WORK LAW.

UNITAR, *see* United Nations Institute for Training and Research.

Unitary State   A centralized government in which local or subdivisional governments exercise only those powers given to them by the central government. It differs from a federal system in which power is constitutionally divided between a central and subdivisional government. The United Kingdom and France are examples of the unitary form. In the United States, local governments, such as cities and counties, stand in a unitary relationship to the state governments that assign specific rights and duties to them. An exception to this is found in those states in which cities are given "home rule" by constitutional provision. *See also* FEDERALISM.

United Nations Admissions, *see* Admission (International Organization).

United Nations Amendment Process, *see* Amendment Process (International Organization).

United Nations Budget, *see* United Nations Finance.

United Nations Capital Development Fund (UNCDF)   An organ of the General Assembly established in 1966 "to assist developing countries in the development of their economies by supplementing existing sources of capital assistance by means of grants and loans. . . . " The creation of the Capital Development Fund capped, under a new title, more than a decade of effort by the underdeveloped countries to establish a Special United Nations Fund for Economic Development (SUNFED proposal) to provide them with capital grants and low-interest, long-term loans. The UNCDF is headed by a twenty-four-member executive board elected by the General Assembly and a managing director appointed by the Secretary-General of the United Nations. Funds to support its operations are contributed by governments and by nongovernmental organizations, and an annual pledging conference is convened by the Secretary-General to elicit these voluntary contributions. *See also* CAPITAL.

United Nations Caucusing Group, *see* Caucusing Group (United Nations).

United Nations Charter   A multilateral treaty which serves as the "constitution" for the United Nations Organization. The Charter was drawn up and signed at San Francisco on June 26, 1945, and was ratified by fifty-one original members and put into effect on October 24, 1945, since known as United Nations Day. The document consists of a preamble and 111 articles that proclaim the purposes and principles of the organization, provide for the establishment of six major organs, and enumerate the procedures and functions of each. *See also* UNITED NATIONS CONFERENCE ON INTERNATIONAL ORGANIZATION.

United Nations Children's Fund (UNICEF) An organization established by the General Assembly in 1946 to provide emergency supplies of food, medicine, and clothing to destitute children in war-ravaged countries. Originally called the United Nations International Children's Emergency Fund (UNICEF), when the General Assembly gave it permanent status its name was changed by deleting the words "International" and "Emergency," but its well-known acronym, UNICEF, was retained. UNICEF has since expanded its operations to include the underdeveloped countries and has increased its activities to include sponsorship of national projects for better education, improved health, and disease control, with matching funds provided by recipient nations. Increasingly it has called upon specialized agencies, such as WHO, UNESCO, and FAO, for advice and help in carrying out its programs. Financing for its programs has come from member governments, from private contributions, from UNICEF holiday greeting card programs, and from Halloween "trick or treat" collections by children in the United States.

United Nations China Membership Issue, *see* Two Chinas Proposal.

United Nations Collective Security System, *see* Collective Security, Sanctions (Collective Security), Security Council.

United Nations Conference on International Organization (UNCIO) The major conference at San Francisco (April 25 to June 26, 1945) that wrote the Charter of the United Nations and approved the Statute of the International Court of Justice. The fifty participating states, together with Poland, became the fifty-one original members of the United Nations. The deliberations at San Francisco were based on the Proposals formulated by the four sponsoring governments (Britain, China, the Soviet Union, and the United States) at the Dumbarton Oaks Conference of 1944. The work of the San Francisco conference resembled that of a constituent body drafting a constitution. It was carried on in four commissions and twelve committees, with final approval recorded at plenary conference sessions. Leadership was provided by the great powers at each stage. The Charter became effective on October 24, 1945 (since designated United Nations Day) when a majority of signers, including the Big Five, had ratified it. Before the meeting of the First General Assembly in January, 1946, the Charter had been ratified by all fifty-one original members. *See also* DUMBARTON OAKS CONFERENCE, YALTA AGREEMENT.

United Nations Conference on Trade and Development (UNCTAD) An organ of the General Assembly established to develop world trade policies. UNCTAD began as a special trade conference attended by 122 states at Geneva in 1964 and was given permanent status by the General Assembly in the same year. The underdeveloped states of the world pushed for its creation as a forum where they could apply pressures on the advanced industrial states to lower their trade barriers to permit expanded trade in primary commodities. Their main objective is to increase foreign exchange earnings to support development programs. UNCTAD is convened in plenary session at least every three years to serve as a center for harmonizing trade and development policies. A fifty-five-member Trade and Development Board initiates policy proposals between UNCTAD sessions, and a secretariat is located at UNCTAD's Geneva headquarters. *See also* GENERAL AGREEMENT ON TARIFFS AND TRADE.

United Nations Development Decade, *see* Second Development Decade.

United Nations Disarmament Commission A body established by the General Assembly in 1952 for the discussion and negotiation of disarmament issues. The United Nations Disarmament Commission since 1958 has included all members of the United Nations. It has been called into plenary session on only two occasions: in 1960 to pressure the Soviets to resume negotiations after their walk-out from Geneva talks over the issue of achieving "parity" in negotiations, and in 1965 to overcome a hiatus in great-power talks resulting from protracted disagreement over the specifics of general and complete disarmament. *See also* CONFERENCE OF THE COMMITTEE ON DISARMAMENT.

United Nations Dispute Settlement Procedures, *see* Dispute Settlement Procedures (United Nations).

United Nations Domestic Jurisdiction Clause, *see* Domestic Jurisdiction Clause.

United Nations Dumbarton Oaks Conference, *see* Dumbarton Oaks Conference.

United Nations Economic and Social Council, *see* Economic and Social Council.

United Nations Educational, Scientific, and Cultural Organization (UNESCO) A specialized agency of the United Nations which promotes cooperation among members in the fields of education, science, and culture. Through recommendations to member governments and through its own activities, UNESCO has carried on exchange programs, promoted teaching and research, and has sought to advance the ideals of equal rights and educational opportunity. UNESCO machinery includes a General Conference, an Executive Board, and a Secretariat, with its headquarters in Paris. *See also* SPECIALIZED AGENCY.

United Nations Emergency Force (UNEF) A special peace-supervising force established by the General Assembly during the Middle East crisis of 1956 to supervise the Israeli-Egyptian cease-fire line. UNEF included contingents from ten countries (Brazil, Canada, Denmark, India, Norway, Sweden, Yugoslavia, Finland, Indonesia, and Colombia) and built up to a peak of about 6,000 officers and men. Principles underlying the establishment of UNEF included: (1) that it be composed of contingents from "neutral" nations; (2) that the United Nations determine the function of the force; (3) that the approval of the host country be secured (Egypt but not Israel agreed to permit UNEF to operate on its territory); (4) that the force be limited to a nonfighting, conciliation role; and (5) that the major costs be financed by a special peace-keeping operations levy on all United Nations members. UNEF functioned continuously from 1956 to 1967 when Egypt's request to withdraw UNEF was followed by a reopening of Arab-Israeli hostilities. *See also* INTERNATIONAL POLICE FORCE.

United Nations Expulsion of Members, *see* Expulsion, Suspension, Withdrawal (International Organization).

United Nations Finance   The function of raising operating funds to expend on overhead costs and the broad-gauged programs carried on under the aegis of the United Nations. Almost all regular budget income comes from contributions assessed upon member states according to a formula that takes account of their national incomes, per capita incomes, and foreign exchange earnings. Each state must pay the major portion of its assessment in dollars, with the balance payable in local currencies. Assessments range from about 30 percent for the largest contributor, the United States, to the established minimum of 0.04 percent required of nearly one-half of the members. Overall operations of the organization are divided into four budgets: (1) the regular budget (general overhead and administrative operating costs); (2) the specialized agencies (WHO, UNESCO, FAO, IBRD, etc.); (3) special voluntary programs (United Nations Development Program, refugees, and UNICEF); and (4) peace-keeping operations (United Nations Emergency Force [UNEF] and United Nations Operation in the Congo [ONUC]).

United Nations Force in Cyprus (UNFICYP)   A peace-supervising force established by the Security Council in 1964 to help end the violence between the Greek and Turkish communities on Cyprus. UNFICYP was assigned the objectives of maintaining law and order on the island, preventing a recurrence of the fighting, and preserving international peace and security. The formula for financing UNFICYP provides that costs be paid by countries supplying troops for the Force, by Cyprus, and by voluntary contributions from United Nations members. The Force includes troop units from Austria, Britain, Canada, Denmark, Finland, Ireland, and Sweden, with special civilian police units contributed by Australia, Austria, Denmark, New Zealand, and Sweden. *See also* INTERNATIONAL POLICE FORCE.

United Nations General Assembly, *see* General Assembly.

United Nations General Debate, *see* General Debate (United Nations).

United Nations Genocide Convention, *see* Genocide Convention.

United Nations High Commissioner for Refugees (UNHCR)   An Office established by the General Assembly in 1951 to afford temporary international protection for refugees pending permanent solutions by member states through resettlement, repatriation, or assimilation. UNHCR was set up to replace the International Refugee Organization (IRO), which had completed the major portion of the task of resettling World War II refugees. The Office of the High Commissioner receives support from the United Nations budget for administrative expenses only, with the financing of all programs dependent upon voluntary national and private contributions. Refugees receiving aid under other United Nations programs, such as the relief of Arab refugees in the Middle East, and those granted the rights of nationals in the country of their residence, do not come under the High Commissioner's jurisdiction. *See also* REFUGEE, UNITED NATIONS RELIEF AND WORKS AGENCY.

United Nations Important Question, *see* Important Question (United Nations).

United Nations Industrial Development Organization (UNIDO)   An agency established by the General Assembly "to promote industrial development . . . and accelerate the industrialization of the developing countries, with particular emphasis on the manufacturing sector." UNIDO began its operations as an "autonomous" organization within the United Nations in 1967. Its responsibilities include intensifying, coordinating, and expediting the efforts of the United Nations in the field of industrial development. A forty-five-member Industrial Development Board, elected by the General Assembly, functions as UNIDO's principal organ and develops principles and policies to guide its program. The Board also supervises activities, creates subsidiary organs when needed, and reports annually to the General Assembly. A secretariat functions at UNIDO's headquarters in Vienna.

United Nations Institute for Training and Research (UNITAR)   An autonomous agency established by the General Assembly in 1963 to train individuals for work in economic and social development, particularly for technical assistance programs. UNITAR programs include granting fellowships to enable individuals from developing countries to upgrade their skills for national or international services, providing experts to teach special courses at colleges and universities in these states, and conducting research on subjects related to economic development. Its governing body consists of a Board of Trustees, who serve as individuals rather than as representatives of states. Trustees are appointed by the Secretary-General in consultation with the Presidents of the General Assembly and the Economic and Social Council. *See also* TECHNICAL ASSISTANCE.

United Nations International Court of Justice, *see* International Court of Justice.

United Nations Operation in the Congo (ONUC)   A military-civilian force established in 1960 to restore peace and order in the former Belgian Congo. Secretary-General Dag Hammarskjöld organized the force (known generally by its French acronym, ONUC) under a mandate granted him by the Security Council when it authorized action by the world organization. ONUC was built into a force of over 20,000, with military personnel furnished by twenty-nine states. In addition, the largest civilian team ever fielded by the United Nations carried out a massive countrywide technical assistance program. Over $400 million was expended between July, 1960, and June, 1964, when ONUC was disbanded. The Congo military operation helped to precipitate a financial crisis that brought the United Nations to the verge of bankruptcy. *See also* UNITED NATIONS FINANCE, INTERNATIONAL POLICE FORCE.

United Nations Original Membership, *see* Yalta Agreement.

United Nations Police Force, *see* International Police Force.

United Nations Regional Commissions   Commissions established by the Economic and Social Council to foster economic cooperation within four major geographical areas of the world. Acting under authority of the Charter (Article 68), ECOSOC in 1947 established an Economic Commission for Europe (ECE) and an Economic Commission for Asia and the Far East (ECAFE), both intended to aid in fostering recovery from World War II. In 1948 ECOSOC recognized an additional role for regional commissions in promoting economic development with the establishment of an Economic Commission for Latin America (ECLA). In 1958 an Economic Commission for Africa (ECA) was founded to help the nations of that continent improve their economic lot. In each case, other states from outside the regions but having a definite interest in the areas are also members of each of the commissions. Efforts to establish a Middle East commission have failed because of a lack of regional harmony. Headquarters for the four commissions are in Geneva, Bangkok, Santiago, and Addis Ababa.

United Nations Relief and Works Agency (UNRWA)   An organization established by the United Nations in 1949 to care for Arab refugees from the Arab-Israeli War of 1948–1949. UNRWA provides food, shelter, education and vocational training, and health services for the refugees, expending more than $800 million in its programs by 1972. The major portion of the annual budget of about $35 million is contributed by the United States. The refugees live in temporary "refugee cities" located in Jordan, Syria, Lebanon, and in Israeli occupied territory. The Arab-Israeli War of 1967 added to UNRWA's responsibilities by creating thousands of new refugees. *See also* REFUGEE, UNITED NATIONS HIGH COMMISSIONER FOR REFUGEES.

United Nations Sanctions, *see* Sanctions (Collective Security).

United Nations Secretariat, *see* Secretariat.

United Nations Secretary-General, *see* Secretary-General.

United Nations Security Council, *see* Security Council.

United Nations Specialized Agencies, *see* Specialized Agency (United Nations).

United Nations Troika Proposal, *see* Troika Proposal (United Nations).

United Nations Trusteeship Council, *see* Trusteeship Council.

United Nations Trust Territory, *see* Trust Territory.

United Nations Uniting for Peace System, *see* Uniting for Peace Resolution.

United Public Workers v. Mitchell, 330 U.S. 75 (1947): Ruled that Congress may prohibit federal employees from participating in political activities. The Court upheld the Hatch Act of 1939, which authorizes the removal of a person from civil service employment for his taking an "active part in political management or political campaigns."

United States Arms Control and Disarmament Agency (USACDA)   An independent agency established in 1961 to conduct research and to develop disarmament policies. USACDA is headed by a Director, appointed by the President with Senate consent, who also serves as principal adviser to the President and the Secretary of State on disarmament matters.

United States Attorney   A federal official whose principal function is to prosecute violations of federal law. A United States Attorney is assigned to each district in which a federal district court is located. He is appointed for a four-year term by the President with the Senate's consent, and is under general supervision of the Department of Justice and the Attorney General of the United States. *See also* DISTRICT ATTORNEY.

United States Code, *see* Code.

United States Commissioner, *see* Federal Magistrate.

United States Government Organization Manual   The official organization handbook of the three branches of the federal government. It lists all federal departments and agencies with detailed descriptions of their powers, duties, and activities. The *Manual* is published annually in July.

United States Information Agency (USIA)   An independent agency established in 1953 that has responsibility for administration of foreign information programs of the United States. The USIA operates a global network of communications media that beam propaganda programs all over the world. The agency works closely with the State Department and related agencies to harmonize its information programs with American foreign policy. *See also* IDEOLOGICAL WARFARE.

United States Intelligence Board, *see* Intelligence (United States).

United States Marshal, *see* Marshal.

United States Postal Service The independent government agency that has the responsibility for operating the United States postal system. The United States Postal Service was created by the Postal Reorganization Act of 1970 to replace the Post Office Department, which had been a major department of the national government, with Cabinet rank, headed by the Postmaster General. Under the Act, the Postal Service Board of Governors appoints postmasters and postal employees, controls rates and classes of mail, and makes general postal operating policy free from political and congressional influence. Civil service status and rights of postal workers were retained under the new Postal Service system. The Postal Service, in addition to carrying the mail, runs a parcel post service, a system of registering, certifying, and insuring mail, sells government bonds, and offers money order, C.O.D., and special delivery services.

United States Reports The official record of cases heard and disposed of by the United States Supreme Court, including the full opinions of the justices. The volumes are issued at the conclusion of the term of the Court but opinions are available in "advance sheets" prior to issuance of the volumes. Two or three volumes of the *Reports* may emerge each year, depending on the volume of business and length of opinions. The volumes are numbered consecutively now, but, prior to 1874, at which time the *Reports* totaled ninety volumes, they were identified by the names of the official court reporters. These include: Dallas, Cranch, Wheaton, Peters, Howard, Black, and Wallace. Thus, a case cited as 1 Cranch 137 (1803), means that the case, decided in 1803, can be found on page 137 of the first volume compiled by Cranch. Since 1874, the volumes are simply numbered, beginning with 91. A case cited as 345 U.S. 123 (1953) will be found on page 123 of volume 345 of the *United States Reports,* and was decided in 1953. All recorded legal decisions in any court may be found in similar fashion by locating the title, volume, and page of the *Report* in which it is given. Reports are available from federal courts of appeals (*Federal Reporter*), district courts (*Federal Supplement*), and highest state courts which are identified by the name of the state, for example, 156 Michigan 124. Commercial companies also put out volumes reporting these cases: *The Supreme Court Reporter* (cited as 57 Sup. Ct. 234) and the *Lawyers' Edition* (cited as 57 L. Ed. 234).

United States Tariff Commission An independent agency that gives information to Congress and the President on American and foreign tariff and trade matters. The six members of the Tariff Commission, three from each of the major parties, are appointed by the President, with the Senate's approval, for six-year terms. *See also* TARIFF.

United States Tax Court A special judicial agency that hears controversies between taxpayers and the Commissioner of Internal Revenue and has jurisdiction over excess profits proceedings. Under the Tax Reform Act of 1969, the Tax Court was designated a court of record under Article I of the Constitution. Prior to this designation it had functioned as a quasi-judicial administrative agency. The Court consists of sixteen judges appointed by the President with the Senate's consent, for twelve-year terms. Each judge heads a division and, although the Court and its judges are located in Washington, D.C., trial sessions are held in various places throughout the country.

United States v. Butler, *see* Agriculture Adjustment Acts of 1933, 1938.

United States v. Classic, 313 U.S. 299 (1941): Upheld the power of Congress to supervise the holding of state primary congressional elections to ensure the right of the people to vote and to have their ballot counted. Classic, a Commissioner of Elections in Louisiana, was convicted for vote fraud under a federal criminal law prohibiting interference with constitutional rights. The Court based its decision on Article I, Section 4, of the Constitution which establishes the regulatory powers of Congress over congressional elections, holding that the primary is an integral part of the election process.

United States v. Curtiss-Wright Export Corp., 299 U.S. 304 (1936): Upheld the validity of a joint resolution of Congress that delegated broad powers to the President to prohibit arms shipments to foreign belligerents. In question was a presidential proclamation levying an embargo on shipment of war matériel to either side in the Gran Chaco war between Bolivia and Paraguay. In the *Curtiss-Wright* case, the Court distinguished between permissible delegations of congressional lawmaking power in domestic areas and those in foreign affairs. The Court noted: "As a member of the family of nations, the right and power of the United States . . . are equal to the right and power of the other nations of the international family. Otherwise the United States is not completely sovereign." *See also* INHERENT POWERS.

United States v. Darby Lumber Co., 312 U.S. 100 (1941): Upheld the Fair Labor Standards Act of 1938, which imposes wage-and-hour regulations upon businesses engaged in or producing goods for interstate commerce and places restrictions upon the use of child labor. *See also* FAIR LABOR STANDARDS ACT.

United States v. Harriss, 347 U.S. 612 (1954): Upheld the constitutionality of the Federal Regulation of Lobbying Act of 1946 against charges that it violates due process, freedom of speech and press, and freedom of petition. *See also* LOBBYIST.

United States v. Johnson, *see* Freedom of Debate.

United States v. Lovett, 328 U.S. 303 (1946): Declared unconstitutional, as a bill of attainder, an act of Congress that named three individuals as ineligible for continued governmental employment, in that the act punished the individuals without judicial trial. *See also* BILL OF ATTAINDER.

United States v. Wong Kim Ark, 169 U.S. 649 (1898): Established that all persons born in the United States are citizens of the United States, even if the parents are aliens ineligible for citizenship. The only major exceptions are children born to foreign diplomats stationed here. The Court held that a Chinese person born in California who went to China for a visit could not be denied readmission to the United States. *See also Jus Soli.*

United World Federalists, *see* World Government.

Uniting for Peace Resolution   An assumption of power by the General Assembly to authorize collective action against an aggressor. The Assembly's new function was made possible by the adoption of the Uniting for Peace Resolution of 1950, which gives the Assembly a backup role to the Security Council when that organ is unable to act because of a veto. Other provisions of the resolution called for summoning the Assembly into "emergency special session" within twenty-four hours in a peace and security crisis, establishment of a Peace Observation Commission and a Collective Measures Committee to aid the Assembly in such situations, and a call for a survey of resources which could be made available by members when needed. *See also* COLLECTIVE SECURITY.

Unit Rule   A rule, applicable prior to 1972 in Democratic national conventions, which provided that state delegations could cast their total votes in a block for a single presidential candidate. The unit rule was not imposed by the national convention; it was merely recognized when properly invoked by state party authorities. In order to broaden grass-roots participation, the Democratic party forbid its use in a major reform of its convention procedure in 1970. *See also* NATIONAL CONVENTION.

Unity of Command   An administrative concept that no person should be subject to the orders of more than one superior. It is related to the idea of "chain of command," which is common to the military services. *See also* HIERARCHY.

Universal Declaration of Human Rights   A proclamation intended to establish a "common standard of achievement for all peoples and all nations" in the observance of civil, political, economic, social, and cultural rights. Prepared by the Commission on Human Rights and the Economic and Social Council, the Universal Declaration was adopted by the General Assembly on December 10, 1948, since designated Human Rights Day. The General Assembly subsequently completed two draft covenants—one containing civil and political, the other economic, social, and cultural rights—intended to make the rights proclaimed in the Universal Declaration effective by national ratification. In addition, nations that accept the first of these covenants may also ratify an Optional Protocol to the Covenant on Civil and Political Rights by which states would be authorized to bring complaints about other violators to an international body. *See also* HUMAN RIGHTS.

Universal Postal Union (UPU)   A specialized agency of the United Nations for integrating national postal services. First established as the General Postal Union by the Berne Treaty of 1874, the UPU adopted its present name in 1878 and entered into an arrangement with the United Nations in 1947. The organization of the Union consists of a Congress that meets every five years, an Executive and Liaison Committee elected by each Congress, a consultative Committee on Postal Research, and an International Bureau located at Berne that functions as a secretariat. The Universal Postal Convention is revised by each Congress; amendment proposals are circulated by the Bureau between Congresses and, following ratification by a sufficient number of members, must be acceded to by the others as a condition of retaining membership. *See also* SPECIALIZED AGENCY.

Universal Set, *see* Set.

Universe, *see* Random, Sampling.

Unstandardized Interview, *see* Interview.

Urban County Plan   A proposed solution to metropolitan area problems that involves the transfer to county governments of functions exercised by several units of government within the county. Several counties in California have taken over the functions of law enforcement, health services, tax assessments and collections, and prisons. Dade County, Florida, has been established as a metropolitan or urban county. Municipalities within that county, including Miami, have transferred to the county power over traffic problems, planning, sewerage, water supply, and other countywide problems. The urban county plan is to be distinguished from city-county consolidation, which contemplates the complete merger of county government with all other units within the county. *See also* METROPOLITAN AREA.

Urban Renewal   Programs conducted by cities to prevent the spread of urban blight, to rehabilitate areas that can be restored, and to clear and redevelop slum areas that are beyond repair. The Housing Act of 1949 and subsequent legislation provide for procedures by which cities can submit programs to obtain federal aid. Aid is provided for planning and clearance programs and for public housing. Federal mortgage insurance is made available to private investors in reconstruction and rehabilitation projects. A major expansion of the program in 1970 includes "new community development," which can take the form of additions to cities, free-standing new communities, or construction within existing cities. *See also* HOUSING ACT.

USACDA, *see* United States Arms Control and Disarmament Agency.

Usage   A custom that, because it is well-established, is regarded as a part of the American constitutional system. Though not precisely provided for in the words of the Constitution, such practices form an important element of the actual operations of government. Among these are such vital components as the role of political parties, the operations of the Electoral College, the presidential Cabinet, and the inner organization of Congress.

Use Tax, *see* Sales Tax.

USIA, *see* United States Information Agency.

Usury   The charging of interest in excess of the maximum rate permitted by law. State usury laws provide for civil and criminal actions against persons or lending institutions charging illegal interest rates.

Utopia   An imaginary human paradise created in the mind and writings of Sir Thomas More. More's ideal commonwealth was located on an island untouched by worldly vices and provided a nearly perfect society. The word "utopia" means literally "no place" and is taken from the title of More's book published in 1516.

VA, *see* Veterans Administration.

Validation, *see* Testing.

Validity, *see* Reliability, Testing.

Valuation, *see* Assessed Valuation.

Value   A concept of what is desirable or good or, in some usages, the good or desired thing itself. Values may thus reflect what a person wants—a goal, a preference, a desired end-state—or they may reflect his concept of what is good and right, what he *ought* rather than what he *wants* to do. Values are internal, subjective concepts that postulate standards of morality, ethics, esthetics, and personal preference. A set of related values held by a person, or shared by a group, is called a *value system*. A *value judgment* is the application of a value to some object or condition, appraising it as more or less preferable in terms of the value. A *norm* is a rule defining a value in terms of expected conduct. In measurement terminology "value" may mean amount or kind, such as a variable having "values" between one and ten. *See also* A PRIORI, NORMATIVE, POLITICAL PHILOSOPHY, POLITICAL THEORY, THEORY.

Value Consensus, *see* Consensus of Values.

Variable   Any characteristic of an object or class of objects that may vary in quantity or quality for different members of the class, or for the same individual at different points in time. If, for example, states are the class of things being studied, national income and governmental form are two among many state characteristics that might be treated as variables. Variation in national income can be measured *quantitatively,* in dollars, while distinctions between forms of government can be measured *qualitatively,* through use of such categories as democracy and dictatorship. Almost any concept may be regarded as a variable if it can be conceived as having at least two different values. Value in this sense does not mean "good" or "bad," but only difference in number or kind. Variables sometimes relate to the differing behaviors of the *same* individuals at different points in time. Commonly, however, political science variables do not refer to *changes* in the behavior of the *same* individuals but to *differences* among *different individuals* in the same class. Thus, legislators, considered as members of a class, may be compared with one another on the basis of such variables as age, geographical region, and political party affiliation. In a research problem the event or condition the investigator wishes to explain or predict is called his *dependent* variable. The factors or conditions he thinks may have explanatory or predictive power are his *independent* variables. The relationship between dependent and independemt variables is not necessarily causal, but causality is usually inferred. An *intervening* variable is an event or condition that affects the operation of the independent variable upon the dependent variable. If, for example, *political propaganda* is the independent variable and *public attitudes* are the dependent variable, *time* may be introduced as an intervening variable by allowing a time interval between the interviewing of different groups of respondents. *Bivariate* analysis is concerned with just two variables; *multivariate* analysis probes relationships among three or more variables. *See also* CLASSIFICATION, CONCEPT, DATA, GENERALIZATION, HYPOTHESIS, PREDICTION, PROPOSITION, SCIENTIFIC METHOD, TENDENCY STATEMENT, THEORY, VALUE.

Veazie Bank v. Fenno, 8 Wallace 533 (1869): Upheld the validity of a 10 percent tax levied by Congress in 1866 upon notes issued by state banks for the purpose of driving them out of circulation. *See also* REGULATORY TAX.

Vector, *see* Field Theory.

Venue   The county or district in which a prosecution is brought for trial and from which jurors are chosen. Venue refers to a particular area, not to the court that has jurisdiction.

Verification, *see* Testing.

Vertical Federalism, *see* Horizontal Federalism.

Veterans Administration (VA)   An independent agency established in 1930 to coordinate the administration of various laws providing benefits for veterans and their dependents. Included are such programs as compensation for service or nonservice connected disabilities or death, vocational rehabilitation, education, home insurance, life insurance, hospitalization, care of disabled veterans, and burial of veterans. The agency is headed by an administrator appointed by the President with the Senate's consent. *See also* VETERANS ORGANIZATIONS.

Veterans of Foreign Wars, *see* Veterans Organizations.

Veterans Organizations Groups organized to promote the interests of former members of the armed forces and their families. The largest and most influential group is the American Legion, with more than 2 million members, followed by the Veterans of Foreign Wars, with over a million members. Both organizations take firm stands on political issues and are basically conservative in outlook. The American Veterans Committee, with less than 30,000 members, supports liberal programs and generally opposes special benefits for veterans. Numerous other veterans organizations are based on religious, ethnic, specific war experiences, or military unit considerations. *See also* PRESSURE GROUP.

Veterans' Preference Special consideration given to veterans in various aspects of the civil service. These include: (1) the addition of five points to the test scores of veterans, ten points to disabled veterans; (2) the waiver of age, physical, and education requirements in some instances; (3) the limitation of competition for some positions to veterans; (4) the provision for special rights with regard to layoffs and dismissals; and (5) the extension of veterans' preference to wives, widows, and mothers of disabled or deceased veterans. These preferences are provided by almost all civil service jurisdictions in the United States.

Veto (Executive) A legislative power vested in a chief executive to return a bill unsigned to the legislative body with reasons for his objections. The Constitution provides that every bill that passes the House and the Senate must be sent to the President before it becomes law. When the President receives a bill, he may: (1) sign it, whereupon it becomes law; (2) not sign it, whereupon it becomes law after ten congressional working days; (3) veto it, and send it back to the house of its origin; or (4) not sign it, whereupon if Congress adjourns within ten days the bill is killed (pocket veto). The President vetoes a bill by writing "veto" (I forbid) across the face of the bill; he then sends it back to Congress with a message setting forth his objections. Congress may amend the bill according to the President's demands and then repass it, or it may reject the President's objection and override the veto by repassing the bill with a two-thirds roll call vote in each house. Governors, too, exercise the veto power and, in all but a few states, may veto individual items of appropriation bills—a power denied to the President. In the states, the number of votes needed to override a gubernatorial veto varies from a simple majority in each house to a two-thirds vote of all members elected to the legislature. *See also* ITEM VETO; POCKET VETO.

Veto (International Organization) A vote that forbids or blocks the making of a decision. Most international institutions operate under the principle of unanimity, which gives each member the authority to veto decisions. In the United Nations, however, the veto power is exercised only by the five permanent members of the

Security Council: Britain, China, France, the United States, and the Soviet Union. On substantive questions, as distinguished from procedural ones on which the veto does not apply, decisions can be made by an affirmative vote of nine of the Council's fifteen members so long as no permanent member vetoes it by casting a negative vote. An abstention from voting by a permanent member does not constitute a veto. The Charter requires that parties to a dispute must abstain from voting when the Council considers pacific settlement procedures. Since Charter amendments must be ratified by all permanent members, failure to ratify would have the same effect as a veto. *See also* SECURITY COUNCIL.

Veto, Item, *see* Item Veto.

Veto, Liberum, *see* Unanimity.

Veto, Pocket, *see* Pocket Veto.

Veto, Security Council, *see* Security Council, Veto (International Organization).

Vice President   The constitutional officer assigned to preside over the Senate and to assume the presidency in case of the death, resignation, removal, or disability of the President. The Vice President is elected on the same ballot with the President and, if no candidate receives a majority of the electoral vote, the Senate chooses the Vice President from the two candidates for that office with the highest number of electoral votes. Although President of the Senate, the Vice President is not considered to be a member, participating only informally, if at all, in its deliberations, and voting only when a tie occurs. *See also* PRESIDENTIAL SUCCESSION, TWENTY-FIFTH AMENDMENT.

Village   A small urban area, called a town or borough in some states, that is a municipal corporation but one with less authority and simpler organization than a city. The term "village" is a legal concept, varying in meaning from state to state in which the designation is used. Village status may be based upon population but many villages are larger than regular cities. Villages usually are governed by a small council and a village president or mayor. Limitations are placed by the state upon the taxing and borrowing powers of villages as well as upon the types of functions that they may perform.

Virginia Plan   A plan, submitted by Edmund Randolph of Virginia to the Constitutional Convention of 1787, that called for scrapping the Articles of Confederation and establishing a new and strong national government. It provided for a two-house legislature based on state population or wealth, a national executive, and a judiciary. Congress would have had power to disallow state legislation and was to be invested with broad power over matters of national concern. *See also* NEW JERSEY PLAN.

Virginia v. Tennessee, 148 U.S. 503 (1893): Denied a suit brought by Virginia to void the boundary line between it and Tennessee on the ground that the line had been established by agreement between the states without the consent of Congress. The Court held that the agreement did not constitute a compact between the states that required the positive approval of Congress. The only compacts or agreements requiring approval are those that tend to increase state power at the expense of the national government. In other instances, Congress may give its approval by implication. *See also* INTERSTATE COMPACT.

Virgin Islands, *see* Naturalization, Territorial Court, Territory.

Visa   A permit to enter a country. Persons seeking admission to the United States must get a visa from a United States consul located abroad. Many countries require visas as well as passports. Visas are usually stamps of approval affixed to the passport by an official of the country to be visited or entered permanently.

Visiting Mission, *see* Trusteeship Council.

VISTA, *see* Volunteers in Service to America.

Viva Voce Vote   A voice vote in a legislative chamber in which the presiding officer determines the outcome from the volume of response from those for and against the measure. *See also* DIVISION, RECORD VOTE, TELLER VOTE.

Vocational Rehabilitation   The training of the physically and mentally handicapped for useful work. The national government provides grants-in-aid to the states for such programs under supervision of the Rehabilitation Services Administration in the Department of Health, Education, and Welfare. Another major program is in the hands of the Veterans Administration which cooperates with various state educational agencies for the training of handicapped veterans.

Voice of America, *see* United States Information Agency.

Voice Vote, *see* Viva Voce Vote

Volunteers in Service to America (VISTA)   A "domestic peace corps" established by the Economic Opportunity Act of 1964 to combat poverty in American communities. VISTA volunteers, paid only a subsistence allowance, work in community action programs, Job Corps and migrant worker camps, Indian reservations, hospitals, and schools. *See also* ECONOMIC OPPORTUNITY ACT.

Vote Certification, *see* Canvassing Board.

Voting, *see* Absentee Voting, Australian Ballot, Cumulative Voting, Independent, Long Ballot, Office-Block Ballot, Party-Column Ballot, Short Ballot, Split Ticket, Straight Ticket, Voting Behavior.

Voting Behavior   A field of study concerned with the ways in which people tend to vote in public elections and the reasons why they vote as they do. Voting behavior studies deal with the influence on voting patterns of such factors as party affiliation, links with family and friends, age, religion, occupation, nationality, place of residence, level of education, personal or business associations, ideological convictions, level of income, general economic well-being, social status, and susceptibility to propaganda as determined by the impact of campaign issues on individual temperaments.

Voting Qualifications   Legal requirements that prospective voters must fulfill to become eligible to vote. Qualifications imposed in all of the states include citizenship, age (eighteen for all elections since the adoption of the Twenty-sixth Amendment in 1971), and residence (although Congress in the Voting Rights Act of 1970 provided that thirty days residence would qualify citizens to vote in presidential elections). Special qualifications involving lengthy residence, tax payments, property ownership, and literacy may no longer be imposed under Supreme Court rulings. Most states, however, disqualify mental incompetents, prison inmates, election-law violators, and vagrants. According to the Fifteenth and Nineteenth Amendments to the Constitution, no person may be disqualified by a state from voting because of race or sex. *See also* DISFRANCHISE, LITERACY TEST, POLL TAX, REGISTRATION, RESIDENCE.

Voting Rights Act of 1965   An act to eliminate restrictions on voting that have been used to discriminate against Negroes. The major provision of the Act automatically suspended the use of literacy or other tests subject to discriminatory manipulation. It authorized the registration of voters by federal registrars in any state or county where such tests were used in the 1964 election and where less than 50 percent of the eligible voters were registered or voted. The states of Alabama, Georgia, Louisiana, Mississippi, South Carolina, Virginia, and parts of North Carolina were mainly affected. Another provision of the Act authorized the Attorney General to bring suit to test the validity of poll taxes in state elections. In 1966, the Supreme Court declared payment of poll taxes as a condition for voting to be unconstitutional (*Harper v. Virginia State Board of Elections,* 383 U.S. 663). Major provisions of the Voting Rights Act of 1965 were upheld by the Supreme Court as a valid exercise of power under the Fifteenth Amendment (*South Carolina v. Katzenbach,* 383 U.S. 301 [1966]). The Act was extended by the Voting Rights Act of 1970.

Voting Rights Act of 1970   An act which continued and expanded upon the efforts of the national government to increase the electorate. The Voting Rights Act of 1970: (1) extended the Voting Rights Act of 1965 for five years; (2) provided for the lowering of the minimum voting age from twenty-one to eighteen in all elections; (3) suspended the use of state literacy tests; (4) prohibited the states from disqualifying voters in presidential elections because of their failure to meet state residence requirements beyond thirty days; and (5) provided for uniform national rules for absentee registration and voting in presidential elections. The Supreme Court in a series of cases in 1970 upheld all provisions of the Act except that which lowered the voting age to eighteen in state and local elections, although the eighteen-year-old provision was upheld for presidential and congressional elections (*Oregon v. Mitchell*, 400 U.S. 112). *See also* TWENTY-SIXTH AMENDMENT, VOTING QUALIFICATIONS.

Wages and Hours Law, *see* Fair Labor Standards Act of 1938.

Wagner Act (National Labor Relations Act of 1935) A major enactment of the New Deal period that guarantees the right of labor to organize and bargain collectively through representatives of its own choosing. The Act established the National Labor Relations Board (NLRB) to administer the Act. The Board is authorized to issue cease and desist orders to employers who commit unfair labor practices as defined by the law and to certify bargaining representatives for unions. *See also NLRB v. Jones and Laughlin Steel Corp.*.

War Hostilities between states or within a state or territory undertaken by means of armed force. A state of war exists in the legal sense when two or more states declare officially that a condition of hostilities exists between them. Beyond this, international jurists disagree as to the kinds of conditions, intentions, or actions that constitute war by legal definition. De facto war exists, however, whenever one organized group undertakes the use of force against another group. The level of hostilities may range from total war utilizing nuclear, chemical, bacteriological, and radiological weapons of mass destruction, to limited war confined to the use of conventional land, sea, and air forces. The objectives of war may range from the total destruction of a state or group to more limited purposes, such as securing a piece of territory or determining a boundary line. It may be fought by well-organized armies or by guerrilla bands ranging through the countryside. The causes of war are many and complex, but unquestionably include political, ideological, economic, religious, and psychological factors. Under international law, the conduct of the belligerents during a war is governed by the rules of warfare developed through custom and broad multilateral treaties. *See also* ACCIDENTAL WAR, BELLIGERENCY, CIVIL WAR, GUERRILLA WAR, INSURGENCY, LIMITED WAR, PREEMPTIVE STRIKE, PREVENTIVE WAR, RULES OF WARFARE, TOTAL WAR, WARS OF NATIONAL LIBERATION.

War Crimes Trials Trials of persons from defeated enemy states to determine their individual, as opposed to national, guilt and punishment for criminal acts committed in the course of war or in bringing on war. The Treaty of Versailles after World War I set a precedent by providing for the trial and punishment of the German Emperor and individuals in the armed forces, although the Allies never carried out the trials. After World War II, twenty-two major German war criminals were tried at Nuremberg by the International Military Tribunal, representing Britain, France, the Soviet Union, and the United States. Charged with crimes against peace, war crimes, and crimes against humanity, twelve defendants were sentenced to death, others received jail sentences, and three were acquitted. Under the Charter of the International Military Tribunal for the Far East, major Japanese war criminals were tried in Tokyo on similar charges by judges representing the eleven countries at war with Japan.

Ward   The division of a city for purposes of electing members to the city council. The ward system is favored in the larger cities, but most cities use an at-large system of electing councilmen, particularly those using the commission or council-manager forms of government. A number of cities now use a combination of both methods, selecting some councilmen from wards and others at large.

War Powers   The authority expressly granted by the Constitution, implied from it, or inherent in the duty of protecting the nation from its enemies. War powers include those granted to Congress to tax and spend for the common defense, to declare war and make rules concerning captures, to raise and support armies and provide a navy, to enact military law, and to oversee the state militias. Moreover, the elastic clause permits Congress to do whatever is necessary and proper in executing these powers. The President, as commander in chief, has the inherent power to do whatever is necessary to protect the nation, subject to judicial scrutiny. In times of crisis, Congress delegates legislative powers to the President as "emergency powers." *See also* COMMANDER IN CHIEF, EMERGENCY POWERS.

Warrant, *see* Arrest Warrant, Search and Seizure.

Warsaw Pact   The twenty-year Eastern European Mutual Assistance Treaty established by the Communist bloc in 1955. Members of the Warsaw Pact include Albania, Bulgaria, Czechoslovakia, East Germany, Hungary, Poland, Romania, and the Soviet Union. The treaty of "Friendship, Cooperation, and Mutual Assistance" established a unified military command for the armed forces of the eight members and provided that each give immediate aid by all means considered necessary, including the use of armed force, to any signatory attacked in Eastern Europe. *See also* ALLIANCE, WARSAW TREATY ORGANIZATION.

Warsaw Treaty Organization (WTO)   A regional military group of Eastern European Communist states established to implement the Treaty of Friendship, Cooperation, and Mutual Assistance concluded in Warsaw in 1955. Membership in the Warsaw Treaty Organization includes all Communist states of East Europe except Yugoslavia and Albania—Bulgaria, Czechoslovakia, East Germany, Hungary, Poland, Romania, and the Soviet Union. The WTO supplements a series of bilateral mutual aid pacts between the Soviet Union and several Communist states concluded between 1943 and 1948. Decisions of the organization are made by a Political Consultative Committee that meets only sporadically, when called by the Soviets, although the Treaty calls for meetings to be held twice annually. Each member nation is represented on the Committee by a high government or party delegate. A military Unified Command anticipated by the Treaty has never been established, and the position of Commander-in-Chief has regularly been filled by Soviet marshals. Subsidiary organs, including a secretariat and a permanent subcommittee to coordinate members' foreign policies, have been set up by the Political Committee. Membership in WTO imposes a responsibility to contribute immediate military assistance to a victim of an armed attack and to consult at once on joint measures to meet the aggression. *See also* WARSAW PACT.

Wars of National Liberation   A doctrine expounded by the Communists, calling for anti-Western or anticapitalist uprisings in the developing world. Although Marx and Lenin alluded to national revolutions fought by Communists to win power, the broader contemporary definition was first expounded by Premier Nikita Khrushchev in 1961. Wars of national liberation are insurgencies undertaken against the established order in the colonial territories and in the nations of Asia, Africa, and Latin America. Communists consider them to be "just wars" to liberate the enslaved masses from economic and political bondage imposed by Western-oriented élite groups. Communist Chinese leaders have also expounded the doctrine of national liberation wars, calling for a general uprising by the peasants in all class-dominated societies. In 1965, Lin Piao, Chinese Vice Premier, outlined a strategy for world conquest that called for gaining control of the "rural" areas of the globe (Africa, Asia, and Latin America) through wars of liberation so that the "cities" of the world (North America and Western Europe) could be strangled, much as the Communists won in China by gaining control over the countryside. *See also* KHRUSHCHEVISM, MAOISM.

Washington, D.C., *see* District of Columbia.

Washington Naval Conference, *see* Washington Treaty for the Limitation of Naval Armaments.

Washington Treaty for the Limitation of Naval Armaments   An agreement reached at the Washington Naval Conference of 1921–1922 by the leading sea powers to limit the size and construction of their capital ships and to establish an agreed power ratio in twenty years. The Washington Treaty of 1922 provided: (1) that battleships would be limited thereafter to 35,000 tons with 16-inch guns, and aircraft carriers were to be limited to 27,000 tons; (2) that new construction of vessels in this class was forbidden for ten years; (3) that replacements of capital ships after 1931 should establish by 1942 a ratio of: Britain 5; the United States 5; Japan 3; France 1.67; and Italy 1.67; and (4) that signatories would limit their naval bases and fortifications in the Pacific area. Efforts to reach agreement at the conference to limit other naval craft, such as submarines, cruisers, and destroyers, failed to achieve a consensus. *See also* RATIO PROBLEM.

Washington v. Texas, *see* Witness.

Watchdog Committee   A committee established by a legislative body for the purpose of overseeing the administration of the laws. In Congress, prior to 1946, each house created a number of select committees to perform this oversight function. In the Legislative Reorganization Act of 1946, Congress vested the "watchdog" responsibility in the standing committees, each responsible for overseeing the execution of laws within its jurisdiction. *See also* INVESTIGATING COMMITTEE.

Water Conservation   The planned use and protection of water resources. Water conservation programs include promoting the navigability of streams, flood control, irrigation, river basin development, pollution control, recreation, reclamation, hydroelectric power, and the use of water for home and industrial consumption. The Bureau of Reclamation of the Department of the Interior, the Soil Conservation Service of the Department of Agriculture, and the United States Army Corps of Engineers play significant and sometimes competing roles in developing the nation's water resources. Since 1970, the Environmental Protection Agency has also participated in programs to protect water purity. *See also* COLORADO RIVER COMPACT, COLUMBIA RIVER COMPACT, CORPS OF ENGINEERS, ENVIRONMENTAL PROTECTION AGENCY.

Watkins v. United States, 354 U.S. 178 (1957): Established that a person may refuse to answer a question put to him by an investigating committee of Congress if the question is not pertinent to the inquiry. The Court upheld Watkins' refusal to answer questions of the House Committee on Un-American Activities regarding certain persons who had at one time been members of the Communist party. For refusing to answer, Watkins was cited for contempt of Congress. The Court reversed his conviction on the ground that the Committee had failed to demonstrate that the questions were pertinent. *See also* INVESTIGATING COMMITTEE.

Ways and Means Committee   A standing committee of the House of Representatives to which all bills for raising revenue are referred. Its twenty-five members study tax and tariff bills and make recommendations to the full House. Occasionally, the Committee itself writes new tax measures.

Weak-mayor Plan   A plan of city government in which the mayor must share his executive authority with other elected officials and the city council. Most cities under the mayor-council plan use the weak-mayor form rather than the strong-mayor plan. The major features of the weak-mayor plan include: (1) a long ballot in which the people choose numerous department heads, boards, and commissions, as well as the mayor, for administrative purposes; (2) a limited power of appointment and removal in the hands of the mayor; (3) the appointment of numerous officials by the council alone; (4) a weak or complete absence of a veto power for the mayor; and (5) direct participation by the council in administrative matters, including preparation of the budget. *See also* MAYOR-COUNCIL PLAN.

Wealth of Nations, *see* Capitalism.

Weather Bureau, *see* Department of Commerce.

Webb-Pomerene Act of 1918   An act that exempts business associations engaged in export trade to foreign lands from the provisions of the antitrust laws. Such organizations must register with and submit reports to the Federal Trade Commission.

Weeks v. United States, *see* Search and Seizure.

Weighted Voting, *see* European Community, International Bank, International Monetary Fund.

Welfare Benefits Termination, *see Goldberg v. Kelly.*

Welfare Program, *see* Department of Health, Education, and Welfare.

Welfare State   A concept that stresses the role of government as the provider and protector of individual security and social good through governmental economic and social programs. This role for government represents a shift from that of a minimal protector of persons and property to that of a positive promoter of human welfare.

Wesberry v. Sanders, 376 U.S. 1 (1964): Held that congressional districts must be substantially equal in population. The Court based its *Wesberry* ruling on Article I, Section 2, of the Constitution, which provides that the House of Representatives shall be chosen "by the People of the several States." While mathematical precision is impossible, said the Court, the Constitution requires that, as nearly as practicable, each man's vote in a congressional election is to be worth as much as any other man's vote. *See also* REDISTRICTING.

West Coast Hotel Co. v. Parrish, 300 U.S. 379 (1937): Supported a minimum wage law of the state of Washington. The Court held that a minimum wage law did not violate freedom of contract under the due process clause of the Fourteenth Amendment.

Western European Union (WEU)   A regional alliance established in 1955 to defend Western Europe from attack, to help control German rearmament, and to cooperate with NATO in the defense of the Atlantic Community. WEU was an expansion of the Brussels Pact to link up that earlier pact's members (Belgium, Britain, France, Luxembourg, and The Netherlands) with two former enemy states (Germany and Italy). The structure of the alliance includes: (1) a Council of the seven Foreign Ministers that may be called into session by any member to consult on threats to the security of Western Europe; (2) an Assembly that meets in Strasbourg and consists of delegations of WEU nations to the Council of Europe's Consultative Assembly; and (3) a secretariat that services the two major organs and the special bodies created to achieve alliance goals.

West Virginia State Board of Education v. Barnette, *see* Jehovah's Witnesses Cases.

WEU, *see* Western European Union.

Whig Party, *see* Republican Party.

Whip   An assistant floor leader who aids the majority or minority floor leaders of each party in each house of Congress. Whips are selected in party caucuses, usually on the recommendation of the floor leaders. Each whip in the House appoints several assistants to aid him, whereas the Senate whips are aided by the secretaries to their respective party policy committees. *See also* MAJORITY FLOOR LEADER.

White Backlash, *see* Racism.

White House Office, *see* Executive Office of the President.

White Primary, *see Smith v. Allwright.*

White Racism, *see* Racism.

WHO, *see* World Health Organization.

Williams v. Florida, *see* Jury.

Williams v. Illinois, *see* Fine.

Williams v. North Carolina, *see* Full Faith and Credit.

Wiretapping   The use of any electronic device to intercept private conversations. After years of confusion over the permissible bounds for the gathering and use of electronic eavesdropping, the Supreme Court ruled that the requirements of the Fourth Amendment's protection against unreasonable searches and seizures must be met (*Berger v. New York,* 388 U.S. 41, *Katz v. United States,* 389 U.S. 347 [1967]). Congress, in the Omnibus Crime Control and Safe Streets Act of 1968, authorized use of telephone taps and bugging devices if a warrant is secured from a judge. In emergency cases involving national security or organized crime, warrants are not required for forty-eight hours under the Act. *See also* SEARCH AND SEIZURE; *Berger v. New York.*

Withdrawal (International Organization), *see* Expulsion, Suspension, Withdrawal.

Witherspoon v. Illinois, *see* Capital Punishment.

Withholding Tax   Provisions of an income or payroll tax system by which the employer deducts a specified percentage from an employee's wage or salary and remits it to the government's tax bureau. Amounts withheld by employers constitute a credit against the employees' total tax liability. *See also* INCOME TAX.

Withinputs, *see* Input.

Without Objection, *see* Unanimous Consent

Witness   A person who presents information or evidence in a trial or investigation. Under the Sixth Amendment and most state constitutions, a person accused of a crime is entitled to confront the witnesses against him and to compel the attendance of witnesses in his favor. In 1965, the Supreme Court ruled that the right of confrontation of witnesses applies in state trials under the due process clause of the Fourteenth Amendment (*Pointer v. Texas,* 380 U.S. 400). The right to compel the attendance of witnesses was similarly applied to the states in 1967 (*Washington v. Texas,* 388 U.S. 14). *See also* CONFRONTATION CLAUSE, SUBPOENA.

WMO, *see* World Meteorological Organization.

Women's Liberation Movement   A contemporary militant feminist movement aimed at achieving status and rights for women in society equal to those of men. Commonly referred to as "Women's Lib," it consists of several national and numerous local organizations and "rap groups." The main goal of the movement is to change society and its culture so that the "dominant-inferior relationship of men to women" can be changed. Particular objectives for the more radical elements of the movement include ending the "power-structured system of patriarchy" by which the father dominates family life, and wiping out "sexism," the conscious or subconscious male chauvinist attitudes that treat women as sex objects. Most liberationists, however, are concerned with less philosophical and more immediate problems, such as ending job and pay discrimination, securing abortion reform, setting up tax-supported child care centers, and securing equal treatment under national, state, and municipal laws. *See also* EQUAL RIGHTS.

Wong Kim Ark Case, *see United States v. Wong Kim Ark.*

Workmen's Compensation   An insurance program, in effect in all states, that provides compensation for workers injured on their jobs and for dependents of workers who are killed in the course of employment. In most states the program is financed entirely by the employer, who must take out private or public insurance for this purpose. Occupational diseases are also covered in many states. An administrative agency is generally established to settle claims arising under the law with appeal to the courts possible. State laws vary with regard to types of employers and occupations covered.

World Bank Group, *see* International Bank, International Development Association, International Finance Corporation.

World Court, *see* International Court of Justice.

World Disarmament Conference   An international meeting of all states concerned with achieving world disarmament to draft a major treaty to accomplish that goal. The first World Disarmament Conference was called by the League of Nations and convened at Geneva from 1932 to 1934 with sixty-one states represented. The calling of a second World Disarmament Conference to be held "not later than 1967" was endorsed by the United Nations General Assembly in 1965, but the conference was never held because of the intransigence of the great powers.

World Government   A concept of a global political entity that would insure peace and security through a supreme authority established over the state system. Most advocates of world government envisage the establishment of a federation having a central authority vested with specifically delegated powers, while the residue of governmental powers would remain with the constituent units. A world law directly applicable and enforceable upon individuals would emanate from the central government. The most active organization promoting the idea of world government is the United World Federalists.

World Health Organization (WHO)   A specialized agency of the United Nations established in 1948 with the basic purpose of "the attainment by all peoples of the highest possible level of health." WHO carries on some of its programs through advisory services which help combat various maladies and aid in the development of national health administrations. Other programs are administered through central WHO facilities and include the holding of international health conventions and the publication of health statistics. WHO machinery includes an annual World Health Assembly, an Executive Board, and a Secretariat that functions under WHO's Director-General at the Geneva headquarters. *See also* SPECIALIZED AGENCY.

World Meteorological Organization (WMO)   A specialized agency of the United Nations established in 1947 to facilitate worldwide cooperation in weather observation and reporting and to encourage research and training in meteorology. The WMO succeeded the 1878 International Meteorological Organization composed of national directors of weather services. The new organization has states rather than individuals as its members, and most states are members. The organization of WMO consists of a World Meteorological Congress that meets every four years with all members represented and each having one vote. An eighteen-member Executive Committee meets annually and functions as an executive body to implement WMO policies. A secretariat headed by a secretary-general services the Geneva headquarters, which functions as an administrative, research, and information center. *See also* SPECIALIZED AGENCY.

World Revolution, *see* Maoism, Trotskyism.

Wriston Committee, *see* Rogers (Foreign Service) Act of 1924.

Writ   An order in writing issued by a court ordering the performance of an act or prohibiting some act. A wide variety of writs exists, ranging from orders to appear in court to orders regarding the execution of the court's judgment. *See also* CERTIORARI, HABEAS CORPUS, INJUNCTION, MANDAMUS.

WTO, *see* Warsaw Treaty Organization.

Xenophilia, *see* Xenophobia.

Xenophobia   Fear or distrust of foreigners and of the policies and objectives of other states. Xenophobia is related to the mass emotions of ethnocentrism and nationalism in that they all involve a relationship between an "in-group" and outsiders that draws distinctions favorable to the former. Xenophobia involves perceptions of other people, not as individuals, but as stereotypes of something feared or hated. Xenophilia, conversely, is the love of anything foreign, an attitude common, for example, among the restless, alienated youth of Eastern Europe. Moreover, both terms may relate to particular foreign groups, as, for example, in the case of Anglophiles (lovers of things British) and Francophobes (distrustful or hateful of the French). *See also* NATIONALISM.

Yalta Agreement   A World War II executive agreement signed at a summit conference of the Big Three (President Franklin D. Roosevelt, Prime Minister Winston Churchill, and Premier Josef Stalin) held at Yalta in the Russian Crimea in February, 1945, to reach agreement on the occupation of Germany, the future of East Europe, a common strategy for the defeat of Japan, and major issues related to the proposed United Nations Organization. Major war-related decisions included: (1) German surrender must be unconditional; (2) German war criminals should be swiftly brought to justice; (3) reparations should be exacted; (4) liberated countries of Eastern Europe should hold free democratic elections; (5) Polish and Russian borders should be shifted westward to the Oder and Neisse rivers at the expense of Germany; and (6) the Soviet Union would join in the war against Japan within three months after the end of the European war. Decisions concerning the proposed United Nations Organization included agreement that: (1) original membership in the new world organization would be open to all states that declared war on the Axis Powers by March 1, 1945; (2) the Soviet Union would receive three memberships in the United Nations (Soviet Union, Ukraine, and Byelorussia) instead of the sixteen demanded by Stalin; (3) a trusteeship system would be set up to replace the League of Nations mandates arrangement; and (4) the veto power in the Security Council would not apply to procedural decisions and could not be used by a party to a dispute to block its consideration. *See also* EXECUTIVE AGREEMENT, ODER-NEISSE LINE.

Yellow Dog Contract, *see* Norris-LaGuardia Act of 1932.

Young Communist League, *see* Communist Party of the Soviet Union.

Young Pioneers, *see* Communist Party of the Soviet Union, Chinese Communist Party.

Youngstown Sheet and Tube Co. V. Sawyer, 343 U.S. 579 (1952): Struck down the President's Executive Order that had authorized seizure of steel mills and their operation by the national government. President Harry S Truman acted under his inherent power as chief executive and commander in chief to safeguard the nation's security during the Korean war, when a strike in the steel mills threatened the supply of weapons, The Court held that the President has no authority under the Constitution to seize private property unless Congress authorizes the seizure, and that the Constitution does not permit the President to legislate. *See also* INHERENT POWERS WAR POWERS.

Zionism   The international movement for the establishment in Palestine of a Jewish national homeland. The movement was established under the leadership of Theodor Herzl in 1897 at the First Zionist Congress. Zionism has been concerned with promoting support for the state of Israel since its creation in 1948, and with the immigration and resettlement of Jews in Israel.

Zoning   The division of a city or other unit of government into districts and the regulation by law of the uses of the land. Zoning is concerned with the nature of buildings (residential, industrial, or commercial), their height and density, and the uses made of particular tracts of land. Zoning laws are enacted under the police power of communities to protect the health, safety, and welfare of the people. A zoning board of appeals is usually created to grant exceptions and variances to persons who might suffer undue hardships under a zoning regulation. *See also* PLANNING.

Zorach v. Clauson, 343 U.S. 306 (1952): Supported New York's released-time program in public schools, under which students are released from classes to attend religious exercises in their respective churches. The Court found no conflict between this practice and the establishment of religion clause in the First Amendment. *See also* SEPARATION OF CHURCH AND STATE.